Dictionary of Contemporary
QUOTATIONS

Edited by Deborah Davis Eisel
and Jill Swanson Reddig

JOHN GORDON BURKE PUBLISHER, INC.

With this volume, i.e. 5, the *Dictionary of Contemporary Quotations* becomes a biennial monographic serial. ISSN 0360-215X *Key Title*: Dictionary of Contemporary Quotations ISBN 934272-06-7

Introduction

The *Dictionary of Contemporary Quotations* is designed to record contemporary quotations which are historically, sociologically, and politically significant. While quotability is a primary criterion of selection, the editors' judgement about a quotations's significance is equally important. Our effort is to record those quotations that deserve being recalled in the future because of the content of the quotations and/or the speaker responsible for it.

This volume represents a cumulation of the semiannual reference service serial published since 1976 under the same title. In addition, sources for 1975 and 1980 have been searched in order to provide a comprehensive listing of quotations for the six year period surveyed.

A quotation cited by the *Dictionary of Contemporary Quotations* includes the following information: name of speaker and descriptive annotation if appropriate; quotation and explanatory amplification if necessary, and quotation source. Quotations are listed under author and subject indexes, though quotations listed in the subject index omit bibliographical source. Sample quotations follow:

AGEE, Philip

The CIA claims that secrecy is necessary to hide what it's doing from the enemies of the United States. I claim that the real reason for secrecy is to hide what the CIA is doing from the American people. (Playboy 22:49 Aug 75)

BARTHOLOMEW, Summer (Miss U.S.A.—1975)

I believe in equal pay for equal jobs, but not communal toilets or anything like that. (Washingtonian 10:21 July 75)

BLAIR, Eric

One feels, as with Napoleon, that he is fighting against destiny, that he can't win, and yet that he somehow deserves to. (writing in the New English Weekly, March 21, 1940). (Village Voice 20:15 July 7, 75)

BLOCH, Robert

I haven't had so much fun since the rats ate my baby sister (upon receipt of the World Fantasy Award for his life work—horror stories). (Los Angeles Times 94:2 Part 1 Nov 4, 75)

More than 175 periodicals and newspapers have been surveyed for this reference work. When a quotation is cited, it is not necessarily the original source of the published quotation. Rather, quotations are cited whenever they seem important enough to be included. In instances where a quotation appears in more than one source, the original source of publication is cited if it can be determined. Otherwise, the published source most widely available to users is cited; as a result, weekly news magazines frequently replace newspapers as the source of quotations.

It is our intention to update this work periodically. We will delete less valuable quotations as we add new material in future editions. For a complete record of quotes, therefore, the user will want to retain all editions of this monograph.

The aim of the *Dictionary of Contemporary Quotations* is to provide a chronological account of what is being said that is important. We hope it will be of help to the student of social science and humanities as well as the student of popular culture. While this book is intended primarily as a reference tool, we think our readers will also enjoy browsing through it. The mixture of profound, banal, humorous, and frightening statements offers an interesting perspective on contemporary society.

The Editors

197263

AUTHORS

AALTO, Alvar. True architecture exists only where man stands in the center. (Newsweek 94:97 July 16, 79)

ABBOUD, A. Robert. Inflation is a product of—and can only be cured by—the people. (New Republic 180:8 June 30, 79)

ABDULLAH, Ismail Sabry. No nation, no matter how rich, can develop another country. (Time 106:42 Dec 22, 75)

ABE, Kobo. In the love for the weak there is always an intent to kill. (New York Times Magazine 86 April 29, 79)

ABE, Kobo. Once a writer throws away his mask he's finished. (New York Times Magazine 78 April 29, 79)

ABOUREZK, James. Anybody who really changed things for the better in this country could never be elected President anyway. (Playboy 26:105-06 Mar 79)

ABOUREZK, James. The bigger the appropriations bill, the shorter the debate. (Playboy 26:106 Mar 79)

ABOUREZK, James. Don't worry about your enemies, it's your allies who will do you in (in politics). (Playboy 26:106 Mar 79)

ABOUREZK, James. I was in a refugee camp in Jordan in 1973. I thought if I closed my eyes I could hear the words Pine Ridge. The Indians and the Palestinians are the same—people without power put against the wall by people with power. (People Weekly 5:15 Jan 19, 76)

ABOUREZK, James. If you want to curry favor with a politician, give him credit for something someone else did. (Washingtonian 15:140 Nov 79)

ABOUREZK, James. In politics, people will do whatever is necessary to get their way. (Playboy 26:106 Mar 79)

ABOUREZK, James. Politics is like the farmer's dog. If you run too fast you get nipped in the ass. If you stand still too long you get screwed. (Politicks & Other Human Interests 1:17 April 25, 78)

ABOUREZK, James. When voting on the confirmation of a Presidential appointment, it's always safer to vote against the son of a bitch, because if he's confirmed, it won't be long before he proves how wise you were. (Playboy 26:106 Mar 79)

ABZUG, Bella. He's a political opportunist, an intellectual mercenary (commenting on her opponent, in the Democratic primary for Senator for New York, Daniel Patrick Moynihan). (Time 108:26 Sept 20, 76)

ABZUG, Bella. I may not look like a Senator, but I think I'm what a Senator should look like. (Time 108:26 Sept 20, 76)

ABZUG, Bella. Like Jimmy Carter, I expect to be born again. I may have lost my seat, but my voice, never. (Washington Post 6:E3 Dec 11, 76)

ABZUG, Bella. Like so many of the dreams of the sixties, the dream of supersonic transport aircraft has faded in the deepening problems of its reality. (Washington Post 29:A15 Jan 5, 76)

ABZUG, Bella. Richard Nixon self-impeached himself. He gave us Gerald Ford as his revenge. (Rolling Stone 227:43 Dec 2, 76)

ABZUG, Bella. Women are still conceived on television and radio as being creatures of consumption who run around squeezing toilet paper and worrying about the taste of their coffee. And that's the role that many of them are prepared to believe they still have to carry forward. (Los Angeles Times 94:2 Part 1 Oct 27, 75)

ACCIARI, Larry. Presidents come and go, but Walter Cronkite—he's an institution. (Newsweek 88:37 July 26, 76)

ACE, Jane. Well, time wounds all heels. (Village Voice 22:20 Dec 26, 77)

ACHESON, Dean. Americans do at the end of the day what they don't like to do at noon. (Time 115:29 June 30, 80)

ACTON, John Emerich Edward Dalberg. I don't hate humanity. I just don't know them personally. (Maclean's 91:23 April 3, 78)

ADAMS, Alice. I don't like good-looking men—one always thinks they'll be dumb. (People Weekly 9:53 April 3, 78)

ADAMS, Ansel. Some people belong to a church—everybody needs something to believe in. Conservation is my point of focus. (Newsweek 94:90 Sept 24, 79)

ADAMS, Cecil. The average oilman has the moral development of a newt. (The Reader (Chicago's Free Weekly) 8:2 April 27, 79)

ADAMS, Henry Brooks. It is impossible to underrate human intelligence—beginning with one's own. (Kansas City Times 109:14B July 8, 77)

ADAMS, Henry Brooks. A teacher affects eternity; he can never tell where his influence stops. (Kansas City Star 97:15B April 6, 77)

ADDAMS, Jane. I do not believe that women are better than men. We have not wrecked railroads, nor corrupted legislatures, nor done many unholy things that men have done; but then we must remember that we have not had the chance. (Working Woman 1:8 Nov 76)

ADDERLEY, Julian (Cannonball). God smiles on certain individuals, and they get the privilege to have certain beautiful, artistic vibrations pass through them. (Time 106:56 Aug 18, 75)

ADE, George. Anybody can win—unless there happens to be a second entry. (Omni 1:131 May 79)

ADE, George. A good musical comedy consists largely of disorderly conduct occasionally interrupted by talk. (Forbes 120:100 July 15, 77)

ADELMAN, Morris A. (economist). The (energy) gap is like the horizon, always receding as you walk, ride, or fly toward it. (Time 110:61 Oct 10, 77)

ADENAUER, Konrad. History is the sum total of the things that could have been avoided. (Kansas City Times 109:12H Dec 9, 76)

ADENAUER, Konrad. An infallible method for conciliating a tiger is to allow oneself to be devoured. (Washingtonian 15:140 Nov 79)

ADJANI, Isabelle. Life is worth being lived but not worth being discussed all the time. (Time 113:67 Feb 12, 79)

ADLER, Alfred. The chief danger in life is that you may take too many precautions. (Kansas City Times 109:14C Jan 24, 77)

ADLER, Mortimer. Only democracy has the justice which comes from granting every man the right to participate in his own government. (Time 110:57 July 25, 77)

ADLER, Mortimer. Philosophy is everybody's business. (Time 110:57 July 25, 77)

ADLER, Mortimer. Political democracy will not work unless it is accompanied by economic democracy. (Time 110:57 July 25, 77)

ADLER, Mortimer. We are hypocrites if we continue to think that the equality of citizenship belongs to all, but not the equality of educational opportunity. (Time 110:57 July 25, 77)

AGEE, Philip. The CIA claims that secrecy is necessary to hide what it's doing from the enemies of the United States. I claim that the real reason for secrecy is to hide what the CIA is doing from the American people. (Playboy 22:49 Aug 75)

AGEE, Philip. The CIA is nothing more than the secret police of American capitalism, plugging up leaks in the political dam night and day so that shareholders of U.S. companies operating in poor countries can continue enjoying their rip-off. (Time 106:62 Aug 4, 75)

AGNELLI, Giovanni. At twenty, it would be fun to retire. It's silly at sixty. At sixty, what can you do anymore? (Esquire 89:38 June 20, 78)

AGNEW, Spiro Theodore. If you've seen one slum, you've seen them all. (New York Times 127:1 section 4 April 2, 78)

AGNEW, Spiro Theodore. I'm in possession of some information, which I won't disclose, that leads me to believe that I would be elected to office if I chose to see to it. I don't think my name needs rehabilitation. I did nothing morally wrong in my eyes (commenting May 1, 1977). (Chicago Tribune 123:16 section 1 May 3, 77)

AGUNGA, John (African witch doctor). Publicity. They lost because they turned coming to me into a publicity gimmick. Witchcraft works only by stealth (commenting on why the Baltimore Orioles lost the race in the American League East despite his spells). (Sports Illustrated 43:12 Oct 20, 75)

AIKEN, George David. I have never seen so many incompetent persons in high office. Politics and legislation have become more mixed and smellier than ever (commenting on the U.S. Senate in his book Aiken: Senate Diary). (New York Times 125:23 June 29, 76)

ALBEE, Dan. The value of an artistic achievement is inversely proportional to the number of people it appeals to. (Omni 1:132 May 79)

ALBERT, Carl. I wanted to get someone I knew we could beat in the next election (commenting on why he recommended Gerald Ford be appointed to replace Spiro Agnew). (Potomac (Sunday Magazine of the Washington Post) 5 Mar 7, 76)

ALBERT, Claude. You have to love the business (journalism) for what it is, not for what you'd like it to be. (Connecticut 41:32 Feb 78)

ALBORNOZ, Claudio Sanchez. I have only one word: peace. We have killed each other too much already. Let us reach understanding under a regime of freedom, all of us putting into it what is necessary from each side of the barricade (exiled former president upon returning to Spain). (New York Times 125:1 April 24, 76)

ALDA, Alan. If I were a politician, I'd be a decent politician. (Newsweek 94:62 Aug 27, 79)

ALDANA, Dave. It's kind of like tumbling around inside a giant clothes dryer (commenting on what it's like falling off a motorcycle at 150 mph). (Sports Illustrated 43:14 Oct 27, 75)

ALDERSON, M. H. If at first you don't succeed, you are running about average. (Reader's Digest 108:122 Feb 76)

ALEXANDER, Shana. (Journalism) offers the maximum of vicarious living with a minimum of emotional involvement. (New York Times Book Review 3 May 6, 79)

ALGREN, Nelson. It's a boomtown. Sixty percent of the people are on welfare. That's my kind of town (about Paterson, New Jersey). (People Weekly 3:68 Feb 17, 75)

ALGREN, Nelson. Never eat at a place called Mom's. Never play cards with a man named Doc. And never lie down with a woman who's got more troubles than you. (Washingtonian 14:152 Nov 78)

ALI, Muhammad. America can no longer afford me. Madison Square Garden and other promoters can't bid against whole countries. (Newsweek 86:59 Sept 29, 75)

ALI, Muhammad. If you want to be equal with me, you can get your own Rolls-Royce, your own house and your own million dollars. (Chicago Sun-Times 32:33 July 16, 79)

ALI, Muhammad. I'm not a Republican or a Democrat. I'm everywhere. I transcend race. I transcend religion. I transcend color. I'm the world's man. I belong to everybody. (W 7:2 April 14, 78)

ALI, Muhammad. It's hard to be humble when you are as great as I am. (Sepia 24:10 April 75)

ALI, Muhammad. Service to others is the rent I pay for my room here on earth. (New York Times 125:16 Section 4 Dec 7, 75)

ALI, Muhammad. Wars on nations are fought to change maps, but wars on poverty are fought to map change. (Playboy 22:68 Nov 75)

ALICE COOPER, . Only Tammy Wynette and Alice Cooper know how hard it is to be a woman. (Playboy 26:26 Oct 79)

ALICE COOPER, . People have the wrong idea of me when they describe me and my music as 'Anti-Establishment'. Bah. I really believe in being Establishment. In fact, I want to be an American Establishment all my own. (Andy Warhol's Interview 7:23 July 75)

ALITO, Noelie. The shortest distance between two points is under construction. (Omni 1:132 May 79)

ALLEN, Agnes. Almost anything is easier to get into than to get out of. (Omni 1:131 May 79)

ALLEN, Agnes. When all else fails, read the instructions. (Omni 1:131 May 79)

ALLEN, Dick. If horses won't eat it, I don't want to play on it. (Esquire 89:30 Mar 28, 78)

ALLEN, Fred. California is a great place to live...if you happen to be an orange. (New West 1:104 Nov 22, 76)

ALLEN, Fred. Television is a triumph of equipment over people, and the minds that control it are so small that you could put them in a gnat's navel with room left over for two caraway seeds and an agent's heart. (CoEvolution Quarterly 16:153 Winter 77/78)

ALLEN, Fred. Television is chewing gum for the eyes. (Playboy 23:150 June 76)

ALLEN, George. Only winners are truly alive. Winning is living. Every time you win, you're reborn. When you lose, you die a little. (Chicago Tribune 76:1 section 2 Mar 17, 78)

ALLEN, Marty. A study of economics usually reveals that the best time to buy anything is last year. (Atlanta 15:26 Jan 76)

ALLEN, Maryon. People in the South love their politics better than their food on the table. (Time 112:32 Oct 9, 78)

ALLEN, Woody. Death is the big obsession behind all the things I've done. (Time 113:64 April 30, 79)

ALLEN, Woody. The difference between sex and death is, with death you can do it alone and nobody's going to make fun of you. (New York Times 125:33 Dec 1, 75)

ALLEN, Woody. Drama stays with people more, like meat and potatoes, while comedy is a dessert, like meringue. (Newsweek 85:87B June 23, 75)

ALLEN, Woody. From childhood I was told never to marry a gentile woman, never to shave on Saturday and, most especially, never to shave a gentile woman on Saturday. (Chicago Sun-Times 32:33 July 16, 79)

ALLEN, Woody. I can't understand why more people aren't bisexual. It would double your chances for a date on Saturday night. (Rolling Stone 272:14 Aug 24, 78)

ALLEN, Woody. I don't believe in an afterlife, although I am bringing a change of underwear. (Life 2:87 Dec 79)

ALLEN, Woody. I have a tough time expressing anger to people. Sometimes I wish I could raise my voice a little, but I just get quiet or become amusing. (Time 113:68 April 30, 79)

ALLEN, Woody. I have an intense desire to return to the womb. Anybody's. (Playboy 26:26 Oct 79)

ALLEN, Woody. I knew I had problems years ago when they asked me what my religion was and I said, 'Jewish with an explanation'. (Newsweek 86:69 Dec 15, 75)

ALLEN, Woody. If my film makes one more person feel miserable, I'll feel I've done my job. (Time 113:69 April 30, 79)

ALLEN, Woody. In terms of human attributes, what really counts is courage. (Time 113:April 30, 79) April 30, 79

ALLEN, Woody. It's not that I'm afraid to die, I just don't want to be there when it happens. (Newsweek 85:87B June 23, 75)

ALLEN, Woody. The lion and the calf shall lie down together, but the calf won't get much sleep. (Time 113:25 Feb 26, 79)

ALLEN, Woody. Love is the answer. But while you're waiting for the answer, sex raises some pretty good questions. (Time 106:47 Dec 15, 75)

ALLEN, Woody. The meaning of life is that nobody knows the meaning of life. (Rolling Stone 216:88 July 1, 76)

ALLEN, Woody. My aim in life is not to be happy. That's not what life is about. I think life is anxiety and turmoil and struggle. (Chicago Tribune 268:4 section 2 Sept 25, 78)

ALLEN, Woody. There have been times when I've thought of suicide, but with my luck it'd probably be a temporary solution. (Time 106:47 Dec 15, 75)

ALLEN, Woody. The universe is merely a fleeting idea in God's mind—and a pretty uncomfortable thought, particularly if you've just made a down payment on a home. (Chicago Sun-Times 31:45 April 18, 78)

ALLEN, Woody (attributed by Marshall Brickman). Showing up is 80 percent of life. (New York Times 126:11 section 2 Aug 21, 77)

ALLMAN, Gregg. I'd like Cher to be pregnant all the time. (Chicago Daily News 13 Dec 30, 77)

ALSOP, Joseph. I'm proud they (CIA) asked me (to aid them) and proud to have done it. The notion that a newspaperman doesn't have a duty to his country is perfect balls. (Time 110:60 Sept 26, 77)

ALSOP, Stewart. A fashionable gentleman who much concerns himself with the fashions of gentlemen is neither fashionable nor a gentleman. (Newsweek 83:108 April 15, 74)

ALTHAM, Keith. (Keith Moon's death) was not suicide. If Keith wanted to do that, he would get into a sports car and drive through a brick wall. (London Times 8096:2 Sept 10, 78)

ALTMAN, Robert. Every time you make a film, you live a full lifetime. (Newsweek 85:46 June 30, 75)

ALTMAN, Robert. If I'd gone through school, gotten a good job and not gotten into films, I'd probably be dead today or a drunk. (Newsweek 85:50 June 30, 75)

ALTMAN, Robert. Making movies is like playing baseball—the fun is the playing. (Time 105:68 June 16, 75)

ALVES, Reuben. Science is what it is not what scientists think they do. (New York Times 128:A8 July 13, 79)

AMALRIK, Andrei. This is not a decision taken freely. I did not want to emigrate to Israel or anywhere else—ever. When a man is born in a country, and is a writer, he does not want to leave—not ever (commenting on his forced emigration to Israel). (New York Times 125:1 April 13, 76)

AMERICAN PETROLEUM INSTITUTE, . In an otherwise nostalgic decade, solar energy has eclipsed apple pie and is giving mom a close race for the title of most popular platitude of the seventies. (Outside 1:11 Jan 78)

AMIN DADA, Idi. Hitler was right about the Jews, because the Israelis are not working in the interests of the people of the world, and that is why they burned the Israelis alive with gas in the soil of Germany. (Newsweek 89:31 Mar 7, 77)

AMIN DADA, Idi. I do not want people in government to play with other people's housewives. (The Observer 9773:10 Dec 17, 78)

AMIN DADA, Idi. I do not want to be controlled by any superpower. I myself consider myself the most powerful figure in the world and that is why I do not let any superpower control me. (Newsweek 89:31 Mar 7, 77)

AMIN DADA, Idi. My face is the most beautiful face in the world. (The Observer 9820: Nov 11, 79)

AMIN DADA, Idi. The problem with me is that I am 50 or 100 years ahead of my time. My speed is very fast. Some ministers had to drop out of my government because they could not keep up. (Newsweek 89:31 Mar 7, 77)

AMIN DADA, Idi. We should not let ourselves be brainwashed by the Western powers that the presence of Soviet technicians in Angola is an indication that the Soviet Union wants to colonize Africa. (Washington Post 21:A1 Dec 26, 75)

AMIN DADA, Idi. When I am criticized by the Western newspapers, it makes me a true son of Africa. (Newsweek 86:41 Aug 4, 75)

AMOUZEGAR, Jamshid (Iran's Interior Minister). The substantive issue is not whether the oil price has gone up too rapidly; the real issue is whether or not the world is willing to realize that the era of cheap and abundant energy is over. (Time 106:31 Sept 15, 75)

ANDERSON, Gary. New York should be saved because without it people would make even more jokes about Los Angeles. (Harper's Weekly 3142:1 Sept 29, 75)

ANDERSON, Jack. The founding fathers intended us to be watchdogs, not lapdogs. (Time 106:78 Nov 24, 75)

ANDERSON, Jack. The networks don't recognize a story until it's in the New York Times. They aren't competent; they're incompetent. (TV Guide 23:7 Nov 15, 75)

ANDERSON, John B. Even inflation has taught us to cheat ourselves of the future. (Sierra Club Bulletin 65:21 May/June 80)

ANDERSON, John B. George Bush is just a tweedier version of Ronald Reagan. (New York Times Magazine 44 Feb 17, 80)

ANDERSON, John B. I am a Republican who dares to wear his heart on the left and his wallet on the right. (The Observer 9837:8 Mar 9, 80)

ANDERSON, John B. I am not running against General Eisenhower. I am running against Jimmy Carter and Ronald Reagan, and I would respectfully suggest that neither is an Eisenhower. (Time 116:36 July 28, 80)

ANDERSON, John B. I am willing to do the things that would make me a one-term President. (New York Times Magazine 36 Feb 17, 80)

ANDERSON, John B. We (Republicans) are a staid and proper bunch. (Rolling Stone 315:48 April 17, 80)

ANDERSON, John B. You cannot become weary in well-doing. (Sierra Club Bulletin 65:23 May/June 80)

ANDERSON, Paul. I have yet to see any problem, however complicated, which, when you looked at it in the right way, did not become still more complicated. (Washingtonian 14:152 Nov 78)

ANDERSON, Paul. Sure, I was once a 97-pound weakling. When I was 4 years old. (Sports Illustrated 43:14 June 16, 75)

ANDERSON, Thomas J. The only secrets the American government has are the secrets it keeps from its own people. (American Opinion 18:17 June 75)

ANDREOTTI, Giulio. In politics there is a clause that is always valid: rebus sic stantibus (circumstances being what they are). (Time 108:54 Dec 13, 76)

ANDRETTI, Mario. I'm my own status symbol. (People Weekly 10:37 Aug 28, 78)

ANGLETON, James. Our generation believed that you go in naked and you leave naked (about working for the CIA). (Time 113:95 April 30, 79)

ANKA, Paul. I didn't want to find a horse's head in my bed (explaining why he allowed Frank Sinatra to first record My Way). (Rolling Stone 257:15 Jan 26, 78)

ANNE, PRINCESS OF GREAT BRITAIN, . I would have won if I hadn't fallen off. And that's been the story of my life (commenting in a book Talking About Horses). (Washington Post 325:D2 Oct 25, 76)

ANNE, PRINCESS OF GREAT BRITAIN, Newspaper strikes are a relief. (People Weekly 3:68 May 26, 75)

ANONYMOUS, . All I know is that horses don't bet on people. They would if they knew how much fun it is. (New York Times Magazine 14 Jan 9, 77)

ANONYMOUS, . Any country that goes to this much trouble to account for every soldier it loses probably ought not to fight a war. (Time 109:18 Mar 28, 77)

ANONYMOUS, . Anybody who believes in astrology was probably born under the wrong sign. (Macleans 90:46 Aug 22, 77)

ANONYMOUS, . The Arabs cannot make war without the Egyptians, but they cannot make peace without the Palestinians. (Time 111:35 Mar 27, 78)

ANONYMOUS, . As long as the bosses pretend they are paying us a decent wage, we will pretend that we are working (Soviet worker's saying). (New York Times 126:25 Section 12 Jan 30, 77)

ANONYMOUS, . Balls, said the Queen—if I had 'em I'd be King. (Film Comment 14:26 Mar/April 78)

ANONYMOUS, . A clean desk is the sign of a sick mind. (Chicago Magazine 27:104 Jan 78)

ANONYMOUS, . The easiest way to change history is to become a historian. (Washingtonian 15:143 Nov 79)

ANONYMOUS, . Get behind a judge on Monday in case you find yourself in front of him on Tuesday. (Los Angeles Times 97:Nov 29, 78)

ANONYMOUS, . He (Robert Byrd) makes the trains run on time but the cars are all empty. (Time 110:14 Oct 10, 77)

ANONYMOUS, . If God had meant for Texans to ski, He would have made bullshit white. (Texas Observer 72:7 Sept 19, 80)

ANONYMOUS, . If the President helps me and my candidates next year, I'll help him in 1980. It's as simple as that. (Christian Science Monitor 70:1 Dec 5, 77)

ANONYMOUS, . If you're bored in New York, you're boring. (Chicago Tribune 193:1 July 11, 76)

ANONYMOUS, . In Cannes, a producer is what any man calls himself if he owns a suit, a tie, and hasn't recently been employed as a pimp. (Village Voice 22:26 June 6, 77)

ANONYMOUS, . Northern Ireland has too many Catholics and twice as many Protestants, but very few Christians. (Time 104:30 Dec 30, 74)

ANONYMOUS, . One man's secret uncontrollable vice is another man's total boring drag. (New York Times 126:2 Section 5 Nov 7, 76)

ANONYMOUS, . The right governs, the left thinks (about French politics). (Time 114:31 Aug 13, 79)

ANONYMOUS, . The socialization of medicine is coming...the time now is here for the medical profession to acknowledge that it is tired of the eternal struggle for advantage over one's neighbor (editorial comment in the Journal of the American Medical Association, 1914). (New York Times Magazine 12 Jan 9, 77)

ANONYMOUS, . A statesman is a dead politician. (Newsweek 94:35 July 2, 79)

ANONYMOUS, . Tennis isn't a matter of life and death—it's more important than that (sign at the John Gardiner Tennis Clinic, Warren, Vermont). (New Times 5:48 Aug 8, 75)

ANONYMOUS, . To err is human; to blame it on the other party is politics. (Washingtonian 15:142 Nov 79)

ANONYMOUS, . Two percent don't get the word. (Washingtonian 15:140 Nov 79)

ANONYMOUS, . A used car is like a bad woman— no matter how good you treat it, it'll give you more trouble than it's worth. (The Reader (Chicago's Free Weekly) 7:11 section 1 April 7, 78)

ANONYMOUS, . The vice-presidency is like a Sally Quinn or Oriana Fallaci interview. Each one thinks it's going to be better for him than it was for the others. (New Times 7:4 Dec 10, 76)

ANONYMOUS, . We do it all for you (McDonald's jingle). (Life 2:86 Dec 79)

ANONYMOUS, . When it comes to organization, Hamilton (Jordan) is a one-man slum. (Esquire 89:78 Mar 28, 78)

ANONYMOUS, . When (John) Connally eats watermelon, (Robert) Strauss spits out the seeds. (New York 9:52 July 5, 76)

ANONYMOUS, . You can hide good luck but not misfortune. (Time 105:44 Jan 20, 75)

ANONYMOUS (A CUBAN), . We don't mind following him blindly because we know Fidel can see everything (commenting on Cuban Prime Minister Fidel Castro). (Chicago Sun-Times 29:2 Nov 8, 76)

ANONYMOUS (AFRICAN AMBASSADOR), . The only way to true majority rule (in Zimbabwe) is by force of arms. (New York Times 128:A3 Nov 30, 78)

ANONYMOUS (AIDE TO GEORGE BUSH), . George is a bit of a jock. (Rolling Stone 311:42 Mar 20, 80)

ANONYMOUS (AMERICAN INDIAN PROTESTER), . They made us many promises, more than I can remember, but they never kept but one; they promised to take our land, and they took it (painted in the offices of the Bureau of Indian Affairs during its occupation by Indian protesters). (New York Times 125:3 Section 4 June 27, 76)

ANONYMOUS (AMERICAN OFFICIAL), . We are so close to a treaty, and yet so far away. (New York Times 128:Nov 16, 78) Nov 16, 78

ANONYMOUS (AN AMERICAN MERCENARY IN RHODESIA), . If I shot a black in Australia or New Zealand or anywhere else in the world, they'd put me in jail for 20 years. Here I can do it legally. (Rolling Stone 245:27 Aug 11, 77)

ANONYMOUS (ATTRIBUTED BY GEORGE F. WILL), . The chance of the bread falling buttered-side-down is directly proportional to the cost of the carpet. (Newsweek 92:120 Nov 27, 78)

ANONYMOUS (BAPTIST MINISTER), . To a lot of churchgoing folks in this country, Billy Graham has become nothing less than the nearest thing to Jesus on this earth. He's sort of like Christ's American son. (Esquire 91:25 April 10, 79)

ANONYMOUS (CALIFORNIA STATE OFFICIAL), . (Jerry Brown) is the only governor with a foreign policy. (New Times 10:16 Jan 9, 78)

ANONYMOUS (COROLLARY TO MURPHY'S LAW), . Everything will take longer than you think it will. (The Reader (Chicago's Free Weekly) 5:2 May 28, 76)

ANONYMOUS (COROLLARY TO MURPHY'S LAW), . If everything appears to be going well, you have obviously overlooked something. (Washingtonian 13:7 Dec 77)

ANONYMOUS (COROLLARY TO MURPHY'S LAW), . If there is a possibility of several things going wrong, the one that will go wrong is the one that will do the most damage. (Washingtonian 13:7 Dec 77)

ANONYMOUS (COROLLARY TO MURPHY'S LAW), . If you play with a thing long enough, you will surely break it. (Washingtonian 13:7 Dec 77)

ANONYMOUS (COROLLARY TO MURPHY'S LAW), . Nothing is as easy as it looks. (The Reader (Chicago's Free Weekly) 5:2 May 28, 76)

ANONYMOUS (EDITORIAL WRITER FOR THE CHICAGO SUN-TIMES), . Chicago redefined clout Tuesday. It's in the hands of the people (upon Jane Byrne's nomination as Chicago's Democratic candidate for mayor). (Chicago Sun-Times 32:43 Mar 1, 79)

ANONYMOUS (EDITORIAL WRITER FOR THE SUNDAY TIMES, SOUTH AFRICAN NEWSPAPER), . As long as this (detention) system survives, men will continue to die mysteriously, and no one will be held accountable. That is what the system was designed to achieve. No South African can say he did not know. (Christian Science Monitor 70:5 Dec 5, 77)

ANONYMOUS (ENVIRONMENTAL PROTECTION AGENCY OFFICIAL), . Sludge is the most serious dilemma we face in wastewater treatment. It's Catch-22. The cleaner we make the water, the more sludge we create. (Wall Street Journal 56:1 Dec 16, 75)

ANONYMOUS (FEDERAL TRADE COMMISSION MEMO), . The current gasoline shortage may be contrived. (Newsweek 93:25 May 28, 79)

ANONYMOUS (FORMER PRESIDENTIAL ADVISER), . The President (Jimmy Carter) has a terminal case of meekness. (Time 113:11 Mar 5, 79)

ANONYMOUS (FRENCH POLITICIAN), . It seems that the more Paris resembles New York, the more anti-American we become. (Christian Science Monitor 71:7 Aug 14, 79)

ANONYMOUS (HAIGHT-ASHBURY DIGGERS SLOGAN), . Today is the first day of the rest of your life. (New Times 9:68 Aug 19, 77)

ANONYMOUS (HEW EMPLOYEE), . Being a Democrat or a Republican is just a party affiliation. 'Don't Make Waves' is a religion. (Harper's 259:22 Aug 79)

ANONYMOUS (INDIAN LEADER), . Guilt feelings have plagued us all. We knew it was a bad investment when we sold it (responding to New York City's threatened bankruptcy with an offer to buy back the land for $24). (Rolling Stone 203:29 Jan 1, 76)

ANONYMOUS (IRANIAN JEWISH SPOKESMAN), . While we will preserve our Jewish tradition, we will also preserve the country's cause, which is, happily, our cause. (New York Times 128:A3 Feb 22, 79)

ANONYMOUS (ITALIAN PROVERB), . A lawsuit is a fruit tree planted in a lawyer's garden. (Washington Post 152:2 May 6, 79)

ANONYMOUS (MEMBER OF JERRY BROWN'S CABINET), . (Jerry Brown) is the hole in the doughnut. You can't put your finger on him, but he's always there. (Harper's 259:14 July 79)

ANONYMOUS (MEMBER OF THE SOUTH MOLUCCAN COMMUNITY), . Before and after each death, they prayed that God would forgive them. After every killing they wept a long time (explaining that the hijackers of a train in the Netherlands are deeply religious men, doing what they think they must). (Chicago Tribune 345:1 Section 1 Dec 11, 75)

ANONYMOUS (MURPHY'S LAW), . If anything can go wrong, eventually it will. (The Reader (Chicago's Free Weekly) 5:2 May 28, 76)

ANONYMOUS (NICARAGUAN WOMAN), . Five earthquakes—what Somoza has done to us, not even five earthquakes could do. (Newsweek 94:45 July 16, 79)

ANONYMOUS (REPORT IN PRAVDA), . People are not punished for their opinions in the U.S.S.R. The only ones who are prosecuted are those who have indulged in propaganda or anti-Soviet agitation, aiming to weaken the political system in force in our country, or those who broadcast manifestly false bombast whose object is to discredit the Soviet Union. (Seven Days 1:30 Mar 28, 77)

ANONYMOUS (RIGHT WING INDIAN POLITICIAN), . We are responsible for creating Indira Gandhi. Don't make Indira a demon, we're the culprits—we let the people down. She's the result of us politicians' playing the fool for 25 years and not solving India's problems. (Washington Post 342:A2 Nov 11, 76)

ANONYMOUS (STATE DEPARTMENT SPOKESMAN), . It will take us two years to repair the damage Scott did in these couple of weeks (commenting on Senator Scott's "fact-finding" tour of the Middle East). (Rolling Stone 199:34 Nov 6, 75)

ANONYMOUS (SWEDISH BANKER), . Our (Swedish) socialists don't care who owns the cow so long as the government gets most of the milk. (Time 111:29 Mar 13, 78)

ANONYMOUS (TEAMSTER UNION MEMBER), . Look at it this way: Our contract expires in April of 1976, right? If Jimmy Hoffa were running for election against Fitzsimmons in July, 1976, Fitzsimmons would have to bust his tail to negotiate a good contract for us, right? With Jimmy Hoffa gone, he don't have to work so hard, does he? (Los Angeles Times 94:14 Part 1 Nov 11, 75)

ANONYMOUS (U.S. DIPLOMAT), . If Torrijos had not worked his charm on the senators, the (Panama Canal) treaties would simply be a dead letter. (Newsweek 91:20 Feb 13, 78)

ANONYMOUS (U.S. OFFICIAL), . What happens when you combine capital and corruption is simply more corruption (about Mexico). (Newsweek 94:27 Oct 1, 79)

ANONYMOUS (WHITE HOUSE AIDE), . (Carter's) mental state is about the same as always. He is still the same dull, dogged, determined, nose-to-the-grindstone fellow we all know. (Time 114:10 July 16, 79)

ANONYMOUS (WHITE HOUSE STAFF MEMBER), . (Jody) Powell is able to speak for Carter without Carter ever having spoken. (Newsweek 90:119 Sept 19, 77)

ANSELMI, Tina (first Italian woman cabinet member). If people outside Italy have the impression that Italy is always on strike, that is because it is. (New York Times 126:21 Section 1 Oct 10, 76)

ANTHONY, Susan B. Failure is impossible. (Chicago Tribune 176:2 section II June 25, 78)

APODACA, Jerry. Let there be no mistake, the West will not become an energy colony for the rest of the nation. (Newsweek 85:65 May 5, 75)

APOLLONIO, Spencer. When four fishermen get together, there's always a fifth. (Down East 22:108 Jan 76)

ARAFAT, Yasir. The future of the United States of America, the American interest in this part of the world, is with the Arab people, not with Israel. (Chicago Sun-Times 32:3 Aug 12, 79)

ARAFAT, Yasir. I have come bearing an olive branch and a freedom fighter's gun. Do not let the olive branch fall from my hand (addressing the United Nations). (Time 104:43 Nov 25, 74)

ARAFAT, Yasir. I have very few cards, but I have the strongest cards. (Time 114:27 Aug 20, 79)

ARAFAT, Yasir. In a sense, Menachem Begin is our best ally. We hope he will increase his aggression and his terrorism so that everybody all over the world will discover the ugly face of this Israeli military junta. (Newsweek 96:47 Sept 8, 80)

ARAFAT, Yasir. Palestine is my wife. (Time 104:36 Nov 11, 74)

ARAFAT, Yasir. Palestine is the cement that holds the Arab world together, or it is the explosive that blows it apart. (Time 104:27 Nov 11, 74)

ARAFAT, Yasir. The Russian bear is thirsty and he sees the water. (The Observer 9833:9 Feb 10, 80)

ARAFAT, Yasir. There is nothing greater than to die for Palestine's return. (Time 111:36 Mar 27, 78)

ARAFAT, Yasir. We (the PLO) do not want to destroy any people. It is precisely because we have been advocating coexistence that we have shed so much blood. (Time 106:42 Dec 8, 75)

ARAFAT, Yasir. When you put a cat in a corner, it will scratch. (The Observer 9772:10 Dec 10, 78)

ARANOFF, Ezra. There's no room for a slow poke in a prize fight. (Chicago Sun-Times 31:6 Mar 6, 78)

ARBOLEYA, Carlos. History will write Miami's (Florida) future in Spanish and English. (Time 112:48 Oct 16, 78)

ARBUS, Diane. I mean it's very subtle and a little embarrassing to me, but I really believe that there are things which nobody would see unless I photographed them. (Town & Country 131:64 Feb 77)

ARCARO, Eddie. It's hard to get up early when you're wearing silk pajamas (commenting on why rich athletes lose their competitive urge). (Chicago Sun-Times 135 Feb 2, 77)

ARCHER, T. D. Carter very definitely was not prolabor. At a labor gathering, he was a labor man. But if you heard him at the chamber of commerce, he was a chamber man. (U.S. News & World Report 81:111 July 5, 76)

ARDEN, Elizabeth. Nothing that costs only a dollar is worth having. (Chicago Tribune 176:2 section II June 25, 78)

AREGOOD, Richard. It's hard to understand all this fuss about John F. Kennedy. After all, Richard Nixon didn't just concentrate on women. He tried to do it to everybody. (More 6:55 July/Aug 76)

AREGOOD, Richard. They say only the good die young. Generalissimo Francisco Franco was 82. Seems about right. (More 6:55 July/Aug 76)

ARLEDGE, Roone. The single biggest problem of television is that everyone talks so much. (Time 110:61 Aug 22, 77)

ARLEN, Michael J. Every civilization creates its own cultural garbage and ours is television (commenting in his book The View from Highway 1). (Washington Post 352:E4 Nov 21, 76)

ARLEN, Michael J. TV is a kind of language that people have learned how to read. (Time 110:44 Dec 5, 77)

ARMSTRONG, Louis. I got a simple rule about everybody. If you don't treat me right, shame on you. (Parade 22 Feb 8, 76)

ARMSTRONG, Neil A. I believe every human has a finite number of heartbeats. I don't intend to waste any of mine running around doing exercises. (Time 114:88 Nov 26, 79)

ARMSTRONG, Neil A. That's one small step for man, one giant leap for mankind (upon stepping on the Moon). (New York Times 128:A12 July 20, 79)

ARNON, Jacob (Former Israeli Finance Ministry director). There comes a point when defense spending becomes so enormous that it presents just as much danger to our survival as do our Arab enemies. (Time 107:49 Jan 5, 76)

ARON, Jean-Paul. Avarice is the predominant French characteristic because of (our) long peasant history. (Newsweek 88:62 Nov 22, 76)

ARON, Raymond. Marxism is the opium of the intellectuals. (Time 114:41 July 9, 79)

ARON, Raymond. There is only one field in which the Soviet Union is successful: the projection of its military power throughout the world. (US News & World Report 85:67 Nov 27, 78)

ARRAU, Claudio. Every concert must be an event, never a routine. (Horizon 20:9 Dec 77)

ARRUPE, Pedro (Superior General of the Jesuits). They can become martyrs, but my priests are not going to leave there (El Salvador) because they are with the people. (Chicago Daily News 12 Aug 9, 77)

ASHBERY, John. I have a feeling that when people say my poetry is difficult, they mean it's complicated. Well, it probably is, but I don't start out to be as complicated as possible. Life is complicated. I in fact try to simplify it as much as I can. (Washington Post 151:B1 May 4, 76)

ASHE, Arthur. I would continue living pretty much as now, except that I would not play tennis as often (in response to 'What would you do with 10 million dollars'). (Money 4:76 Nov 75)

ASIMOV, Isaac. A lot of people can write. I have to. (Time 113:80 Feb 26, 79)

ASIMOV, Isaac. There's nothing wrong with middle age, but it comes hard to a person who is a child prodigy by profession. (Time 115:K6 May 12, 80)

ASIMOV, Isaac. We are the only creatures ever to inhabit the Earth who have truly seen the stars. (Omni 2:90 April 80)

ASIMOV, Isaac. Women tend to be dirtier but less clever than men. I don't know why, but they can be surprisingly vulgar (about women and limericks). (Time 111:74 April 24, 78)

ASPIN, Les. It's a kind of mongoose-cobra relationship (about the press and the CIA). (Time 111:12 Jan 9, 78)

ASPINALL, Wayne. The conservation extremists demand too much of our public land for their own private use. (American Opinion 18:150 July/Aug 75)

ASSAD, Hafez. Sadat is a traitor to his own people and the Arab nation. (Newsweek 93:25 April 2, 79)

ASSAD, Hafez. Step-by-step might be all right if the steps were giant steps, but they are tortoise steps. (Time 106:29 Dec 8, 75)

ASTAIRE, Fred. I don't dance—ever—and I don't intend to ever again. (Chicago Tribune 1:25 section 1 Jan 1, 78)

ASTOR, Nancy. I married beneath me. All women do. (The Observer 9822:35 Nov 25, 79)

AUCHINCLOSS, Louis. I am neither a satirist nor a cheerleader. I am strictly an observer. (New York Times Book Review 7 Sept 23, 79)

AUDEN, Wystan Hugh. Among those whom I like, I can find no common denominator; but among those whom I love, I can: all of them make me laugh. (Reader's Digest 107:78 Nov 75)

AUDEN, Wystan Hugh. Biographies of writers, whether written by others or themselves, are always superfluous and usually in bad taste. A writer is a maker, not a man of action. (The American Book Review 1:8 April/May 78)

AUDEN, Wystan Hugh. Had one to name the author who comes nearest to bearing the same kind of relation to our age as Dante, Shakespeare and Goethe bore to theirs, Kafka is the first one would think of. (Time 111:80 Jan 30, 78)

AUDEN, Wystan Hugh. I do not know of anyone in the United States who writes better prose (about M. F. K. Fisher). (Bon Appetit 23:127 Nov 78)

AUDEN, Wystan Hugh. Literary confessors are contemptible, like beggars who exhibit their sores for money, but not so contemptible as the public that buys their books. (Time 114:98 Nov 19, 79)

AUDEN, Wystan Hugh. Poetry makes nothing happen. (Washingtonian 13:166 Dec 77)

AUDEN, Wystan Hugh. A suffering, a weakness, which cannot be expressed as an aphorism should not be mentioned. (Time 114:98 Nov 19, 79)

AUDEN, Wystan Hugh (attributed by Peter Conrad). The economic vice of Europeans is avarice, while that of Americans is waste. (Time 115:40 Mar 31, 80)

AUERBACH, Jerold S. Equal justice under law (often means) unequal justice under lawyers. (Time 111:59 April 10, 78)

AUMONT, Jean-Pierre. Marriages are not eternal, so why should divorce be? (W 6:2 July 8, 77)

AUTH, Tony. Once in a while when they're expecting a chuckle, I knee them in the groin (explaining his personal cartooning philosophy). (Guardian Weekly 118:17 Jan 1, 78)

AUTRY, Gene. I'm gonna die with my boots on. (Chicago Tribune Magazine 62 Dec 3, 78)

AUTRY, Gene. We had no violence when I did the westerns, just fist fights and comedy. (Newsweek 85:9 Mar 3, 75)

AYCKBOURN, Alan. There are very few people on top of life, and the rest of us don't like them very much. (Newsweek 128:4 section 2 Mar 25, 79)

AYERS, Brandt. It is much too soon to think of Jimmy Carter as another Jefferson. (Village Voice 21:39 Dec 6, 76)

AZEVEDO, Pinheiro de. People power becomes tyranny when it is not united under a body of law. (Time 106:30 Dec 1, 75)

BAAR, James A. Regardless of what you say or do, some of the people will hate you all of the time. (Wharton Magazine 2:16 Fall 77)

BABENCO, Hector. Brazil is a country that can only be understood by metaphors, where the reality of things violently exceeds fiction. (New York Times 127:10 April 30, 78)

BACALL, Lauren. I agree with the Bogart theory that all an actor owes the public is a good performance. (The Observer 9777:11 Jan 14, 79)

BACON, Francis (British Painter). After all, as existence in a way is so banal, you may as well try to make a kind of grandeur it rather than be nursed to oblivion. (Time 105:34 April 14, 75)

BACON, Mary. We are not just a bunch of illiterate Southern nigger killers. We are good white Christian people working for a white America. When one of your wives or one of your sisters gets raped by a nigger, maybe you'll get smart and join the Klan. (Sepia 24:12 Sept 75)

BAEZ, Joan. I hate getting older, losing my youth. But there's a good side of it. I've left a lot of neuroses behind—stage fright, insecurities, terrors, phobias—that had me dissolved into a puddle of nothing. For anybody who's listening, they don't have to go on forever. (Chicago Tribune 184:17 July 3, 77)

BAGNOLD, Enid. I wasn't a born writer, but I was born a writer. (Human Behavior 7:17 May 78)

BAGNOLD, Enid. The state of the world depends on one's newspaper. (Washington Post 351:C1 Nov 21, 75)

BAILEY, F. Lee. I defend crime; I'm not in favor of it. (Boston 70:72 Dec 78)

BAILEY, Pearl. I never ask myself how I do what I do. After all, how does it rain? (W 7:8 June 9, 78)

BAILEY, Pearl. There's a period of life when we swallow a knowledge of ourselves and it becomes either good or sour inside. (Chicago Tribune 176:2 section II June 25, 78)

BAKER, Bobby. It's very important for the American people to know who's buying their politicians. (Chicago Sun-Times 31:8 July 7, 78)

BAKER, Howard Henry. I don't understand all the fuss over the Gallup poll (with Reagan leading Ford). President Ford is going to veto it anyway. (Newsweek 86:23 Dec 22, 75)

BAKER, Howard Henry. In Washington I'm thought of as a conservative, but in Tennessee I'm thought of as a Bolshevik. (Time 107:15 Aug 9, 76)

BAKER, Howard Henry. (Jimmy Carter is) a yellow-pad President. (Time 114:22 July 23, 79)

BAKER, Howard Henry. There are animals crashing around in the forest. I can hear them but I can't see them (about the Watergate investigation). (Time 114:24 Nov 12, 79)

BAKER, Howard Henry. We do more with someone who shoots a cop than someone who assassinates an ambassador. (Time 113:11 Mar 5, 79)

BAKER, Joy (wife of Howard Baker). Politics has nullified my personality. (Time 106:55 Dec 1, 75)

BAKER, Russell. A $10 million windfall? At today's prices, I'd feel almost as rich as I did one day in 1936 when I found a dime on the sidewalk and blew the whole wad on 20 Mary Jane candy bars, a box of jujubes and a double feature. Nowadays, I'd use the $10 million to buy a new suit, subscribe to the opera, get a front-end alignment for my car and take my wife to dinner in a New York restaurant. This would probably use up the whole $10 million, but if there were a few hundred thousand left over, I'd squirrel it away in a sock for my old age, hoping that some evening, when I have been long locked away in a nursing home, it would still have the purchasing power to bribe my caretaker to sneak out to the nearest fast food joint and bring me back a chocolate ice-cream soda (in response to 'What would you do with 10 million dollars'). (Money 4:76 Nov 75)

BAKER, Russell. Inanimate objects are classified scientifically into three major categories—those that don't work, those that break down, and those that get lost. (Washingtonian 15:140 Nov 79)

BAKER, Russell. Like most writers, I don't read much, at least not good stuff. You can either write or you can read. (Esquire 91:76 Jan 30, 79)

BAKER, Russell. Misery no longer loves company. Nowadays it insists upon it. (Washingtonian 14:152 Nov 78)

BAKER, Russell. Televiso ergo sum—I am televised, therefore I am. (Time 116:9 Sept 22, 80)

BAKHTIAR, Shapour. We have replaced an old and corrupt dictatorship with a dictatorship accompanied by anarchy. (The Observer 9787:1 Mar 25, 79)

BALANCHINE, George. Ballet is woman. (Time 111:64 Feb 6, 78)

BALANCHINE, George. God made men to sing the praises of women. They are not equal to men; they are better. (Time 116:93 Sept 15, 80)

BALANCHINE, George. I am the mother in this world of dance. (Time 115:87 May 19, 80)

BALANCHINE, George. In England you have to be dignified; if you are awake it is already vulgar. (The Observer 9813:14 Sept 23, 79)

BALANCHINE, George (attributed by Merrill Ashley). A new ballet is like putting on a new coat. You have to move around in it awhile before it is comfortable. (Time 111:65 Feb 6, 78)

BALDWIN, James. It (language) is the most vivid and crucial key to identity. (Saturday Review 6:14 Oct 13, 79)

BALDWIN, James. Love does not begin and end the way we seem to think it does. Love is a battle, love is a war; love is a growing up. (Cosmopolitan 188:268 Feb 80)

BALDWIN, James. The range (and rein) of accents on that damp little island make England coherent for the English and totally incomprehensible for everyone else. (Saturday Review 6:14 Oct 13, 79)

BALDWIN, Roger. I'm a crusader and crusaders don't stop. (Chicago Tribune 52:1 secton 3 Feb 21, 79)

BALL, George W. (Lyndon Johnson) did not suffer from a poor education, he suffered from the belief that he had a poor education. (Washingtonian 11:102 June 76)

BALTZELL, Edward Digby, Jr. I believe in inherited wealth. Society needs to have some people who are above it all. (Town & Country 132:97 July 78)

BALTZELL, Edward Digby, Jr. The masses who have no roots are far less dangerous to a society than an elite with no roots. (Town & Country 132:97 July 78)

BALTZELL, Edward Digby, Jr. When class authority declines, money talks. (Town & Country 132:97 July 78)

BANI-ASSADI, Hossein. Islam has no kings. (New York Times 128:12 Feb 25, 79)

BANISADR, Abolhassan. In our campaign against the U.S., the hostages are our weakness, not our strength. (Time 115:31 Mar 21, 80)

BANKHEAD, Tallulah. Cocaine isn't habit-forming. I should know—I've been using it for years. (Playboy 26:26 Oct 79)

BANKHEAD, Tallulah. I don't know what I am, dahling. I've tried several varieties of sex. The conventional position makes me claustrophobic. And the others give me either a stiff neck or lockjaw. (Playboy 24:203 Dec 77)

BANKHEAD, Tallulah. My heart is as pure as the driven slush. (San Francisco Chronicle This World 1978:40 Jan 29, 78)

BANKS, Ernie. I like my players to be married and in debt. That's the way you motivate them. (New York Times 125:3 Section 5 April 11, 76)

BARBER, John. If the gait was stiff the larynx was in superlative order (commenting on the London performance of 72-year-old Bing Crosby). (Washington Post 201:B2 June 23, 76)

BARBOUR, Hugh R. There is nothing like a good negative review to sell a book. (Newsweek 90:69 Oct 31, 77)

BARDEN, Charles (executive director of the Texas Air Control Board). We prefer economic growth to clean air. (Rolling Stone 225:33 Nov 4, 76)

BARDOT, Brigitte. I leave before being left. I decide. (Chicago Tribune 176:2 section II June 25, 78)

BARDOT, Brigitte. It's better to be old than dead. (The Observer 9812:10 Sept 16, 79)

BARDOT, Brigitte. Men are beasts and even beasts don't behave as they do. (Viva 4:26 Feb 77)

BARKAN, Al. We're (AFL-CIO) going to have the best-organized, best-financed political force in the history of organized labor. No one else will have what we have. All we need is a candidate. (Time 107:10 Mar 1, 76)

BARKLEY, Alben. Three months is a generation in politics. (Time 106:9 July 14, 75)

BARNARD, Christiaan. Compared with Harlem, Soweto is paradise. (New York Times Book Review 79 April 30, 78)

BARNARD, Christiaan. There is one message I would give to young doctors and that is that the goal of medicine is not to prolong life. It is to alleviate suffering and improve the quality of life. (Chicago Tribune 64:14 Mar 5, 78)

BARON, Alan. We have divided the presidential election process from the governing process. (Time 115:27 Jan 28, 80)

BAROODY, J. M. Zionism is racism because it is built on exclusivity. The Jews believe they are a superior race, a chosen people. They believe their home should be in Palestine, the Promised Land. Since when was God in the real-estate business? (Newsweek 86:52 Nov 24, 75)

BARRAGAN, Luis. Art is made by the alone for the alone. (Time 115:50 May 12, 80)

BARROW, Willie. It's easier being black than being a woman. (Sepia 26:12 Sept 75)

BARRYMORE, John. There's something about a closet that makes a skeleton terribly restless. (Kansas City Times 109:14B July 8, 77)

BARTH, John. God was a pretty good novelist; the only trouble was that He was a realist. (New York Times Book Review 33 April 1, 79)

BARTH, John. My books are allowed to know one another, as children of the same father, but they must lead their lives independently. (Time 114:96 Oct 8, 78)

BARTHOLOMEW, Summer (Miss U.S.A.--1975). I believe in equal pay for equal jobs, but not communal toilets or anything like that. (Washingtonian 10:21 July 75)

BARUCH, Bernard Mannes. To me, old age is always 15 years older than I am. (Rocky Mountain News 241:90 Dec 19, 79)

BARUCH, Bernard Mannes (attributed by William Flanagan). I buy low and sell high (when asked how he had made a fortune in the stock market). (New York 10:56 May 2, 77)

BARYSHNIKOV, Mikhail. I am happy in America but I am still a Russian and I hope one day I may go back to dance in Russia. (People Weekly 4:86 Dec 1, 75)

BARYSHNIKOV, Mikhail. I have no doubts about what I did, but I have regrets. I left behind my friends, my public, my theater and Leningrad, my city, the most beautiful in the world. Now I have a divided soul. (Newsweek 85:64 May 19, 75)

BARYSHNIKOV, Mikhail. With Balanchine I grew up. (Newsweek 94:82 July 2, 79)

BARZINI, Luigi. We (Italians) might be the first developed country to turn itself back into an underdeveloped country. (Time 111:63 April 3, 78)

BASIE, William (Count). I'll be here until they take me away. (Detroit 2:86 May 79)

BATTISTA, O. A. The fellow who says he'll meet you halfway usually thinks he's standing on the dividing line. (Washingtonian 15:140 Nov 79)

BATTLE, Bill. Class is, when they run you out of town, to look like you're leading the parade (commenting after being forced out as head football coach at Tennessee). (Sports Illustrated 45:18 Dec 13, 76)

BAULER, (Paddy). Chicago ain't ready for reform yet. (Harper's Weekly 3168:8 Aug 23, 76)

BAULER, (Paddy). Take care of the voters first, then you can take care of yourself. (Chicago Daily News 5 Aug 22, 77)

BAUMAN, Robert E. Anytime the House is in session the American people are probably in danger. (New York Times 125:31 April 6, 76)

BAYH, Birch Evans. I am tired of the oil companies determining the price of everything we use that is made from petroleum. I want to break up the monopolistic control they have from the time they punch a hole in the ground to putting gas in the tank. (Newsweek 86:81 Oct 27, 75)

BAYH, Birch Evans. If there is one symbol of the Establishment ripping off the people, it is the oil companies. (Time 107:56 June 28, 76)

BEAME, Abraham David. I believe it would be an act of hypocrisy on my part to participate in any welcoming ceremony with any chief of state who has been a party to the United Nations resolution which seeks to revive a new form of racism as a substitute for the principles of understanding and peaceful negotiations upon which this world body was formed. (New York Times 125:4 Oct 28, 75)

BEAME, Abraham David. No New Yorker should take Rupert Murdoch's New York Post seriously any longer. It makes Hustler magazine look like the Harvard (Law) Review. (Rolling Stone 249:33 Oct 6, 77)

BEARD, Peter. Nixon is what America deserved and Nixon is what America got. (Photograph 5:5 April 78)

BEATON, Sir Cecil. I think you have to have a strange note of badness if you are to have, to possess goodness (when asked what similarities exist between stars of yesteryear and today). (Los Angeles Times 97:2 part 2 Aug 7, 78)

BEATON, Sir Cecil. Perhaps the world's second worst crime is boredom; the first is being a bore. (Time 115:89 Jan 28, 80)

BEAUMARCHAIS, DE, Pierre Augustine Caron De. It is not necessary to understand things in order to argue about them. (Kansas City Times 109:14B July 8, 77)

BEAUMONT, Marie-Claude (French automobile racer). Auto racing is a matter of mathematics—timing. Sex has nothing to do with winning a race. You see, the timekeeper's clock ticks at the same speed for a man or a woman. (Chicago Daily News 298:29 Section 3 Dec 18, 75)

BEAUVOIR, Simone De. I cannot be angry at God, in whom I do not believe. (The Observer 9776:10 Jan 7, 79)

BEAUVOIR, Simone De. In itself, homosexuality is as limiting as heterosexuality: the ideal should be to be capable of loving a woman or a man; either, a human being, without feeling fear, restraint, or obligation. (Ms 6:16 July 77)

BEAUVOIR, Simone De. One is not born a woman, one becomes one. (Ms 6:16 July 77)

BECKER, Jules. It is much harder to find a job than to keep one. (Washingtonian 14:152 Nov 78)

BECKETT, Samuel. All I want to do is sit on my ass and fart and think of Dante. (Newsweek 91:96 June 5, 78)

BECKETT, Samuel. I turned to writing plays to relieve myself of the awful depression that prose led me into. Life at that time was too demanding, too terrible, and I thought theatre would be a diversion. (The Observer 9759:29 Sept 10, 78)

BECKETT, Samuel. There's man all over for you, blaming his boots for the faults of his feet. (Philadelphia 69:187 Sept 78)

BEGIN, Menachem. Europe's rivers are still red with Jewish blood. This Europe cannot teach us how to maintain our security. (Christian Science Monitor 70:5 Dec 2, 77)

BEGIN, Menachem. Jerusalem will remain undivided for all generations until the end of the world. (The Observer 9762:15 Oct 1, 78)

BEGIN, Menachem. The life of every man who fights in a just cause is a paradox. He makes war so that there should be peace. He sheds blood so that there should be no more bloodshed. That is the way of the world. A very tragic way beset with terrors. There is no other. (Time 107:27 May 30, 77)

BEGIN, Menachem. This region isn't Switzerland. (The Observer 9795:9 May 20, 79)

BEGIN, Menachem. When I am called a terrorist and Arafat is called a guerilla, I think it is the apex of injustice. (Time 107:31 May 30, 77)

BEHAN, Brendan. I have never seen a situation so dismal that a policeman couldn't make it worse. (Cleveland 4:118 Aug 75)

BEHAN, Brendan. I think anything is all right provided it is done in private and doesn't frighten the horses. (Cleveland 4:118 Aug 75)

BELAFONTE, Harry. When African countries got independence, I thought there would be a new morality in the world. The next thing I knew Nigerians were shooting Biafrans, and Idi Amin was on the scene. I thought, 'My God, we're not better than the rest.' There are no super-blacks any more than super-whites. They're only people. (Sepia 26:10 Feb 77)

BELL, Griffin. Former cabinet officers shouldn't be seen or heard. (The Tennessean 74:4 Aug 20, 79)

BELL, Griffin. I think we have too many crimes, and I definitely have the view that we have too many laws. (Time 108:16 Dec 27, 76)

BELL, Helen Choate. The French are a low lot. Give them two more legs and a tail, and there you are. (New York 10:88 Jan 31, 77)

BELL, Terrence H. We need to liberalize vocational education—and vocationalize liberal education. (Money 5:48 April 76)

BELLA, Ben. It is an illusion to think you can have a revolution without prisons. (New York Times 128:3 section 4 July 8, 79)

BELLOW, Saul. Being a writer is a rather dreamy thing. And nobody likes to have the diaphanous tissues torn. One has to protect one's dream space (on learning that he had won the Nobel Prize for Literature). (New York Times 126:A10 Oct 22, 76)

BELLOW, Saul. The child in me is delighted. The adult in me is skeptical (upon receiving the Nobel Prize for Literature). (Chicago Sun-Times 29:2 Oct 22, 76)

BELLOW, Saul. I know you think I'm a square, Freifeld, but there's no name for the shape I'm in. (Newsweek 86:39 Sept 1, 75)

BELLOW, Saul. I see politics—ultimately—as a buzzing preoccupation that swallows up art and the life of the spirit. (Newsweek 86:39 Sept 1, 75)

BELLOW, Saul. One can't tell writers what to do. The imagination must find its own path. But one can fervently wish that they—that we—would come back from the periphery. We do not, we writers, represent mankind adequately (excerpt from his Nobel lecture on literature in Stockholm). (New York Times 126:1 Dec 13, 76)

BELLOWS, Jim. Newspapers were 15 years too late in awakening to TV. If newspapers had done their jobs, TV Guide would not have been successful, and newspapers would have had more readers than advertisers. (Washington Journalism Review 1:29 April/May 78)

BENCHLEY, Nathaniel. Contrary to popular opinion there is not a college education in that bottle; you don't get smarter with every drink you take. (Writer's Digest 58:28 Oct 78)

BENCHLEY, Robert. I have tried to know absolutely nothing about a great many things, and I have succeeded fairly well. (Rocky Mountain News 31:64 April 23, 80)

BENCHLEY, Robert. There may be said to be two classes of people in the world: those who constantly divide the people of the world into two classes and those who do not. (Washingtonian 14:152 Nov 78)

BENCHLEY, Robert. Traveling with children corresponds roughly to traveling third class in Bulgaria. (Time 113:76 June 25, 79)

BENES, Bernardo. God gave us our geography and Fidel Castro gave us our biculturalism (about Miami). (Miami Magazine 27:27 Nov 75)

BENES, Bernardo. It is up to Jimmy Carter to say, 'Yes, I believe in human rights' (on President Castro's offer to let political prisoners to come to the United States). (New York Times 128:B1 Nov 23, 78)

BENNETT, Arnold. The price of justice is eternal publicity. (Time 113:85 April 30, 79)

BENNY, Jack. I'm a simple guy. For a comedian I'm surprisingly normal. I have never been to a psychiatrist and I've only been married once. (Newsweek 85:63 Jan 6, 75)

BERGMAN, Ingmar. Possessiveness is neurotic, but this is how I am. (New West 2:24 April 25, 77)

BERGMAN, Ingrid. I don't dream about my past. I accept my age and make the best of it. (Time 107:44 Jan 19, 76)

BERGMAN, Ingrid. A kiss is a lovely trick designed by nature to stop speech when words become superfluous. (Viva 4:26 May 77)

BERGSON, Henri. Think like a man of action, and act like a man of thought. (Kansas City Star 97:4B Feb 6, 77)

BERHANGER, Elio. Fashion has become like an old prostitute. Nobody even uses the word elegance anymore. (W 7:Mar 17, 78) Mar 17, 78

BERKOWITZ, David. Whatever it is has left me, I've mellowed. (Chicago Sun-Times 32:5 Feb 23, 79)

BERLE, Milton. The best way a new comic can start is to have funny bones. (People Weekly 9:96 April 3, 78)

BERLIN, Irving. There wasn't anyone in show business who will be missed as much as Bing Crosby, not only as a performer, but also as a person. (New York Times 126:42 Oct 16, 77)

BERNARDIN, Joseph. If the concept of a woman's freedom requires that she have the right to destroy her offspring, then that concept of freedom is brutal and unworthy... Freedom cannot be freedom from personal responsibility. Freedom follows from responsible action. (US News and World Report 81:27 Sept 27, 76)

BERNSTEIN, Al. Obesity can't be laughed off. (Chicago Sun-Times 31:6 Sept 17, 78)

BERNSTEIN, Carl. Let me say no one has successfully challenged the accuracy of this book (The Final Days) or any single assertion in it. (Meet the Press 20:9 April 18, 76)

BERRA, Yogi. In baseball, you don't know nothing. (New West 4:116 April 9, 79)

BERRA, Yogi. You can observe a lot just by watching. (Omni 1:131 May 79)

BERRIGAN, Daniel. (The Pope's) views of women are old-fashioned, and they are probab)y not going to change. We can't have apartheid at the altar. (Time 114:34 Oct 15, 79)

BERRIGAN, Daniel. When we get locked up now, there's a sigh of ennui (on the declining state of civil disobedience). (Time 111:67 Mar 20, 78)

BERTOLUCCI, Bernardo. To make a film it is not necessary to know anything technical at all. It will all come with time. (Texas Monthly 4:40 Aug 76)

BESTON, Henry. Peace with the earth is the first peace. (Blair & Ketchum's Country Journal 3:88 Aug 76)

BEVERIDGE, Albert J. The Philippines are ours forever. They are not capable of self-government. How could they be? They are not of a self-governing race (comments made in 1900). (July 4, 1976 special edition magazine of the Washington Post 142 July 4, 76)

BHUTTO, Zulfikar Ali. Democracy demands reciprocity. (Time 106:26 Dec 29, 75)

BHUTTO, Zulfikar Ali. A politician is like a spring flower: he blossoms, he blooms, and a time comes for him to fade. (Time 107:38 May 2, 77)

BIDEN, Joseph. Half the people don't know the difference between SALT and pepper. (Time 113:37 April 16, 79)

BIGGS, Barton. (James McIntyre) is a nice, naive, not terribly bright lawyer from Georgia...without a questioning bone in his body. (Esquire 89:8 May 23, 78)

BIKO, Steve. Being Black is not a matter of pigmentation, but is a reflection of a mental attitude. Merely by describing yourself as Black you have started to fight against all the forces that seek to use your blackness as a stamp that makes you out as a subservient being. (Encore 6:15 Dec 27, 77)

BILLINGS, Josh. Consider the postage stamp: its usefulness consists in the ability to stick to one thing till it gets there. (Kansas City Times 109:14B July 8, 77)

BILLINGTON, James. Violence is not only "as American as cherry pie," it is likely to remain a la mode for some time to come. (Newsweek 86:13 Oct 6, 75)

BIRLEY, Rhoda. Mothers are a great bore. (W 5:13 July 23, 76)

BISHOP, Elizabeth. Poetry shouldn't be used as a vehicle for any personal philosophy. (Chicago Tribune 155:1 section 5 June 4, 78)

BISMARCK, Otto, fuerst von. The less people know about how sausages and laws are made, the better they'll sleep at night. (Washingtonian 15:140 Nov 79)

BISSELL, Richard M. I believe they worked without pay for the most part (on the role of the Mafia in the CIA Castro murder plots). (Rolling Stone 195:28 Sept 11, 75)

BLACK, Shirley Temple. I admired Mrs. Roosevelt enormously for two things in particular: her capacity for hard work and her overwhelming interest in the field of human rights. (Chicago Tribune 254:33 Sept 11, 77)

BLACK, Shirley Temple. I'm pleased to be the first woman in 200 years to hold this job. I'm energetic, I'll work hard and I look forward to shaking up anything I see that needs shaking up (commenting on her nomination to be U.S. Chief of Protocol). (Washington Post 201:B2 June 23, 76)

BLACK ELK, . Sometimes I think it might have been better if we had stayed together and made them kill us all. (Quest/78 2:113 Sept/Oct 78)

BLACKBURN, Ben B. If it was up to me, we would go back to public hanging and we would not have trouble collecting rent (advocating public hanging as a remedy for public housing tenants who fall behind in their rent). (Chicago Sun-Times 28:5 Nov 11, 75)

BLACKMUN, Harry. There is another world out there, the existence of which the (Supreme) Court, I suspect, either chooses to ignore or fears to recognize. And so the cancer of poverty will continue to grow. (Writing on the decision not to require government financing of abortions). (Time 110:6 July 4, 77)

BLACKMUR, R. P. Literature exists to remind the powers that be, simple and corrupt as they are, of the turbulence they have to control. (New York Times Book Review 32 Sept 23, 79)

BLAIR, Eric. Any life when viewed from the inside is simply a series of defeats. (Toronto Globe and Mail 136:5 section 5 Nov 17, 79)

BLAIR, Eric. If you want a picture of the future, imagine a boot stamping on the human face— forever...and remember that it is forever. (Omni 2:94 April 80)

BLAIR, Eric. One feels, as with Napoleon, that he is fighting against destiny, that he can't win, and yet that he somehow deserves to. (writing in the New English Weekly, March 21, 1940). (Village Voice 20:15 July 7, 75)

BLAKE, Eubie. I don't drink, don't carouse and don't fool around with women. These things are all bad for you. (W 9:16 Dec 19, 80)

BLAKE, Eubie. I don't know nothing else but how to write and play music, and I'll never quit until the man counts eight, nine, ten and waves me out. (Newsweek 91:87 June 5, 78)

BLAKE, Eubie. When she (Alberta Hunter) sang the blues, you felt so sorry for her you would want to kill the guy she was singing about. (Newsweek 90:101 Oct 31, 77)

BLASS, Bill. Design is like the theatre—the bug bites you early. (Bookviews 1:36 June 78)

BLOCH, Robert. I haven't had so much fun since the rats ate my baby sister (upon receipt of the World Fantasy Award for his life work—horror stories). (Los Angeles Times 94:2 Part 1 Nov 4, 75)

BLOCK, Herbert L. If it's good, they'll stop making it. (Time 113:25 Feb 26, 79)

BLOCK, Herbert L. (Jimmy Carter) looks a little like both Jack Kennedy and Eleanor Roosevelt. (Time 110:92 Dec 12, 77)

BLOOM, Robert. Nobody wants to be a skunk at a garden party (explaining why his office concealed Bert Lance's past). (Rolling Stone 251:61 Nov 3, 77)

BLUMENTHAL, W. Michael. Most bureaucratic regulations look like Chinese to me—and I can read Chinese. (Washingtonian 12:11 Aug 77)

BOCUSE, Paul. The only place for them (women) is in bed. Anyone who doesn't change his woman every week or so lacks imagination. (Newsweek 86:53 Aug 11, 75)

BOCUSE, Paul. Your best American restaurants are the Steak Houses,...the ones with the meat in the window. I love a steak with a baked Idaho potato. Delicious. (Christian Science Monitor 70:22 Dec 8, 77)

BOGART, Humphrey (attributed by Lauren Bacall). I think you (Noel Coward) are wonderful and charming, and if I should ever change from liking girls better, you would be my first thought. (People Weekly 6:49 Dec 13, 76)

BOGERT, Jeremiah M. We've found that frauds often keep a spotless record while too often many otherwise sound business people get careless with credit. (Business Week 2410:76 Dec 8, 75)

BOHANNAN, Paul. Margaret Mead was, in fact, a centipede; she had that many shoes. (Time 112:57 Nov 27, 78)

BOHR, Niels. But horseshoes have a way of bringing you luck even when you don't believe in them. (Village Voice 21:25 June 28, 76)

BOK, Derek. If you think education is expensive—try ignorance. (Town & Country 133:140 May 79)

BOLKAN, Florinda T. The only thing I'm afraid of is getting bored. (W 8:12 Feb 2, 79)

BOND, Julian. Don't let Jimmy Carter pull the peanut butter over your eyes. (Wilson Library Bulletin 51:25 Sept 76)

BOND, Julian. I don't think you'll have to worry that this mental midget, this hillbilly Hitler from Alabama is anywhere near becoming the nominee of the Democratic party. (Rolling Stone 192:33 July 31, 75)

BOND, Julian. I think Jimmy Carter wants to be president more than any other person I've ever known. And that is just terrifying. (Christian Science Monitor 68:12 July 21, 76)

BOND, Julian. It bothers me to think that a year from now an occasion will come up when some response is called for from him (Jimmy Carter) as President and I have no way of knowing what it would be. (Newsweek 88:25-26 July 19, 76)

BOND, Julian. It is almost as though we were climbing a molasses mountain dressed in snowshoes, while everyone else rides a rather rapid ski lift to the top (about Black unemployment). (Chicago Tribune 320:18 Nov 16, 77)

BOND, Julian. There's no new right. There's a new left of unbelievably queasy liberals. (Newsweek 90:42 Nov 7, 77)

BOND, Langhorne. The best fertilizer in a pasture is the footprint of the owner. (Chicago Sun-Times 32:2 June 27, 79)

BONNER, Yelena (wife of Andrei Sakharov). It (The Master of Margarita) is the perfect theatre for the Moscow intelligentsia. It doles out the truth in small doses, never big enough to cause trouble. (Newsweek 89:42 June 13, 77)

BOONE, Pat. I just can't get it into my head that a cabinet man can tell a bad joke in private and get fired, and then John Dean can tell the same joke to millions and get paid for it (commenting on the Earl Butz resignation). (New York Times 125:11 Oct 6, 76)

BOONE, Pat. I think my life is a vindication of what Middle America wants. (TV Guide 26:34 April 1, 78)

BOONE, Pat. Jimmy Carter is a Christian, but he's a McGovern-type Christian, proabortion, prohomosexuality and prolegalizing marijuana. (Rolling Stone 222:14 Sept 23, 76)

BOORSTIN, Daniel J. The contemporary time is always the best time to live. It is a mistake to say the best age is one without problems. (Time 106:53 Sept 1, 75)

BOORSTIN, Daniel J. The courage we inherit from our Jeffersons and Lincolns and others is not the Solzhenitsyn courage of the true believer, but the courage to doubt. (Time 111:21 June 26, 78)

BOORSTIN, Daniel J. Just as the printing press five centuries before had begun to democratize learning, now the television set would democratize experience, incidentally changing the very nature of what was newly shared. (Esquire 89:48 April 25, 78)

BOORSTIN, Daniel J. Our national politics has become a competition for images or between images, rather than between ideals. (Time 113:84 April 9, 79)

BOORSTIN, Daniel J. We suffer primarily not from our vices or our weaknesses, but from our illusions. (Time 114:133 Nov 12, 79)

BOOTH, Arch. I find these figures impossible to accept (in response to a Peoples Bicentennial Commission's sponsored survey reflecting wide public disenchantment with American business). (Harper's Weekly 3140:9 Sept 12, 75)

BORGE, Victor. I would put it all in escrow and allocate it toward future payments for fuel for the family car (in response to 'What would you do with 10 million dollars'). (Money 4:77 Nov 75)

BORGES, Jorge Luis. America is still the best hope. But the Americans themselves will have to be the best hope too. (Time 107:51 July 5, 76)

BORGES, Jorge Luis. (American students) read only what they must to pass, or what the professors choose. Otherwise they are totally dedicated to television, to baseball and to football. (Time 107:47 June 21, 76)

BORGES, Jorge Luis. (I am) very glad about the military coup—it will be a pleasure to be free of hoodlums and gangsters and to be governed again by officers and gentlemen (commenting upon his announcement to return to Argentina). (New York Times 125:15 May 1, 76)

BORGES, Jorge Luis. I had a country. I am ashamed of my country today. (Time 106:47 Dec 1, 75)

BORGES, Jorge Luis. I have never met a man who was both intelligent and Peronist. (Vogue 168:310 Dec 78)

BORGES, Jorge Luis. I think most people are more important than their opinions. (The Times 8067:39 Feb 5, 78)

BORGES, Jorge Luis. When the literature of the second half of the 20th century is studied, the names will be different than we hear now. They will have found hidden writers. People who won Nobel prizes will be forgotten. I hope I will be forgotten. (Washington Post 140:D1 April 23, 76)

BORROWS, Lee (resident of Harlem). That 'Roots' ain't nothin. If they ever told it like it was, the riots would start again. (Rolling Stone 235:33 Mar 24, 77)

BOSCHWITZ, Rudy. First he appoints himself to the job, and then he doesn't show up for work (about Wendell Anderson). (US News & World Report 85:33 Nov 20, 78)

BOTHA, Pieter W. I believe SWAPO is not interested in elections. They are only interested in foisting their ideas on the people of SouthWest Africa at the point of a gun. (New York Times 128:A13 Nov 20, 78)

BOTSTEIN, Leon. The English language is dying, because it is not taught. (Time 106:34 Aug 25, 75)

BOULANGER, Nadia. Education is to bring people to be themselves, and at the same time, know how to conform to the limits. (New York Times 126:D25 Sept 11, 77)

BOULANGER, Nadia. I've been a woman for a little more than 50 years, and I've gotten over my original astonishment (upon being asked how it felt to be the first female conductor of the Boston Symphony in 1938). (New York Times 129:C5 Oct 23, 79)

BOULANGER, Nadia. One works or one cannot work—that would be death. (New York Times 129:C5 Oct 23, 79)

BOULDING, Kenneth E. Politics is a ritualistic dialectic—a bit like a football game. It doesn't really matter who wins, but you have to pretend it does in order to be part of the whole divine comedy. (Denver 5:48 July 76)

BOULDING, Kenneth E. The purpose of education is to transmit information from decrepit old men to decrepit young men. (Omni 2:31 April 80)

BOUMEDIEANE, Houari. Europe and the U.S. have plundered the natural wealth of the Third World. We should consider whatever contribution the industrialized countries make (to be) a simple restitution of a tiny part of the debt contracted by their odious exploitation. (Newsweek 86:37 Sept 15, 75)

BOURKE-WHITE, Margaret. Know your subject thoroughly, saturate yourself with your subject, and your camera will take you by the hand. (Blair & Ketchum's Country Journal 4:78 June 77)

BOUTON, Jim. You see, you spend a good piece of your life gripping a baseball and in the end it turns out that it was the other way around all the time. (New West 4:116 April 9, 79)

BOUZA, Anthony. When you watch (ghetto) mothers take their kids to school, en route to a menial job, amid the drunks and junkies, you think maybe there is hope and the human spirit can triumph (commenting upon his retirement from the New York City police department after 23 years). (People Weekly 6:62 Dec 13, 76)

BOVEE, Christian. Kindness is a language the dumb can speak and the deaf can hear and understand. (Forbes 120:116 July 1, 77)

BOWEN, Elizabeth. All your youth you want to have your greatness taken for granted; when you find it taken for granted, you are unnerved. (Kansas City Star 97:15C Sept 22, 76)

BOYLE, Charles. If not controlled, work will flow to the competent man until he submerges. (Time 113:25 Feb 26, 79)

BOYLES, Tiny. Getting beat up is like eating hot food. After the first bite you don't feel the rest. (Oui 8:52 May 79)

BRADLEY, Bill. First, I was suspicious of an advertising industry that manufactures needs, then sells products to foster those needs. Second, some offers were coming to me as a "white hope", and that offended me. Third, basketball was an important part of my life. I wanted to keep it pure. Hair sprays and deodorants and popcorn poppers were not basketball (on why he never made TV commercials). (Sports Illustrated 46:22 April 18, 77)

BRADLEY, Thomas. This isn't a local issue solely between New York and the Ford Administration—all of us are involved (regarding aid to New York City). (Los Angeles Times 94:10 Part 1 Nov 8, 75)

BRAGG, W. L. The essence of science lies not in discovering facts but in discovering new ways of thinking about them. (Omni 1:29 April 79)

BRAINE, John. I believe absolutely in Christian sexual morality, which means that I believe in premarital virginity. Virgins don't get V.D., don't have abortions, don't have illegitimate babies, and aren't forced to get married. And no man, no matter how progressive, has ever objected to his bride being a virgin. (Kansas City Times 97:17C Oct 12, 76)

BRAND, Stewart. I thought the sixties went on too long. (Outside 1:68 Dec 77)

BRAND, Stewart. (Jerry Brown) is willing to look at new ideas and he has the courage to take risks. I think it's because he did time in a seminary. (Outside 1:69 Dec 77)

BRAND, Stewart. My expectation is that the sky will fall. My faith is that there's another sky behind it. (Omni 2:50 Dec 79)

BRANDEIS, Louis. The most important thing we (judges) do is not doing. (Time 113:92 Jan 22, 79)

BRANDEL, Fernand. The preserve of the few, capitalism is unthinkable without society's active complicity. (World Issues 3:30 Oct/Nov 78)

BRANDO, Marlon. Acting is an empty profession. I do it for the money because for me there is no pleasure. (Time 107:74 May 24, 76)

BRANDO, Marlon. Carter has done something no other President has done: He has brought into the sharpest contrast the hypocrisy of the U.S. in respect to human rights. (Playboy 26:126 Jan 78)

BRANDO, Marlon. I would like to conduct my life and be a part of society that is as good as grass grows. I'd like to be a blade of grass in concert with other blades of grass. Ants do well, sharks and cockroaches. They survive. I'm for survival. (Chicago Tribune 343:4 Section 1 Dec 8, 75)

BRANDO, Marlon. If there are men who have a clean soul, he's (Tennessee Williams) one of them. (Playboy 26:140 Jan 78)

BRANDO, Marlon. If you're rich and famous you don't have any trouble getting laid. (Players 3:32 Feb 77)

BRANDO, Marlon. The principal benefit acting has offered me is the money to pay my psychiatrists. (Los Angeles 23:181 Nov 78)

BRANDO, Marlon. There are so many Jews in creative and executive positions. And Hollywood showed you the crude stereotype of every minority and race—the nigger, the Indian, the Mexican, these portraits reinforced the very attitudes that kept those people down. Many of the people responsible for this were Jews. Didn't they remember what it was like to be down themselves? (Chicago Tribune 343:4 Section 1 Dec 8, 75)

BRANDT, Willy. If I had had a shooting iron with me then I would have put an end to it (commenting on his despair during the sex-and-spy scandal revelations that led to his downfall as Chancellor). (Washington Post 349:A12 Nov 19, 75)

BRAUDEL, Fernand (French historian). A historian never judges. He is not God. The power the historian has is to make the dead live. It is a triumph over death. (Time 109:78 May 23, 77)

BREAUX, John. If these do-gooders have their way you'll need a permit to turn on a faucet in the bathroom (commenting on environmentalists' causes). (Outside 1:17 Dec 77)

BRECHT, Bertolt. Because things are the way they are things will not stay the way they are. (Philadelphia Magazine 68:305 Nov 77)

BRECHT, Bertolt. Grub first, art after. (New York Times Magazine 22 Jan 23, 77)

BRECHT, Bertolt. I hope that because of my life, the powerful will sleep less comfortably (on his epitaph). (Guardian Weekly 120:17 April 29, 79)

BREL, Jacques. Dying is man's only natural act. (Atlas World Press Review 25:49 Dec 78)

BRENAN, Gerald. Miracles are like jokes. They relieve our tension suddenly by setting us free from the chain of cause and effect. (Time 113:147 Feb 5, 79)

BRENAN, Gerald. We are closer to the ants than to the butterflies. Very few people can endure much leisure. (Time 113:147 Feb 5, 79)

BRENAN, Gerald. When the coin is tossed, either love or lust will fall uppermost. But if the metal is right, under the one will always lie the other. (Time 113:147-48 Feb 5, 79)

BRENAN, Gerald. Words are as recalcitrant as circus animals and the unskilled trainer can crack his whip at them in vain. (Time 113:148 Feb 5, 79)

BRESLIN, Catherine. A freelancer lives at the end of a sawed-off limb. (Time 111:77 April 10, 78)

BRESLIN, Jimmy. If this is what happens when you let them out of the kitchen, I'm all for it (commenting on Gael Greene's first novel Blue Skies, No Candy). (New York Times 126:52 Nov 16, 76)

BRESLIN, Jimmy. Nobody ever drank more than Kevin (Cash)—he was a real newspaperman. (Time 107:34 Jan 12, 76)

BRESLIN, Jimmy. One of the truly great things about being brought up in New York City is that it allows you to go through life with an open mind. (Chicago Tribune 194:1 July 12, 76)

BRESSLER, Marvin. There is no crisis to which academics will not respond with a seminar. (Washingtonian 15:140 Nov 79)

BREWSTER, Kingman. A diplomat does not have to be a eunuch. (W 7:37 Sept 15-22, 78)

BREZHNEV, Leonid I. Building Detente requires no little political courage. (Newsweek 93:41 Jan 22, 79)

BREZHNEV, Leonid I. God will not forgive us if we fail (about Strategic Arms Limitation Talks). (New York Times 128:1 June 17, 79)

BREZHNEV, Leonid I. Modern economics, politics and public affairs are so complex that they can be mastered only by collective understanding. (New York Times 128:A3 Nov 8, 78)

BREZHNEV, Leonid I. Relaxation of international tension by no means eliminates the struggle of ideas. (American Legion Magazine 100:9 Feb 76)

BREZHNEV, Leonid I. Time is passing quickly. When meeting young workers, collective farmers, students and servicemen, I realize at times that events which, in effect, are not that distant are legendary to them. (Newsweek 96:47 July 7, 80)

BRICKMAN, Marshall. Open marriage is nature's way of telling you you need a divorce. (Cosmopolitan 188:268 Feb 80)

BRIDENBAUGH, Dale G. From what I've seen, the magnitude of the risks and the uncertainty of the human factor and the genetic unknowns have led me to believe that there should be no nuclear power (commenting after his resignation as manager for performance evaluation and improvement at a General Electric Company plant in California). (New York Times 125:12 Feb 3, 76)

BRIGGS, John. When it comes to politics, anything is fair. (Village Voice 23:62 Oct 16, 78)

BROCK, Bill. If the (1980) election focuses on Carter and his record, Carter will lose. (Time 116:13 July 28, 80)

BROCK, Bill. Reagan has this remarkable ability to project decency, a sense of knowing where he is and where he is going. (Time 116:13 July 28, 80)

BROCK, Bill. This (Republican) party is a new party—we are on our way up. (Time 116:10 July 28, 80)

BROCK, Lou. If you can perceive a goal and then make it happen, you live a dream. (Newsweek 94:49 Aug 27, 79)

BRODER, David S. Anybody who wants the presidency so much that he'll spend two years organizing and campaigning for it is not to be trusted with the office. (Time 113:25 Feb 26, 79)

BRODER, David S. At least half the Carter Cabinet were good bets to be there, no matter which Democrat was nominated and elected. (Washington Post 46:2 Special Section: The Carter Presidency Jan 20, 77)

BRODER, David S. He (Richard Strout) must get out of bed every day as if it's his first chance to set the world right. (Time 111:83 Mar 27, 78)

BRODER, David S. The warning flags are flying for front-runner Jimmy Carter. He has simply not been able to consolidate his position in the way a genuinely strong candidate should (commenting on the upcoming Presidential race, 5/23/76). (New Times 7:68 Sept 3, 76)

BROGAN, D. W. Democracy is like a raft. It never sinks, but damn it, your feet are always in the water. (Time 107:25 May 2, 77)

BROOKE, Edward William. A dreamer, a genius, a most exciting woman (about Sarah Caldwell). (Time 106:65 Nov 10, 75)

BROOKE, Edward William. If my years in public life have taught me anything, it is that nothing in this nation is separate but equal. Nothing could be worse for our country and our children than the resurrection of this immoral and illegal doctrine. (Sepia 25:10 June 76)

BROOKS, Jim. Businessmen commit a fraud when they say they're interested in anything but profit. (New West 1:17 Dec 20, 76)

BROOKS, Mel. Everything we do in life is based on fear, especially love. (Playboy 26:26 Oct 79)

BROOKS, Mel. I don't think in terms of results. I think: what next insanity can I shock the world with. (Maclean's 91:10 April 17, 78)

BROOKS, Mel. To be the funniest has always been my aim. Not the most philosophical, not the most profound, but the funniest. (Newsweek 85:55 Feb 17, 75)

BROOKS, Richard. (Diane Keaton) has more artistic courage than anyone I know. (Time 110:72 Sept 26, 77)

BROONZY, Bill (Big). It's all folk music, cause horses don't sing (in response to Studs Terkel's question, are the Blues folk music). (Stereo Review 37:62 July 76)

BROUN, Heywood Hale. If anyone corrects your pronunciation of a word in a public place, you have every right to punch him in the nose. (Kansas City Times 109:14B July 8, 77)

BROUN, Heywood Hale. Sport is a preparation for more sport and not a businessmen's ROTC. (New York Times Book Review 8 July 29, 79)

BROWN, Don. (Bluegrass) becomes an addiction—just like any other grass, I suppose. (Time 110:45 July 4, 77)

BROWN, Edmund Gerald, Jr. All I guarantee is a lot of hard work and to tell you what is working and what is not. (Encore American & Worldwide News 5:4 June 21, 76)

BROWN, Edmund Gerald, Jr. Are you kidding? Just being governor is a pain in the ass (when asked once if he had Presidential aspirations). (Newsweek 85:25 June 9, 75)

BROWN, Edmund Gerald, Jr. California is the place where the rest of the country and the rest of the world look for leadership and I want to keep it that way. (San Francisco Chronicle This World 1978:29 Feb 26, 78)

BROWN, Edmund Gerald, Jr. Communications erodes provincialism. (Esquire 89:64 Feb 78)

BROWN, Edmund Gerald, Jr. The first rule of politics is to be different. (Newsweek 93:24 April 23, 79)

BROWN, Edmund Gerald, Jr. Government isn't a religion. It shouldn't be treated as such. It's not God; it's human, fallible people feathering their nest most of the time. (Time 105:34 April 14, 75)

BROWN, Edmund Gerald, Jr. I think it's time for the President, certainly the next President, to say no to nuclear power. (New York Times 128:A18 April 26, 79)

BROWN, Edmund Gerald, Jr. I think Jimmy Carter ought to take the Paraquat out of whatever it is in. (San Francisco Chronicle This World 1978:2 May 21, 78)

BROWN, Edmund Gerald, Jr. If work is more interesting and challenging, people should be paid less. Those are the people who get great psychic rewards: their lives are better because they have the privilege of interesting work. (Potomac (Sunday Magazine of the Washington Post) 5 May 30, 76)

BROWN, Edmund Gerald, Jr. If you want a Governor who makes decisions, then you are going to get a Governor who makes mistakes. (Time 112:21 Sept 25, 78)

BROWN, Edmund Gerald, Jr. I'm not conservative—I'm just cheap. (Time 107:9 May 31, 76)

BROWN, Edmund Gerald, Jr. In California, you've got to realize one thing: you don't mess around with a man's cars or his guns. (New West 3:54 Dec 18, 78)

BROWN, Edmund Gerald, Jr. In this business a little vagueness goes a long way. (New Times 6:18 May 28, 76)

BROWN, Edmund Gerald, Jr. Information is the equalizer; it breaks down the hierarchy. A lot of institutions are living in a world that is rapidly passing them by. (Esquire 89:65 Feb 78)

BROWN, Edmund Gerald, Jr. Issues are the last refuges of scoundrels. (Washingtonian 15:140 Nov 79)

BROWN, Edmund Gerald, Jr. The nation is not governable without new ideas. (Time 114:21 Nov 12, 79)

BROWN, Edmund Gerald, Jr. People are ready to make sacrifices for the betterment of this country, but only on a basis that we all bear up the burdens and bear under them on an equal basis, and that is not happening today. (Meet The Press 19:2 Oct 5, 75)

BROWN, Edmund Gerald, Jr. The power of the executive is like a chess game; there are very few moves that one can make. (Gold Coast Pictorial 13:9 Feb 77)

BROWN, Edmund Gerald, Jr. The reason why everybody likes planning is because nobody has to do anything. (The Coevolution Quarterly 10:23 Summer 76)

BROWN, Edmund Gerald, Jr. There is a limit to the good things we have in this country. We're coming up against those limits. It's really a very salutary exercise to learn to live with them. (Time 106:18 Dec 8, 75)

BROWN, Edmund Gerald, Jr. We must sacrifice for the future, or else we steal from it. (The Tennessean 74:6 April 11, 79)

BROWN, Edmund Gerald, Jr. You don't have to do things. Maybe by avoiding doing things you accomplish a lot. (New York Times 125:17 April 26, 76)

BROWN, Edmund Gerald, Jr. You lean a little to the left and then a little to the right in order to always move straight ahead (on the art of governing). (Time 112:89 Oct 2, 78)

BROWN, Elaine. I may not be saying 'off the mother-fucking pigs' anymore, but I'm still talking about serious political change. Who cares who takes credit? The Panthers? The Democrats? As long as the work gets done. (Ms 4:109 Mar 76)

BROWN, George, Jr. It is time to take a giant step backward (in suggesting the use of dirigibles instead of airplanes in air travel). (Rolling Stone 201:32 Dec 4, 75)

BROWN, George S. If any citizen of this country is so concerned about his mail being read or is concerned about his presence at a meeting being noted, I'd say we ought to read his mail and we ought to know what the hell he has done. (Chicago Sun-Times 30:10 Mar 29, 77)

BROWN, George S. They own, you know, the banks in this country, the newspapers. Just look at where the Jewish money is. (Time 104:16 Nov 25, 74)

BROWN, Harold. A lesson we learned from Viet Nam is that we should be very cautious about intervening in any place where there's a poor political base for our presence. (Time 109:24 May 23, 77)

BROWN, Harold. (Russia) has shown no response to U.S. restraint—when we build, they build; when we cut, they build. (Newsweek 93:104 June 25, 79)

BROWN, Phyllis George. A smart woman will suggest things to a man and let him take the credit. (New Woman 10:12 May/June 80)

BROWN, Rita Mae. I want the American public to discover the difference between the Republican Party and the Democratic Party is the difference between syphillis and gonorrhea. (Seven Days 1:26 Mar 14, 77)

BROWN, Sam. Never offend people with style when you can offend them with substance. (Washingtonian 14:152 Nov 78)

BROWN, Sam. Never trust anybody over 30. (Chicago Sun-Times 31:26 June 4, 78)

BROWN, Willie. Jerry (Brown) likes Jimmy (Carter) about as well as I like Lester Maddox. (New York Times 125:36 section 1 Sept 19, 76)

BROWNMILLER, Susan. It (rape) is nothing more or less than a conscious process of intimidation by which all men keep all women in a state of fear. (Time 106:48 Oct 13, 75)

BRUCE, Lenny. I only said it, man. I didn't do it. (Oui 7:51 Feb 78)

BRYANT, Anita. God says that someone who practices homosexuality shall not inherit the Kingdom of God. God is very plain on that. (Ms 6:50 July 77)

BRYANT, Anita. Heaven knows, I wouldn't want to deny anyone their human rights, but I'm not denying their right to be human (commenting on her fight against homosexual rights in Miami). (New Times 8:46 April 15, 77)

BRYANT, Anita. If gays are granted rights, next we'll have to give rights to prostitutes and to people who sleep with St. Bernards and to nailbiters. (More 8:13 Mar 78)

BRYANT, Anita. If homosexuality were the normal way, God would have made Adam and Bruce. (Rolling Stone 243:41 July 14, 77)

BRYNNER, Yul. If you've got just a plain fat head under your hair, don't shave it or you'll look like a melon. (The Observer 9783:11 Feb 28, 79)

BRZEZINSKI, Zbigniew. America still provides to most people in the world the most attractive social *condition* (even if not the model), and that remains America's special strength. (Time 107:8 June 14, 76)

BRZEZINSKI, Zbigniew. A big country like the U.S. is not like a speedboat on a lake. It can't veer suddenly to the right or left. It's like a large ship. There's continuity to its course. (Time 111:18 May 29, 78)

BRZEZINSKI, Zbigniew. By the time we're through, the world will have been reordered. (W 7:33 Nov 10, 78)

BRZEZINSKI, Zbigniew. Pessimism is a luxury that policymakers can't afford because pessimism, on the part of people who try to shape events, can become a self-fulfilling prophecy. (Time 112:26 Aug 21, 78)

BRZEZINSKI, Zbigniew. Power is very intangible. It's nothing to be liked for its own sake. But...if you use power in a responsible way, then power is something one can enjoy. (Washington Post 61:B1 Feb 4, 77)

BRZEZINSKI, Zbigniew. We live in a world in which there will be many local conflicts, in which all the major powers will exercise self-restraint, because they have to exercise self-restraint in the nuclear...it will be a sign of the maturity of the American people and of the growing wisdom of the American people if we adjust ourselves to the notion that in our age there is a twilight zone between war and peace and that this twilight zone of limited wars is going to be very much a feature of our lifetime. (Washington Post 21:C3 Dec 26, 76)

BUCHAN, Alastair. Respectability depends on whose side you're on. To the Turks, Lawrence of Arabia was a terrorist. (Time 104:44 Nov 25, 74)

BUCHAN, John. The charm of fishing is that it is the pursuit of what is elusive but attainable, a perpetual series of occasions for hope. (New York Times 126:2 Section 5 Nov 7, 76)

BUCHWALD, Art. As the economy gets better, everything else gets worse. (Book Digest 6:32 Dec 79)

BUCHWALD, Art. Benedict Arnold has been misunderstood. A great general, a ladies' man par excellence and one of the big spenders of the time, he might have been the father of our country if Congress hadn't passed him over for promotion. (People Weekly 6:21 July 12, 76)

BUCHWALD, Art. The day you leave Russia is the happiest day of your life. (Book Digest 4:30 Sept 77)

BUCHWALD, Art. I don't mind 800 million Chinese drinking a bottle (of Coca-Cola) a day, but I don't want them to bring back the empties. (Time 113:69 Feb 19, 79)

BUCHWALD, Art. I doubt that I would do anything different from what I am doing right now. First of all, I can't eat any more than I am right now. Second, I would not buy anything more, because I find possessions a pain in the ass. Third, I have a very good relationship with all my relatives and if I started giving them money, I know they would hate me in their hearts. Come to think of it, I am going to have to review your kind offer. I don't want it. It would only screw up my life, which is screwed up enough as it is (in response to 'What would you do with 10 million dollars'). (Money 4:76 Nov 75)

BUCHWALD, Art. In this country, when you attack the Establishment, they don't put you in jail or a mental institution. They do something worse. They make you a member of the Establishment. (Time 110:67 Dec 5, 77)

BUCHWALD, Art. In 80 percent of the countries in the world today, guys like myself would be in jail. (Book Digest 4:27 Sept 77)

BUCHWALD, Art. It isn't the bad lawyers who are screwing up the justice system in this country—it's the good lawyers...If you have two competent lawyers on opposite sides, a trial that should take three days could easily last six months. (Time 111:58 April 10, 78)

BUCHWALD, Art. There is entirely too much talk about going to war these days. (The Observer 9835:9 Feb 24, 80)

BUCHWALD, Art. Whether it's the best of times or the worst of times, it's the only time you've got. (Time 112:67 Sept 4, 78)

BUCHWALD, Art. The women's liberation movement has affected my sex life: I haven't had any since it started. (Playboy 25:102 May 78)

BUCK, Pearl. One faces the future with one's past. (Chicago Tribune 176:2 section II June 25, 78)

BUCKLEY, Pat. Women were born to be taken care of by men—I do think that's the law of the universe. (W 6:1 Oct 14, 77)

BUCKLEY, William Frank, Jr. All adventure is now reactionary. (Time 109:87 May 23, 77)

BUCKLEY, William Frank, Jr. The General Assembly long ago abdicated the authority to cause uproar. Do you get mad at the Bronx Zoo? We shouldn't pull out of the United Nations. We shouldn't stop debating in the General Assembly. But we should stop voting in it—permanently (upon the anti-Zionist vote in the UN General Assembly). (New York Times 125:17 Nov 12, 75)

BUCKLEY, William Frank, Jr. If people would just take my advice, everything would go well. (W 7:2 April 14, 78)

BUCKLEY, William Frank, Jr. Reagan is both too fatalistic and too modest to be a crusader. He doesn't have that darkness around the eyes of a George McGovern. (Time 106:20 Nov 24, 75)

BUCKLEY, William Frank, Jr. We should be big enough to grant a little people what we ourselves fought for 200 years ago (commenting on the Panama Canal). (San Francisco Chronicle This World 1978:2 Jan 22, 78)

BUCY, Fred. Nothing is ever accomplished by a reasonable man. (Book Digest 6:30 Dec 79)

BUJOLD, Genevieve. Caesar was Cleopatra's guru and Guinness was mine. (Newsweek 85:32 Jan 6, 76)

BUKOVSKY, Vladimir. China today is Russia 20 or 30 years ago. She is following in our footsteps, which are those of totalitarianism. (American Legion Magazine 102:16 Mar 77)

BUKOVSKY, Vladimir. If I were to answer what sustains us in this struggle, first and foremost is trust, faith in people, faith in the future, and faith in the human values for which we stand (commenting at the White House on Soviet dissidents). (New York Times 126:A4 Mar 2, 77)

BUNDY, McGeorge. The history of the Vietnam war, properly understood, will testify not to the dangers of excessive presidential power but to the perils of secretiveness (comment made at the end of his own role in the war in October 1973). (July 4, 1976 special edition magazine of the Washington Post 146 July 4, 76)

BUNDY, McGeorge. One of the things we've always valued about Henry Ford is candor. (Harper's 254:32 Mar 77)

BUNTING, Josiah. The (West Point honor) code is an anachronism but a good anachronism. (Time 107:20 June 7, 76)

BUNUEL, Luis. Sex without sin is like an egg without salt. (New Times 5:5 Nov 28, 75)

BURDEN, Chris. Learn how to make counterfeit money. Some of it is really beautiful (advice for budding artists). (Chicago Magazine 27:22 Jan 78)

BURGER, Warren Earl. I will never hire a woman clerk. A woman would have to leave work at 6 p.m. and cook dinner for her husband. (New Woman 10:12 May/June 80)

BURGER, Warren Earl. If law-school graduates, like cars, could be recalled for failure to meet commercial standards, the recall rate would be very high on those who go into the courts without substantial added training. (US News & World Report 85:73 Aug 21, 78)

BURGER, Warren Earl. Perhaps without knowing all the reasons, they were ahead of many others in seeing that something was missing in modern life (commenting on American youth of the '60s). (Washington Post 176:A4 May 29, 76)

BURGER, Warren Earl. The very discussion of independence reminds us how much each freedom is dependent on other freedoms. (American Legion Magazine 99:36 Nov 75)

BURGER, Warren Earl. We may be well on our way to a society overrun by hordes of lawyers, hungry as locusts, and brigades of judges in numbers never before contemplated. (Time 109:40 June 27, 77)

BURGESS, Anthony. The element of suppression has to exist in any state, but a democracy looks to a sophisticated citizenry that regards the suppression of intolerance as the duty of the individual soul. (Time 111:49 May 8, 78)

BURGESS, Anthony. We need beauty queens more than politicians. (The Observer 9809:10 Aug 26, 79)

BURGESS, Anthony. Women cannot help moving, and men cannot help being moved. (Playboy 24:346 Dec 77)

BURGESS, Frank Gelett. If in the last few years you hadn't discarded a major opinion or acquired a new one, check your pulse. You may be dead. (Forbes 120:80 Aug 1, 77)

BURNHAM, Daniel. Make no little plans. (Chicago 26:160 Dec 77)

BURNS, Arthur Frank. The ultimate consequence of inflation could well be a significant decline of economic and political freedom for the American people. (Time 111:33 Jan 9, 78)

BURNS, Arthur Frank. While I have not yet reached the conclusion that Federal financial assistance is necessary (to New York City), I am closer to such a conclusion than I have been in the past. (New York Times 125:1 Nov 12, 75)

BURNS, George. If you tear yourself down, people feel sorry for you, and if they feel sorry for you, they like you. (New York Times Book Review 12 Feb 10, 80)

BURNS, George. If you want to live a long time you have to smoke cigars, drink martinis and dance close. (Chicago Sun-Times 32:6 Nov 27, 79)

BURNS, George. Now, they say, you should retire at 70. When I was 70 I still had pimples. (Time 112:69 Aug 7, 78)

BURNS, George. To be perfectly honest, I don't think acting is very hard. They say the most important thing is to be able to laugh & cry. Well, if I have to cry, I think of my sex life, and if I have to laugh, I think of my sex life. (Chicago Tribune 312:31 Section 1 Nov 7, 76)

BURNS, George. Too bad that all the people who know how to run the country are busy driving taxicabs and cutting hair. (Life 2:117 Dec 79)

BURNS, George. When I do go, I plan to take my music with me. I don't know what's out there, but I want to be sure it's in my key. (Playboy 22:48 Dec 75)

BURNS, GEORGE (ATTRIBUTED BY DAVID STEINBERG), . (Critics are) eunuchs at a gang-bang. (New Times 10:38 Jan 9, 78)

BURNS, JOHN, . We expect very little of our (state) legislatures, and they continually live up to our expectations. (Time 111:101 May 29, 78)

BURROUGHS, John. If you want to see birds, you must have birds in your heart. (Outside 1:11 Dec 77)

BURROUGHS, William S. What you want to do is eventually what you will do anyway. Sooner or later. (Village Voice 22:44 May 16, 77)

BURTON, John C (New York City's Deputy Mayor for Finance). It's time that financial types developed a greater tolerance for imprecision, because that's the way the world is. (Time 109:49 Jan 24, 77)

BURTON, Richard. Clint (Eastwood) is in the great line of Spencer Tracy and James Stewart and Bob Mitchum. They have a kind of dynamic lethargy. They appear to do nothing and they do everything. (Esquire 89:45 Mar 14, 78)

BURTON, Richard. I only see a movie when I can't avoid it. (W 5:16 July 23, 76)

BURTON, Richard. I was a homosexual once but not for long. It didn't work, so I gave it up. (People Weekly 3:68 June 23, 75)

BURTON, Richard. I was a star from the moment I first walked on the stage. (Chicago Tribune 284:2 section 2 Oct 11, 77)

BURTON, Richard. We actors, madmen, are capable of experiencing not just the moment but the nostalgia and anticipation of it. (People Weekly 13:64 April 21, 80)

BUSBY, Steve. I throw the ball harder than Nolan Ryan. It just doesn't get there as fast. (Sports Illustrated 43:6 Aug 4, 75)

BUSH, Earl (press aide to Richard J. Daley). Don't print what he says; print what he means (about Richard J. Daley). (Chicago Sun-Times 33:2 Oct 17, 80)

BUSH, George. Everyone says they are going to reinvent the wheel, that their Vice President is going to be in on developing North-South strategy and other great projects. But it never happens. Two years later, you wake up and find he's still going to funerals. (Time 116:12 July 28, 80)

BUSH, George. I am a non-politician, as of now. (Meet the Press 20:9 Feb 22, 76)

BUSH, George. I can feel it in my bones. I'm going to be President. (Time 115:26 Feb 4, 80)

BUSH, George. I'll prevail over Reagan because it is right that I prevail. (New York 13:44 Jan 21, 80)

BUSH, George. John Anderson is not a national candidate. He's an anomaly. Time 115:24 Mar 17, 80)

BUTHELEZI, Gatsha (Zulu Chief). I shudder for my country, and I shudder for all its people. The whole white population will, in the final analysis, be answerable for the sins that are committed in their name by those they have elected to determine not only their destiny but ours. (Town & Country 131:51 June 77)

BUTHELEZI, Gatsha (Zulu Chief). South Africa is one country. It has one destiny. Those who are attempting to divide the land of our birth are attempting to stem the tide of history. (New York Times 125:4 April 23, 76)

BUTLER, Nicholas Murray. An expert is one who knows more and more about less and less. (Kansas City Times 109:14B

BUTLER, Samuel. In practice it is seldom very hard to do one's duty when one knows what it is, but it is sometimes exceedingly difficult to find this out. (Kansas City Star 97:4B Oct 10, 76)

BUTZ, Earl Lauer. He no playa the game, he no maka the rules (in response to Pope Paul's stand on birth control). (People Weekly 3:56 Sept 29, 75)

BUTZ, Earl Lauer. I don't know why we have to look at every bird that comes down the line. If GM inspected every piston ring the way we inspect chickens, a new Chevrolet would cost $20,000 (responding to consumer pressure for more rigorous government food inspection). (Mother Jones 1:10 Dec 76)

BUTZ, Earl Lauer. I'll tell you why you can't attract coloreds. Because coloreds only want three things. You know what they want? I tell you what coloreds want. It's three things: first, a tight pussy; second, loose shoes; and third, a warm place to shit. That's all (responding to a question from Pat Boone and explaining why the Republican Party didn't attract more blacks—reported by John Dean). (Rolling Stone 223:57 Oct 7, 76

BUTZ, Earl Lauer. In California, Mexican farmworkers are no longer allowed to use the short-handled hoes they have for generations; now they are required to use long-handled American-type hoes. This is not because the workers or the farmers want the change; but apparently because the city people, driving by, feel more comfortable watching the workers using the kind of hoes that look good through car windows. (Mother Jones 1:6 July 76)

BUTZ, Earl Lauer. It was stupid—like General Motors breaking into Ford to steal Edsel plans (commenting on Watergate, in the long term). (People Weekly 5:84 April 19, 76)

BUTZ, Earl Lauer. Oh hell, John, everybody was out by then. You know...it's like the dog who screwed a skunk for a while, until it finally shouted, I've had enough (commenting to Pat Boone and John Dean regarding the lukewarm reception of Robert J. Dole by the delegates of the Republican National Convention). (Rolling Stone 223:57 Oct 7, 76)

BUTZ, Earl Lauer. Our capitalism is no longer capitalism; it is a weakened mixture of government regulations and limited business opportunities. (American Legion Magazine 99:21 Dec 75)

BYRD, Robert. The nation cannot afford to have as director of the Office of Management and Budget a man whose personal problems are so great that they detract from the performance of his duties. (Newsweek 90:22 Oct 3, 77)

BYRD, Robert. The Senate is very much like a violin. The sound will change with the weather, the dampness, the humidity. The Senate is a place of great moods. (Time 110:14 Oct 10, 77)

BYRD, Robert. West Virginians have always had five friends—God Almighty, Sears Roebuck, Montgomery Ward, Carter's Little Liver Pills and Robert C. Byrd. (Time 111:12 Jan 23, 78)

BYRNE, Jane. Diamonds are a girl's best friend, and Federal grants are second. (Newsweek 96:24 Sept 29, 80)

BYRNE, Jane. If they care to come with me and accept the fact I'm a candidate, I am willing to work with them (about Chicago's Regular Democratic Organization). (Chicago Sun-Times 32:1 Mar 1, 79)

BYRNE, Jane. I'm a Democrat, I believe in the Democratic Party. (New York Times 128:1 Mar 1, 79)

BYRNE, Jane. With the Irish, you know, only the strongest survive. (New York Times Magazine 77 Mar 9, 80)

CAAN, James. You know the kind of actor I am? I'm the sort who says before each movie, 'Oh God, give me a break'. (Time 105:80 April 7, 75)

CABELL, James Branch. There is no memory with less satisfaction in it than the memory of some temptation we resisted. (Forbes 120:100 July 15, 77)

CADDELL, Patrick. I'm less influential than I'd like to think I am, and a lot more than I deserve. (Time 114:14 Aug 6, 79)

CADDELL, Patrick. Clearly, God is a Democrat. (Boston 68:115 Sept 76)

CADDELL, Patrick. I don't know any politician in America who could run against himself and win. (Time 115:18 April 7, 80)

CAEN, Herb. What others call kooks we look upon as characters in a charade we smile at (about California). (New York Times 128:A18 Nov 30, 78)

CAGNEY, James. Once a song-and-dance man, always a song-and-dance man. Those few words tell as much about me professionally as there is to tell. (Time 107:42 Jan 26, 76)

CALDER, Alexander. The underlying sense of form in my work has been the system of the universe, or part thereof. For that is a rather large model to work from. (Washington Post 343:C11 Nov 12, 76)

CALDER, Alexander. Why do I live in Paris? Because in Paris it's a compliment to be called crazy. (Time 108:63 Nov 22, 76)

CALDWELL, Taylor. Women irritate me. I've met a few intelligent women—not many. They're usually after a man, that's all. (New Woman 10:12 May/June 80)

CALIFANO, Joseph A., Jr. If you put a cookie jar on the shelf and leave a kid in the room, he's going to get at that jar. We've got a lot of people out there eating cookies (on the existing welfare system). (US News & World Report 84:43 Jan 9, 78)

CALIFANO, Joseph, A. Jr. Of course, we recognize the right to dissent. That's what our boys in Vietnam are fighting for. But this shows that the overwhelming majority of American college students and the American public stand fully behind the President in his policy in Vietnam (commenting in 1965 when he accepted for President Johnson an 8-foot petition with 2,500 signatures from students and faculty at American University protesting the Vietnam War). (Washington Post 21:C2 Dec 26, 76)

CALIFANO, Joseph A., Jr. Writing things clearly does not necessarily mean writing them short. (Washingtonian 13:11 Nov 77)

CALLAGHAN, James. I believe all good people should be in bed by 11 o'clock at night. (The Observer 9775:9 Dec 31, 78)

CALLAGHAN, James. I was brought up to believe that free collective bargaining was the milk of the gospel. (But) if I went into the witness box today, having watched its operation over many years, I could not with honesty declare that it produced either justice for the weak or fairness between different groups. (Time 110:43 Sept 19, 77)

CALLAGHAN, James. Spain's self-inflicted isolation is brought about not just by a single act of brutality, but by injustices over a generation or more. (Time 106:37 Oct 13, 75)

CALLAHAN, Daniel. There's no guarantee that high IQ people produce better people or a better society. It is not the retarded kids of the world who produce the wars and destruction. (Time 115:49 Mar 10, 80)

CALLAS, Maria. I hate to be pitied, and I never pitied anyone. (Time 110:56 Sept 26, 77)

CALLAS, Maria. To be an opera singer, you have to be an actress. (Newsweek 90:67 Nov 7, 77)

CALLEY, William Laws, Jr. I think I've always been a pacifist. (Washington Post 205:H1 June 27, 76)

CALLEY, William Laws, Jr. I was a coward. I couldn't have backed out (from the My Lai attack) if I wanted to because I believed in this nation. (People Weekly 4:31 Nov 24, 75)

CALLOWAY, Cab. Women, horses, cars, clothes. I did it all. And do you know what that's called. It's called living. (Sepia 26:10 Jan 77)

CAMERON, Clyde (Australian Labor and Immigration Minister). I'm not going to allow a degenerate who could influence the young and weak-minded to enter this country and stage this sort of exhibition here (about Alice Cooper). (Time 105:53 April 7, 75)

CAMERON, John. In order to get a loan you must first prove you don't need it. (Washingtonian 14:154 Nov 78)

CAMERON, John. When your opponent is down, kick him. (Town & Country 133:140 May 79)

CAMERON, Simon. An honest politician is one who, when he is bought, will stay bought. (Village Voice 21:16 Nov 8, 76)

CAMPBELL, William J. The grand jury is the total captive of the prosecutor, who, if he is candid, will concede that he can indict anybody, at any time, for almost anything, before any grand jury. (Time 110:61 July 4, 77)

CAMUS, Albert. Alas, after a certain age every man is responsible for his face. (CoEvolution Quarterly 17:30 Spring 78)

CAMUS, Albert. Illness is a convent which has its rule, its austerity, its silences, and its inspirations. (Time 112:74 July 10, 78)

CAMUS, Albert. Not only is there no solution but there aren't even any problems. (Time 112:74 July 10, 78)

CANBY, Vincent. Bland has always been big in television. (New York Times 126:15 section 2 Nov 13, 77)

CANETTI, Elias. ...I have succeeded in grabbing this century by the throat. (New York Times Book Review 58 April 29, 79)

CANETTI, Elias. To be the last man to remain alive is the deepest urge of every real seeker after power. (New York Times Book Review 58 April 29, 79)

CAPONE, Alphonse. It rains in Chicago and snows too. But after all home is home. (Chicago 24:186 Dec 75)

CAPONE, Alphonse. Let the worthy citizens of Chicago get their liquor the best way they can. I'm sick of the job. It's a thankless job and full of grief. (Chicago 24:186 Dec 75)

CAPONE, Alphonse. They blamed everything but the Chicago Fire on me. (Chicago 24:186 Dec 75)

CAPONE, Alphonse. When I sell liquor, it's called bootlegging; when my patrons serve it on silver trays on Lake Shore Drive, it's called hospitality. (Aspen 3:43 Spring 77)

CAPOTE, Truman. He's a sphinx without a secret (commenting on Andy Warhol). (People Weekly 5:15 May 10, 76)

CAPOTE, Truman. He's like a good brand of cereal—nothing is wrong, but nothing is particularly appetizing (commenting on Nelson Rockefeller). (People Weekly 5:15 May 10, 76)

CAPOTE, Truman. I mean I can create any kind of social world I want, anywhere I want. (New York 9:49 Feb 9, 76)

CAPOTE, Truman. I say I'm a homosexual who has had heterosexual experiences. (W 5:8 July 23, 76)

CAPOTE, Truman. I'm the greatest genius of all time. (W 5:6 April 30, 76)

CAPOTE, Truman. It is not writing; it is only typing (about Jack Kerouac). (Village Voice 22:52 Oct 31, 77)

CAPP, Al. If the strip (Li'l Abner) had any message at all, maybe that was it—leave the goddam world alone and we'll do fine (commenting on the end of Li'l Abner which ran for 43 years). (Newsweek 40:50 Oct 17, 77)

CAPP, Al. The martyrs at Kent State were the kids in National Guard uniforms. (Newsweek 90:50 Oct 17, 77)

CAPUTO, Philip J. The impetus or the impulse that makes people heroic in wars is the very thing that can make them monsters. (Chicago Tribune Magazine 23 Mar 19, 78)

CARAMANLIS, Constantine. So we Greeks have been from ancient times: we are skillful at making idols, not that we may worship them, but that we may have the pleasure of destroying them. (Time 110:51 Dec 5, 77)

CARDIN, Pierre. Chanel never influenced fashion one bit. (W 8:5 Mar 16, 79)

CARDIN, Pierre. I have to do things differently from anyone else. For that, they say I am crazy. (Chicago Tribune 286:24 Oct 13, 77)

CARDIN, Pierre. The jean. The jean is the destructor. It is a dictator. It is destroying creativity. The jean must be stopped. (People Weekly 5:41 June 28, 76)

CAREW, Rodney. I baby my bats, treat them like my kids, because using a bat is how I make my living. (Time 110:53 July 18, 77)

CAREY, Hugh. A hard worker but he is perceived otherwise (about Ted Kennedy). (New York Times 128:A18 Nov 22, 78)

CAREY, Hugh. I cannot deny that there is a contagion in New York which is about to sweep across the nation. (Time 106:9 Oct 20, 75)

CAREY, Hugh. I had only two hands all year and one was holding Abe Beame's. (Rolling Stone 207:30 Feb 26, 76)

CAREY, Hugh. It is not becoming of a President to create animosity among the people by pitting one section of the country against another (in response to President Ford's stand on aid to New York City). (Los Angeles Times 94:10 Part 1 Nov 8, 75)

CAREY, Hugh. It isn't fair when the President of the United States hauls off and kicks the people of the city of New York in the groin, and I'm going to fight back. (New York Times 125:1 Oct 31, 75)

CAREY, Hugh. My impression was that he (Jimmy Carter) has the Eleanor Roosevelt teeth and she (Rosalynn Carter) has the Eleanor Roosevelt brain. (Chicago Tribune 326:2 section 5 Nov 21, 76)

CAREY, Hugh. My mind doesn't govern my conscience, my conscience governs my mind. (New York Times 127:A1 April 6, 78)

CARLSON, Norman A. Until the behavioral sciences can give us clues as to what motivates the criminal offender, we cannot assure rehabilitation. All we can do is offer offenders the opportunity to rehabilitate themselves. (Behavior Today 7:4 Jan 5, 76)

CARLSON, Phil. Don't ever try to eat where they don't want to feed you. (Washingtonian 15:140 Nov 79)

CARMICHAEL, Stokely. The only position for women in the movement is prone. (New York Times Magazine 91 April 10, 77)

CARPENTER, Elizabeth. If John Connally had been around at the Alamo, he would have organized Texans for Santa Anna. (Texas Monthly 4:10 Sept 76)

CARR, Jesse. Being powerful is like being a lady. If you have to tell people you are, you ain't. (Newsweek 88:77 Sept 27, 76)

CARSWELL, James. Whenever man comes up with a better mousetrap, nature invariably comes up with a better mouse. (Omni 1:132 May 79)

CARTER, Billy. Ah cain't drink this here Reengold beer. The next vice president of the United States is the man who brings me a Pabst Blue Ribbon. (Washington Star 193:1 Section D July 13, 76)

CARTER, Billy. Bunch of damned hypocrites down there at that Baptist church. The only time I ever go is when one of the kids is baptized. (Chicago Tribune 326:5 Section 1 Nov 21, 76)

CARTER, Billy. I drink liquor out of a cup instead of out of the bottle now (commenting on how his life has been affected by his brother's candidacy for the Presidency). (Washington Post 323:B3 Oct 23, 76)

CARTER, Billy. I found out water can be drunk straight. (Chicago Sun-Times 32:2 April 24, 79)

CARTER, Billy. I know more about Libya than the whole State Department put together. I'm going to succeed just by treating them like folks. (Time 116:34 July 28, 80)

CARTER, Billy. I'm not the Carter that doesn't tell a lie. (Newsweek 88:24 Dec 6, 76)

CARTER, Billy. Jimmy will never tell me to change. His staff may bitch. But to hell with his damn staff. (Newsweek 90:37 Nov 14, 77)

CARTER, Billy. Marijuana is like Coors beer. If you could buy the damn stuff at a Georgia filling station, you'd decide you wouldn't want it. (Newsweek 90:33 Nov 14, 77)

CARTER, Billy. There's a helluva lot more Arabians than there is Jews. (Time 116:34 July 28, 80)

CARTER, Billy. Yes sir, I'm a real Southern boy. I got a red neck, white socks, and Blue Ribbon beer. (Chicago Tribune 326:5 Section 1 Nov 21, 76)

CARTER, Don. One of the advantages bowling has over golf is that you seldom lose a bowling ball. (Sports Illustrated 43:8 Aug 11, 75)

CARTER, Hodding, III. The thing you have to remember about Southerners is that we're always generous and forgiving—with our friends. (New York 9:28 July 26, 76)

CARTER, James Earl. All personal expenses are paid for out of my own pocket. (We are not) mooching off the American taxpayers (reacting to criticism of the fact that his married son and family live in the White House). (Time 109:10 Mar 14, 77)

CARTER, James Earl. The American people and our government will continue our firm commitment to promote respect for human rights not only in our own country but also abroad (to Andrei Sakharov). (Newsweek 89:17 Feb 28, 77)

CARTER, James Earl. Any claims or allegations that American Jewish leaders or anyone else urged me to ask Andy (Young) for his resignation are absolutely and totally false. (New York Times 129:B1 Sept 24, 79)

CARTER, James Earl. As is the case in time of war there is potential war profiteering in the impending energy crisis. This could develop with the passing months as the biggest rip-off in history. (New York Times 126:A16 Oct 14, 77)

CARTER, James Earl. Christ says don't consider yourself better than someone else because one guy screws a whole bunch of women while the other guy is loyal to his wife. (Chicago Sun-Times 29:2 Sept 21, 76)

CARTER, James Earl. Civil service reform will be the centerpiece of government reorganization during my term in office. (Washington Post Magazine 11 Dec 3, 78)

CARTER, James Earl. The corrosive effects of inflation eat away at ties that bind us together as a people. (New York Times 128:1 Jan 26, 79)

CARTER, James Earl. Doubts are the stuff of great decisions, but so are dreams. (Time 113:24 Mar 26, 79)

CARTER, James Earl. The duty of our generation of Americans is to renew our nation's faith—not focused just against foreign threats, but against the threat of selfishness, cynicism and apathy. (Time 113:10 Feb 5, 79)

CARTER, James Earl. A good old boy is somebody who's compatible with the group. I feel just as much at home around Billy's (his brother's) filling station as I do in the black Baptist Church, as I do with the big-shot Texas businessman. (New Times 7:72 July 23, 76)

CARTER, James Earl. (Hubert Humphrey) has been an inspiration and a conscience to us all. His greatest personal attribute was that he really knew how to love. (Time 111:21 Jan 23, 78)

CARTER, James Earl. I am against any creation of a separate Palestinian state. (Chicago Sun-Times 32:3 Aug 12, 79)

CARTER, James Earl. I can't resign from the human race because there's discrimination, and I don't intend to resign from my own church because there's discrimination. (Time 108:22 Nov 22, 76)

CARTER, James Earl. I guarantee I will not fight inflation with your jobs (to bulding trades tent meeting, San Diego, October 79). (Newsweek 94:48 Oct 22, 79)

CARTER, James Earl. I have never detected or experienced any conflict between God's will and my political duties. (Time 111:13 June 26, 78)

CARTER, James Earl. I have never met an Arab leader that in private professed the desire for an independent Palestinian state. (New York Times 128:21 Sept 1, 79)

CARTER, James Earl. I have nothing against a community that's made up of people who are Polish, Czechoslovakians, French Canadians or blacks who are trying to maintain the ethnic purity of their neighborhood. This is a natural inclination on the part of the people. (Guardian Weekly 117:15 Sept 11, 77)

CARTER, James Earl. I look on Senator Mondale, who will be the next Vice President, as my top staff person. (Newsweek 89:16 Jan 10, 77

CARTER, James Earl. I remember in this room last May someone asked me if my administration was all image and no substance, or style and no substance. Lately the criticisms have been that there is too much substance and not enough style. (New York Times 127:1 section 4 Oct 30, 77)

CARTER, James Earl. I think I earn it (referring to his $200,000 salary). (New York Times 126:A12 May 13, 77)

CARTER, James Earl. I think the government ought to stay out of the prayer business... (New York Times 128:2 April 8, 79)

CARTER, James Earl. I think the President is the only person who can change the direction or attitude of our nation. (Encore American & Worldwide News 5:4 June 21, 76)

CARTER, James Earl. I think the world economy is stable. (The Observer 9816:11 Oct 14, 79)

CARTER, James Earl. I would have a fairly steady stream of visitors, just average Americans...to come in and spend a night with us at the White House and eat supper with us. (Rolling Stone 234:39 Mar 10, 77)

CARTER, James Earl. I'd rather commit political suicide than hurt Israel. (Time 110:30-33 Oct 17, 77)

CARTER, James Earl. If I ever lie to you, if I ever betray you, then I want you to leave me (to political supporters). (Time 106:26 Oct 13, 75)

CARTER, James Earl. If Kennedy runs, I'll whip his ass. (Chicago Tribune 3:6 June 13, 79)

CARTER, James Earl. In war, we offer our very lives as a matter of routine. We must be no less daring, no less steadfast, in the pursuit of peace. (Time 113:12 Mar 26, 79)

CARTER, James Earl. Inflation has become embedded in the very tissue of our economy. (Time 111:66 April 24, 78)

CARTER, James Earl. (Jerry Brown) is California's way of celebrating the Year of the Child. (US News & World Report 86:6 May 14, 79)

CARTER, James Earl. The most important skill for any President is leadership. A national leader, to be effective, must have the ability to lead this country and the vision to know where it must be led. (American Legion Magazine 102:20 Feb 77)

CARTER, James Earl. My name is Jimmy Carter and I'm running for President of the United States. (Washington Post 224:A16 July 16, 76)

CARTER, James Earl. No one should mistake the energy problem for what it is—a fundamental crisis that threatens Americans and America's way of life. (Time 109:63 May 23, 77)

CARTER, James Earl. No poor, rural, weak, or black person should ever have to bear the additional burden of being deprived of the opportunity of an education, a job, or simple justice. (New York 9:57 July 19, 76)

CARTER, James Earl. Our people want a President to be both tough and gentle, both statesman and politician, both dreamer and fighter. You expect him to have the drive to reach the White House, and the wisdom and patience to govern wisely. (TV Guide 24:22 July 24, 76)

CARTER, James Earl. (Republicans are) men of narrow vision who are afraid of the future and whose leaders are inclined to shoot from the hip. (Time 116:13 July 28, 80)

CARTER, James Earl. The survival of Israel is not a political issue. It is a moral imperative. (Time 107:13 June 21, 76)

CARTER, James Earl. There are many things in life that are not fair. (Village Voice 23:11 Jan 2, 78)

CARTER, James Earl. There is nothing for nothing. (Newsweek 96:55 July 14, 80)

CARTER, James Earl. We are now free of that inordinate fear of Communism which once led us to embrace any dictator who joined us in our fear. (Time 107:9 June 6, 77)

CARTER, James Earl. We must face a time of national austerity. (US News & World Report 85:17 Nov 6, 78)

CARTER, James Earl. When I chop down this cherry tree it will be the first time I've chopped down a tree and told the truth about it (upon receiving the Atlanta Press Club's I-cannot-tell-a-lie-award). (Atlanta 16:28 June 28, 76)

CARTER, James Earl. When I finish my term, I want black people to say that I did more for them in my presidency than any other President in their lifetime. (Sepia 26:12 April 77)

CARTER, James Earl (Attributed by Robert Shrum). I'd be a pretty pathetic nominee if I wasn't able to get rid of Strauss as national chairman. (New York 9:54 July 5, 76)

CARTER, Lillian. How could Jimmy criticize me? I am his momma. (Life 2:140 Dec 79)

CARTER, Lillian. I don't know of anybody in my hometown who's destitute. I wouldn't let them be. (Chicago Tribune 225:1 section 5 Aug 13, 78)

CARTER, Lillian. I don't know why he (President Ford) ever chose Dole when there are so many capable men. I think he's a hatchet man, although he denies it. If he wins and should ever become President, I think I'm going to move to South America. (Washington Post 329:B3 Oct 29, 76)

CARTER, Lillian. I tried it once and it gave me diarrhea (about Billy Beer). (Chicago Daily News 13 Dec 30, 77)

CARTER, Lillian. I was born loving everybody. (Time 110:74 Oct 10, 77)

CARTER, Lillian. I'm not a city person, I'm a country hick. (Newsweek 88:39 July 26, 76)

CARTER, Lillian. Jimmy's not sexy, he's my son. (People Weekly 13:114 Mar 3, 80)

CARTER, Lillian. Marriage ain't easy but nothing that's worth much ever is. (Chicago Sun-Times 32:33 July 16, 79)

CARTER, Lillian. Sometimes when I look at all my children, I say to myself, 'Lillian, you should have stayed a virgin'. (Time 116:93 Sept 15, 80)

CARTER, Rosalynn. I don't mind being called tough. I am strong, and I do have definite ideas and opinions. In the sense that 'tough' means I can take a lot, stand up to a lot, it's a fair description (responding to being called the Steel Magnolia). (People Weekly 6:25 Nov 15, 76)

CARTER, Rosalynn. I find myself in the eye of history. I have influence. And I know it. (New York Times Magazine 39 June 3, 79)

CARTER, Rosalynn. I have always been more political than (Jimmy). (Time 114:13 Aug 6, 79)

CARTER, Rosalynn. I've always worked hard, and that's why they call me 'The Steel Magnolia'. (Maclean's 89:8 Nov 29, 76)

CARTER, Rosalynn. Jimmy taught me a long time ago that you do the best you can and don't worry about the criticisms. Once you accept the fact that you're not perfect then you develop some confidence. (Newsweek 94:47 Nov 5, 79)

CARTER, Rosalynn. The President of the United States cares what I think. (Time 113:22 May 7, 79)

CARTER, Rosalynn. When people ask me about Jimmy being a Baptist, and indicate they feel no Baptist can run the country, I just remind them that Harry Truman was a Baptist, and I think he did a great job. (W 5:16 July 23, 76)

CARTER, Rubin (Hurricane). The kindest thing I can say about my childhood is that I survived it. (Chicago Sun-Times 28:86 Dec 16, 75)

CARTIER-BRESSON, Henri. The camera is a weapon. It's not a propaganda means, but it's a way of shouting the way you feel.... It's an affirmation. It's like the last three words of 'Ulysses' of James Joyce. It's 'Yes, yes, yes!'. (Christian Science Monitor 69:25 Jan 10, 77)

CARTIER-BRESSON, Henri. For me the camera is an instrument of intuition and spontaneity, the master of the instant. (The Times 8104:5 Nov 5, 78)

CARTLAND, Barbara. Being 18 is like visiting Russia. You're glad you've had the experience, but you'd never want to repeat it. (The Observer 9764:14 Oct 15, 78)

CARTLAND, Barbara. I'm the only author with 200 virgins in print. (Town & Country 131:144 Dec 77)

CASALS, Pablo. The truly important things in life— love, beauty and one's own uniqueness—are constantly being overlooked. (Forbes 119:312 May 15, 77)

CASH, Johnny. I guess the record shows I'm far from perfect—but I want to keep trying. (US News & World Report 84:60 Feb 27, 78)

CASSIDY, Shaun. I'm no different from what I was before, except that people ask for my autograph and tear off my clothes. (Chicago Sun-Times 31:6 April 18, 78)

CASTANEDA, Jorge. We would like to see the U.S. treat us (Mexico) as an adult country capable of managing our own affairs. (Newsweek 94:26 Oct 1, 79)

CASTRO, Fidel. I don't think the contradictions between capitalism and socialism can be resolved by war. This is no longer the age of the bow and arrow. It's the nuclear age, and war can annihilate us all. The only way to achieve solutions seems to be for the different social systems to coexist. (Seven Days 1:17 June 20, 77)

CASTRO, Fidel. Men are very fragile. We disappear and go up in smoke for almost any reason. (Time 107:51 Jan 5, 76)

CATER, Douglass. If power corrupts, being out of power corrupts absolutely. (Book Digest 6:32 Dec 79)

CEAUSESCU, Nicolae. We are an independent Rumania and we will always remain an independent Rumania. (New York Times 128:A10 Nov 30, 78)

CERF, Bennett. Everyone has a streak of pure, unadulterated ham. Many won't admit it. I revel in it. (Time 110:68 Aug 22, 77)

CEZANNE, Paul. I am the primitive of the method I have invented. (Newsweek 40:78 Oct 17, 77)

CEZANNE, Paul. Painting from nature is not copying the object; it is realizing one's sensations. (Time 110:85 Oct 17, 77)

CHABROL, Claude. I ask audiences to contemplate a character, not identify with him. (Time 106:76 Sept 29, 75)

CHAGALL, Marc. I love life more now than I did as a boy, and I will go on loving it more until my last moments. (Time 110:40 July 18, 77)

CHAGALL, Marc. Me, I do not understand Chagall. (Time 109:95 May 23, 77)

CHAGALL, Marc. My greatest weakness is America. (People Weekly 6:18 Aug 2, 76)

CHAMBERS, Marilyn. Maybe I'll make a Mary Poppins movie and shove the umbrella up my ass. (Playboy 26:26 Oct 79)

CHAMFORT, Nicholas. The success of many books is due to the affinity between the mediocrity of the author's ideas and those of the public. (Kansas City Times 109:14B July 8, 77)

CHANCELLOR, John. Eric (Sevareid) never told people what he thought, but what he learned. (Time 110:111 Dec 12, 77)

CHANCELLOR, John. Television is good at the transmission of experience. Print is better at the transmission of facts. (Time 115:71 Feb 25, 80)

CHANDLER, A. B. (Happy). We Americans are a peculiar people. We are for the underdog no matter how much of a dog he is. (Reader's Digest 107:78 Nov 75)

CHANDLER, Raymond. Bogart can be tough without a gun. Also he has a sense of humor that contains that grating undertone of contempt. Bogart is the genuine article. (American Film 1:68 April 76)

CHANDLER, Raymond. Every story I write is a fire for you to warm your hands by. (Chicago Tribune 254:4 section 3 Sept 11, 78)

CHANDLER, Raymond. If my books had been any worse, I should not have been invited to Hollywood...if they had been any better, I should not have come. (Bookviews 1:21 April 78)

CHANEL, Coco. Youth is something very new: twenty years ago no one mentioned it. (Chicago Tribune 176:2 section II June 25, 78)

CHAPLIN, Charles Spencer. I am known in parts of the world by people who have never heard of Jesus Christ. (Chicago Tribune 58:12 Feb 27, 78)

CHAPLIN, Charles Spencer. I can't understand Karl Marx, so how can I be a Communist? (Guardian Weekly 118:5 Jan 1, 78)

CHAPLIN, Charles Spencer. I never thought of the tramp in terms of appeal. He was myself, a comic spirit, something within me that I said I must express. (Chicago Tribune 360:2 Dec 26, 77)

CHAPLIN, Charles Spencer. Life is a tragedy when seen in close-up, but a comedy in long-shot. (Guardian Weekly 118:5 Jan 1, 78)

CHAPLIN, Charles Spencer. My prodigious sin was and still is, being a nonconformist. Although I am not a Communist, I refused to fall in line by hating them. (Guardian Weekly 118:5 Jan 1, 78)

CHAPLIN, Charles Spencer. One cannot do humor without great sympathy for one's fellow man. As the tramp I think I endeared myself through his terrific humility.... (Chicago Tribune 360:2 Dec 26, 77)

CHAPMAN, Marshall. As far as I'm concerned, feminists have done to women what the Baptists did to religion. (Stereo Review 41:90 Dec 78)

CHAPMAN, Robert W. A quotation, like a pun, should come unsought, and then be welcomed only for some propriety or felicity justifying the intrusion (from "The Art of Quotation"). (Writer's Digest 57:11 May 77)

CHARLES, PRINCE OF WALES, . Falling madly in love with someone is not necessarily the starting point to getting married. (Cosmopolitan 188:268 Feb 80)

CHARLES, PRINCE OF WALES, . I've fallen in love with all sorts of girls—and I fully intend to go on doing so. It's very important to find the right partner. In my position, obviously, the last thing I could possibly entertain is getting divorced. (Los Angeles Times 94:2 Part 1 Nov 12, 75)

CHARLES, PRINCE OF WALES, . Much of British management does not seem to understand the human factor. (The Observer 9783:11 Feb 25, 79)

CHARLES, PRINCE OF WALES, . What I really need is a good wife. (The Observer 9797:10 June 3, 79)

CHARLES, PRINCE OF WALES, . Women's liberationists rather annoy me because they tend to argue all the time and start calling you a male chauvinist pig and, frankly, it becomes rather uncivilized. (Los Angeles Times 94:2 Part 1 Nov 18, 75)

CHARO, . It doesn't bother me if I'm called dumb but I do resent it if I'm called slow. You should see how quickly I learned the way to the bank. (The Star 4:2 Aug 30, 77)

CHAVEZ, Cesar. We will win in the end. We learned many years ago that the rich may have the money, but the poor have the time. (Newsweek 86:67B Sept 22, 75)

CHAYEFSKY, Paddy. Television is democracy at it's ugliest. (New York Times 126:18 Section 2 Nov 14, 76)

CHEEVER, John. Actually, male or female, what a writer has to have are an extraordinary memory, a marvelous ear, and a passion for bringing disparities together. MS 5:77 April 77)

CHEEVER, John. Fiction is our most intimate and acute means of communication. (US News & World Report 86:92 May 21, 79)

CHEEVER, John. If you are an artist, self-destruction is quite expected of you. (Time 112:125 Oct 16, 78)

CHEEVER, John. It (plot) is a calculated attempt to hold the reader's interest at the sacrifice of moral conviction. (Esquire 90:35 Nov 21, 78)

CHEEVER, John. Literature is much more a conversation than a discourse. (US News & World Report 86:92 May 21, 79)

CHENEY, Richard B. Basically, I am skeptical about the ability of government to solve problems, and I have a healthy respect for the ability of people to solve problems on their own. (Washington Post 336:A3 Nov 6, 75)

CHER, . I left him for a woman: me (commenting on her divorce from Sonny Bono). (People Weekly 4:35 Dec 29/Jan 5, 76)

CHESTERTON, Gilbert Keith. Optimism: the noble temptation to see too much in everything. (Kansas City Times 109:14B July 8, 77)

CHEVALIER, Maurice. Old age is a wonderful thing...when you consider the alternative. (Saturday Evening Post 251:40 Mar 79)

CHILD, Julia. Life itself is the proper binge. (Cosmopolitan 180:178 May 76)

CHILES, Lawton M., Jr. Half of the reporters in town are looking on you as a Pulitzer Prize to be won (about being a senator). (Time 111:10-11 Jan 23, 78)

CHILES, Lawton M., Jr. Secrecy in government has become synonymous, in the public mind, with deception by the government. (Christian Science Monitor 67:3 Nov 4, 75)

CHRISTIE, Agatha. If I could write like Elizabeth Bowen, Muriel Spark or Graham Greene, I should jump to high heaven with delight, but I know that I can't. (Time 110:127-32 Nov 28, 77)

CHURCH, Frank. If we are to preserve freedom and keep constitutional government alive in America, it cannot be left to a President and his agents alone to decide what must be kept secret. Congress, if it is to check the abuse of executive power, must retain its right to inquiry and independent judgement. (Washington Post 73:A15 Feb 17, 76)

CHURCH, Frank. I've accomplished about all I can in a senatorial career. If SALT II is grounds for my defeat, so be it. (Human Events 39:2 June 16, 79)

CHURCH, Frank. The Presidency is no place for on-the-job training. I've always advocated the politics of substance, not the politics of style. (Encore American & Worldwide News 5:4 June 21, 76)

CHURCHILL, Sir Winston. Don't argue the difficulties. They argue for themselves. (Christian Science Monitor 69:15 June 27, 77)

CHURCHILL, Sir Winston. Foster Dulles is the only case I know of a bull who carries his china shop with him. (Time 111:83 Feb 27, 78)

CHURCHILL, Sir Winston. It (democracy) is the worst system—except for all those other systems that have been tried and failed. (Time 106:63 July 14, 75)

CHURCHILL, Sir Winston. Russia is a riddle wrapped in an enigma. (Village Voice 22:77 Nov 28, 77)

CHURCHILL, Sir Winston. You don't make the poor richer by making the rich poorer. (To The Point International 3:39 Nov 1, 76)

CHURCHILL, Sir Winston (attributed by Michael Korda). Willie (W. Somerset Maugham) may be an old bugger, but by God, he's never tried to bugger me. (Newsweek 94:105 Nov 5, 79)

CIARDI, John. Early to bed and early to rise probably indicates unskilled labor. (Kansas City Star 97:2D Feb 20, 77)

CIARDI, John. Love is the word used to label the sexual excitement of the young, the habituation of the middle-aged, and the mutual dependence of the old. (Chicago Tribune 212:1 section II July 31, 78)

CLAIBORNE, Craig. I think that some people, and I suspect a great number of people, are born with the gustatory equivalent of perfect pitch. (New York Times 126:C6 Nov 22, 76)

CLARK, Alan. Librarians are standing in their graves. (New York Times 128:26 April 8, 79)

CLARK, Alex. It's always darkest just before the lights go out. (Washingtonian 14:152 Nov 78)

CLARK, Joe. If I walked on water, people would say it was because I couldn't swim. (New York Times 129:2 section E Feb 17, 80)

CLARK, Joseph. A leader should not get too far in front of his troops or he will be shot in the ass. (Washingtonian 15:140 Nov 79)

CLARK, Kenneth. Integration is a painful job. It is social therapy, and like personal therapy it is not easy. (Time 106:14 Sept 22, 75)

CLARK, Ramsey. The Democratic Party is a party in name only, not in shared belief. (Time 116:12 Aug 25, 80)

CLARKE, Arthur C. Any sufficiently advanced technology is undistinguishable from magic. (Omni 2:87 April 80)

CLARKE, Arthur C. Experience has shown that the most important results of any technological breakthrough are those that are not obvious. (American Film 2:67 Oct 76)

CLARKE, Arthur C. The facts of the future can hardly be imagined ab initio by those who are unfamiliar with the fantasies of the past. (Omni 2:94 April 80)

CLARKE, Arthur C. The only way to find the limits of the possible is by going beyond them to the impossible. (Omni 2:85 April 80)

CLARKE, Arthur C. The time may come when men control the destinies of the stars. (Time 114:27 July 26, 79)

CLARKE, Arthur C. When a distinguished but elderly scientist says that something is possible he is almost certainly right. When he says it is impossible, he is very probably wrong. (Omni 2:82 April 80)

CLAY, William. Whenever I see certain elements in the press show favoritism to a Black man running for a position of power, I know there's a nigger in the woodpile somewhere. (Sepia 26:10 May 76)

CLEAVER, Eldridge. Black people need to realize very fundamentally that they are full and equal citizens of the U.S. We can no longer 'fence straddle' about where we are going. We're as much a part of the United States as any Rockefeller. (Sepia 25:12 Sept 76)

CLEAVER, Eldridge. A black pig, a white pig, a yellow pig, a pink pig—a dead pig is the best pig of all. We encourage people to kill them (in 1970). (Newsweek 85:40 Mar 17, 75)

CLEAVER, Eldridge. If it came down to the choice between a woman and a radio, I'd choose a radio. It brings the outside world in. (Sepia 24:12 June 75)

CLEAVER, Eldridge. Prison holds no terror for me (upon his return to the US from self imposed exile). (Washington Post 348:A15 Nov 18, 75)

CLEAVER, Kathleen. I'm older and wiser. I've lost my romanticism about revolution in America. I don't say it's inconceivable, but I know that none of us who believed ourselves to be revolutionaries in the '60s can conceive of the form a revolution would take in America. (Christian Science Monitor 68:2 Dec 22, 75)

CLEMENS, Samuel Langhorne. The best way to cheer yourself up is to try to cheer somebody else up. (Kansas City Times 109:12H Dec 9, 76)

CLEMENS, Samuel Langhorne. Never put off till tomorrow what you can do the day after tomorrow. (San Francisco Chronicle This World 1978:40 Jan 29, 78)

CLEMENS, Samuel Langhorne. Only kings, editors, and people with tapeworms have the right to use the editorial 'we'. (Omni 1:131 May 79)

CLEMENS, Samuel Langhorne. There is something fascinating about science. One gets such wholesale returns of conjecture out of such trifling investments of fact. (Omni 2:37 April 80)

CLEMENTS, Bill. My opponent is in for a real fracas. If he thinks it's going to be some kind of cakewalk, I will assure you he's gotten hold of a hot enchilada. (D Magazine 5:21 June 78)

CLEVELAND, Grover. While the people should patriotically and cheerfully support their government, its functions do not include the support of the people (inaugural address—1893). (Christian Science Monitor 69:14 Jan 20, 77)

CLIFFORD, Clark. Jimmy Carter has the best mind of any President I have known. (Time 110:16 Oct 3, 77)

CLINE, Ray S. The First Amendment is not the central purpose of our Constitution. (More 8:Feb 78) Feb 78

CLINE, Ray S. The only unrestricted intelligence organization in this country is the American press. (Time 106:10 Aug 4, 75)

CLOSE, Del (Director of Chicago's Second City). Laughter is a response to a gestalt formation where two previously incompatible or dissimilar ideas suddenly form into a new piece of understanding—the energy released during that reaction comes out in laughter. (New Times 10:42 Jan 9, 78)

COBB, Irvin S. I'd rather be late for supper in this world tonight than be in some other world on time for breakfast in the morning. (Kansas City Times 109:11B Feb 4, 77)

COCA, Imogene. I've never figured out why we work so well together, except that we both laugh at exactly the same time. (about herself and Sid Caesar). (Time 110:98 Sept 19, 77)

COCHRANE, Elizabeth. Life can be a great adventure and I'm going to make it one. (Amer Legion Magazine 100:16 June 76)

COCKBURN, Alexander. Descriptions of sin are what we want at the breakfast table, not admonitions against it. (Village Voice 23:13 Jan 9, 78)

COCKBURN, Claud. Never underestimate the effectiveness of a straight cash bribe. (Village Voice 21:39 Oct 4, 76)

COFFIN, William Sloane. If you get an Evangelical with a social conscience you've got one of God's true saints. (Time 110:58 Dec 26, 77)

COHEN, Mark B. Nothing can so alienate a voter from the political system as backing a winning candidate. (Washingtonian 14:152 Nov 78)

COHEN, Richard. The best stories never check out. (The Nation 231:663 Dec 20, 80)

COHEN, William. Congress is designed to be slow and inefficient because it represents the total diversity of this country. (Time 105:22 June 9, 75)

COHN, Roy. I only hope that this country remains a place where Steve (Rubell) and I can build what's become a great institution in America and in the world. (W 8:12 Feb 2, 79)

COHODAS, Howard L. If it looks too good to be true, it is too good to be true. (Washingtonian 15:151 Nov 79)

COLBERT, Jean Baptiste. The art of taxation consists in so plucking the goose as to obtain the largest possible amount of feathers with the smallest possible amount of hissing. (Time 111:19 April 17, 78)

COLBY, William Egan. America got into Viet Nam and then decided that there are some things we can't do. Well, I think we didn't do it right. But I think we could have done it. (Time 107:17 Jan 19, 76)

COLBY, William Egan. By the way, *did* you ever work for the CIA? (to Bob Woodward upon agreeing to issue an official denial that Woodward had ever worked for the CIA). (New York 8:50 July 28, 75)

COLBY, William Egan. (Daniel Schorr) carried out his obligation to the first amendment to the Constitution and to himself as a newsman and should not be punished (commenting the release of the secret House report on United States intelligence operations). (New York Times 125:39 Mar 31, 76)

COLBY, William Egan. From the draft of the committee report that I have seen and the news stories about it, I believe it is totally biased and a disservice to our nation (referring to the report by the House Select Committee on Intelligence). (New York Times 125:1 Jan 27, 76)

COLBY, William Egan. I have definitional problems with the word violence. I don't know what the word violence means. (Rolling Stone 196:32 Sept 25, 75)

COLBY, William Egan. I'm convinced it's possible to run a secret agency as part of a constitutional society. (Time 107:17 Jan 19, 76)

COLE, Edward N. Kick the hell out of the status quo. (Time 109:87 May 16, 77)

COLETTE, Sidonie Gabrielle Claudine. It is not a bad thing that children should occasionally, and politely, put parents in their place. (Chicago Tribune 176:2 section II June 25, 78)

COLICOS, John. Over the years I have discovered that villains are like blonds—they have more fun (commenting on playing a TV villain). (Chicago Tribune 227:18 Aug 15, 78)

COLLINS, John Churton. Half the mistakes in life arise from feeling where we ought to think, and thinking where we ought to feel. (Rocky Mountain News 319:72 Mar 6, 80)

COLLINS, Judy. Aging does have its rewards. (Newsweek 93:79 Mar 12, 79)

COLSON, Charles Wendell. I would do anything that Richard Nixon asks me to do. (Time 103:13 Mar 11, 74)

COLSON, Charles Wendell. The only good guys to emerge from Watergate are those self-justified, upright fellows writing their own accounts. Since everyone has written a book, the sum of all the books is that no one was guilty, just everyone else.... (National Review 30:474 April 14, 78)

COMFORT, Alex. Nobody is safe being prejudiced against what they themselves are going to become (commenting on aging). (New York Times 126:24 Oct 25, 76)

COMINS, David H. People will accept your idea more readily if you tell them Benjamin Franklin said it first. (Washingtonian 14:152 Nov 78)

COMMONER, Barry. Our system today no more resembles free enterprise than a freeway resembles a dirt road. (Time 114:19 Aug 13, 79)

COMMONER, Barry. When you fully understand the situation it is worse than you think. (Life 2:170 Dec 79)

COMPTON-BURNETT, Ivy. We must use words as they are used or stand aside from life. (Time 111:36 Jan 2, 78)

CONABLE, Barber. Arthur (Burns) is a great politician. He is a master of the pregnant pause. He knows when to clean his pipe. He can answer the most complicated questions with 'I doubt it', and the world is thunderstruck with his wisdom. When he comes to testify before any committee (of Congress), the whole committee shows up. He has the same effect on the members that Henry Kissinger had. He seems to be right. (Time 110:13 Dec 26, 77)

CONABLE, Barber. The country still views him (Gerald Ford) as the guy who is filling the gap between Watergate and the next election. (Newsweek 86:23 Dec 22, 75)

CONABLE, Barber. The trouble with Carter is he's listening only to God—and God doesn't pay taxes. (Time 111:11 May 1, 78)

CONDON, Richard. I'm a man of the marketplace as well as an artist. I am a pawnbroker of myth. (New York Times Magazine 45 Sept 2, 79)

CONNALLY, John. He (Ronald Reagan) communicates with his constituents, and they fill in the blanks. He leaves a thought with people that they can flesh out. (Time 116:13 July 28, 80)

CONNALLY, John Bowden. All hat and no cattle (about George Bush). (Kansas City Times 112:A15 July 23, 80)

CONNALLY, John Bowden. I don't subscribe to the notion that everyone around President Nixon was tarnished. (New York 12:8 July 9, 79)

CONNALLY, John Bowden. I have very few close friends. (Time 114:21 Sept 10, 79)

CONNALLY, John Bowden. I hope as long as I live I never lose the desire to participate in public affairs. I've seen the system work today and it has made me more deeply committed to preserving the system (upon his acquittal on bribery charges). (Harper's Weekly 3123:4 May 2, 75)

CONNALLY, John Bowden. The power of this country, in spite of all the misconceptions that exist, is in the Congress of the United States and not in the White House. (US News & World Report 86:30 July 2, 79)

CONNALLY, John Bowden. There's a little larceny in the hearts of all of us. (New York 12:8 July 9, 79)

CONNALLY, John Bowden (attributed by Henry Alfred Kissinger). You will be measured in (Washington D.C.) by the enemies you destroy. The bigger they are, the bigger you are. (Time 114:45 Oct 8, 79)

CONNALLY, Mark (son of John Connally). I've seen the political life and I don't want it. (W 5:16 July 23, 76)

CONNER, Caryl. All avocados in all stores will always be rock-hard the day you want to make guacamole. (Washingtonian 14:26 Dec 78)

CONNOLLY, Cyril. Imprisoned in every fat man a thin one is wildly signalling to be let out. (Newsweek 85:74B Jan 20, 75)

CONNOLLY, Cyril. Nothing dates like hate. (Village Voice 22:52 Oct 31, 77)

CONRAD, Joseph. The sea is not my subject. Mankind is my subject. (Newsweek 93:74 Feb 19, 79)

COOKS, Stoney (aide to Andrew Young). Liberals want to do it for you. Southerners want to do it with you (commenting on the Carter administration's attempt to involve minorities in the government). (New York Times Magazine 19 Feb 6, 77)

COOLEY, Denton. A successful surgeon should be a man who, when asked to name the three best surgeons in the world, would have difficulty deciding on the other two. (Atlantic 244:56 Sept 79)

COOLIDGE, Calvin. I think the American public wants a solemn ass as a President. And I think I'll go along with them. (New York Times 128:C26 Feb 23, 79)

COOPER, Chester L. There are a lot of ambitious guys who are neither bright nor able, yet they do well. The guy who's willing to cancel his wife's birthday party is the guy who's likely to become an assistant secretary of state. (Washington Post 205:C4 June 27, 76)

COOVER, Robert. You make a million or you don't even get printed. (New Times 8:53 Aug 19, 77)

COPLAND, Aaron. Conducting is a real sport. You can never guarantee what the results are going to be, so there's always an element of chance. That keeps it exciting. (Time 112:96 Sept 18, 78)

COPLAND, Aaron. The ideal listener, above all else, possesses the ability to lend himself to the power of music. (Washington Post 352:G1 Nov 21, 76)

CORCORAN, Thomas. Whenever this town loses positive direction, it means something is struggling to be born in the nation—there is a wind coming (about Washington, D.C.). (Time 106:9 Sept 1, 75)

CORRIGAN, Mairead. Our world is rushing towards disaster. But it's not too late to prove the power of love...we've got to prove that the way of nonviolence can bring social change (from her Nobel Peace Prize acceptance speech). (Los Angeles Times 97:4 part 1 Dec 11, 77)

CORRY, Carolyn M. Paper is always strongest at the perforations. (Omni 1:132 May 79)

CORSARO, Frank. Of course my productions are vulgar. Theater itself is vulgar. (Esquire 90:63 Sept 26, 78)

COSELL, Howard. I think the Moscow Games will be a disaster—and the last Olympics. (Newsweek 88:51 Aug 9, 76)

COSELL, Howard. Indiana should be No. 1. They probably have a bigger payroll than the New York Knicks. (Chicago Tribune 123:3 Section 3 May 2, 76)

COSTA-GAVRAS, . Film is the only way now to reach out to people all around the world. The time of the book is over. (Village Voice 20:106 Dec 8, 75)

COSTANZA, Midge. I'd like to take the two of them (Anita Bryant and Phyllis Schlafly) and make bookends. (New York Times 127:22 April 4, 78)

COUGHLIN, J. Walter (secret service agent for President Johnson). Once, the President and I rode up and down on the White House elevator 21 times because the door wouldn't open, he fired me 42 times before we got out. I finally said, 'I tell you what, Mr. President, you get me off this thing and I'll quit.'. (Los Angeles Times 94:2 Part 1 Nov 5, 75)

COULSON, Gail. In South Africa all of us, for one reason or another, are living behind bars—blacks and whites, good guys, bad guys, everybody. (Chicago Sun-Times 29:40 June 19, 76)

COUNTRYMAN, Vernon (Harvard professor). The bar is still dominated by shortsightedness and self-interest. Spotting change there is like watching a glacier move. (Time 110:52 Aug 8, 77)

COURT, Margaret. I will not play any more tournament tennis. If I had been meant to play tennis again, God would have led me to it (commenting upon her permanent retirement from tennis). (New York Times 125:42 April 23, 76)

COUSINS, Norman. History is an accumulation of error. (Saturday Review 5:13 April 15, 78)

COUSINS, Norman. A hospital is no place for a person who is seriously ill. (Time 115:71 June 30, 80)

COUSINS, Norman. I am no pessimist. I doubt that any man knows enough to be a pessimist. (Saturday Review 5:12 April 15, 78)

COUSINS, Norman. Infinity converts the possible into the inevitable. (Saturday Review 5:18 April 15, 78)

COUSINS, Norman. Life is an adventure in forgiveness. (Saturday Review 5:12 April 15, 78)

COUSTEAU, Jacques Yves. I don't know what to expect. I wouldn't do it if I did. But we know there is something there, and now our task is to find out what (commenting on his search for the legendary lost continent of Atlantis off Greece). (People Weekly 4:76 Nov 17, 75)

COUSTEAU, Jacques Yves. Today I don't swim at all because I haven't the time to go 10 to 12 miles offshore to find clean water. (Washington Post 226:B2 July 19, 77)

COWLEY, Malcolm. Conrad Aiken remained just a heavy drinker until he died at 84. By that time he had possibly consumed more gin than anyone else in the world. (Writer's Digest 58:26 Oct 78)

COWLEY, Malcolm. No complete son-of-a-bitch ever wrote a good sentence. (Inquiry 1:28 July 24, 78)

COWLEY, Malcolm. One compensation of age is simply sitting still. (Life 1:77 Dec 78)

COZZENS, James Gould. The longer I watch men and life, the surer I get that success whenever more than minor comes of luck alone. By comparison, no principles, ideas, goals, and standards of conduct matter much in an achieving of it. (New York Times 127:39 July 30, 78)

CRAMER, Jerome. Schools are now asked to do what people used to ask God to do. (Time 115:59 June 16, 80)

CRANE, Philip. If you asked central casting in Hollywood for somebody to play the role of President, they'd send you John Connally. (US News & World Report 86:29 July 2, 79)

CRANE, Philip. It is suicidal to pay the bills for an organization (the United Nations) whose goal has become world revolution, the stimulation of terrorist violence, and the destruction of the West. (American Opinion 18:29 Nov 75)

CRANE, Philip. It's always better to stand on your principles and lose than to lose your principles and win. (Newsweek 93:37 Mar 19, 79)

CRANSON, Maurice. (Government is) a necessary evil that allows for tyranny by the collectivity over the individual. (Time 110:57 July 25, 77)

CRAWFORD, Joan. Growing old is no fun. Frankly, if they (senior citizens) say they enjoy it, I think they're either lying through their teeth or they've grown senile. (Chicago Sun-Times 30:6 July 21, 77)

CRESPI, Consuelo. In Italy now you want to feel rich and look poor. (Time 111:53 May 15, 78)

CRICHTON, Michael. I find facts inhibiting....The more you know, the more you are obliged to the truth. I much prefer not to know. (New York Times 128:17 section 2 Jan 28, 79)

CRICHTON, Michael. I think we can all agree that American medicine, the way it is now, is not successful. But there's no evidence that the Government can run anything. If you like the Post Office, you'll like socialized medicine. (Time 111:91 Jan 9, 78)

CRISP, Mary D. We are about to bury the rights of over 100 million American women under a heap of platitudes. (New York Times 129:B1 July 10, 80)

CRISP, Quenton. The English think incompetence is the same thing as sincerity. (New York Times 126:7 section 12 Jan 30, 77)

CROCE, Arlene. Reviewing should function like a Food and Drug Administration, even if that function is largely futile. Time 111:71 Jan 9, 78

CRONKITE, Walter. It is not the reporter's job to be a patriot or to presume to determine where patriotism lies. His job is to relate the facts. (Time 115:60 Feb 11, 80)

CRONKITE, Walter. The very constraint against taking positions is a mark of the professional in journalism, not letting opinions impact on reporting. I've spent a lifetime suppressing them. (Time 115:78 May 12, 80)

CROSBY, Bing. Family life is the basis for a strong community and a great nation. (National Catholic Reporter 12:8 July 2, 76)

CROSBY, Bing. He was an average guy who could carry a tune (on his epitaph). (Newsweek 90:102 Oct 24, 77)

CROSBY, Bing. It (show business) has been my life for 50 years. It's been a long, long pull and I've had great results. I can't complain if it stops tomorrow. (Newsweek 90:101 Oct 24, 77)

CROSS, George L. We want to build a university the football team can be proud of. (Chicago Sun-Times 32:69 Nov 8, 79)

CROUCH, Dee. At 18,000 feet, you're roughly half as smart as you are at sea level. The lore is that you don't come back from the mountain as smart as when you go up (commenting on the effect of high altitude on the human brain by the doctor with the American Bicentennial Expedition to Mt. Everest). (New York Times 126:44 Oct 23, 76)

CRUZ, Francisco Rodriguez. The biggest crime in Cuba is to think. (Newsweek 95:31 May 26, 80)

CULVER, John C. Teddy (Kennedy) doesn't want to be President; he just doesn't want anybody else to be President. (Newsweek 94:29 Sept 24, 79)

CUMMINGS, Sam. The arms business is founded on human folly. That is why its depths will never be plumbed, and why it will go on forever. (Esquire 90:64 Mar 1, 78)

CUMMINGS, Sam. The plainest print cannot be read through a solid gold sovereign—or a ruble or a golden eagle (about attempts to control arms exports). (Esquire 89:64 Mar 1, 78)

CUMMINGS, Sam. There are huge new markets opening up; soon there will be the rearming of China, as everybody knows. And then Russia. And then Europe again. There's no end to it. (Esquire 89:69 Mar 1, 78)

CUNNINGHAM, Imogen. In my professional life as a portrait photographer, I've found very often people can't face themselves. They can't live with the faces they were born with. It's not a nice occupation to try to please people with their faces. (Art in America 65:42 May/June 77)

CURTIS, Carl Thomas. In the whole history of the world, whenever a meateating race has gone to war against a non-meateating race, the meat eaters won. It produces superior people. (Washingtonian 11:22-23 Dec 75)

CURTIS, John. Between owners and players, a manager today has become a wishbone. (Sports Illustrated 47:18 July 18, 77)

CURTIS, Tony. There's simply no other way for a man to feel his manliness, his kingliness if you will, than to be loved by a beautiful woman. (The Observer 9778:10 Jan 21, 79)

CZAPKO, Laura. No child throws up in the bathroom. (Omni 1:131 May 79)

DALEY, Richard J. But then you can never go as low as a newspaper. A newspaper is the lowest thing there is. (Newsweek 85:55 May 5, 75)

DALEY, Richard J. He's a young man with his whole future in front of him. You can't blame anyone for being a candidate. (Newsweek 88:46 July 26, 76)

DALEY, Richard J. If anything happens to me, you guys stick together. I'm telling you—you guys stick together or everything we've worked for together will be for nothing. (Chicago Sun-Times 32:8 Mar 4, 79)

DALEY, Richard J. It is amazing what they will be able to do once they get the atom harassed. (Chicago Sun-Times 32:57 Mar 21, 79)

DALEY, Richard J. The police are not here to create disorder. They are here to preserve disorder (commenting during the 1968 Democratic Convention in Chicago). (Time 108:46 Jan 3, 77)

DALEY, Richard J. These organizations are fine and legitimate. But what is the matter with (the police) having people in there? (Explaining the secret infiltration of civic organizations by the Chicago Police Department). (Chicago Tribune 316:1 Section 1 Nov 12, 75)

DALEY, Richard J. Together we must rise to higher and higher platitudes. (Time 108:46 Jan 3, 77)

DALI, Salvador. The difference between a madman and me is that I am not mad. (Time 115:76 Mar 3, 80)

DALTREY, Roger. The last thing I wanted to do was have a fist fight with Pete Townshend. Unfortunately, he hit me first with a guitar. (Creem 7:38 Nov 75)

DANN, Mike. (Jackie) Gleason's one of the most versatile people in the business. He's so brilliant, he's always depressed and bored. Maybe that's why he never seemed to enjoy performing. (Chicago Tribune Magazine 17 Mar 26, 78)

DARBOUZE, FATHER, . Dying of hunger and being executed by the government are the same thing. (Newsweek 96:31 July 7, 80)

DASMANN, Raymond F. We are hooked like junkies, dependent on the drug of wasteful consumption. (New York Times 126:A18 Dec 1, 76)

DAVIES, Denzil. Oil is a wasting asset, and if you don't invest (its revenues) in profitable assets, you'll be left with nothing. (Newsweek 96:60 July 14, 80)

DAVIES, Gavin. Like even the best wonder drug, North Sea oil has side effects we (British) don't like. (Newsweek 96:60 July 14, 80)

DAVIS, Angela. I'm not pessimistic about change in this country. I'm convinced that this country will one day be socialist.   (New York 11:43 April 17, 78)

DAVIS, Bette. I divide women into two categories. The female and the broad. Me? I'm a broad. (Time 112:Oct 23, 78) Oct 23, 78

DAVIS, Bette. I was always eager to salt a good stew. The trouble is that I was expected to supply the meat and potatoes as well.   (Viva 5:29 Oct 77)

DAVIS, Bette. My contention is that producers won't make repulsive films if the public don't got to see them.   (The Observer 9813:9 Sept 23, 79)

DAVIS, Bette. You've got to know someone pretty well to hate them.   (Village Voice 21:105 July 19, 76)

DAVIS, Cullen. You don't know how good it feels to get out of jail.   (Kansas City Times 111:1 Jan 23, 79)

DAVIS, Edward Michael. America is on the verge of a crime wave like the world has never seen before.   (Coronet 13:70 Nov 75)

DAVIS, Edward Michael. I always felt the federal government really was out to force me to hire 4-foot-11 transvestite morons.   (Los Angeles Times 96:1 part 2 Aug 7, 77)

DAVIS, Edward Michael. I think one of the greatest dangers that faces people in this country is the tyrants who would come in and solve your crimes by putting a rock festival in every park.   (Rolling Stone 206:13 Feb 12, 76)

DAVIS, Edward Michael. Now I don't think you can necessarily equate Farm Workers with people with unusual sexual preference, but I suppose you could call them united fruit workers.   (Rolling Stone 236:45 April 7, 76)

DAVIS, Edward Michael. When Brutus gave it to him (Caesar) in the back with that knife, you know if Brutus had a gun they would have talked about gun control. But they didn't pull in knife control or we'd all have to be eating spaghetti all the time. (Rolling Stone 201:32 Dec 4, 75)

DAVIS, Ossie. She was in the nature of a primeval force. She was there and everybody knew it. Universal. You celebrate her like you celebrate a beautiful sunset (about Josephine Baker). (Washington Post 340:B1 Nov 9, 76)

DAY, Dorothy. The best thing to do with the best things in life is to give them up.   (Life Special Report: Remarkable American Women 1776-1976 39 76)

DAYAN, Ehud. Moshe Dayan has exchanged our settlements for peanuts from Jimmy Carter. (People Weekly 10:148 Nov 13, 78)

DAYAN, Moshe. I, Moshe Dayan, as an individual am not a coward. But as a Jew I am a very frightened man.   (Time 110:30 Oct 17, 77)

DAYAN, Moshe. Of course, if you want to make peace, you don't talk to your friends. You talk to your enemies. But the question is whom do we want to make peace with—not just who are our enemies (explaining his objections to negotiating with the PLO).   (Newsweek 40:33 Oct 17, 77)

DAYAN, Moshe. They (guerrillas) may kill two, five, ten civilians, but they will not destroy the peace treaty with Egypt.   (New York Times 128:4 April 23, 79)

DAYAN, Moshe. You cannot get the Arab opinion by sitting and talking to Jews.   (The Observer 9810:10 Sept 2, 79)

DEAN, John Wesley, III. I don't have a friend. If I ever get one, I'll come back (responding after being asked to list the name of a reference for a library card application).   (New York Times 126:58 Nov 3, 76)

DEAN, John Wesley, III. I don't want to be known as the all-time snitch.   (People Weekly 6:122 Dec 13, 76)

DEAN, John Wesley, III. Last summer I reread *1984*, and after several years at the Nixon White House, it made fascinating, almost frightening reading.   (Ms 4:63 Oct 75)

DEAN, John Wesley, III. Prisons are emotional zoos filled with paranoids, manic depressives, homosexuals, schizophrenics and assorted fruits and vegetables without labels.   (Newsweek 40:9 July 4, 77)

DEAN, John Wesley, III. Washington is a much better place if you are asking questions rather than answering them.   (Washingtonian 14:153 Nov 78)

DEBUTTS, John (Chairman of the Board, AT&T). We believe competition works to the disadvantage of the average (telephone) user, and where it does, we are determined to fight it. (American Legion Magazine 99:17 Aug 75)

DE CASSERES, Benjamin. My studies in speculative philosophy, metaphysics, and science are all summed up in the image of a mouse called man running in and out of every hole in the cosmos hunting for the absolute cheese. (Harper's Weekly 3164:19 June 28, 76)

DE CHIRICO, Giorgio. I paint what I see with my eyes closed.   (New York Times 128:B5 Nov 22, 78)

DE CHIRICO, Giorgio. Modernism is dying in all the countries of the world. Let us hope it will soon be just an unhappy memory.   (New York Times 128:B5 Nov 22, 78)

DECROW, Karen Lipshultz. I like the companionship of men. I don't want to cut myself off from half the human race.   (New York Times 125:15 Oct 28, 75)

DECROW, Karen Lipshultz. I wasn't a feminist. I just wanted more money (regarding her '67 decision to join the National Organization for Women).   (New York Times 125:15 Oct 28, 75)

DEDERICH, Charles. Anything less than changing the world is Mickey Mouse to me.   (Chicago Tribune 337:2 section 2 Dec 3, 78)

DEDERICH, Charles. Nonviolence was a position. We can change positions anytime we want to (about Synanon).   (Chicago Tribune 337:3 section 2 Dec 3, 78)

DE GAULLE, Charles. There is no point in taking special precautions when those who want to kill me are as incompetent as those who are supposed to protect me.   (Time 106:23 Oct 6, 75)

DE GAULLE, Charles. Treaties fade as quickly as young girls and roses.   (New York Times Magazine 42 April 27, 80)

DE GAULLE, Charles. We may as well go to the moon, but that's not very far. The greatest distance we have to cover still lies within us. (Omni 2:36 April 80)

DE GAULLE, Sandra. Everyone in the world loves him except the Americans (about Richard Nixon). (W 9:4 Dec 5, 80)

DELACROIX, Eugene. A taste for simplicity cannot endure for long. (Time 113:57 Jan 8, 79)

DE LAURENTIIS, Dino. To make a movie is not like to make a book. A movie is much, much more—not just pushing a pencil in a room. (Los Angeles Times Calendar 60 Nov 28, 76)

DELISLE, Paul (maitre d' of Sans Souci Restaurant). Once we had the Texan. He learned to eat fine French food. The Georgian—he can learn too. (Time 108:25 Nov 22, 76)

DELLUMS, Ronald V. There are not many Vietnamese constituents in America and that is why it took 12 years to develop a broad base of support against that war. But it won't take 25 million black people 12 years to mobilize against American involvement in Angola. (Chicago Sun-Times 28:6 Dec 22, 75)

DE MARCO, Frank. That would be like hearing from a call girl who gave you a dose (when asked if he had heard from ex-president Nixon lately—his former tax client). (Rolling Stone 202:36 Dec 18, 75)

DE MILLE, Agnes. Dance today is terrifying. (Los Angeles Times Calendar 70 June 11, 78)

DE MILLE, Agnes. I am a theater woman. I am not a saint. (W 6:24 Dec 9, 77)

DE MILLE, Agnes. If there was the Resurrection, and He danced, I don't think I'd see Him in Swan Lake if I could avoid it. (Soho Weekly News 6:29 Nov 2, 78)

DE MILLE, Agnes. The theater gives us one rule: don't be a bore. (W 6:24 Dec 9, 77)

DEMPSTER, Nigel. If you can't take it (gossip), then don't give it. (Viva 4:105 Oct 76)

DENIRO, Robert. I'm spending about $600 a week talking to my analyst. I guess that's the price of success. (The Star 4:2 July 26, 77)

DENIRO, Robert. There is a certain combination of anarchy and discipline in the way I work. (Time 110:60 July 25, 77)

DENIRO, Robert. You have to earn the right to play a character. (New York Times 126:13 Section 2 Mar 6, 77)

DENVER, John. (Alaska is) not a state it's an experience. (Chicago Tribune 228:16 Aug 16, 78)

DENVER, John. I epitomize America. (Rolling Stone 231:40 Jan 27, 77)

DEREK, John. I always get along fine with my women, as soon as they recognize that I am God. (New Woman 10:12 May/June 80)

DERROW, Martin. Ronald Reagan is the prototype American politician of the '70s: mindless, witless, positionless and worthless. (Time 106:4 Dec 15, 75)

DERSHOWITZ, Alan. If he (Warren Burger) were one of the Founding Fathers, he would have voted against the Bill of Rights. (Saturday Review 6:20 Dec 79)

DERSHOWITZ, Alan. Judges are the weakest link in our system of justice, and they are also the most protected. (Newsweek 91:76 Feb 20, 78)

DERSHOWITZ, Alan. Screw is a despicable magazine, but that's what the First Amendment was designed to protect. (Newsweek 90:53 Nov 7, 77)

DESAE, Morarji. An expert seldom gives an objective view. He gives his own view. (Time 111:47 Feb 27, 78)

DEVORE, Irven. Males are a vast breeding experiment run by females. (Time 110:63 Aug 1, 77)

DEVRIES, Peter. I love being a writer. What I can't stand is the paperwork. (New York Times Book Review 35 July 15, 79)

DE VRIES, Peter. Reality is impossible to take neat, we must dilute it with alcohol. (Writer's pigest 58:29 Oct 78)

DIBNAH, Stanley. The novel of recent years has become so candid that there are now not many books which are unacceptable to adult readers. (The Observer 9767:13 Nov 5, 78)

DICKENS, Charles. There are books of which the backs and covers are by far the best parts. (Time 106:87 Dec 8, 75)

DICKEY, James. Flight is the only truly new sensation that men have achieved in modern history. (New York Times Book Review 15 July 15, 79)

DICKINSON, Angie. I dress for women—and I undress for men. (Time 112:79 Aug 14, 78)

DICKSTEIN, Morris. The history of the sixties was written as much in the Berkeley Barb as in the New York Times. (New West 4:52 Jan 1, 79)

DIDION, Joan. California is a place in which a boom mentality and a sense of Chekhovian loss meet in uneasy suspension. (New York Times Magazine 36 June 17, 79)

DIDION, Joan. I think nobody owns land until their dead are in it. (Chicago Tribune 176:2 section II June 25, 78)

DIETRICH, Marlene. Never marry an actress (to Eddie Fisher). (Newsweek 86:67 Nov 17, 75)

DIETRICH, Marlene. Once a woman has forgiven her man, she must not reheat his sins for breakfast. (Cosmopolitan 188:268 Feb 80)

DIGGS, Charles C. As an American, I regret that the United States has allowed the Soviet Union to become identified as the principal supporter of African liberation. (New York Times 125:6 Jan 12, 76)

DIMAGGIO, Joe. I can't take it anymore. I'm not in good enough shape (announcing his retirement as a player in oldtimers' games). (Sports Illustrated 43:12 Sept 1, 76)

DIRKSEN, Everett. The oil can is mightier than the sword. (Washingtonian 14:153 Nov 78)

DISRAELI, Benjamin. A man is occasionally thankful when he says 'thank you'. (Kansas City Times 109:16C Feb 14, 77)

DISRAELI, Benjamin. Travel teaches toleration. (Time 110:68 Oct 10, 77)

DIXON, Paul Rand. I understand there are Arabs who are not dirty (responding when asked to retract a racial slur directed at Ralph Nader). (Rolling Stone 235:35 Mar 24, 77)

DOBIE, J. Frank. The average Ph.D. thesis is nothing but a transference of bones from one graveyard to another. (Rocky Mountain News 37:70 May 29, 80)

DOBLER, Conrad. I can say with a clear conscience that I have never knowingly bit another football player. For one thing, I believe in good hygiene (in response to charges that he had bitten a rival player). (Sports Illustrated 43:12 Sept 29, 75)

DOBLER, Conrad. Religiously speaking, it is an advancement from a Cardinal to a Saint (commenting on his trade from St. Louis to New Orleans football teams). (Sports Illustrated 49:10 Aug 7, 78)

DOBLER, Conrad. Well, 35 million TV viewers know that Karras has a lot of class. And all of it is third (after Alex Karras described him as the dirtiest player in pro football). (Sports Illustrated 43:14 Oct 27, 75)

DOCTOROW, E. L. In an age that celebrates facts, the writer who begins to break down the line between fact and fiction represents the reassertion of the authority and perception of the individual mind. (New York Times Book Review 3 Jan 27, 80)

DOCTOROW, E. L. There is no longer any such thing as fiction or nonfiction; there's only narrative. (New York Times Book Review 3 Jan 27, 80)

DODGSON, Charles Lutwidge. If you limit your actions in life to things that nobody can possibly find fault with, you will not do much. New York Times Book Review 29 June 17, 79)

DOLAN, Terry. The Republican Party is a fraud. It's a social club where rich people go to pick their noses. (Time 114:21 Aug 20, 79)

DOLCI, Danilo. We in Sicily are still parched by the sun, plagued by poverty and milked by the Mafia. (New York Times 127:49 Oct 30, 77)

DOLE, Robert J. George Meany could run for President. But why should he step down? (Wall Street Journal 56:1 Sept 7, 76)

DOLE, Robert J. If you liked Richard Nixon, you'll love Bob Dole. (Christian Science Monitor 68:17 Sept 10, 76)

DOLE, Robert J. It may turn out that 1974 was the good year for a Republican to be on the ballot. (Time 105:9 Feb 17, 75)

DOLE, Robert J. A Republican has to have a sense of humor because there are so few of us. (Time 108:26 Aug 30, 76)

DOLE, Robert J. Thank goodness whenever I was in the Oval Office I only nodded (commenting on the Watergate tapes). (Christian Science Monitor 68:17 Sept 10, 76)

DOLE, Robert J. With all respect, Connally, Goldwater and Rockefeller are great men but they don't indicate any forward thrust in our party. We've got to start building from the bottom up instead of the top down. (Time 108:30 Aug 30, 76)

DONAHUE, Mark. That last lap, I really didn't want it to end; I wanted it to go on and on (spoken during his short retirement). (Time 106:47 Sept 1, 75)

DONLEAVY, J. P. Authors don't have any respect at all in terms of a profession in America—and this is quite a good and stimulating thing. (Newsweek 94:95 Oct 22, 79)

DONLEAVY, J. P. Nearly everybody who pans my books doesn't get anywhere in the literary trade. (Newsweek 94:95 Oct 22, 79)

DONLEAVY, J. P. Writing is turning one's worst moments into money. (Playboy 26:135 May 79)

DORFMAN, Dan. To lie to the press on a public matter is, in effect, to lie to the people. (New York 10:9 May 9, 77)

DORNFELD, Arnold (attributed by Mike Royko). If your mother says she loves you, check it out (on the journalist's responsibility). (Town & Country 132:173 Sept 78)

DOTY, William R. Connally will always be remembered for his bright Nixon button and his weakness for milk shakes. (Texas Monthly 3:8 Aug 75)

DOUGLAS, Norman. It takes a wise man to handle a lie; a fool had better remain honest. (Kansas City Star 97:14C Dec 22, 76)

DOUGLAS, William Orville. The great and invigorating influences in American life have been the unorthodox; the people who challenge an existing institution or way of life, or say and do things that make people think. (Kansas City Times 109:14C Jan 22, 77)

DOUGLAS, William Orville. I have been bothered with incessant and demanding pain which depletes my energy to the extent that I have been unable to shoulder my full share of the burden (upon his resignation from the Supreme Court in a letter to President Ford). (New York Times 125:2 Nov 13, 75)

DOUGLAS, William Orville. I haven't been much of a proselytizer on the court. I've got the theory that the only soul I had to save was my own. (Time 115:83 Jan 28, 80)

DOUGLAS, William Orville. A lifetime diet of the law alone turns judges into dull, dry husks. (Newsweek 86:46 Nov 24, 75)

DOUGLAS, William Orville. The press has a preferred position in our constitutional scheme not to enable it to make money, not to set newsmen apart as a favored class, but to bring fulfillment to the public's right to know. (New York Times 127:2 section 4 Aug 6, 78)

DOUGLASS, Bobby. If you want to keep your beer real cold, put it next to Jim Fink's heart. (Chicago Tribune Magazine 14 July 31, 77)

DRINAN, Robert. Politics is the formation of public morality. (Chicago Tribune 261:20 Sept 17, 80)

DRUCKER, Peter F. Capital formation is shifting from the entrepreneur who invests in the future to the pension trustee who invests in the past. (New York Times 125:15 Section 3 May 16, 76)

DRUCKER, Peter F. In all recorded history there has not been one economist who had to worry about where the next meal would come from. (New York Times 125:15 Section 3 May 16, 76)

DRUCKER, Peter F. Look at governmental programs for the past fifty years. Every single one—except for warfare—achieved the exact opposite of its announced goal. (New York Times 125:15 Section 3 May 16, 76)

DRUCKER, Peter F. The main impact of the computer has been the provision of unlimited jobs for clerks. (New York Times 125:15 Section 3 May 16, 76)

DRUCKER, Peter F. The only things that evolve by themselves in an organization are disorder, friction and malperformance. (The Wharton Magazine 1:14 Fall 76)

DRUCKER, Peter F. So much of what we call management consists in making it difficult for people to work. (New York Times 125:15 Section 3 May 16, 76)

DRUCKER, Peter F. The wonder of modern institutions is not that they work so badly, but that anything works at all. (The Wharton Magazine 1:14 Fall 76)

DRYANSKY, G. Y. Paris is becoming more vulgar, New York more refined. (W 8:8 Jan 19, 79)

DUBOS, Rene. Each civilization has its own kind of pestilence and controls it only by reforming itself. (Skeptic 19:29 May/June 77)

DUBOS, Rene. There is a universal tendency, if we can manage it, to do something a little different from what other people are doing. (Omni 2:126 Dec 79)

DUBUS, Andre. Romance dies hard, because its very nature is to want to live. (Boston 69:236 Dec 77)

DUCHAMP, Marcel. I was interested in ideas—not in merely visual products. I wanted to put painting once again at the service of the mind. (New York Times 128:1 section 7 Feb 11, 79)

DUDNEY, Bob. The country would have recovered from the death of John Kennedy, but it hasn't recovered yet from the death of Lee Harvey Oswald and probably never will. (Esquire 85:62 Feb 76)

DUFFY, Sean. The chance of a meaningful relationship with a member of the opposite sex is inversely proportional to their amount of beauty. (Omni 1:132 May 79)

DUGGAN, B. To every Ph.D. there is an equal and opposite Ph.D. (Washingtonian 14:153 Nov 78)

DUGGER, Ronnie. To be from Texas will always have a kind of gusto to it. (New York Times 129:B12 Oct 15, 79)

DUKAKIS, Michael S. If, in fact, I had a windfall of $10 million tax free, I would hire someone to handle all the stupid requests like yours (in response to 'What would you do with 10 million dollars'). (Money 4:77 Nov 75)

DUKE, David. Black people have organizations that fight for black power, and Jews look out for each other. But there isn't anyone except the Klan who will fight for the rights of white people. (Newsweek 90:45 Nov 14, 77)

DUNAWAY, Faye. I've always thought that acting is an art of creating accidents. (W 5:15 Nov 26, 76)

DUNCAN, Isadora. With what a price we pay for the glory of motherhood. (Chicago Tribune 176:2 section II June 25, 78)

DUNDEE, Chris. Middle age is when you start for home about the same time you used to start for somewhere else. (Sports Illustrated 44:10 Mar 29, 76)

DUNDES, Alan. Football is a healthy outlet for male-to-male affections just as spin the bottle and post office are healthy outlets for adolescent heterosexual needs. (Time 112:112 Nov 13, 78)

DUNNE, Finley Peter. A fanatic is a man that does what he thinks the Lord would if He knew all the facts. (Forbes 120:186 Oct 15, 77)

DUNNE, John Gregory. Hollywood is the only place where you fail upwards. (US 1:12 Feb 21, 78)

DURANT, Will. One of the lessons of history is that nothing is often a good thing to do and always a clever thing to say. (Washingtonian 14:153 Nov 78)

DURANT, Will. The primary things in my own life have been a wife, a house and some children roaming around us once in a while. (People Weekly 4:62 Dec 8, 75)

DURANT, Will. We are living in a time when woman thinks she has been emancipated, but I'm afraid that's a complimentary way of saying she's been industrialized. (Chicago Sun-Times 28:30 Nov 6, 75)

DURANTE, Jimmy. There's a million good-lookin' guys, but I'm a novelty. (New York Times 129:1 Jan 30, 80)

DURKIN, John. I may not be the smoothest item to come down the turnpike. (Time 106:28 Sept 29, 75)

DURKIN, John. In New Hampshire today, the Ayatullah Khomeini could beat Carter. (Time 113:52 April 9, 79)

DURY, Ian. Sex is about as important as a cheese sandwich. (Chicago Sun-Times 31:6 June 20, 78)

DUTTON, Fred. George Wallace is a more truly democratic candidate than Ford, Humphrey or Jackson. He wants everyone to vote, while they hope to narrow down the voting public. (W 4:11 Dec 12, 75)

DUTTON, Fred. Lawyers have become secular priests. (Time 111:58 April 10, 78)

DUTTON, Fred. Washington is like a woman who is always waiting to be seduced. (Time 109:26 Feb 7, 77)

DYLAN, Bob. I didn't consciously pursue the Bob Dylan myth. It was given to me—by God. Inspiration is what we're looking for. You just have to be receptive to it. (People Weekly 4:26 Nov 10, 75)

DYLAN, Bob. Money doesn't exist because I don't recognize it. (New Times 10:45 Feb 6, 78)

DYLAN, Bob. Rock and roll ended with Little Anthony and the Imperials. (Rolling Stone 257:42 Jan 26, 78)

DYLAN, Bob. Somebody called me the Ed Sullivan of rock and roll. I don't know what that means, but it sounds right. (TV Guide 24:4 Sept 11, 76)

DYSON, Freeman. The only certainty in (the) remote future is that radically new things will be happening. (Omni 2:40 June 80)

EARHART, Amelia. There are two kinds of stones, as everyone knows, one of which rolls. (Chicago Tribune 176:2 section II June 25, 78)

EASTLAND, James O. I didn't know that guy was a nigger (about Anwar Sadat). (New Times 8:15 June 24, 77)

EASTWOOD, Clint. Everybody talks about love, but the thing that keeps marriage together for me is friendship. (Chicago Tribune Magazine 174:25 Aug 1, 76)

EATON, Cyrus S. I've been going to Cuba for 60 years. I think our policy is wrong there, just as it was in Vietnam (discussing his planned invitation to visit Cuba). (Los Angeles Times 95:2 Part 1 Dec 26, 75)

EATON, Cyrus S. We must either learn to live with the Communists or resign ourselves to perish with them. (Time 113:93 May 21, 79)

EATON, Richard. Life is subject to change without notice. (More 8:9 June 78)

EBAN, Abba Solomon. Better to be disliked than pitied. (New York 9:38 July 26, 76)

EBAN, Abba Solomon. You cannot have peace without risks. (Time 111:37 Mar 6, 78)

ECHEVERRIA ALVAREZ, Luis. I would like to have as my successor a person who would continue with the reforms I have begun and carry them much further. (Time 105:35 Feb 10, 75)

ECKARDT, Wolf Von. The only lift you get from this building is when you take the elevator from the basement to the second floor. (Washingtonian 10:88 Aug 75)

ECKHARDT, Nadine. Most politicians are just little men who couldn't get it up in high school. (Newsweek 86:38 Oct 13, 75)

ECKHART, Johannes. God becomes and disbecomes. (Human Behavior 7:33 May 78)

ECKSTINE, Billy. If your popularity is based on a gimmick, like plunking a guitar with your teeth to taunting the audience with obscenities, better grab the money and run. You'll never last. (Chicago Tribune 235:12 Aug 23, 77)

EDDINGTON, Arthur. The stuff of the universe is mind stuff. (Human Behavior 7:32 May 78)

EDER, Richard. A critic may write for an institution, but he shouldn't be one. (Village Voice 22:97 Mar 28, 77)

EDISON, Thomas Alva. Anything that won't sell, I don't want to invent. (New York Times Book Review 7 Feb 25, 79)

EDISON, Thomas Alva. The day will come when science will create a machine as a force which is so terrible, so infinitely horrifying, that even man, a bellicose being who brings suffering, torment, and death upon his fellows, at the risk of bringing these torments upon himself will shudder with fear and renounce war forever. (Atlas World Press Review 23:13 Nov 76)

EDISON, Thomas Alva. Deafness has been of great advantage to me as my business is thinking. (Newsweek 93:104 Mar 26, 79)

EDWARDS, James B. I don't believe the South will buy Jimmy Carter. He is nothing more than a Southern-talking George McGovern. (New York Times 125:51 June 29, 76)

EDWARDS, Shelton. The way to get somewhere in politics is to find a crowd that's going some place and get in front of it. (Time 112:16 Aug 28, 78)

EGGLESTON, Justine Judd. I got tired of people calling me a dirty Jew so I figured I'd settle in the one country (Israel) where dirty Jew means you need a bath. (The Jerusalem Post 828:11 Sept 14, 76)

EHRLICH, Paul. The petrochemical industry is at about the intellectual and moral level of the people who sell heroin to high school kids. (Outside 1:10 July/Aug 78)

EHRLICHMAN, John D. I have done my time. I don't think he (Richard Nixon) is ever going to stop doing his time. (Time 111:67 May 15, 78)

EHRLICHMAN, John D. If I wanted to do some candidate a dirty trick, I'd endorse him. Maybe I'll go campaign for Lowell Weicker. (New Times 6:14 June 11, 76)

EHRLICHMAN, John D. Narcotics suppression is a very sexy political issue. (Playboy 23:174 Nov 76)

EHRLICHMAN, John D. We operate in this country, and in the media and the courts, on a situational ethics base. (Time 106:21 Dec 1, 75)

EIKERENKOETER, Frederick J. I indulge myself shamelessly and so should you. (Cosmopolitan 179:66 Sept 75)

EINSTEIN, Albert. An empty stomach is not a good political adviser. (Kansas City Times 109:14B May 11, 77)

EINSTEIN, Albert. Everything should be made as simple as possible, but not simpler. (Newsweek 93:100 April 16, 79)

EINSTEIN, Albert. God may be subtle, but He isn't mean. (The Observer 9785:9 Mar 11, 79)

EINSTEIN, Albert. Let every man be respected as an individual and no man idolized. (Parade 4 July 1, 79)

EINSTEIN, Albert. Nationalism is an infantile disease. It is the measles of mankind. (Chicago Tribune 281:2 section 2 Oct 8, 78)

EINSTEIN, Albert. Princeton is a wonderful little spot. A quaint and ceremonious village of puny demigods on stilts. (Philadelphia Magazine 66:116 Aug 75)

EINSTEIN, Albert. Sit with a pretty girl for an hour, and it seems like a minute; sit on a hot stove for a minute, and it seems like an hour—that's relativity. (Rocky Mountain News 235:104 Dec 13, 79)

EINSTEIN, Albert. To punish me for my contempt for authority, Fate made me an authority myself. (Chicago Tribune 281:1 section 2 Oct 8, 78)

EINSTEIN, Albert. To the village square we must carry the facts of atomic energy. From there must come America's voice (commenting in 1946). (Newsweek 85:23 Feb 24, 75)

EINSTEIN, Albert. When a man after long years of searching chances upon a thought which discloses something of the beauty of this mysterious universe, he should not therefore be personally celebrated. He is already sufficiently paid by his experience of seeking and finding. (New York Times 128:18 section 4 Nov 10, 78)

EINSTEIN, Albert. With fame I become more and more stupid, which of course, is a common phenomenon. There is far too great a disproportion between what one is and what others think one is. With me, every peep becomes a trumpet solo. (Time 113:75 Feb 19, 79)

EINSTEIN, Albert. The world needs heroes and it's better they be harmless men like me than villains like Hitler. (Newsweek 92:43 Nov 27, 78)

EINSTEIN, Albert (attributed by Yousuf Karsh). Curiosity has its own reason for existence. (Parade 7 Dec 3, 78)

EISELEY, Loren. (Man's) basic and oldest characteristic is that he is a creature of memory, a bridge into the future, a time binder. Without this recognition of continuity, love and understanding between the generations becomes impossible. (Time 110:61 July 25, 77)

EISELEY, Loren. There is but one way into the future: the technological way. (Time 110:61 July 25, 77)

EISELEY, Loren. We are changelings...who have slept in wood nests or hissed in the uncouth guise of waddling amphibians. We have played such roles for infinitely longer ages than we have been men. (Washington Post 232:B3 Oct 23, 76)

EISENHOWER, David. Journalists aren't nearly as interesting as they think they are. (Esquire 87:35 July 77)

EISENHOWER, Dwight David. It has been the tough-minded optimist whom history has proved right in America. (Newsweek 85:18 Feb 24, 75)

EISENHOWER, Dwight David. It is difficult for me to see a single qualification that the man has for the presidency. I think he is shallow, vain and untrustworthy—on top of which he is indecisive (commenting on Robert Kennedy). (Esquire 90:39 Aug 15, 78)

EISENHOWER, Dwight David. The path to America's future lies down the middle of the road. (Time 116:32 July 28, 80)

EISENHOWER, Dwight David. These are not bad people... All they are concerned about is to see that their sweet little girls are not required to sit in schools alongside some big overgrown Negroes. (Time 109:66 Mar 28, 77)

EISENHOWER, Mamie Geneva (Doud). I let Ike run the country and I ran the home. (New York Times 126:26 Section 1 Nov 14, 76)

EKLAND, Britt. I say I don't sleep with married men, but what I really mean is that I don't sleep with happily married men. (The Observer 9812:10 Sept 16, 79)

ELDRIDGE, Paul. Man is always ready to die for an idea, provided that idea is not quite clear to him. (Washingtonian 15:141 Nov 79)

ELGIN, Duane S (futurologist). Once you discover that space doesn't matter, or that time can be traveled through at will so that time doesn't matter, and that matter can be moved by consciousness so that matter doesn't matter—well, you can't go home again. (New York 10:55 Dec 27, 76/Jan 3, 77)

ELIOT, George. Blessed be the man who, having nothing to say, abstains from giving wordy evidence of the fact. (Kansas City Star 97:38 July 14, 77)

ELIOT, George. I have the conviction that excessive literary production is a social offense. (Kansas City Times 109:33 Mar 15, 77)

ELIOT, Thomas Stearns. Those who say they give the public what it wants begin by underestimating public taste and end by debauching it. (American Film 5:83 Nov 79)

ELLICK, Thomas. If anyone is looking for a replacement for John Wayne as the personification of America, (John Connally) is it. (Time 114:58 July 16, 79)

ELLISON, Jessie. New York should be saved because we live there even when we live somewhere else. (Harper's Weekly 3142:1 Sept 29, 75)

ELLISON, Ralph. People who want to write sociology should not write a novel. (Newsweek 91:21 Feb 20, 78)

EMERSON, Eric. The second is never as good as the first. (Omni 1:131 May 79)

EMERSON, Ralph Waldo. Every hero becomes a bore at last. (Time 111:57 June 19, 78)

EMERSON, Ralph Waldo. To be great is to be misunderstood. (Forbes 119:312 May 15, 77)

EMERSON, William A., Jr. A foolish consistency is the hobgoblin of small committees. (Wilson Library Bulletin 52:534 Mar 78)

EMERSON, William A., Jr. New Yorkers are an endangered species. (Newsweek 86:9 Dec 29, 75)

EMERY, Fred J. Regulation is the substitution of error for chance. (Washingtonian 15:141 Nov 79)

EMMINGER, Otmar. Inflation is like a dictator. It must be fought before it becomes established, or it is too late. (Time 113:35 June 11, 79)

EPHRON, Nora. For a lot of women, the women's movement has just given them a political rationalization for their fear of success. (Christian Science Monitor 69:2 Dec 10, 76)

EPHRON, Nora. For those of us who believe that Hustler is a truly obscene magazine, it is a difficult moment. It is one of those cases that makes you search for some loophole (commenting on the Hustler pornography case). (New York Times Magazine 18 Mar 6, 77)

EPHRON, Nora. We have lived in an era when happiness was a warm puppy, and the era when happiness was a dry martini, and now we have come to an era when happiness is knowing what your uterus looks like. (Human Behavior 7:17 May 78)

EPSTEIN, Joseph. A few things ought to be said on behalf of the 1970's—not the least among them that they weren't the 1960's. (Time 115:39 Jan 7, 80)

EPSTEIN, Thomas A. With extremely few exceptions, nothing is worth the trouble. (Omni 1:131 May 79)

ERHARD, Werner. Belief is a disease. (Book Digest 3:141 July 76)

ERHARD, Werner. The goal of the (EST) training is 'getting it,' but you don't 'get it' in the training. You get that you've got it in the training. (Newsweek 85:46 Feb 17, 75)

ERHARD, Werner. The point is, until its time comes, nothing you do will work. And when its time comes, what you do will work and you will do what works. (Newsweek 92:78 Aug 28, 78)

ERHARD, Werner. What the Buddhists were saying is this: true nothing is what is. EST is because EST is nothing. (Chicago 25:21 Oct 76)

ERHARD, Werner. You are perfect exactly the way you are. (Life 2:86 Dec 79)

ERISH, Andrew. America is 90 percent corn. (New York Times 128:23 Nov 25, 78)

ERVIN, Samuel James. Nobody I know wanted to see Nixon go to jail, (but) there's an old saying that mercy but murders, pardoning those that kill. (Newsweek 85:24 Jan 13, 75)

ERVIN, Samuel James. The statute of limitations has already run out on all my past indiscretions. And more unfortunately, I have lost all capacity to commit any more. (Chicago Sun-Times 29:24 June 16, 76)

ESQUERRA, Maria Antonia (Chicana nun). The theology of liberation in North America will be written by the oppressed. (Time 106:34 Sept 1, 75)

ESTES, Billie Sol. You win by losing, hold on by letting go, increase by diminishing, and multiply by dividing. These are the principles that have brought me success.   (New York Times 128:23 Feb 25, 79)

EVANS, Chick. I just hate to think of dying, to not wake up tomorrow and think of another way to hit that golf ball.   (Quest 2:120 Mar/April 78)

EVANS, Dale. I cannot sit in judgment of anyone. I have been forgiven a great deal myself. But there are some things that God just does not condone—and homosexuality is just one of them. It says so many times in the Bible.   (San Francisco Chronicle This World 1978:2 Aug 6, 78)

EVANS, Medford. It usually takes disciplined organization to dislodge entrenched power.   (American Opinion 18:29 Nov 75)

EVANS, Roy. He (John Connally) likes deep rugs and rich people.   (Time 107:12 Feb 16, 76)

EVANS, Walker. Photography isn't a matter of taking pictures. It's a matter of having an eye.   (Chicago Tribune 226:2 section 6 Aug 14, 77)

EVTUSHENKO, Evgenii Aleksandrovich. Distrust is the mother of war and political racism.   (Atlas World Press Review 23:10 Nov 76)

EYSENCK, H. J. Scientists, especially when they leave the particular field in which they have specialized, are just as ordinary, pig-headed and unreasonable as anybody else.   (Omni 2:49 Dec 79) .

FABER, Harold. If there isn't a law, there will be.   (Book Digest 6:32 Dec 79)

FAHD, PRINCE OF SAUDI ARABIA, . If Iran goes, God help us.   (The Observer 9777:11 Jan 14, 79)

FAIRLIE, Henry. All over Washington, people are now speed-reading the Koran.   (Parade 6 Feb 17, 80)

FAIRLIE, Henry. The once rambunctious American spirit of innovation and adventurousness is today being paralyzed by the desire to build a risk-free society.   (Time 114:71 Oct 22, 79)

FALLACI, Oriana. I doubt very much that my future as an interviewer of powerful people in the United States is a brilliant future if Mr. Kissinger goes on being the President of the United States.   (Esquire 83:105 June 75)

FALLACI, Oriana. An interview is a love story for me. It's a fight. It's a coitus.   (Time 106:70 Oct 20, 75)

FALLOWS, James. I came to think that Carter believes fifty things, but no one thing.   (New York Times 128:23 April 26, 79)

FALLOWS, James. I'm inclined to doubt this government can be changed, by Carter or any other President.   (Time 112:91 Dec 4, 78)

FALWELL, Jerry. Not only should we register them (Communists), but we should stamp it on their foreheads and send them back to Russia. This is a free country.   (Washington Post 275:B3 Sept 6, 77)

FALWELL, Jerry. Textbooks are Soviet propaganda.   (Kansas City Star 113:1E Dec 7, 80)

FARENTHOLD, Frances Tarlton (Sissy). The right to an abortion has become a class issue, a race issue, a privacy issue and even a consumer issue, but it is above all, our issue (commenting on the National Women's Political Caucus).   (San Francisco Chronicle This World 1977:2 Sept 18, 77)

FARLEY, Lin. A feminist is a woman who knows she's oppressed, who responds to that oppression by fighting it, and who realizes that she can change nothing alone; she is a sister. She believes in herself and the power of women, she sees the necessity for struggle and she likes to win, in other words, she is completely un-feminine.   (New York Times 125:32 Nov 8, 75)

FARRELL, James T. There's one good kind of a writer—a dead writer.   (Chicago Sun-Times 32:53 Aug 24, 79)

FASSBINDER, Rainer Werner. I long for a little naivete but there's none around.   (Film Comment 12:2 Jan/Feb 76)

FAULK, John Henry. I was taught that the first ten amendments were sacrosanct, that they're the engine by which this society runs and I admire people who cherish them and loathe and despise people who would circumvent and destroy them. So it took no act of courage to do what I did. It was an act of principle. What else would you do? I like to think all American people would do the same thing if they felt the way I did.   (Los Angeles Times Calendar 94:30 Nov 9, 75)

FAULKNER, William. I believe that man will not merely endure: he will prevail (commenting in his 1950 Nobel Prize acceptance speech).   (New York Times Magazine 42 Dec 5, 76)

FAULKNER, William. I gave the world what it wanted—guts and genitals.   (True 57:14 Dec 75)

FAULKNER, William. The past is never dead; it is not even past.   (Newsweek 89:87 Feb 21, 77)

FAWCETT-MAJORS, Farrah. God balances things out. My theory is that God gives you either straight white teeth with lots of cavities or crooked, stained teeth with no cavities. I have lots of cavities.   (Chicago Tribune 78:33 Mar 19, 78)

FAWCETT-MAJORS, Farrah. I thought Marilyn Monroe was the most beautiful woman in the world and Elizabeth Taylor breathtaking. But when I see myself on the screen I say: Oh, shoot! What are they talking about.   (Chicago Tribune 243:12 Aug 31, 77)

FEATHER, William. Loneliness is something you can't walk away from.   (Forbes 119:312 May 15, 77)

FEATHER, William. No plan is worth a damn unless somebody makes it work.   (Forbes 120:186 Oct 15, 77)

FEENEY, Leonard. The first American girl who 'made good' according to God's exact standards (about Elizabeth Seton).   (Time 106:53 Sept 22, 75)

FEIN, Leonard. Israel is squandering recklessly its most critical and natural resource—the good will that many people around the world, and in this country in particular, feel for this gutsy country.   (Time 114:43 July 23, 79)

FEISAL, KING OF SAUDI ARABIA, . If anyone feels wrongly treated, he has only himself to blame for not telling me. What higher democracy can there be.   (Time 105:22 April 7, 75)

FELD, Eliot. Each time I make a dance, it's like being a virgin. (People 11:45 May 14, 79)

FELDMAN, Marty. Humor is like sex. Those who do it don't talk about it. (People Weekly 6:103 Dec 27/Jan 3, 77)

FELDMAN, Marty. I always feel like a con artist after everything I've done. (Chicago Tribune 207:7 July 26, 77)

FELDMAN, Marty. Well, any melodrama inverted is good material for a comedy. (Chicago Tribune 207:7 July 26, 77)

FELIX, Virginia. Decision makers are those who have the greatest vested interest in the decision. (Omni 1:132 May 79)

FELLINI, Federico. I don't have problems with actors—they have problems with me. (Time 107:76 May 17, 76)

FELLINI, Federico. I know for sure that wherever he goes he will continue to be himself, to speak his voice and to begin from the beginning with exalting sensation (commenting on Ingmar Bergman's self-imposed exile from Sweden). (Washington Post 143:B3 April 26, 76)

FENSON, Mel. We're aimed at people interested in the sport of hunting—hunting for animals or hunting for people (commenting as Marketing Director on the aims of the periodical Soldier of Fortune). (Mother Jones 1:10 Dec 6, 77)

FERNANDES, Millor (Brazilian playwright). The horrendous state of our prisons is what prevents them from being occupied by members of our highest society. (New York Times 126:8 May 24, 77)

FERNANDES, Millor (Brazilian playwright). In a democracy we are all equal before the law. In a dictatorship we are all equal before the police. (New York Times 126:8 May 24, 77)

FERRIS, Earle. There's nothing neither good nor bad that can't be made more so. (Washingtonian 15:143 Nov 79)

FIEDLER, Leslie. There can be no terror without the hope for love and love's defeat. (New York Arts Journal 9:15 April/May 78)

FIELD, Marshall, V. They all started out with nothing in those days, and the biggest crooks won. I was just lucky to come from a line of successful crooks. (Esquire 89:96 Mar 28, 78)

FIELDS, W. C. I was in love with a beautiful blonde once—she drove me to drink—'tis the one thing I'm indebted to her for. (Aspen 3:52 Feb 77)

FIELDS, W. C. There comes a time in the affairs of men when you must take the bull by the tail and face the situation. (San Francisco Chronicle This World 1978:40 Jan 29, 78)

FIELDS, W. C. Women are like elephants. They're nice to look at but I wouldn't want to own one. (Viva 5:26 Dec 77)

FINCH, Peter. Acting is fascinating and not an ignoble profession. No one lives more than the actor. (Time 108:53 Jan 24, 77)

FINK, Stanley. There are times when reasonable people come to no solution. (New York 10:9 July 25, 77)

FINLEY, Charles Oscar. I always wanted to be a player, but I never had the talent to make the big leagues. So I did the next best thing: I bought a team. (Time 106:42 Aug 18, 75)

FINLEY, Charles Oscar. I've never seen so many damned idiots as the owners in sport. (Time 106:42 Aug 18, 75)

FITZGERALD, F. Scott. Having once found the intensity of art, nothing else that can happen in life can ever again seem as important as the creative process. (Forbes 120:186 Oct 15, 77)

FITZGERALD, F. Scott. I talk with the authority of failure—Ernest (Hemingway) with the authority of success. (Time 111:89 April 3, 78)

FITZGERALD, F. Scott. The test of a first-rate intelligence is the ability to hold two opposed ideas in the mind at the same time, and still retain the ability to function. (New York Times Book Review 23 Mar 4, 79)

FITZGERALD, F. Scott. There never was a good biography of a good novelist. There couldn't be. He is too many people, if he's any good. (Writer's Digest 56:6 Dec 76)

FITZGERALD, Zelda. A vacuum can only exist, I imagine, by the things which enclose it. (Chicago Tribune 176:2 section II June 25, 78)

FITZHUGH, Gilbert W. The Republicans fight like cats and go home and sulk. The Democrats fight like cats, and suddenly there are more cats. (Time 107:11 Aug 23, 76)

FITZSIMMONS, Frank E. For those who would say it's time to reform this organization, that it is time that the officers quit selling out the membership of their union, I say to them, go to hell. (Newsweek 87:49 June 28, 76)

FITZSIMMONS, Frank E. Personally, I don't think George Meany would know a trade unionist if he tripped over one. (Chicago Tribune 310:3 Section I Nov 6, 75)

FITZSIMMONS, Frank E. The Teamsters are without peer as an organization dedicated to the service of mankind. (New York Times Magazine 31 Nov 7, 76)

FITZSIMMONS, Frank E. When Hoffa left here (for prison) he said he'd be back in 90 days. That's Hoffa. His ego was as big as this floor. (People Weekly 4:22 Dec 29/Jan 5, 76)

FLAHERTY, Joe. It seems that in the baseball world Martin is someone with whom you have an affair or a fling but never a relationship. (Village Voice 21:17 July 12, 76)

FLANAGAN, Fionnula. The one thing you must not commit with the Irish is to succeed. (TV Guide 26:22 April 29, 78)

FLANNER, Janet. I'm not one of those journalists with a staff. I don't even have a secretary. I act as a sponge. I soak it up and squeeze it out in ink every two weeks. (New York Times 28:B10 Nov 8, 78)

FLANNER, Janet. She (Elsa Maxwell) was built for crowds. She has never come any closer to life than the dinner table. (New York Times 128:B10 Nov 8, 78)

FLEENER, Terre. What the Jewish people endured does not give them the right to visit violence on other people. (Chicago Sun-Times 32:100 July 1, 79)

FLEISHMAN, Stanley. There are more citizens in jail in the United States today for publishing books, magazines, newspapers, and films than there are in all the countries of the world put together. (American Film 2:4 June 77)

FLEMING, John. Show me your books, and I'll tell you who you are. (Esquire 89:71 Feb 78)

FLOOD, Curt. Being black is always having people being cautious about what they call you. (Esquire 89:46 Mar 1, 78)

FLOOD, Curt. I am a man, not a consignment of goods to be bought and sold. (Esquire 89:42 Mar 1, 78)

FLYNT, Althea. I told him 'God may have walked into your life, but $20 million a year just walked out' (to Larry Flynt upon his conversion). (New York 11:56 Jan 9, 78)

FLYNT, Larry. If I'm guilty of anything it's bad taste. I don't think people ought to be put in jail for having bad taste. (Newsweek 89:34 Feb 21, 77)

FLYNT, Larry. If you ask me, yes, I am a born-again Christian. But I am going to continue publishing pornography, and anybody who doesn't like it can go kiss a rope. (New York Times 127:A16 Feb 2, 78)

FLYNT, Larry. I've been all the way to the bottom. There's only one way to go now, and that's up. I'm going to be hustling for the Lord. (Time 110:112 Dec 5, 77)

FLYNT, Larry. We are genuine entertainment with no pretensions. We have proved that barnyard humor has a market appeal. (Time 109:51 Feb 21, 77)

FOLEY, Thomas S. There is a mood in this country that government action is not necessarily always the perfect solution to social problems. (US News & World Report 84:24 Jan 23, 78)

FONDA, Henry. I don't feel I'm totally a man of integrity. But if there is something in the eyes, a kind of honesty in the face, then I guess you could say that's the man I'd like to be, the man I want to be. (Time 112:118 Oct 9, 78)

FONDA, Jane. Conservation is the religion of the future. (Life 2:170 Dec 79)

FONDA, Jane. I think that every movie is political. (New Times 10:58 Mar 20, 78)

FONDA, Jane. It is time to look at crime in the suites, not just in the streets. (Time 114:31 Oct 8, 79)

FONDA, Jane. Putting Energy Secretary James Schlesinger in charge of nuclear power is like putting Dracula in charge of a blood bank. (New York 12:43 May 28, 79)

FONDA, Jane. (Robert Redford is), and remains, a bourgeois in the worst sense of the word. (Chicago Tribune 314:28 Nov 10, 77)

FONDA, Peter. I'm heir to nothing but a legend, which is full of ...air. (Chicago Tribune Magazine Nov 6, 77) Nov 6, 77

FONTAINE, Joan. The physical side of being a woman is detestable. (The Observer 9767:13 Nov 5, 78)

FONTANA, Robert S. Even if everyone quits smoking today, we could still look forward to a legacy of maybe 50,000 lung cancer deaths a year for the next 20 years (commenting on the early findings of a two-year lung cancer study). (New York Times 125:20 Mar 27, 76)

FONTEJN, Abraham J (chief of Netherlands' police force). There is one basic approach and that is never give in (summarizing his government's response to terrorism). (Chicago Tribune 39:2 Section 2 Feb 6, 76)

FORBES, Malcolm S. A bore is someone who persists in holding his own views after we have enlightened him with ours. (Reader's Digest 108:261 May 76)

FORBES, Malcolm S. I'd say capitalism's worst excess is in the large number of crooks and tinhorns who get too much of the action. (Playboy 26:108 April 79)

FORBES, Malcolm S. People who never get carried away should be. (Town & Country 130:166 Nov 76)

FORD, Charlotte. I worked for charity all my life, and now it's kind of fun to work for money. (Rolling Stone 237:53 April 21, 77)

FORD, Elizabeth (Bloomer). A liberated woman is one who feels confident in herself, and is happy in what she is doing. She is a person who has a sense of self. I think it all comes down to freedom of choice. (New York Times 125: Nov 8, 75)

FORD, Elizabeth (Bloomer). People stop me all the time to urge that my husband run for the presidency, but I'm doing my best to discourage him. (W 7:2 Sept 29, 78)

FORD, Gerald Rudolph. Detente means moderate and restrained behavior between two superpowers—not a license to fish in troubled waters. (American Legion Magazine 99:36 Nov 75)

FORD, Gerald Rudolph. Eurocommunism is not, as their propagandists say, Communism with a human face. It is Stalinism in a mask and tyranny in disguise. (New York Times 127:2 Oct 30, 77)

FORD, Gerald Rudolph. (Governor Ronald Reagan) doesn't dye his hair; he's just prematurely orange. (Esquire 83:56 Jan 75)

FORD, Gerald Rudolph. Having become Vice President and President without expecting or seeking either, I have a special feeling toward these high offices. To me, the presidency and vice presidency were not prizes to be won, but a duty to be done. (Time 108:22 Aug 30, 76)

FORD, Gerald Rudolph. I am going to be heard from. (Time 107:14 May 30, 77)

FORD, Gerald Rudolph. I can tell you—and tell you now—that I am prepared to veto any bill that has as its purpose a federal bailout of New York City to prevent a default. (New York Times 125:1 Oct 30, 75)

FORD, Gerald Rudolph. I did not take the sacred oath of office to preside over the decline and fall of America. (American Legion Magazine 99:21 Dec 75)

FORD, Gerald Rudolph. I don't think the United States should ever involve itself in the internal situation in any country. (New York 9:33 Feb 23, 76)

FORD, Gerald Rudolph. I don't use the word detente any more. I think what we ought to say is that the United States will meet with the superpowers, the Soviet Union and with China and others, and seek to relax tensions so that we can continue a policy of peace through strength. (New York Times 125:20 Mar 2, 76)

FORD, Gerald Rudolph. I learned a long time ago in politics, never say never. (New York Times 128:17 April 22, 79)

FORD, Gerald Rudolph. I share your deep appreciation about the increased irreverence for life (commenting in a speech to the 41st Eucharistic Congress). (Rolling Stone 222:14 Sept 23, 76)

FORD, Gerald Rudolph. I'm a better President than a campaigner. (Time 107:16 June 28, 76)

FORD, Gerald Rudolph. Instead of being amiable I can get a little firm with a different tone of my voice and with a little sterner look on my face, but I don't go into an outburst because I think, really, when you go into an outburst, you sort of lose control of your capability to analyze something (commenting on how he shows his anger without creating a scene). (Los Angeles Times 95:2 Part 1 Jan 23, 76)

FORD, Gerald Rudolph. It's good for America to see that you can get a fair trial in Washington (to Robert S. Strauss upon the acquittal of John Connally). (New York 8:48 Aug 25, 75)

FORD, Gerald Rudolph. Most of the important things that happen in the world happen in the middle of the night. (San Francisco Chronicle This World 1978:2 Feb 26, 78)

FORD, Gerald Rudolph. My motto towards the Congress is communication, conciliation, compromise and cooperation. (Time 104:27 Dec 2, 74)

FORD, Gerald Rudolph. A President should never promise more than he can deliver and a President should always deliver everything that he's promised. (Time 108:15 Oct 4, 76)

FORD, Gerald Rudolph. There is no Soviet domination of Eastern Europe and there never will be under a Ford Administration. (Chicago Sun-Times 29:2 Oct 8, 76)

FORD, Gerald Rudolph. To the great people of the government of Israel. Excuse me—of Egypt. (Remark at a dinner given in his honor by visiting Egyptian President Anwar Sadat). (Rolling Stone 201:32 Dec 4, 75)

FORD, Gerald Rudolph. Unfortunately the United States did not carry out its commitment in the supplying of military hardware and economic aid to South Vietnam. I wish we had. I think if we had, this present tragic situation in South Vietnam would not have occurred. (Harper's Weekly 3123:4 May 2, 75)

FORD, Gerald Rudolph. We cannot improve this agency by destroying it (commenting on the CIA at the installation ceremony for George Bush as director). (New York Times 125:1 Jan 31, 76)

FORD, Gerald Rudolph. We skiers know that falling down isn't important; it's getting up again. (New York 10:104 Nov 14, 77)

FORD, Gerald Rudolph. You can be certain that I have just begun to fight. America's armed forces today are second to none. And I will take whatever steps are necessary to see that they remain second to none. (Los Angeles Times 94:3 Part 1 Nov 3, 75)

FORD, Henry. History is more or less bunk. (Time 111:74 Jan 9, 78)

FORD, Henry. Thinking is the hardest work there is—which is probably the reason why so few engage in it. (Forbes 121:96 Feb 6, 78)

FORD, Henry, II. Never complain, never explain. (New York Times 128:19 Mar 26, 79)

FORD, Henry, II. This country developed in a particular way because of the automobile, and you can't just push a button and change it. (Time 105:71 Feb 10, 75)

FORD, Jack. I'll be so glad when this is all over and my father is no longer President (commenting on politics and political campaigning). (Washington Post 48:G2 Jan 22, 76)

FORD, Steve. Sometimes I'm for it and sometimes I'm against it (on the legalization of marijuana). (Rolling Stone 200:29 Nov 20, 75)

FOREMAN, George. Boxing is like jazz. The better it is, the less people appreciate it. (Sepia 25:12 Sept 76)

FOREMAN, Percy. Man's inhumanity to man is only exceeded by woman's inhumanity to woman. (Newsweek 88:93 Nov 8, 76)

FORSTER, E. M. If I had to choose between betraying my country and betraying my friend, I hope I should have the guts to betray my country. (Time 115: June 2, 80)

FORTAS, Abe. The law of revenge has its roots in the deep recesses of the human spirit, but that is not a permissible reason for retaining capital punishment. (New York Times Magazine 9 Jan 23, 77)

FOSTER, Jodie. Acting has spared me from being a regular everyday kid slob. (Time 107:49 Feb 23, 76)

FOSTER, Jodie. I've never studied acting. My technique is pure instinct. I'm not bragging, but certain kids have the timing and ability to mimic—and others don't. That's the way it is. And it's important not to be self-conscious. (Chicago Tribune 148:4 section 6 May 29, 77)

FOWLES, John. Cherish the poet; there seemed many great auks till the last one died. (The American Book Review 1:21 Dec 77)

FOWLES, John. Fiction is a removing activity. The ghost that haunts all writers is, 'Am I betraying reality?'. (W 6:12 Oct 14, 77)

FRAIN, Andy. Never trust a man with a mustache or a man who carries an umbrella. (The Reader (Chicago's Free Weekly) 7:14 Jan 27, 78)

FRAMPTON, Peter. I'm not for women's liberation like staunch fem libbers are, but if the old lady is tired and there's a sink full of washing up, I'll do it, you know? (Playboy 25:102 May 78)

FRANCO, Francisco. I ask forgiveness from all, as I give my most heartfelt forgiveness to those who declared themselves my enemies. I believe and hope that I had no enemies other than those who were enemies of Spain—Spain, which I will love until the last moment and which I promised to serve until my dying breath, which is near. (New York Times 125:17 Nov 21, 75)

FRANCO, Francisco. My God, how hard it is to die. (Newsweek 86:66 Nov 24, 75)

FRANK, Mark R. One's ability to perform a given task competently decreases in proportion to the number of people watching. (Omni 1:132 May 79)

FRANKEL, Charles. Scholarship must be free to follow crooked paths to unexpected conclusions. (Time 113:8 May 14, 79)

FRANKEL, Charles. Whatever happens in government could have happened differently, and it usually would have been better if it had. (The Reader (Chicago's Free Weekly) 5:2 May 28, 76)

FRANKLIN, Bonnie. When I was little, my mother always told me my beauty comes from within. Any idiot knows that means you're ugly.   (The Star 4:2 Aug 30, 77)

FRASER, Douglas. The President is a nice man, an intelligent man and he likes his job. But he doesn't have any fire in his belly.   (Chicago Sun-Times 32:2 April 27, 79)

FRASER, Malcolm. Receiving Skylab is an honor we would happily have foregone.   (New York Times 128:B1 July 13, 79)

FRAZIER, Joe. I want him like a hog wants slop (commenting on wanting to fight Muhammad Ali).   (New York Times 125:12 Section 5 May 30, 76)

FREIFELD, Sam. Saul Bellow is a great writer who is smaller than life.   (Chicago 28:176 Dec 79)

FREMONT-SMITH, Eliot. Booksellers are good at drinking; librarians are better.   (Village Voice 20:49 June 9, 75)

FRENCH, Marilyn. Men believe men are central to women's lives, and they're not—even when they become economically central, even psychologically, when we have to please them. Children are the center of a woman's life. Work is always central. When you have children, they become your work, your opus.   (Chicago Tribune 8:9 section 5 Jan 8, 78)

FRESCO, Catherine B. If you knew what you were doing, you'd probably be bored.   (Washingtonian 15:141 Nov 79)

FREUD, Sigmund. The first human who hurled a curse instead of a weapon against his adversary was the founder of civilization.   (Rocky Mountain News 244:58 Dec 22, 79)

FREUD, Sigmund. My cigar is not a symbol. It is only a cigar.   (Washingtonian 12:112 April 77)

FREUD, Sigmund. One is very crazy when in love.   (Playboy 26:26 Oct 79)

FRIEDAN, Betty. The women's liberation movement was only a waystation. The questions we face now cannot be solved by women alone. Thinking must come in cooperation with old people, young people, heart-attack prone executives, trade unionists, blacks and other minorities. I feel a great anxiety now about the collision between the increased aspirations of women and the erosion of support for affirmative action programs and equal rights.   (Chicago Tribune 320:11 Section 5 Nov 16, 75)

FRIEDBERG, A. Alan. Boston is a city with champagne tastes and beer pocketbooks.   (Time 114:82 July 16, 79)

FRIEDMAN, Milton. Governments never learn. Only people learn.   (The Observer 9840:11 Mar 30, 80)

FRIEDMAN, Milton. In this day and age, we need to revise the old saying to read, Hell hath no fury like a bureaucrat scorned.   (Newsweek 86:47 Dec 29, 75)

FRIEDMAN, Milton. Inflation is the one form of taxation that can be imposed without legislation.   (American Opinion 18:37 April 75)

FRIEDMAN, Milton. Let me propose that we take as our major motto what I would like to see as an 11th commandment: that everyone shall be free to do good at his own expense.   (American Legion Magazine 103:12 Aug 77)

FRIEDMAN, Milton. New York City's financial crisis was possibly the best thing to happen in this country in a long time.   (University Daily Kansan 86:1 Dec 5, 75)

FRIEDMAN, Milton. There is no such thing as a free lunch. That is the sum of my economic theory. The rest is elaboration.   (Reader's Digest 112:190 Feb 78)

FRIENDLY, Fred. The news is the one thing networks can point to with pride. Everything else they do is crap, and they know it.   (Time 115:74 Jan 14, 80)

FRIENDLY, Fred. TV still basically indexes rather than reports the news.   (Time 115:70 Feb 25, 80)

FRITCHEY, Clayton. President Carter says he doesn't 'panic in a crisis.' But that's not the problem. The problem is that he panics without a crisis.   (Time 114:116 Nov 19, 79)

FROMME, Lynette (Squeaky). Anybody can kill anybody.   (Time 106:19 Sept 15, 75)

FROMME, Lynette (Squeaky). I can't be rehabilitated because I haven't done anything wrong.   (Time 106:19 Dec 29, 75)

FROST, Robert. Half the world is composed of people who have something to say and can't, and the other half who have nothing to say and keep on saying it.   (Kansas City Star 97:38 July 14, 77)

FROST, Robert. Home is the place where you have to go there, they have to take you in.   (Rocky Mountain News 134:44 Sept 3, 79)

FUENTES, Carlos. Mexicans have always asked themselves why a people so close to God should be so near the United States.   (W 5:9 Oct 29, 76)

FUENTES, Carlos. There are two things one never should do after fifty: change wives and give interviews.   (Nuestro 2:36 Nov 78)

FUGETT, Jean. I always thought of Pittsburgh as a dirty city, a crude city and a blue-collar town. And that's exactly what I think of their football team (commenting after the Super Bowl game).   (New York Times 125:3 Section 5 Jan 25, 76)

FULBRIGHT, James William. A great nation is peculiarly susceptible to the idea that its power is a sign of God's favor, conferring upon it a special responsibility for other nations—to make them richer and happier and wiser, to remake them, that is, in its own shining image. Power confuses itself with virtue and tends also to take itself for omnipotence (comments made in the 1960s).   (July 4, 1976 special edition magazine of the Washington Post 146 July 4, 76)

FULBRIGHT, James William. If once the press was excessively orthodox and unquestioning of Government policy, it has now become almost sweepingly iconoclastic.   (Time 106:78 Nov 24, 75)

FULBRIGHT, James William. It is one of the perversities of human nature that people have a far greater capacity for enduring disasters than for preventing them, even when the danger is plain and imminent.   (American Legion Magazine 98:20 Jan 75)

FULLER, Curtis. But there's only one Count Basie. That's all there'll ever be.   (Detroiter 66:38 June 75)

FULLER, R. Buckminster. The future is a choice between Utopia and oblivion.   (Analog Science Fiction/Science Fact 99:97 Oct 79)

FULLER, R. Buckminster. Sometimes I think we're alone. Sometimes I think we're not. In either case, the thought is quite staggering.   (Omni 2:39 April 80)

FURNESS, Betty. I'd invest $9 million in Big Mac bonds. It might not really help New York City, but it would not hurt. And if I never saw the money again, what's the difference? I'd still have my $1 million, a figure I can cope with. I would see that some of it got into the hands of a number of people whose problems can be solved with money. I'd try to find one person whose dreams aren't ever going to come true because of lack of money, and I'd pay for those dreams. And then I'd go to Bloomingdale's (in response to 'What would you do with 10 million dollars').   (Money 4:76 Nov 75)

GABIN, Jean. You are a young me (about Marlon Brando).   (Look 1:96 Mar 5, 79)

GABO, Naum. Today is the deed.   (Guardian Weekly 117:21 Sept 4, 77)

GABOR, Zsa Zsa. I have never hated a man enough to give his diamonds back.   (Cosmopolitan 188:268 Feb 80)

GABOR, Zsa Zsa. Macho does not prove mucho.   (Washingtonian 15:143 Nov 79)

GABOR, Zsa Zsa. A man in love is incomplete until he has married. Then he's finished.   (Village Voice 22:20 Dec 26, 77)

GABOR, Zsa Zsa. You're never too young to be younger.   (Oui 8:82 Jan 78)

GALBRAITH, John Kenneth. Anyone who says he isn't going to resign, four times, definitely will.   (Town & Country 133:140 May 79)

GALBRAITH, John Kenneth. Capitalism will survive.   (New York Times Book Review 31 Sept 30, 79)

GALBRAITH, John Kenneth. I'm opposed to tax decreases. If the last one had worked Jerry Ford would still be President.   (San Francisco Examiner 1977:2 section B May 1, 77)

GALBRAITH, John Kenneth. (Money) ranks with love as man's greatest source of joy. And it ranks with death as his greatest source of anxiety. It differs from an automobile, a mistress, and cancer in being equally important to those who have it and those who don't. So when you watch people in a supermarket, you're seeing people in touch with their deepest emotions.   (Chicago Tribune 131:1 section 3 May 11, 77)

GALBRAITH, John Kenneth. No ethic is as ethical as the work ethic.   (Cosmopolitan 188:264 June 80)

GALBRAITH, John Kenneth. The study of money, above all other fields of economics, is one in which complexity is used to disguise or evade the truth, not reveal it. Much discussion involves priestly incantation, the same type used by doctors and lawyers to pretend to a sort of difference that excludes other people.   (Chicago Tribune 131:1 section 3 May 11, 77)

GALBRAITH, John Kenneth. The (tax) revolt of the affluent, which now has politicans so frightened, is not a violent thing. The response in the ghettoes if life there is allowed further to deteriorate might be different.   (New York Times 128:A23 Jan 12, 79)

GALELLA, Ron. I photograph the Kennedys because, like it or not, they are the royalty of America.   (Boston 70:123 Dec 78)

GALLAGHER, Bill. The first thing they cut were night classes to teach English to migrants. You have to ask whether the motives are fiscal or political. It seems to me that we have our priorities backward—we are paying the banks, and trying to deal with the needs of the people last.   (Maclean's 88:84 Oct 6, 75)

GALLICO, Paul. In place of great literary fame, I've millions of people who care about what I write and who like me. What the hell more do I want?   (Newsweek 88:57 July 26, 76)

GALLUP, George. I could prove God statistically.   (Omni 2:42 Nov 79)

GALVIN, William. Instead of bemoaning what Government does to business, Reagan attacked what Government is doing to people. It's a strategy, and one which, as a Democrat, frightens me.   (Time 116:29 July 28, 80)

GANDHI, Indira (Nehru). The freedom of the people cannot be allowed to come in the way of the freedom of the masses.   (People Weekly 4:33 Dec 29/Jan 5, 76)

GANDHI, Indira (Nehru). I am one of the sights of Delhi.   (Time 114:61 July 16, 79)

GANDHI, Indira (Nehru). I have no recollection of games, children's parties or playing with other children. All my games were political ones—I was, like Joan of Arc, perpetually being burned at the stake.   (Time 106:16 July 7, 75)

GANDHI, Indira (Nehru). The people do not care about all that emergency business that is in the newspapers all the time. The poor people are with me. They know that I have always been their friend.   (New York Times 128:A10 Nov 9, 78)

GANDHI, Indira (Nehru). The steps we have taken are to strengthen our democracy (upon suspending civil liberties and imposing press censorship).   (Newsweek 86:42 Aug 4, 75)

GANDHI, Indira (Nehru). We should be vigilant to see that our march to progress is not hampered in the name of the Constitution.   (New York Times 125:5 Section I Dec 28, 75)

GANN, Paul. We're only asking the government to live within our means (favoring California's Proposition 4).   (Newsweek 94:45 Sept 24, 79)

GANNETT, Lewis. The great days in New York were just before you got there.   (Country Journal 5:10 Dec 78)

GARDNER, Brian. Polluters must be made to pay so much that the fines—continuously leveled until the pollution stops—are so high that not to pollute is a cheaper alternative.   (New Scientist 76:516 Nov 24, 77)

GARDNER, John. Instead of the United States being run by a well-knit behind-the-scenes power group, it is whipsawed by a great multiplicity of special interests.   (American Legion Magazine 102:20 Feb 77)

GARLAND, Judy. I have gone through hell, I tell you, a hell no one, no person, no man, no beast, not even a fire hydrant could endure.   (Newsweek 85:52 May 26, 75)

GARN, Jake. I frankly don't give a damn if a 14-legged bug or the woundfin minnow live or die.   (Outside 1:10 July/Aug 78)

GARRY, Charles. Mark Lane knew about everything; the guns, the drugs, the suicide pact—and he never told anyone.   (Newsweek 92:52 Dec 4, 78)

GARSON, Barbara. Elizabeth Gurley Flynn's autobiography reminded me with a jolt that it wasn't until the time of the Stokely Carmichaels, imitated by the Tom Haydens, that women on the left had to fight to get the floor or to get up off of the floor.   (Ms 4:92 Feb 76)

GARVEY, Ed. When you talk about civil liberties in professional sports, it's like talking about virtue in a whorehouse.   (Village Voice 20:37 Dec 8, 75)

GASICH, Welko (Vice President of Northrop Aircraft Corporation). Until we have a bona fide world police force, it's still Dodge City and everyone wants a rifle over his door.   (Time 105:44 March 3, 75)

GASS, Istvan (Hungarian soccer star). It's not serious work. I don't do anything. In fact, I've never seen a gun (on his job as a soldier).   (Sports Illustrated 43:12 Sept 1, 75)

GAULD, Joseph. The rod (physical discipline) is only wrong in the wrong hands.   (Time 107:51 Aug 9, 76)

GAUSSEN, Gerard. Mrs. (Estee) Lauder represents what we French admire most about Americans—brains and heart.   (Chicago Tribune 22:33 Jan 22, 78)

GEISEL, Theodor. Adults are obsolete children and the hell with them.   (Time 113:93 May 7, 79)

GENTRY, Dave Tyson. True friendship comes when silence between two people is comfortable.   (Reader's Digest 107:56B Sept 75)

GETTY, Jean Paul. I suffer no guilt complexes or conscience pangs about my wealth. The Lord may have been disproportionate, but that is how He—or nature, if you like—operates.   (Time 107:41 May 24, 76)

GETTY, Jean Paul. If you can count your money, you don't have a billion dollars.   (Newsweek 87:55 June 14, 76)

GETTY, Jean Paul. The meek shall inherit the earth, but not its mineral rights.   (Time 113:25 Feb 26, 79)

GETTY, Jean Paul. Remember, a billion dollars isn't worth what it used to be.   (Newsweek 94:166 Nov 19, 79)

GETZ, Stan. (Jimmy) Carter is playing it real safe and having only chamber quartets and opera. Let the peanut farmer break out a little and get some jazz at the White House.   (Chicago Tribune 212:33 July 31, 77)

GIAMATTI, A. Bartlett. The university must be a tributary to a larger society, not a sanctuary from it.   (Time 112:89 Oct 2, 78)

GIANNINI, Giancarlo. For an actor, it's always difficult to have a wife. It's not hard to be without one.   (W 8:22 Feb 2, 79)

GIBBS, Philip. It's better to give than to lend, and it costs about the same.   (Kansas City Star 97:38 July 14, 77)

GIELGUD, John (attributed by Leslie Caron). Never show your good side—show your faults (instruction to actors).   (New York Times 126:31 section 2 Aug 28, 77)

GILES, Warren. (Charlie) Finley wouldn't think God could make a good (baseball) commissioner.   (Chicago Tribune 185:12 July 4, 78)

GILL, Brendan. The rich have no need to pronounce words correctly. They can leave all that to their lawyers and accountants.   (Andy Warhol's Interview 8:60 Dec 78)

GILLESPIE, Dizzy. It took me all my life to learn the biggest music lesson of them all—what not to play.   (Sepia 25:10 Dec 76)

GILLESPIE, Marcia Ann. I did not stand up for my rights as a black person in America to be told that I have to sit down because I'm a woman.   (Time 114:99 Oct 29, 79)

GILMORE, Gary Mark. Death is the only inescapable, unavoidable, sure thing. We are sentenced to die the day we're born.   (Chicago Sun-Times 29:2 Nov 17, 76)

GILMORE, Gary Mark. I believe I was given a fair trial. The sentence is proper, and I'm willing to accept it with dignity, like a man (pleading with the Utah Supreme Court to allow him to be executed by a firing squad on schedule).   (Chicago Sun-Times 29:2 Nov 11, 76)

GILMORE, Gary Mark. Let's do it.   (Chicago Daily News 13 Dec 30, 77)

GILMORE, Gary Mark. You sentenced a man to die—me—and when I accept this most extreme punishment with grace and dignity, the people of Utah want to back down and argue with me about it. You're silly (a note delivered from his death row cell to the Utah State Supreme Court).   (New York Times 126:25 Nov 9, 76)

GINGRICH, Arnold. To stand out, for a man or a magazine, it is necessary to stand for something. Otherwise you stand still.   (Newsweek 88:78 July 19, 76)

GINSBERG, Allen. Art is shapely.   (The American Book Review 1:8 April/May 78)

GINSBERG, Allen. I like a varied audience—little old ladies, homosexuals, weirdos.   (Time 113:81 Mar 5, 79)

GINZBURG, Alexander. The Russian (people) do not believe in Communism.   (US News & World Report 86:17 June 18, 79)

GIONO, Jean. Reality pushed to its extreme ends in unreality.   (Village Voice 21:93 Sept 27, 76)

GIROUD, Francoise. If an atom bomb fell on France, (Valery Giscard d'Estaing) would be there to congratulate himself that there had not been two.   (Time 110:120 Nov 28, 77)

GISCARD D'ESTAING, Valery. The foreign policy of France is not made and will not be made in the newsrooms of some of the international information media. France, her people and her laws have no lessons to receive from anyone, and I invite those who wish to be our friends to refrain from giving us their lessons (commenting about international criticism on the French handling of the release of Abu Daoud, the Palestinian suspected of planning the 1972 Munich Olympic attack on Israeli athletes).   (Christian Science Monitor 69:9 Jan 19, 77)

GISCARD D'ESTAING, Valery. Nuclear energy is at the crossroads of the two independences of France: the independence of her defense and the independence of her energy supply.   (Time 110:31 Aug 15, 77)

GISCARD D'ESTAING, Valery. The present world crisis is not just a passing perturbation but in reality represents a permanent change. If we examine the major graphic curves that are drawn for the future by the phenomena of our times, you see that all of these curves lead to catastrophe. (Time 106:53 Sept 1, 75)

GISCARD D'ESTAING, Valery. You do not fear freedom for yourself, do not then fear it for your friends and allies. (New York Times 125:2 May 19, 76)

GISH, Lillian. Films are the greatest force ever to move the hearts and minds of the world. The Observer 9772:10 Nov 78)

GISH, Lillian. I don't think actresses have the right to marry and ruin a man's life. (Chicago Sun-Times 32:33 July 16, 79)

GISH, Lillian. I've had the best life of anyone I know, or knew, Dear. And I knew some amazing people. Guardian Weekly 120:19 May 6, 79

GISH, Lillian. Movies have to answer a great deal for what the world is today. (Time 105:44 Feb 3, 75)

GIULINI, Carlo Maria. I always think I am a very small man. When I shave myself, I look in the mirror and see behind me Beethoven and Brahms. (Time 111:63 April 3, 78)

GIVENCHY, Hubert De. After I open a collection and see people trying on my clothes and treating them roughly, I suffer. My dresses are like my family. (Time 110:67 Sept 26, 77)

GLADSTONE, William Ewart. He (Bismarck) made Germany great and Germans small. (Harpers 260:8 Feb 80)

GLASSMAN, James K. As a sit-in veteran and small businessman myself, I'm convinced that entrepreneurship is the last refuge of the trouble-making individual. (Washington Monthly 8:44 Oct 76)

GLEASON, Jackie. I drank because it removed the warts and blemishes. Not from me but from the people I associated with. It sort of dimmed the lights. (Chicago Tribune Magazine 17 Mar 26, 78)

GLEASON, Jackie. Thin people are beautiful, but fat people are adorable. (People Weekly 5:29 May 3, 76)

GLENN, John. Our objective is to prevent the people of this country from getting economically raped (arguing against the decontrol of petroleum prices). (Time 106:61 Oct 13, 75)

GLENVILLE, Peter. Compared to ordinary men with ordinary ambitions, Larry (Olivier) was a sea monster. (New York Times Magazine 62 Mar 25, 79)

GOCKLEY, David. Sarah is an administrator only in the sense that no one else can administrate her (about Sarah Caldwell). (Time 106:65 Nov 10, 75)

GODART, Suzanne. Keep a girl in jeans from 4 to 14, and you'll wind up with a Butch on your hands. (W 9:8 Jan 18, 80)

GOEBBELS, Joseph. The Jews are re-emerging. Anyone in a position to do so should kill Jews off like rats. In Germany, thank God, we have already done a fairly complete job. I trust that the world will take its cue from this (from his diary, 1945). (Newsweek 91:49 Jan 16, 78)

GOEBBELS, Joseph. Nothing is easier than leading the people on a leash. I just hold up a dazzling campaign poster and they jump through it. (The Guardian Weekly 115:17 Oct 10, 76)

GOEBBELS, Joseph. Whoever can conquer the streets will one day conquer the state, for every form of power politics and any dictatorially run state has its roots in the streets. (Los Angeles Times Book Review 1 June 11, 78)

GOELET, Robert G. I can't think of anything I'd rather be doing than serving as president of the museum. I have a personal weakness for fish and birds; I'm nuts for fossils, and I have a healthy respect for poisonous snakes. (New York Times 125:15 Dec 1, 75)

GOLD, Herbert. Never trust a newspaper over 10. (New West 4:52 Jan 1, 79)

GOLD, Herbert. The rubber-stamp expression is a rubber stamp even the first time it is pressed into our brains. (Newsweek 93:11 Feb 5, 79)

GOLDBERG, Arthur Joseph. We need a world in which it is safe to be human. (Kansas City Times 109:28 Jan 4, 77)

GOLDBERGER, Paul. Other cities consume culture, New York creates it. (Town & Country 131:14 Sept 77)

GOLDSMITH, James. We (British) have reached the state where the private sector is that part of the economy the Government controls and the public sector is the part that nobody controls. (The Observer 9787:11 March 25, 79)

GOLDSTEIN, Al. A hard-on is its own redeeming value. (Penthouse 8:106 Jan 77)

GOLDSTEIN, Al. When it comes to pornography, I know two kinds of people: those who don't know what they're talking about, and those who don't know what they're missing. (Washington Post 353:D3 Nov 22, 76)

GOLDWATER, Barry Morris. A book should not be charged the same rate for mailing as a brick. (New York Times 126:16 Section 4 Jan 30, 77)

GOLDWATER, Barry Morris. Eternal vigilance is the price of liberty. (Texas Observer 70:2 Aug 11, 78)

GOLDWATER, Barry Morris. He let this country down, he let his party down. And that's the last time I want to talk about Nixon, ever (summarizing his feelings about Richard Nixon). (People Weekly 5:9 Mar 22, 76)

GOLDWATER, Barry Morris. I don't care if I'm called a Democrat or a Republican as long as I'm in bed with people of the same thinking. (Rolling Stone 227:43 Dec 2, 76)

GOLDWATER, Barry Morris. I don't object to a woman doing anything in combat as long as she gets home in time to cook dinner. (Viva 5:29 Oct 77)

GOLDWATER, Barry Morris. I have always said if you put Reagan in one hand and Ford in the other hand and turn the lights out, you wouldn't know who the hell you had in either hand, because of their political philosophy. (Meet the Press 20:5 May 2, 76)

GOLDWATER, Barry Morris. I think there are some things which we don't want to know. Nothing could make the Soviets happier than to see our wonderful intelligence system destroyed (in suggesting that Congressional probes of the CIA be called off). (Rolling Stone 201:32 Dec 4, 75)

GOLDWATER, Barry Morris. I would have said that we should fight for the (Panama) canal if necessary. But the Viet Nam years have taught me that we wouldn't. So we might as well hand it over. (Time 110:11 Aug 22, 77)

GOLDWATER, Barry Morris. If he (William Scott) were any dumber, he'd be a tree. (New Times 6:17 April 16, 76)

GOLDWATER, Barry Morris. There are only so many lies you can take, and now there has been one too many. Nixon should get his ass out of the White House—today (after leaving a conference with Nixon before his resignation as president). (Time 104:21 Aug 19, 74)

GOLDWATER, Barry Morris. This is a great country where anybody can grow up to be President— except me. (Chicago Tribune 245:20 Sept 2, 77)

GOLDWATER, Barry Morris, Jr. Without a sense of privacy, the Bill of Rights' guarantees cease to function. (Time 110:17 July 18, 77)

GOLDWIN, Robert. The cause I push is a kind of elevated common sense. (Time 105:22 March 3, 75)

GOLDWYN, Samuel. If ya wanna send a message, call Western Union. (Mother Jones 2:61 Sept/Oct 77)

GOLDWYN, Samuel. A verbal contract isn't worth the paper it's written on. Washingtonian 14:154 Nov 78

GOMEZ, Lefty. If you don't throw it, they can't hit it. (Washingtonian 15:141 Nov 79)

GONCALVES, Vasco dos Santos. Emotion is not incompatible with lucidity. (Time 105:40 May 5, 75)

GONCALVES, Vasco dos Santos. It is not simple to be a member of a government team whose duration is expressed in days. (Time 106:14 Sept 1, 75)

GOODE, William J. Success is sexy (about women). (Esquire 91:51 April 24, 79)

GOODMAN, Benny. Everything I own, whatever I have accomplished, all that I am, really, I owe to music. (People Weekly 9:80 Jan 23, 78)

GOODMAN, Ellen. It has begun to occur to me that life is a stage I'm going through. (Time 114:125 Dec 10, 79)

GOODMAN, Julian. As the pioneering network, as the first network, we like to think of ourselves as the network with some class (commenting on NBC). (Washington Post 352:K7 Nov 21, 76)

GOODWIN, Richard N. He's not even an accidental president. He's a double-misfortune president— president by grace of the criminal code and modern electronics (about Gerald R. Ford). (New York 8:43 Aug 18, 75)

GORDIMER, Nadine. The facts are always less than what really happened. (Time 110:93 Sept 19, 77)

GORDON, Ruth (actress). In the old days, ptomaine poisoning was a cover-all. If you missed a show and you were young, it meant you were having an abortion. If you were old, it meant you were having a face-lift. (Time 107:40 April 5, 76)

GOTBAUM, Victor. (John Lindsay) was elegant where the rest of us had a piece of vulgarity in us. From the start, he was a made-to-order whipping boy. (Chicago Tribune 22:2 section 2 Jan 22, 78)

GRABLE, Betty. There are only two reasons for my success, and I'm standing on them. (New Orleans 10:108 Aug 76)

GRACE PATRICIA, CONSORT OF RANIER III, PRINCE OF MONACO, . It's her (daughter Princess Caroline's) happiness that counts. I don't care if she's marrying a commoner. (Forbes 122:26 Oct 2, 78)

GRAFF, Henry. Vance is a practitioner of turtle diplomacy. (Time 111:14 April 24, 78)

GRAHAM, Benjamin. Never having to balance your checkbook (a definition of financial success). (Money 5:37 July 76)

GRAHAM, Benjamin. (The stock market is) a Falstaffian joke that frequently degenerates into a madhouse. (Money 5:36 July 76)

GRAHAM, Bill. San Francisco is not a part of America. (Chicago Daily News Panorama 4 Jan 22/23, 77)

GRAHAM, Billy. I believe I have demonic forces opposed to me wherever I preach. (The Observer 9832:9 Feb 3, 80)

GRAHAM, Billy. I stopped in San Clemente last month and spent an hour with him. He's more like his old self before he became President. He's joking, he's kidding, he's laughing a lot. (Los Angeles Times 95:2 Part 1 Dec 15, 75)

GRAHAM, Billy. I was shocked and surprised. This was a Nixon I didn't know (commenting on the language used on some of the Nixon tapes). (Los Angeles Times 95:2 Part 1 Dec 15, 75)

GRAHAM, Billy. In her own way she (Ethel Waters) did as much for race relations as any American in the 20th Century. (Chicago Tribune 245:5 Sept 2, 77)

GRAHAM, Billy. Most Houstonians will spend eternity in Hell. (Texas Monthly 6:154 Feb 78)

GRAHAM, Billy. Nixon in my judgement was a true intellectual. (Chicago Tribune Magazine 46 Nov 6, 77)

GRAHAM, Billy. The pressures of being a well-known clergyman are unbelievable, and I'd like to escape to heaven if I could. (Chicago Tribune Magazine 32 Nov 6, 77)

GRAHAM, Billy. Transcendental Meditation is evil because...it opens space within you for the devil. (Ms 6:50 July 77)

GRAHAM, Katharine. This company (The Washington Post) is not now and never has been antiunion. (Newsweek 86:44 Dec 22, 75)

GRAHAM, Martha. Dance is my passion—it's all I really know besides love; a little of both. (Washington Post 65:C3 Feb 8, 77)

GRANT, Cary. My formula for living is quite simple. I get up in the morning and go to bed at night. In between times, I occupy myself as best I can. (Los Angeles Times Calendar 39 June 11, 78)

GRASS, Gunter. If you don't face it, it means two things: you lost the war and you've also lost the ability to make clear why it happened. (Time 112:77 Nov 13, 78)

GRASSO, Ella. In Connecticut, I'm just an old shoe (describing how she was elected Governor of Connecticut). (Time 104:10 Nov 18, 74)

GRAY, Francine du Plessix. Women are the only exploited group in history who have been idealized into powerlessness. (Time 111:76 Jan 30, 78)

GRAZIANO, Rocky. The singin's easy. Memorizin' the words is hard (upon his New York City night club singing debut). (Sports Illustrated 43:14 Aug 18, 75)

GREELEY, Andrew. (Busing) is not designed to bring justice to blacks or to improve education. It is intended rather to punish whites for their past racial prejudice. You punish whites by playing chess with their children. (Chicago Tribune 33:3 section 3 Feb 2, 78)

GREELEY, Andrew. Only a charlatan or a lunatic would be hopeful about the present state of Catholicism. (Psychology Today 10:51 June 76)

GREEN, Mark (lawyer). While piously proclaiming an interest in the public good, the bar's Canons of Ethics have operated as Canons of Profits. (Time 110:52 Aug 8, 77)

GREENBERG, David. An oldtimer is someone who can remember when a naughty child was taken to the woodshed instead of to a psychiatrist. (American Opinion 18:29 Nov 75)

GREENBERG, Mike. Half of San Antonio's population is of Mexican descent; the other half just eats that way. (Chicago 24:112 Sept 75)

GREENBERG, Stanley. Writing isn't an exact science. It is more like chasing a butterfly you're not sure you want to catch. (Writer's Digest 56:5 May 76)

GREENE, Bob. Indeed, Hugh Hefner is beginning to seem more and more like everyone's kindly and slightly bewildered uncle. (Newsweek 86:13 Sept 29, 75)

GREENE, Graham. God forbid people should read our books to find the juicy passages. (The Observer 9816:11 Oct 14, 79)

GREENE, Graham. There is far more religious faith in Russia than in England. (The Observer 9850:13 June 8, 80)

GREENFELD, Josh. Cinema is a form of Danish. (Time 111:97 April 10, 78)

GREENFELD, Josh. New Jersey looks like the back of an old radio. (Time 111:97 April 10, 78)

GREENFIELD, Jeff. You will get what you want if you vote for the candidate who says exactly the opposite of what you most deeply believe. (Penthouse 10:123 Nov 78)

GREENFIELD, Meg. The wages of interracial living is not mass suicide and murder. (Newsweek 92:132 Dec 4, 78)

GREENSPAN, Alan. When I met Ayn Rand, I was a free enterpriser in the Adam Smith sense, impressed with the theoretical structure and efficiency of markets. What she did was to make me see that capitalism is not only efficient and practical, but also moral. (Newsweek 85:61 Feb 24, 75)

GREER, Germaine. Everyone I know is either married or dotty. (The Observer 9790:10 April 15, 79)

GREER, Germaine. I love men like some people like good food or wine. (The Observer 9782:10 Feb 18, 79)

GREER, Germaine. It's sheer myth that feminists are anti-child—we're the only people who're going to give children a better deal. (People Weekly 5:72 Jan 26, 76)

GREER, Germaine. Security is when everything is settled, when nothing can happen to you; security is a denial of life. (Redbook 148:57 Mar 77)

GREGOIRE, Menie. Every French male born is convinced that, by definition, he is an expert lover. Many wives tell me that they go to see pornographic movies with their husbands as a way of delicately indicating to them that they don't know as much about lovemaking as they think they do. (Macleans 88:72 Nov 3, 75)

GRIFFIN, Mickey. It's high time the rednecks came back to Washington. There are a hell of a lot more rednecks out there than people who eat crepes suzette. (Rolling Stone 193:27 Aug 14, 75)

GRIFFITH, Calvin. He's the P.T. Barnum of baseball. (about Charles Oscar Finley). (Time 106:42 Aug 18, 75)

GROPPI, James E. Right now, the bus will be my church and the people who board it my parishioners (commenting on his status as a bus driver in Milwaukee after his excommunication from the Catholic Church). (Chicago Sun-Times 29:8 Nov 12, 76)

GROSS, Alan. If you see a Gucci loafer in L.A. today, you're looking at the foot of a lawyer. (Chicago 28:288 May 79)

GRUBER, Jack. Integration is not something you win at, it's something you work at. (Time 110:21 Oct 31, 77)

GUARE, John. Innocence is ignorance where you're not getting caught. (Village Voice 22:35 Aug 15, 77)

GUCCI, Aldo. We are not businessmen, we are poets. (Town & Country 131:193 Dec 77)

GUERRINA, Allan B. In any group of eagles, you will find some turkeys. (Washingtonian 15:140 Nov 79)

GUEST, Lucy Cochrane (C.Z.). I think manners are the most important thing in life. (Mother Jones 2:10 Aug 77)

GUEVARA, Nacha. In life the things you want always arrive after you've stopped waiting. (Chicago Sun-Times 32:8 section 4 July 1, 79)

GUGGENHEIM, Peggy. I don't like art today, I think it has gone to hell. (W 8:24 Oct 12, 79)

GUNTHER, John. All happiness depends on a leisurely breakfast. (Washingtonian 14:154 Nov 78)

GURFEIN, Murray. A cantankerous press must be suffered by those in authority in order to preserve freedom of expression and the right of the people to know. (Time 114:59 Dec 31, 79)

GURNEY, Edward John. Everybody who knows me knows I have a very poor memory. (Rolling Stone 195:28 Sept 11, 75)

GURNEY, Edward John. I have a feeling of great relief that this long ordeal is finally over, a feeling of great satisfaction that we've beaten these mean, vicious people from the Government. They destroyed a United States Senator, blackened my name and besmirched my character (commenting on his acquittal from the last charge against him in a political shakedown case). (New York Times 126:19 Oct 28, 76)

GUTHRIE, Arlo. The difference between Anita Bryant and me may be that she definitely feels that God is on her side, and I have to keep questioning whether I'm on His (upon becoming a Franciscan lay brother). (Mother Jones 3:9 Sept/Oct 78)

GUTHRIE, Arlo. The world has shown me what it has to offer...It's a nice plce to visit, but I wouldn't want to live there. (Rolling Stone 268:36 June 29, 78)

GUTHRIE, Janet. I am a racing driver who happens to be a woman. (New York Times 125:6 Section 5 April 18, 76)

GUTHRIE, Woody. You can't write a good song about a whorehouse unless you been in one. (Los Angeles Times Calendar 82 Mar 26, 78)

HAGEDORN, Tom. As far as I'm concerned, environmentalists and food stamp cheaters are the same thing. (Potomac (Sunday Magazine of the Washington Post) 4 Mar 7, 76)

HAGEN, Walter. You only get one trip through life, so don't forget to stop and smell the flowers. (Newsweek 85:71 April 21, 75)

HAGGARD, Merle. I was born the running kind, with leaving always on my mind. (Village Voice 25:8 July 2, 80)

HAIG, Alexander M. The arms race is the only game in town. (Esquire 90:31 Sept 26, 78)

HAIG, Alexander M. Military service and public service are not unakin. (The Observer 9776:10 Jan 7, 79)

HAIG, Alexander M. The next war could be a come-as-you-are party. (Esquire 90:31 Sept 26, 78)

HAILE SELASSIE I, EMPEROR OF ETHIOPIA, . Death changes everything, sweeps everything away. Even mistakes. (Newsweek 86:32 Sept 8, 75)

HALAS, George. You can have a session with your girl friend. What's that last you? Twenty minutes, half an hour? Or you can go out and get stiff with the boys. A few hours, right? But to win a game in the National Football League. That lasts a whole week. (Chicago Daily News 13 Dec 30, 77)

HALDANE, J. B. S. I suspect that there are more things in heaven and earth than are dreamed of, or can be dreamed of, in any philosophy. (Times Literary Supplement 3952:1502 Dec 23, 77)

HALDEMAN, Harry Robbins. I'll approve of whatever will work and am concerned with results—not methods. (Time 103:12 Mar 11, 74)

HALES, E. E. Y. Hell is where you are free to be yourself, and nothing but yourself (commenting in his novel Chariot of Fire). (Time 109:92 Mar 7, 77)

HALEY, Jack. I don't believe there's no business like show business. (Newsweek 93:90 June 18, 79)

HALIBURTON, Thomas C. The great secret of life is to learn lessons, not to teach them. (Kansas City Star 97:14C Dec 22, 76)

HALL, Daryl. It's socially immoral for a white person to act like a black person. (Creem 9:34 Aug 77)

HALL, Donald. Less is more, in prose as in architecture. (Writer's Digest 58:8 Nov 78)

HALL, John. The colleges would do better to get rid of the nights and return to Saturday afternoon football the way God and Grantland Rice created it (commenting on college football being played at night). (Sports Illustrated 45:16 Nov 1, 76)

HALL, Keith W. The word 'necessary' seldom is. (Washingtonian 15:141-42 Nov 79)

HALL, Monty. You can learn more about America by watching one half-hour of Let's Make a Deal than you can by watching Walter Cronkite for an entire month. (Time 115:85 Feb 18, 80)

HALSTON (COSTUME DESIGNER), . A designer is only as good as his clientele. We only suggest things. It is fashionable people who make fashion. (People Weekly 7:65 June 20, 77)

HAND, Learned. In a pitilessly consistent democracy, judges would not be making law at all. (Time 113:91 Jan 22, 79)

HANSEN, George. Firearms are not the problem. People are. (American Opinion 18:29 Sept 75)

HARDEN, Frank. Every time you come up with a terrific idea, you find that someone else thought of it first. (Washingtonian 14:154 Nov 78)

HARDING, Warren Gamaliel. Our most dangerous tendency is to expect too much of government, and at the same time to do for it too little (inaugural address—1921). (Christian Science Monitor 69:14 Jan 20, 77)

HARLOW, Bryce N. Our only protection against the presidency is the character of the president. (Washingtonian 11:103 June 76)

HARRELL, John R. The black man's angry, the yellow man's angry. Everybody's angry but the white man, and he's asleep. (Time 114:8 Nov 5, 79)

HARRELSON, Ken. Baseball is the only sport I know that when you're on offense, the other team controls the ball. (Sports Illustrated 44:14 Sept 6, 76)

HARRIMAN, Averell. As I look back, what I regret most was that I wasn't able to influence Johnson to abandon the war in Vietnam. To see that war go on, to find him listening to people with such a completely wrong point of view. Every day there were those whispering in his ear, 'No president ever lost a war.' That was red meat for a Texan. (Potomac (Sunday Magazine of the Washington Post) 72 Dec 7, 75)

HARRIMAN, Averell. I've had much more fun out of life since I became a Democrat. (Potomac (Sunday Magazine of the Washington Post) 4 Jan 11, 76)

HARRIMAN, Averell. People read into 'detente' a situation that doesn't exist. They get 'detente' mixed up with 'rapprochement'. Detente means the relaxation of tensions between nations. My experience is that the Russians are suspicious as hell, but Brezhnev is absolutely committed to peace. It takes patience. If we let the Pentagon have its way, we'll have war. (Potomac (Sunday Magazine of the Washington Post) 72 Dec 7, 75)

HARRIMAN, Averell. The Russians are not nuts, they are not crazy people, they're not Hitler. But they are trying to dominate the world by their ideology and we are killing the one instrument which we have to fight that ideology, the CIA. (W 4:16 Nov 16, 75)

HARRINGTON, Michael. I think that we should offer Jimmy Carter our hand to help him fulfill the promises he made. And if he doesn't take our hand, we should give him a shove.   (Mother Jones 2:30 July 77)

HARRINGTON, Michael. We've created a kind of gray, shadowy atmosphere which is 'just don't get us involved.' Well, I think the guy on the street expects us to solve real problems and not just generate the impression of looking busy when we're not doing anything that counts.   (People Weekly 4:12 Nov 17, 75)

HARRIS, David. People are ready for a congressman who went to jail before he went to Washington instead of after (commenting on what effect his 20 month jail term for resisting induction would have on his bid for the congressional seat of Pete McCloskey).   (People Weekly 5:72 Jan 12, 76)

HARRIS, Fred. The basic issue in 1976 is privilege. It's time to take the rich off welfare.   (Newsweek 86:24 Dec 22, 75)

HARRIS, Fred. If I had it to do over I would have started out the way I wound up, as more of an iconoclast. There was a feeling when I went to the Senate that if you want to have any influence you had to go along. The truth is just the opposite of that.   (Washington Post 21:A6 Dec 26, 75)

HARRIS, Fred. Our current economic problems are not a failure of the system, they are a failure of economic leadership.   (Village Voice 20:28 July 7, 75)

HARRIS, Fred. Sometimes it seems we are willing to prop up any two-bit dictator who can afford the price of a pair of sunglasses.   (Time 106:25 Dec 22, 75)

HARRIS, Fred. These huge corporations say they favor free enterprise. Well, I want to give them a big dose of it. It's time the J. Paul Gettys, the Nelson Rockefellers and these great big corporations started haulin' their part of the freight. Why, did you know there was one year Rockefeller didn't pay any income taxes. We oughta sue that man for nonsupport.   (Newsweek 86:25 Dec 22, 75)

HARRIS, Fred. We've got to dismantle the monster (about the CIA).   (Time 106:24 Sept 29, 75)

HARRIS, Fred. You couldn't call it victory because we didn't run that well. But we ran just well enough to keep going so it really wasn't defeat. We didn't know what to call it and we just decided to call it quits (commenting on his decision to end his bid for the Democratic nomination for President).   (New York Times 125:14 April 9, 76)

HARRIS, James A. Twenty-three percent of school children are failing to graduate, and another large segment graduate as functional illiterates. If 23 percent of anything else failed—23 percent of the automobiles did not run, 23 percent of the buildings fell down, 23 percent of stuffed ham spoiled—we'd look at the producer. The schools, here, are not blameless.   (Harper's Weekly 3123:4 May 2, 75)

HARRIS, Louis. Gerald Ford is viewed as more of a man of integrity, for example, than Jimmy Carter is (commenting on the results of his polling of public opinion).   (ABC News Issues and Answers 1 April 18, 76)

HARRIS, Patricia Roberts. If my life has had any meaning at all, it is that those who start out as outcasts can wind up as being part of the system. Maybe others can forget what it was like to be excluded from the dining rooms in this very building, Senator, but I shall not forget (testifying before the Senate Committee on her scheduled nomination for Secretary of Housing and Urban Development).   (New York Times 126:22 Jan 11, 77)

HARRIS, Patricia Roberts. Poverty is not so much the absence of money as the absence of aspiration, of the knowledge that it is possible to go anywhere else.   (Skeptic 19:10 May/June 77)

HARRIS, Sydney J. Any philosophy that can be 'put in a nutshell' belongs there.   (Washingtonian 14:154 Nov 78)

HARRIS, Sydney J. The art of living consists in knowing which impulses to obey and which must be made to obey.   (Kansas City Times 109:28 Jan 4, 77)

HARRIS, Sydney J. It is not criminals, but laws that are the worst enemy of Law.   (Chicago Daily News 8 May 5, 77)

HARRIS, Sydney J. The paradox in games is that most games are no fun unless you take them seriously; but when you take them seriously, they cease being games.   (Chicago Daily News 8 May 5, 77)

HARRISON, Elizabeth (former wife of Rex Harrison). Rex is the only man in the world who would disdainfully send back the wine in his own home.   (Time 106:41 Dec 29, 75)

HARRISS, Joseph. Parisians have always recognized the human need for the superfluous.   (Time 110:38 July 18, 77)

HART, Gary. Exxon seems to have the idea that it can solve America's energy problems almost totally at Colorado's expense.   (Newsweek 96:58 July 14, 80)

HART, Gary. The race (between Ronald Reagan and Gerald Ford) all boils down to a contest between the philosophies of Herbert Hoover and Calvin Coolidge.   (New York 8:97 Dec 8, 75)

HART, Gary. To get the government off your back, get your hands out of the government's pockets.   (Newsweek 90:36 Nov 7, 77)

HASKINS, Caryl. It's funny that we often value what is rare and specialized. What is truly precious is what is common and unspecialized.   (Washington Post 70:H7 Feb 13, 77)

HASSAN II, KING OF MOROCCO, . I am convinced that the march has fulfilled its mission and reached its goal, and we must therefore return to our point of departure (commenting upon Morocco's march into the Spanish Sahara).   (New York Times 125:1 Nov 10, 75)

HASSAN II, KING OF MOROCCO, . I do not want to frustrate my subjects because a people is not a toy.   (Time 106:28 Nov 10, 75)

HASTINGS, James F. I came up to age 49 without having a great deal to show for it. Taking a look around at the next 12 to 14 years of productive life, I decided I couldn't spend it here under the circumstances and frustrations I see in this legislative body (upon his mid-term resignation as a U.S. congressman).   (Washington Post 22:A1 Dec 27, 75)

HATCHER, Richard. We've created a Frankenstein's monster with a Southern drawl, a more cultured version of the old Confederate at the schoolhouse door. (Time 107:14 April 19, 76)

HATEM, Abu. We will force the United States to recognize (us). Without the Palestine Liberation Organization there is not going to be any peace in the Middle East. (New York Times 128:A3 June 11, 79)

HATFIELD, Mark. It's in the realm of the unconscionable. It raises the greatest probability and potential of introducing nuclear weaponry into conventional warfare (commenting on the neutron bomb). (New York Times 126:4 section 4 July 17, 77)

HAUGHTON, James (Cook County Hospital Director). The residents and interns (who struck the Cook County Hospital for 18 days) are the same young people who tore up colleges five years ago. (Chicago Tribune 231:5 Section 2 Nov 17, 75)

HAUPTMANN, Bruno Richard. I have said it all, I am innocent. There is nothing else I could tell. (New York 9:76 Nov 22, 76)

HAUSER, Philip M. (Chicago) has lace pants in the front, and soiled drawers behind. (Chicago Tribune 71:1 Mar 12, 78)

HAWKINS, Erick. Dance is the most beautiful metaphor of existence in the world. (New York Times 128:12 section 2 July 1, 79)

HAYAKAWA, Samuel Ichiye. Before World War II in Japan they killed off all the older politicians. All that were left were the damn fools who attacked Pearl Harbor. I think that this country needs elder statesmen too. (Time 107:21 June 21, 76)

HAYAKAWA, Samuel Ichiye. (Children are) recent immigrants in our midst. (Esquire 91:16 April 24, 79)

HAYAKAWA, Samuel Ichiye. I guess they're entitled to remain as sick as they like as long as they like (commenting on homosexuals). (Rolling Stone 244:47 July 28, 77)

HAYAKAWA, Samuel Ichiye. I lust after women in my heart every hour on the hour. But being so busy in campaigning, I have to settle for that. (New York Times Magazine 30 Oct 31, 76)

HAYAKAWA, Samuel Ichiye. I must say, I find senators much more interesting people than professors...Professors are too damned specialized. (Chicago Tribune 117:2 section 1 April 27, 77)

HAYAKAWA, Samuel Ichiye. I think it's too much to expect of an elected official to condemn himself to a fully ascetic life, as if he were a priest. But whatever he does he must do with utmost discretion. (Los Angeles 21:86 Oct 76)

HAYAKAWA, Samuel Ichiye. If you have ceased to be ready to face the frightening, then you become old. We weren't put on earth to behave like barnacles. (Time 110:26 Oct 10, 77)

HAYAKAWA, Samuel Ichiye. Let gas go to $1.50, even $2 per gallon. A lot of poor don't need gas because they are not working. (Time 113:12 May 28, 79)

HAYAKAWA, Samuel Ichiye. Republicans are people who, if you were drowning 50 feet from shore, would throw you a 25-foot rope and tell you to swim the other 25 feet because it would be good for your character. Democrats would throw you a 100-foot rope and then walk away looking for other good deeds to do. (Time 107:8 June 14, 76)

HAYAKAWA, Samuel Ichiye. There is only one thing age can give you, and that is wisdom. (New West 1:17 July 5, 76)

HAYDEN, Thomas. During the 1960s, we fought the pigs. Now we fight the high price of bacon. (Newsweek 90:36 Nov 7, 77)

HAYDEN, Thomas. I don't believe that any defense contract ought to be cut in the face of mass unemployment. (US News & World Report 18:12 Nov 3, 75)

HAYDEN, Thomas. If it weren't for the Bill of Rights people like me would be in jail instead of running for office (commenting on his bid for the Senate). (Los Angeles Times 95:3 Part 1 Jan 5, 76)

HAYDEN, Thomas. The radicalism of the '60's became the fascism of the '70's (responding to heckling from left-wing radicals during a speech on his current campaign for U.S. Senator). (Wall Street Journal 56:14 Dec 17, 75)

HAYES, Helen. An audience simply cannot go on reacting indefinitely to a play that doesn't know where it's going. (W 4:10 July 11, 75)

HAYES, Helen. There is no racial or religious prejudice among people in the theater. The only prejudice is against bad actors, especially successful ones. (Time 114:85 Dec 17, 79)

HAYES, Woody. Football is about the only unifying force left in America today. (Life 2:87 Dec 79)

HAYES, Woody. It isn't the size of the dog in the fight, but the size of the fight in the dog that counts. (Forbes 120:80 Aug 1, 77)

HAYES, Woody. When you fight in the North Atlantic, you train in the North Atlantic. (TV Guide 26:45 Nov 18, 78)

HEALEY, Denis. Mrs. Thatcher is doing for monetarism what the Boston Strangler did for door-to-door salesmen. (The Observer 9825:10 Dec 16, 79)

HEARST, Austine. After 40, a woman needs a lover and a good facelift. And after 50, cash. (W 7:2 Oct 27, 78)

HEARST, Patricia Campbell. I was sick of the middle-class life I was leading. The SLA members seemed to have some purpose to their lives. (Los Angeles Times 94:3 Part 1 Oct 26, 75)

HEARST, Patricia Campbell. I'd really like to travel again—anywhere but Italy. There's too much kidnapping there. (Time 112:45 July 24, 78)

HEATH, Edward. I started out studying music but very quickly went downhill and into politics. (Time 116:93 Sept 15, 80)

HEATH, Edward. She couldn't take down a scoop if you gave it to her at dictation speed (about the London Observer's political correspondent, Nora Beloff). (Village Voice 20:17 Sept 8, 75)

HEBERT, F. Edward. Russell Long could cut your toenails without taking your shoes off. (New Orleans 13:62 Nov 78)

HEFFERAN, Colien. The woman who once saw marriage as a form of security now finds that she can provide her own security. (US News & World Report 85:83 Nov 27, 78)

HEFNER, Hugh Marston. If a man has a right to find God in his own way, he has a right to go to the Devil in his own way also. (Playboy 26:82 Jan 79)

HEFNER, Hugh Marston. If I told you, for example that Playboy, in its 22 years, was one of the major things that contributed to the women's movement, you might find it a mindboggler, but it happens to be true. (Chicago Tribune 124:1 Section 1 May 3, 76)

HEFNER, Hugh Marston. I'm not primarily an entrepreneurial businessman. I'm primarily a playboy philosopher. (Chicago Tribune 124:1 Section 1 May 3, 76)

HEGEL, Georg Wilhelm Friedrich. Peoples and governments have never learned anything from history, or acted on principles deductible from it. (New York Times 127:32 section 2 April 9, 78)

HEIDE, Wilma Scott. I do not refer to myself as a housewife for the reason that I did not marry a house. (Viva 4:26 Aug 77)

HEIDEGGER, Martin. He who does not know what homesickness is, cannot philosophize. (Time 107:59 June 7, 76)

HEINFELDEN, Curt. The scenery only changes for the lead dog. (Washingtonian 15:143 Nov 79)

HELION, Jean (French painter). I looked through my studio window and I found that the outside world was more beautiful than my picture. (Time 106:78 Oct 20, 75)

HELLER, Joseph. If I could be clever on demand, I'd still be in advertising. (Life 2:16 June 79)

HELLER, Joseph. I've come to look upon death the same way I look upon root-canal work. Everyone else seems to get through it all right, so it couldn't be too difficult for me. (Playboy 22:76 June 75)

HELLER, Joseph. No one governs. Everyone performs. Politics has become a social world. (New York Times 128:15 section 6 Mar 4, 79)

HELLMAN, Lillian. I cannot and will not cut my conscience to fit this year's fashions (referring to the activities of the House Un-American Activities Committee). (Time 106:77 Oct 6, 75)

HELLMAN, Lillian. I don't understand personal salvation. It seems to me a vain idea. (Rolling Stone 233:55 Feb 24, 77)

HELLMAN, Lillian. I think (Watergate and the McCarthy Era) are deeply connected, with Mr. Nixon being the connection, the rope that carries it all through. (New York Times 125:28 Nov 7, 75)

HELLMAN, Lillian. If I had to give young writers advice, I would say, Don't listen to writers talking about writing or about themselves. (Time 110:40 Sept 5, 77)

HELLMAN, Lillian. In looking about me, in looking at me, I have long believed that few people grow wiser with the years. (New York Times Book Review 3 Mar 25, 79)

HELLMAN, Lillian. Nobody can argue any longer about the rights of women. It's like arguing about earthquakes. (Rolling Stone 233:56 Feb 24, 77)

HELLMAN, Lillian. We have no national memory. (Time 113:28 April 23, 79)

HELM, Levon. Music is medicine, and if the doctor is going to make house calls, he better know how to play. (Newsweek 90:102 Oct 31, 77)

HELMS, Jesse. If Environmental Action had its way, the American people would starve and freeze to death in the dark. (Chicago Sun-Times 31:2 June 5, 78)

HELMS, Jesse. It's very clear that the Russians have taken us to the cleaners. If this is the best the Administration can do, I suggest a SALT-free diet. (Time 113:39 May 21, 79)

HELMS, Richard McGarrah. I think he was yielding to that human impulse of the greater good (explaining why the CIA scientist in charge of the Chemical Weapons Division did not destroy shellfish toxin as ordered by President Nixon). (Rolling Stone 199:34 Nov 6, 75)

HELMS, Richard McGarrah. If I ever do decide to talk, there are going to be some very embarrassed people in this town, you can bet on that (commenting after testifying to the Watergate Committee on CIA involvement in domestic intelligence operations). (Newsweek 85:21 Feb 24, 75)

HELMS, Richard McGarrah. We're not in the Boy Scouts (about the Central Intelligence Agency). (Atlantic 244:36 Aug 79)

HEMENWAY, Russell. He's (Jimmy Carter) the first president in recent history that would occupy the most important office in the world without any commitment to anybody. (New York 9:8 July 12, 76)

HEMINGWAY, Ernest. The first and final thing you have to do in this world is to last in it and not be smashed by it. (Kansas City Times 109:1A Feb 3, 77)

HEMINGWAY, Ernest. If she (Marlene Dietrich) had nothing but her voice, she could break your heart with it. (Book Digest 5:99 April 78)

HEMINGWAY, Ernest. Make a thing as true as possible, and it will live. (New York Times Book Review 30 July 23, 78)

HEMINGWAY, Margaux. I love men's clothes, but that doesn't make me a weirdo. (Los Angeles Times 95:22 Part 4 Dec 12, 75)

HEMINGWAY, Mary. Books are helpful in bed. But they are not responsive (commenting on widowhood). (People Weekly 6:49 Dec 13, 76)

HEMINGWAY, Mary. I'm too old to waste my time being sentimental. (Time 110:41 July 25, 77)

HENDERSON, Vivian Wilson. We have programs for combatting racial discrimination, but not for combatting economic class distinctions. (Time 107:71 Feb 9, 76)

HENDRIX, Jimi. It's funny the way most people love the dead. Once you are dead, you are made for life. (Rolling Stone 227:81 Dec 2, 76)

HENRY, Julia. Incentive...that's the word for life. (W 7:24 Dec 8, 78)

HENRY, Orville. He's such a nice guy. But if they had a Naive Bowl, he would coach both sides (about TCU's football coach Jim Shofner). (Sports Illustrated 43:20 Nov 10, 75)

HENSHAW, Paul C. Gold is how you survive when everything else is down the drain. (New West 1:11 July 5, 76)

HEPBURN, Katharine. Acting really isn't a very high-class way to make a living, is it? (The Observer 9779:10 Jan 21, 79)

HEPBURN, Katharine. First God made England, Ireland and Scotland. That's when He corrected His mistakes and made Wales. (Time 112:69 Aug 7, 78)

HEPBURN, Katharine. Sometimes I wonder if men and women really suit each other. Perhaps they should live next door and just visit now and then. (Cosmopolitan 188:268 Feb 80)

HERNDON, Terry. He seemed like a nice little guy with a lot of chutzpah (upon meeting President Carter). (Newsweek 96:27 July 14, 80)

HEROLD, Don. Many people have character who have nothing else. (Chicago Sun-Times 32:25 July 14, 79)

HERZBERG, Donald. Never leave hold of what you've got until you've got hold of something else. (Washingtonian 14:155 Nov 78)

HERZOG, Werner. You should look straight at a film; that's the only way to see one. Film is not the art of scholars but of illiterates. (New York Times 126:D19 Sept 11, 77)

HESTON, Charlton. Acting is the oldest profession, no matter what claims are made by the other trade. (People 10:102 Sept 4, 78)

HEWITT, Don. People are finding that truth is more fascinating than fiction. (US News & World Report 85:52 Nov 20, 78)

HIGGINSON, John. We now know there are a hundred causes of cancer, and eighty of them are cigarettes. (Texas Monthly 6:174 June 76)

HILL, Clinton J. If I had reacted just a little bit quicker, I could have (saved Kennedy), I guess, and I'll live with that to my grave. (Chicago Tribune 341:16 Section 1 Dec 7, 75)

HILL, E. V. Life lived at its best is full of daily forgivin' and forgettin'. (Time 114:65 Dec 31, 79)

HILLMAN, Sidney. Politics is the science of how who gets what, when and why. (Rocky Mountain News 62:36 June 23, 80)

HINCKLE, Warren. I never know what I am going to do. That's why I'm so valuable (upon the cessation of City of San Francisco Magazine which he edited). (Village Voice 21:28 Feb 16, 76)

HINES, Jack, Jr. (restaurant cashier). Hollywood is the sinkhole of Los Angeles. (Time 110:16 Aug 15, 77)

HITCHCOCK, Alfred Joseph. All actors should be treated like cattle. (Chicago Sun-Times 32:1 section 3 Mar 4, 79)

HITCHCOCK, Alfred Joseph. Conversation is the enemy of good wine and food. (Time 112:99 Oct 9, 78)

HITCHCOCK, Alfred Joseph. I wouldn't be able to sleep nights if I thought I had to spend even $10 million on a picture...When you work with a smaller budget, you're forced to use ingenuity and imagination and you almost always come up with a better picture. (Chicago Tribune 339:16 Dec 5, 77)

HITCHCOCK, Alfred Joseph. Most people make mystery films. I don't. I make films of suspense. A surprise in a film takes 10 seconds, suspense takes up an hour. (Chicago Daily News 92:29 April 9, 76)

HITCHCOCK, Alfred Joseph. There is no terror in a bang, only in the anticipation of it. (Village Voice 23:1 Jan 23, 78)

HITCHCOCK, Alfred Joseph. Well, I think it's below one's dignity to be an actor (commenting on why he will not appear in films of other directors). (Washington Post 266:L1 Aug 28, 77)

HITCHENS, Ivon. My pictures are painted to be listened to. (The Observer 9787:14 Mar 25, 79)

HITLER, Adolf. You know, everybody has a price—and you'd be surprised how low it is. (New York Times Book Review 23 July 24, 77)

HO CHI MINH, . It is better to sniff French dung for a while than to eat China's all our lives. (New York Times 128:1 section 4 Feb 25, 79)

HOCHMAN, Sandra. I'd rather be hung from clotheslines and washed in laundromats than read in libraries (commenting on her poetry to be printed on clothing and bedsheets). (W 5:2 May 14, 76)

HOCHMANN, John L. After all, publishing is a business, literature is a happy accident. (New York Times Book Review 35 July 30, 78)

HOCKNEY, David. I'm a Puritan at heart. I also think I'm the world's most overrated, overpaid artist. (Newsweek 90:73 Nov 14, 77)

HODEL, Donald. (Environmentalism is) a crusade to stop all development in this country. (Wall Street Journal 56:1 Dec 17, 75)

HOFFA, James Riddle. I don't cheat nobody. I don't lie about nobody. I don't frame nobody. I don't talk bad about people. If I do, I tell 'em. So what the hell's people gonna try to kill me for? (Playboy 22:73 Dec 75)

HOFFA, James Riddle. The only guy who needs a bodyguard is a liar, a cheat, a guy who betrays friendship. (Time 106:63 Nov 24, 75)

HOFFER, Eric. I hang onto my prejudices. They are the testicles of my mind. (New York Times 128:9 section 7 Jan 28, 79)

HOFFER, Eric. I was never in a hurry in my life. I could hang on to an idea for years, chew on a sentence for months, and I had time to catch fleeting insights. (Los Angeles Times 97:1 part 4 Feb 3, 78)

HOFFER, Eric. The mystery of our time is the inability of decent people to get angry. At present, anger and daring have become the monopoly of a band of mindless juvenile terrorists. (New York Times 128:28 section 7 Jan 28, 79)

HOFFMAN, Abbie. I don't trust (Jerry Brown). He has more colors than a Panamanian patio at sunset. (Time 113:81 June 11, 79)

HOFFMAN, Abbie. It's hard to convince a girl's parents that a revolutionary fugitive with a vasectomy is a good deal. (Village Voice 21:22 May 3, 76)

HOFFMAN, Abbie. I've adopted a much more orthodox Communist view. I used to say I was an anarchist or maybe a hedonistic Communist, but around the world people understand the force that's fighting for them is Communism. It means the end of sex, love, dope, art, individuality and doing things you want to do. (New York Times 125:76 Section 1 Dec 7, 75)

HOFSTADER, Douglas. It always takes longer than you expect, even when you take Hofstader's Law into account. (Omni 1:131 May 79)

HOFSTADTER, Richard. The United States was the only country in the world that began with perfection and aspired to progress. (Wisconsin Trails 17:5 Winter 76)

HOLLAND, Jack. The tragedy of Northern Ireland is that it is now a society in which the dead console the living. (New York Times Magazine 39 July 15, 79)

HOLLOW, Norman. In the olden days the Indian peoples defended themselves with bows and arrows. Now, politics is the only way our rights can be developed. (New York Times 125:1 Section 1 Dec 21, 75)

HOLMES, Oliver Wendell. The life of the law has not been logic; it has been experience. (Christian Science Monitor 69:27 Aug 3, 77)

HOLMES, Oliver Wendell. Put not your trust in money. Put your money in trust. (Cleveland 6:36 Mar 77)

HOLMES, Oliver Wendell. Taxes are the price that society pays for civilization. (Time 112:60 Sept 25, 78)

HOLTZ, Lou. God did not put Lou Holtz on this earth to coach pro football (announcing his resignation as the coach of the New York Jets). (New York Times 126:B15 Dec 10, 76)

HOLTZMAN, Elizabeth. Government follows Newton's law of physics. Objects stay at rest until they're pushed. (Newsweek 96:27 Sept 8, 80)

HOOKS, Benjamin Lawson. If we don't solve this race problem, this country isn't going to ever rest in peace. (Newsweek 88:46 Nov 22, 76)

HOOKS, Benjamin Lawson. There's a great lie abroad that black people don't want to work. I have an idea. You give us the jobs and we'll give you the welfare and see how you like that for a while. (Time 111:67 Mar 13, 78)

HOOKS, Benjamin Lawson. We are not looking for Jimmy Carter or any other white man to deliver black people but for black people to deliver themselves. (Sepia 26:10 June 77)

HOOVER, Herbert Clark. Fishing...brings meekness and inspiration, reduces our egotism, soothes our troubles and shames our wickedness. It is discipline in the equality of men—for all men are equal before fish. (New York Times 126:2 Section 5 Nov 7, 76)

HOOVER, John Edgar. The cure for crime is not the electric chair but the high chair. (Chicago Sun-Times 29:76 July 9, 76)

HOOVER, John Edgar. I regret to say that we of the FBI are powerless to act in cases of oral-genital intimacy, unless it has in some way obstructed interstate commerce. (New York 13:14 Oct 6, 80)

HOPE, Bob. I don't think I'd do anything if it were a sacrifice. (Rolling Stone 311:47 Mar 20, 80)

HOPE, Bob. I think we're running out of perversions to put in film, and I'm looking forward to it (on pornographic movies). (Los Angeles Times 96:2 Part 1 Dec 30, 76)

HOROWITZ, Rachel. If you're a public employee and your job depends on public officials, you have to be in politics. (Newsweek 96:27 July 14, 80)

HOROWITZ, Vladimir. You can't be serious 24 hours a day. You have to take half an hour or an hour a day to be childish. (Time 112:88 Oct 16, 78)

HOUDE, Camillien. A mob is like a river—it never runs uphill. (Macleans 90:63 July 11, 77)

HOUSEMAN, John. There is no question but that Marlon Brando would have been America's Olivier if he had continued in the classical theater. (W 4:11 Dec 12, 75)

HOVING, Walter (Chairman of Tiffany's). Give the customer what Tiffany likes, because what it likes, the public ought to like. (Chicago Tribune 188:29 Aug 7, 77)

HOWAR, Barbara. I just can't bring myself to believe this country will ever elect a president with orange hair (commenting on Ronald Reagan's election prospects). (Potomac (Sunday Magazine of the Washington Post) 4 Feb 8, 76)

HOWAR, Barbara. I'm now fast approaching the age when a woman doesn't fan herself in public. (W 5:8 June 25, 76)

HOWARD, Robert T. The family hour seems to have become just another cop-out used by creative people to explain their failure. (Los Angeles Times 94:13 Part 4 Nov 4, 75)

HOWE, Sir Geoffrey. Finance must determine expenditure; expenditure must not determine finance. (The Observer 9799:9 June 17, 79)

HOWE, Sir Geoffrey. Nineteen seventy-eight has been the year of the bloody-minded. (The Observer 9775:9 Dec 31, 78)

HOWLETT, Michael. With Daley, you know, it was Daley who always came first; the other guy always came third with Daley, no matter who the other guy was. (Who came second?) Nobody. That was Daley's percentage. (Chicago Tribune 233:2 section 2 Aug 21, 77)

HOY, Wayne. If you go slow enough, long enough, you'll be in the lead again. (Washingtonian 15:143 Nov 79)

HOYLE, Fred. There is a coherent plan in the universe, though I don't know what it's a plan for. (Omni 2:40 April 80)

HUA, Kuo-Feng. Great disorder across the land leads to great order. (Time 108:19 Jan 10, 77)

HUA, Kuo-Feng. Peace cannot be got by begging. War cannot be averted by yielding. (The Observer 9819:9 Nov 4, 79)

HUA, Kuo-Feng. We have such people (dissidents) in a miniscule number. We still have them. Unfortunately, they exist—like thieves, bribe-takers, spectators and other criminals exist. Both are inflicting harm to our society and that is why they should bear punishment in complete accordance with the demands of Soviet law. (San Francisco Chronicle This World 1977:2 Sept 18, 77)

HUBBARD, Elbert. A conservative is a man who is too cowardly to fight and too fat to run. (Human Behavior 6:13 May 77)

HUBBARD, Elbert. Do not take life too seriously—you will never get out of it alive. (Human Behavior 6:13 May 77)

HUBBARD, Elbert. Never explain. Your friends do not need it and your enemies will not believe you anyway. (Kansas City Star 97:4B Oct 10, 76)

HUBBARD, Elbert. This will never be a civilized country until we spend more money for books than we do for chewing gum. (Human Behavior 6:12 May 77)

HUBBARD, Harry. Making Texans stand in line for gas is like making Kansans stand in line for wheat. (Newsweek 94:22 July 2, 79)

HUBBARD, Kin. It must be great to be rich and let the other fellow keep up appearances. (Human Behavior 7:71 Sept 78)

HUBBARD, Kin. We're all pretty much alike when we get out of town. (Human Behavior 7:71 Sept 78)

HUDSON, Rock. Inside this hulk you see before you is a frustrated song-and-dance man just screaming to get out. (Time 107:41 Feb 2, 76)

HUFSTEDLER, Shirley. A man cannot be very kind unless he is also very strong. (New York Times Magazine 104 June 8, 80)

HUFSTEDLER, Shirley. There is a little nonsense and sloth in the seams and marrow of all human industry. (New York Times Magazine 94 June 8, 80)

HUGO, Richard. In the world of imagination, all things belong. (New York Times Book Review 11 Mar 25, 79)

HULL, Bobby. The idiot owners, the incompetent coaches, the inept players are dragging the game into the mud. They're destroying it with their senseless violence. The game is no pleasure anymore, it's an ordeal (about hockey). (Chicago Daily News 39 April 23, 76)

HULL, Ma. When God sees fit to take me, I want him to take me providing my own way. (Atlanta 16:47 June 76)

HUMPHREY, Hubert Horatio. The biggest corruption in politics, friends, is not money. It's publicity. (New York 9:100 May 10, 76)

HUMPHREY, Hubert Horatio. Compassion is not weakness and concern for the unfortunate is not socialism. (Time 111:25 Jan 23, 78)

HUMPHREY, Hubert Horatio. The greatest gift of life is friendship and I have received it. (Time 110:23 Nov 7, 77)

HUMPHREY, Hubert Horatio. Happiness is contagious, just exactly like being miserable. People have to believe that they can do better. They've got to know that there's somebody that wants to help and work with them, somebody that hasn't tossed in the towel. (Time 111:25 Jan 23, 78)

HUMPHREY, Hubert Horatio. I do not want a great political party which nearly lost its soul in Vietnam to sell its soul on busing. (New Times 6:29 Feb 20, 76)

HUMPHREY, Hubert Horatio. I guess maybe I am the freest man I have ever been in my life. I seek nothing. I want nothing except one thing: I am going to tell it like it is. (Encore American & Worldwide News 5:4 June 21, 76)

HUMPHREY, Hubert Horatio. I have a feeling he (Walter Mondale) was born under the right star. (Chicago Tribune Magazine 26 Sept 18, 77)

HUMPHREY, Hubert Horatio. I have no intention to enter any primaries; I will enter no primaries. I am not a candidate for president. I authorize no group to work in my behalf. (Meet The Press 19:3 Nov 2, 75)

HUMPHREY, Hubert Horatio. I want the President to be as considerate of New York City and of New York State as he is of countries all over the world. Within the same week that he said no help for New York, he sends us up a program for $5 billion of additional military aid in support assistance for the Middle East. (Meet The Press 19:2 Nov 2, 75)

HUMPHREY, Hubert Horatio. I would rather be honestly wrong than to be a deliberate hypocrite. (New Times 10:72 Feb 6, 78)

HUMPHREY, Hubert Horatio. If I believe in something, I will fight for it with all I have. But I do not demand all or nothing. I would rather get something than nothing. Professional liberals want glory in defeat. The hardest job for a politician today is to have the courage to be moderate. (Time 111:22-24 Jan 23, 78)

HUMPHREY, Hubert Horatio. Life was not meant to be endured, but enjoyed. (New Times 10:51 Feb 6, 78)

HUMPHREY, Hubert Horatio. A man with no tears is a man with no heart. (Chicago Tribune 263:2 Sept 20, 77)

HUMPHREY, Hubert Horatio. Oh, my friend, it isn't what they take away from you that counts—it's what you do with what you have left. (Newsweek 89:43 July 25, 77)

HUMPHREY, Hubert Horatio. One thing I don't need at this stage of my life is to be ridiculous, so I'm not going to do it (explaining his decision not to enter the New Jersey primary). (New York Times 125:A1 April 30, 76)

HUMPHREY, Hubert Horatio. Politics isn't a matter of making love. It's making choices. (Newsweek 91:22 Jan 23, 78)

HUMPHREY, Hubert Horatio. The Senate is a place filled with goodwill and good intentions, and if the road to hell is paved with them, then it's a pretty good detour. (Newsweek 91:23 Jan 23, 78)

HUMPHREY, Hubert Horatio. The time has arrived for the Democratic Party to get out of the shadow of states' rights and walk forthrightly into the bright sunshine of human rights (at the 1948 Democratic National Convention). (Time 111:22 Jan 23, 78)

HUMPHREY, Hubert Horatio. We made judgements about that part of the world based on our experience in Europe. We were a world power with a half-world knowledge. (Time 105:20 May 12, 75)

HUNDLEY, William G. The worst defense lawyers I know are those who become convinced their clients are innocent. (Time 111:89 Mar 6, 78)

HUNG, Tran Van (Vietnamese refugee). We are shrubs, planted in a new place, needing care and water to grow again. (Newsweek 94:52 July 2, 79)

HUNGATE, William. The electorate knows more and believes less and expresses it louder than at any time in history. (Wall Street Journal 56:1 April 28, 76)

HUNT, Everette Howard. No one is entitled to the truth. (Rolling Stone 239:40 May 19, 77)

HUNT, Haroldson Lafayette. Money is just something to make bookkeeping convenient. (Time 104:44 Dec 9, 74)

HUNT, Nelson Bunker. People who know how much they're worth aren't usually worth that much. (Time 115:56 May 12, 80)

HUNTER, Ross. Every one of us in Hollywood is overpaid. (W 8:2 Mar 16, 79)

HUSSEIN, KING OF JORDAN, . It's amusing. The Americans have changed Presidents six times since I've been King. And they talk to the Arabs about stability? (People Weekly 6:122 Dec 13, 76)

HUSTON, John. (Charles Bronson is) a hand grenade with the pin pulled. (Time 111:52 Jan 9, 78)

HUTTON, Barbara. All the unhappiness in my life has been caused by men. (New York Times 128:1 May 13, 79)

HUXLEY, Thomas. It is the customary fate of new truths to begin as heresies and to end as superstitions. (Omni 2:36 June 80)

HYDE, Henry. There are one million children who are thrown away like Kleenex because someone thinks they are not as valuable as a snail darter (opposing abortions). (Time 114:27 July 9, 79)

IACOCCA, Lee A. The free-enterprise system has gone to hell. (Time 114:74 Oct 8, 79)

IACOCCA, Lee A. I don't want to mislead anyone or to spread false hope—unemployment is awful. From the bottom of the trough we're in, it's a long climb back to business as usual. Even with all the qualification, however, things are getting better, not worse. (Harper's Weekly 3123:4 May 2, 75)

IACOCCA, Lee A. I never invent anything any more. Everything I do is to meet a law. (Time 114:71 Oct 22, 79)

IACOCCA, Lee A. This year the public will have a choice, the likes of which it hasn't had in years. The difference between our cars and GM's is like the difference between a four-foot blonde and a seven-foot brunette. (Wall Street Journal 57:1 Oct 29, 76)

IANNI, Francis (American Sociologist). As in business, politics and education, there will be equal opportunities in crime. You can't have Bella Abzugs without Bonnie Parkers. (Time 106:8 Dec 1, 75)

IBARRURI, Dolores (Spanish Civil War activist). It is better to die on your feet than live on your knees. (Time 109:50 May 23, 77)

ICHORD, Richard. Once you have done the budget, once you get the statistics, it is much like getting down the unvirtuous woman. Once you get her down, you can do anything you want to. (Rolling Stone 242:60 June 30, 77)

IGUINIZ, Javier (Peruvian economist). The growth of capitalism is the same as the growth of world poverty. (Time 106:34 Sept 1, 75)

IRANI, C. R. The only protection for a free press is the courage to demand it. (Chicago Tribune 233:4 section 2 Aug 21, 77)

IRWIN, Robert. I'm essentially illiterate. I've arrived at all my ideas by sitting on a rock scratching my ass. (ARTnews 76:50 Summer 77)

ISLEY, Fred (Manager of public relations, Xerox Corporation). I don't know if the public's negative attitude makes a difference to corporations (in response to a Peoples Bicentennial Commission's sponsored survey reflecting wide public disenchantment with American business). (Harper's Weekly 3140:9 Sept 12, 75)

JACKSON, Glenda. Acting is an opportunity to meet other people's minds that you can't get anywhere else. (W 5:12 Nov 26, 76)

JACKSON, Glenda. I'm waiting for the day when I wake up and life is a breeze. I used to think that happened when you grew old. But it doesn't. That's just a fantasy. (Chicago Tribune 57:10 section 6 Feb 26, 78)

JACKSON, Glenda. Sarah Bernhardt believed in the human will above all things. I can empathize with that. Because I do believe that things can be changed; and by changed, I mean improved, not simply altered. (Ms 4:53 Feb 76)

JACKSON, Henry Martin. I think my positions that I have taken are liberal in the best traditions of the Democratic Party. (Meet the Press 20:1 Mar 14, 76)

JACKSON, Henry Martin. It is a misguided social experiment and it is failing and we ought to stop it (about busing). (Christian Science Monitor 252:24 Nov 24, 75)

JACKSON, Jack. No rule is ever so good, or so well written, or covers so many contingencies, that it can't be replaced by another, much better, more appropriate rule (with the exception of this rule). (Washingtonian 14:26 Dec 78)

JACKSON, Jesse. The absence of (George) Wallace is not the presence of justice. (Time 107:30 May 17, 76)

JACKSON, Jesse. Affirmative action is a moot point if you don't learn to read and write. (Time 114:42 Aug 6, 79)

JACKSON, Jesse. Apartheid is violence by definition. (Newsweek 94:36 Aug 13, 79)

JACKSON, Jesse. I suggest to you boys you are not a man because you make a baby. You are a man because you protect a baby (urging pupils at Martin Luther King Junior High School to develop pride through education). (Chicago Tribune 302:3 Section 1 Oct 30, 75)

JACKSON, Jesse. In a hot war we (Blacks) die first; in a cold war, we starve first. (Newsweek 94:27 Sept 3, 79)

JACKSON, Jesse. It used to be the Klan in white robes who were the killers, now we've gone from Southern rope to Northern dope. (Sepia 25:10 Feb 76)

JACKSON, Jesse. Many of us allow our children to eat junk, watch junk, listen to junk, talk junk, play with junk, and then we're surprised when they come out to be social junkies. (Life 2:86 Dec 79)

JACKSON, Jesse. People in South Africa only have the Bible as a constitution. (Chicago Sun-Times 32:32 July 20, 79)

JACKSON, Jesse. A school system without parents at its foundation is just like a bucket with a hole in it. (Time 112:46 July 10, 78)

JACKSON, Jesse. We too often condemn blacks who succeed and excel, calling them Uncle Toms. The ideal ought to be for all of us to succeed and excel. (Sepia 25:12 Sept 76)

JACKSON, Jesse. What does it matter if we have a new book or an old book, if we open neither? (Time 112:46 July 10, 78)

JACKSON, Maynard. If Richard Nixon were black, he would be catching so much hell, he would rather be in jail. (Sepia 24:10 Jan 75)

JACKSON, Reggie. Hitting is better than sex. (Esquire 89:98 Mar 1, 78)

JACKSON, Reggie. I don't mind getting beaten, but I hate to lose. (Sepia 26:10 Mar 77)

JACKSON, Reggie. I represent both the overdog and the underdog in society. (Rolling Stone 283:48 Sept 6, 79)

JACKSON, Robert. We (judges) are not final because we are infallible, but we are infallible because we are final. (Time 113:91 Jan 22, 79)

JACOBS, Andy. (Ralph) Nader has become a legend in his own mind. (Time 112:21 Aug 7, 78)

JAGGER, Bianca. What do I really want as a woman? I want it all. (Playboy 26:186 Jan 79)

JAGGER, Mick. I should think not, judging from Elvis. No, rock 'n' roll music is for adolescents. It's a dead end (responding when asked Can rock stars move toward middle age?). (Los Angeles Times 96:2 part I Sept 15, 77)

JAGGER, Mick. I'd rather be dead than sing Satisfaction when I'm 45. (People Weekly 7:58 May 2, 77)

JAGGER, Mick. Keith and I are two of the nicest people we know. (Creem 10:55 Jan 79)

JAGGER, Mick. Politics, like the legal system, is dominated by old men. (Life 2:117 Dec 79)

JAMES, Henry. (Anthony Trollope's) great, his inestimable merit was a complete appreciation of the usual. (Time 109:57 May 16, 77)

JAMES, Henry (attributed by William L. Shirer). It's a complex fate, being an American. (New York Times Book Review 25 July 24, 77)

JAMES, William. A great many people think they are thinking when they are merely rearranging their prejudices. (Kansas City Times 109:18C July 30, 77)

JAMISON, Judith. Every dancer lives on the threshold of chucking it. (New York Times Magazine 148 Dec 5, 76)

JANEWAY, Eliot. The dollar has become like a hydrant at an international convention of dogs. (Esquire 90:59 Nov 21, 78)

JANEWAY, Eliot. The thrill of making a fast buck follows only the thrill of love at first sight. Everyone needs to take an occasional fling with money...and with love. (Chicago Tribune 95:14 April 5, 77)

JANOV, Arthur. The world is having a nervous breakdown. Valium is the only glue that holds it together. (Rolling Stone 219:19 Aug 12, 76)

JARVIS, Howard. Everyone is entitled to my opinion. (Time 111:21 June 19, 78)

JARVIS, Howard. I didn't promise anybody that Prop 13 would reduce rent. (Newsweek 93:71 June 4, 79)

JARVIS, Howard. The only way to cut government spending is not to give them the money to spend in the first place. (New West 3:32 July 3, 78)

JARVIS, Felton (Elvis Presley's Producer). It's like someone just came up and told me there aren't going to be any more cheeseburgers in the world (commenting on Elvis Presley's death). (Country Music 7:36 Dec 77)

JAVITS, Marion. I am his mistress. His work is his wife (explaining that she and her husband lead separate lives). (People Weekly 5:70 Feb 2, 76)

JAY, Peter. All I would ask of Americans is that you go on being yourselves—valiant without being fanatical, individualistic without being foolhardy, skeptical without being cynical, openminded without being indecisive, generous without being naive, patriotic without being nationalistic, and good without being perfect. (New York Times 126:46 Oct 13, 77)

JAY, Peter. As a journalist, I have sat for 10 years listening to government spokesmen beating the drum, justifying the unjustifiable, explaining the inexplicable, defending the indefensible. They were doing their jobs, but you could feel the atmosphere of sorrowful skepticism rising. (Chicago Tribune 200:10 July 19, 77)

JAY, Peter. One of the daunting things in the modern world is that the management of this planet would be mind-boggling even if there were only one philosopher-king. (The Times 8059:32 Dec 4, 77)

JEFFERSON, Thomas. Every man has two countries—his own and France. (Time 110:103 Nov 28, 77)

JEFFERSON, Thomas. I like the dreams of the future better than the history of the past. (Time 111:74 Jan 9, 78)

JEFFERSON, Thomas. Nature has given to man no other means (than the press) of sifting out the truth either in religion, law, or politics. (Time 114:74 July 16, 79)

JEFFERSON, Thomas. Our peculiar security is the possession of a written constitution. Let us not make it a blank paper by construction. (New York Times Magazine 118 Oct 9, 77)

JEFFERSON, Thomas. Were it left to me to decide whether we should have government without newspapers or newspapers without government, I should not hesitate a moment to prefer the latter. (Macleans 91:50 July 24, 78)

JENKINS, Robin. It is not the goodness of saints that makes us feel there is hope for humanity: it is the goodness of obscure men. (New York Times Book Review 14 Feb 3, 80)

JENNER, Bruce. If you want to use the decathlon as a test of total athletic ability, then I guess I'm the world's greatest athlete. It's as good a test as any, I guess. But that sure doesn't help me when I stand up at a tee and try to hit a golf ball. Then I'm just another guy who can't hit straight. (Sports Illustrated 47:6 Aug 15, 77)

JENNINGS, Waylon. Honesty is something you can't wear out. (Country Music 7:55 Jan/Feb 79)

JEROME, Jerome K. It is always the best policy to speak the truth, unless of course you are an exceptionally good liar. (Kansas City Star 97:26 May 2, 77)

JEROME, Jerome K. It is impossible to enjoy idling thoroughly unless one has plenty of work to do. (Rocky Mountain News 79:86 July 10, 80)

JESSYE, Eva. I am no longer the only raisin in the rice pudding. (New York Times 129:76 Oct 7, 79)

JIMENEZ, Janey. Just like a bull in the correo, Patty (Hearst) never really had a chance. She was doomed from the beginning. (Chicago Tribune 324:4 section 5 Nov 20, 77)

JOHN, Elton. People in England are so bloody nosey. (The Observer 9820:10 Nov 11, 79)

JOHN PAUL I, POPE, . The danger for modern man is that he would reduce the earth to a desert, the person to an automaton, brotherly love to planned collectivization, often introducing death where God wishes life. (San Francisco Chronicle This World 2 Sept 3, 78)

JOHN PAUL I, POPE, . Divorce is the sword of Damocles hanging over conjugal love: its presence generates uncertainty, fear, suspicion. (Time 112:80 Sept 11, 78)

JOHN PAUL I, POPE, . I don't have the wisdom or heart of Pope John or the preparation and culture of Pope Paul—but I am in their place...I hope you will help me with your prayers. (Newsweek 92:40 Sept 4, 78)

JOHN PAUL I, POPE, . If I hadn't been a bishop, I would have wanted to be a journalist. (Time 112:80 Sept 11, 78)

JOHN PAUL I, POPE, . If St. Paul returned to the world now as a journalist he would not only direct Reuters but seek time on television. (The Observer 9758:9 Sept 3, 78)

JOHN PAUL I, POPE, . If someone had told me I would be Pope one day, I would have studied harder. (The Observer 9761:14 Sept 24, 78)

JOHN PAUL I, POPE, . Many have forgotten that a theologian is not only he who speaks of God, but he who speaks to God (chastising theologians who he felt had lost their fidelity to the church). (Newsweek 92:42 Sept 4, 78)

JOHN PAUL I, POPE, . Those who treat theology as a human science rather than a sacred science, or exaggerate their freedom lack faith. (Time 112:66 Sept 4, 78)

JOHN PAUL II, POPE, . It is the right of the faithful not to be troubled by theories and hypotheses that they are not expert in judging or that are easily simplified or manipulated by public opinion. (Time 114:68 Oct 22, 79)

JOHN PAUL II, POPE, . Our times demand not to enclose ourselves in inflexible borders, especially when human good is concerned. (New York Times 128:1 June 11, 79)

JOHN PAUL II, POPE, . Priesthood is forever—we do not return the gift once given. (Time 114:21 Oct 15, 79)

JOHN PAUL II, POPE, . There is but one thing more dangerous than sin: the murder of man's sense of sin. (New York Times 128:7 April 2, 79)

JOHN PAUL II, POPE, . Violence always delays the day of justice (to the IRA). (The Observer 9814:1 Sept 30, 79)

JOHNS, Glynnis (actress). For me, most relationships with men have been like pregnancies—they last about nine months. (Chicago Tribune 226:2 section 5 Aug 14, 77)

JOHNSON, Al (Patricia Hearst's defense attorney). I remember when the Chowchilla kidnapping occurred. Patty (Hearst) said she wondered how long it would take the FBI to indict the 26 children for the crime. (People Weekly 6:40 Dec 13, 76)

JOHNSON, Claudia Alta (Taylor). The First Lady is an unpaid public servant elected by one person: her husband. (Washington Post 266:K7 Aug 28, 77)

JOHNSON, Claudia Alta (Taylor). A politician ought to be born a foundling and remain a bachelor. (Time 106:56 Dec 1, 75)

JOHNSON, Claudia Alta (Taylor). The South is the future. It is the political pivot of the country now. It's very gratifying to see Jimmy Carter become President, to see the South finally win out after all these years. (Washington Post 351:E3 Nov 20, 76)

JOHNSON, Flora. There is nothing like death. Everything that approaches it is metaphor. (Chicago 25:115 July 76)

JOHNSON, Haynes. As work and space expand and collide they breed their own reaction. (Washington Post 252:A3 Aug 14, 77)

JOHNSON, Haynes. Jimmy Carter met the press and they were his (commenting after Carter's first press conference as President). (Time 109:11 Feb 11, 77)

JOHNSON, James P. Mr. Chairman, I think the record should show that for the first time since McKinley, we have a Republican President worth shooting (upon hearing of Lynette "Squeaky" Fromme's attack on President Ford). (Newsweek 86:22 Sept 15, 75)

JOHNSON, Lyndon Baines. Boys, it is just like the Alamo. Somebody should have by God helped those Texans. I'm going to Viet Nam. (Time 105:28 May 12, 75)

JOHNSON, Lyndon Baines. I never believed that Oswald acted alone, although I can accept that he pulled the trigger. (Skeptic 9:55 Sept/Oct 75)

JOHNSON, Lyndon Baines. I never trust a man unless I've got his pecker in my pocket. (Village Voice 21:16 Nov 8, 76)

JOHNSON, Lyndon Baines. I'd druther have him (J. Edgar Hoover) inside the tent pissin' out than outside pissin' in. (Washingtonian 13:221 Mar 78)

JOHNSON, Lyndon Baines. If Walter Cronkite would say on television what he says on radio, he would be the most powerful man in America. (Newsweek 93:91 April 30, 79)

JOHNSON, Lyndon Baines. If you don't blow your horn, somebody will steal it. (TV Guide 25:A4 Dec 24, 78)

JOHNSON, Lyndon Baines. If you have a mother-in-law with only one eye, and that eye is in the middle of her forehead, you don't keep her in the living room (in response to why he had not told Congress more of what he knew to be the truth about Vietnam). (Village Voice 20:17 June 23, 75)

JOHNSON, Lyndon Baines. I'm not going to be the first President to lose a war. (Time 105:28 May 12, 75)

JOHNSON, Lyndon Baines. Killing, rioting, and looting are contrary to the best traditions of this country. (Texas Monthly 3:93 Dec 75)

JOHNSON, Lyndon Baines. The most important thing a man has to tell you is what he is not telling you. (Time 114:13 Aug 20, 79)

JOHNSON, Lyndon Baines. The thing I feared from the first day of my presidency was actually coming true. Robert Kennedy had openly announced his intention to reclaim the throne in the memory of his brother. (Esquire 90:42 Aug 15, 78)

JOHNSON, Nicholas. Most of what I did as a government official was try to encourage more competition, by having smaller enterprises that would truly compete, by removing barriers to entry, by relieving the dependence of business on large government payments and I was opposed at every step and turn of the way, by businessmen. (The Reader (Chicago's Free Weekly) 10:15 Nov 28, 75)

JOHNSON, Philip. All cultures that can be called cultures have built monuments. (Time 113:59 Jan 8, 79)

JOHNSON, Philip. As birds have beautiful plumage, so do we try to have beautiful buildings. There is no other purpose. (Time 113:56 Jan 8, 79)

JOHNSON, R. W. Any solution to a problem changes the problem. (Washingtonian 15:141 Nov 79)

JOHNSON, Samuel. No man but a blockhead ever wrote except for money. (Time 111:75 April 10, 78)

JOHNSON, Samuel. When a man knows he is to be hanged in a fortnight, it concentrates his mind wonderfully. (New York Times 126:28 section 1 April 24, 77)

JOHNSON, Sterling. In the heroin business, the Mexicans are the short-order cooks. The French are the chefs. (Rolling Stone 204:30 Jan 15, 76)

JOHNSON, Wanda. Once I became a member of the inner circle, I realized he was a madman, completely insane (about Jim Jones). (New York Times 128:B1 Nov 21, 78)

JOHNSTON, Jill. All women are lesbians except those who don't know it yet. (Ms 4:80 Nov 75)

JOHNSTON, Jill. Feminism at heart is a massive complaint. Lesbianism is the solution. (Time 106:39 Sept 8, 75)

JONES, Bertram Hays. Football plays are like accounting problems. They baffle you at first, but once you've learned the system they're easy. (People Weekly 6:36 Dec 27/Jan 3, 77)

JONES, Charles. A shift of power (toward Congress) that started because of Nixon's arrogance has continued because of Carter's artlessness. (Time 111:8 Jan 23, 78)

JONES, David. Man is the only maker, neither beast nor angel share this dignity with him. (New York Times 128:9 section 7 Feb 18, 79)

JONES, Franklin P. One thing in which the sexes are equal is in thinking that they're not. (Reader's Digest 108:261 May 76)

JONES, James Thurman. I am God; there is no other God and religion is the opium of the people. (New York Times 128:A17 Nov 21, 78)

JONES, John. I do write poetry but it is no good and I tear it up. (Guardian Weekly 119:4 Nov 12, 78)

JONES, Mary Harris (Mother Jones). I asked a man in prison once how he happened to be there and he said he had stolen a pair of shoes. I told him if he had stolen a railroad he would be a United States Senator. (July 4, 1976 special edition magazine of the Washington Post 134 July 4, 76)

JONES, Preston. I think I'm a story-teller playwright. But whatever the story is, for me it would always involve "time" because time is not the sun going up and down every day. It is not a clock. It is not a calendar. Time is an eroding, infinite mystery. Time is, in fact, a son-of-a-bitch. (New York Times 126:3 section 2 Oct 17, 76)

JONES, Reginald. One of the aspects of the free enterprise system is that you should be allowed to succeed, and you should also be allowed to fail (about Chrysler Corporation). (Time 114:100 Nov 12, 79)

JONES, Stephan. I can almost say I hate this man because he has destroyed everything I've worked for (about Jim Jones). (New York Times 128:B1 Nov 22, 78)

JONES, Thomas. Friends may come and go, but enemies accumulate. (Washingtonian 14:155 Nov 78)

JONG, Erica. Everyone has talent. What is rare is the courage to follow the talent to the dark place where it leads. (Los Angeles Times 97:6 part 4 Feb 3, 78)

JONG, Erica. I cannibalized real life. (Newsweek 85:71 May 5, 75)

JONG, Erica. If Jackie Kennedy did not exist, the press would have to invent her. (In The Know 1:9 Nov 75)

JONG, Erica. It seems to me that sooner or later, all intelligent women become feminists. (New York Times 125:32 Nov 8, 75)

JONG, Erica. Perhaps all artists were, in a sense, housewives: tender of the earth household. (Chicago Tribune 176:2 section II June 25, 78)

JONG, Erica. You don't have to beat a woman if you can make her feel guilty. (Viva 4:28 April 77)

JORDAN, Barbara. I'm neither a Black politician, nor a woman politician. Just a politician. A professional politician. (Essence 8:99 Sept 77)

JORDAN, Barbara. My faith in the Constitution is whole—complete—total. (Newsweek 88:70 July 4, 76)

JORDAN, Hamilton. Historically, I think there probably is an inferiority complex associated with being southern. (Esquire 89:79 Mar 28, 78)

JORDAN, Hamilton. If after the inauguration you find a Cy Vance as Secretary of State and Zbigniew Brzezinski (of Columbia University) as head of national security, then I would say we failed. And I'd quit. But that's not going to happen. (Christian Science Monitor 69:3 Dec 6, 76)

JORDAN, Hamilton. If Jimmy Carter were running against Charlie Kirbo, I'd vote for Charlie. (Time 107:17 July 12, 76)

JORDAN, Hamilton. If the gossip columnists don't get me, I'll be around. That's on the record. (US News & World Report 84:33 Feb 27, 78)

JORDAN, Hamilton. If the President had to fire all but one of us, he probably would keep Stu (Eizenstat). (Time 111:14 April 3, 78)

JORDAN, Hamilton. I'm a chauvinist that tries to do better. (Esquire 89:84 Mar 28, 78)

JORDAN, Hamilton. I'm here for as long as he wants me. (New York Times 128:B1 July 23, 79)

JORDAN, Hamilton. One of my strengths is that I know my weaknesses. (Time 114:42 Aug 6, 79)

JORDAN, Hamilton. Perhaps the strongest feeling in this country today (1972) is the general distrust and disillusionment of government and politicians at all levels. (New York Times 128:A17 July 19, 79)

JOUBERT, Joseph. Space is to place as eternity is to time. (Omni 2:39 April 80)

JUAN CARLOS I, KING OF SPAIN, . No human life should be put in danger when just and disinterested solutions are offered and when cooperation and understanding are sought among peoples. (New York Times 125:23 Nov 3, 75)

JUNG, Carl Gustav. Nothing has a stronger influence on their children than the unlived lives of the parents. (Boston 70:97 June 78)

JUNOT, Philippe. Society's ills come from people having lost the taste for enjoyment. (Rolling Stone 271:16 Aug 10, 78)

KAEL, Pauline. Hollywood is the only place where you can die of encouragement. (After Dark 13:20 Sept 80)

KAFKA, Franz. A book must be the axe for the frozen sea inside us. (Time 111:82 Jan 30, 78)

KAFKA, Franz. In the fight between you and the world, back the world. (Washingtonian 14:154 Nov 78)

KAFKA, Franz. Writing is a sweet and wonderful reward, but for what? In the night it became clear to me, as clear as a child's lesson book, that it is the reward for serving the devil. (Time 111:80 Jan 30, 78)

KAHN, Alfred. All life is a concatenation of ephemeralities. (Barron's 59:5 Feb 19, 79)

KAHN, Alfred. If you can't explain what you're doing in simple English, you are probably doing something wrong. (Time 111:63 May 8, 78)

KAHN, J. Kesner. Free market competition, freely advertised, is consumerism at its best. (American Opinion 18:18 June 75)

KAHN, J. Kesner. When politicians come up with a solution for your problem, you have two problems. (American Opinion 18:21 May 75)

KAHN, Roger. His (Jackie Robinson) race was humanity, and he did a great deal for us. (TV Guide 25:14 Aug 6, 77)

KAIDA, Ivan Ivanovich. First, I was a man without a country, then I was a man without land. Now I am truly rich, for I have both. (Down East 22:35 April 76)

KAIDA, Yuju. Women company employees are like desserts. If you consider company work as a meal, men employees are the main dishes, and women employees are desserts. If a company has to slash the cost of food, the first thing it has to cut is a dessert. (Los Angeles Times 95:4 Part 1-A Dec 8, 75)

KANE, Walter. It is tragic that Howard Hughes had to die to prove that he was alive. (Newsweek 87:25 April 19, 76)

K'ANG-HSI, 1654-1722 (CHINESE EMPEROR), . In history one needs the facts, not hollow words or literary elegance. (Newsweek 91:75 May 22, 78)

KAPILOFF, Larry. I believe that politics is 90 percent the profession of cowards. (San Diego Magazine 31:88 May 79)

KARSH, Yousuf. Photography is the voice of humanity. And that voice must be heard. (Parade 6 Dec 3, 78)

KASELIONIS, Simas. Writers aren't like mushrooms—you can't grow them. (Chicago 24:23 Aug 75)

KAUFMAN, George. Satire is what closes Saturday night. (Time 107:72 Feb 2, 76)

KAUFMAN, Irving. It is not enough for justice to be declared. The judge must assure that justice is done. (Time 113:92 Jan 22, 79)

KAUNDA, Kenneth. An African in Zimbabwe does not need a communist to tell him that he is not free. (To The Point International 4:10 June 20, 77)

KAUNDA, Kenneth. A new Zimbabwe (Rhodesia) can only be born out of the barrel of a gun. (Time 110:30 July 18, 77)

KAUNDA, Kenneth. Not every white man is bad. (The Observer 9769:13 Nov 19, 78)

KAVANAGH, Patrick. Whatever will live must touch the heart of the mob in some way. (Washington Post 102:A17 Mar 17, 77)

KAYE, Peter F. (Ford campaign spokesman). Mondale is a 100 per cent bona fide liberal. It gives us a tangible target. We're not just running against this peanut farmer who walks on water. (Rolling Stone 221:16 Sept 9, 76)

KEATS, John. I think we may class the lawyer in the natural history of monsters. (Time 111:56 April 10, 78)

KEENE, David (Reagan aide). Fighting the Ford (presidential campaign) operation is kind of like fighting the Spanish Armada. They're bigger, but they don't maneuver very well. (Wall Street Journal 56:1 July 19, 76)

KELLEY, Clarence M. If we are to have any degree of success in solving the cases now confronting us in terrorist, espionage, and other major security matters, we must have all the tools available to us—including electronic surveillance (suggesting before a Palm Beach, California civic group that Congress authorize the use of wiretaps and bugs for the FBI). (Christian Science Monitor 68:2 Mar 22, 76)

KELLEY, Ken. But history is nothing but a chronology of oppressors oppressing the oppressed. (Rolling Stone 216:38 July 1, 76)

KELLEY, Stanley. Last guys don't finish nice. (Town & Country 133:140 May 79)

KELLY, Edward J. (Mayor of Chicago, 1933-1947). Franklin Roosevelt was the best precinct captain I ever had. (Harper's Weekly 3168:8 Aug 23, 76)

KELLY, Gene. Musicals are my real love. I didn't want to make pictures with messages. I just wanted to make people happy and bring joy. (Christian Science Monitor 70:42 Dec 5, 77)

KENNEDY, Caroline. His face seemed swollen and his sideburns reached his chin (writing about Elvis Presley's corpse). (Chicago Daily News 13 Dec 30, 77)

KENNEDY, Edward Moore. I *know* I cannot run for President now, and I've accepted that. It took a certain discipline and adjustment, but I've settled this with myself. (Encore American & Worldwide News 5:4 June 21, 76)

KENNEDY, Edward Moore. I am glad to be an underdog. (The Observer 9836:9 Mar 2, 80)

KENNEDY, Edward Moore. I hope to gain the Democratic nomination in 1980. But I also hope to do more—to help give the Democratic Party back its timeless truth. (Newsweek 96:21 July 7, 80)

KENNEDY, Edward Moore. I think Mr. Carter has created Ronald Reagan. (The Observer 9856:12 July 20, 80)

KENNEDY, Edward Moore. I would be much happier if Carter were successful. (New York Times Magazine 29 June 24, 79)

KENNEDY, Edward Moore. If and when needed, anti-trust laws are ready and able to promote a diverse and competitive press. (Esquire 91:6 Feb 27, 79)

KENNEDY, Edward Moore. If someone in my position doesn't realize the danger, he'd be a fool. But anybody who lets that danger paralyze him is useless (concerning the danger of assassination). (Time 106:18 Sept 15, 75)

KENNEDY, Edward Moore. My father always said: 'If it's on the table, eat it'. (The Observer 9813:9 Sept 23, 79)

KENNEDY, Edward Moore. The people I respected most in the Senate—Phil Hart, for example—said you measure accomplishments not by climbing mountains, but by climbing molehills. (Chicago Tribune 72:6 section 1 Mar 13, 77)

KENNEDY, Edward Moore. The press made Jimmy Carter, and now they're trying to destroy him. I'm going to set my own course. (Time 112:10 Aug 21, 78)

KENNEDY, Edward Moore. Tip O'Neill can communicate more with a wink and a nod than most politicians can in a two-hour speech. (Saturday Evening Post 251:14 Mar 79)

KENNEDY, Edward Moore. We cannot afford a foreign policy based on the pangs of unrequitted love. (The Tennessean 74:7 Jan 30, 80)

KENNEDY, Edward Moore. Whatever contributions the Kennedys have made are very much tied into the incredible importance and power of that force in our lives, the family. (New York Times Magazine 15 June 17, 79)

KENNEDY, Eugene. We not only romanticize the future; we have also made it into a growth industry, a parlor game and a disaster movie all at the same time. (New York Times Magazine 68 Dec 2, 79)

KENNEDY, Florynce Rae. If men could get pregnant, abortion would be a sacrament. (Viva 5:28 Nov 77)

KENNEDY, Florynce Rae. If the ass is protecting the system, ass-kicking should be undertaken regardless of the sex, ethnicity, or charm of the ass involved. (Ms 1:89 Mar 73)

KENNEDY, Florynce Rae. Most lawyers are like whores. They serve the client who puts the highest fee on the table. (Ms 1:89 Mar 73)

KENNEDY, Florynce Rae. There are a few jobs that actually require a penis or vagina. All other jobs should be open to everybody. (Ms 1:55 Mar 73)

KENNEDY, Florynce Rae. There's no sex to a brain. (Human Behavior 7:17 May 78)

KENNEDY, Joan. If Ted is elected President of the United States, I will commit myself to the ongoing struggle for women's equality with everything I have and everything I am. (New York Times 129:14 Feb 24, 80)

KENNEDY, John Fitzgerald. And so, my fellow Americans, ask not what your country can do for you; ask what you can do for your country (inaugural address—1961). (Christian Science Monitor 69:14 Jan 20, 77)

KENNEDY, John Fitzgerald. Domestic policy can only defeat us; foreign policy can kill us. (New York Times Magazine 50 Sept 9, 79)

KENNEDY, John Fitzgerald. He's got no class (about Richard Nixon). (Time 111:20 Mar 6, 78)

KENNEDY, John Fitzgerald. I know that when things don't go well, they like to blame the President, and that is one of the things presidents are paid for. (Rocky Mountain News 185:60 Oct 24, 79)

KENNEDY, John Fitzgerald. If somebody is going to kill me, they are going to kill me. (New Leader 61:15 Nov 6, 78)

KENNEDY, John Fitzgerald. If we are strong, our strength will speak for itself. If we are weak, words will be no help. (Kansas City Times 109:28 Jan 4, 77)

KENNEDY, John Fitzgerald. Let every nation know, whether it wishes us well or ill, we shall pay any price, bear any burden, meet any hardship, support any friend or oppose any foe to assure the survival and the success of liberty. (Time 105:43 April 7, 75)

KENNEDY, John Fitzgerald. My father always told me that steel men were sons-of-bitches, but I never realized till now how right he was (in the 1962 steel-price confrontation). (Chicago Tribune 147:2 section 2 May 29, 77)

KENNEDY, John Fitzgerald. The worse I do, the more popular I get. (Time 115:31 May 5, 80)

KENNEDY, John Fitzgerald (attributed by David Reckford). Those who make peaceful revolution impossible make violent revolution inevitable. (The Observer 9785:13 Mar 11, 79)

KENNEDY, Joseph P., III. There's no question being a Kennedy can open a lot of doors, but it's also opened a few I didn't want to walk through. (Newsweek 88:24 July 12, 76)

KENNEDY, Robert Francis. At least one half of the days that he (John F. Kennedy) spent on this earth were days of intense physical pain. (Newsweek 96:69 July 14, 80)

KENNEDY, Robert Francis (attributed by Bill Moyers). I have myself wondered if we did not pay a very great price for being more energetic than wise about a lot of things, especially Cuba. (Washington Post 228:A5 July 21, 77)

KENNEDY, Rose. I first met my husband when I was 10 or 12 years old. Unlike many of the kids today, I married for love...the money—that came later. (W 7:2 Feb 3, 78)

KENNEDY, Rose. I never thought I'd live to see the day a Kennedy would have eggs and tomatoes thrown at him in Boston. (Washington Post 48:G2 Jan 22, 76)

KENNEDY, Rose. The temptation to be the one to kill the third Kennedy brother is just too great (on why she doesn't want Ted Kennedy to run for President). (New York Times Magazine 29 June 24, 79)

KEROUAC, Jack. Walking on water wasn't built in a day. (The American Book Review 1:8 April/May 78)

KERR, Clark. Have plenty of football for the alumni, sex for the students, and parking for the faculty. (Washingtonian 15:142 Nov 79)

KERR, Clark. Naderism has taken over education. (Time 110:75 Nov 14, 77)

KERR, Jean. Marrying a man is like buying something you've been admiring for a long time in a shop window. You may love it when you get it home, but it doesn't always go with everything else in the house. (Chicago Tribune 65:1 section 5 Mar 5, 78)

KESEY, Ken. Always stay in your own movie. (New Times 9:68 Aug 19, 77)

KESEY, Ken. He (Timothy Leary) is caught like a bone in the throat of the prison system—they can't swallow him and they can't spit him out. (Chicago Sun-Times 29:9 April 14, 76)

KETCHAM, Brian (architect of New York City's Transportation Control Plan). Everyone is looking for a technological bandaid for the automobile air pollution problem. The answer is walking. It's so logical, it's absurd. (Wall Street Journal 57:12 Oct 29, 76)

KEYNES, John Maynard. My only regret in life is that I did not drink more champagne. (Money 5:53 April 76)

KEYSERLING, Hermann A. The greatest American superstition is belief in facts. (Kansas City Times 109:26 Jan 25, 77)

KHALKHALI, Ayatollah. Even if this traitor Shah hides himself in a corner of the White House, we shall get him out and kill him. (The Observer 9801:9 July 1, 79)

KHAN, Naved N. Bloomingdale's is more than a store. It is a way of life. (Time 106:4 Dec 22, 75)

KHOMEINI, Ayatollah Ruhollah. All western governments are just thieves. Nothing but evil comes from them. (Time 115:22 Jan 7, 80)

KHOMEINI, Ayatollah Ruhollah. Criminals should not be tried. They should be killed. (Newsweek 93:52 April 23, 79)

KHOMEINI, Ayatollah Ruhollah. Dictatorship is the greatest sin in the religion of Islam. Fascism and Islamism are absolutely incompatible. (Time 114:57 Oct 22, 79)

KHOMEINI, Ayatollah Ruhollah. From its very inception, Islam has been afflicted by the Jews. (Newsweek 93:42 Jan 29, 79)

KHOMEINI, Ayatollah Ruhollah. God has given us all the rules of the game. (Newsweek 93:38 Feb 26, 79)

KHOMEINI, Ayatollah Ruhollah. It is impossible to solve Iran's political problems without the disappearance of the Pahlevi dynasty. (US News & World Report 85:46 Nov 20, 78)

KHOMEINI, Ayatollah Ruhollah. A Moslem woman must be at the man's disposition for anything he may desire, and she may not refuse him without a religiously valid reason. When she is married to a Moslem man, she becomes his chattel. (New Woman 10:12 May/June 80)

KHOMEINI, Ayatollah Ruhollah. The people of Iran want to be martyrs. (The Observer 9826:9 Dec 23, 79)

KHOMEINI, Ayatollah Ruhollah. To vote for anything but an Islamic republic would be a sin. (Chicago Sun-Times 32:27 Mar 7, 79)

KHOMEINI, Ayatollah Ruhollah. We have the ideology to distinguish right from wrong, and we should not hesitate to tell misguided people, here and abroad, what is wrong with them. (Time 114:25 Dec 10, 79)

KHOMEINI, Ayatollah Ruhollah. We (Iran) did not need these armaments in the past; we will not be in need of them in the future (about U.S. arms). (US News & World Report 85:46 Nov 20, 78)

KHOSROWDAD, Manouchechr. We know that if the Shah leaves the Communists will come marching. (Newsweek 93:36 Jan 22, 79)

KHRUSHCHEV, Nikita Sergeevich. Call it what you will, incentives are the only way to make people work harder (responding to a charge that the Soviet Union was going capitalist). (Time 106:63 July 14, 75)

KHRUSHCHEV, Nikita Sergeevich. Life is short. Live it up. (Viva 4:25 July 77)

KHRUSHCHEV, Nikita Sergeevich. Politicians are the same the world over: they promise to build a bridge even where there is no river. (Village Voice 22:23 Aug 29, 77)

KHRUSHCHEV, Nikita Sergeevich. The survivors (of a nuclear attack) would envy the dead. (Harper's 259:36 Aug 79)

KIDD, Bruce. We should stop preaching about sport's moral values. Sport, after all, isn't Lent. It's a pleasure of the flesh. (Chicago Tribune 76:1 section 2 Mar 17, 78)

KILLENS, John O. Let's stop titillating white people. No matter what we black folks do, we always wind up as entertainers. (Sepia 26:10 May 76)

KILPATRICK, James J. Find out where the people want to go, then hustle yourself around in front of them. (Washingtonian 15:143 Nov 79)

KIMBALL, Spencer W. (President of the Mormon Church). Too many people have forgotten the first commandment—be fruitful and multiply. (SA, The Magazine of San Antonio 1:9 Jan 78)

KING, Billie Jean. Amateur athletes have become the pawn of manipulators and big business. (The Nation 221:654 Dec 20, 75)

KING, Billie Jean. Don't go to college if you want to make your living in sports. (New York Times 127:5 section 5 Mar 26, 78)

KING, Billie Jean. Tennis is still a rich suburban game. Whites identify with tennis and hockey. Blacks identify with basketball and music. (Chicago Tribune 27:1 section 4 Jan 27, 78)

KING, Clennon. It shows how beautiful Southern people are—they may growl and grimace, but they're the sweetest white folks on earth (commenting on the decision by the Plains Baptist Church to integrate). (Newsweek 88:81 Nov 22, 76)

KING,, Coretta Scott. America's jobless cannot "wait". Not only because waiting is no solution and not only because waiting has social consequences that are frightening to contemplate, but because to do nothing when we have the capacity to act is morally and socially wrong. (Newsweek 88:13 Aug 16, 76)

KING, Coretta Scott. I don't have the facts, but at this stage I say it appears there was a conspiracy in the death of my husband. (Los Angeles Times 94:12 Part 1 Nov 28, 75)

KING, Coretta Scott. There are so many monuments to war, so many testaments to sorrow, I wish America—through a national holiday and the center—would help build one monument of peace (referring to the Dr. Martin Luther King, Jr. Center for Social Change). (Chicago Tribune Magazine 11:40 Jan 11, 76)

KING, Coretta Scott. There is a spirit and a need and a man at the beginning of every great human advance. Each of these must be right for that particular moment of history, or nothing happens. (Chicago Tribune 176:2 section II June 25, 78)

KING, Donald. I have risen to the top in the promotion business just as I climbed to the top in the numbers game: by wits and grits and bullshit. (Cleveland 4:90 Nov 75)

KING, Jonathan. There are tremendous fortunes to be made from this new technology (referring to recombinant DNA 'gene-splitting' experiments), and in this case safety and private profit are incompatible. (Christian Science Monitor 70:14 Dec 8, 77)

KING, Larry L. One receives an inverse ratio of romantic opportunities to that which one needs. (Viva 4:72 76)

KING, Martin Luther, Jr. I'm not fearing any man. Mine eyes have seen the glory of the coming of the Lord. (Playboy 23:127 June 76)

KING, Martin Luther, Sr. Nothing that a man does takes him lower than when he allows himself to fall so far as to hate anyone. (Newsweek 96:92 Sept 15, 80)

KING, Martin Luther, Sr. Surely the Lord sent Jimmy Carter to come on out and bring America back where she belongs. (Washington Post 224:A1 July 16, 76)

KINGMAN, David Arthur. There's no way to be a nice guy and play professional athletics. You have to just go out and be mean. (Chicago Tribune Magazine 21 April 19, 78)

KIPLING, Rudyard. A woman is only a woman but a good cigar is a smoke. (Washingtonian 12:110 April 77)

KIRBO, Charles. He's (Jimmy Carter) got faults, like all of us. He's ambitious. But he's not greedy, and he's considerate. (Time 107:17 July 12, 76)

KIRBO, Charles. I may be wrong, and I may be biased, but I'm sure as hell not uncertain (commenting on his status as advisor to President Carter). (New York Times Magazine 15 Mar 20, 77)

KIRBO, Charles. Once he (John Connally) gets across that Texas line—he's not much. (Newsweek 88:25 Aug 2, 76)

KIRKLAND, Lane. All sinners belong in the church; all citizens owe fealty to their country; and all true unions belong in the American Federation of Labor and Congress of Industrial Organizations. (New York Times 129:B1 Nov 20, 79)

KIRKLAND, Lane. Any jackass can draw up a balanced budget on paper. (US News & World Report 88:90 May 19, 80)

KIRKLAND, Lane. Carter is your typical, smiling, brilliant, backstabbing, bullshitting, southern nut-cutter. (New Times 7:13 Sept 3, 76)

KIRKPATRICK, Lyman B., Jr. The heart of the matter is that the American people will tolerate what must be done to protect the nation as long as it does not seem to destroy what it is protecting (commenting on what the public will allow from the U.S. Intelligence Community). (Forbes 121:30 Jan 9, 78)

KIRKUP, Jon. The sun goes down just when you need it the most. (Washingtonian 14:154 Nov 78)

KISSINGER, Henry Alfred. The absence of alternatives (in the Middle East) clears the mind marvelously. (Time 111:35 Jan 2, 78)

KISSINGER, Henry Alfred. All the Russians can offer is war, but we can bring the peace (commenting on the Mideast situation). (Time 109:16 Jan 24, 77)

KISSINGER, Henry Alfred. The American body politic is basically healthy. Our people want to believe in their government. (Time 106:35 Oct 27, 75)

KISSINGER, Henry Alfred. Among the many claims on American resources, I would put those of Vietnam in alphabetical order. (Newsweek 89:47 May 16, 77)

KISSINGER, Henry Alfred. Cambodia's agony unfolded with the inevitability of a Greek tragedy. (Newsweek 94:59 Oct 22, 79)

KISSINGER, Henry Alfred. The cold war was not so terrible and detente was not so exalting. (The Observer 9833:9 Feb 10, 80)

KISSINGER, Henry Alfred. Competing pressures tempt one to believe that an issue deferred is a problem avoided; more often it is a crisis invited. (Time 114:82 Oct 15, 79)

KISSINGER, Henry Alfred. Each success only buys an admission ticket to a more difficult problem. (Wilson Library Bulletin 53:513 Mar 79)

KISSINGER, Henry Alfred. For God's sake, how many swan songs can a lame duck deliver? (commenting on his many farewell ceremonies). (Rolling Stone 234:39 Mar 10, 77)

KISSINGER, Henry Alfred. High office teaches decision making, not substance. It consumes intellectual capital; it does not create it. (Time 114:81 Oct 15, 79)

KISSINGER, Henry Alfred. I am not here (at the 1980 Republican Convention) as a job seeker. (Time 116:14 July 28, 80)

KISSINGER, Henry Alfred. I don't stand on protocol. If you'll just call me excellency (Responding to a newsman who asked how to address the new Secretary of State). (Chicago Tribune 333:1 Section 2 Nov 28, 76)

KISSINGER, Henry Alfred. I have always thought of foreign policy as bipartisan. (Chicago Tribune 233:6 Section 2 Aug 21, 77)

KISSINGER, Henry Alfred. I think Metternich was an extremely skilled diplomat, but not very creative. (Time 107:33 Jan 12, 76)

KISSINGER, Henry Alfred. I will think of you with affection—tinged by exasperation (speaking before the National Press Club). (Time 108:53 Jan 24, 77)

KISSINGER, Henry Alfred. If we do not meet the Russian challenge now at modest cost we will find it necessary to do so further down the road when it will be more costly and more dangerous (commenting on why U.S. aid is needed in Angola). (Christian Science Monitor 21:9 Dec 24, 75)

KISSINGER, Henry Alfred. Intellectuals condemn society for materialism when it is prosperous and for injustice when it fails to ensure prosperity. (Time 107:49 June 20, 77)

KISSINGER, Henry Alfred. It is idiotic to talk about negotiations if we are really serious. The only thing we are doing that is positive, that puts pressure on the enemy, is killing Viet Cong—we would have to stop killing Viet Cong during negotiations and right then we would lose the only bargaining counter we have (comments made in January of 1967). (July 4, 1976 special edition magazine of the Washington Post 141 July 4, 76)

KISSINGER, Henry Alfred. It is necessary for the Western democracies to recapture the sense that they can control their own destiny. (Time 106:36 Oct 27, 75)

KISSINGER, Henry Alfred. It is true that I enjoyed my celebrity status in my previous position, but I can prove that when I left Washington I wore exactly the same size crown as when I arrived. (New York Times 169:A3 May 23, 77)

KISSINGER, Henry Alfred. It was hard to avoid the impression that Nixon, who thrived on crisis, also craved disasters. (Time 114:59 Oct 1, 79)

KISSINGER, Henry Alfred. It's true, as Secretary of State-designate Cy Vance has said, that there will always be a place for me at the State Department. But it's awfully cold down in the basement. (Christian Science Monitor 29:2 Jan 13, 77)

KISSINGER, Henry Alfred. The longer I am out of office, the more infallible I appear to myself. (San Francisco Chronicle This World 1977:2 Oct 16, 77)

KISSINGER, Henry Alfred. The main point...in the mechanics of my success comes from the fact that I have acted alone. (Esquire 89:41-42 Mar 14, 78)

KISSINGER, Henry Alfred. Most administrations come to office believing that they are saving the world. This one believes it created the world (commenting on the Carter administration). (Chicago Sun-Times 30:3 May 4, 77)

KISSINGER, Henry Alfred. My impression is that there is unanimity on the course that we are pursuing. It would be a tragedy if during this election year we did not find some means to put some restraint on our domestic debates in the field of foreign policy. (Los Angeles Times 95:1 Part 1 Jan 20, 76)

KISSINGER, Henry Alfred. My megalomania, of course, reaches levels in which an admission of inadequacy is next to inconceivable (responding to a question of whether or not it is harder to conduct diplomatic negotiations in an election year). (Wall Street Journal 56:1 June 25, 76)

KISSINGER, Henry Alfred. Nelson Rockefeller was the greatest American I have ever known. (Newsweek 93:27 Feb 5, 79)

KISSINGER, Henry Alfred. No communist country has solved the problem of succession. (Time 113:59 Mar 12, 79)

KISSINGER, Henry Alfred. One had the sense that if (Charles de Gaulle) moved to a window, the center of gravity might shift, and the whole room might tilt everybody into the garden. (Time 114:82 Oct 15, 79)

KISSINGER, Henry Alfred. One thing I don't want around me is a military intellectual. I don't have to worry about you on that score (to Alexander Haig). (Look 1:58 June 11, 79)

KISSINGER, Henry Alfred. One thing I have never understood is how he became a politician. He really dislikes people. He hated to meet new people (about Richard Nixon). (Time 106:39 Oct 27, 75)

KISSINGER, Henry Alfred. Power is the greatest aphrodisiac of all. (Maclean's 91:72 Mar 6, 78)

KISSINGER, Henry Alfred. Sadat is the greatest (statesman) since Bismarck. (Esquire 91:30 Jan 30, 79)

KISSINGER, Henry Alfred. The Shah (of Iran) was—despite the travesties of retroactive myth—a dedicated reformer. (Time 114:77 Oct 15, 79)

KISSINGER, Henry Alfred. A statesman who too far outruns the experience of his people will fail in achieving a domestic consensus, however wise his policies. (On the other hand), a statesman who limits his policies to the experience of his people is doomed to sterility. (Time 108:32 Nov 8, 76)

KISSINGER, Henry Alfred. There are times when the national interest is more important than the law (commenting on suggestions that the U.S. cut off military aid to Turkey for making illegal use of American arms in Cyprus). (New York Times Magazine 13 Oct 31, 76)

KISSINGER, Henry Alfred. There cannot be a crisis next week. My schedule is already full. (Time 109:16 Jan 24, 77)

KISSINGER, Henry Alfred. There were some personality disputes which neither of us handled with the elegance and wisdom that perhaps was necessary (commenting on his relationship with former Secretary of Defense James Schlesinger). (New York Times 125:8 Nov 11, 75)

KISSINGER, Henry Alfred. To me women are no more than a pastime, a hobby. Nobody devotes too much time to a hobby. (Ms 6:50 July 77)

KISSINGER, Henry Alfred. Two years from now nobody will give a damn if I am up, down or sideways. (Time 106:29 Nov 17, 75)

KISSINGER, Henry Alfred. We are all the president's men, and have got to behave that way. (Meet the Press 20:6 April 18, 76)

KISSINGER, Henry Alfred. We are making remarkable progress toward an agreement—and toward a nervous breakdown. It's going to be a race to see which will be achieved first (about Middle East peace negotiations). (Time 106:19 Sept 8, 75)

KISSINGER, Henry Alfred. We are not going around looking for opportunities to prove our manhood. (Ms 4:63 Oct 75)

KISSINGER, Henry Alfred. We must resist the myth that government is a gigantic conspiracy. We cannot allow the intelligence services of the country to be dismantled. (Washington Post 355:1 Nov 25, 75)

KISSINGER, Henry Alfred. We now face the challenge of the early '80s with forces designed in the '60s. (Chicago Sun-Times 32:2 Aug 1, 79)

KISSINGER, Henry Alfred. We should have bombed the hell out of them the minute we got into office (a week after the 1973 Vietnam peace agreement). (Rolling Stone 188:35 June 5, 75)

KISSINGER, Henry Alfred. You can give odds of a million to one with Jimmy the Greek because one thing is certain: under no circumstances will I accept a position in a new Administration. It's time for younger men to be given a chance. (New York Times 126:10 Nov 9, 76)

KITT, Eartha. There is no greater reward in life than love. The rewards are so tremendous. Even if you don't get love from the person you're giving it to, you get it from somewhere else. (Sepia 26:10 May 76)

KLEIN, Lawrence. What really scares me is signs of a worldwide slowdown at a time when the economies of the West have become increasingly synchronized. (Time 108:77 Nov 22, 76)

KLORES, Stanley. The ordination of women to the priesthood is against the will of God (commenting upon his decision to leave the Protestant Episcopal Church for the Catholic church on the issue of women becoming priests). (Chicago Sun-Times 29:48 Oct 6, 76)

KLUGE, Alexander. German (movie) directors are like airplanes always circling the airport but never landing. (Time 111:53 Mar 20, 78)

KNEECE, Jack. They say Louisiana is somewhat like a banana republic, say Guatemala. That's not true. They speak better English in Guatemala. (New Orleans 9:15 May 75)

KNIEVEL, Evel. What I said after the accident about quitting isn't true. That was my body talking over my mind. I plan to try again (recuperating after he and motorcycle failed to clear 13 London buses). (Ms 4:62 Oct 75)

KNIGHT, Andrew (Editor of The Economist, London). We are a government of opposition, no matter who is in power. (W 4:2 Sept 19, 75)

KNIGHT, Damon. If there is a universal mind, must it be sane? (Village Voice 23:37 Aug 21, 78)

KNOPF, Alfred A. It's peculiar. The older I become the more radical I become. (W 4:2 Oct 31, 75)

KNOWLES, John H. Over 99 percent of us are born healthy and made sick as a result of personal misbehavior and environmental conditions. (Time 111:65 June 12, 78)

KNOWLES, John H. A sense of humor is the prelude to faith and laughter is the beginning of prayer. (New York Times 128:A22 Mar 7, 79)

KOCH, Edward I. It happens that intellectual honesty is not the coin of the realm in politics. (New York Times 129:B1 Oct 23, 79)

KOCH, Edward I. Jerry Brown is not a flake. (New York 12:16 Mar 12, 79)

KOCH, Edward I. New York is a place of bounding, exuberant diversity. (Christian Science Monitor 70:7 Jan 4, 78)

KOCH, Edward I. You're not a nice guy if you have a gun, even if you are a nice guy. (Time 115:63 Mar 3, 80)

KOHLER, Jerry. I'd just as soon die in Viet Nam as in the library. (Salina (Kansas) Journal 10 May 27, 76)

KOJAK, Theo. Hindsight is the only exact science. (Philadelphia 68:113 July 77)

KOKONIEN, Vladimir. The group do nothing to help people achieve self-perfection. They lack glamour, novelty and sparkle. They are unattractive and they have no originality (upon rejecting the Rolling Stones' request to perform in the USSR). (People Weekly 3:66 April 21, 75)

KOON, Larry. Women are best suited for secretarial work, decorating cakes and counter sales, like selling lingerie. (New Woman 10:12 May/June 80)

KORDA, Michael. Accuracy has never been my strongest point. (Chicago Tribune 332:1 section 3 Nov 28, 79)

KORDA, Michael. Gossip, unlike river water, flows both ways. (Reader's Digest 106:114 June 76)

KORFF, Baruch. I fully believe that every detractor of President Nixon will come before the bar of justice, whether in this lifetime or later. (Los Angeles Times 94:2 Part 1 Oct 27, 75)

KOSINSKI, Jerzy. I go to discos for the same reason I visit bars and hospital emergency rooms. They are all graveyards. (W 8:2 June 22, 79)

KOSLOW, Ron. What marijuana was to the Sixties, real estate is to the Seventies. (Esquire 93:17 Feb 80)

KOVIC, Ron. The government took the best years of my life away from me and millions of other young men. I just think they're lucky I wrote a book instead of buying a gun. (People Weekly 6:58 Dec 27/Jan 3, 77)

KOWAL, Charles (American astronomer). I enjoy learning things, but a university is the last place in the world to learn anything. (Time 106:75 Oct 27, 75)

KRAMER, Hilton. The way things are going, one expects to hear any day now that virginity is back in style. (New York Times 125:1 Section 2 May 23, 76)

KRAUS, Karl. The devil is an optimist if he thinks he can make people worse than they are. (Inquiry 1:25 Jan 23, 78)

KRAUSE, Charles. In the jungle, a press card is just another piece of paper. (Washingtonian 15:142 Nov 79)

KREMENTZ, Jill. Can I call you back? (in response to the question 'Is photography art?'). (Andy Warhol's Interview 7:11 Nov 75)

KRIEL, Anneline (Miss World of 1975). (South Africa is) a great country and a lot of changes are going on. In all the government buildings the black and white separate signs are down and in the major hotels and restaurants too. (Washington Post 337:B5 Nov 7, 75)

KRISTOFFERSON, Kris. Sam (Peckinpah) is like an old dog you sometimes have to apologize for. (Time 110:73 July 4, 77)

KRISTOL, Irving. Being frustrated is disagreeable, but the real disasters of life begin when you get what you want. (Book Digest 6:28 Dec 79)

KRISTOL, Irving. Many middle-class reformers will find to their surprise, that the populace is going to be quick to bite the hand that aims to feed it. The populace doesn't want to be fed; it wants more freedom to graze on its own. (Esquire 89:76 May 23, 78)

KROC, Ray. If you think small, you'll stay small. (Chicago 28:12 Mar 79)

KRUGER, James T. (South African Minister of Justice). I am not glad and I am not sorry about Mr. Biko. He leaves me cold. (Newsweek 90:41 Sept 26, 77)

KRUGER, James T. (South African Minister of Justice). It remains a fact that a happy person cannot be a communist (asking for reform of his country's race laws). (Rolling Stone 222:14 Sept 23, 76)

KUAN, Han-Ch'ing. What characterizes the current world situation is decidedly not an irreversible process of detente but the approaching danger of a new world war. (American Legion Magazine 99:21 Dec 75)

KUBRICK, Stanley. All you can do is either pose questions or make truthful observations about human behavior. The only morality is not to be dishonest. (Time 106:78 Dec 15, 75)

KUBRICK, Stanley. The essence of dramatic form is to let an idea come over people without its being plainly stated. (Time 106:72 Dec 15, 75)

KUCINICH, Dennis. I'm not antibusiness, just pro-people. The private sector has not been denied a forum here (in Cleveland), only control. (New York Times 128:A15 Nov 13, 78)

KUGEL, Yerachmiel. Ethics is not a branch of economics. (St. Louis Post-Dispatch 99:2G July 24, 77)

KUHN, Annette. To be 75, sailing, cracking a bone, and wanting to go sailing again as soon as this trifle is healed—that's my idea of a good life. (Village Voice 20:79 July 28, 75)

KUHN, Maggie (head of the Gray Panthers). What distresses me is that both old and young people are hooked on drugs. Old people are sedated into vegetables with tranquilizers, but the pushers of those drugs—doctors and pharmaceutical houses—are never sent to jail. They have a license to rip off old people and they rip them off every chance they get. (People Weekly 4:30 Oct 27, 75)

KUNG, Hans. The Pope needs a think tank, no, a brain trust, around him, instead of the court theologians who now surround him. (Chicago Daily News 5 June 1, 77)

KUNSTLER, William. Although I couldn't pull the trigger myself, I don't disagree with murder sometimes, especially political assassinations, which have been a part of political life since the beginning of recorded history. (Washington Post 55:C18 Jan 29, 76)

KUPFERBERG, Tuli. What is a beatnik? Why, it's exactly everything that Herbert Hoover hates. (New York 12:82 May 7, 79)

KURSAWA, Akira. I have discovered human beings really are weak, capable of saying only good things about themselves. (W 10:

KY, Nguyen Cao. I was not corrupt. Perhaps that is the only thing I regret. I realized after 14 months in this country the value of money, whether it's clean or dirty. (New York Times 125:55 July 1, 76)

KY, Nguyen Cao. Never believe what any Vietnamese tells you, including me (commenting in 1966). (Newsweek 85:17 May 19, 75)

KY, Nguyen Cao. Remember, we lost the war not because of your fault but because of bad leadership. Tell your children and grandchildren we are exiled because of Nguyen Van Thieu. Remember that name. He is the most despicable man in the world (visiting Vietnamese refugees in Camp Pendleton, California). (Newsweek 85:17 May 19, 75)

KY, Nguyen Cao. We Vietnamese are the newest refugees in your history. We know your country is a land of immigrants. Your sons and daughters fought to keep Vietnam free, and we Vietnamese wish to earn your respect and friendship. We wish not to be hawks or doves, but eagles. (Los Angeles Times 94:9 Part 6 Nov 9, 75)

KYRIAZI, Gary. More than ever, people need a place to scream. (Time 110:34 July 4, 77)

LABUE, Charles. A natural child is always conceived as soon as one is adopted. (Omni 1:132 May 79)

LACASSAGNE, Jean (19th century French criminologist). Societies have the criminals they deserve. (Time 110:25 July 11, 77)

LACOVARA, Philip. Nixon having resigned without formal prosecution has carried into his retirement a presumption of formal innocence, which was ratified by Ford's pardon. He is accepted in polite society—not as the felon he unquestionably was. (Newsweek 86:25 Oct 27, 75)

LADD, Cheryl. Jaclyn (Smith) is the only girl I know that has the body of a go-go dancer and the mind of an angel. (Chicago Tribune 76:18 Mar 17, 78)

LAFFER, Arthur. The U.S. is the fastest 'undeveloping' country in the world. (Time 114:36 Aug 27, 79)

LAIRD, Melvin. Conservation alone is a slow walk down a dead-end street. (Time 110:62 Oct 10, 77)

LAKER, Freddie. The man that doesn't change his mind doesn't think. (The Observer 9804:9 July 22, 79)

LAMARR, Hedy. Any girl can be glamorous. All you have to do is stand still and look stupid. (Chicago Sun-Times 30:21 Jan 28, 78)

LANCE, Thomas Bertram. Folks are serious about three things—their religion, their family, and most of all, their money. (Time 108:20 Dec 6, 76)

LANCE, Thomas Bertram. He (Jimmy Carter) campaigns liberal, but he governs conservative. (Washington Post 61:A3 Jan 31, 77)

LAND, Edwin. Anything worth doing is worth doing to excess. (Time 107:66 May 9, 77)

LAND, Edwin. I am addicted to at least one good experiment a day. (Time 115:68 Mar 17, 80)

LANDERS, Ann. I believe people want some spiritual leadership. It shows in the primaries; Jimmy Carter. He speaks openly about his religion. They see in him something that offers hope. (Washington Post 146:B1 April 29, 76)

LANDERS, Ann. Love is the most precious thing in all the world. Whatever figures in second place doesn't even come close. (New York 9:68 Feb 16, 76)

LANDON, Melville. Levity is the soul of wit. (San Francisco Chronicle This World 1978:40 Jan 29, 78)

LANDOR, Walter Savage. Men cannot bear to be deprived of anything they are used to; not even of their fears. (Kansas City Star 97:4B Oct 10, 76)

LANDRY, Tom. God doesn't make any losers. (Chicago Sun-Times 32:32 April 21, 79)

LANDRY, Tom. Nothing funny ever happens on the football field. (Time 111:75 Jan 16, 78)

LANE, Frank. Monday got about $125,000 from the Cubs last season and struck out 125 times. He got paid $1,000 a strikeout. This year he'll probably get $250,000 from the Dodgers, which means he's gotten a raise to $2,000 a strikeout. (Sports Illustrated 46:10 Mar 14, 77)

LANGLOIS, Henri. Most people advance through life walking backward. Those artists who face forward are likely to be put in jail—or the madhouse. (New York Times 126:D13 Jan 23, 77)

LAO-TSE (CHINESE PHILOSOPHER), . You should govern a great nation as you fry a small fish, with little stirring about. (Chicago Tribune 117:2 section 1 April 27, 77)

LAPHAM, Lewis H. Democracy means that you and I must fight. Democracy means a kind of Darwinism for ideas. (Time 111:84 Jan 23, 78)

LAPHAM, Lewis H. I take for granted Jefferson's dictum that money, not morality, constitutes the principle of commercial nations. (Harper's 254:32 Feb 77)

LARKIN, Philip. I see life more as an affair of solitude diversified by company than as an affair of company diversified by solitude. (The Observer 9825:35 Dec 16, 79)

LASCH, Christopher. The mother's power originates in the imposition of her own madness on everybody else. (New York Times Magazine 14 May 13, 79)

LASCH, Christopher. Radicalism in the United States has no great triumphs to record. (Time 110:67 Aug 15, 77)

LASSER, Louise. The best and worst thing that happened to me in 1976 was that I lived through it. (Rolling Stone 235:35 Mar 24, 77)

LASSER, Louise. When you are a celebrity, you are totally a victim. (Time 111:56 June 19, 78)

LASZLO, Ervin. The materialistic growth ethic is not an immutable expression of human nature. (Time 107:56 April 26, 76)

LAUGHLIN, Tom. Never trust a man with ideas. (New York 8:51 Aug 4, 75)

LAUGHLIN, Tom. The youth of this country have only two heroes: Ralph Nader and Billy Jack. (New York 8:51 Aug 4, 75)

LAUREN, Ralph. I can do anything I want. (W 7:8 Dec 8, 79)

LAWRENCE, David Herbert. The essential American soul is hard, stoic, isolate and a killer. (Time 111:53 Jan 9, 78)

LAWRENCE, David Herbert. Never trust the artist. Trust the tale. (Esquire 89:93 June 20, 78)

LAWTON, George E. If it is important to give the human animal a good start in life, it is just as important to see that he makes a good finish. (Saturday Evening Post 251:98 Mar 79)

LAXALT, Paul D. Our polls show that every prospective bride is a drag on the (Republican) ticket, except Jerry Ford. That would be a political marriage made in heaven. (Time 116:12 July 28, 80)

LAXALT, Paul D. We are finding that conservatives throughout this country are going to marshal together and present, I think, a formidable political challenge, and comes the general election, personally I think that Ronald Reagan has the potential of putting together the same basic elements against Jimmy Carter that Richard Nixon did in 1972. (Meet the Press 20:3 May 16, 76)

LAYNE, Bobby. Living in a small town (Lubbock) in Texas ain't half bad—if you own it. (Kansas City Times 111:10 Nov 17, 78)

LAZAR, Swifty. The problem with dull parties is the people who make them up. (W 7:17 Nov 24, 79)

LEACHMAN, Cloris. Fat people pollute the esthetic environment. (People Weekly 5:29 May 3, 76)

LEAR, Amanda. I hate to spread rumors, but what else can you do with them. (Interview 8:32 Mar 78)

LEAR, Amanda. I've come to realize that as soon as you get rich and famous, you stop picking up the bills. And as long as you're poor and struggling, you have to pay for everything. (Interview 8:32 Mar 78)

LEAR, Norman. Sex and violence are a smokescreen. There are interests in this country that don't care to have fun made about the problems existing in society (concerning the censorship of television). (Time 106:43 Aug 25, 75)

LEAR, Norman. TV executives don't make decisions based on their own sense of showmanship. They make decisions based on fear. (Emmy 1:12 Winter 79)

LEAR, Norman. When I give advice to rising starlets I say, just remember, Hollywood is the land of the definite maybe. (US 1:81 June 14, 77)

LEARY, Timothy. I don't have one nostalgic bone in my body for the 1960's. I have no desire to go back to Woodstock and spend three days in the mud on 'downers'. (New York Times 126:23 Oct 19, 76)

LEARY, Timothy. I don't like hippies. I don't like communes. I despise heroin. I've never participated in an orgy. It may ruin my reputation, but I'm particularly monogamous. (Los Angeles Times 96:15 part V Jan 30, 77)

LEARY, Timothy. I think climate, atmosphere and environment are tremendously important in your consciousness and your evolution. Southern California is the growing edge of the human species. It is also a media center, where I can transmit my messages. This is where the migrants and the mutants and the future people come, the end point of terrestial migration. (Los Angeles Times 96 Part V:18 Jan 30, 77)

LEARY, Timothy. Successful hippies are on their way to running this country. (People Weekly 6:77 Dec 27/Jan 3, 77)

LEARY, Timothy. There's no way you're going to have full employment in this country without a war or space migration... Only in space can we take steps in our evolution... Only there will we be able to expand intelligence and the human life span.. (Los Angeles Times 96:18 part V Jan 30, 77)

LEARY, Timothy. We needed drugs like LSD once to make us aware that we could alter our consciousness, do our own rewiring... Today I see drugs like LSD as primitive and at one point necessary evolutionary steps that are rapidly outmoded, like fossil fuels. (Los Angeles Times 96:1 part V Jan 30, 77)

LEARY, Timothy. You have to remember, the truth is funny. (Cleveland 8:17 Nov 79)

LEBOWITZ, Fran. Contrary to popular opinion the hustle is not a new dance step—it is an old business procedure. (Andy Warhol's Interview 9:70 Feb 79)

LEBOWITZ, Fran. Having been unpopular in high school is not just cause for book publication. (New York Times Book Review 39 June 17, 79)

LEBOWITZ, Fran. If God had meant for everything to happen at once, he would not have invented desk calendars. (Time 111:K3 May 29, 78)

LEBOWITZ, Fran. The outdoors is what you have to pass through to get from your apartment into a taxicab. (People 10:71 Sept 4, 78)

LEBOWITZ, Fran. Rome is a very loony city in every respect. One needs but spend an hour or two there to realize that Fellini makes documentaries. (Andy Warhol's Interview 7:46 July 75)

LEBOWITZ, Fran. Sleep is death without the responsibility. (Time 111:K3 May 29, 78)

LE BRIS, Michel. God is dead, Marx is dead, and I'm not doing all that well myself. (To the Point International 4:20 Aug 8, 77)

LEBRON, Lolita. Until my last breath I will fight for the liberation and freedom of Puerto Rico. (New York Times 128:1 Sept 12, 79)

LE CARRE, John. I can't live elsewhere; this country (England) is the source for me. I understand the choreography here. (Time 110:72 Oct 3, 77)

LE CARRE, John. People are very secretive creatures—secret even from themselves. (The Observer 9833:9 Feb 10, 80)

LEE, Bill (pitcher for the Boston Red Sox). I'm mad at Hank Aaron for deciding to play one more season. I threw him his last home run and thought I would be remembered forever. Now I'll have to throw him another. (Christian Science Monitor 68:31 May 3, 76)

LEFEBVRE, Marcel. The church is full of thieves, mercenaries and wolves. During the past 20 years, the Vatican has become the friend of our enemies. (Time 110:64 July 11, 77)

LEFEBVRE, Marcel. The rite of Mass today is a bastard rite. The sacraments today are bastard sacraments. We want to have prayers like our ancestors. We want to keep the Catholic faith. (Time 108:63 Sept 20, 76)

LEFEBVRE, Marcel. Rome, and not I, is in error. (Guardian Weekly 120:6 Jan 28, 79)

LEFEVRE, William M. There are only two emotions in Wall Street: fear and greed. (Time 111:42 May 1, 78)

LE GUIN, Ursula. If science fiction becomes respectable, it may die. (Newsweek 86:74 Dec 22, 75)

LEHMAN, Ernest. If writer's block is soluble in alcohol, so is the liver. (Writer's Digest 58:26 Oct 78)

LEHMEN, Ernest. Very few people realize, when they go to a movie theatre and want to be entertained, what sort of blood has flowed in order that they might have a good time. (Chicago Tribune 282:18 section 6 Oct 9, 77)

LEHRER, Tom. When Henry Kissinger can get the Nobel Peace Prize, what is there left for satire? (Chicago Sun-Times 33:76 July 9, 80)

LEIBOWITZ, Irv. When hammering a nail, you will never hit your finger if you hold the hammer with both hands. (Omni 1:132 May 79)

LEMON, Bob. I had my bad days on the field, but I didn't take them home with me. I left them in a bar along the way (commenting at his induction into the Baseball Hall of Fame). (Sports Illustrated 45:7 Aug 23, 76)

LENIN, Vladimir Il'ich. The propagandist transmits many ideas to one or more persons; the agitator transmits only one or a few ideas, but transmits them to a whole lot of people. (New York Times 127:4 section 4 April 2, 78)

LENNON, John. As usual, there's a great woman behind every idiot (upon winning his permanent residence status in the U.S.). (Newsweek 88:44 Aug 9, 76)

LEONARD, Bill. This is the major leagues. They didn't turn the Sistine Chapel over to the first guy who walked in off the street. They turned it over to Michelangelo (Defending network television's policy of rejecting news documentaries from outside sources). (TV Guide 23:6 Nov 15, 75)

LEONARD, Sugar Ray. The era of the trainer or manager talking for the fighter is over. They're not going to do his fighting, so they shouldn't be doing his talking, either. (Sports Illustrated 49:10 July 17, 78)

LEONE, Mama. No one ever filed for divorce on a full stomach. (Viva 4:26 May 77)

LEOPOLD, Aldo. The first prerequisite of intelligent tinkering is to save all the pieces. (Washingtonian 13:149 Sept 78)

LESHER, Richard. We surveyed our members as to what's troubling them. Number one is government. Number two is government. Number three is government and number four is government. (W 7:2 April 4, 78)

LEVESQUE, Rene. The quality of a civilized society is the treatment it affords minorities. (New York Times 128:23 April 5, 79)

LEVI, Edward. I would like to be remembered as one who, in a transition period, helped the President in his efforts to restore faith in the operations of government and particularly in the administration of justice. (Time 108:72 Dec 20, 76)

LEVI-STRAUSS, Claude. Age removes the confusion, only possible in youth, between physical and moral characteristics. (Time 111:99 April 24, 78)

LEVIN, S. Jay. Stocks do not move unless they are pushed. (Book Digest 6:32 Dec 79)

LEVINE, James. The audience experience should come from listening, not from noticing the conductor having an eight and a half minute sustained orgasm. (Chicago Tribune 38:14 Feb 7, 78)

LEVY, Bernard-Henri. Between the barbarity of capitalism, which censures itself much of the time, and the barbarity of socialism, which does not, I guess I might choose capitalism. (Time 111:30 Mar 13, 78)

LEVY, Bernard-Henri. The only successful revolution of this century is totalitarianism. (Time 110:29 Sept 12, 77)

LEVY, Bernard-Henri. Solzhenitsyn is the Shakespeare of our time, the only one who knows how to point out the monsters. (Time 110:29 Sept 12, 77)

LEWIS, Anthony. In making a prison for others, the Afrikaners have imprisoned themselves. (Chicago Daily News 14 Dec 3-4, 77)

LEWIS, C. S. All that is not eternal is eternally out of date. (Time 110:92 Dec 5, 77)

LEWIS, C. S. A young man who wishes to remain a sound atheist cannot be too careful of his reading. God is, if I may say it, very unscrupulous. (New York Times 126:B1 Dec 20, 76)

LEWIS, Jerry. Only the man who does nothing makes no mistakes. (Boston 69:74 Sept 77)

LEWIS, Jerry Lee. That dead son of a gun is still riding on my coattails (about Elvis Presley). (New York Times Magazine 45 Mar 25, 79)

LEWIS, Joe E. You're not really drunk if you can lie on the floor without hanging on. (Playboy 26:26 Oct 79)

LEWIS, Jonathan. Most politicians get elected by being all things to all people. Jerry (Brown) survives by being nothing to everyone. (Harper's 259:14 July 79)

LIBERMAN, Alexander. All serious art is against convention. (New York Times Magazine 61 May 13, 79)

LIDBERG, A. A. Distribute dissatisfaction uniformly. (Washingtonian 15:140 Nov 79)

LIDDY, G. Gordon. Before going to prison I believed that criticism of the criminal justice system for its treatment of the poor was so much liberal bleating and bunk. I was wrong. (Connecticut 40:48 Feb 77)

LIDDY, G. Gordon. The criminal justice system is breaking down because we, as a nation, have for too long neglected to nourish its heart—the court systems of our country. (Connecticut 40:48 Feb 77)

LIDDY, G. Gordon. I have found within myself all I need and all I ever shall need. I am a man of great faith, but my faith is in George Gordon Liddy. I have never failed me. (Chicago Tribune 257:20 Sept 14, 77)

LIDDY, G. Gordon. I think in all fairness to the man, you'd have to put him right up there with Judas Iscariot (about John Dean). (More 5:11 July 75)

LIDDY, G. Gordon. When the prince approaches his lieutenant, the proper response of the lieutenant to the prince is Fiat volutas tua, (thy will be done)...I think I delayed things substantially. The prince was prince for a longer period of time (when asked if he would do that kind of work again for a President and if he felt he had taken the blame for Watergate in vain). (Rolling Stone 250:53 Oct 20, 77)

LIEBERMANN, Rolf. Running an opera is like running a restaurant. If the boss is not there, the food gets bad and the service even worse. (Time 108:58 Sept 20, 76)

LIEBLING, A. J. Freedom of the press belongs to those who own one. (American Film 3:67 July/Aug 78)

LIEBLING, A. J. The people who have something to say don't talk; the others insist on talking. (Washingtonian 15:142 Nov 79)

LILIENTHAL, David E. If a great number of countries come to have an arsenal of nuclear weapons, then I'm glad I'm not a young man and I'm sorry for my grandchildren (commenting at hearings of the Senate Government Operations Committee). (New York Times 125:2 Jan 20, 76)

LILLY, Doris. Gossip and manure are only good for one thing—and that's spreading. Gossip doesn't mean a damn thing unless you spread it around. (W 4:2 Aug 22, 75)

LINCOLN, Abraham. Sitting here, where all the avenues to public patronage seem to come together in a knot, it does seem to me that our people are fast approaching the point where it can be said that seven-eighths of them are trying to find out how to live at the expense of the other eighth. (Mother Jones 3:29 Jan 78)

LINCOLN, Abraham. So this is the little lady who made this big war (comment upon meeting Harriet Beecher Stowe). New York Times 126:1 Section 10 Nov 7, 76)

LINDBERGH, Anne Morrow. Writing is thinking. It is more than living, for it is being conscious of living. (Time 103:101 Mar 11, 74)

LINDBERGH, Anne Morrow (attributed by Julie Nixon Eisenhower). Life is a gift, given in trust—like a child. (Christian Science Monitor 69:21 June 23, 77)

LINDBERGH, Charles Augustus. I do not want to be a member of the generation that through blindness and indifference destroys the quality of life on our planet. (Washington Post 161:G2 May 15, 77)

LINDBERGH, Charles Augustus. It was the combination of an undeveloped science with an art, resulting in adventure for the mind and body that brought stimulation to the spirit (commenting on aviation). (Washington Post 161:G2 May 15, 77)

LINDBERGH, Charles Augustus. I've had enough fame for a dozen lives; it's not what it's cracked up to be. (New York Times Magazine 12 May 8, 77)

LINDBERGH, Charles Augustus. Life is like a landscape. You live in the midst of it, but can describe it only from the vantage point of distance. (Washington Post 161:G2 May 15, 77)

LINDGREN, Lynn (Ms All-Bare America). I like to expose myself to a diversity of reactions and outcomes (in reply to why she wanted the title of Ms All-Bare America). (Philadelphia Magazine 66:143 Oct 75)

LINDSAY, John Vliet. Every public official should be recycled occasionally (commenting on his post-mayoral activities—as lawyer and TV host). (Chicago Tribune 117:14 section 1 April 27, 77)

LINDSAY, John Vliet. Flattery isn't harmful unless inhaled. (Chicago Tribune 22:1 section 2 Jan 22, 78)

LINDSAY, John Vliet. If you want gratitude, get yourself a dog. (Chicago Tribune 22:2 section 2 Jan 22, 78)

LINEWES, David. We are an information-spoiled society. It's been so easy to collect that we just keep on collecting. Tens of millions of names are being pushed around from one organization to another for whatever purposes they want them, and we don't know anything about it. (Time 110:17 July 18, 77)

LIPPMANN, Walter. I think there is a stopping point between globalism and isolationism. The test of statesmanship is to find those stopping points and to act accordingly (comments in a critique of Vietnam policy in 1965). (July 4, 1976 special edition magazine of the Washington Post 149 July 4, 76)

LIPPMANN, Walter. When all think alike, no one is thinking. (Book Digest 6:28 Dec 79)

LIPPMANN, Walter. You are just a puzzled man making notes about what you think. (Time 112:84 July 10, 78)

LIPSEN, Chuck. Folklore has it that the oldest profession is prostitution. I always thought it was lobbying. (W 6:2 Sept 16, 77)

LISAGOR, Peter. Hubert Humphrey could have gotten a better deal in bankruptcy court (about the 1968 Democratic National Convention). (Washington Journalism Review 1:37 April/May 78)

LISAGOR, Peter. Washington is a place where the truth is not necessarily the best defense. It surely runs a poor second to the statute of limitations. (Time 108:71 Dec 20, 76)

LITTLE RICHARD, . Real women don't want to climb telephone poles. (New Woman 10:12 May/June 80)

LODGE, John Davis. Man is born into the world as a pig and is civilized by women. (W 6:2 Feb 18, 77)

LOEB, William. I think the total sum of his (Gerald Ford's) incompetency, his failure to lead and to a certain extent his deviousness would in the vernacular sum up to that phrase (that the President of the United States is a jerk), yes. (Meet the Press 20:2 Feb 15, 76)

LOGAN, Ben. TV is hydraulic. You push down violence and up pops exploitative sex. (Newsweek 91:54 Feb 20, 78)

LOMBARDI, Vince. Winning isn't everything. It is the only thing. (Newsweek 94:166 Nov 19, 79)

LOMBARDO, Guy. The reason we have lasted so long is that we play music for lovers rather than acrobats. (Newsweek 90:126 Nov 14, 77)

LOMBARDO, Guy. When I go, I'll take New Year's Eve with me. (Newsweek 90:126 Nov 14, 77)

LONG, Earl. Mr. Luce is like a man who owns a shoe store and buys all the shoes to fit himself. Then he expects other people to buy them. (Esquire 89:97 Jan 78)

LONG, Russell. Entertainment is to the selling business the same thing as fertilizer is to the farming business—it increases the yield (commenting on the three martini lunch). (Forbes 121:26 Feb 20, 78)

LONG, Russell. Those who defame us, curse us, abuse us and lie about us, would be in one hell of a fix without us (about energy producers). (Time 114:84 Nov 26, 79)

LONGWORTH, Alice Roosevelt. Fill what's empty. Empty what's full. And scratch where it itches. (Washingtonian 15:142 Nov 79)

LONGWORTH, Alice Roosevelt. He was the best company there ever was (about John L. Lewis). (New York Times 124:15 Section 4 Aug 17, 75)

LONGWORTH, Alice Roosevelt. The secret of eternal youth is arrested development. (Washington Post 103:1 section C Feb 24, 80)

LOOS, Anita. Gentlemen don't prefer blondes. If I were writing that book today, I'd call it 'Gentlemen Prefer Gentlemen'. (Newsweek 85:72 May 12, 75)

LOPES, Dave. I don't know where I got the power (to hit a key home run), but maybe it was from the Big Dodger in the Sky. (Chicago Daily News 3 Dec 30, 77)

LOPEZ REGA, Jose. I have written a few pages of the prologue in the book of our national destiny. My opponents and the anti-patriots will make it their task to fill an entire volume of fiction (upon being removed from his job as personal secretary to President Isabel Peron). (The Guardian Weekly 113:7 July 19, 75)

LORD, Winston. The Trilateral Commission doesn't secretly run the world. The Council on Foreign Relations does that. (W 7:9 Aug 4, 78)

LOREN, Sophia. I will be a very wise and serene old lady. As I get older, I get quieter, because now I know myself better. (Chicago Tribune 15:33 Jan 15, 78)

LOREN, Sophia. I'm a giraffe. I even walk like a giraffe, with a long neck and legs. It's a pretty dumb animal, mind you. (The Observer 9788:39 April 1, 79)

LOREN, Sophia. The mob that adores you is the most wonderful tribute there can be. (Newsweek 96:63 Oct 6, 80)

LOREN, Sophia. Success has not changed me. I have become more mature with time, but I am that same girl I was 20 years ago. (Time 116:53 July 28, 80)

LOREN, Sophia. We actors are the damned of the earth. (The Observer 9862:12 Aug 31, 80)

LOUGHRIGE, Alan Craig. The middle of the road is the best place to get run over. (Washingtonian 15:142 Nov 79)

LOUIS, Joe. You can run, but you can't hide. (Mother Jones 3:65 Dec 77)

LOVAT, Tom. Last night I sat down and tried to think about the highlights from last year and I fell asleep (Utah football coach commenting on his 1-10 season). (Sports Illustrated 43:14 Sept 15, 75)

LOVELL, James, Jr. I'm convinced that the last human sound on this continent won't be a bang, but a burp (commenting on what will happen if people don't eat less and exercise more. (Sports Illustrated 44:12 May 3, 76)

LOVELL, James, Jr. We will fly women into space and use them the same way we use them on Earth—and for the same purpose. (Ms 6:49 July 77)

LOWE, Nick. (Grace Slick) is like somebody's mom who's had a few too many drinks at a cocktail party. (Time 111:46 June 26, 78)

LOWELL, James. A wise skepticism is the first attribute of a good critic. (Kansas City Star 97:24 Mar 29, 77)

LOWELL, Robert. Almost all good women poets are either divorced or lesbian. (San Francisco Chronicle 111:19 May 25, 77)

LOWNES, Victor. This company is doing a good business, if we can only stop pissing away the profits. (Time 106:61 Aug 4, 75)

LOWREY, Bette. Inflation is just a high priced depression. (Cleveland 4:15 May 75)

LOY, Myrna. Nobody seems to like each other anymore. (Viva 5:108 Oct 77)

LUCAS, Bill. If he can help us by getting people out, I don't care if he's 120 years old (about Jim Bouton). (Newsweek 92:80 Sept 18, 78)

LUCAS, George. I'm not out to be thought of as a great artist. It's a big world and everybody doesn't have to be significant. (Time 115:73 May 19, 80)

LUCE, Clare Boothe. There aren't many women now I'd like to see as President—but there are fewer men. (Newsweek 94:95 Oct 22, 79)

LUCE, Clare Boothe (attributed by Paul Dickson). No good deed goes unpunished. (Playboy 25:22 May 78)

LUCE, Henry. He seduces me. When I'm with him I feel like a whore (when asked how he felt about John Kennedy). (Esquire 89:114 Jan 78)

LUCE, Henry. I thought it was Time's job to make people unhappy and Life's job to make them happy. (Esquire 89:100 Jan 78)

LUCE, Henry. Make money, be proud of it; make more money, be prouder of it. (Washington Journalism Review 1:22 April/May 78)

LUCIANO, Ron. What I really hate about umpiring is that we can never win. We don't walk off a field with a grin on our faces. (Newsweek 86:43 Sept 1, 75)

LUDLAM, Charles. My work is eclectic not ethnocentric. It is a Rosetta Stone of theatrical conventions. (Village Voice 20:120 Nov 17, 75)

LUEDERS, Edward. Solitude leads to amplitude. (Country Journal 5:105 Aug 78)

LUKACS, John. I believe human nature doesn't change. I believe very strongly in original sin. I also take a dim view of the pursuit of justice as being the superior value of Western civilization. I think truth is more important than justice. (Washington Post 26:C3 Dec 31, 76)

LULE, Yusufu. Our strength and our success will depend on our unity. (Newsweek 93:42 April 23, 79)

LUMBARD, J. Edward. In areas of doubt and conflicting considerations, it is thought better to err on the side of free speech. (American Legion Magazine 102:22 June 77)

LYNCH, James. If we do not live together, we will die—prematurely—alone. (Guardian Weekly 117:17 Sept 18, 77)

LYND, Staughton. The best way to be a radical in America would be to be so much a part of the situation in which you were that you didn't need to be a radical. You could just live the situation as opposed to coming in and organizing it. (New York Times Magazine 70 Aug 14, 77)

MAAZEL, Lorin. Too many concerts are given by too many orchestras. You get the professionalism of mediocrity, and it grinds on like some kind of dreadful machine that never stops. (People Weekly 5:28 Jan 12, 76)

MABLEY, Moms. A woman is a woman until the day she dies, but a man's a man only as long as he can. (Sepia 24:10 Jan 75)

MACARTHUR, Douglas. Duty, honor, country: Those three hallowed words reverently dictate what you want to be, what you can be, and what you will be...The long gray line has never failed us (at the U.S. Military Academy at West Point, May 12, 1962). (Washington Post 208:B1 July 1, 77)

MACARTHUR, Douglas. It's the orders you disobey that make you famous. (Time 112:89 Sept 11, 78)

MACARTHUR, John D. Anybody who knows what he's worth, isn't worth very much (upon being asked how much he was worth). (Chicago Tribune 340:2 Section 1 Dec 5, 76)

MACARTHUR, John D. It's no fun being rich anymore. People are too damned jealous and suspicious of you. They figure anybody that makes as much money as I allegedly have must have cheated somebody. (Parade 10 Aug 28, 77)

McARTHUR, Robert. Never imply that they care whether your socks match; and never forget that they do. (Washingtonian 14:46 Jan 79)

MACCAFFERY, Desmond. A biographer is an artist who is on oath. (Time 114:86 July 2, 79)

McCARTHY, Eugene Joseph. He (Fritz Mondale) has the soul of a vice-president. (Village Voice 21:14 Oct 11, 76)

McCARTHY, Eugene Joseph. If you're in the peanut business you learn to think small (about Jimmy Carter). (New York 9:9 Aug 2, 76)

McCARTHY, Eugene Joseph. If you've been in this business for 28 years, you don't like to leave the institutions in worse shape than you found them (explaining his rationale for staying in politics). (New York Times Magazine 102 Oct 24, 76)

McCARTHY, Eugene Joseph. Jimmy Carter says he talks to Jesus five times a day. Some of us think he really shouldn't have to bother the Lord that often. He should be able to make some decisions on his own. (New York 9:9 Aug 2, 76)

McCARTHY, Eugene Joseph. Kissinger won a Nobel Peace Prize for watching a war end that he was for. (New York Times Magazine 100 Oct 24, 76)

McCARTHY, Eugene Joseph. The most important member of the Executive Branch is the press secretary. I will appoint Mort Sahl. He's the only newspaper reader I know in America. I'll have him sit on the White House steps in the morning and catch the New York Times when it's thrown over the fence—and the Washington Post. He will throw the latter back immediately. (Washington Post 56:D3 Jan 30, 76)

McCARTHY, Eugene Joseph. The only thing that saves us from the bureaucracy is inefficiency. An efficient bureaucracy is the greatest threat to liberty. (Time 113:67 Feb 12, 79)

McCARTHY, Eugene Joseph. The polls show that 10 percent of the public are ready to vote for me even though they don't know I'm running. We hope that figure won't drop when they learn I'm in the race. (New York 9:9 Aug 2, 76)

MCCARTHY, Eugene Joseph. The Republican Party is a lower form of plant life, like moss on a rock. It has very low vitality—green in the summer, slightly gray in the winter—but it never dies. If the Republicans had any decency, they'd just go away. (New York Times Magazine 13 Oct 24, 76)

MCCARTHY, Eugene Joseph. The selling of arms is now one of the principal occupations of the Defense Department. (Center Report 8:11 Dec 75)

MCCARTHY, Eugene Joseph. The two-party system has given this country the war of Lyndon Johnson, the Watergate of Nixon, and the incompetence of Carter. Saying we should keep the two-party system simply because it is working is like saying the Titanic voyage was a success because a few people survived on life rafts. (Chicago Tribune 253:5 section 2 Sept 10, 78)

MCCARTHY, Eugene Joseph. Vice-presidential candidates just clutter up the campaign. We should not ask the country to make two judgements. Everyone knows Vice-Presidents have no influence on Presidents, once elected. Presidents' wives have much more influence. Perhaps we should have the candidates' wives debate. (New York Times 126:2 section 1 Oct 10, 76)

MCCARTHY, Eugene Joseph. Work is the only kind of property many people have in America. (Center Report 8:12 Dec 75)

MCCARTHY, Eugene Joseph (attributed by Daniel Patrick Moynihan). No one ever was associated with (Lyndon Johnson) who was not in the end somehow diminished. (The Observer 9796:34 May 27, 79)

MCCARTHY, Mary. It really takes a hero to live any kind of spiritual life without religious belief. (The Observer 9816:35 Oct 14, 79)

MCCARTHY, Mary. One has to believe that love is eternal, even if one knows it is not. (The Observer 9816:35 Oct 14, 79)

MCCARTNEY, Linda. Our kids keep asking, what is Daddy going to do when he grows up? (People Weekly 5:35 June 7, 76)

MCCARTNEY, Paul. You cannot reheat a souffle (commenting on promoter Sid Bernstein's attempt to reunite the Beatles). (Rolling Stone 225:33 Nov 4, 76)

MCCLOSKEY, Paul N. I don't believe there are any reasoning powers behind the programmed articulation of Ronald Reagan and I would like to test this thesis in open debate. (Los Angeles Times 94:2 Part 1 Nov 26, 75)

MCCOLOUGH, C. Peter. Businessmen's ethics are not any worse than those of the public as a whole. It's just that the businessman is more accountable than any other level of society and is much more likely to be caught in any dereliction of duty or responsibility. (W 6:12 Oct 14, 77)

MCCORMACK, Mike. One man's conservation is all to frequently another man's unemployment. (Time 110:27 Dec 12, 77)

MCCREE, Wade. Washington is the only town in the world where sound travels faster than light. (Chicago Sun-Times 31:6 June 20, 78)

MCCULLERS, Carson. I have more to say than Hemingway, and, God knows, I say it better than Faulkner. (Time 106:E3 July 21, 75)

MCGOFF, John. I am not now, nor have I ever been, an agent or front for any foreign government, including the Republic of South Africa. (New York Times 128:A12 July 19, 79)

MCGOVERN, George Stanley. Any candidate who says or implies that by supporting him the voters can stop the buses will prove as President to be either a liar or a violator of the Constitution. (Los Angeles Times 94:7 Part 1 Nov 24, 75)

MCGOVERN, George Stanley. He who tugs Uncle Sam's beard too hard risks reprisal from the mightiest nation on the face of this earth. (The Observer 9822:9 Nov 25, 79)

MCGOVERN, George Stanley. I do not want a great political party which nearly lost its soul in Vietnam to sell its soul on the issue of busing. (Los Angeles Times 94:7 Part 1 Nov 24, 75)

MCGOVERN, George Stanley. I think it's going to be a fascinating experience...to be required, after twenty years away from the classroom, to systematically organize my thoughts on foreign policy. (Los Angeles Times 96sPart I:2 Jan 14, 77)

MCGOVERN, George Stanley. I will not vote for the illusion of arms control. (New York Times 128:A6 July 10, 79)

MCGOVERN, George Stanley. I will support Jimmy Carter with the same enthusiasm with which he supported the Democratic ticket in 1972. (Time 107:29 May 17, 76)

MCGOVERN, George Stanley. In this campaign, the Democratic Party and its candidates must demand an orderly withdrawal of American forces from Korea within a specified time. It would take no more than a year to leave; it might take as long as the decade of Vietnam to stay and bleed and die and lose. This time let us make peace before the making of a war. (Los Angeles Times 94:4 Part 1 Oct 26, 75)

MCGOVERN, George Stanley. The liberals are giving up too soon on the kind of economic and social change that we were trying to bring about in 1972—they want a winner, almost no matter who it is. (American Legion 101:42 July 76)

MCGOVERN, George Stanley. The longer the title, the less important the job . (Town & Country 133:141 May 79)

MCGOVERN, George Stanley. Marching in mindless lockstep is the lowest form of party loyalty. (Village Voice 22:34 May 16, 77)

MCGOVERN, George Stanley. Thoughtful Americans understand that the highest patriotism is not a blind acceptance of official policy, but a love of one's country deep enough to call her to a higher standard. (Life 2:117 Dec 79)

MCGOVERN, George Stanley. Warren (Beatty) not only cares about issues, but his judgment is very perceptive. (Time 112:73 July 3, 78)

MCGOVERN, George Stanley. We are defending a corrupt dictatorship, as we did to that last shameful day in Saigon (about the Republic of Korea). (Los Angeles Times 94:4 Part 1 Oct 26, 75)

MCGOVERN, George Stanley. We can mark it down that the ghost of Joe McCarthy still stalks this land (commenting on the treatment of Theodore Sorensen as Carter's nominee for the directorship of the CIA). (Seven Days 1:45 Feb 28, 77)

MCGUIRE, Al. I don't know why people question the academic training of a student-athlete. Half the doctors in the country graduated in the bottom half of their class.   (Sports Illustrated 44:16 Oct 4, 76)

MCGUIRE, Al. I want my teams to have my personality—surly, obnoxious and arrogant. (Sports Illustrated 43:14 June 16, 75)

MCGUIRE, Al. The only thing in this country that blacks really dominate, except poverty, is basketball.   (Chicago Tribune 63:1 section 5 Mar 3, 78)

MCHARG, Ian. Give us your poor and oppressed and we will give them Harlem and the Lower East Side, Bedford-Stuyvesant, the South Side of Chicago, and the North of Philadelphia—or, if they are very lucky, Levittown.   (July 4, 1976 special edition magazine of the Washington Post 34 July 4, 76)

MACHEL, Samora (President of Mozambique). We cannot tolerate a bourgeoisie in Mozambique, even a black one.   (Time 107:26 May 3, 76)

MCHUGH, Vicki (aide to Rosalynn Carter). I traveled in a Rolls long before Jimmy Carter became President and I don't plan to stop now.   (W 7:33 Nov 10, 78)

MCINTYRE, Bruce. If the (Washington) Post experience says anything, maybe it's this: being a so-called union-busting paper doesn't interfere with greatness.   (More 8:8 Mar 78)

MCKAY, Robert. If war is too important to be left to the generals, surely justice is too important to be left to lawyers.   (Time 111:66 April 10, 78)

MCKUEN, Rod. The best remedy for a cold is to go to bed with a good book, or a friend who's read one.   (Viva 4:26 Feb 77)

MCKUEN, Rod. Having been born a bastard, I feel it has given me a head start on all those people who have spent their lives becoming one.   (Time 106:30 Dec 29, 75)

MCKUEN, Rod. People are not born bastards. They have to work at it (commenting on his lifelong search to find his father).   (People Weekly 5:15 June 28, 76)

MACLAINE, Shirley. He (Ronald Reagan) is a true velvet fascist, really smooth.   (Chicago Sun-Times 29:12 Feb 17, 76)

MACLAINE, Shirley. He says his lust is in his heart. I hope it's a little lower (about Jimmy Carter). (Life 2:86 Dec 79)

MACLAINE, Shirley. I want women to be liberated and still be able to have a nice ass and shake it. (People Weekly 5:27 May 10, 76)

MACLAINE, Shirley. Sure, I'd play a hooker again, if she got to be Secretary of State.   (New York Times 125:5 Section 2 April 18, 76)

MACLAINE, Shirley. We're bisexual up to the age of 3, but what society won't admit is that we're bisexual most of our lives.   (W 6:2 Sept 2, 77)

MACLAINE, Shirley. When you know who you are and you realize what you can do, you can do things better at 40 than when you're 20.   (Time 107:39 Feb 16, 76)

MACLEISH, Archibald. Freedom is still the last great revolutionary cause.   (Chicago Tribune 163:2 section 2 June 11, 78)

MACLEISH, Archibald. What we know to be man is in these stacks (about the Library of Congress). (New York Times 129:B14 Oct 4, 79)

MCLUHAN, Marshall. Most clear writing is a sign that there is no exploration going on. Clear prose indicates an absence of thought.   (Time 106:36 Aug 25, 75)

MCLUHAN, Marshall. North America looks, as usual, grim.   (Mother Jones 1:9 Nov 76)

MCLUHAN, Marshall. Only the vanquished remember history.   (Forbes 120:120 Aug 15, 77)

MCLUHAN, Marshall. Television is not a visual medium.   (CoEvolution Quarterly 16:86 Winter 77/78)

MCLUHAN, Marshall. That was the human family sitting down together. It passed history unexpectedly (about Anwar Sadat's first visit to Israel).   (Time 110:44 Dec 5, 77)

MCLUHAN, Marshall. To discuss the dignity of an unborn life is ludicrous (when) the Apocalypse is at hand.   (New York Times A25 Oct 1, 76)

MCLUHAN, Marshall. TV is addictive. It's a drug. (Washington Post 161:H1 May 15, 77)

MACMILLAN, Harold. A foreign secretary is forever poised between a cliche and an indiscretion. (Kansas City Star 97:4B Jan 30, 77)

MCNAMARA, Robert Strange. It's not a frustration that my speeches have less impact on the U.S. It's a frustration that the U.S. has not, I think, given proper weight to the developing countries, even in its own narrow national interest.   (New York Times 125:1 Section 3 Nov 30, 75)

MCNAUGHTON, Andrew. The patient who is suffering from cancer doesn't care if he gets his Laetrile from an angel or a devil.   (Maclean's 89:28 Jan 76)

MACNEIL, Robert. TV has created a nation of news junkies who tune in every night to get their fix on the world.   (Time 115:65 Feb 25, 80)

MCNULTY, Franklin L. With adequate integrity, guts can be located.   (Parade 4 May 27, 79)

MACRAE, Norman. An anti-growth cult is being taught to a generation of idealistic kids as if it was high moral philosophy or even a religion.   (Time 106:17 Nov 10, 75)

MADDOX, Lester Garfield. The reason he (Jimmy Carter) says he never lies is because he thinks the truth originates with him.   (Newsweek 88:25 July 19, 76)

MADDOX, Lester Garfield. There are two Jimmy Carters, one running for president and one governor of Georgia, and let me tell you one thing: if Richard Nixon had gotten his training from Jimmy Carter, he never would have gotten caught.   (Rolling Stone 204:30 Jan 15, 76)

MADDOX, Lester Garfield. The thing I don't like about New York is the tendency to reward bums and penalize hard work.   (Rolling Stone 203:29 Jan 1, 76)

MADISON, James. Liberty is to faction what air is to fire.   (Time 112:73 Oct 23, 78)

MADSON, Carlisle. The purchase of any product can be rationalized if the desire to own it is strong enough.   (Washingtonian 15:140 Nov 79)

MAGNUSON, Warren. Why, if we passed the Ten Commandments, President Ford would veto them. He'd say there were too many or they interfered with foreign policy or something.   (Potomac (Sunday Magazine of the Washington Post) 4 Jan 11, 76)

MAGRUDER, Jeb Stuart. I lost my moral compass. (Newsweek 85:49 May 5, 75)

MAGUIRE, Daniel. Turning the other cheek is an ideal like a horizon to turn to. It is not a practical guide for the police in the Bronx. (Time 112:59 Sept 18, 78)

MAHEU, Robert. I can summarize my attitude about employing more Negroes very simply. I think it is a wonderful idea for somebody else, somewhere else. I know this is not a very praiseworthy point of view, but I feel that Negroes have already made enough progress to last the next hundred years. (Newsweek 87:32 April 19, 76)

MAILER, Norman. Ego is the word of the century. (New York Times Magazine 110 Dec 2, 79)

MAILER, Norman. Hemingway knew in advance, with a fine sense of timing, that he would have to campaign for himself, that the best tactic to hide the lockjaw of his shrinking genius was to become the personality of our time. (Time 111:89 April 3, 78)

MAILER, Norman. It is easier not to pay one's mother than not to pay a creditor. (Chicago Sun-Times 32:6 Feb 28, 79)

MAILER, Norman. It's hard to get to the top in America, but it's even harder to stay there. (Time 113:74 April 2, 79)

MAILER, Norman. I've made an ass of myself so many times I often wonder if I am one. (New York Times Magazine 53 Sept 9, 79)

MAILER, Norman. My talent is making money, not managing it. (Kansas City Times 111:Jan 25, 79) Jan 25, 79

MAILER, Norman. (Thomas Wolfe was) the greatest five-year-old who ever lived. (New York Times Book Review 3 Dec 2, 79)

MAILER, Norman. A writer of the largest dimension can alter the nerves and marrow of a nation. (New York Times Magazine 54 Sept 9, 79)

MAIN, Michael. For every action there is an equal and opposite government program. (Omni 1:132 May 79)

MAKARIOS III, Archbishop. I would consort with the devil himself if it would keep Cyprus and its people independent. (Time 110:32 Aug 15, 77)

MAKAROVA, Natalia. Even the ears must dance. (Newsweek 85:65 May 19, 75)

MAKAROVA, Natalia. I am an erotic woman and that's what dance is. (Newsweek 85:64 May 19, 75)

MALAMUD, Bernard. I write to know the next room of my fate. (Time 114:86 July 2, 79)

MALCOLM X, . This thing with me will be resolved by death and violence. (Playboy 23:127 June 76)

MALDONADO, Jose. For the usurper Juan Carlos, we forsee a war without mercy. Instead of climbing carpeted stairs to the throne, he will be forced to mount the scaffold. Regicide awaits him. (Time 106:57 Nov 24, 75)

MALINOWSKI, Bronislaw. Every historical change creates its mythology. (Time 109:86 May 23, 77)

MALLE, Louis. Being a director is like being a thief. You steal bits and pieces of the lives around you, and you put them into a movie. (New York Times 126:C6 Nov 19, 76)

MALLE, Louis. It always surprised me that people consider me a French director. I don't like the French. They get on my nerves. They are so pompous and have no humor... They don't adjust to modern civilization at all. (W 6:2 Jan 7, 77)

MALLE, Louis. Making a film is a life cycle—like being born, taking first steps, developing relationships. And the end of the shooting is like death in many ways. (Rolling Stone 262:39 April 6, 78)

MALLE, Louis. Pretty Baby is a picture about child prostitution in which everybody else is the victim. (Chicago 27:12 June 78)

MALRAUX, Andre. A minor living art is far more vital than a major dead one. (New York Times Magazine 17 Jan 23, 77)

MALRAUX, Andre. There cannot be another Michelangelo in today's society because our faith in man is too weak. (Time 105:40 May 12, 75)

MALRAUX, Andre. There is no such thing as death. There is only I who am dying (commenting on death in his novel The Royal Way). (Washington Post 355:C5 Nov 24, 76)

MAMET, David. I want to change the future of American theatre. (Village Voice 21:101 July 5, 76)

MAMET, David. Intellectually, I'd like to think of them (critics) as running-dog conspirators against the institution of art. But they're just jack-offs like the rest of us. (More 7:31 July/Aug 77)

MANDEL, Morris. Always put off until tomorrow what you shouldn't do at all. (Reader's Digest 106:145 April 75)

MANDELSTAM, Osip. Poetry is respected only in this country (Russia)—people are killed for it. There's no place where more people are killed for it. (New York Times Book Review 34 Mar 4, 79)

MANKIEWICZ, Frank Fabian. The higher the tuition, the fewer days they spend in school. (Washingtonian 14:154 Nov 78)

MANKIEWICZ, Frank Fabian. The Rockefeller report was the first report that was a smear and whitewash at the same time. (Rolling Stone 192:33 July 31, 75)

MANKIEWICZ, Frank Fabian. Since we are not yet serious about guns, let us at least withhold the most costly target (the President). (Newsweek 86:34 Oct 6, 75)

MANKIEWICZ, Herman. There but for the grace of God goes God (about Orson Welles). (American Film 4:70 Feb 79)

MANKIEWICZ, Tom. Whatever Jimmy Carter is asking us to be, Superman is already. (Time 110:64 Aug 1, 77)

MANN, Herbie. Don't let your taste get in the way of reaching a broader audience. (Newsweek 93:57 April 2, 79)

MANSFIELD, Katherine. Whenever I prepare for a journey, I prepare as though for death. Should I never return, all is in order. This is what life has taught me. (Human Behavior 7:16 May 78)

MANSFIELD, Mike. The crisis you have to worry about most is the one you don't see coming. (US News & World Report 88:42 Oct 31, 77)

MANSFIELD, Mike. There is a time to stay and a time to go. Thirty-four years is not a long time but it is time enough (commenting on his retirement from the Senate). (New York Times 125:12 Mar 5, 76)

MANSFIELD, Mike. Treaties are not forever (urging that the United States quit its defense treaty with Taiwan and recognize China). (Chicago Sun-Times 29:2 Nov 22, 76)

MANTLE, Mickey. There was a great, dark mystery about it when I first came here from Oklahoma. I still get goose-pimples just walking inside it. Now I think this is about the prettiest ball park I ever saw (commenting at the reopening of Yankee Stadium). (New York Times 125:1 April 16, 76)

MAO, Tse-Tung. After my death, the rightists may seize power. They will use my words to raise their own banner. (But) they will not rule for long (in a letter to his wife at the start of the Cultural Revolution). (New York Times 127:2 section 4 Feb 5, 78)

MAO, Tse-Tung. All reactionaries are paper tigers. (Newsweek 88:45 Sept 20, 76)

MAO, Tse-tung. By the end of this year, the victory of Socialism will be assured (in 1955). (New York Times 128:1 section 4 Dec 3, 78)

MAO, Tse-Tung. Every Communist must grasp the truth, Political power grown out of the barrel of a gun. Our principle is that the party commands the gun and the gun must never be allowed to command the party. (Newsweek 88:40 Sept 20, 76)

MAO, Tse-Tung. I am alone with the masses. (Time 108:38 Sept 20, 76)

MAO, Tse-Tung. (I am) only a lone monk walking the world with a leaky umbrella. (Time 108:37 Sept 20, 76)

MAO, Tse-Tung. If the Americans do not recognize us in 1,000 years, they will recognize us in 1,001 years. (New York Times 126:3 section 4 Aug 21, 77)

MAO, Tse-tung. Let a hundred schools of thought contend. Let a hundred flowers blossom (in 1956-57). (New York Times 128:1 section 4 Dec 3, 78)

MAO, Tse-Tung. The most important thing is to be strong. With strength, one can conquer others, and to conquer others gives one virtue. (Time 108:41 Sept 20, 76)

MAO, Tse-tung. Once all struggle is grasped, miracles are possible. (New York Times 128:1 section 4 Dec 3, 78)

MAO, Tse-Tung. Revolution is a drama of passion. We did not win the People over by appealing to reason but by developing hope, trust, fraternity. (Time 108:41 Sept 20, 76)

MAO, Tse-Tung. Sometimes we have only to fart to stir Americans into moving a battleship or two or even a whole fleet. (Time 108:44 Sept 20, 76)

MAO, Tse-Tung. What's wrong with taping a conversation when you happen to have a tape recorder with you? Most people in America love playing with tape recorders. (about Richard Nixon). (Rolling Stone 193:27 Aug 14, 75)

MARCEAU, Marcel. I am a silent witness of my time. (Christian Science Monitor 69:22 Feb 2, 77)

MARCHESI, Joseph. Only an immigrant can appreciate America (upon revisiting Ellis Island, where he arrived as an immigrant in 1919). (New York Times 125:24 section I May 30, 76)

MARCHETTI, Victor. Ours is not yet a totalitarian government, but it is an elitist democracy—and becoming more so every year. (Inquiry 1:24 Feb 6, 78)

MARCOS, Ferdinand E. I would like to return the Filipino to what he was before he was altered and modified by the softness of Western and other ways. (Time 107:21 Jan 5, 76)

MARCOS, Ferdinand E. It is easier to run a revolution than a government. (Time 107:35 June 6, 77)

MARCOS, Ferdinand E. Not only the occurrences in Vietnam, but the aspirations of the new nations in Asia seem to have brought about a changed situation which challenges the historic commitment of the United States to the peace and stability of the region. (Washington Post 365:A19 Dec 7, 75)

MARCOVICCI, Andrea. I like to play women who want something for themselves and will fight for it. (Time 110:53 Aug 22, 77)

MARCUS, Stanley. A businessman can make no worse mistake than to try to use the muscle of the advertising dollar to try to influence the news. (Atlantic 241:38 April 78)

MARGARET ROSE, PRINCESS OF GREAT BRITAIN, . Things have come to a pretty pass when somebody of our type murders his nanny. They're so hard to come by these days (commenting on Lord Lucan, accused of murdering his children's nanny). (Town & Country 131:97 Mar 77)

MARGOLIS, Susan. Today the gifted as well as the deranged among us are struggling to be famous the way earlier Americans struggled to be saved. (Time 111:56 June 19, 78)

MARK, Sir Robert. The real art of policing a free society or a democracy is to win by appearing to lose or at least to win by not appearing to win. (The Observer 9701:13 July 17, 77)

MARK, Sir Robert (chief of London's police force). To be perfectly blunt about it, what we are saying is that we are prepared to sacrifice the life of the hostages, if it comes to that. The only way to deal with these people is to make no deals at all (commenting on the British response to terrorists). (Chicago Tribune 39:2 Section 2 Feb 6, 78)

MARLEY, Bob. It takes a revolution to make a solution. (To the Point International 4:17 Sept 12, 77)

MARQUEZ, Gabriel Garcia. The famous Latin American 'literary boom' is a lie; what is real is the Cuban Revolution. (Seven Days 1:41 March 14, 77)

MARQUIS, Don. If you make people think they're thinking, they'll love you; but if you really make them think, they'll hate you. (Rocky Mountain News 250:50 Dec 28, 79)

MARSH, Jean. I think poetry is like a diary: people don't tend to write anything in it until something awful happens. (Newsweek 91:32 Feb 13, 78)

MARSH, Jean. I wouldn't have wanted to be an upstairs *or* a downstairs woman: I would have wanted to be a man. The women weren't allowed to do anything (commenting on English life in the television program Upstairs, Downstairs). (Atlanta 16:28 June 76)

MARSH, Jean. We're not sent into this life to be alone, but two-by-two, like in the ark. (W 7:41 Oct 13, 78)

MARSHALL, George C. Anybody who makes a real decision after 4:00 in the afternoon should have his head examined. (Book Digest 5:32 June 78)

MARSHALL, John. The peculiar circumstances of the moment may render a measure more or less wise, but cannot render it more or less constitutional. (New York Times Magazine 38 Oct 9, 77)

MARSHALL, Thurgood. (I am) appalled at the ethical bankruptcy of those who preach a right to life that means a bare existence in utter misery for so many. (Time 110:6 July 4, 77)

MARSHALL, Thurgood. The Ku Klux Klan never dies. They just stop wearing sheets because sheets cost too much. (Time 112:91 Dec 4, 78)

MARTIN, Abe. Beauty is only skin deep, but it's a valuable asset if you're poor or haven't any sense. (Human Behavior 7:70 Sept 78)

MARTIN, Abe. Being an optimist after you've got everything you want doesn't count. (Human Behavior 7:70 Sept 78)

MARTIN, Abe. What this country needs is a good five-cent cigar. (Human Behavior 7:70 Sept 78)

MARTIN, Billy. I can't change now. I guess it's like being a gunfighter. Once you start, you do it for life—until somebody comes along and shoots you down. (Newsweek 85:61 April 7, 75)

MARTIN, Billy. The two of them (George Steinbrenner and Reggie Jackson) deserve each other. One's a born liar; the other's convicted. (New York Times 127:1 section 5 July 30, 78)

MARTIN, Mary. Growing old is boring. It's boring to lose your hair or your eyesight or to go to the dentist and have teeth put in. Though I can't help thinking I'm still 19. I wouldn't have missed my life for anything, but I wouldn't go back for anything. (New York Times 126:52 Sept 8, 77)

MARTIN, Mary. He's (Richard Rodgers) the one person I will never, never wash out of my hair. (New York Times 128:C15 Dec 4, 78)

MARTY, Martin E. A saint has to be a misfit. A person who embodies what his culture considers typical or normal cannot be exemplary. (Time 106:48 Dec 29, 75)

MARVIN, Lee. There's too much damned violence on the screen. I don't go for it. Some of those producers and directors need some sense bashed into their heads. (The Star 4:2 Aug 30, 77)

MARX, Groucho. I never forget a face, but in your case I'll make an exception. (Viva 5:80 Sept 77)

MARX, Groucho. I wouldn't belong to any club that would have me for a member. (New York Times 126:40 Aug 21, 77)

MARX, Groucho. Military intelligence is a contradiction in terms. (San Francisco Chronicle This World 1978:40 Jan 29, 78)

MARX, Groucho. Nixon is a scoundrel. He belongs in the penitentiary. That's where he belongs. And that's where he'd be if a deal hadn't been made. (Parade 4 Nov 9, 75)

MARX, Groucho. Not since 'David Copperfield' have I read such a stirring and inspiring life story (commenting on his own book Groucho and Me). (New York Times 126:52 Nov 16, 76)

MARX, Karl. The first freedom of the press consists in this: that it is not a trade (writing in the Neve Rheinische Zeitung, May 19, 1842). (Village Voice 24:26 April 2, 79)

MARX, Minnie. Where else can people who don't know anything make a living (commenting on show business). (Newsweek 91:76 May 22, 78)

MARZULLO, Vito. It's not that I lie. It's just that I don't know the difference sometimes. (Chicago Sun-Times 31:2 Sept 27, 78)

MASON, James. Talking about my leading ladies is difficult for me if I'm going to be honest. Any opinion I give is bound to offend somebody. So when I want to tread cautiously, I tell people that the best actress I ever worked with was Margaret Rutherford. (People Weekly 4:74 Oct 13, 75)

MASON, Tony. The thing is that 90% of the colleges are abiding by the rules, doing things right. The other 10%, they're going to the bowl games. (Sports Illustrated 43:14 Oct 27, 75)

MASTERS, William Howell. Males have made asses of themselves writing about female sexual experience. (Newsweek 85:74 May 5, 75)

MATA-HARI, . The dance is a poem and each movement a word. (Interview 15 May 76)

MATHIAS, Charles McCurdy. People tend to want to follow the beaten path. The difficulty is that the beaten path doesn't seem to be leading anywhere. (Time 106:12 Dec 8, 75)

MATHIAS, Charles McCurdy. That's what the American system is all about: to keep power divided, to prevent a small core from either pole suddenly thrusting its decisions on the country. (Time 107:17 Aug 23, 76)

MATHIS, Andrew W. It's bad luck to be superstitious. (Omni 1:131 May 79)

MATLOVICH, Leonard P. They gave me a medal for killing two men and discharged me for loving one. (Chicago Sun-Times 28:36 Aug 18, 75)

MATURE, Victor. Apparently, the way to a girl's heart is to saw her in half. (Playboy 26:26 Oct 79)

MAUGHAM, William Somerset. Only a mediocre person is always at his best. (Forbes 120:80 Aug 1, 77)

MAUGHAM, William Somerset. People ask you for criticism, but they only want praise. (Rocky Mountain News 141:44 Sept 10, 79)

MAUGHAM, William Somerset. The unfortunate thing about this world is that good habits are so much easier to get out of than bad ones. (Kansas City Times 109:14C Jan 22, 77)

MAULDIN, Bill. We have more provincialism and bigotry and superstition and prejudice per square mile than almost any other nation. (Rolling Stone 225:56 Nov 4, 76)

MAYER, Jean. The ability to arrive at complex decisions is the hallmark of the educated person. (People Weekly 6:44 Nov 15, 76)

MAYS, Benjamin. If this (country) is a melting pot, I don't want the Negro to melt away. (Time 111:49 Feb 13, 78)

MAYS, Willie. I think I was the best baseball player I ever saw. (Newsweek 93:68 Feb 5, 79)

MEAD, Margaret. At least 50 percent of the human race doesn't want their mother-in-law within walking distance. (Newsweek 92:75 Nov 27, 78)

MEAD, Margaret. For the first time the young are seeing history being made before it is censored by their elders (in defense of TV). (Time 112:57 Nov 27, 78)

MEAD, Margaret. I expect to die someday but I'll never retire. (Change 9:12 Sept 77)

MEAD, Margaret. One reason women live longer than men is that they can continue to do something they are used to doing, whereas men are abruptly cut off, whether they are admirals or shopkeepers. (Time 110:68 Aug 8, 77)

MEAD, Margaret. Women, it is true, make human beings, but only men can make men. (Chicago Tribune 176:2 section II June 25, 78)

MEANS, Jacqueline. We have spent so many years meeting and debating on this when we could have been doing other things. I'm glad it's over so that I can be able to get to work with the ministry (commenting on the ordination of women in the Protestant Episcopal Church). (Christian Science Monitor 69:26 Jan 10, 77)

MEANY, George. Everything in this world that affects life, liberty and happiness is the business of the American trade union movement. (American Legion Magazine 100:9 Feb 76)

MEANY, George. The fight against inflation must be on the basis of the equality of sacrifice, not the sacrifice of equality. (Time 113:9 Feb 5, 79)

MEANY, George. Foreign policy is too damned important to be left to the Secretary of State. (Time 106:7 Sept 8, 75)

MEANY, George. They say Carter is the first businessman ever to sit in the White House. But why did they have to send us a small businessman? (Time 112:62 Nov 27, 78)

MEDLIN, James. The most healthy thing in L.A. is to do nothing. (New West 3:116 Oct 9, 78)

MEHTA, Asoka. Socialism is an attractive goal, but concentration of power is as dangerous as concentration of capital. (Time 111:30 Mar 13, 78)

MEIGHEN, Arthur. We are not in the same boat, but we are pretty much in the same waters. (New York Times 129:E5 section 4 Nov 4, 79)

MEIR, Golda. Don't be humble, you're not that great. (New York Times Book Review 39 June 17, 79)

MEIR, Golda. I may not have been a great prime minister, but I would have been a great farmer. (Chicago Tribune 306:18 Nov 2, 77)

MEIR, Golda. I wouldn't accept the West Bank and Gaza as part of Israel if they were offered on a silver platter. (Village Voice 25:8 Oct 8, 80)

MEIR, Golda. It's a sad world. A very sad world. But I'm an optimist. For an Israeli to be a pessimist is a luxury we can't afford. We would have to sit down and die, and that's all. But we don't want to. So we go on. Things will change. You'll see. (New York Times 126:20 section 2 Aug 14, 77)

MEIR, Golda. Naturally he (Moshe Dayan) has his faults, and like his virtues they are not small ones. (Time 106:102 Nov 24, 75)

MEIR, Golda. We are angriest at the Arabs not because they kill us, but because they force us to kill them. (Mother Jones 1:44 July 76)

MEKAS, Jonas. Avant-garde film doesn't want to and can't be part of any business. (Village Voice 20:72 July 7, 75)

MELATO, Mariangela. She's like 25 men. I've never seen so monstrous a vitality (about Lina Wertmueller). (Time 107:58 Feb 16, 76)

MELLON, Paul. One of the main things money provides is privacy. (Time 111:79 May 8, 78)

MENCKEN, Henry Louis. For every human problem, there is a neat, plain solution—and it is always wrong. (Washingtonian 14:155 Nov 78)

MENCKEN, Henry Louis. No one ever went broke underestimating the intelligence of the American people. (More 6:14 May 76)

MENCKEN, Henry Louis. One horse laugh is worth ten thousand syllogisms. (New York Times Book Review 27 Sept 7, 80)

MENKE-GLUCKERT, Peter. Environment has become the Viet Nam of the middle class. (Time 107:48 April 25, 77)

MENNINGER, Karl. 'Insane' is an expression we psychiatrists don't use until we get to court. Insanity is a question of public opinion. (Time 106:57 Oct 20, 75)

MENNINGER, Karl. The jail is a horrible institution manned by amateurs and politicians. (Los Angeles Times 96:2 part 1 Oct 2, 77)

MENNINGER, Karl. Sex and sexuality never made anyone ill and never made anyone feel guilty. It is the hate and destructiveness concealed in them which produce strange aberrations and bitter regret. (Playboy 24:203 Dec 77)

MENOTTI, Gian Carlo. I am almost 66, and I have to start fighting the shadow of death. When I see darkness coming, I turn on the stage lights and don't worry about the cost of electricity. (Time 107:75 June 6, 77)

MERCOURI, Melina. I have been playing a woman with a past since I was five years old. (Time 107:93 June 6, 77)

MERMAN, Ethel. (Cole Porter) sang like a hinge. (Time 114:97 Oct 1, 79)

MEROLA, Gaetano. Chicago is merely a place to change trains. (New York Times 128:C9 Nov 21, 78)

MEYER, Russ. My films are like a reptile you beat with a club. You think you've killed it, but then you turn around and it gets you in the ankle. (Washington Post 340:B1 Nov 9, 76)

MEYERS, Victor Aloysius (former Lieutenant Governor of California). Habitually I go without a vest so that I can't be accused of standing for the vested interests. (New York Times 125:27 April 26, 76)

MEYNER, Helen. Let the best man win, whomever she may be. (Life 2:140 Dec 79)

MIDLER, Bette. (Fans) make me think that maybe there's more to me than I know. (Newsweek 94:37 July 2, 79)

MIDLER, Bette. I adore deceit and don't give a damn about being misrepresented (in interviews). But I will not be made to sound boring to the thousands that are convinced I am, if not Jackie O, certainly the next best thing. (Newsweek 94:37 July 2, 79)

MIDLER, Bette. I want to be a legend. (TV Guide 25:22 Dec 3, 77)

MIDLER, Bette. The worst part of having success is to try finding someone who is happy for you. (Chicago Sun-Times 29:32 Mar 3, 76)

MIKULSKI, Barbara A. America is not a melting pot. It is a sizzling cauldron. The ethnic worker is fooled into thinking that blacks are getting everything. (Chicago Tribune 8:2 section 2 Jan 8, 78)

MIKULSKI, Barbara A. Pete Preppy looks through his yearbook, calls up Mike Macho, and says, "Got anyone good for State?" "Sure," answers Mike. "Try Tom Terrifico." (On "the old boy network" of hiring practices in Washington, D.C.). (Time 109:17 Mar 28, 77)

MIKULSKI, Barbara A. Some people like to raise flowers; I like to raise hell, I want to be the Amelia Earhart of Congress. I want to fly into the areas of the unknown, like she did, for the fun of it. (Time 108:48 Nov 15, 76)

MIKVA, Abner J. My definition of a liberal is someone who can look at an idea and see that it doesn't work, even if it was a liberal idea. (Chicago Tribune 222:4 section 3 Aug 10, 78)

MIKVA, Abner J. Someone once said that politics is like poker—it's only fun when you play for a trifle more than you can afford to lose. (Chicago Sun-Times 31:5 Nov 9, 78)

MILLAY, Edna St. Vincent. It is not true that life is one damn thing after another; it's one damn thing over and over. (Viva 4:25 July 77)

MILLER, Ann. All my life I've tried to be an eight-by-ten glossy. (Newsweek 85:52 May 26, 75)

MILLER, Ann. No matter what you've achieved, if you're not loved (by a man), Honey, you ain't nothin' but a hound dog. (New Woman 10:12 May/June 80)

MILLER, Arnold (U.M.W. President). Julius Caesar had his Brutus but I've got about a hundred Brutuses. The problems I have are not with the membership, it's with the elected officials and the staff. (Time 109:54 Feb 7, 77)

MILLER, Arthur. I always doubted that writers ever really understand more than anyone else. All you can hope is that maybe you feel a little more. (The Observer 9812:35 Sept 16, 79)

MILLER, Arthur. I think a play ought to cast a shadow; it ought to be something you can walk around. (New York Times 128:6 section 2 June 17, 79)

MILLER, Arthur. I think that you don't take seriously any art that's not dealing finally with whether we are doomed or not. (Christian Science Monitor 69:30 Aug 8, 77)

MILLER, Arthur. I've always written in the back of my head for the great unwashed. (New York Times 128:6 section 2 June 17, 79)

MILLER, Arthur. The paranoia of stupidity is always the worst, since its fear of destruction by intelligence is reasonable. (Forbes 121:28 April 3, 78)

MILLER, Arthur. Part of being a playwright is being an actor. One way or another, whether surreptitiously or not, a good playwright is an actor. (Connecticut 41:115 Jan 78)

MILLER, Arthur. There is no solution for him, or us, if we choose him (Ted Kennedy). (Chicago Sun-Times 32:6 July 20, 79)

MILLER, Arthur. Violence is the last refuge of scoundrels (commenting on TV violence). (Christian Science Monitor 69:30 Aug 8, 77)

MILLER, Bill (director of administration for the Denver Water Department). The bad news is that if the drought keeps up within a few years we'll all be drinking reclaimed sewer water. The good news is that there won't be enough to go around. (Chicago Sun-Times 30:2 Mar 4, 77)

MILLER, George William. Don't rationalize mediocrity. (Time 112:62 July 17, 78)

MILLER, George William. Inflation (is) a clear and present danger. (New York Times 128:10 section 4 Aug 12, 79)

MILLER, George William. There is no penalty for overachievement. (Time 112:62 July 17, 78)

MILLER, Henry. Death itself doesn't frighten me because I don't believe it's the end. All my intuitive feelings are that this cannot be the only world. It's too damn short, too ugly and too meaningless. (People Weekly 10:62 Aug 21, 78)

MILLER, Henry. I owe everything to the French. I am more close to France than America even though I lived there only 10 years, from 1929 to 1939. Those years in France meant everything to me and formed my whole career. (New York Times 126:62 Nov 23, 76)

MILLER, Henry. I'm going to beat those bastards (when asked how he would write his epitaph). (People Weekly 10:62 Aug 21, 78)

MILLER, Henry. To the person who thinks with his head, life is a comedy. To those who think with their feelings, or work through their feelings, life is a tragedy. (Soho News 5:3 Jan 26, 78)

MILLER, Marvin. The fact that Miss Little was vindicated doesn't mean anything about the judicial system of this state or of the United States. The real reason she was vindicated was the international outcry about Joan Little. (The Guardian Weekly 113:4 Aug 23, 75)

MILLER, Patricia Robertson. The airlines spell safety with a dollar sign and the FAA practices regulation by death. (Chicago Sun-Times 32:48 Aug 1, 79)

MILLETT, Kate. Male chauvinist is a simple, idiotic way of describing him (Ayatollah Khomeini). (The Observer 9786:10 Mar 18, 79)

MILLS, Chuck. I give the same halftime speech over and over. It works best when my players are better than the other coach's players. (Sports Illustrated 45:20 Oct 25, 76)

MILLS, Chuck. When it comes to football, God is prejudiced—toward big, fast kids (commenting on religion and football). (New York Times 125:3 Feb 1, 76)

MILLS, Wilbur Daigh. I'd go for days at a time and not remember what I'd done. Especially 1974, I don't remember much of 1974 at all. (New York Times 128:B1 Dec 4, 78)

MILLS, Wilbur Daigh. I'm not the man of steel I thought I was. (Ms 4:62 Oct 75)

MILNES, Richard Monckton. My exit is the result of too many entrees. (Writer's Digest 58:11 Oct 78)

MINGUS, Charles. Don't call me a jazz musician. The word jazz means nigger, discrimination, second-class citizenship, the back-of-the-bus bit. (Time 113:77 Jan 22, 79)

MINOR, Gregory C. My reason for leaving is a deep conviction that nuclear reactors and nuclear weapons now present a serious danger to the future of all life on this planet (commenting on why he resigned from his position as a managing engineer at a General Electric Company nuclear reactor plant). (New York Times 125:12 Feb 3, 76)

MINOR, Robert. The winning entry is never as good as your own. (Omni 1:131 May 79)

MINOW, Newton. The most important educational institution in the country is not Harvard or Yale or Caltech—it's television. (Time 113:50 May 28, 79)

MINOW, Newton. There is no contract you can't get out of for money. (Wilson Library Bulletin 53:507 Mar 79)

MIRO, Joan. Fools do not make art. (New York Arts Journal 7:8 Nov/Dec 77)

MISRACH, Richard. The primary illusion of photography is fact—its apparent literal transcription of the world. Thus, it becomes interesting when a body of photographs describes a world that is both convincing and authentic, and at the same time nonexistent. (Outside 1:35 Jan 78)

MITCHELL, Arthur. That's what Dance Theater of Harlem is: classical ballet with soul. (Time 107:56 Mar 8, 76)

MITCHELL, Clarence M., Jr. Lyndon B. Johnson was the greatest American President on civil rights. (New York Times 128:28 April 15, 79)

MITCHELL, John. All that crap, you're putting it in the paper? It's all been denied. Katie Graham's gonna get her tit caught in a big fat wringer if that's published. (Village Voice 23:11 Jan 2, 78)

MITCHELL, John. Henceforth, don't call me, I'll call you (on release from Federal prison). (New York Times 128:23 Jan 20, 78)

MITCHELL, John. It could have been a hell of a lot worse. He could have sentenced me to spend the rest of my life with Martha Mitchell (commenting on his Watergate-related jail sentence). (Newsweek 85:15 Mar 3, 75)

MITCHELL, John. It's nice to be back in Alabama (upon entering prison at Maxwell Air Force Base). (New York Times 126:1 June 23, 77)

MITCHELL, John. Watch what we do, not what we say (commenting in 1969 on the direction of the Nixon administration). (Time 104:50 Aug 19, 74)

MITCHUM, Robert. I do films for the greatest return, for the least effort. (The Times 8042:3 Aug 7, 77)

MITFORD, Nancy. Sisters stand between one and life's cruel circumstances. (Ms 6:65 Sept 77)

MIX, Tom (attributed by Heywood Hale Broun). Straight shooters always win. (Travel & Leisure 11:138 Feb 80)

MIYAZAWA, Kiichi (Foreign Minister of Japan). What you have lost is not a war but a cause, and your credibility has not really suffered because it is widely known that the people you were trying to help could not really help themselves. (Newsweek 85:84 May 5, 75)

MOGULL, Artie (President of United Artists Records). I'll make two predictions: big bands will not come back, and Dolly Parton will continue to be the only girl singer with big tits to sell records. (Rolling Stone 243:41 July 14, 77)

MOHAMMED REZA PAHLEVI, SHAH OF IRAN, . I will not rule. I will reign. (The Observer 9777:11 Jan 14, 79)

MOHAMMED REZA PAHLEVI, SHAH OF IRAN, . I'm not just another dictator. I'm a hereditary monarch. (Village Voice 23:19 Aug 21, 78)

MOHAMMED REZA PAHLEVI, SHAH OF IRAN, . In a man's life, women count only if they're beautiful and graceful and know how to stay feminine. (Washingtonian 10:21 July 75)

MOHAMMED REZA PAHLEVI, SHAH OF IRAN, . Nobody can overthrow me—I have the power. (US News & World Report 84:37 June 26, 78)

MOHAMMED REZA PAHLEVI, SHAH OF IRAN, . Those who believe in the Iranian Constitution, the monarchical regime, and the principles of the White Revolution must join the new party. Those who do not are traitors who must either go to prison or leave the country. (Village Voice 20:36 June 30, 75)

MOHAMMED REZA PAHLEVI, SHAH OF IRAN, . Who would believe that I should work 10 hours a day for 37 years to help my country only to see it go back to the point where I began? (The Observer 9781:11 Feb 11, 79)

MOHAMMED REZA PAHLEVI, SHAH OF IRAN, . Why can't the press see what Marx is doing behind Muhammad's banner? (Newsweek 93:41 Jan 29, 79)

MONACO, James. Film has come of age as an art, probably because television now receives the brunt of contempt from the remaining proponents of an elite culture. (New York Times Book Review 11 April 1, 79)

MONAGHAN, Jim. I guess every day in New Orleans is like a B-movie. (New Orleans 10:30 Jan 76)

MONDALE, Joan. Fritz (Walter Mondale) says I never make a decision without consulting him. He's right. I consult—and then do what I want to. (Time 107:25 July 26, 76)

MONDALE, Joan. The issue is Watergate or waterbed. The Democrats do it to their secretaries but the Republicans do it to the country. (Time 108:24 Oct 11, 76)

MONDALE, Walter Frederick. Everybody thinks it's easy to be appointed. It's the toughest of all. You have to get 100 percent of the vote. (Time 107:22 July 26, 76)

MONDALE, Walter Frederick. For a workingman or woman to vote Republican this year is the same as a chicken voting for Colonel Sanders. (Rolling Stone 225:33 Nov 4, 76)

MONDALE, Walter Frederick. I saw where Joe Califano gave up $500,000 a year to become HEW secretary; Mike Blumenthal, $400,000 to become Treasury secretary; and Cy Vance, $250,000 to become secretary of state. As far as I can tell, I'm the only one who took the job because I needed the money. (Chicago Tribune 64:29 section 1 Mar 5, 78)

MONDALE, Walter Frederick. If you are sure you understand everything that is going on, you are hopelessly confused. (Book Digest 6:28 Dec 79)

MONDALE, Walter Frederick. It shows above all that Americans are no good at all at killing, lying and covering up and I'm glad that's the case (on CIA assassination attempts on foreign leaders). (Washington Post 351:1 Nov 21, 75)

MONDALE, Walter Frederick. There is no way on earth people can take the Vice-president of the United States seriously (originally quoted by columnist Jim Klobuchar in the Minneapolis Tribune in 1974). (Rolling Stone 221:16 Sept 9, 76)

MONDALE, Walter Frederick. There must be some fundamental changes in America's intelligence activities or they will fundamentally change America. (Foreign Policy 23:58 Summer 76)

MONDALE, Walter Frederick. You should know that my position has always been that I have not been an advocate of busing to achieve racial balance. What I have resisted is the repeal of the 14th Amendment that prohibits discrimination in our school system. I think that is the only honorable and legal position that can be taken. (Washington Post 224:A13 July 16, 76)

MONKS, John (Oklahoma State Representative). In every country the Communists have taken over, the first thing they do is outlaw cockfighting (opposing a bill that would outlaw cockfighting in Oklahoma). (Ms 6:49 July 77)

MONNET, Jean. The world is divided into those who want to become someone and those who want to accomplish something. (Time 113:47 Mar 26, 79)

MONNIER, Valentine. I'm not a big deal yet, but I will be. (Interview 8:7 June 78)

MONROE, Marilyn. I think I made his back feel better (about John F. Kennedy). (Time 106:11 Dec 29, 75)

MONTAGU, Ashley. The idea is to die young as late as possible. (Town & Country 133:141 May 79)

MONTAGU, Ashley. Most psychiatrists need to have their heads examined. Analysis, it has been said, is the study of the id by the odd. (Chicago Tribune 142:3 section 5 May 22, 77)

MONTANER, Carlos Alberto. The U.S. is a neurotic Midas who homogenizes everything he touches. (Atlas World Press Review 23:39 Nov 76)

MOON, Keith. Some of the things I've done, I couldn't have anything but the reputation of being a lunatic. (Newsweek 92:93 Sept 18, 78)

MOON, Sun Myung. Are Americans that foolish? Can they really be brainwashed by Rev. Moon, a Korean? I know your answer is no. My answer is no, too. No American is so foolish (commenting before congressmen on charges that the Korean evangelist has mind control over young people and forces them to maintain him in luxury). (Chicago Tribune 353:15 Section 4 Dec 19, 75)

MOON, Sun Myung. God has been very good to me. (Newsweek 92:81 Dec 4, 78)

MOON, Sun Myung. God sent me to America in the role of a doctor. (People Weekly 6:35 Dec 27/Jan 3, 77)

MOON, Sun Myung. Kings and queens and heads of state will someday bow at my feet. I will conquer and subjugate the world. (Potomac (Sunday Magazine of the Washington Post) 6 May 30, 76)

MOON, Sun Myung. The time will come when my words will serve as law. (New York 10:97 Mar 7, 77)

MOON, Sun Myung. Without me, on earth everything will be nullified. (New West 4:62 Jan 29, 79)

MOORE, Clayton. The Lone Ranger was honest, he was a gentleman and he used perfect diction. If I may say so without boasting, I am a great American. (Newsweek 91:29 Jan 23, 78)

MOORE, George C. No, we never gave it a thought (in response to whether the FBI had ever discussed the constitutional or legal authority for its Cointelpro Program). (New York Times 125:1 section 4 May 2, 76)

MOORE, Henry. Looking at sculpture teaches people to use their inborn sense of form, to improve their own surroundings, to make life marvelous. (Chicago Tribune 237:1 section 3 Aug 25, 78)

MOORE, Henry. Sculpture should always at first sight have some obscurities and further meanings. People should want to go on looking and thinking. (Mankind 6:43 May 78)

MOORE, Henry. Some people ask me why I live and work in the country. Space, light and distance are three good reasons. (Mankind 6:10 May 78)

MOORE, Henry. Stonehenge is not a building, it is a carving. (Quest 2:26 Nov 78)

MOORE, Jonathan. We're not getting as conservative as much as we are becoming less liberal. (US News & World Report 84:24 Jan 23, 78)

MOORE, Marianne. A writer is unfair when he is unable to be hard on himself. (Writer's Digest 58:6 Feb 78)

MOORE, Mary Tyler. Behind each beautiful wild fur there is an ugly story. It is a brutal, bloody and barbaric story. The animal is not killed—it is tortured. I don't think a fur coat is worth it. (Chicago Sun-Times 28:3 Nov 18, 75)

MOORE, Mary Tyler. Worrying is a necessary part of life. (Chicago Tribune 32:16 Feb 1, 78)

MOORE, Roger. My real attitude toward women is this, and it hasn't changed because of any movement or anything: basically, women like to be treated as sex objects. (Playboy 25:102 May 78)

MOORE, Sara Jane. I did indeed willfully and knowingly attempt to murder Gerald R. Ford, the President of the United States, by use of a handgun and would now like to enter a plea of guilty. (New York Times 125:1 Dec 13, 75)

MOREAU, Jeanne. Age does not protect you from love. But love, to some extent, protects you from age. (People Weekly 3:66 Feb 3, 75)

MORGAN, Charles, Jr. If I were in New York and I were on the other side of the law...I would think about moving somewhere else fast. (New York Times Magazine 41 Mar 25, 79)

MORGAN, Charles, Jr. If Moses had gone to Harvard Law School and spent three years working on the Hill, he would have written the Ten Commandments with three exceptions and a savings clause. (Rolling Stone 205:30 Jan 15, 76)

MORGAN, Marabel. It is only when a woman surrenders her life to her husband, reveres and worships him, and is willing to serve him, that she becomes really beautiful to him. (Ms 7:64 June 3, 79)

MORGAN, Marabel. Love never makes demands. Love is unconditional acceptance of him and his feelings. (Cosmopolitan 188:268 Feb 80)

MORGAN, Ted. One has come to America to get a sense of life's possibilities. (Philadelphia 69:179 Nov 78)

MORLEY, Robert. Commercials are the last things in life you can count on for a happy ending. (Time 111:53 Feb 6, 78)

MORO, Aldo. I believe I have done my duty to the end (upon the announcement of the resignation of his cabinet). (New York Times 125:1 May 1, 76)

MORRIS, Richard B. The United States is still the last best hope of man. (US News & World Report 81:73 July 5, 76)

MORRIS, Roger. Detente is now suffering from the fact that it was deliberately obscured as diplomacy and oversold as politics. (New York Times Magazine 7 May 30, 76)

MORRISON, Toni. What is curious to me is that bestial treatment of human beings never produces a race of beasts. (New York Times Magazine 40 May 20, 79)

MORROW, Dwight. One of the troubles is that we judge ourselves by our motives and others by their actions. (Christian Science Monitor 70:47 Dec 7, 77)

MORROW, Lance. Celebrities are intellectual fast food. (Time 111:57 June 12, 78)

MORROW, Lance. It bewilders Americans to be hated. (The Observer 9829:9 Jan 13, 80)

MORROW, Lance. When fame ceases to bear any relation to worth or accomplishment, then the whole currency of public recognition is debased. (Time 111:56 June 19, 78)

MORTON, Rogers Clark Ballard. Governor Reagan's announcement (of choosing Senator Schweicker as his running mate) appears to be an effort to exchange the second highest office in the land for a handful of delegates. (Newsweek 88:17 Aug 9, 76)

MORTON, W. C., Jr. If rats are experimented upon, they will develop cancer. (Omni 1:131 May 79)

MOSES, Robert. If you elect a matinee idol as mayor, you get a musical-comedy administration. (New York 10:58 Sept 5, 77)

MOSS, Frank. There comes a certain point when physicians, like other lawbreakers, must be put in jail (commenting on Medicaid and Medicare fraud). (Newsweek 88:24 Aug 9, 76)

MOSS, Stirling. Bald heads are cheap to run and they need very little maintenance. (Kansas City Times 97:17C Oct 12, 76)

MOTHER TERESA, . I am unworthy (upon winning the Nobel Peace Prize). (New York Times 129:1 Oct 18, 79)

MOTHER TERESA, . Jesus said love one another. He didn't say love the whole world. (The Observer 9836:9 Mar 2, 80)

MOTHER TERESA, . Loneliness and the feeling of being unwanted is the most terrible poverty. (Time 106:49 Dec 29, 75)

MOTHER TERESA, . Those countries with legalized abortions are the poorest countries in the world. (The Observer 9825:10 Dec 16, 79)

MOTHERWELL, Robert. Every intelligent painter carries the whole culture of modern painting in his head. It is his real subject, of which anything he paints is both an hommage and a critique. (Los Angeles Times Calendar 96:86 July 31, 77)

MOTHERWELL, Robert. I think art is one of the few things that bestows very deep meanings to human existence. (Connecticut 41:119 Jan 78)

MOUNTBATTEN, Louis. I can't think of a more wonderful thanksgiving for the life I have had than that everyone should be jolly at my funeral. (The Observer 9810:10 Sept 2, 79)

MOUNTBATTEN, Louis. I loathe all manifestations of extremism and I believe we should strive, above all else, for the dignity and human rights of mankind, regardless of race, color and creed. (Time 114:33 Sept 10, 79)

MOUNTBATTEN, Louis. If the Third World War is fought with nuclear weapons, the fourth will be fought with bows and arrows. (Maclean's 88:73 Nov 17, 75)

MOWAT, Farley. Everything outrages me that outrages nature—and most of what modern man does outrages nature. (People Weekly 13:65 Mar 31, 80)

MOYERS, Bill D. Dick Goodwin was no saint, not close, but if there's a hereafter, I'd rather spend it with Goodwin than with Gabriel. (New York 8:38 Aug 18, 75)

MOYERS, Bill D. He's smiling like a Christian with four aces (about Jimmy Carter). (New York 9:52 July 26, 76)

MOYERS, Bill D. It isn't wisdom or intelligence that influences a President, it's opportunity. (Newsweek 91:22 April 17, 78)

MOYERS, Bill D. Nixon systematically robbed the country of its ability and willingness to trust the President. (Newsweek 83:80 April 15, 74)

MOYERS, Bill D. Of all the myths of journalism, objectivity is the greatest. (National Review 31:1021 Aug 12, 79)

MOYERS, Bill D. TV personalities are like celluloid. They're very perishable. (Newsweek 83:80 April 15, 74)

MOYNIHAN, Daniel Patrick. As the lights go out in the rest of the world, they shine all the brighter here. (Time 107:28 Jan 26, 76)

MOYNIHAN, Daniel Patrick. Even our sense of peoplehood grows uncertain as ethnic assertions take their implacable toll on the civic assumption of unity. (Time 106:16 Nov 10, 75)

MOYNIHAN, Daniel Patrick. For some time now, the United Nations has been showing a seemingly compulsive urge so to outrage those very principles on which it was founded, as to suggest that a sinister transmutation has occurred in an organism that yet enough remembers its own beginnings as to be revulsed by what it has become and somehow to seek expatriation in bringing on its own doom (upon the UN vote to equate Zionism with racism). (Wall Street Journal 56:12 Nov 10, 75)

MOYNIHAN, Daniel Patrick. The great corporations of this country were not founded by ordinary people. They were founded by people with extraordinary energy, intelligence, ambition, aggressiveness. All those factors go into the primordial capitalist urge. (Time 111:27 June 19, 78)

MOYNIHAN, Daniel Patrick. I don't think there's any point in being Irish if you don't know that the world is going to break your heart eventually. (New York Times Book Review 15 April 30, 78)

MOYNIHAN, Daniel Patrick. I would consider it dishonorable to leave this post (as chief United States delegate to the U.N.) and run for any office, and I hope it would be understood that if I do, the people, the voters to whom I would represent myself in such circumstances, would consider me as having said in advance that I am a man of no personal honor to have done so. (Chicago Tribune 326:4 Section 1 Nov 21, 76)

MOYNIHAN, Daniel Patrick. If the U.N. didn't exist, it would be impossible to invent it. (Time 107:27 Jan 26, 76)

MOYNIHAN, Daniel Patrick. If welfare reform meant putting arsenic in children's milk, there would be local officials who would settle for that as long as it meant full federal funding. (Rolling Stone 235:35 Mar 24, 77)

MOYNIHAN, Daniel Patrick. It is no accident, I fear, that this racist murderer (Idi Amin), as one of our leading newspapers (the New York Times) called him this morning, is the head of the Organization of African Unity. (Newsweek 86:51 Oct 13, 75)

MOYNIHAN, Daniel Patrick. Most politicians have a right to feel morally superior to their constituencies. (Rolling Stone 219:43 Aug 12, 76)

MOYNIHAN, Daniel Patrick. Nixon understood more about liberals than liberals ever understood about him. (The Observer 9796:33 May 27, 79)

MOYNIHAN, Daniel Patrick. The only reason people in America are starving is because they are idiots, and if they are idiots they deserve to. (Boston 68:82 Sept 76)

MOYNIHAN, Daniel Patrick. (The multinational corporation) is arguably the most creative international institution of the 20th century. (Time 106:62 July 14, 75)

MOYNIHAN, Daniel Patrick. There is no nation so poor that it cannot afford free speech, but there are few elites which will put up with the bother of it. (Time 107:28 Jan 26, 76)

MOYNIHAN, Daniel Patrick. The time may have come when the issue of race could benefit from a period of 'benign neglect' (to Richard Nixon in 1970). (Newsweek 94:90 Nov 19, 79)

MOYNIHAN, Daniel Patrick. Totalitarianism is bad, gangsterism is worse, but capitulationism is the worst of all. (Time 107:26 Jan 26, 76)

MOYNIHAN, Daniel Patrick. What kind of a prick are you? (to Ron Gollobin, reporter for WCVB-TV, Boston). (More 7:6 Jan 77)

MOYNIHAN, Daniel Patrick. When a person goes to a country and finds their newspapers filled with nothing but good news, he can bet there are good men in jail. (University Daily Kansan 87:4 Feb 16, 77)

MOYNIHAN, Daniel Patrick. Work is no longer considered to be a form of punishment as applied to women. A liberal constituency no longer finds work unattractive. (Time 110:8 Aug 15, 77)

MUCHOW, David. Budgeting is a black art practiced by bureaucratic magicians. (Chicago Sun-Times 29:2 Nov 19, 76)

MUDD, Roger. One of the problems with broadcast journalists is that we have been convinced, sometimes against our better judgment, that we are not reporters but show-business people. (Newsweek 96:64 July 14, 80)

MUDDY WATERS, . Those whites can play instruments real fine. But there's something missing in the singing. They just don't eat enough pinto beans; they haven't had enough hard times. (Sepia 25:5 Feb 76)

MUGGERIDGE, Malcolm. It is only believers in the Fall of Man who can really appreciate how funny men are. (The Observer 9762:15 Oct 1, 78)

MUGGERIDGE, Malcolm. (Journalism) is the ideal profession for those who find power fascinating and its exercise abhorrent. (Time 114:73 Aug 13, 79)

MUGGERIDGE, Malcolm. Western society suffers from a largely unconscious collective death wish. (Time 114:86 Sept 10, 79)

MUHAMMAD, Wallace D. I doubt if the Pope knows as much about Scripture as I do. I may not be the best orator, I may not have gone very far in school, but I am the boldest nigger you ever saw. (Newsweek 85:71 June 30, 75)

MUIR, Bill. If the meek are going to inherit the earth, our offensive linemen are going to be land barons. (Sports Illustrated 44:24 May 10, 76)

MUIR, Robert. The single most important quality Karen Anne Quinlan has is life. This court will not authorize that life to be taken away from her. (New Times 5:40 Nov 28, 75)

MUNRO, Ross H. Communist countries never expel correspondents for telling lies. (New York Times 127:11 Nov 27, 77)

MURDOCH, Iris. A bad review is even less important than whether it is raining in Patagonia. (The Observer 9770:12 Nov 26, 78)

MURDOCH, Rupert. I cannot avoid the temptation of wondering whether there is any other industry (than newspaper publishing) in this country which seeks to presume so completely to give the customer what he does not want. (Time 107:46 May 30, 77)

MURPHY, Gerald. Only the invented part of life was satisfying, only the unrealistic part. (Newsweek 83:76 April 15, 74)

MURPHY, Jack (Director of public relations for Exxon). We're not really surprised. But you can just say we have no comment (in response to a Peoples Bicentennial Commission's sponsored survey reflecting wide public disenchantment with American business). (Harper's Weekly 3140:9 Sept 12, 75)

MURPHY, Thomas A. (Chairman of General Motors Corporation). For years the motto of organized labor was said to be the single word 'more'. It has not changed, but now we also hear talk of 'less'—not less wages, not less benefits, but less work. The public will see—must see—that less work not balanced by increased productivity really means more cost.   (Business Week 2409:45 Dec 1, 75)

MURPHY, Thomas Aquinas. There's a desire today for more security and for a risk-free society. But that becomes a choiceless society, not a free society.   (Time 111:70 Mar 27, 78)

MURROW, Edward R (attributed by Charles Kuralt). Just because you speak in a voice loud enough to be heard over television by 16 million people, that doesn't make you any smarter than you were when you spoke loudly enough to be heard only at the other end of the bar.   (Mpls 42 Jan 77)

MURTAUGH, Danny. A bad call (in baseball) is one that goes against you.   (TV Guide 26:14 May 6, 78)

MUSE, Clarence. The public believed in the Negro's voice, but not in his intelligence.   (Time 114:123 Oct 29, 79)

MUSGRAVE, Thea. In art you have to follow your hunch. You can't play it safe.   (Time 110:72 Oct 10, 77)

MUSSOLINI, Benito. It is not impossible to govern Italians. It is merely useless.   (Time 116:29 July 7, 80)

MUZOREWA, Bishop Abel. I do not want Zimbabwe ever to become another banana republic.   (Time 113:36 April 30, 79)

MUZOREWA, Bishop Abel. I question whether God himself would wish me to hide behind the principles of non-violence while innocent persons were being slaughtered.   (The Observer 9767:13 Nov 5, 78)

MUZOREWA, Bishop Abel. We are not here in a spirit of give and take—we have come here to take, to take our country (comment made at the Geneva Conference on Rhodesia).   (Chicago Sun-Times 29:2 Oct 30, 76)

MYERSON, Bess. You can't be beautiful and hate.   (Forbes 122:200 Oct 30, 78)

MYRDAL, Gunnar. It is natural for the ordinary American when it sees something wrong to feel not only that there should be a law against it but also that an organization should be formed to combat it.   (Time 112:34 Aug 7, 78)

NABOKOV, Vladimir. Anonymous praise hurts nobody.   (New York Times Book Review 27 July 31, 77)

NABOKOV, Vladimir. Great novels are above all great fairy tales. Literature does not tell the truth but makes it up.   (Newsweek 90:42 July 18, 77)

NABOKOV, Vladimir. I am an American writer, born in Russia and educated in England, where I studied French literature before spending 15 years in Germany.   (Washington Post 212:C4 July 5, 77)

NADER, Ralph. I start with the premise that the function of leadership is to produce more leaders, not more followers.   (Time 108:41 Nov 8, 76)

NADER, Ralph. If nuclear power is so safe, why won't the insurance industry insure it?   (Newsweek 85:24 Feb 24, 75)

NADER, Ralph. I'll tell you what the real problem is. We ask people to think, instead of asking them to believe. And history has always gone to those who ask people to believe.   (New York Times Magazine 52 Jan 18, 76)

NADER, Ralph. The speed of exit of a civil servant is directly proportional to the quality of his service.   (Town & Country 133:141 May 79)

NADER, Ralph. There is not an energy crisis. There is an energy monopoly crisis, too many of the energy decisions are being made by a few large corporations instead of by a broader aggregate of consumer determinants.   (Meet the Press 21:3 April 17, 77)

NADER, Ralph. This (the Three Mile Island accident) is the beginning of the end of nuclear power in this country.   (Time 113:8 April 9, 79)

NAGY, Ivan. Ballet is the original women's liberation profession. It is created for females.   (Time 112:61 Sept 11, 78)

NAIPAUL, V. S. Africa has no future.   (New York Times Book Review 36 May 13, 79)

NAIPAUL, V. S. There is a certain 'scum' quality in Latin America. They imagine that if you kill the right people everything will work. Genocide is their history.   (New York Times Book Review 36 May 13, 79)

NAM DUCK WOO (DEPUTY PRIME MINISTER OF SOUTH KOREA), . There is not one developing country in the world where Western democracy really works.   (Time 107:32 June 6, 77)

NAMATH, Joe. I can't wait until tomorrow. Why not? Cause I get better looking every day.   (New York Times 126:2 Section 5 Nov 7, 76)

NAMATH, Joe. I love football. I really love football. As far as I'm concerned, it's the second best thing in the world.   (Playboy 24:346 Dec 77)

NASH, Graham. Serious musicians who read music don't understand what goes on with hippies.   (People Weekly 8:57 Dec 12, 77)

NASH, Ogden. Marriage is the alliance of two people, one of whom never remembers birthdays and the other never forgets them.   (Cosmopolitan 188:268 Feb 80)

NASH, Ogden. People who have what they want are fond of telling people who haven't what they want that they really don't want it.   (Kansas City Times 109:14C Jan 22, 77)

NASH, Ogden. Progress might have been all right once, but it's gone on too long.   (Reader's Digest 106:98 Feb 75)

NASSER, Gamal Abdel. Blow for blow, slap for slap. I don't act, I react.   (Newsweek 105:32 June 9, 75)

NASSER, Gamal Abdel. Sadat's greatest ambition is to own a big automobile and have the government pay for the gasoline (commenting on Sadat as Vice President of Egypt).   (Time 105:31 June 9, 75)

NAVRATILOVA, Martina. My wish is to have enough money so that I never have to play another set of tennis if I don't want to.   (San Francisco Chronicle This World 1978:2 Mar 12, 78)

NEEDHAM, Richard J. Men are foolish, they think money should be taken from the rich and given to the poor. Women are sensible, they think money should be taken from the rich and given to them.   (Toronto Globe and Mail 134:6 July 13, 77)

NEEDHAM, Richard J. You should treat your children as strangers whom you happen to like. If, that is, you happen to like them. (Toronto Globe and Mail 134:6 July 13, 77)

NEFF, Donald. To state it crudely, it appears that since the U.S. cannot negotiate peace in the Middle East, it will buy it. (Time 106:18 Aug 25, 75)

NEIZVESTNY, Ernst. A man should stand on his own two feet, even if he has only one leg. (New York Times 128:C19 Dec 1, 78)

NELSON, Gaylord. Meeting with Carter, you have the impression you're with a computer taking in information and not giving you any reaction. You don't feel you've met with anybody. (New Times 9:50 Nov 25, 78)

NELSON, Willie. My definition of music is anything that sounds good to the ear. If a peanut rolling across the floor sounds good, that's music. (Wall Street Journal 56:1 July 1, 76)

NELSON, Willie. To me, a hippie is a redneck with hair, and a redneck is a hippie with his hair cut off. It's not so much a difference in hair as attitude as to whether a guy is hip or not hip, whether he'd rather talk to you or fight you. (Texas Observer 68:13 Aug 6, 76)

NELSON, Willie. To me, a redneck is someone who likes to fight. Whiskey makes you want to fight and marijuana makes you want to listen to music. And marijuana and beer together is probably the greatest truth serum ever. (Texas Observer 68:13 Aug 6, 76)

NELSON, Willie. To write songs, I usually need a reason. Like not having any money. (Newsweek 92:53 Aug 14, 78)

NERUDA, Pablo. I am writing these quick lines for my memoirs only three days after the unspeakable events took my great comrade, President Allende, to his death. The aggressors' version is that they found clear signs of suicide on his lifeless body. The version published abroad is different. The President of the Republic of Chile was riddled and ripped to pieces by the machine guns of Chile's soldiers, who had betrayed Chile once more (from his book Memoirs). (New York Times 126:C19 Jan 7, 77)

NESMITH, Jeff. Life is a great big monopoly game to Carter, and every piece has to fit in its place—including the press. (Newsweek 88:82 Nov 22, 76)

NESSEN, Ron. I'm a Ron, but not a Ziegler. (Time 104: Dec 9, 74)

NESSEN, Ron. Press conferences force more policy decisions than anything else. (Time 106:32 May 5, 75)

NESSEN, Ron. Yes, I think the phone has reached there. They even have indoor toilets (commenting on President Ford's trip to Elkins, West Virginia). (Los Angeles Times 94:2 Part 1 Nov 6, 75)

NETTLETON, Lois. I'm terribly chauvinistic about this city. Smell the air—it's sexy. Chicago is vital, and it continues to improve. (Chicago Tribune 266:8 section 2 Sept 23, 77)

NEUHAUS, Richard John. Religion had become a silly imitation of what was happening in the marketplace. Christianity lost its nerve to challenge the culture. (Newsweek 86:64 Sept 29, 75)

NEUMAN, Alfred E. Today, it takes more brains and effort to make out the Income Tax Form than it does to make the income. (Mad Magazine 175:1 June 75)

NEW YORK TIMES, . The question on Tuesday is not whether there might have been better candidates than those nominated by the two major parties. The only question before the American people is whether they have been given a choice of leadership and prospective policies worthy of their vote. We find the choice clear-cut. We cast our vote for Jimmy Carter. (New York Times 126:18 Section 4 Oct 31, 76)

NEWELL, Guy. The cancer problem has not been solved, but it has never been more solvable. (American Legion Magazine 102:7 May 77)

NEWFIELD, Jack. Justice is a meat grinder. (Chicago Tribune 46:1 Section 7 Feb 15, 76)

NEWMAN, Edwin. I believe some silence is helpful to thought. And I believe to some extent radio and television discourage thought and reflection. (Chicago Tribune 1:23 Jan 1, 78)

NEWMAN, Paul. I figure that on my tombstone, it's going to say, 'He was a terrific actor until one day his eyes turned brown'. (Chicago Tribune 319:31 section 1 Nov 14, 76)

NEWMAN, Paul. If you don't have enemies, you don't have character. (First Run 2 June 10, 79)

NEWMAN, Paul. Racing is the best way I know to get away from all the rubbish of Hollywood. (The Observer 9799:9 June 17, 79)

NEWMAN, Paul. There's no way that what people see on celluloid has anything to do with me. (Chicago 25:86 July 76)

NEWMAN, Susan. Making movies has nothing to do with acting. (Time 111:52 Feb 6, 78)

NEWTON, C. M. When you're hired, you're fired—the date just hasn't been filled in yet. (New York Times 125:12 Section 5 May 30, 76)

NGUYEN-VAN-THIEU (FORMER PRESIDENT OF SOUTH VIETNAM), . A coalition (government) is like a sugar-coated poison pill. When the sugar melts, the poison kills you. (Time 105:12 April 14, 75)

NGUYEN-VAN-THIEU (FORMER PRESIDENT OF SOUTH VIETNAM), . I am resigning, but I am not deserting. (Time 105:13-14 May 5, 75)

NIEBUHR, Reinhold. Man's capacity for justice makes democracy possible, but man's inclination to injustice makes democracy necessary. (Rocky Mountain News 122:54 Dec 17, 80)

NIEH, Jung-chen (Chinese Politburo member). All correct ideas are subject to changes on the basis of time, location and conditions. Otherwise they will become metaphysical ideas. (Time 110:54 Sept 19, 77)

NIES, John. The effort expended by the bureaucracy in defending any error is in direct proportion to the size of the error. (Washingtonian 14:155 Nov 78)

NIETZSCHE, Friedrich Wilhelm. If a man really has strong faith he can indulge in the luxury of skepticism. (Kansas City Star 97:24 Aug 2, 77)

NIKOLAIS, Alwin. Whatever I do reflects the fact that I am an American. It reflects the freedom, the history and the creativity that is possible here. (New York Times 128:13 section 2 Dec 23, 79)

NIN, Anais. One must thrust out of a finished cycle in life, and that leap is the most difficult to make—to part with one's faith, one's love, when one would prefer to renew the faith and recreate the passion. (Kansas City Star 97:15C Sept 22, 76)

NIN, Anais. A real writer does not need the publicity that is granted with equal fervor to a toothpaste. A real writer only wants his book to be read by those who want to read it, and if there are 100 of them, it is enough to keep his work alive and sustain his productivity. (Washington Post 42:D4 Jan 16, 77)

NISBET, Robert. The doctrine of a benevolent state grows stronger. Very big government is not going to disappear. (Newsweek 90:34 Nov 7, 77)

NIVEN, David. Actors don't retire, they just get offered fewer parts. (W 6:18 July 8, 77)

NIVEN, David. I have a face that is a cross between two pounds of halibut and an explosion in an old clothes closet. (W 6:18 July 8, 77)

NIVEN, David. I've taken up the Bible again, somewhat in the spirit of W.C. Fields—looking for loopholes. (The Observer 9774:7 Dec 24, 78)

NIXON, Patricia Ryan. I gave up everything I've ever loved (commenting in 1960 on the price of political life). (Good Housekeeping 187:158 Aug 78)

NIXON, Patricia Ryan. If they had been my tapes, I would have burned or destroyed them because they were like a private diary, not public property. (Village Voice 23:62 Aug 7, 78)

NIXON, Richard Milhous. As Brazil goes, so will the rest of the Latin American continent (commenting in 1971). (Time 108:30 Nov 29, 76)

NIXON, Richard Milhous. Call it paranoia, but paranoia for peace isn't that bad (commenting on the wiretapping of government officials and journalists to discover leaks of confidential information during the Vietnam war). (New York Times 126:A1 May 20, 77)

NIXON, Richard Milhous. Henry (Kissinger) likes to say outrageous things....he was fascinated by the celebrity set and he liked being one himself. (Time 109:41 May 23, 77)

NIXON, Richard Milhous. History will justifiably record that my handling of the Watergate crisis was an unmitigated disaster. (Chicago Sun-Times 32:35 Sept 17, 79)

NIXON, Richard Milhous. I brought myself down. I have impeached myself. (New York Times 127:38 April 30, 78)

NIXON, Richard Milhous. I let down my friends. I let down the country....I let the American people down....(But) if they want me to get down and grovel on the floor, no. Never (commenting in his first David Frost interview on Watergate). (Wall Street Journal 56:1 May 5, 77)

NIXON, Richard Milhous. I should have had you for my lawyer and I might still be president (to Edward Bennett Williams upon the acquittal of John Connally). (New York 8:48 Aug 25, 75)

NIXON, Richard Milhous. If it hadn't been for Martha, there'd have been no Watergate. (Washingtonian 13:11 Nov 77)

NIXON, Richard Milhous. If the United States doesn't stand up for our friends when they are in trouble, we're going to wind up without any friends. (New York Times 128:B6 July 12, 79)

NIXON, Richard Milhous. I'm not a loveable man (on his explanation of why the press kept picking on him). (Time 110:23 Sept 12, 77)

NIXON, Richard Milhous. In our own lives, let each of us ask—not just what will government do for me, but what can I do for myself (inaugural address—1973). (Christian Science Monitor 69:14 Jan 20, 77)

NIXON, Richard Milhous. It is quite obvious that there are certain inherently governmental actions which, if undertaken by the sovereign in protection of...the nation's security, are lawful, but which if undertaken by private citizens are not (commenting to the Senate Intelligence Committee on his authorization of covert CIA efforts to prevent Chilean President Allende's election in 1970). (Wall Street Journal 56:1 Mar 12, 76)

NIXON, Richard Milhous. Knowing a little about everything won't work. Knowing a great deal about important things is essential (for Presidents). (Time 112:16 Aug 28, 78)

NIXON, Richard Milhous. The media has abdicated its fact gathering to nonbelieving young people, who seem to want to break down our values. (Chicago Sun-Times 28:58 Nov 18, 75)

NIXON, Richard Milhous. My political life is over. (New York Times 128:A5 Dec 1, 78)

NIXON, Richard Milhous. The next President's qualifications should be tested against foreign policy. If he fails there, we all fail. (Time 114:27 Sept 10, 79)

NIXON, Richard Milhous. One thing I really hate is exercise for exercise's sake. (Philadelphia 69:131 April 78)

NIXON, Richard Milhous. Only three men in America understand the use of power. I do. John Connally does. And I guess Nelson does. (American Opinion 18:21 May 75)

NIXON, Richard Milhous. Presidents come and go, but the Supreme Court, through its decisions, goes on forever. (Playboy 26:111 April 79)

NIXON, Richard Milhous. Some people say I didn't handle it properly and they're right. I screwed it up. And I paid the price (about Watergate). (New York Times 128:A5 Dec 1, 78)

NIXON, Richard Milhous. There is one thing solid and fundamental in politics—the law of change. What's up today is down tomorrow. (Time 104:40 Aug 19, 74)

NIXON, Richard Milhous. (Watergate) was worse than a crime, it was a blunder. (The Observer 9771:14 Dec 3, 78)

NIXON, Richard Milhous. We are a compromised country at the moment (1975). (Ladies' Home Journal 92:40 Dec 75)

NIXON, Richard Milhous. We are now in a war called peace. (Time 114:27 Sept 10, 79)

NIXON, Richard Milhous. We have very little leadership in our country today (1975). (Ladies' Home Journal 92:52 Dec 75)

NIXON, Richard Milhous. When news is concerned, nobody in the press is a friend—they are all enemies. (Time 111:104 April 17, 78)

NIXON, Richard Milhous. Writing is the toughest thing I've ever done. (Rolling Stone 227:43 Dec 2, 76)

NIXON, Richard Milhous (attributed by Robert J. Dole). It's always hard to lose the close ones—if it's a big one—but when it's close, everyone is looking around, you know, the cannibals come out and try to assess what happened. (Mother Jones 2:7 Jan 77)

NIZER, Louis. Having fought for the 1st amendment before *Penthouse* was born I wish (the first amendment) was in better hands than a magazine that specializes in close ups of women's orifices (spoken as the attorney for Rancho La Costa in its $630 million libel suit against *Penthouse* magazine.) (Los Angeles Times 94:22 Part 1 Nov 14, 75)

NIZER, Louis. I would rather trust 12 jurors with all their prejudices and biases than I would a judge. I think the reason democracy works is because as you multiply judgements, you reduce the incidence of error. (Chicago Tribune Magazine 31 Feb 5, 78)

NKOMO, Joshua. I do not think the British know what genuine majority rule is. (The Observer 9806:10 Aug 5, 79)

NKOMO, Joshua. There's no such thing to me as whites. (The Observer 9760:13 Sept 17, 78)

NKOMO, Joshua. We are not the beasts and villains we are painted to be. (The Observer 9818:11 Oct 28, 79)

NOLAN, John T. If you outsmart your own lawyer, you've got the wrong lawyer. (Washingtonian 15:142 Nov 79)

NORMAN, Edward. Truth does not cease because people give up believing it. (The Observer 9767:13 Nov 5, 78)

NORODOM SIHANOUK, KING OF CAMBODIA (ABDICATED 1955), . When they no longer need me, they will spit me out like a cherry pit (about the Khmer Rouge). (Time 106:38 Sept 22, 75)

NORRIS, Clarence (the sole surviving |Scottsboro Boy|). The lesson to Black people, to my children, to everybody, is that you should always fight for your rights even if it costs you your life. Stand up for your rights, even if it kills you (commenting on his struggle to clear his name upon being pardoned by the state of Alabama). (New York Times 126:1 Oct 26, 76)

NORRIS, Kathleen. If ambition doesn't hurt you, you haven't got it. (Kansas City Star 97:4B Feb 6, 77)

NORRIS, William. Dammit, rebuilding the cities will be one of the great growth industries of the future. It will replace the auto as the big provider of jobs—if we Americans can ever get ourselves organized. (Time 111:61 April 3, 78)

NORRIS, William. We talk a lot about human rights, but I don't know of any human right that is more important than a job. (Time 111:61 April 3, 78)

NOTO, Lore. Critics are beasts, highly-disturbed people, basically frustrated, totally insincere, and brutalized by the profession they're in. The public should be warned: critics may be harmful to your health. (More 7:31 July/Aug 77)

NOVA, Leo. The other person's attitude depends on which direction the money moves between you. (Omni 1:131-32 May 79)

NOVICK, Julius. It is a well-known and infuriating fact of life that in any relationship, if one party really and truly does not give a damn, that party will inevitably have the upper hand. Indifference is power (ask any cat). (Village Voice 21:81 Feb 14, 77)

NOYES, Eliot F (industrial designer). Familiarity breeds acceptance. (Time 110:71 Aug 1, 77)

NUREEV, Rudolf. I do not try to dance better than anyone else. I only try to dance better than myself. (Newsweek 85:32 Jan 6, 76)

NUREEV, Rudolf. I'm 40 years old. It's time to indulge, to be foolish if I wish. (Saturday Review 5:54 Nov 11, 78)

NYE, Blaine. It's not whether you win or lose but who gets the blame (commenting on his football philosophy). (Sports Illustrated 45:16 Nov 15, 76)

NYERERE, Julius Kamberage. South Africa is no different from Rhodesia. The struggle by blacks in both countries is exactly the same—for majority rule. So what happens in Rhodesia will happen in South Africa. (People Weekly 6:40 Dec 27/Jan 3, 77)

NYIREGYHAZI, Ervin. Music is a wonderful way of life but a terrible career. (Stereo Review 41:61 July 78)

NYRO, Laura. I've always loved the country for the seasons and the city for people and ideas. (Ms 4:4 Mar 76)

OATES, Joyce Carol. Sometimes my work is very savage, very harsh. But so is life. My material is not sordid, it's just a realistic reflection of a society that is in turmoil. (People Weekly 6:66 Nov 15, 76)

OBEY, David R. Joe McCarthy made me an independent, Stevenson made me a Liberal, and Eisenhower made me a Democrat. (New York Times 128:B20 Mar 1, 79)

OBEY, David R. Politics is the only thing I really cared about, except the Green Bay Packers. (New York Times 128:B20 Mar 1, 79)

O'BRIAN, Hugh. There is quite enough grief when one is alone. Why compound it by getting married? (upon his founding Marriage Anonymous). People Weekly 5:72 Jan 26, 76)

O'BRIAN, Jack. (Truman Capote is) Jackie Susann with an education. (Time 107:68 June 28, 76)

OCCHIOGROSSO, Peter. Sonny Rollins is the Vladimir Nabokov of the tenor saxophone. (Soho Weekly News 6:27 Nov 2, 78)

OCHS, Adolph Simon. When a tabloid prints it, that's smut. When the Times prints it, that's sociology. (Time 110:75 Aug 15, 77)

O'CONNELL, David (one of the IRA's leading tacticians). Put your faith in the Provos and Ireland will be free. We will abolish British rule, we will smash it. (New York Times 125:7 April 26, 76)

O'CONNOR, Flannery. Anybody that admires Thomas Wolfe can be expected to like good fiction only by accident. (New York Times Book Review 3 Dec 2, 79)

O'CONNOR, Flannery. (Fame) is a comic distinction shared with Roy Rogers's horse and Miss Watermelon of 1955. (Time 113:86 Mar 5, 79)

O'CONNOR, Flannery. For a fiction writer, to believe nothing is to see nothing. (Ms 8:39 July 79)

O'CONNOR, Flannery. What (Graham Greene) does, I think, is try to make religion respectable to the modern unbeliever by making it seedy. (Time 113:86 Mar 5, 79)

O'CONNOR, John J. Exposure to television is not necessarily fatal. (New York Times 127:33 section 2 Nov 27, 77)

OGDEN, David A. If you don't appreciate the amount of luxuries your budget can afford, you are getting paid far too much. (Omni 1:132 May 79)

OGILVEY, David. The consumer is not a moron. She is your wife. (Viva 4:26 Aug 77)

O'KEEFFE, Georgia. I'll paint what I see but I'll paint it big to say what is to me the wideness and wonder of the world as I live it. (Newsweek 88:76 Nov 22, 76)

OKUN, Arthur M. Society can transport money from rich to poor only in a leaky bucket. (Time 115:83 April 7, 80)

OKUN, Arthur M. The world is not safe for incumbents. (New York Times 128:15 section 3 June 24, 79)

OLDENBURG, Claes. I am for art that coils and grunts like a wrestler. I am for art that sheds hair. I am for art you can sit on. I am for art you can pick your nose with or stub your toe on. (Time 113:57 Jan 8, 79)

OLDENBURG, Claes. To give birth to form is the only act of man that has any consequence. (Chicago 25:18 Nov 76)

O'LEARY, John. There isn't a gasoline shortage. There's a driving surplus. (Time 113:66 June 25, 79)

OLIANSKY, Joel. TV writing is the country of the blind where the one-eyed man is king. (1977 Writer's Yearbook 61)

OLIVIER, Laurence. Acting great parts devours you. (The Observer 9788:9 April 1, 79)

OLIVIER, Laurence. Acting is a masochistic form of exhibitionism. (Los Angeles Times Calendar 33 Feb 26, 78)

OLIVIER, Laurence. I am an actor because that is all I am qualified to do. (Los Angeles Times Calendar 33 Feb 26, 78)

OLIVIER, Laurence. I love comedy every bit as much as tragedy, perhaps more, because the whole scene of humanity is under its roof. (New York Times Magazine 60 Mar 25, 79)

OLIVIER, Laurence. I think I would have liked to have been a farmer. Earth and greasepaint are a very good mix. (Time 106:58 Dec 29, 75)

OLIVIER, Laurence. I'm not sure what I'm like and I'm not sure I want to know. (New York Times Magazine 56 Mar 25, 79)

OLIVIER, Laurence. Living is strife and torment, disappointment and love and sacrifice, golden sunsets and black storms. (Los Angeles Times Calendar 35 Feb 26, 78)

OLIVIER, Laurence. My worst performance was as Father Christmas. I didn't fool my children. They said, 'We know you're not Daddy' Christmas. You're Daddy. (New York Times 125:41 Dec 10, 75)

OLIVIER, Laurence. Probably every great actor in history was the son of a clergyman. (Chicago Tribune 201:20 July 20, 79)

OLIVIER, Laurence. You can't just run. You have to look as if you're running (about acting). (New York Times Magazine 20 Mar 25, 79)

O'MALLEY, Frank Ward. Life is just one damned thing after another. (Viva 4:25 July 77)

ONASSIS, Jacqueline Lee (Bouvier) Kennedy. I always wanted to be some kind of writer or newspaper reporter. But after college—I did other things. (New York Times 126:A10 Jan 14, 77)

O'NEAL, Tatum. She (Shirley Temple) wasn't very good. She was fine when she was 6 or 7. But did you notice how she couldn't act when she was 14? (Chicago Tribune 148:5 section 6 May 29, 77)

O'NEILL, Eugene. Born in a hotel room—and God damn it—died in a hotel room. (New York Times 128:5 section D Nov 26, 78)

O'NEILL, Eugene. Life is a tragedy, hurrah. (New York Times 128:l5 section 6 Mar 4, 79)

O'NEILL, Thomas P. (Tip). If this were France, the Democratic Party would be five parties. (Time 112:42 Nov 20, 78)

O'NEILL, Thomas P. (Tip). Since the day he commuted Nixon, he hasn't done anything right (commenting on Congressional rapport with Gerald Ford). (Time 104:27 Dec 2, 74)

ONO, Yoko. Keep your intentions in a clear bottle and leave it on the shelf when you rap. (Chicago Tribune 176:2 section II June 25, 78)

OPPENHEIMER, J. Robert. The optimist thinks this is the best of all possible worlds, and the pessimist knows it. (Town & Country 133:141 May 79)

ORBEN, Robert. I feel that if God had really wanted us to have enough oil, He never would have given us the Department of Energy. (Time 113:71 Feb 26, 79)

ORLANS, Harold. Logic is a game men play as cats play with balls of string, whereas reality is a game the gods play with us. (Change 9:34 April 77)

O'ROURKE, Joseph. The antiabortionists are antifree, antiwomen and anti-Christian. (Time 114:27 July 9, 79)

ORTON, Joe. All classes are criminal today. We live in an age of equality. (After Dark 11:51 Dec 78)

OSBORN, Kenneth Barton. There are icebergs, and we are the Titanic (about the Central Intelligence Agency). (Playboy 22:58 Aug 75)

OSBORNE, John. Asking a working writer what he thinks about critics is like asking a lamppost what it feels about dogs. (Time 110:77 Oct 31, 77)

OTIS, Amos (baseball player). Trying to sneak a pitch past him (Rod Carew) is like trying to sneak the sunrise past a rooster. (Time 110:53 July 18, 77)

O'TOOLE, John E. Most packaged goods are minor products (and) the consumer's most effective response to a disparity between an advertising claim and reality is never to buy the product again. When you buy a political candidate as a result of his advertising, you're stuck with the purchase for four years—with results that can be far more devastating than not getting your teeth as white as you had hoped. (TV Guide 24:23 July 24, 76)

OUTHIER, Louis. You don't get fat from a good kitchen—only from a bad one. (W 4:11 Nov 28, 75)

OWEN, David. The government (of Rhodesia) under the Constitution may well be multiracial, but the power structure will be white. (New York Times 128:3 April 8, 79)

OZARK, Danny. Mike Anderson's limitations are limitless. (Sports Illustrated 43:14 June 16, 75)

OZAWA, Seiji. Slave (Mstislav Rostropovich) doesn't interpret, he feels. His music is really his character. He is conducting his life. (Time 110:84 Oct 24, 77)

PACKWOOD, Robert. We haven't got an obligation to bail those liars out (in accusing New York City officials of deliberately lying to the Senate Banking Committee). (Chicago Tribune 304:2 Section 1 Oct 31, 75)

PAGE, Geraldine. The sadness I feel is that half my life or more is over, the list of films so short, and the people won't see all of what I could have shown them. (Los Angeles Times Calendar 27 Sept 3, 78)

PAGNOL, Marcel. The most difficult secret for a man to keep is the opinion he has of himself. (Reader's Digest 107:166 Oct 75)

PAIGE, Satchel. Don't look back. Something might be gaining on you. (Maclean's 90:96 Nov 14, 77)

PAIGE, Satchel. Go very gently on the vices such as carrying on in society. The social rumble ain't restful. (Maclean's 90:96 Nov 14, 77)

PAIGE, Satchel. How old would you be if you didn't know how old you was? (Chicago Tribune 37:2 section 2 Feb 6, 78)

PAIGE, Satchel. If your stomach disputes you, lie down and pacify it with cool thoughts. (Maclean's 90:96 Nov 14, 77)

PAIGE, Satchel. Keep the juices flowing by jangling around gently as you move. (Maclean's 90:96 Nov 14, 77)

PALME, Olof. I am deeply sorry if he leaves Sweden, partly because of his artistic ability and partly because he is a good friend (commenting on Ingmar Bergman's plans to leave Sweden permanently). (New York Times 125:3 April 24, 76)

PANDIT, Vijaya Lakshmi (aunt of Indira Gandhi). The essence of democracy has always been the right to dissent. And it was working in India, though slowly, and perhaps awkwardly. One can't govern simply by clapping into jail everyone who disagrees. Please understand that I'm very proud of Indira. But the good career she has begun is being threatened by all this sorry business of muzzling people and stifling dissent. (New York Times 126:11 Section 1 Oct 31, 76)

PANNENBERG, Wolfhart. The greatest deception (of our era is the idea that) political change can satisfy a religious need. (Time 107:65 Mar 8, 76)

PANZA DI BIUMO, Giuseppe. For me, art is the visualization of philosophy. (Newsweek 86:69 Aug 11, 75)

PAPP, Joseph. The true dramatist of our time is a poet; the true poet, a dramatist. (New York Times 128:C24 Dec 1, 78)

PARINGAUX, Roland-Pierre (French journalist). The two parts of Viet Nam are like Sparta and Byzantium; they are like two ingredients of a sweet and sour sauce, difficult to mix so that it will remain tasty for all. (Time 105:10 May 12, 75)

PARK, Tongsun. I want to tell you what I have done in Washington constitutes an American success story on a small scale. (New York Times 127:1 section 4 April 9, 76)

PARK, Tongsun. I'm glad it's all over. They were talking about 150 Congressmen; now it's narrowed to three. The whole thing (Koreagate scandal) was just a syndrome following Watergate. (W 7:33 Nov 10, 78)

PARK, Tongsun. Some people enjoy making other people happy. I like to entertain. I am concerned that we have no Perle Mesta. We should have somebody in the private sector who plays the role of catalyst to bring people together. I like to do my share. (People Weekly 6:30 Nov 15, 76)

PARKER, Charlie. Romance without finance ain't got no chance. (The Animator 4:1 Fall 76)

PARKER, Dorothy. An author really hasn't made it until he no longer shows his books to his friends. (Writer's Digest 56:11 Dec 78)

PARKER, Gail Thain. We must not be misled by snobbery into thinking that there is only one way to become educated. (Time 111:90 April 10, 78)

PARKER, Tim. Originality begets conformity. (Omni 1:132 May 79)

PARKINS, Tom. Anything that happens enough times to irritate you will happen at least once more. (Omni 1:132 May 79)

PARKINSON, C. Northcote. Expenditure rises to meet income. (Washingtonian 14:155 Nov 78)

PARKINSON, C. Northcote. Nonsense expands so as to fill the space available (Corollary to Parkinson's Law). (Wilson Library Bulletin 52:219 Nov 77)

PARKINSON, C. Northcote. Work expands to fill the time allotted to it, or, conversely, the amount of work completed is in inverse proportion to the number of people employed. (The Reader (Chicago's Free Weekly) 5:2 May 28, 76)

PARKS, Gordon. Huddie was meant for music and born for trouble. (New York 9:66 May 10, 76)

PARTON, Dolly. I know my hair is out of the '60s, my clothes are '50s and the shoes I wear are from the '40s. But I like looking like I came out of a fairy tale. (Los Angeles Times 95:32 Part 4 Dec 26, 75)

PARTON, Dolly. If people think I'm a dumb blonde because of the way I look, then they're dumber than they think I am. (Ms 7:16 June 79)

PARTON, Dolly. A real important thing is that, though I rely on my husband for love, I rely on myself for strength. (Chicago Sun-Times 32:33 July 16, 79)

PARTON, Dolly. When I sit back in my rocker, I want to have done it all. (Time 109:73 April 18, 77)

PARTRIDGE, Eric. I always wanted to become a writer, and I consider myself to be one. (Time 110:76 Oct 17, 77)

PASTORE, John O. I've always been weary of people who stayed on too long—stalwarts in their day who end up being held up by their staff. I don't want to mention any names. I wouldn't let that happen to me. (People Weekly 4:76 Oct 27, 75)

PASTORE, John O. This has become a Government by veto. We've got the minority dragging the majority around by the nose. (Time 106:64 Sept 22, 75)

PATMAN, Wright (attributed by James T. Molloy). Next to the church, credit unions do more good for the people than any other institution. (Chicago Sun-Times 29:22 Mar 10, 76)

PATON, Alan. Sometimes, you think of apartheid as a fort. Often it is seen as a prison. But it is really a grave the Afrikanner has dug for himself. (New York Times 127:32 Oct 30, 77)

PATTERSON, L. Ray. The concern of the public (about crime) is not so much for vindictive retribution, but for some retribution. (Time 112:54 Sept 18, 78)

PATTON, Edward L. Almost everyone who views the (Alaska) pipeline agrees that it is not a visual abomination. In fact, I predict that it will be a leading tourist attraction. (Outside 1:7 Sept 77)

PATTON, George S. In war, just as in loving, you've got to keep on shoving. (Playboy 26:26 Oct 79)

PAUL, Jerry. This system doesn't want justice. It wants convictions. That's why, given enough money, I can buy justice. I can win any case in this country, given enough money (upon winning acquittal for Joan Little in her murder trial). (Chicago Tribune 296:4 Section 1 Oct 23, 75)

PAUL VI, POPE, . In reality, it is not enough to be free from something. One must be free for someone or something. (American Legion Magazine 101:15 Dec 76)

PAUL VI, POPE, . The real reason (for the ban on women priests) is that Christ, giving the church its fundamental constitution, its theological anthropology subsequently always followed by church tradition, ordained it thus: That in a choir of human voices there shall be tenors and sopranos. (Chicago Tribune 31:8 section 1 Jan 31, 77)

PAULUCCI, Jeno F. It pays to be ignorant, for when you're smart you already know it can't be done. (New York Times 126:5 Section 3 Nov 7, 76)

PAULUCCI, Jeno F. The meek have to inherit the earth—they sure don't know how to market it. (New York Times 126:5 Section 3 Nov 7, 76)

PAZ, Octavio. The soul has become a department of sex, and sex has become a department of politics. (Newsweek 94:137 Nov 19, 79)

PEKAR, Harvey. A person who can't relate to comic books is like somebody who can't relate to opera. They're both culturally deprived. (Cleveland 5:153 July 76)

PELE, . God has been kind to me. Three World Cups and now a championship in America. I can die now. (Newsweek 90:73 Sept 12, 77)

PENDEN, Bill. Atomic energy is a future idea whose time is past. Renewable energy is a future idea whose time has come. (Atlas World Press Review 24:38 April 77)

PENN, Irving. I rate myself out of combat—as something between a painter and an old-time photographer. But if I were to define myself, I'd say I was the least specialized of all photographers. I need a balanced diet. (New York Times Magazine 21 Sept 4, 77)

PENNY, J. C. Intelligence is the effort to do the best you can at your particular job; the quality that gives dignity to that job, whether it happens to be scrubbing a floor, or running a corporation. (Forbes 120:186 Oct 15, 77)

PEPPER, Claude. Mandatory retirement arbitrarily severs productive persons from their livelihood, squanders their talent, scars their health, strains an already overburdened Social Security system and drives many elderly persons into poverty and despair. (Time 110:67 Aug 8, 77)

PERCY, Charles. The Rock of Gibraltar has sunk (upon Jane Byrne's nomination as Chicago's Democratic candidate for mayor). (Chicago Sun-Times 32:5 Mar 1, 79)

PERCY, Charles. We have to get the (Republican) Party out of the country clubs, out of a Caucasian atmosphere, away from the Anglo-Saxon approach. As long as the Republican Party takes a Neanderthal point of view, I don't see why it deserves to win. (Time 110:93 Dec 12, 77)

PERCY, Walker. Every novelist I know is miserable. (New York Times Book Review 31 June 29, 80)

PERES, Shimon. Stroking a tiger (the P.L.O.) will not make it a pussycat. (Time 109:24 April 18, 77)

PERETZ, Martin. You know, the thing I really disliked most about Chavez was the way he established himself as a tool of the Kennedy elite. (Boston Magazine 67:66 July 75)

PEREZ, Carlos Andres (President of Venezuela). The increase of petroleum prices is by no means a selfish act of OPEC members for the exclusive benefit of their countries. It represents the irrevocable decision to dignify the terms of trade, to revalue raw materials and other basic products of the third world. (New York Times 126:3 Nov 29, 76)

PEREZ, Manuel Benitez. Bullfighting is an animal inside me, and it is one that I cannot dominate—it dominates me. (Newsweek 96:12 Sept 8, 80)

PERKINS, Frances (former Secretary of Labor). Being a woman has only bothered me in climbing trees. (Life Special Report: Remarkable American Women 1776-1976 21 1976)

PERKINS, Maxwell. Editors are extremely fallible people, all of them. Don't put too much trust in them (to Taylor Caldwell). (Esquire 89:65 July 18, 78)

PERKINS, Maxwell. It is always better to give a little less than the reader wants, than more (to Ray Stannard Baker). (Esquire 89:65 July 18, 78)

PERKINS, Maxwell. You have to throw yourself away when you write (to Elizabeth Lemmon). (Esquire 89:65 July 18, 78)

PERLS, Fritz. Learning is discovering that something is possible. (Omni 2:36 Nov 79)

PERON, Maria Estela Martinez Isabel. The country is suffering internal and external aggression from journalistic terrorism and defamatory rumors. My state of health is not a sufficient reason to try unethically and against the popular will to strip me of my legitimate authority. (Washington Post 337:A13 Nov 7, 75)

PERON, Maria Estela Martinez Isabel. If I have to apply five turns of the screw each day for the happiness of Argentina, I will do it. (Time 106:40 Sept 29, 75)

PERRY, Joe. The only aging rock star is a dead one. (Creem 10:30 Dec 78)

PETER, Laurence J. Bureaucracy defends the status quo long past the time when the quo has lost its status. (San Francisco Chronicle This World 1978:40 Jan 29, 78)

PETER, Laurence J. The cream rises until it sours. (San Francisco Chronicle This World 1978:40 Jan 29, 78)

PETER, Laurence J. If two wrongs don't make a right, try three (Nixon's principle). (Washingtonian 14:155 Nov 78)

PETER, Laurence J. If you don't know where you are going, you will probably end up somewhere else. (San Francisco Chronicle This World 1978:40 Jan 29, 78)

PETER, Laurence J. In a hierarchy, every employee tends to rise to the level of his own incompetence. (The Reader (Chicago's Free Weekly) 5:2 May 28, 76)

PETER, Laurence J. In the country of the blind, the one-eyed King can still goof up. (San Francisco Chronicle This World 1978:40 Jan 29, 78)

PETER, Laurence J. Most hierarchies were established by men who now occupy the upper levels, thus depriving women of an equal opportunity to achieve their levels of incompetence. (San Francisco Chronicle This World 1978:40 Jan 29, 78)

PETERS, Charles. In Washington, bureaucrats confer, the President proclaims and the Congress legislates, but the impact on reality is negligible, if evident at all. (Time 115:14 June 30, 80)

PETERSON, Esther. If a man fights his adversaries, he's called determined. If a woman does it, she's frustrated. (National Observer 16:18 June 13, 77)

PHAN HIEN (DEPUTY PRIME MINISTER OF VIETNAM), . We are ready to do our best to facilitate departures. (The Observer 9804:9 July 22, 79)

PHILBY, Kim. John Foster Dulles was a strong personality with views as narrow as a small-gauge railway. (Esquire 89:53 Mar 28, 78)

PHILBY, Kim. Now I can abandon my earlier reserve and call him an idle, ignorant, ungenerous old fraud. (Esquire 89:55 Mar 28, 78)

PHILIPSON, Morris. The commercial publisher says of his book, this is no good but it'll make a lot of money. The university publisher says, this is good and it won't make money. (New York Times 125:33 June 30, 76)

PHILLIPS, Howard. We hope that Ronald Reagan will not be the third President to work for Henry Kissinger. (Time 116:14 July 28, 80)

PHILLIPS, Kevin. I don't see how the (Republican) party can survive a Carter victory because it would wrap up the Southern opportunity for growth. When you take that away, you take away the future of the whole party. (Wall Street Journal 56:14 Oct 11, 76)

PICASSO, Jacqueline. Living with Picasso was like living with a blowtorch; he was a consuming flame. (Time 108:70 Nov 8, 76)

PICASSO, Pablo. After Matisse, Chagall is the only artist who really knows color. (Art News 76:48 Summer 77)

PICASSO, Pablo. Art is lies that tell the truth. (More 8:34 June 78)

PICASSO, Pablo. Every child is an artist. The problem is how to remain an artist once he grows up. (Time 108:68 Oct 4, 76)

PICASSO, Pablo. For me there are only two kinds of women—goddesses and doormats. (People Weekly 13:37 May 26, 80)

PIERCE, Webb. One drink is too many and a million is not enough. (Country Music 5:63 April 77)

PIERSON, L. R. If you're coasting, you're going downhill. (Washingtonian 14:155 Nov 78)

PILEGGI, Nicholas. The best thing that ever happened to the Mafia is that none of them went to the Columbia School of Journalism or read Clay Felker on the importance of the media—so they retain some insight about the way the world really works. (More 7:22 Jan 77)

PINERO, Miguel. I'd like to die with my back against the wall and two guns smokin'. (Andy Warhol's Interview 7:27 Nov 77)

PINIELLA, Lou (New York Yankee outfielder). I cussed him out in Spanish, and he threw me out in English (commenting on an argument he once had with umpire Armando Rodriguez). (Sports Illustrated 43:12 Sept 1, 75)

PINOCHET, Augusto. When people don't listen to words, they'll listen to deeds. (The Times 8126:10 Mar 23, 80)

PIPPIN, Horace (folk artist). Pictures just come to my mind and then I tell my heart to go ahead. (Newsweek 90:60 Aug 22, 77)

PIRANDELLO, Luigi. Life is little more than a loan shark: it exacts a very high rate of interest for the few pleasures it concedes. (The Reader (Chicago's Free Weekly) 7:2 Dec 23, 77)

PIRIE, (Mrs) John T., Jr. Great chefs are reluctant to come to the Midwest. They still fear the Indian's tomahawk. (Town & Country 129:159 Dec 75)

PISIER, Marie-France. People wear resort clothes but actually Hollywood is an enormous factory. People work ten times harder than anywhere else. (Newsweek 89:47 May 16, 77)

PITMAN, Keith A. All generalizations are untrue. (Washingtonian 14:26 Dec 78)

PLANT, Robert. The lifestyle of rock 'n' roll is to live well and take a good woman. (Creem 9:49 July 77)

POGO (CARTOON CHARACTER), . We have met the enemy and they is us. (Philadelphia 69:188 Sept 78)

POIROT, Paul L. Multiplying wealth is by far the fastest way to help the poor. Dividing the wealth and subsidizing poverty is the fastest way to starve everyone. (American Opinion 18:29 Nov 75)

POLYKOFF, Shirley. If I've only one life, let me live it as a blonde! (advertising slogan). (New York 9:37 Aug 23, 76)

POPE, Generoso, Jr. A Pulitzer Prize ain't going to win us (the National Enquirer) two readers. (Newsweek 85:62 April 21, 75)

PORTER, Katherine Anne. Dullness, bitterness, rancor, self-pity, baseness of all kinds can be most interesting material for a story provided these are not also the main elements in the mind of the author. (Newsweek 91:75 May 22, 78)

PORTER, Sir George. If sunbeams were weapons of war, we would have had solar energy centuries ago. (Omni 2:37 June 80)

PORTILLO, Jose Lopez. Mexico is neither on the list of United States priorities nor on that of United States respect. (New York Times 128:A8 Nov 20, 78)

PORTILLO, Jose Lopez. We will have to be tied by geography as long as the world goes round; we already are tied by history; we also would like to be tied by good will. (American Legion Magazine 102:34 April 77)

POST, Emily. An overdose of praise is like 10 lumps of sugar in coffee; only a very few people can swallow it. (Kansas City Times 109:14C Jan 22, 77)

POULSEN, Brad. When anything is used to its full potential, it will break. (Omni 1:132 May 79)

POUND, Ezra. At seventy, I realized that instead of being a lunatic, I was a moron. (Horizon 21:96 Mar 78)

POWELL, Jody. After getting kicked out (of the Air Force Academy) for cheating, politics seemed like the next best thing. (Time 109:23 June 6, 77)

POWELL, Jody. How many times did Jimmy Carter say during the campaign he was a fiscal conservative—50,000 times? That's the mistake people have made all along—not believing he means what the hell he says. (Newsweek 89:44 May 16, 77)

POWELL, Jody. I probably had a political philosophy at one point, but I don't think about political philosophy any more. (Time 109:17 June 6, 77)

POWELL, Paul. I can smell the meat a-cookin'. If you can't get a meal, take a sandwich (advice to lawmakers). (Chicago 27:11 June 78)

PRENDERGAST, George Washington. I never took a dime from the public till; it's all been honest graft. (Change 8:60 Aug 76)

PRESLEY, Elvis. I don't know anything about music. In my line I don't have to. (Creem 11:30 Feb 80)

PRICE, Reynolds. The classical world decided wisely that any human accorded the honors of a hero must be, above all, dead. (Saturday Review 5:17 Dec 78)

PRINZE, Freddie. Hollywood is one big whore. It breeds decadence. (Playboy 24:110 June 77)

PRIOLO, Paul. What that guy (Jerry Brown) does is enough to make a grown Republican cry. (The Times 8102:9 Oct 22, 78)

PRITCHETT, V. S. It is the role of the poet to look at what is happening in the world and to know that quite other things are happening. (New York Times Book Review 50 June 3, 79)

PRITCHETT, V. S. There are rules for old men who are in love with young girls, all the stricter when the young girls are in love with them. It has to be played as a game. (Time 114:127 Nov 12, 79)

PRITIKIN, Nathan. Although our results need confirmation, we believe they are the first evidence demonstrating reversal of human arteriosclerosis by diet. (Chicago Tribune 120:11 Section 1 April 29, 76)

PRIZEMAN, John. Collecting books is like collecting other people's minds, like having people on the shelves—only, you can just put them away when you want to. (Esquire 89:76 Feb 78)

PROXMIRE, William. If New York has one quality, it is the fantastic brass—that ability to con you into buying the Brooklyn Bridge. (San Francisco Chronicle This World 1978:2 Aug 6, 78)

PROXMIRE, William. Sunlight remains the world's best disinfectant (summing up his feelings on truth in lending and opening the Federal Reserve System to public scrutiny). (New York Times 126:62 Sept 9, 77)

PUZO, Mario. (Film writing) is the most crooked business that I've ever had any experience with. You can get a better shake in Vegas than you can in Hollywood. (Time 112:72 Aug 28, 78)

PUZO, Mario. I find that the only thing that really stands up, better than gambling, better than booze, better than women, is reading. (Time 111:72 June 26, 78)

PUZO, Mario. I never knew anybody so determined to be unhappy (about Joseph Heller). (New York Times 128:16 section 6 Mar 4, 79)

PUZO, Mario. A novelist should never take the movie business seriously. (New York Times 128:40 section 7 Feb 18, 79)

QADDAFI, Muammar. If he (Billy Carter) runs for President, we will do what we can to support him. (Life 3:108 Feb 80)

QADDAFI, Muammar. People are getting killed everywhere by their leaders. (The Observer 9799:9 June 17, 79)

QADDAFI, Muammar. She does not interfere in politics (commenting on his wife's best quality). (Life 3:108 Feb 80)

QUANT, Mary. Good taste is death, vulgarity life. (Life 2:83 Nov 79)

QUARRY, Jerry. This will surprise some people because I was at it so long, but the truth of the matter is that I hated boxing. It is a cruel, vicious sport—nothing more than two people trying to kill each other—and the more vicious it gets, the more people like it. I'm not an animal. Maybe that's why I didn't become champion (commenting on embarking on a career as a singer). (New York Times 125:3 Section 5 Jan 4, 76)

QUIN, Percy Edwards. A man must sometimes rise above principle. (Washingtonian 15:143 Nov 79)

QUINLAN, Thomas. Church is like a saloon. The doors swing in and the doors swing out. If you don't believe, get the hell out. (Chicago Tribune 198:4 July 17, 77)

QUINN, Sally. An attitude of sexuality is as pervasive in Cuba as the presence of Fidel Castro. You can feel sex in the atmosphere, on the street, in conversation, in people's actions. The Cubans seem to be thinking of it much of the time. (The Guardian Weekly 116:50 April 3, 77)

QUINN, Sally. Washington society is ruled with unwavering severity by a handful of aging widows, dowagers and old maids who subsist on fortunes inherited from robber-baron husbands or corrupt political daddies. (Atlanta 16:124 Jan 77)

RABIN, Yitzhak. For me, peace means reconciliation of the Arab countries with the existence of Israel as a Jewish state. (Newsweek 88:47 Dec 20, 76)

RADNER, Gilda. I grew up in front of a television set, and now I'm growing old inside one. (Chicago Tribune 322:3 section 6 Nov 18, 79)

RADZIWILL, Lee. I do hope to get married someday. (W 8:12 Oct 12, 79)

RAHIM, Abdur. The war (in Afghanistan) is like a good love affair. All the action happens at night. (Time 113:44 May 14, 79)

RAHV, Philip. Nothing can last in America more than ten years. (Time 110:67 Aug 15, 77)

RAILSBACK, Thomas F. I'm concerned that candidates can often be packaged like wieners, and the best-looking wiener sometimes wins. (Chicago Sun-Times 28:3 Nov 3, 75)

RAM DASS, . If I'm saving the whale, why am I eating tuna fish? (New Times 11:39 Sept 4, 78)

RAND, Ayn. The state of today's culture is so low that I do not care to spend my time watching and discussing it. (Time 107:32 Jan 12, 76)

RAND, Sally. What in heaven's name is so strange about a grandmother dancing nude? I bet lots of grandmothers do it. (Chicago Sun-Times 28:12 Dec 16, 75)

RANDALL, Tony. I knew the auto wouldn't last. (Chicago Tribune 170:14 June 19, 79)

RANDALL, Tony. People don't call you mad or eccentric if you are well-heeled. It's only when you're poor that they call you a nut.... (Chicago Tribune 170:14 June 19, 79)

RANDALL, Tony. (Television is) producing such crap that the public is going to get tired of it very, very fast. It's garbage. But crap is my real word for it. I am supposed to be an intelligent, educated man, but I can't find a better word for it. (Chicago Tribune 153:22 June 3, 78)

RANDLE, Sonny (football coach at the University of Virginia). We've stopped recruiting young men who want to come here to be students first and athletes second. (Sports Illustrated 43:12 Sept 1, 75)

RAPPOLT, Richard T. It's easier to get people off of heroin than coffee. (Rolling Stone 234:39 Mar 10, 77)

RATTIGAN, Terrence. I could never see why craftsmanship should be equated with insincerity. (The Times 8059:35 Dec 4, 77)

RATTIGAN, Terrence. What a lovely world we're in, if only we'd let ourselves see it. (Guardian Weekly 117:4 Dec 11, 77)

RAUSCHENBERG, Robert. Ideas aren't real estate; they grow collectively, and that knocks out the egotistical loneliness that generally infects art. (Time 108:60 Nov 29, 76)

RAUSCHENBERG, Robert. Painting relates to both art and life. I try to act in the gap between the two. (Chicago 26:112 Dec 77)

RAVEL, Jean-Francois. Stalinism is the essence of Communism. (Time 107:32 Feb 2, 76)

RAVENAL, James C. The American Century is over. The era of American dominance and control, heralded by Henry Luce and established in the wake of World War II, lasted only 25 years. Of course, everyone knows that it is over. But our policy-makers have not absorbed this message, and our nation has not begun to adjust to its implications and consequences. (Foreign Policy 22:89 Spring 76)

RAVITZ, Justin Charles. I understand the function of American media. Essentially, they exist to please their advertisers. (Mother Jones 2:51 Sept/Oct 77)

RAY, Dixie Lee. Anything that the private sector can do, government can do it worse. (Mother Jones 6:31 May 77)

RAY, Dixie Lee. A nuclear power plant is infinitely safer than eating, because 300 people choke to death on food every year. (Rolling Stone 235:35 Mar 24, 77)

RAY, Elizabeth. I can't type. I can't file. I can't even answer the phone. (Life 2:86 Dec 79)

RAY, Man. I have always preferred inspiration to information (commenting on photography). (ARTnews 76:52 Jan 77)

RAY, Man. I would like to go to only one funeral, mine. (Andy Warhol's Interview 7:23 Feb 76)

RAY, Man. The pursuit of liberty and the pursuit of pleasure—that takes care of my whole art. (Newsweek 88:53 Nov 29, 76)

RAY, Man. The streets are full of admirable craftsmen, but so few practical dreamers. (ARTnews 76:52 Jan 77)

RAY, Man. There is no progress in art any more than there is progress in making love. There are simply different ways of doing it. (New York Times Book Review 1 Feb 26, 78)

RAYBURN, Sam. If you want to get along, go along. (Washingtonian 14:155 Nov 78)

RAYBURN, Sam. No one has a finer command of language than the person who keeps his mouth shut. (Lawrence Daily Journal-World 120:24 Aug 29, 78)

RAYBURN, Sam. Son, always tell the truth. Then you'll never have to remember what you said the last time. (Chicago Sun-Times 32:32 June 28, 79)

RAYBURN, Sam. The three most important words in the English language are wait a minute. (Time 107:15 Aug 9, 76)

RAYBURN, Sam. A whore's vote is just as good as a debutante's. (D Magazine 6:86 June 79)

READ, David H. C. The worst sin is dullness. (Time 114:65 Dec 31, 79)

REAGAN, Maureen. I am the most vociferous of all his detractors in our family regarding his candidacy (commenting on her father's candidacy for President). (Los Angeles Times 94:2 Part 1 Nov 13, 75)

REAGAN, Nancy. I'm in favor of the death penalty—I think it saves lives. (Rolling Stone 207:30 Feb 26, 76)

REAGAN, Nancy. My life began with Ronnie. (Newsweek 86:38 Oct 13, 75)

REAGAN, Ronald. As a matter of fact, Nancy never had any interest in politics or anything else when we got married (denying charges that his wife is the real political power in the family). (Rolling Stone 219:19 Aug 12, 76)

REAGAN, Ronald. The (Carter) administration doesn't know the difference between being a diplomat and a doormat. (US News & World Report 86:54 May 7, 79)

REAGAN, Ronald. The coils woven in that city (Washington, D.C.) are entrapping us all and, as with the Gordian knot, we cannot untie it. We have to cut it with one blow of the sword. (Encore American & Worldwide News 5:4 June 21, 76)

REAGAN, Ronald. Eighty percent of air pollution comes from plants and trees. (Time 116:18 Aug 25, 80)

REAGAN, Ronald. The entire graduated-income-tax structure was created by Karl Marx. (New York 13:28 April 28, 80)

REAGAN, Ronald. Human beings are not animals, and I do not want to see sex and sexual differences treated as casually and amorally as dogs and other beasts treat them. I believe this could happen under the ERA. (Ms 4:78 Nov 75)

REAGAN, Ronald. I always grew up believing that if you build a better mousetrap, the world will beat a path to your door. Now if you build a better mousetrap the government comes along with a better mouse. (Chicago Tribune 323:1 Section 1 Nov 19, 75)

REAGAN, Ronald. I believe that government is the problem, not the answer. (Washington Post 137:A5 April 20, 76)

REAGAN, Ronald. I don't believe in the old tradition of picking someone at the opposite end of the political spectrum because he can get some votes you can't get yourself (on choosing a running mate, July 9, 1976). (Newsweek 88:14 Aug 9, 76)

REAGAN, Ronald. I don't have an ideology. I think ideology is a scare word. Ideology is Marxism and Leninism, Hitlerism or something of the kind. (Meet the Press 21:8 May 1, 77)

REAGAN, Ronald. I don't know of anyone today that has less influence in this country than business. (Washington Post 353:A14 Nov 23, 75)

REAGAN, Ronald. I don't think my positions have changed at all. (New York 13:28 April 28, 80)

REAGAN, Ronald. I finally figured out this politics. It's like show business. You start with a big opening act, coast, and close with a great crescendo. (Time 106:16 Nov 24, 75)

REAGAN, Ronald. I have included in my morning and evening prayers every day the prayer that the Federal Government not bail out New York. (Time 116:18 Aug 25, 80)

REAGAN, Ronald. I sometimes think Adam and Eve were Russians. They didn't have a roof over their head, nothing to wear, but they had one apple between them and they thought that was Paradise. (Chicago Tribune 323:1 Section 1 Nov 19, 75)

REAGAN, Ronald. I think an image has been created that I don't care about the underprivileged. Anyone who knows me knows that's not true; I'm a pushover for a hard-luck story. (Newsweek 94:21 Oct 1, 79)

REAGAN, Ronald. I worry about Kissinger. He needed someone like Nixon to keep him on that tough track. He has to have someone around who can keep him from giving away the store. (Time 106:22 Nov 17, 75)

REAGAN, Ronald. If we get the federal government out of the classroom, maybe we'll get God back in. (The Washingtonian 11:97 July 76)

REAGAN, Ronald. I'm beginning to wonder if the symbol of the United States pretty soon isn't going to be an ambassador with a flag under his arm climbing into the escape helicopter. (Time 113:11 Mar 5, 79)

REAGAN, Ronald. (In movies) I was usually the steady, sincere suitor—the one the girl finally turned to. (Time 116:14 July 28, 80)

REAGAN, Ronald. The Latin American countries have a respect for *macho.* I think if the United States reacts with firmness and fairness, we might not earn their love, but we would earn their respect. (Time 107:12 May 17, 76)

REAGAN, Ronald. Let's face it, the first enemy in Angola is obviously Ronald Reagan. (Harper's Weekly 3152:11 Jan 9, 76)

REAGAN, Ronald. Middle age is when you're faced with two temptations and you choose the one that will get you home by 9:30 (commenting on the 27th anniversary of his 39th birthday). (Washington Post 65:C6 Feb 8, 77)

REAGAN, Ronald. The minimum wage has caused more misery and unemployment than anything since the Great Depression. (Time 116:11 Sept 1, 80)

REAGAN, Ronald. Of the four wars in my lifetime, none came about because the U.S. was too strong. (The Observer 9853:12 June 29, 80)

REAGAN, Ronald. Once you've seen one redwood, you've seen them all. (New York Times Magazine 71 July 4, 76)

REAGAN, Ronald. The problem isn't a shortage of fuel, it's a surplus of government. Newsweek 94:21 Oct 1, 79

REAGAN, Ronald. Take away the arms of the citizenry and where is its defense. (Time 106:24 Nov 24, 75)

REAGAN, Ronald. This is not a campaign; it's a crusade. (Tennessean 75:7 July 16, 80)

REAGAN, Ronald. Thou shalt not criticize other Republicans. (Time 116:13 July 28, 80)

REAGAN, Ronald. Treaties invite nationalization. (Time 107:19 May 17, 76)

REAGAN, Ronald. The trouble with (the Carter) administration is that for everybody they got in, it was a step up. They never had it so good. (Time 115:16 June 30, 80)

REAGAN, Ronald. Unemployment insurance is a prepaid vacation plan for freeloaders. (Time 116:16 Aug 25, 80)

REAGAN, Ronald. We could pave the whole country and put parking stripes on it and still be home by Christmas (about winning the Vietnamese War). (New York 13:28 April 28, 80)

REAGAN, Ronald. You can vote with your feet in this country. If a state is mismanaged you can move (commenting on the possibility that some states might substitute inadequate programs for the Federal ones he would like to eliminate). (New York Times 125:1 Jan 17, 76)

REAGAN, Ronald. You know, politics has been called the second oldest profession. Sometimes there is a similarity to the first. (Chicago Tribune 323:1 Section 1 Nov 19, 75)

REASONER, Harry. Confirming my long-time nonsexist grace and courtesy, I suggest we just do it alphabetically by last names (commenting on the billing of the co-anchor news team of Harry Reasoner and Barbara Walters). (New York Times 125:63 April 23, 76)

REBOZO, Charles Gregory. Never again. (In response to the question if he plans to dabble in politics). (W 5:2 Feb 6, 76)

REDFORD, Robert. Health food may be good for the conscience, but Oreos taste a hell of a lot better. (Chicago Tribune 27:12 Jan 27, 78)

REDFORD, Robert. If you stay in Beverly Hills too long you become a Mercedes. (Time 107:58 Mar 29, 76)

REDFORD, Robert. I've always had a very low regard for cynicism; I think it is the beginning of dying. (Time 107:55 Mar 29, 76)

REDGRAVE, Vanessa. California is a place with lots of warm weather and lots of cold people. (US 1:80 June 28, 77)

REED, Lou. I'm like an Elvis Presley with brains, or Bob Dylan with looks. (Time 111:79 April 24, 78)

REEVE, Christopher. Women keep asking me if I really am Superman. My reply to them is, 'only if you're Lois Lane'. (W 7:33 Nov 10, 78)

REEVES, Richard. The GOP has been reduced to aging Sinclair Lewis characters, white Protestants, small tycoons, and shopkeepers from small places. (New York 9:8 Aug 30, 76)

REEVES, Richard. Howard Jarvis is a nut, but in my heart I know he's right. (Esquire 89:33 May 23, 78)

REEVES, Richard. I'm not enamored of his (William Safire) political viewpoint, which is sometimes to the right of Genghis Khan. But, hell, I read him because I have to. He's not predictable. (Time 110:101 Oct 3, 77)

REEVES, Richard. New Yorkers are so optimistic that there's going to be some kind of bailout. There's no such thing as a bailout. The options now are total disaster or Washington taking control of the city. It's really the beginning of the end of local government in this country. (W 4:29 Nov 14, 75)

REEVES, Richard. The people of New York have no political leader. (New York 8:33 Aug 4, 75)

REEVES, Richard. Politics is sex in a hula-hoop. (New York 9:99 June 14, 76)

REEVES, Richard. (Television is) our new environment and, like the weather, it often determines whether we stay home or not. (Esquire 89:57 April 25, 78)

REEVES, Richard. Television, of course, is dangerous. But that does not mean it is necessarily bad. (Esquire 89:57 April 25, 78)

REICH, Steve. You must love music or be a duck. (Ear 4:8 Feb 78)

REICH, Walter. If brainwashing is accepted as a defense, we're in for a brainwashing ourselves in regard to our concept of guilt and innocence (commenting on F. Lee Bailey's defense of Patricia Hearst). (New York Times 125:14 section 4 Feb 22, 76)

REINHARDT, Ad. The eyes are in the head for a reason. (Art in America 65:72 Mar/April 77)

REMARQUE, Erich Maria. Not to laugh at the 20th century is to shoot yourself. (Time 111:94 April 3, 78)

RESTON, James. Old men running for the Presidency of the United States are like old men who take young brides. It's an exciting idea for a while but it seldom works. New York Times 128:25 Jan 26, 79

RESTON, James. Washington has no memory. (The Observer 9811:9 Sept 9, 79)

REXROTH, Kenneth. The one country I feel at home in is Japan. I don't feel at home here. I don't like a country where traffic cops are armed to the teeth (commenting on life in the U.S.). (Washington Post 14:15 Dec 19, 76)

REYNOLDS, Burt. I want to lead a quiet, pseudointellectual life and go out and direct a picture two times a year. You can only hold your stomach in for so many years. (Time 111:54 Jan 9, 78)

REYNOLDS, Burt. I'm trying very subtly and subliminally to ease myself away from Billy Clyde Puckett and toward Cary Grant. I may be the most unsophisticated Cary Grant in 20 years, but I'm going to get there. (Time 111:54 Jan 9, 78)

RHODES, Frank H. T. The great universities are those in which people grow by contact with others in ever-widening circles. (Time 110:51 Nov 14, 77)

RHODES, James. They are the worst type of people we harbor in America, worse than brown shirts and the Communist element (concerning the Kent State demonstrators). (Rolling Stone 195:28 Sept 11, 75)

RHODES, John J. If the Republicans split this year I think Republicans will deserve the fate they will get, which is resounding defeat. (Meet the Press 20:3 May 9, 76)

RHODES, John J. What the hell would he (Gerald Ford) want to spend the next four years of his life as Vice President for? (Time 116:18 July 28, 80)

RHYS, Jean. If you want to write the truth, you must write about yourself. (Newsweek 93:103 May 28, 79)

RIBMAN, Ronald. Criticism is like an Indian gauntlet. One has to run through it to survive. Critics create an environment of mediocrity. (More 7:31 July/Aug 77)

RICE, Kathleen Brown. Contrary to his reputation, he is not a flake, and he does have a sense of humor (about Jerry Brown). (New York Times 128:C5 Mar 6, 79)

RICH, Lee. Public broadcasting has become a joke. They spend more time fighting with each other than they do putting shows on the air. (Emmy 1:13 Winter 79)

RICHARD, Cliff. Just because someone isn't married doesn't mean he's homosexual. (People Weekly 13:55 Feb 18, 80)

RICHARD, Ivor. The U.N. will not abolish sin, but it can make it more difficult for the sinner. (US News & World Report 87:62 Sept 17, 79)

RICHARDS, Paul. I don't communicate with players. I tell them what to do. I don't understand the meaning of communication. (New York Times 125:3 Section 5 July 11, 76)

RICHARDSON, Elliot Lee. I may be at this very moment entering the Guiness Book of Records as the most sworn-in of Americans. If I hadn't been moving so fast from place to place, I might well have become the most sworn-at of Americans. (New York Times 125:29 Feb 3, 76)

RICHARDSON, Elliot Lee. There was a time when the seas seemed endless and the skies vast enough to swallow any of the mistakes and errors of man. The world used to be big and men could afford to be small. Now the world is small and men must be big. (Reader's Digest 112:196 Feb 78)

RICHARDSON, Elliot Lee. You don't have to be Jewish to like being on the Supreme Court. (National Review 27:1330 Dec 5, 75)

RICHARDSON, Sir Ralph. You've got to perform the role hundreds of times. In keeping it fresh one can become a large, madly humming, demented refrigerator. You go mad (on being in a hit play). (Time 112:75 Aug 21, 78)

RICKOVER, Hyman G. I never start to like a man until I tell him off three or four times a day. (People Weekly 7:36 June 20, 77)

RIDGEWAY, Matthew B. Candidates are no better or worse than those who choose and elect them, and therein lies the answer to what we are to become. (American Legion Magazine 101:21 Aug 76)

RIDING, Alan. Never commit yourself fully to anyone; always leave numerous options open; be all things to all men, and, keep your true sentiments well hidden (rule number 1 of long-term survival in Mexican politics). (New York Times Magazine 130 Sept 16, 79)

RIEGLE, Donald. Henry Kissinger is pregnant with America's foreign policy, and we're all waiting for him to give birth. (Potomac (Sunday Magazine of the Washington Post) 4 Feb 8, 76)

RIESMAN, David. The question is not whether leadership is obsolete but whether democracy is governable. (Time 114:26 Aug 6, 79)

RIESMAN, David. The road to the board room leads through the locker room. (Time 111:59 June 26, 78)

RIFKIND, Simon. (Judicial) impartiality is an acquired taste, like olives. You have to be habituated to it. (Time 114:49 Aug 20, 79)

RIGGS, Bobby. Gals are super, but I haven't changed my opinion of them: I still like them best in the bedroom and the kitchen. (Playboy 25:102 May 78)

RIMBAUD, Arthur. My greatest fear is that people will see me as I see them. (Newsweek 83:103 Mar 25, 74)

RINFRET, Pierre A. Consensus is the security blanket of the insecure. (Challenge 19:42 May/June 76)

RINGER, Barbara A. The basic human rights of individual authors throughout the world are being sacrificed more and more on the altar of the technological revolution. (American Legion Magazine 99:21 Dec 75)

RINGER, Robert. The women behind the (women's liberation) movement want the same thing all group leaders want and have wanted through history: ego assuagement. (Playboy 25:110 May 78)

RITTER, John. Luckily, as an actor I can still be an adolescent. (People 11:32 June 11, 79)

RIVERS, Joan. My favorite city in the world is New York. Sure it's dirty—but like a beautiful lady smoking a cigar. (Reader's Digest 113:266 Nov 78)

RIVERS, Larry. Is photography art? Art is everything. (Andy Warhol's Interview 7:12 Nov 75)

RIZZO, Frank Lazzaro. A conservative is a liberal who was mugged the night before. (American Opinion 18:29 Nov 75)

RIZZO, Frank Lazzaro. If you want fiction, read the news pages; if you want facts, read the comic pages. (Philadelphia 69:253 Nov 78)

RIZZO, Frank Lazzaro. Just wait, after November you'll have a front row seat because I'm gonna make Attila the Hun look like a faggot (to several friends). (Philadelphia Magazine 66:118 Oct 75)

RIZZO, Frank Lazzaro. Male chauvinist? I'm sure that title don't fit me because I was a leader with men. (Los Angeles Times 96:2 part 1 Oct 10, 77)

RIZZO, Frank Lazzaro. The streets are safe in Philadelphia. It's only the people who make them unsafe (when asked his opinion on crime in the streets). (Los Angeles Times 96:2 part 1 Oct 10, 77)

RIZZO, Frank Lazzaro. This city could never pay Frank Rizzo back for what I've done—slept on floors, no holidays, no vacation. I knew I was the difference between destruction and disorder. (Time 113:66 June 25, 79)

RIZZO, Frank Lazzaro. We need excellence in public education and if the teachers can't do it, we'll send in a couple of policemen. (Time 110:40 Oct 24, 77)

RIZZO, Frank Lazzaro. When I see the American flag, my blood still runs cold. (New York Times 128:29 section 2 Jan 21, 79)

ROBBINS, Harold. I'm the best novelist in the world. (Book Digest 7:22 Aug 80)

ROBERTS, Dale. He is a man of letters—all of them lower case. (Writer's Digest 58:11 Oct 78)

ROBESON, Paul. American democracy is Hitler Fascism. (Newsweek 86:58 Oct 6, 75)

ROBESON, Paul (attributed by John E. Mitchell). My problem is not to counteract the white man's prejudice against the Negro. That does not matter. I have set myself to educate my brother to believe in himself. (Time 107:5 Feb 23, 76)

ROBINSON, Frank. It's nice to come into town and be referred to as the manager of the Cleveland Indians instead of as the first black manager. (Sepia 26:10 Jan 76)

ROCHBERG, George. The business of art is to praise God. (Newsweek 93:73 Feb 19, 79)

ROCKEFELLER, David. Although I work downtown, my family does have something of a stake in a small parcel of land which abuts Fifth Avenue (commenting on Rockefeller Center and his ties to the Fifth Avenue area in New York City). (New York Times 126:A13 Oct 22, 76)

ROCKEFELLER, David. Basically I operate on the principle that you should never do something for yourself that you can get someone else to do for you. (Penthouse 12:64 Oct 80)

ROCKEFELLER, David. One of the great threats to the banking system is excessive disclosure. If banks are required to disclose information on the financial condition of the people we loan money to, this could be very embarrassing and seriously hurtful to our customers. It could make banks so cautious that we wouldn't loan money to anybody except to the triple-A, blue-chip customer. (People Weekly 5:29 May 24, 76)

ROCKEFELLER, John Davison. A friendship founded on business is better than a business founded on friendship. (Kansas City Times 109:12H Dec 9, 76)

ROCKEFELLER, John Davison, III. I don't have a whole lot of faith in what the oil companies say. (Time 114:61 July 16, 79)

ROCKEFELLER, John Davison, III. The name Rockefeller does not connote a revolutionary, and my life situation has fostered a careful, cautious attitude that verges on conservatism. I am not given to errant causes. (Newsweek 92:38 July 24, 78)

ROCKEFELLER, John Davison III (attributed by an aide). I am too rich to steal. (Time 110:81 Oct 24, 77)

ROCKEFELLER, Nelson Aldrich. After much thought, I have decided further that I do not wish my name to enter into your consideration for the upcoming Republican Vice-Presidential nominee (letter to President Ford). (New York Times 125:26 Nov 4, 75)

ROCKEFELLER, Nelson Aldrich. Being a Rockefeller is like living in a goldfish bowl. The goldfish get used to it and so do we. (New York Times 128:26 Jan 28, 79)

ROCKEFELLER, Nelson Aldrich. The best part about being Vice President is presiding over the Senate. Where else could I have Barry Goldwater addressing me as 'Mr. President?'. (Time 106:10 Sept 29, 75)

ROCKEFELLER, Nelson Aldrich. Congressional actions in the past few years, however well intentioned, have hamstrung the presidency and usurped the presidential prerogative in the conduct of foreign affairs. (Christian Science Monitor 68:2 May 11, 76)

ROCKEFELLER, Nelson Aldrich. Free enterprise is the greatest and most productive system man has ever created. In a modest way, I have been a beneficiary. (Los Angeles Times 95:2 Part 1 Dec 7, 75)

ROCKEFELLER, Nelson Aldrich. I don't think I'm cut out to be a number 2 type of guy. (Newsweek 93:29 Feb 5, 79)

ROCKEFELLER, Nelson Aldrich. I think the Republican Party is only going to be an effective party if it reflects the best interests of the American people, and traditionally that is in the center. That is where our country has always been. That is where the Republican Party has won. (Time 106:19 Nov 17, 75)

ROCKEFELLER, Nelson Aldrich. I would like to apologize to the Senate of the United States, to its members, and particularly to Senator Jackson for my remarks in an off-the-record meeting. There is no question it was a mistake (apologizing for suggesting that two members of Senator Henry M. Jackson's staff had Communist ties). (New York Times 125:19 April 28, 76)

ROCKEFELLER, Nelson Aldrich. It depends on who you're talking to. If you're talking to the head of the KGB and you happen to be overheard, and you're Jane Fonda or somebody else, there's no reason you shouldn't be overheard if somebody has the capability to overhear you—which I don't know if they do or not (commenting on electronic surveillance by the National Security Agency). (Rolling Stone 201:32 Dec 4, 75)

ROCKEFELLER, Nelson Aldrich. It's already too late to do anything about it (South Vietnam). I guess a lot of Vietnamese are going to die. For us, we go on living. (Time 105:6 July 28, 75)

ROCKEFELLER, Nelson Aldrich. The President (Gerald Ford) is an awfully nice person. He is not by nature a gut fighter. He hasn't had to be. He has been a reconciler. (ABC News Issues and Answers 2 May 2, 76)

ROCKNE, Knute. You show me a good and gracious loser, and I'll show you a failure! (Argosy 384:15 Nov 76)

ROCKWELL, Geo. Making something perfectly clear only confuses everybody. (Down East 22:108 Jan 76)

RODGERS, Richard. When the lyrics are right, it's easier for me to write a tune than to bend over and tie my shoelaces. Time 115:83 Jan 14, 80

RODIA, Simon. I had in mind to do something big and I did (about the Watts Towers). (Travel & Leisure 8:67 Oct 78)

RODRIGUEZ, Chi Chi. After all these years it's still embarrassing for me to play on the American golf tour. Like the time I asked my caddie for a sand wedge and he comes back 10 minutes later with a ham on rye (commenting on his Puerto Rican Spanish accent). (Sports Illustrated 44:8 Mar 8, 76)

ROEMER, Michael. You can't learn to die as though it were a skill. People die in the way they have lived. Death becomes the expression of everything you are, and you can bring to it only what you have brought to your life. (Time 107:69 May 3, 76)

ROGERS, Ginger. If you don't stand for something, you will stand for anything. (Parade 9 June 18, 78)

ROGERS, Will. Any man who thinks civilization has advanced is an egoist. (Time 104:92 Oct 7, 74)

ROGERS, Will. Everything is funny as long as it is happening to somebody else. (Kansas City Star 97:2A April 10, 77)

ROGERS, Will. There is good news from Washington today. The Congress is deadlocked and can't act. Newsweek 85:23 June 9, 75

ROGERS, Will. The trouble with practical jokes is that very often they get elected. Rocky Mountain News 36:50 May 28, 80

ROGERS, William D. Making foreign policy is a little bit like making pornographic movies. It's more fun doing it than watching it. (Chicago Sun-Times 29:9 June 29, 76)

ROHATYN, Felix. I feel like somebody who tries to check into a hospital and keeps getting referred to the cemetery (about New York funding problems). (Time 106:10 Nov 10, 75)

ROHATYN, Felix. We ought to change the sign on the Statue of Liberty to read, 'this time around, send us your rich'. (Newsweek 92:88 Nov 27, 78)

ROLLINS, Sonny. Music is an open sky. (Soho Weekly News 6:27 Nov 2, 78)

ROMERO, Oscar Arnulfo. They can kill me, but the voice of justice will never be stilled. (Newsweek 95:47 April 7, 80)

RONSTADT, Linda. I'm so disorganized, what I really need is a good wife. (People Weekly 4:54 Nov 17, 75)

ROONEY, Mickey. Be friends first. If you say 'I love you' in the beginning, it's like using your three best jokes at the start of your act. You have nowhere to go from there (advice on how to ensure a happy marriage). (Los Angeles Times 97:2 part 1 Sept 4, 78)

ROONEY, Mickey. I'm the only man who has a marriage license made out To Whom It May Concern. (Time 114:104 Oct 29, 79)

ROONEY, Mickey. A lot of people have asked me how short I am. Since my last divorce, I think I'm about $100,000 short. (Chicago Sun-Times 31:6 June 22, 78)

ROOSEVELT, Eleanor. No one can make you feel inferior without your consent. (San Francisco Chronicle This World 1978:40 Jan 29, 78)

ROOSEVELT, Franklin Delano. Government has the definite duty to use all its power and resources to meet new social problems with new social controls. (Newsweek 92:27 Nov 27, 78)

ROOSEVELT, Franklin Delano. If you treat people right they will treat you right—90 percent of the time. (Kansas City Times 109:14C Jan 14, 77)

ROOSEVELT, Franklin Delano. Nothing just happens in politics. If something happens you can be sure it was planned that way. (Oui 7:107 May 78)

ROOSEVELT, Franklin Delano. The only way to do anything in the American government is to bypass the Senate (returning from Yalta). (Chicago Tribune 147:2 section 2 May 29, 77)

ROOSEVELT, Franklin Delano. Our true destiny is not to be ministered unto but to minister to ourselves and to our fellow men (inaugural address—1933). (Christian Science Monitor 69:14 Jan 20, 77)

ROOSEVELT, Franklin Delano. When you get to the end of your rope, tie a knot and hang on. (Kansas City Star 97:2F June 5, 77)

ROOSEVELT, James. My uncle Teddy stole it, my father Franklin kept it going, and as far as I'm concerned they can now give it back (commenting on the Panama Canal). (Rolling Stone 262:36 April 6, 78)

ROOSEVELT, Theodore. All the great masterful races have been fighting races. (Newsweek 93:84 April 2, 79)

ROOSEVELT, Theodore. Black care rarely sits behind a rider whose pace is fast enough. (Time 113:81 April 9, 79)

ROREM, Ned. I have suffered far less from being a homosexual than I have from being a composer. (People Weekly 10:40 Aug 21, 78)

ROSE, Don. One of the reasons I have been in politics so long is to see that there are no more Donovans. (Chicago Sun-Times 32:3 Mar 1, 79)

ROSE, Pete. Singles hitters drive Fords. Home-run hitters drive Cadillacs. (New West 4:116 April 9, 79)

ROSE, Richard. Even an atheist must be a Protestant atheist or Catholic atheist in order to have status in the society (commenting on life in Northern Ireland). (Time 104:30 Dec 30, 74)

ROSENBERG, Harold. In linking art to the modern consciousness, no artist is more relevant than Steinberg. (Time 111:92 April 17, 78)

ROSENBERG, Harold. Steinberg's art is a parade of fictitious personages, geometric shapes, items of household equipment, personified furniture, each staged in a fiction of what it is—or in a dream of being something else. (Esquire 89:82 April 25, 78)

ROSENBLOOM, Carroll. I never did really care for working. I don't know why anyone would work if they didn't have to. (Esquire 90:112 Nov 21, 78)

ROSENFIELD, Paul. (Tuesday Weld is) too much a '60's character to be a 70's star, but she'll always work: When they need an eccentric, they call Tuesday. (Chicago Tribune 22:1 section 5 Jan 22, 78)

ROSENTHAL, A. M. I don't care if you screw an elephant, just don't cover the circus. (New West 4:17 Mar 26, 79)

ROSENTHAL, Arthur J. If I had a book on the bestseller list I'd suspect I was doing something wrong (commenting on his role as director of the Harvard University Press). (New York Times 125:33 June 30, 76)

ROSENTHAL, Benjamin. Kissinger prefers to deal with great men and world leaders, partly because it makes for better history writing. But he must deal with Congress because we reflect the will of the American people. (Time 105:13 Mar 10, 75)

ROSSELLINI, Roberto. I believe that the cinema has failed in its mission of being the art of our century. (Newsweek 89:75 July 13, 77)

ROSSINI, Gioacchino. Give me a laundry list, and I will set it to music. (Time 112:97 Oct 9, 78)

ROSSITER, Clinton. The essence of (Franklin) Roosevelt's Presidency was his airy eagerness to meet the age head on. (Time 114:11 July 16, 79)

ROSSY, Paul (former vice chairman, Swiss Banking Commission). God, after all, created Switzerland for one purpose—to be the clearinghouse of the world. (Time 110:74 July 18, 77)

ROSTEN, Leo. Any man who hates dogs and babies can't be all bad (about W. C. Fields). (TV Guide 26:29 Dec 30, 78)

ROSTROPOVICH, Mstislav. The cello is like an imperfect woman whom you love for her imperfections. Through the cello I can speak with my own personal voice, without intermediaries between me and the audience. (Newsweek 40:75 Oct 17, 77)

ROSTROPOVICH, Mstislav. I don't even know why my hands do certain things sometimes. They just grab for the notes. (Time 110:83-84 Oct 24, 77)

ROSTROPOVICH, Mstislav. Music and art are a whole spiritual world in Russia. In Russia when people go to a concert, they don't go to it as an attraction, as an entertainment, but to feel life. (New York Times Magazine 15 April 18, 76)

ROSTROPOVICH, Mstislav. When I play for an audience, I feel that I am making my confession to those people. (New York Times Magazine 66 April 18, 76)

ROTH, Philip. The road to hell is paved with works-in-progress. (New York Times Book Review 1 July 15, 79)

ROTH, Philip. When you publish a book, it's the world's book. The world edits it. (New York Times Book Review 13 Sept 2, 79)

ROTH, William V., Jr. Public confidence and trust in the federal government are low not only because of Watergate or our experience in Vietnam, but also because too many politicians have promised more than the government can deliver. (Chicago Tribune 311:1 Section 1 Nov 7, 75)

ROTHKO, Mark. There is no such thing as a good painting about nothing. (Texas Monthly 7:166 April 79)

ROTHSCHILD, Emma. For the last 20 years, America's influence on Europe has had more to do with food and animal feed than with high politics or low diplomacy. (New York Times 127:19 section E April 16, 78)

ROTHSCHILD, Marie-Helene De. I'm not a bit ashamed of being rich. I think it's very healthy to have big parties now and again, like they did in history. Time 105:48 June 9, 75

ROWAN, Carl. Carter turned out to be not a populist but a small-town businessman. Time 115:73 June 9, 80

ROWEN, Phyllis. When you grow as a designer, you realize that nothing is forever. (Architectural Digest 32:122 Nov/Dec 75)

ROWSE, A. L. I've always thought of myself as a parallel to D.H. Lawrence. (The Times 8062:35 Jan 1, 78)

ROWSE, A. L. Most people's opinions are of no value at all. (The Observer 9809:10 Aug 26, 79)

ROWSE, A. L. This filthy 20th century. I hate its guts. (Time 112:K9 Nov 13, 78)

ROYKO, Mike. Daley is quite good at getting himself elected, but beyond that, he's not much of a political genius anymore. (Newsweek 88:35 Nov 22, 76)

ROYKO, Mike. The motto of the (Chicago) City Council is: never do today what somebody else can do today or tomorrow. (Chicago Sun-Times 32:2 Nov 26, 78)

ROYSTER, Vermont. When things go wrong somewhere, they are apt to go wrong everywhere. (Washingtonian 14:155 Nov 78)

ROZELLE, Pete. Sporting events give people time off from the problems of the world. (US News & World Report 85:62 Oct 16, 78)

ROZELLE, Pete. The world knows no less rational person than a losing bettor (commenting in opposition to efforts to legalize betting on professional football). (Time 108:69 Sept 20, 76)

RUBIN, Jerry. I'm famous. That's my job. (Christian Science Monitor 68:30 April 26, 76)

RUBIN, Jerry. Most men act so tough and strong on the outside because on the inside, we are scared, weak, and fragile. Men, not women, are the weaker sex. (Chicago Tribune 75:24 Mar 16, 78)

RUBINSTEIN, Artur. Composing a concert is like composing a menu. I believe in musical digestion. (Time 113:52 April 9, 79)

RUBINSTEIN, Artur. I need to be surrounded by (beautiful women). They don't have to be anything special, I can enjoy looking at the legs of a stupid woman. (People Weekly 3:66 April 21, 75)

RUBINSTEIN, Artur. I'm not a drug fiend, I'm not a drunkard, but I am the laziest man I ever met. (Time 105:39 Feb 10, 75)

RUBINSTEIN, Artur. Most people ask for happiness on condition. Happiness can only be felt if you don't set any condition. (Kansas City Star 97:15C Sept 22, 76)

RUBINSTEIN, Artur. To get as old as I am (91) one must drink a glass of whiskey every morning, smoke a long cigar and chase beautiful girls. (People Weekly 10:144 Nov 20, 78)

RUBINSTEIN, Artur. When I was young I used to have successes with women because I was young. Now I have successes with women because I am old. Middle age was the hard part. (Chicago Tribune 37:1 section 2 Feb 6, 78)

RUBINSTEIN, Artur. You can't generalize about art. A man has no right to the title of artist if he can be compared to another. A condition of the artist is to be a unique personality. (Chicago Tribune Magazine 18 Jan 23, 77)

RUBINSTEIN, Michael. The ultimate blasphemy must be censorship. (The Observer 9701:13 July 17, 77)

RUCKELSHAUS, Jill. It occurred to me when I was 13 and wearing white gloves and Mary Janes and going to dancing school, that no one should have to dance backwards all their lives. (Chicago Sun-Times 30:21 Jan 28, 78)

RUCKELSHAUS, Jill. When you write stories about the women's movement now, don't look for us in the street. We have gone to the statehouse (to the National Press Club). (Time 107:15 Jan 5, 76)

RUDA, Edwin (Artist). I find it incredible that after 25,000 years of art and 5,000 years of written history—after all that visual hindsight and explication—the gulf between image and word persists the way it does. Only 25 years ago abstract painters were being asked why they painted the way they did; now the question seems to be: why paint at all? (Artforum 14:33-34 Sept 75)

RUDKIN, David. The play should liberate itself from the personal origins of the author. (Village Voice 22:89 June 27, 77)

RUE, Arnold. I'm always suspicious about anyone from Texas who talks about energy (about John Connally). (New York Times 128:D18 June 12, 79)

RUMI (SUFI MYSTIC), . Men's minds perceive second causes, but only prophets perceive the action of the First Cause. (Human Behavior 7:33 May 78)

RUMSFELD, Donald. The absence of a reprimand should not be taken as an endorsement of inelegant phraseology (commenting at a Pentagon news conference on the controversial statements of General George S. Brown). (New York Times 126:26 Oct 19, 76)

RUMSFELD, Donald. If you try to please everybody, somebody is not going to like it. (The Washingtonian 12:107 Feb 77)

RUNYON, Damon. All life is six-to-five against. (New York 9:36 Nov 1, 76)

RUNYON, Damon. Man's only weapon against a woman is his hat. He should grab it and run. (Viva 4:28 April 77)

RUNYON, Damon. The race is not always to the swift, nor the battle to the strong, but that's the way to bet. (Omni 1:131 May 79)

RUSK, Dean. Americans have a way of doing at the end of the day what they don't want to do at noon. (Time 110:95 Nov 21, 77)

RUSK, Dean. I don't believe in a code of ethics in the journalism profession, and I don't believe in equal time between the media. If there are abuses toward freedom of the press, then let us correct them thru free speech. (Los Angeles Times 94:2 Part 1 Oct 26, 75)

RUSSELL, Bertrand. I believe myself that romantic love is the source of the most intense delights that life has to offer. (Chicago Tribune 212:1 section II July 31, 78)

RUSSELL, John Robert (Duke of Bedford). You Americans have this lovely notion about English royalty. You think the prince marries the princess and they go off to live happily ever after in a beautiful castle. In reality the prince is trying to get that lovely 300-year-old roof to stop leaking. (People Weekly 5:60 May 24, 76)

RUSSELL, Mark. President Ford has thrown the word detente out, and I'm glad he did, because nobody could define it in the first place. Except me. Detente is like going to a wife-swapping party and coming home alone. (Chicago Tribune Magazine 193:20-21 July 11, 76)

RUSSELL, Rosalind. Flops are a part of life's menu, and I'm never a girl to miss out on any of the courses. (Time 108:102 Dec 13, 76)

RYAN, Cornelius. The mathematics of self-pity can be raised to infinity. (Time 114:83 Aug 6, 79)

RYAN, Eddie. The amount of time it takes to deliver a letter is directly proportional to the price of the stamp. (Omni 1:132 May 79)

RYAN, John. Bribes are just bad business. (Mother Jones 2:50 July 77)

RYKIEL, Sonia. Every woman must create her own ambience; it is not I or Yves St. Laurent but the woman who has to create herself and be a unique person. (Time 110:54 Nov 7, 77)

RYOR, John (National Education Association president). It's just about as useless as a back pocket in a shirt (commenting on the value of the U.S. Office of Education). (Chicago Sun-Times 29:2 Nov 10, 76)

RYUN, Jim. Christ spoke to me. He said I had fought a good fight, run a good race and it was finished (commenting on how he decided to retire). (New York Times 125:5 Section 5 Mar 7, 76)

SADAT, Anwar. The approach of Carter is really something like mine. He is a villager, he is also at ease, and he is also a true believer. (Esquire 91:33 Jan 30, 79)

SADAT, Anwar. The dogs can go on barking—but they will not stop the caravan (about Arab critics of the Egypt-Israeli Peace Treaty). (Time 113:22 May 28, 79)

SADAT, Anwar. I am really startled till this moment that the barrier of distrust that has been between us (Egypt and Israel) during the last 30 years has been broken down in 35 hours. Amazing. Really. (Time 111:31 Jan 2, 78)

SADAT, Anwar. I have dealt with three presidents, Nixon, Ford and this Carter. I can say that everything is improving. (Time 111:32 Jan 2, 78)

SADAT, Anwar. I like the way Americans put their feet up on the desk. (Time 111:27 Jan 2, 78)

SADAT, Anwar. No one ever knows what I am thinking, not even my own family. I go alone. (Time 111:22 Jan 2, 78)

SADAT, Anwar. The Russians had a Central Committee meeting last summer and decided they could support me but never trust me. I said that was okay—I couldn't trust them either. (Los Angeles Times 94:5 Part 2 Nov 4, 75)

SADAT, Anwar. They wanted to exert pressure and to bring me to my knees, but I don't go down on my knees except before God Almighty (speaking about the Soviet Union). (New York Times 125:1 Mar 15, 76)

SADLOWSKI, Ed. I guess maybe I'm a romantic, but I look on the American labor movement as a holy crusade, which should be the dominant force in this country to fight for the workingman and the underdog and make this a more just society. (New York Times Magazine 33 Dec 19, 76)

SADLOWSKI, Ed. There's a fire in the steelworkers union, and I'm not gonna piss on it. (Rolling Stone 202:48 Dec 18, 75)

SAFFIOTTI, Umberto. Cancer in the last quarter of the 20th century can be considered a social disease, a disease whose causation and control are rooted in the technology and economy of our society. (Time 106:67 Oct 20, 75)

SAFIRE, William. Gerald Ford's Presidency was unique in this century for not producing a single memorable phrase. (New York Times Magazine 90 Nov 19, 78)

SAFIRE, William. I think that one of Nixon's great contributions to civil liberties was getting caught doing what the two presidents before him got away with. (Book Digest 4:28 July 77)

SAFIRE, William. (Jimmy Carter is) the best U.S. President the Soviet Union ever had. (Time 114:116 Nov 19, 79)

SAFIRE, William. My business (is) writing informed polemics—with a satisfying zap. (Newsweek 93:94 April 23, 79)

SAHL, Mort. In the forties, to get a girl you had to be a GI or a jock. In the fifties, to get a girl you had to be Jewish. In the sixties, to get a girl you had to be black. In the seventies, to get a girl you've got to be a girl. (Chicago 26:77 April 77)

SAHL, Mort. The more you stay the same, the more they say you've changed. (Newsweek 92:16 Dec 11, 78)

SAINT JAMES, Margo. (We've already) got legalized prostitution: marriage. (Washington Post 138:B7 April 21, 76)

SAINT JOHN, Adela Rogers. Poor little man, they made him out of lemon Jello and there he is. He's honest and he's hard-working. But he's not great (commenting on Robert Redford). (Chicago Sun-Times 29:8 Oct 26, 76)

SAINT LAURENT, Yves. Fashions fade, style is eternal. (Andy Warhol's Interview 5:13 April 75)

SAINT LAURENT, Yves. Haute couture is opera. It is dreams and phantoms and magic. (Time 110:47 Aug 8, 77)

SAIQUA (PALESTINIAN ORGANIZATION), . Sadat has committed the ugliest treason in the history of the Arab nation, so the blood of the traitor must be shed. He will be followed to the farthest corners of the world until his death sentence is carried out (upon Anwar Sadat's visit to Israel). (Chicago Tribune 325:2 section 1 Nov 21, 77)

SAKATA, Michita. Security is like sun, water or air. When they are plentiful you don't appreciate their value. (Newsweek 86:53 Oct 6, 75)

SAKHAROV, Andrei Dmitrievich. Every spectator or athlete who comes to the Olympics will be giving indirect support to Soviet military policies. (New York Times Magazine 31 June 8, 80)

SAKHAROV, Andrei Dmitrievich. I hope this prize is not only an acknowledgement of my personal merits, but of the merits of all those who fight for human rights (commenting on his Nobel Peace Prize). (People Weekly 4:26 Oct 27, 75)

SAKHAROV, Andrei Dmitrievich. I regard this as a challenge to world public opinion. I have always been trusted and I do not believe there are grounds to think that I have committed a state crime (upon the denial of permission to travel to Oslo, Norway to receive the Nobel Peace Prize). (Los Angeles Times 94:16 Part 1 Nov 13, 75)

SAKHAROV, Andrei Dmitrievich. Thermonuclear warfare has already become a dark reality of modern times, like Auschwitz, the Gulag and Famine. (Time 106:44 Oct 20, 75)

SAKHAROV, Andrei Dmitrievich. To keep one's self-respect, one must act in accordance with the general human longing for peace, for true detente, for genuine disarmament (in his message accepting the Nobel Peace Prize). (New York Times 125:10 Dec 11, 75)

SALANT, Richard S. In view of the adversary situation in which Dan Schorr is placed in pending government investigations, he has agreed with CBS that he will be relieved of all reporting duties for an indefinite period. (Los Angeles Times 83:10 Part 1 Feb 24, 76)

SALINGER, J. D. Some of my best friends are children. In fact, all of my best friends are children. (Washington Star 323:1 section D Nov 19, 78)

SALK, Jonas. The best thing to do (for people worried about cancer-causing substances) is quit reading the newspaper. (Chicago Sun-Times 29:54 Mar 17, 76)

SALMORE, Stephen. In the 1960s, the burden of proof against change rested with those accepting the status quo. In the 1970s, the burden of proof rests with those who want change. (US News & World Report 84:25 Jan 23, 78)

SAMUELS, John S., III. Texas is sort of an opera. (New York Times 128:17 section 2 Jan 21, 79)

SANCHEZ, Robert. In looking backward, we must renew our faith in God. In looking forward, we must renew our faith in men. (National Catholic Reporter 12:8 July 2, 76)

SANDBURG, Carl. A baby is God's opinion that the world should go on. (Kansas City Star 97:2D Feb 20, 77)

SANDBURG, Carl. Life is like an onion: you peel it off one layer at a time and sometimes you weep. (San Francisco Chronicle This World 1978:40 Jan 29, 78)

SANDBURG, Carl. Ordering a man to write a poem is like commanding a pregnant woman to give birth to a redheaded child. You can't do it—it's an act of God. (Reader's Digest 112:189 Feb 78)

SANDBURG, Carl. Slang is language that takes off its coat, spits on its hands, and goes to work. (Kansas City Times 109:17C July 15, 77)

SANDERS, Ed. Just because you're paranoid doesn't mean they're not trying to get you. (The Reader (Chicago's Free Weekly) 7:4 section 1 April 7, 78)

SANDERSEN, Ann. When I'm in New York I'm homesick for Aspen, and when I'm in Aspen I'm homesick for Aspen. (Outside 1:25 Sept/Oct 78)

SANTAYANA, George. Fanatics are those people who know what they are doing is what God would be doing if He only had all the facts. (Time 112:94 Oct 9, 78)

SANTAYANA, George. Our dignity is not in what we do, but in what we understand. (Kansas City Star 97:4B Oct 10, 76)

SANTAYANA, George. Sometimes we have to change the truth in order to remember it. Time 106:57 July 28, 75

SARAGAT, Giuseppe. Along-side the body of (Aldo) Moro lies the body of the first Italian republic. (Time 111:32 May 22, 78)

SAROYAN, William. I would rather write, even pompously, than celebrate meaninglessness. (New York Times Book Review 20 July 15, 79)

SAROYAN, William. 1977 was one hell of a year. I didn't die. (People Weekly 9:94 Jan 23, 78)

SARRIS, Andrew. We New Yorkers are the most naive and provincial people in the world to put so much faith not in princes and priests, but in a mere publication (about the New York Times). (Village Voice 20:63 Aug 11, 75)

SARTRE, Jean-Paul. We can only see the somber recesses in our selves if we try to become transparent to others. (Chicago Tribune 282:4 section 7 Oct 9, 77)

SASSOON, Vidal. I call myself a lucky barber. (The Observer 9786:10 Mar 18, 79)

SAVALAS, Telly. I am a loud, extraverted friendly person, but never rude. (Time 107:38 June 28, 76)

SAVITCH, Jessica. The thing you need most in this business (TV journalism) is stamina. (Ms 8:86 Aug 79)

SAVORY, Allen (former Rhodesian MP). The prime minister (Ian Smith) has the rare ability to make people believe things they know for a fact are untrue. (People Weekly 5:46 June 7, 76)

SAWYER, Charles. The United States, like Atlas, is holding up the world. But who holds up Atlas? American business. (Time 113:85 April 23, 79)

SCAMMON, Richard. There's nothing wrong with the Republican Party that double-digit inflation won't cure. (Guardian Weekly 119:17 Nov 12, 78)

SCHAFLY, Phyllis. The atomic bomb is a marvelous gift given to America by a wise god. (The Times 8142:8 July 13, 80)

SCHARY, Dore. Critics are like mayors of New York; nobody really wants to like them. (More 7:31 July/Aug 77)

SCHEER, Robert. The journalist's job is to get the story by breaking into their offices, by bribing, by seducing people, by lying, by anything else to break through that palace guard. (Time 107:56 April 4, 77)

SCHEUCH, Erwin. (Helmut) Schmidt is an above-average average German. (Time 113:32 June 11, 79)

SCHINDLER, Rabbi Alexander. The world isn't used to your (Jimmy Carter's) open diplomacy. It stiffens the back of Israel and raises the expectations of the Arabs, which, once frustrated, will retard rather than bring peace.   (Time 110:11 July 18, 77)

SCHLAFLY, Phyllis. Ask yourself: When you are rescued from the third floor of a burning building, do you want to be carried down the ladder by a man or a woman?   (National NOW Times 11:6 Aug 78)

SCHLAFLY, Phyllis. 'Equal parenting' does not work—the maternal tuning in never turns off.   (National NOW Times 11:6 Aug 78)

SCHLAFLY, Phyllis. What's so wrong about that (baby-selling)? If I hadn't been blessed with babies of my own, I would have been happy to have paid thousands of dollars for a baby (commenting in support of the decriminalization of baby-selling).   (Ms 6:50 July 77)

SCHLESINGER, Arthur, Jr. Chappaquiddick is to Kennedy what polio was to FDR. It will make him a better President.   (Chicago Sun-Times 32:6 July 20, 79)

SCHLESINGER, Arthur, Jr. 'Gay' used to be one of the most agreeable words in the language. Its appropriation by a notably morose group is an act of piracy.   (Time 111:36 Jan 2, 78)

SCHLESINGER, Arthur, Jr. The higher loyalty, it has always seemed to me, is to truth, public enlightenment, and history.   (Atlantic 244:28 Aug 79)

SCHLESINGER, Arthur, Jr. History can be a high-risk occupation.   (The Observer 9769:13 Nov 19, 78)

SCHLESINGER, Arthur, Jr. I will support the Democratic ticket, but actually I think they're both a couple of stiffs (commenting on the 1976 Democratic and Republican candidates).   (W 5:14 Nov 12-19, 76)

SCHLESINGER, Arthur, Jr. If it is necessary for a biographer of Robert Kennedy to regard him as evil, then I am not qualified to be his biographer.   (Time 112:74 Sept 4, 78)

SCHLESINGER, Arthur, Jr. It is evident that what pretends to be a Democratic administration has deliberately and methodically chosen Republican policies.   (Washington Post 102:3 June 24, 79)

SCHLESINGER, Arthur, Jr. John Kennedy was a realist brilliantly disguised as a romantic; Robert Kennedy, a romantic stubbornly disguised as a realist.   (Newsweek 92:78 Sept 4, 78)

SCHLESINGER, Arthur, Jr. One attacked injustices because he found them irrational; the other because he found them unbearable (about John and Robert Kennedy).   (New York Times 128:A23 Nov 23, 78)

SCHLESINGER, James Rodney. The American role in maintaining a worldwide military balance is better understood in Moscow than it is in this country.   (American Legion Magazine 98:20 Jan 75)

SCHLESINGER, James Rodney. Any time the President of the United States asks one to do a job that's doable, it's one's obligation to do it (explanation of why he agreed to help create a national energy policy).   (Time 107:60 April 4, 77)

SCHLESINGER, James Rodney. I would sleep right near the nuclear plant; there is no question about that. It is a comfortable neighbor (affirming his confidence in the safety of nuclear power).   (New York Times 126:40 July 11, 77)

SCHLESINGER, James Rodney. They (the oil companies) are just as much victims of the shortage as we are; indeed, more the victims.   (Chicago Sun-Times 32:64 June 14, 79)

SCHMIDT, Helmut. He (Jimmy Carter) is making (foreign) policy from the pulpit.   (Time 107:14 May 9, 77)

SCHMIDT, Helmut. Talking with him (Ludwig Erhard) is like trying to nail Jell-O to the wall.   (Time 113:32 June 11, 79)

SCHMIDT, Helmut. We Germans are in the heart of Europe. In any new war, we have everything to lose and nothing to gain.   (Newsweek 96:37 July 14, 80)

SCHMITT, Harrison. Space represents the kind of resource for the human spirit that North America was three hundred years ago: a new stimulus for the spirit of freedom.   (Omni 2:82 June 80)

SCHNEIDERS, Greg. For all his flaws and faults, as a manager he (Nixon) did a good job.   (Washingtonian 13:11 Nov 77)

SCHNEIDERS, Greg. He (Jimmy Carter) is the opposite of macho. He's soft on the outside and hard on the inside.   (Washington Post 352:B3 Nov 19, 76)

SCHORR, Alvin (director of New York City's Community Service Society). Poor people are losing more money to which they are entitled by law because of callous and hostile welfare administration than they are getting from all the fraud that is charged. There is a welfare Watergate to be looked into, but the poor have no special prosecutor.   (Business Week 2466:49 Jan 17, 77)

SCHORR, Daniel. All news is an exaggeration of life.   (Village Voice 20:134 May 26, 75)

SCHORR, Daniel. I think I ended up simply being indigestible (commenting on why he resigned from CBS).   (Washington Post 303:G1 Oct 3, 76)

SCHORR, Daniel. I'm fighting for freedom of the press, and maybe I should also be fighting for freedom *from* the press.   (Newsweek 88:17 Oct 11, 76)

SCHORR, Daniel. The joys of martyrdom are considerably overrated.   (Time 107:62 Mar 8, 76)

SCHORR, Daniel. To betray a source would be to betray myself, my career and my life. I cannot do it (commenting in his testimony before the Pike committee).   (Time 108:76 Oct 11, 76)

SCHRADER, Paul. I like to fire a movie like a bullet. Then I stay with it until it hits its target.   (Chicago Sun-Times 31:1 section 3 Mar 12, 78)

SCHREINER, Olive. We are men or women in the second place, human beings in the first.   (Ms 6:94 Aug 77)

SCHROEDER, Patricia. We need some nannies around here for the boys. We need some warm milk, we need some cookies, and then maybe we can have a little better decorum in this body and be able to deal with a little more substance (about the House of Representatives).   (Time 111:13 Mar 27, 78)

SCHROEDER, Patricia. When men talk about defense, they always claim to be protecting women and children, but they never ask the women and children what they think. (New York Times Book Review 35 Feb 17, 80)

SCHULLER, Robert. The church is in the business of retailing religion. (Time 105:38 Feb 24, 75)

SCHULTZE, Charles. If you can't measure output, then you measure input. (Washingtonian 14:155 Nov 78)

SCHUMACHER, Ernst F. As a good friend says, most of the modern economics as taught is a form of brain damage. (The Reader (Chicago's Free Weekly) 6:27 Mar 25, 77)

SCHUMACHER, Ernst F. It's impossible to discuss economic problems without concepts like temptation and seduction. In economics this is translated into free consumer choice. (The Reader (Chicago's Free Weekly) 6:27 Mar 25, 77)

SCHUMACHER, Ernst F. People always called me a crank, but I didn't carry any resentment about that because it is an excellent thing, a crank. It is not expensive, it is relatively nonviolent, and it causes revolutions. (Christian Science Monitor) 69:1 June 27, 77)

SCHUMACHER, Ernst F. Production by the masses, rather than mass production. (Newsweek 90:72 Sept 19, 77)

SCHUMACHER, Ernst F. They're spending their time rearranging the deck chairs on the Titanic (commenting on his fellow economists). (The Reader (Chicago's Free Weekly) 6:27 Mar 25, 77)

SCHUMAN, William. In my own music, I'm alone, absolutely alone. (New York Times 129:19 section D Aug 3, 80)

SCHWAB, Charles M. Personality is to a man what perfume is to a flower. (Kansas City Times 109:1 April 15, 77)

SCHWARTZ, Delmore. No reputation is more than a snowfall. (Times Literary Supplement 3969:2 April 28, 78)

SCHWEIKER, Richard. Detente is dead and the Soviets killed it. (The Observer 9828:10 Jan 6, 80)

SCHWEITZER, Albert (attributed by Norman Cousins). We are at our best when we give the doctor who resides within each patient a chance to go to work. (Newsweek 94:99 Sept 24, 79)

SCOTT, George C. The actor is never rewarded in film. Film stardom is a peripheral and distorted kind of fulfillment. (New York Times Magazine 12 Jan 23, 77)

SCOTT, George C. Most actors, maybe all actors, are not really all that fascinating or brilliant people, aside from their ability to perform on stage or for the camera. If you ask me, they're dull. (Chicago Tribune 89:16 Mar 30, 78)

SCOTT, Hugh. I had a will to believe (in Nixon's innocence), but they didn't show me all the documents. I was led into making statements on incomplete evidence. I was trying to be fair when I was personally deeply disturbed. (Washington Post 365:A3 Dec 5, 75)

SCOTT, Hugh. The worst mistake I made was supporting the Carswell nomination (reflecting on his three decades in Congress). (Washington Post 365:A3 Dec 5, 75)

SCOTT, Ulric. An Independent-Republican is an elephant that is trying to forget. (Time 106:8 Dec 1, 75)

SCOTT, Wendell. Auto racing, I'm sad to say, is still a white man's sport. It's a shame that a woman got to qualify for Indy before a black man did. (New York Times 126:36 June 1, 77)

SCOTT, William. The only reason we need zip codes is because niggers can't read. (Politicks and Other Human Interests 1:15 Mar 28, 78)

SCOTT, William. What's this Gaza stuff? I never have understood that (to Israeli Prime Minister Yitzhak Rabin). (Rolling Stone 199:34 Nov 6, 75)

SCRANTON, William W. The only universality that one can honestly associate with the Universal Declaration of Human Rights is universal lip service. (New York Times 126:10 Nov 25, 76)

SEALE, Bobby. Those who know don't talk; and those who talk don't know. (New York Times Magazine 53 Nov 20, 77)

SEAMAN, Barbara. (A feminist is) a woman who is for women, which does not mean being against men. (New York Times 125:32 Nov 8, 75)

SEARS, John. Politics is motion and excitement. (Time 114:22 Nov 12, 79)

SEARS, John. You never really win anything in politics. All you get is a chance to play for higher stakes and perform at a higher level. (Time 115:32 Jan 21, 80)

SEEGER, Pete. TV must become our council fire, our town hall. (CoEvolution Quarterly 16:153 Winter 77/78)

SEGOVIA, Andres. Artists who say they practice eight hours a day are liars or asses. (The Observer 9839:10 Mar 23, 80)

SEIB, Charles. The pettiness and unfairness of gossip masquerading as news is one reason the Washington press is seen by many Americans as vindictive, destructive and often irrelevant. (Time 111:70 Mar 20, 78)

SEIDENBAUM, Art. A city worrying about image enhancement is like a man considering a wig; each faces the world with a shining inferiority complex. (Wall Street Journal 56:14 June 25, 76)

SELLERS, Peter. The older I get, the less I like the film industry and the people in it. In fact, I'm at a stage where I almost loathe them. (Time 115:73 Mar 3, 80)

SELYE, Hans. Stress is the nonspecific response of the body to any demand. (Human Nature 1:58 Feb 78)

SENGHOR, Leopold Sedar. Africa will teach rhythm to a world dead with machinery and cannon. (Time 116:5 July 7, 80)

SEVAREID, Eric. The chief cause of problems is solutions. (Town & Country 133:141 May 79)

SEVAREID, Eric. (One should learn) to retain the courage of one's doubts, as well as one's convictions, in this world of dangerously passionate certainties. (Time 110:111 Dec 12, 77)

SEVAREID, Eric. People see (Walter) Cronkite as they used to see Eisenhower—the fellow next door who'd invite you to his backyard barbecue, and a world statesman at the same time. (Time 115:68 Feb 25, 80)

SEVAREID, Eric. The problem is not so much finding out what the news is, it's making sense of it. (TV Guide 25:A55 Dec 13, 77)

SEVAREID, Eric. There is an immense amount of biased listening and inaccurate listening (commenting on TV news audiences). (TV Guide 25:A55 Dec 13, 77)

SEVAREID, Eric. We are a turbulent society but a stable republic. The mind goes blank at the thought of a world without one such power. (Time 110:111 Dec 12, 77)

SEXTON, Anne. Creative people must not avoid the pain that they get dealt. (Time 110:124 Nov 28, 77)

SEXTON, Anne. I wonder if the artist ever lives his life—he is so busy recreating it. (The American Book Review 1:4 Dec 77)

SEYMOUR, Steven. Translations are like women. When they are pretty, chances are they won't be very faithful. (Rolling Stone 260:16 Mar 9, 78)

SHAFAT, Gershon. Kissinger is a disaster. His priorities are: one, Kissinger; two, the President; three, the U.S. Israel is nowhere among them. (Time 106:23 Aug 25, 75)

SHAFFER, Floyd. I believe it would be healthier if the church could laugh because I believe that God laughs. (Newsweek 86:64 Sept 29, 75)

SHALES, Tom. The Ayatollah Khomeini has the world by the networks. (Time 114:64 Dec 3, 79)

SHANKER, Albert. Power is a good thing. It is better than powerlessness. (Time 106:17 Sept 22, 75)

SHANKER, Albert. Teaching is no longer seen as a woman's job. Teaching is seen as a tough, exciting place where things are happening. (Ms 6:85 July 77)

SHANNON, William V. What is actually happening is often less important than what appears to be happening. (Book Digest 6:30 Dec 79)

SHAPIRO, Joseph H. Aesthetics is to art what ornithology is to birds. (Chicago 26:178 Sept 77)

SHAPIRO, Joseph H. Great art is so complex and has so many levels of meaning it carries its own equivocation. (Chicago 26:17 Sept 77)

SHAPIRO, Joseph H. Nowhere is a man's imagination so fertile as in the discovery of new ways to say no to a man who asks for money. (Chicago 26:178 Sept 77)

SHARPE, Cornelia. I think sex is the greatest thing since Coca-Cola. (Viva 2:21 Sept 75)

SHAW, George Bernard. (Charlie Chaplin is) the one genius created by the cinema. (Time 111:63 Jan 2, 78)

SHAW, George Bernard. Gambling promises the poor what property performs for the rich—something for nothing. (Rocky Mountain News 333:70 Mar 20, 80)

SHAW, George Bernard. A government that robs Peter to pay Paul can always depend upon the support of Paul. (San Francisco Chronicle This World 1978:40 Jan 29, 78)

SHAW, George Bernard. The man who has never made a mistake will never make anything else. (Kansas City Times 109:26 Jan 25, 77)

SHAW, George Bernard. My method is to take utmost trouble to find the right thing to say, and then to say it with the utmost levity. (Kansas City Star 97:15B April 6, 77)

SHAW, George Bernard. The test of a man's or a woman's breeding is how they behave in a quarrel. (Forbes 119:312 May 15, 77)

SHAW, George Bernard. When a stupid man is doing something he is ashamed of, he always decides it is his duty. (Los Angeles Times Calendar 64 April 30, 78)

SHAW, Henry Wheeler. As scarce as truth is, the supply has always been in excess of the demand. (Rocky Mountain News 44:78 June 5, 80)

SHAWN, William (attributed by Brendan Gill). Liebling wants to live like a stockbroker, but he doesn't want to be a stockbroker. (Andy Warhol's Interview 8:60 Dec 78)

SHCHARANSKY, Anatoly. I am happy that I have lived honestly and in peace with my conscience, and never lied even when I was threatened with death. (Guardian Weekly 119:7 July 23, 78)

SHEED, Wilfrid. Criticism is what every reviewer would like to write if he had the time. (New York Times 128:9 section 7 Jan 21, 79)

SHEED, Wilfrid. One reason the human race has such a low opinion of itself is that it gets so much of its wisdom from writers. (New York Times 128:9 section 7 Jan 21, 79)

SHEED, Wilfrid. Suicide is the sincerest form of criticism life gets. (The Tennessean 74:11 June 27, 79)

SHEEHAN, George A. To know running is to know life. (New York Times Book Review 30 Dec 3, 78)

SHEEN, Fulton J. Freedom is the right to do what you ought to do. (Time 114:84 Dec 24, 79)

SHEEN, Martin. I don't believe in God, but I do believe that Mary was His mother. (Rolling Stone 303:48 Nov 1, 79)

SHEPHERD, Cybill. If you kept seeing Robert Redford stark naked on the screen, would he be a superstar today? No way. Or Gene Hackman showing everything? Their million dollar days would be over. I want to be in a movie where all the men take their clothes off and I don't. (People Weekly 6:122 Dec 13, 76)

SHERO, Fred. We know that hockey is where we live, where we can best meet and overcome pain and wrong and death. Life is just a place where we spend time between games. (Penthouse 8:68 April 77)

SHERRILL, Henry Knox. Far too many people in the church have very great convictions about very small things. (Newsweek 95:93 May 26, 80)

SHERROD, William Forrest (Blackie). Sportswriting is just like driving a taxi. It ain't the work you enjoy. It's the people you run into. (Texas Monthly 3:93 Dec 75)

SHIELDS, Gerald R. It is obvious that the photocopying issue is to be decided soon and that the odds favor turning libraries into some sort of reprint warehouse for publisher's products. (Library Journal 100:2307 Dec 15, 75)

SHIELDS, Mark. I don't think Carter and self-doubt have ever met. (Washingtonian 11:103 June 76)

SHIELDS, Mark. Jerry Brown is the Renee Richards of American politics. (Newsweek 93:25 Jan 22, 79)

SHOR, Toots. Any bum who can't get drunk by midnight, ain't tryin (commenting on a midnight curfew imposed on nightclubs, bars and restaurants during World War II). (New York Times 126:36 Jan 25, 77)

SHOR, Toots. A good saloonkeeper is the most important man in the community. (Time 106:44 Sept 22, 75)

SHOR, Toots. I don't want to be a millionaire, I just want to live like one. (New York Times 126:36 Jan 25, 77)

SHORE, Dinah. Bing (Crosby) sings like all people think they sing in the shower. (Newsweek 90:101 Oct 24, 77)

SHRIVER, Eunice. Mistakes were obviously made in terms of the investigation, but I'm satisfied with their conclusions (on the Warren Commission). (Christian Science Monitor 68:8 Dec 3, 75)

SHUTTLEWORTH, John. We are still much too preoccupied with taking our machines out into the woods, instead of making a place for the forest in our hearts. (The Mother Earth News 35:7 Sept 75)

SIDEY, Hugh. Bureaucrats are the only people in the world who can say absolutely nothing and mean it. (Time 108:13 Nov 29, 76)

SIDEY, Hugh. Carter must understand that in this city (Washington) we cut red tape lengthwise. (Time 108:13 Nov 29, 76)

SIDEY, Hugh. The measurement of the gestation period of an original thought in a bureaucracy is still pending. (Time 108:13 Nov 29, 76)

SIDEY, Hugh. One must always remember that freedom from action and freedom from purpose constitute the philosophical bases of creative bureaucracy. (Time 108:13 Nov 29, 76)

SIDEY, Hugh. When a bureaucrat makes a mistake and continues to make it, it usually becomes the new policy. (Time 108:13 Nov 29, 76)

SIDLIN, Murry. Young people are visually sophisticated but often musically illiterate. (Time 110:75 Oct 17, 77)

SIKINGER, Maximilian. It's better to be a hungry coyote than to be a satisfied dog. (Village Voice 22:32 May 9, 77)

SILBERMAN, Laurence. The legal process, because of its unbridled growth, has become a cancer which threatens the vitality of our forms of capitalism and democracy. (Time 111:56 April 10, 78)

SILLS, Beverly. My voice has served me very well, and I would like to be able to put it to bed, so that it can go quietly and with pride (upon her announcement that she would retire in 1980). (Time 111:82 Jan 23, 78)

SILLS, Beverly. She (Maria Callas) was a pioneer and an inspiration. (Newsweek 90:93 Sept 26, 77)

SILLS, Beverly. We have taste, and if we like something we should be verbal about it. We are behind Europe in only one way and that is in government subsidization (commenting on why Americans should be proud of their own culture). (Washington Post 68:C3 Feb 11, 76)

SILLS, Beverly. When I go on the talk shows, I project what I am—an intelligent and well-educated girl from Brooklyn. (New York Times 126:39 section 2 Oct 10, 76)

SIMELS, Steve. David Bowie (is) the single worst thing to happen to rock music since the deaths of Brian Jones, Janis Joplin, and Jimi Hendrix. (Stereo Review 35:71 Dec 75)

SIMELS, Steve. John Denver (is) Johnny Mathis disguised as a hillbilly. He has never written a decent song, his voice is an Irish tenor only a whit less offensive than Dennis Day's, and, as far as I can tell, his only function is to provide adolescent girls with records to cry over in the privacy of their bedrooms. (Stereo Review 35:72 Dec 75)

SIMON, George T. Only God can make a tree and only men can play good jazz. (National NOW Times 11:12 Aug 78)

SIMON, John. The culture of the nation's capital would seem to be a capital joke. (New York 8:76 May 12, 75)

SIMON, John. Every era gets the leader it deserves; John Wayne is ours. (Newsweek 93:77 June 25, 79)

SIMON, John. (Glenda Jackson) has the looks of an asexual harlequin. (Time 110:34 Dec 26, 77)

SIMON, John. I always thought Miss (Liza) Minelli's face deserving—of first prize in the beagle category. (Time 110:34 Dec 26, 77)

SIMON, John. I love plays, but I love them in a different way. I'm not blind. I don't gush. I love the theater as it might be. (Time 110:34 Dec 26, 77)

SIMON, Neil. When it's 105 in New York City, it's 78 in LA. When it's 20 below in New York City, it's 78 in LA. Of course, there are 11 million interesting people in New York City and only 78 in LA (commenting upon moving to Hollywood). (Chicago Tribune 247:2 section 5 Sept 4, 77)

SIMON, William E. Bad politicians are sent to Washington by good people who don't vote. (Atlanta 16:130 Aug 76)

SIMON, William E. Corporations are people, too (proposing a new tax break for big businesses). (Rolling Stone 195:28 Sept 11, 75)

SIMON, William E. In the United States today, we already have more government than we need, more government than most people want, and certainly more government than we are willing to pay for. (Vital Speeches 42:72 Nov 15, 75)

SIMON, William E. I've lived through the Saturday Night Massacre and the Sunday Night Massacre. Only Butz and me are left. We'll probably go on Monday. (Los Angeles Times 94:2 Part 1 Nov 6, 75)

SIMON, William E. My education in the energy realm was not complete until I truly understood the nature of the oil hysteria of the liberal Democrats. It is a symbolic mania sheltered by a profound refusal to look at the facts. (US News & World Report 84:24 April 24, 78)

SIMON, William E. The Republican Party today is inert, flattened into a jellied inconsistency by a half century of compromises of principle. It may even deserve to die. (US News & World Report 84:24 April 24, 78)

SIMON, William E. Show me a good loser and I'll show you a loser. (Washingtonian 11:24 April 76)

SIMON, William E. Surely this (Carter) Administration will go down in history as the worst stewards of the American economy in our lifetime. (Time 116:14 July 28, 80)

SIMON, William E. Washington is the only city where sound travels faster than light. (Atlanta 16:130 Aug 76)

SIMON, William E. We're going to have a taxpayers' revolt if we don't begin to make the tax system more simple, more understandable, so that everyone knows that everybody is paying his fair share. (Chicago Tribune 11:1 Section 1 Jan 11, 76)

SIMON, William E. We're going to sell New York to the Shah of Iran. It's a hell of an investment (during New York City's financial crisis). (Time 105:21 May 26, 75)

SIMONE, Nina. Jazz lets black people know, everytime they hear it, that they have their hands on the pulse of life. (Sepia 26:10 June 77)

SIMONET, Henri. France has an African policy which is not ours. (New York Times 127:19 section 4 June 4, 78)

SIMONS, Frank. There is but one way for a newspaperman to look on a politician, and that is down. (Chicago Sun-Times 32:6 April 7, 79)

SIMPSON, David. In the first century A.D., Petronius declared painting dead. In 1934 Moholy-Nagy declared painting dead. In 1970—probably earlier—Robert Morris declared painting dead. Three of many. (Artforum 14:34 Sept 75)

SINATRA, Frank. (Bing Crosby) was the father of my career, the idol of my youth and a dear friend of my maturity. (Time 110:106 Oct 24, 77)

SINATRA, Frank. Hell hath no fury like a hustler with a literary agent. (Newsweek 87:19 Jan 26, 76)

SINATRA, Frank. I am a symmetrical man, almost to a fault. (New York 13:32 April 28, 80)

SINATRA, Frank. I'm for anything that gets you through the night, be it prayer, tranquilizers or a bottle of Jack Daniels. (Playboy 26:26 Oct 79)

SINATRA, Frank, Jr. I rued the day that the Beatles were unfortunately born into this world. They are, in my mind, responsible for most of the degeneration that has happened, not only musically, but in the sense of youth orientation politically, too. They are the people who made it first publicly acceptable to spit in the eye of authority. (Rolling Stone 249:34 Oct 6, 77)

SINCLAIR, John. You can't make a revolution if you have to make a living. (Newsweek 90:26 Sept 5, 77)

SINCLAIR, Upton. I tried to touch America's conscience and all I did was hit it in the stomach (commenting on the effect of his novel The Jungle). (Philadelphia 67:65 Nov 76)

SINGER, Isaac Bashevis. Fiction can entertain and stir the mind; it does not direct it. (Time 112:82 July 3, 78)

SINGER, Isaac Bashevis. I never forget that I am only a storyteller. (Time 112:129 Oct 16, 78)

SINGER, Isaac Bashevis. I'm a pessimist with cheerfulness. It's a riddle even to me, but this is how I am. (Chicago Tribune 291:20 Oct 18, 78)

SINGER, Isaac Bashevis. I'm before everything else a writer, not just Jewish, and I'm not doing it with some illusion that I'm going to do great things. I just feel that I have to tell a story. (Chicago Tribune 281:4 section 2 Oct 8, 78)

SINGER, Isaac Bashevis. Literature is the memory of humanity. (US News & World Report 85:60 Nov 6, 78)

SINGER, Isaac Bashevis. A Marxist has never written a good novel. (New York Times Magazine 42 Nov 26, 78)

SINGER, Isaac Bashevis. The supernatural is like the ocean, while the so-called natural is only a little island on it. And even this little island is a great riddle. (New York Times 128:18 section 4 Dec 3, 78)

SINGER, Isaac Bashevis. A writer, like a woman, never knows why people like him, or why people dislike him. We never know. (Time 112:69 Aug 7, 78)

SINGER, Isaac Bashevis. Writers were not born to change the world. (Time 112:82 July 3, 78)

SINGLAUB, John K. I don't know if it's capriciousness, inconsistency or naivete, but I have a feeling that with the present Administration there isn't anybody in charge (commenting on the Carter administration). (Los Angeles Times 97:2 part 1 June 2, 78)

SIRICA, John J. I hope no political party will ever stoop so low as to embrace the likes of Richard Nixon again. (The Tennessean 74:10 section F May 13, 79)

SIRICA, John J. Nixon should have been indicted. (Chicago Tribune 119:2 section 2 April 29, 79)

SITWELL, Edith. The public will believe anything, so long as it is not founded on truth. (Kansas City Star 97:2D Feb 20, 77)

SKELTON, Red. I trust God, my wife, and myself. People take kindness for weakness, and generosity has the form of a sucker. (Chicago Tribune 241:12 Aug 29, 77)

SKINNER, Cornelia Otis. A woman's virtue is man's greatest invention. (Time 114:76 July 23, 79)

SLATER, Jim. As you get better at a thing it gets less interesting. (The Observer 9761:14 Sept 24, 78)

SLOAN, Hugh, Jr. There's a strong parallel between the Carter and Nixon White Houses. I don't think there's going to be another Watergate. But you're relying on a group of eager young people who are going to make mistakes. (Chicago Tribune 52:16 Feb 21, 77)

SLOANE, Harvey. He's maturing like good Kentucky bourbon (about Jimmy Carter). (Time 107:10 May 24, 76)

SMELSER, Neil. Californians believe the best is behind them. (Time 110:23 July 18, 77)

SMITH, Alexis. Women who are only involved with how they look are always dull. (Chicago Tribune 123:16 section 1 May 3, 77)

SMITH, Charles Merrill. In a democracy you can be respected though poor, but don't count on it. (Time 113:25 Feb 26, 79)

SMITH, Donald N (President of Burger King). The individual choice of garnishment of a burger can be an important point to the consumer in this day when individualism, in my mind, is an increasingly important thing to people. (Rolling Stone 237:53 April 21, 77)

SMITH, Howard K. The Cubans may be hostile to America, but they love Americans. (TV Guide 25:13 Feb 26, 77)

SMITH, Ian Douglas. Everything is fine in Rhodesia. (The Observer 9812:10 Sept 16, 79)

SMITH, Ian Douglas. I am not prepared to think in terms of color (speaking about black v. white rule in Rhodesia). (Time 108:61 Nov 15, 76)

SMITH, Ian Douglas. I do not believe in black majority rule in Rhodesia—not in a thousand years. (People Weekly 5:45 June 7, 76)

SMITH, Ian Douglas. I don't accept anybody as a mediator. When you are dealing with your future, in other words your life, I don't think you can place this in the hands of anybody (rejecting Secretary of State Henry Kissinger's suggestion that Harold Wilson could act as a mediator in the Rhodesian crisis). (New York Times 125:B1 May 21, 76)

SMITH, Ian Douglas. I have got to admit that things haven't gone quite the way I wanted. (The Observer 9797:10 June 3, 79)

SMITH, Ian Douglas. No African rule in my lifetime. The white man is the master of Rhodesia, has built it, and intends to keep it (comment made in 1964). (Washington Post 295:A10 Sept 25, 76)

SMITH, Ian Douglas. We may lose in the end, but I think it's better to lose while you're standing up and fighting than crawling out on your knees (commenting on his fight to continue white rule in Rhodesia). (People Weekly 5:47 June 7, 76)

SMITH, Ian Douglas. We never have had a policy in Rhodesia to hand over our country to any black majority and, as far as I am concerned, we never will (commenting in March, 1976). (Time 108:37 Oct 11, 76)

SMITH, James. There ain't no sense in dying before your time is come. (Quest 2:114 Mar/April 78)

SMITH, Maggie. I'm always very relieved to be somebody else, because I'm not sure at all who I am. (New York Times 128:C26 Sept 12, 79)

SMITH, Margaret Chase. We live together. I don't make any apologies (explaining her relationship with William C. Smith, Jr.). (Newsweek 86:58 Oct 6, 75)

SMITH, Patti. As far as I'm concerned, being any gender is a drag. (Playboy 26:26 Oct 79)

SMITH, Patti. I want every faggot, grandmother, five-year-old and Chinaman to be able to hear my music and say YEAH. (Time 107:76 Jan 5, 76)

SMITH, Patti. Jesus died for somebody's sins but not mine. (Philadelphia 69:185 Sept 78)

SMITH, Patti. Not even boot camp is as tough as being in rock and roll. (Chicago Tribune 340:3 Section 6 Dec 13, 76)

SMITH, Red. Writing is very easy. All you do is sit in front of a typewriter keyboard until little drops of blood appear on your forehead. (Writers' Digest 55:4 Nov 75)

SMITH, Sam. He stood on his own (about Elvis Presley). (New York Times Magazine 45 Mar 25, 79)

SMITH, W. Eugene. I carry a torch with my camera. (Life 1:56 Dec 78)

SMITH, W. Eugene. I torture myself to make it all come out as deep and honest as I can. (Life 1:49 Dec 78)

SNOW, C. P. Literary intellectuals at one pole—at the other, scientists...Between the two a gulf of mutual incomprehension. (Omni 1:39 Mar 79)

SNOW, C. P. Money is not so important as a pat on the head. (The Observer 9723:11 Dec 18, 77)

SOARES, Mario. Troikas never work. They haven't worked since Roman times. (Time 106:25 Aug 18, 75)

SOBEL, Nathan. There's no such thing as organized crime in this city (New York City). There's a little of it in Las Vegas, but that's it. (New York 9:38 July 19, 76)

SOBY, James Thrall. Only a few artists in history have been able to create so strange and so original a world as Giorgio De Chirico. (New York Times 128:B5 Nov 22, 78)

SOEDER, Karin (Sweden's first woman Foreign Minister). Men care about power because for them power is linked to sexual performance. Women achieve positions of power out of a need to do something, not because we need reassurance. (Atlas World Press Review 24:48 Mar 77

SOFFER, Gerald. All the signs suggest that life exists on Mars, but we can't find any bodies. (Omni 2:40 April 80)

SOLTI, Sir Georg. Chicago should erect a statue to me for what I have done. (Chicago 26:152 Dec 77)

SOLZHENITSYN, Aleksandr Isaevich. Communism is unregenerate; it will always present a mortal danger to mankind. It is like an infection in the world's organism: it may be dormant, but it will inevitably attack with a crippling disease. (Time 115:49 Feb 18, 80)

SOLZHENITSYN, Aleksandr Isaevich. The entire period from 1945 to 1975 can be viewed as another world war that was lost by the West without a battle. (Time 115:48 Feb 18, 80)

SOLZHENITSYN, Aleksandr Isaevich. For us in Russia Communism is a dead dog, while for many people in the West it is still a living lion. (The Observer 9782:10 Mar 18, 79)

SOLZHENITSYN, Aleksandr Isaevich. Hastiness and superficiality are the psychic disease of the 20th century. (Time 111:33 June 19, 78)

SOLZHENITSYN, Aleksandr Isaevich. I can set your minds at ease. There will be no nuclear war. Why do the Soviets need war when they can break off nation after nation, piece by piece, from the West? (Time 106:56 July 21, 75)

SOLZHENITSYN, Aleksandr Isaevich. Mr. Kissinger always has an emergency exit available to him. He can transfer to a university to lecture to credulous youngsters about the art of diplomacy. But the government of the United States will have no emergency exit. (Chicago Tribune 343:4 Section 1 Dec 8, 75)

SOLZHENITSYN, Aleksandr Isaevich. Now they (Russian leaders) don't say we're going to bury you anymore. They say detente. (Newsweek 83:46 July 14, 75)

SOLZHENITSYN, Aleksandr Isaevich. The Soviet Union's economy is on such a war footing that even if it were the unanimous opinion of all members of the Politburo not to start a war, this would no longer be in their power. (New York Times 125:26 Mar 3, 76)

SOLZHENITSYN, Aleksandr Isaevich. To defend oneself, one must also be ready to die; there is little such readiness in a society raised in the cult of material well-being. (Time 111:18 June 26, 78)

SOLZHENITSYN, Aleksandr Isaevich. When changes occur in the Soviet regime, the whole orbit of life on earth will change.   (The Observer 9783:11 Feb 25, 79)

SOLZHENITSYN, Aleksandr Isaevich. Whenever the tissue of life is woven of legalistic relations, there is an atmosphere of moral mediocrity, paralyzing man's noblest impulses.   (Time 111:33 June 19, 78)

SOMERS, Al. The key to success is a good eye, an even temper and being boss of your game. You should also know where the nearest exit is, and remember to tell the scorekeeper where you want the body sent.   (People Weekly 9:38 Feb 27, 78)

SOMERS, Suzanne. If you've got it, bump it with a trumpet.   (Playboy 26:26 Oct 79)

SOMOZA DEBAYLE, Anastasio. I am a tied donkey fighting with a tiger.   (Chicago Sun-Times 32:1 July 8, 79)

SOMOZA DEBAYLE, Anastasio. I was born in Nicaragua, I am Nicaraguan, and I will live here forever. Those who want me to go will have to push me out by force.   (Chicago Tribune 20:16 Jan 20, 79)

SOMOZA DEBAYLE, Anastasio. Nicaraguan people will never forget the treason of their Costa Rican friends against their Nicaraguan brothers.   (New York Times 128:5 section 4 July 15, 79)

SONTAG, Susan. Nobody ever discovered ugliness through photographs. But many, through photographs, have discovered beauty.   (Vogue 168:185 June 78)

SONTAG, Susan. Style is the principle of decision in a work of art, the signature of the artist's will.   (Vogue 168:185 June 78)

SONTAG, Susan. There are some elements in life— above all, sexual pleasure—about which it isn't necessary to have a position.   (Village Voice 21:77 Mar 22, 76)

SOREL, Edward. At what I do, I am the best there is.   (Guardian Weekly 119:17 Nov 12, 78)

SOREL, Edward. For the past 15 years I've been making cartoons that in one way or another suggest that America is educated by incompetents, governed by hypocrites, and ruled by the military industrial complex.   (Guardian Weekly 119:17 Nov 12, 78)

SORENSEN, Theodore Chaikin. To continue fighting for this post, (the directorship of the CIA) which would be my natural inclination, would only handicap the new administration if I am rejected, or handicap my effectiveness if confirmed.   (The Guardian Weekly 116:7 Jan 23, 77)

SOUSA, John Philip. Jazz will endure as long as people hear it through their feet instead of their brains.   (Los Angeles Times Calendar 82 Mar 26, 78)

SPARK, Muriel. People who have hope are sad because they are so often disappointed.   (New York Times Book Review 47 May 20, 79)

SPAULDING, Jim. When newspapers write about themselves, they lie.   (New West 3:65 Jan 16, 78)

SPEAR, Michael. Launching a new towns program in the early 1970's was like asking the Wright brothers to test their airplane in a hurricane and then concluding, when it crashed, that the invention did not work.   (Time 112:84 Oct 16, 78)

SPIELBERG, Steven. Directing a movie with Truffaut on the set is like having Renoir around when you're still painting by numbers.   (Time 108:50 Aug 30, 76)

SPIELBERG, Steven. The most expensive habit in the world is celluloid, not heroin, and I need a fix every few years.   (Time 113:97 April 26, 79)

SPIELBERG, Steven. My advice to anyone who wants to be a movie director is to make home movies. I started out by shooting 8 millimeter home movies with neighbors and friends.   (Texas Monthly 4:38 Aug 76)

SPIKOL, Art. The fact is that most people don't drive cars that reflect what they are: they drive the closest thing they can find to what they'd like to be.   (Philadelphia Magazine 66:198 Nov 75)

SPINKS, Leon. You can take a man out of the ghetto, but you can't take the ghetto out of a man.   (The Observer 9760:13 Sept 17, 78)

SPITZ, Mark. I was a porpoise out of water. I was not prepared for the adulation I received. I could not handle the world.   (The Times 8063:30 Jan 8, 78)

SPIVEY, Victoria. Musicians today are sloppier than I ever seen them. And the most of them, the worst notes they make, the greater they seem to become.   (Sepia 26:10 Nov 75)

SPOCK, Benjamin. Fathers ought to form a union and win the right to go home early if their children are sick.   (The Observer 9786:10 Mar 18, 79)

SPROLES, Judy. If there is an opinion, facts will be found to support it.   (Omni 1:132 May 79)

STAFFORD, Jean. I write for myself and God and a few close friends.   (Time 113:78 April 9, 79)

STALLONE, Sylvester. Actors are a walking, throbbing mass of unhealed scar tissue by the time they get anywhere.   (Chicago Sun-Times 32:3 section 3 Nov 5, 78)

STALLONE, Sylvester. I make my living with my mind. My muscles I consider merely machinery to carry my mind around.   (Chicago Tribune 210:16 July 29, 77)

STANDISH, David. The blues hasn't died out; it's turned white.   (Chicago 27:236 Jan 78)

STAPLETON, Ruth Carter. I am not going to be the Billy Graham of the Carter administration.   (People Weekly 5:16 June 28, 76)

STAPLETON, Ruth Carter. If Jesus loves Larry Flynt, who am I to turn my back?   (Life 2:87 Dec 79)

STARGELL, Willie. They give you a round bat and they throw you a round ball. And they tell you to hit it square (commenting on baseball).   (New York Times 127:4 section 5 April 2, 78)

STARR, Kevin O. An obsession with self-fulfillment proved one of the dangers of the California dream.   (Esquire 89:62 Feb 78)

STARR, Kevin O. Perhaps if we find a way to save our Presidents, we can find a way to save ourselves.   (Newsweek 86:34 Oct 6, 75)

STARR, Kevin O. There is no stable intellectual tradition in California except utopianism.   (Esquire 89:134 Feb 78)

STEFFENS, Lincoln. I have seen the future, and it works (commenting on Bolshevism after a trip to Russia in 1919).   (Newsweek 83:76 April 15, 74)

STEICHEN, Edward. The mission of photography is to explain man to man and each man to himself. (Camera 35 20:37 July 76)

STEIN, Benjamin. L.A. is the original in a gigantic Xerox machine that is spreading its copies everywhere. It is, thus, in a certain sense the center of the universe. (Esquire 89:64 Feb 78)

STEIN, Gertrude. Considering how dangerous everything is, nothing is really frightening. (Human Behavior 7:17 May 78)

STEIN, Gertrude. Everybody gets so much information all day long that they lose their common sense. (Chicago Tribune 176:2 section II June 25, 78)

STEIN, Gertrude. Money is always there but the pockets change; it is not in the same pockets after a change, and that is all there is to say about money. (Time 106:E8 Oct 13, 75)

STEIN, Gertrude. Nothing can, or will, happen in Africa. (New York Times Book Review 10 July 1, 79)

STEIN, Gertrude. One of the great things about not going to movies is that you get lots of surprises. (Film Comment 12:2 Jan/Feb 76)

STEIN, Gertrude. We are always the same age inside. (Omni 2:38 April 80)

STEINBECK, John. Competing with Hemingway isn't my idea of good business. (Time 106:48 Dec 1, 75)

STEINBECK, John. Here is no sentiment, no contest, no grandeur, no economics. From the sanctity of this occupation, a man may emerge refreshed and in control of his own soul. He is not idle. He is fishing, alone with himself in dignity and peace. It seems a very precious thing to me. (New York Times 126:2 section 5 Nov 7, 76)

STEINBECK, John. The profession of book writing makes horse racing seem like a solid, stable business. (Time 112:68 Aug 28, 78)

STEINBERG, Saul. The doodle is the brooding of the hand. (Time 112:88 Oct 16, 78)

STEINBERG, Saul. The life of the creative man is led, directed and controlled by boredom. (Time 111:92 April 17, 78)

STEINBERG, Saul. Performance bores me. What interests me is the invention. I like to make a parody of bravura. (Time 111:92 April 17, 78)

STEINBERG, Saul. Unlike writing, drawing makes up its own syntax as it goes along. The line can't be reasoned in the mind. It can only be reasoned on paper. (Time 111:92 April 17, 78)

STEINBERG, William. Great conductors do not dance. (Newsweek 91:93 May 29, 78)

STEINEM, Gloria. The average secretary in the U.S. is better educated than the average boss. (Time 112:61 Sept 11, 78)

STEINEM, Gloria. Feminism means that each woman has power over her own life and can decide what to do for herself. (Chicago Tribune 338:1 Dec 4, 78)

STEINEM, Gloria. The first problem for all of us, men and women, is not to learn, but to unlearn. (Human Behavior 7:17 May 78)

STEINEM, Gloria. If a magazine were published with similar attitudes toward blacks or Jews, it would be immediately shut down by public opinion (commenting on Hustler magazine). (New York Times Magazine 18 Mar 6, 77)

STEINEM, Gloria. A pedestal is as much a prison as any small space. (Playboy 26:26 Oct 79)

STEINEM, Gloria. Today a woman without a man is like a fish without a bicycle. (New York 9:26 Aug 9, 76)

STEINER, George. The world of Auschwitz lies outside speech as it lies outside reason. (Time 111:53 May 1, 78)

STEINFELS, Peter. Rather than getting the government they want, the people should want the government they get; they should be retutored to fit its current capacities. (Newsweek 94:74 July 2, 79)

STENGEL, Charles Dillon (Casey). If you walk backward you'll find out that you can go forward and people won't know if you're coming or going. (Newsweek 86:47 Aug 11, 75)

STENGEL, Charles Dillon (Casey). Oldtimers weekends and airplane landings are alike. If you can walk away from them they're successful (after the annual Oldtimers Day at Shea Stadium). (Sports Illustrated 43:10 July 14, 75)

STERN, Isaac. You don't realize how close it is to you, how much it is a part of your body, until it is gone (about the violin). (New York Times Magazine 15 Aug 12, 79)

STERNBACH, Leo Henryk. I am not a victim of capitalistic exploitation. If anything, I am an example of capitalistic enlightenment (commenting on his discovery of Valium and Librium and selling of the patent to his employer Hoffman-La Roche at $1 per drug). (Parade 8 June 27, 76)

STEVENS, John Paul. It's always been my philosophy to decide cases on the narrowest grounds possible and not to reach out. (New York Times 125:1 Dec 9, 75)

STEVENS, John Paul. Judges should impose on themselves the discipline of deciding no more than is before them. (American Legion Magazine 100:9 Feb 76)

STEVENS, John Paul. One of the strongest arguments against regulating obscenity through criminal law is the inherent vagueness of the obscenity concept. (Chicago Tribune 161:12 section 1 June 10, 77)

STEVENS, Robert S. Ronald Reagan badly ruined the Republican party in California. (New West 1:8 April 26, 76)

STEVENSON, Adlai, II. By the time a man is nominated for the Presidency of the United States, he is no longer worthy to hold the office. (Washingtonian 15:143 Nov 79)

STEVENSON, Adlai, II. An editor is someone who separates the wheat from the chaff and then prints the chaff. (Texas Observer 68:7 Dec 24, 76)

STEVENSON, Adlai, II. A free society is one where it is safe to be unpopular. (Human Behavior 7:68 May 78)

STEVENSON, Adlai, II. Good government cannot exist side by side with bad politics: the best government is the best politics. (Kansas City Star 97:4B Jan 30, 77)

STEVENSON, Adlai, II. The government must be the trustee for the little man, because no one else will be. The powerful can usually help themselves—and frequently do. (Human Behavior 7:68 May 78)

STEVENSON, Adlai, II. I have been tempted to make a proposal to our Republican friends: that if they stop telling lies about us, we would stop telling the truth about them. (Human Behavior 7:68 May 78)

STEVENSON, Adlai, II. I have often thought that if I had any epitaph that I would rather have more than another, it would be to say that I had disturbed the sleep of my generation. (Newsweek 90:120 Oct 24, 77)

STEVENSON, Adlai, II. It is better to light one candle than to curse the darkness. (New York Times Magazine 45 July 4, 76)

STEVENSON, Adlai, II. The journey of a thousand leagues begins with a single step. So we must never neglect any work of peace within our reach, however small. (Human Behavior 7:69 May 78)

STEVENSON, Adlai, II. Man does not live by words alone, despite the fact that sometimes he has to eat them. (Human Behavior 7:69 May 78)

STEVENSON, Adlai, II. Nixon is the kind of politician who would cut down a redwood tree, then mount the stump for a speech on conservation. (Human Behavior 7:68 May 78)

STEVENSON, Adlai, II. Since the beginning of time, governments have been mainly engaged in kicking people around. The astonishing achievement of modern times in the Western world is the idea that the citizens should do the kicking. (Human Behavior 7:68 May 78)

STEVENSON, Adlai, II. There was a time when a fool and his money were soon parted, but now it happens to everybody. (New York Times 128:A19 June 11, 79)

STEVENSON, Adlai, II. You can tell the size of a man by the size of the thing that makes him mad. (Texas Observer 7 June 18, 76)

STEVENSON, Adlai, III. I don't think ideas are incompatible with political reality. (Time 113:18 Feb 26, 79)

STEVENSON, Adlai, III. I've been called my great-grandfather's grandson, my father's son and at times even my wife's husband. Now, they're calling me Mayor Daley's pet rock. (Chicago Tribune 198:1 July 16, 76)

STEVENSON, Adlai, III. The nation was never exalted to high levels of endeavor by reorganization plans and zero-based budgeting. In fact, the strong Presidents may have been least occupied by matters of management. A great President has an agenda for the nation. (Time 113:18 Feb 26, 79)

STEVENSON, Robert Louis. Politics is perhaps the only profession for which no preparation is thought necessary. (Rocky Mountain News 134:44 Sept 3, 79)

STEWART, James. The most important thing about acting is to approach it as a craft, not as an art and not as some mysterious type of religion. (Chicago Tribune 105:25 section 1 April 17, 77)

STEWART, P. L. When you are in it up to your ears, keep your mouth shut. (Omni 1:132 May 79)

STIEGLITZ, Alfred. Let all the art in the world be destroyed. It will rise again, for the art spirit is inherent in man. (Los Angeles Times Book Review 96:10 July 31, 77)

STIMSON, Henry. Gentlemen do not read each other's mail. (Maclean's 89:72 April 5, 76)

STOESSINGER, John G. The President holds our future in his hands. His personality may be our destiny. (Time 114:20 Dec 31, 79)

STOKES, Geoffrey. Attica is full of Hurricane Carters who were never champions. Or championed. (Village Voice 20:106 Dec 8, 75)

STOKOWSKI, Leopold. Every rehearsal must be better than the last. Every concert must be better than the last. We must never be satisfied because upwards in quality is quality without limit. (Chicago Tribune 261:4 section 6 Sept 18, 77)

STOKOWSKI, Leopold. The history of popular music shows that it is the true art form of the people. (Newsweek 90:94 Sept 26, 77)

STOKOWSKI, Leopold. I don't believe in tradition. It is a form of laziness. (Time 110:55 Sept 26, 77)

STOKOWSKI, Leopold. Music appeals to me for what can be done with it. (Time 110:54 Sept 26, 77)

STOLL, Cal. We finally got Nebraska where we want them—off the schedule. (Sports Illustrated 43:5 Aug 25, 75)

STOLLEY, Richard. Young sells better than old, pretty sells better than ugly, music sells better than television, television better than movies, and politics doesn't sell at all. (New York 10:15 Sept 12, 77)

STONE, David. One man's 'simple' is another man's 'huh'? (Omni 1:132 May 79)

STONE, Isidor Feinstein. The biggest menace to American freedom is the intelligence community. (Wilson Library Bulletin 51:25 Sept 76)

STONE, Isidor Feinstein. The First Amendment gives newspapermen a status and a mandate, an honored place in society, that cannot be matched in England, much less on the European continent. It is peculiarly American. I feel as though I survived an Ice Age and helped to keep this heritage intact. (Chicago Tribune 26:3 section 2 Jan 26, 78)

STONE, Isidor Feinstein. (Jimmy Carter) seems to me a conventional moderate conservative, Southern agro-businessman who got elected posing as a barefoot boy populist; a good man, who's doing some things on which he deserves support, but limited in everything but his ambition, which got him to the White House. But he seems more and more the tinkering, fuss-budget engineer. There's no music in him. He can fool people for a while, but he really doesn't know how to inspire. He just doesn't have the gift of greatness, the capacity to speak to the hearts and souls of men. (Chicago Tribune 26:3 section 2 Jan 26, 78)

STONE, Richard. One privilege of home ownership is the right to have lousy taste and display it. (Time 111:24 April 17, 78)

STOPPARD, Tom. I suppose my purpose as a playwright, if such a thing can be stated at all, has been to marry the play of ideas with comedy or farce. (Los Angeles Times Calendar 46 Jan 9, 77)

STOTESBURY, E. T. A good servant should never be in the way and never out of the way. (Town & Country 131:95 Mar 77)

STOUT, Rex. Writing any kind of fiction is a sort of explosion. When the explosion has taken place, there's no use going around looking at the debris. (Newsweek 86:65 Nov 10, 75)

STRACHEY, Lytton. It is perhaps as difficult to write a good life as to live one. (Time 114:83 July 2, 79)

STRACHEY, Lytton. Uninterpreted truth is as useless as buried gold. (Time 114:86 July 2, 79)

STRAUSS, Robert S. Everybody in government is like a bunch of ants on a log floating down a river. Each one thinks he is guiding the log, but it's really just going with the flow. (Time 111:47 April 17, 78)

STRAUSS, Robert S. I didn't come to town yesterday on a load of watermelons. (Newsweek 94:5 July 16, 79)

STRAUSS, Robert S. If you're in politics, you're a whore anyhow. It doesn't make any difference who you sleep with. (Texas Monthly 6:132 Feb 78)

STRAUSS, Robert S. I'm not going to deliver a candidate to the party, I'm going to deliver a party to the candidate. (New York 9:50 July 5, 76)

STRAUSS, Robert S. It's a little like makin' love to a gorilla. You don't quit when you're tired—you quit when the gorilla's tired (when asked whether he planned to quit as chairman of the Democratic National Committee). (Chicago Tribune 36:2 section 2 Feb 5, 78)

STRAUSS, Robert S. There ain't but one good job in this government, and you got it (to Jimmy Carter). (Time 116:12 Sept 22, 80)

STRAUSS, Robert S. The three most overrated things in Washington are Bob Strauss, home cooking, and Hamilton Jordan's private life. (Chicago Tribune 52:12 Feb 21, 78)

STRAUSS, Robert S. You know, it's awfully easy to tell people to go to hell. But it's another thing to get them there. (Newsweek 94:47 July 16, 79)

STRAVINSKY, Vera. When people ask me what I want for my birthday, I always say, 'Time, time, time'. (W 7:2 April 14, 78)

STRAVINSKY, IGOR FEDOROVICH, . If everything would be permitted to me, I would feel lost in this abyss of freedom. (New York Times 126:D25 Sept 11, 77)

STROESSNER, Alfredo. Human rights is a Trojan horse of international Communism. (Mother Jones 3:8 June 78)

STROUT, Richard. (American Democracy is) the only governmental vehicle on earth that has two steering wheels: one for the President, one for the Congress. You never can tell who's driving. (Time 111:83 Mar 27, 78)

STURM, Joanna. Grandmother (Alice Roosevelt Longworth) certainly is a feminist, but she'd never admit it. She feels it's tacky to identify yourself with a group, and to become overemotional. It's a question of esthetics. (Chicago Tribune 226:29 Aug 14, 77)

STYRON, William. I think a great novel could even come out of Beverly Hills. (New York Times Book Review 18 May 27, 79)

SUSANN, Jacqueline. I don't have any peers, as far as writers go. (After Dark 8:35 Aug 75)

SUSKIND, Sigmund. Cheating (in colleges) is not endemic, it's epidemic. (Time 107:29 June 7, 76)

SUTTON, Willie. I always figured that being a good robber was like being a good lawyer. (Village Voice 21:118 Sept 13, 76)

SWANSON, Gloria. It's hereditary, all in the genes. But no one can have skin like a baby's bottom if they're going to stuff that hole in their face with chocolate and banana splits. (Chicago Tribune 320:11 Section 5 Nov 16, 75)

SWAYDUCK, Edward. When we examine Ford's political and legislative record, we must ask the crucial question: Is Ford really an Edsel. (Washingtonian 11:294 Dec 75)

SWEARINGEN, John E. The President has made an emotional appeal to defend a tax program that is indefensible. His energy program involves the largest peacetime tax increase ever imposed on our citizens. (New York Times 126:A1 Oct 14, 77)

SYMINGTON, Stuart. (Charles Finley) is one of the most disreputable characters to enter the American sports scene. (New York Times 125:2 Section 5 Sept 19, 76)

SZASZ, Thomas. Just as (mental) illness is not a crime, so crime is not an illness. (TV Guide 28:32 May 17, 80)

SZATHMARY, Louis. If an American chef is pinching anything at 4 A.M., it is his wife's behind (when asked if French chefs were at market at 4 A.M. pinching tomatoes). (Chicago Sun-Times 31:41 Mar 6, 78)

SZENT-GYOERGYI VON NAGYRAPOLT, Albert. Discovery consists of seeing what everybody has seen and thinking what nobody has thought. (Omni 2:45 Dec 79)

TALBERT, Bob. Resisting temptation is easier when you think you'll probably get another chance later on. (Reader's Digest 107:166 Oct 75)

TALBERT, Diron. There ain't but one time to go fishin' and that's whenever you can. (The Washingtonian 11:116 Sept 76 (1))

TALBOTT, Basil, Jr. Chicago may have nominated its first mayor who goes to a beauty shop, but she is in the city's oldest tradition. (Chicago Sun-Times 32:5 section 2 Mar 4, 79)

TALESE, Gay. Lawyers have become the third force in publishing. I see them as the new enemy. (Time 115:51 Mar 17, 80)

TALMADGE, Betty. If you love the law and you love good sausage, don't watch either of them being made. (The Reader (Chicago's Free Weekly) 7:23 Nov 25, 77)

TALMADGE, Betty. There's not much difference between selling a ham and selling a political idea. (Time 112:23 July 31, 78)

TALMADGE, Herman. At no time did I maintain a cash hoard in the pocket of an overcoat or anywhere else. (New York Times 128:2 section 4 July 15, 79)

TALMADGE, Herman. I took my personal problems to the bottle rather than to my Maker. (Time 113:59 Mar 12, 79)

TALMADGE, Herman. The people of Georgia did not elect me to be a bookkeeper. (New York Times 128:A16 July 12, 79)

TALMADGE, Herman. Virtually everything is under federal control nowadays except the federal budget. (American Legion Magazine 99:17 Aug 75)

TANEN, Ned (former Hollywood agent). There's no orphan like the movie that doesn't work; a hit movie has 90 fathers. (New York Times Magazine 18 Aug 7, 77)

TANNER, Chuck. Having Willie Stargell on your ball club is like having a diamond ring on your finger. (Time 114:108 Oct 29, 79)

TANNER, Jack. An editor has no friends. (Challenge 19:5 Mar/April 76)

TANNER, Jack. Fame is empty. But it is better to find that out afterwards. (Challenge 19:5 Mar/April 76)

TANNER, Jack. Nothing could discredit capitalism more than a decision by the Russians to try it. (Challenge 19:4 Mar/April 76)

TANNER, Jack. A person without character always does what is right. (Challenge 19:5 Mar/April 76)

TANNER, Jack. What is counted as truth in one age is counted as myth in the next. (Challenge 19:4 Mar/April 76)

TANNER, Jack. When God created the world, He said it was good. That was His second mistake. (Challenge 19:5 Mar/April 76)

TARTIKOFF, Brandon. Hollywood is like Harvard. Once you're accepted, you can't flunk out. (New Times 10:31 Jan 9, 78)

TATI, Jacques. Comedians speak with their legs. (Times Literary Supplement 3969:460 April 28, 78)

TAWIL, Raymonde. We (Palestinians) are like grass. The more you cut it, the more it will grow. (Time 111:36 Mar 27, 78)

TAYAC, Turkey (Chief of the Piscataway Indians). They don't know about Indians any more than a buzzard knows about ice cream (about the Bureau of Indian Affairs). (Washingtonian 10:103 May 75)

TAYLOR, Elizabeth. I do feel sorry for Amy Carter, I know the problems she'll have. (Newsweek 88:66 Aug 9, 76)

TAYLOR, Elizabeth. I love Richard for the extravagant thought but he doesn't have to spoil me any more—just love me (upon the sale of her $1 million pink diamond ring purchased as a wedding gift. (Los Angeles Times 94:2 Part 1 Nov 8, 75)

TAYLOR, Elizabeth. I'm confident that he's (Jimmy Carter) a short-term President. (Chicago Tribune 212:44 July 31, 79)

TAYLOR, Elizabeth. When people say: she's got everything, I've only one answer: I haven't had tomorrow. (Chicago Tribune 176:2 section II June 25, 78)

TEAGUE, Freeman, Jr. Nothing is so simple it cannot be misunderstood. (Omni 1:132 May 79)

TEASDALE, Sara. Art can never mean to a woman what it does to a man. Love means that. (New York Times Book Review 9 Dec 23, 79)

TELLER, Edward. I am forever described as the father of the H-bomb. I would much prefer to be known as the father of two wonderful children. (Outside 1:13 Oct 77)

TELLER, Edward. Nuclear power is not an option—it is a part of the fight for the survival of freedom. (New York Times 129:A30 Dec 12, 79)

TENG, Hsiao-Ping. If the masses feel some anger, we must let them express it. (The Observer 9771:14 Dec 3, 78)

TENG, Hsiao-Ping. It doesn't matter whether you climb Mount Everest by its North slope or its South slope as long as you get to the top. (Newsweek 93:36 Feb 5, 79)

TENG, Hsiao-Ping. You can sign all the treaties you want, but you cannot trust the Russians. (Chicago Tribune 38:3 section 3 Feb 7, 79)

TERKEL, Studs. Dissent is not merely the right to dissent—it is the duty. (National Catholic Reporter 12:7 July 2, 76)

TERKEL, Studs. I would like to see the end of institutional brutalities and stupidities. I would like to see the abolition of the CIA, which symbolizes those things, and I would like people to look at the FBI as the secret police system it is, rather than something sacred. (Chicago Tribune 343:4 Section 1 Dec 8, 75)

TERKEL, Studs. Take it easy, but take it. (Studs Terkel Program June 16, 76)

TERKEL, Studs. Working people are brighter than we think. Their jobs may be drab, but they transcend them. (Time 111:77 Jan 30, 78)

TERRELL, Douglas. In Europe, it's easy to instill pride (in the Army); on the border they can see the enemy. In the States, they see McDonald's. (Newsweek 96:35 July 14, 80)

THARP, Twyla. Art is the only way to run away from home without leaving home. (Ms 5:66 Dec 76)

THARP, Twyla. Dancing is like bank robbery, it takes split-second timing. (Ms 5:68 Dec 76)

THARP, Twyla. I sometimes find structure a riot. (Chicago Tribune 198:3 section 6 July 17, 77)

THATCHER, Margaret Hilda. Britain's progress toward socialism has been an alternation of two steps forward with half a step back. (Time 105:30 Feb 10, 75)

THATCHER, Margaret Hilda. The British government is wholly committed to genuine black majority rule in Rhodesia. (Chicago Sun-Times 32:25 Aug 2, 79)

THATCHER, Margaret Hilda. Foreign policy is simply a matter of national self-interest. (New York Times Magazine 56 April 29, 79)

THATCHER, Margaret Hilda. I am controversial. That means I stand for something. (Time 115:34 Jan 7, 80)

THATCHER, Margaret Hilda. I never read books. (The Observer 9774:7 Dec 24, 79)

THATCHER, Margaret Hilda. I represent the workers, not the shirkers. (Look 1:44 June 11, 79)

THATCHER, Margaret Hilda. If a Tory does not believe that private property is one of the main bulwarks of individual freedom, then he had better become a socialist and have done with it. (Time 105:30-31 Feb 24, 75)

THATCHER, Margaret Hilda. If you want anything said, ask a man; if you want anything done, ask a woman. (New York Times Magazine 52 April 29, 79)

THATCHER, Margaret Hilda. I'm not a consensus politician, or a pragmatic politician, but a conviction politician. (Newsweek 93:52 April 9, 79)

THATCHER, Margaret Hilda. It is important not to be so obsessed with yesterday's danger that we fail to detect today's. (The Observer 9822:9 Nov 25, 79)

THATCHER, Margaret Hilda. I've got fantastic stamina and great physical strength, and I've a woman's ability to stick to a job and get on with it when everyone else walks off and leaves it. (Time 85:30 Feb 17, 75)

THATCHER, Margaret Hilda. No one would remember the Good Samaritan if he'd only had good intentions. He had money as well. (The Observer 9829:9 Jan 13, 80)

THATCHER, Margaret Hilda. Opportunity means nothing unless it includes the right to be unequal. (The Illustrated London News 263:26 Nov 75)

THATCHER, Margaret Hilda. Patience is not one of my obvious virtues. (The Observer 9832:9 Feb 3, 80)

THATCHER, Margaret Hilda. There can be no liberty unless there is economic liberty. (Village Voice 24:35 May 14, 79)

THATCHER, Margaret Hilda. We are not short of summits. The only thing we are short of is the results from summits. (The Observer 9723:11 Dec 18, 77)

THATCHER, Margaret Hilda. We (Conservatives) believe that you get a responsible society when you get responsible individuals. (New York Times Magazine 36 April 29, 79)

THATCHER, Margaret Hilda. What Britain needs is an iron lady. (Newsweek 93:50 May 14, 79)

THATCHER, Margaret Hilda. You cannot have national welfare before someone has created national wealth. (Time 112:61 Sept 11, 78)

THEROUX, Paul. Travel is glamorous only in retrospect. (The Observer 9815:10 Oct 7, 79)

THEROUX, Paul. You are not what you eat; but where you eat is who you are. (Travel & Leisure 7:76 Aug 77)

THOMAS, Bob. Hemingway had a very strong opinion that writers should not stay in journalism too long. He felt it damaged your sensitivity. I suspect he is right. (Writers Digest 56:27 May 76)

THOMAS, Caitlin (wife of Dylan Thomas). Dylan wanted us to be young and unwise forever—to be permanently naughty children. He managed this by killing himself with booze, but I was left to grow old. (Time 106:46 Dec 15, 75)

THOMAS, Dylan. I've had eighteen straight whiskies. I think that is the record. (Writer's Digest 58:11 Oct 78)

THOMAS, Lewis. These are bad times for reason, all around. Suddenly, all of the major ills are being coped with by acupuncture. If not acupuncture, it is apricot pits. (Time 109:97 May 23, 77)

THOMAS, Lewis. We do not, in any real way, run the (world). It runs itself, and we are part of the running. (Time 111:85 May 29, 78)

THOMAS, Lowell. After the age of 80, everything reminds you of something else. (Time 112:62 Nov 27, 78)

THOMAS, Lowell. The best years have been all of my years. (Newsweek 96:9 July 7, 80)

THOMAS, Marlo. A man has to be Joe McCarthy to be called ruthless. All a woman has to do is put you on hold. (New York Times Book Review 35 Feb 17, 80)

THOMAS, Marlo. Nothing is either all masculine or all feminine except sex. (People Weekly 8:50 Dec 19, 77)

THOMPSON, Hunter S. I don't plan to give up any of my guns until the cops give up theirs. (The California Aggie 96:6 Mar 2, 78)

THOMPSON, Hunter S. I don't think incompetence is any excuse for being a dumb President. (The California Aggie 96:6 Mar 2, 78)

THOMPSON, Hunter S. I'm basically a lazy person. And proud of it. (The California Aggie 96:6 Mar 2, 78)

THOMPSON, Hunter S. There's no such thing as a 'nice' reporter. That's like saying somebody's a nice liberal. (W 5:11 Sept 3, 76)

THOMPSON, James. It is better to make fun of yourself than let your opponent do it for you. (San Francisco Chronicle This World 1977:2 Oct 16, 77)

THOMPSON, Lord Roy Herbert. I am in business to make money, and I buy more newspapers to make more money to buy more newspapers. (New York Times 125:28 Aug 5, 76)

THOMPSON, Lord Roy Herbert. My favorite music is the sound of radio commercials at $10 a whack. (New York Times 125:28 Aug 5, 76)

THOMPSON, Lord Roy Herbert. No leisure, no pleasure, just work (commenting on the secret of his success). (New York Times 125:28 Aug 5, 76)

THOMPSON, Mike. Franklin Roosevelt couldn't be nominated today. A Bruce Jenner could beat him. (Time 115:26 Jan 28, 80)

THOMSON, Campbell. If it ever was true that a hospital was a charity organization, it no longer is true. (San Francisco Examiner 1977:1 May 1, 77)

THOMSON, Meldrim. Henry Kissinger is the cunning architect of America's planned destruction. (American Opinion 18:27 Oct 75)

THOMSON, Virgil. Music in any generation is not what the public thinks of it but what the musicians make of it. (New York Times 127:13 section 2 July 2, 78)

THURBER, James. One martini is all right, two is too many, three is not enough. (Rocky Mountain News 327:86 Mar 14, 80)

THURBER, James. There is no safety in numbers, or in anything else. (Washingtonian 14:155 Nov 78)

THURMOND, Strom. There are not enough laws on the books of the nation, nor can there be enough laws, to break down segregation in the South (commenting in 1948 as he accepted the presidential nomination of the Dixiecrat Party). (Washington Post 264:A3 Aug 27, 77)

TISELIUS, Arne. The world is full of people who should get the Nobel Prize but haven't got it and won't get it. (Time 112:81 Sept 25, 78)

TITO, Josip Broz. Frankly speaking, I would not like to live in America. True, there is democracy, in some respects even too much, while in others there is none. (San Francisco Chronicle This World 1978:2 Mar 12, 78)

TOKLAS, Alice B. The young men of today seem mostly to be interested in the manner rather than the matter. (Chicago Tribune 176:2 section II June 25, 78)

TOLSON, Clyde. I hopes that someone shoots and kills the son of a bitch (about Robert Kennedy). (Newsweek 92:79 Sept 4, 78)

TOLSTOY, Leo. Happy families are all alike. Every unhappy family is unhappy in its own way (from Anna Karenina). (New York Times 127:29 section 2 Feb 5, 78)

TOLSTOY, Leo (attributed by Woody Allen). Any man over 35 for whom death is not the main consideration is a fool. (Newsweek 85:87B June 23, 75)

TOMLIN, Lily. I worry about kids today. Because of the sexual revolution they're going to grow up and never know what dirty means. (Time 109:71 Mar 28, 77)

TOMLIN, Lily. If love is the answer, could you rephrase the question? (Cosmopolitan 188:268 Feb 80)

TOMLIN, Lily. Of all the actors working now, he (Richard Pryor) is the one who has the most instant rapport with his audience. (Time 110:66 Aug 22, 77)

TOMLIN, Lily. Sometimes I worry about being a success in a mediocre world. (New Times 9:47 Jan 9, 78)

TOMLIN, Lily. Why is it we are always hearing about the tragic cases of too much, too soon? What about the rest of us? Too little, too late. (Time 109:71 Mar 28, 77)

TOMLIN, Lily. Why is it when we talk to God, we're said to be praying, but when God talks to us, we're schizophrenic? (Time 109:71 Mar 28, 77)

TONSOR, Stephen. New Deal liberals are as dead as a dodo. The only problem is they don't know it. (Newsweek 90:34 Nov 7, 77)

TOOMEY, Bill. We would be naive to place track and field ahead of world events. Sports cannot live outside reality. (Time 115:16 Jan 28, 80)

TOON, Malcolm (United States Ambassador to Russia). I am not in a position to explain why the Soviets have or have not done certain things. I have never been able to explain what makes them tick. (People Weekly 6:34 Dec 13, 76)

TORRIJOS, Omar. In truth, the (Panama Canal Zone) treaty is like a little pebble which we shall be able to carry in our shoe for 23 years, and that is better than the stake we have had to carry in our hearts. (Time 110:10 Aug 22, 77)

TOSCANINI, Arturo. I kissed my first woman and smoked my first cigarette on the same day; I've never had time for tobacco since. (Kansas City Star 97:26 May 2, 77)

TOUREL, Jennie. You see, it isn't just boiled potatoes, what I do. (Stereo Review 35:80 Nov 75)

TOWER, John. You can argue shades of difference all day, yet there is little philosophical difference between Gerald Ford and Ronald Reagan. The important thing is that Mr. Ford is an 'electable' conservative while Mr. Reagan would lose to the Democratic candidate this fall. (Wall Street Journal 56:1 April 29, 76)

TOWNSEND, Peter. It isn't enough any more to write books: publishers expect you to sell them. (W 7:39 Nov 10, 78)

TOWNSHEND, Pete. The way all societies are is that some people get, and some people don't. (Rolling Stone 325:35 June 26, 80)

TOYNBEE, Arnold. The Englishman's truly distinctive disease is his cherished habit of waiting until the 13th hour. (Time 106:30 Aug 4, 75)

TOYNBEE, Arnold. To be able to fill leisure intelligently is the last product of civilization. (Chicago Tribune 67:1 section 5 Mar 8, 78)

TRACHTENBERG, Alan. Ellis Island represented the opening American act of one of the most remarkable dramas in all of history: the conversion of agricultural laborers, rural homemakers and traditional craftsmen into urban industrial workers. (Time 109:63 Mar 28, 77)

TRAIN, Russell E. Economic, social and environmental costs and benefits of the continued use (of mercurial pesticides) are not sufficient to outweigh the risk to man or the environment (commenting on the EPA immediate ban on production of virtually all pesticides containing mercury). (New York Times 125:1 Feb 19, 76)

TRAN-VAN-HUONG, . Thieu ran away from destiny; it has now come to me. (Time 105:15 May 5, 75)

TREVINO, Lee. Pressure is playing for ten dollars when you don't have a dime in your pocket. (Esquire 93:44 Feb 80)

TREZZA, Alphonse. The best (publishers') customer in the world is a library. You know why? They don't have the brains to cancel the subscription. (Library Journal 102:1339 June 15, 77)

TRILLING, Lionel. The particular concern of literature of the last two centuries has been with the self in its standing quarrel with culture. (Newsweek 86:69 Nov 17, 75)

TROLLOPE, Anthony. Nothing surely is so potent as a law that may not be disobeyed. It has the force of the water drop that hollows the stone. (Time 109:57 May 16, 77)

TROY, Frosty. He's George Wallace without racism (about Fred Harris). (Time 106:24 Dec 22, 75)

TRUDEAU, Margaret. I was not so much a hippy as a failed hippy; a hippy without a cause. (Guardian Weekly 120:18 June 17, 79)

TRUDEAU, Margaret. If I don't feel like wearing a bra I don't wear one. I'd never let my nipples show at a state function, though—I'd be frightened the old men would have heart attacks. (Rolling Stone 238:40 May 5, 77)

TRUDEAU, Margaret. It takes two to destroy a marriage. (Cosmopolitan 188:268 Feb 80)

TRUDEAU, Pierre Elliott. The atmosphere of Watergate has polluted the atmosphere of other democratic countries. Nobody trusts anybody anymore. (American Legion Magazine 98:32 May 75)

TRUDEAU, Pierre Elliott. He did not talk like a fanatic when he talked about world leaders. Within the framework of his ideology, he's a man of world stature (commenting on Fidel Castro after a visit to Cuba). (New York Times 125:3 Jan 30, 76)

TRUDEAU, Pierre Elliott. I'm saying that Canadians as a whole have been trying to get more out of society than they've been putting into it. (American Legion Magazine 102:22 June 77)

TRUDEAU, Pierre Elliott. Most Canadians understand that the rupture of their country would be a crime against the history of mankind. (Time 111:32 Feb 13, 78)

TRUDEAU, Pierre Elliott. The Tory future is worse than the Liberal past. (New York Times 128:3 May 20, 79)

TRUFFAUT, Francois. (Alfred Hitchcock) considers documentary and reportage the two inherent enemies of the cinema of fiction. (New York Times 128:19 section 2 Mar 4, 79)

TRUFFAUT, Francois. I am reproached because my men (in films) aren't adults, but in my life, I have not met many men who are adults. (Rolling Stone 293:43 June 14, 79)

TRUFFAUT, Francois. In love, women are professionals, men are amateurs. (Rolling Stone 293:43 June 14, 79)

TRUFFAUT, Francois. They (tomorrow's films) will resemble the men who make them, and the number of spectators will be about equal to the number of the director's friends. They will be an act of love. (Print 30:85 May/June 77)

TRUMAN, Harry S. The C students run the world. (Time 108:32 Nov 8, 76)

TRUMAN, Harry S. He (Douglas MacArthur) doesn't have a staff, he has a court. (Newsweek 85:90 May 12, 75)

TRUMAN, Harry S. Hell, he (Dwight Eisenhower) probably never paid a medical bill in his life (commenting on Eisenhower's dislike of welfare programs). (Newsweek 85:90 May 12, 75)

TRUMAN, Harry S. I never did give anybody hell. I just told the truth, and they thought it was hell. (Time 105:45 June 9, 75)

TRUMAN, Harry S. I vote for the better man. He is the democratic nominee. (Washington Post Magazine 5 Dec 3, 78)

TRUMAN, Harry S. (John Kennedy) had his ear so close to the ground it was full of grasshoppers. (Time 111:89 Mar 20, 78)

TRUMAN, Harry S. The only things worth learning are the things you learn after you know it all. (Reader's Digest 106:145 April 75)

TRUMAN, Harry S. That Richard Nixon, boys, is a no-good lying son of a bitch (commenting during one of his Presidential press conferences). (Newsweek 85:89 May 12, 75)

TRUMAN, Harry S. You know what makes leadership? It is the ability to get men to do what they don't want to do, and like it. (Time 108:49 Nov 8, 76)

TRUMAN, Harry S. You want a friend in this life, get a dog. (New West 3:33 Dec 4, 78)

TUCKER, Carol. Competition, you know, is a lot like chastity. It is widely praised, but alas, too little practiced (commenting on her plans as assistant agriculture secretary to seek a healthy shot of competition for the nation's food industry). (Chicago Sun-Times 30:2 April 19, 77)

TUCKER, Sophie. From birth to age 18, a girl needs good parents. From 18 to 35, she needs good looks. From 35 to 55, she needs a good personality. From 55 on, she needs good cash. (Chicago Sun-Times 30:21 Jan 28, 78)

TURNER, R. E. (Ted). If being against stuffiness and pompousness and bigotry is bad behavior, then I plead guilty. (Time 110:84 Sept 19, 77)

TURNER, R. E. (Ted). Lots of sex for everybody, that's a solution to the world's problems. (Playboy 25:67 Aug 78)

TWEED, William Marcy (Boss). I've tried to do some good, even if I have not had good luck. (New York 9:38 July 19, 76)

TYRRELL, R. Emmett, Jr. A new Government took office in Washington, not via bayonets and tanks as is the custom in some of the world's capitals (but) in the Democratic Way...via hyperbole, sham, melodrama and public-spirited mendacity (commenting on the Carter inauguration). (Time 109:93 Mar 7, 77)

UDALL, Morris King. A boss is a political leader who is on somebody else's side. (ABC News Issues and Answers 1 April 25, 76)

UDALL, Morris King. I am against vice in every form, including the Vice Presidency (responding to questions concerning the possibility of his accepting a vice presidential nomination). (New York Times 125:21 April 1, 76)

UDALL, Morris King. I am saying we have to make fundamental changes in this country, that we are at the end of an era of cheap energy and resources, that the 70's and 80's are going to be a time of adaptation. (Meet the Press 19:3 Nov 30, 75)

UDALL, Morris King. Obviously the Ford administration is very bad for this country. A Reagan administration would be much worse. I don't anticipate having any trouble supporting a Democratic candidate, whoever it is. (Meet the Press 20:6 April 4, 76)

UDALL, Morris King. (Ronald Reagan and George Wallace) are the twin horsemen of the radical right. (Chicago Sun-Times 29:70 Feb 6, 76)

UDALL, Morris King. The voters are the people who have spoken—the bastards (consoling his campaign workers with a story of what a politician, beaten in a close, hard-fought election once said). (Chicago Sun-Times 29:14 July 14, 76)

UDALL, Morris King. We fought a good fight, now we're here to help Jimmy Carter celebrate his victory (at the Democratic National Convention). (New York Times 125:2 July 11, 76)

UDALL, Morris King. You're not part of Anchorage society if you support a preservationist bill. (Saturday Review 6:20 Feb 17, 79)

UEMURA, Naomi (mountain climber). In an age when technology enables you even to reach the moon, an adventure is only possible where there is no technology. (Time 109:87 May 23, 77)

ULLMANN, Liv. A good director is the same all over the world. A good director is one who provides the inspiration and courage for you to use what is inside you. (Washington Post 77:K9 Feb 20, 77)

ULLMANN, Liv. You must put more in your life than a man. (Time 113:65 Jan 29, 79)

UNITED JEWISH APPEAL, . Speak now, so that we never again pay the price of silence. (appeared as part of an advertisement in the New York Times and the New York Post). (Time 105:39 May 12, 75)

UNITED STATES. CONGRESS. SENATE. SELECT COMMITTEE ON INTELLIGENCE OPERATIONS, . There is no inherent Constitutional authority for the President or any intelligence agency to violate the law. (New York Times 125:14 Section 4 May 2, 76)

UNRUH, Jesse. As a Governor, Reagan was better than most Democrats would concede, though not nearly as good as most Republicans like to think. (Time 106:19 Nov 24, 75)

UNRUH, Jesse. If I had slain all my political enemies, I wouldn't have any friends today. (New West 1:8 Sept 13, 76)

UNRUH, Jesse. Money is the mother's milk of politics. (US News & World Report 85:50 Sept 18, 78)

USERY, William J. Even though I don't have a teamsters card, I belong to this club because I believe in it. (Newsweek 87:49 June 28, 76)

USTINOV, Peter. An optimist is someone who knows exactly how sad and bad the world can be. (The Observer 9826:9 Dec 23, 79)

USTINOV, Peter. I just don't know what my image is and I don't want to know. If you arrive at the point where the man looking back at you in the mirror is more important than the man who is looking into the mirror, then you might as well pack up. (Christian Science Monitor 70:25 Dec 7, 77)

USTINOV, Peter. Pessimism was a Victorian luxury. I think nowadays you have to be optimistic—even if the facts are completely opposed to your viewpoint and ridiculous and unrealistic. (Christian Science Monitor 70:25 Dec 7, 77)

USTINOV, Peter. The time to write memoirs is when total recall has not yet invaded the cavities of the mind left empty by the inaction of retirement. (Christian Science Monitor 70:24 Dec 7, 77)

VAKY, Viron Peter. No negotiation, mediation or compromise can be achieved any longer with a Somoza government. (New York Times 128:A14 July 12, 79)

VALENTI, Jack. I sleep each night a little better, a little more confidently, because Lyndon Johnson is my President. (New York Times 126:1 section 4 Aug 21, 77)

VALLEE, Jacques. The theory of space and time is a cultural artifact made possible by the invention of graph paper. (CoEvolution Quarterly 16:82 Winter 77/78)

VALLEE, Rudy. I thought my freshman English instructor at Yale was crazy when he said life was cold, cruel, rotten, hard and it stinks. But I found out he was right. (Washington Post 333:B7 Nov 3, 75)

VALLI, Frankie. There's nothing wrong with the world, only the people in it. And the same goes for music. (New York 8:62 Aug 4, 75)

VANCE, Cyrus R. In pursuing a human rights policy, we must always keep in mind the limits of our power and of our wisdom. (New York Times 126:2 section 1 May 1, 76)

VANCE, Cyrus R. Our Export-Import Bank is continuing on schedule (to Korea) with its credit and its guarantee of $1 billion for the purchase of nuclear power plants. (New York Times 129:7 Nov 4, 79)

VAN DE WETERING, Janwillem. I've meditated for thousands of hours now, and I still don't know nothing. It's disgusting. (Chicago Tribune 291:1 section 2 Oct 18, 79)

VANDERBILT, Amy. One face to the world, another at home makes for misery. (Chicago Tribune 176:2 section II June 25, 78)

VANDERBILT, Gloria. A woman can never be too thin or too rich. (Chicago Sun-Times 32:3 Dec 18, 80)

VANDERBILT, William K. Inherited wealth is a real handicap to happiness. It is as certain a death to ambition as cocaine is to morality. (Times Literary Supplement 3960:198 Feb 17, 78)

VAN DERBUR, Marilyn (former Miss America). The vital, successful people I have met all had one common characteristic. They had a plan. (People Weekly 6:23 Dec 13, 76)

VAN DOREN, Mark (attributed by Robert Giroux). A classic is a book that is never out of print. (New York Times Book Review 23 Jan 6, 80)

VEECK, Bill. Baseball is the only orderly thing in a very unorderly world. If you get three strikes, even Edward Bennett Williams can't get you off. (Sports Illustrated 43:14 June 2, 75)

VEECK, Bill. I'd like to be devious, but I can't find it in myself. (Chicago 27:99 July 78)

VELLECA, Carl. The people will always know where to find me (commenting on his candidacy for Concord, Massachusetts' selectman which originated from his home at the Massachusetts Correctional Institution). (New York Times 125:18 April 26, 76)

VIDAL, Gore. Any man who can win a contemporary presidential campaign ought not to be President. (Rolling Stone 319:42 May 15, 80)

VIDAL, Gore. As now set up, the best one can hope for in a President is that he not be entirely insane. (Rolling Stone 319:42 May 15, 80)

VIDAL, Gore. Beside Carter and Reagan he (John Anderson) looks like Lincoln. Beside Lincoln he looks like Anderson. (Rolling Stone 319:42 May 15, 80)

VIDAL, Gore. Better the zero of Carter than the minus of Kennedy. (Rolling Stone 319:42 May 15, 80)

VIDAL, Gore. Each writer is born with a repertory company in his head. Shakespeare had perhaps 20 players, and Tennessee Williams has about five and Samuel Beckett one—and perhaps a clone of that one. I have ten or so, and that's a lot. (Time 111:47 April 17, 78)

VIDAL, Gore. I no more want to see the world end than Swift wanted to eat Irish babies. (Bookviews 1:22 June 78)

VIDAL, Gore. I would pay off those publications that report the doings and expenditures of Madame Onassis. Never to read about her again would not only be socially beneficial but would, I am sure, stem the rising tide of world communism (in response to 'What would you do with 10 million dollars'). (Money 4:76 Nov 75)

VIDAL, Gore. In writing and politicking, it's best not to think about it, just do it. (Bookviews 1:24 June 78)

VIDAL, Gore. It is not enough to succeed, a friend must also fail. (In The Know 1:47 June 75)

VIDAL, Gore. Most American writers I find phony, but it's a phony country. (Bookviews 1:24 June 78)

VIDAL, Gore. Reagan may not be all man, but he sure is all boy. Just what the country needs. (Rolling Stone 319:42 May 15, 80)

VIDAL, Gore. Sex is politics. (Playboy 26:177 Jan 78)

VIDAL, Gore. To understand Mary Hartman is to understand America. If Tiberius had watched the show, he would still be alive today. (Time 108:51 Aug 30, 76)

VIDAL, Gore. Truman (Capote) has made lying an art. A *minor* art. (Viva 5:105 Oct 77)

VIDELA, Jorge Rafael. A terrorist is not only someone with a gun or a bomb, but anyone who disseminates ideas contrary to Western and Christian civilization. (Mother Jones 3:38 July 78)

VIDOR, King. Good films, like good wine, improve with age. (New York Times 126:C6 Jan 14, 77)

VIDOR, King. I don't think one can sum up Russia in one word, but 'grim' might do. (W 8:12 Oct 12, 79)

VIORST, Judith. Brevity may be the soul of wit, but not when someone's saying 'I love you'. (Chicago Tribune 176:2 section II June 25, 78)

VIVA, . I'm so gullible that Hitler probably could have led me around by the nose. (W 4:10 July 11, 75)

VIZINCZEY, Stephen. No girl, however intelligent and warmhearted, can possibly know or feel half as much at 20 as she will at 35. (Time 111:99 April 24, 78)

VOIGT, Jon. The real dream (of America) is that with independence there is more strength and more beauty. (Rolling Stone 292:50 May 31, 79)

VOIGT, Jon. Things don't have to be about politics to be political. (Rolling Stone 292:50 May 31, 79)

VOLCKER, Paul A. The standard of living of the average American has to decline. (New York Times 129:1 Oct 18, 79)

VOLLBRACHT, Michaele. The fashion industry is like someone with a BB gun: they aim at you, they don't kill you, but they hurt you a hell of a lot. (Village Voice 22:63 Mar 14, 77)

VOLLBRACHT, Michaele. If you have to talk about fashion, then you are not in it. (Village Voice 22:63 Mar 14, 77)

VON BRAUN, Werner. I look forward to the day when mankind will join hands to apply the combined technological ingenuity of all nations to the exploration and utilization of outer space for peaceful uses. (Time 109:72 June 27, 77)

VON HAYEK, Friedrich. You can have economic freedom without political freedom, but you cannot have political freedom without economic freedom. (Village Voice 24:35 May 14, 79)

VON HOFFMAN, Nicholas. If he (William Paley) is remembered at all, it will be as the man who gave America 'Hee Haw'. (New York 12:109 April 30, 79)

VON HOFFMAN, Nicholas. Professionalism is a cheap and easy way of disciplining labor. (More 8:25 Feb 78)

VONNEGUT, Kurt. Hunter Thompson's disease,...an incurable, fatal malady suffered by those who feel that Americans can be as easily led to beauty as to ugliness, to truth as to public relations, to joy as to bitterness. (New Times 7:25 Dec 10, 76)

VONNEGUT, Kurt. The work (of writing fiction) is exceedingly tedious. It is like making wallpaper by hand for the Sistine Chapel. (Cosmopolitan 187:213 July 79)

VORONEL, Nina. Soviet life is so absurd that when I write realistically, it becomes the theatre of the absurd. (New York Times 125:28 Nov 7, 75)

VORSTER, John. It's fast reaching the state where we feel that the United States wants to prescribe to us (South Africa) how we should run our country internally and that is of course unacceptable to us. It is a fool who doesn't listen to advice but nobody can allow outsiders however well-intentioned, whatever their motives, to meddle in their internal affairs. (San Francisco Chronicle This World 1977:2 Sept 25, 77)

VOZNESENSKY, Andrei. When Man put on clothes for the first time, he challenged the Lord and became His equal. (Vogue 168:193 Feb 78)

VREELAND, Diana. Air conditioning is like power and love. In the wrong hands, it'll kill you. (W 7:13 July 7, 78)

VREELAND, Diana. Either one's life is attractive or it isn't. (Town & Country 129:79 June 75)

VREELAND, Diana. It was a small revolution and not bloody thank God. But it was a revolution, and for the first time youth went out to life, instead of waiting for life to come to them, which is the difference between the '60s and any other decade I've lived in (commenting on the flower children). (Chicago Tribune 226:4 section 5 Aug 14, 77)

VREELAND, Diana. Show me a fashionable woman, and I will show you a woman who accomplished something. (Newsweek 91:3 Jan 2, 78)

WADE, Richard. If you put the top 50 liberals inside a room to stop Henry Jackson, they'd have no troops for the job. Liberals have influence but no power. (Time 107:23 April 5, 76)

WAGNER, Richard. A poet is nothing if not someone who knows without having made a study. (New York Times Book Review 9 April 1, 79)

WAGNER, Robert. A person's state of happiness is almost directly related to the amount of gas in his tank. (New York Times 128:A10 July 13, 79)

WAGNER, Winifred. If Hitler walked through the door today, I would be just as glad and happy to see and have him here as ever. (Time 106:33 Aug 18, 75)

WAITS, Tom. Reality is for those who can't face drugs. (Playboy 26:26 Oct 79)

WAIYAKI, Munyha (Kenyan foreign Minister). We believe that the man (Jimmy Carter) is basically honest. He may not have had too much experience in government, but we don't hold it against him. This was one thing that was said about Africans not too long ago. (Newsweek 88:54 Nov 22, 76)

WALD, Jeffrey. I don't *think* I made her a star. I *know* I did (about Helen Reddy). (People Weekly 3:64 May 12, 75)

WALD, Richard. California understands the real purpose of television is to collect a crowd of advertisers. (Esquire 89:62 Feb 78)

WALDEN, Phil (President of Capricorn Records). That's the old American way—if you got a good thing, then overdo it. (Rolling Stone 216:10 July 1, 76)

WALDHEIM, Kurt. The post of Secretary General is at the same time one of the most fascinating and one of the most frustrating jobs in the world, encompassing, as it does, the height of human aspiration and the depth of human frailty. (New York Times 126:12 Dec 9, 76)

WALKER, Alexander (British critic). She (Lina Wertmueller) is a female misogynist masquerading as a political crusader.   (Time 107:58 Feb 16, 76)

WALKER, Jimmy. A reformer is a guy who rides through a sewer in a glass-bottomed boat.   (New York Times 129:A15 July 7, 80)

WALLACE, Clinton. Money is the means by which you can purchase everything but happiness and health, and will pay your ticket to all places but Heaven.   (National Review 30:282 Mar 3, 78)

WALLACE, Cornelia. I don't believe George needs a family. He just needs an audience.   (Parade 5 April 2, 78)

WALLACE, Cornelia. I'm the Rocky Stallone of Alabama politics.   (New York Times 127:A8 Aug 7, 78)

WALLACE, George Corley. Being a southerner is not as much geographical now as it is a state of mind. When I say southern I mean this: people are beginning to realize that big government is not good for the people.   (Encore American & Worldwide News 5:4 June 21, 76)

WALLACE, George Corley. I don't mind dictatorships abroad provided they are pro-American.   (Time 106:15 Oct 27, 75)

WALLACE, George Corley. I draw the line in the dust and toss the gauntlet before the feet of tyranny. And I say, segregation now. Segregation tomorrow. Segregation forever.   (New York 8:36 July 28, 75)

WALLACE, George Corley. Let 'em call me a racist in the press. It don't make any difference. Hell, I want 'em to. 'Cause if you want to know the truth, race is what's gonna win this thing for us.   (Sepia 26:10 Feb 76)

WALLACE, George Corley. Segregation is a moot question, and integration is the law of the land. It is a moot question, and therefore we don't want to go back, nor make any attempt to change what is now a fact accomplished.   (Meet the Press 20:5 Mar 28, 76)

WALLACE, George Corley. The Supreme Court has to write a hundred pages on what pornography is. The average man who works in a steel mill can tell you right off whether that's filth or not.   (Newsweek 85:44 April 21, 75)

WALLACE, George Corley. The viewpoints I expressed eight years ago now are expressed by all the candidates. They are expressed by a majority of the American people, and they are going to prevail in 1976 whether I'm around or not.   (Christian Science Monitor 68:3 Dec 5, 75)

WALLACE, George Corley. We told you years ago that the U.N. was a no-'count outfit.   (Time 106:41 Nov 24, 75)

WALLACE, Mike. There are no indiscreet questions, there are only indiscreet answers.   (Washington Post 190:L2 June 10, 79)

WALPOLE, Horace. You must renounce imagaination forever if you hope to succeed in plagiarism. Forgery is intention, not invention.   (Philadelphia 68:61 Aug 77)

WALTERS, Barbara. I always told people that if I ever had a million dollars my dream was to stay up every night reading trashy novels and sleep until noon.   (Time 107:51 May 3, 76)

WALTERS, Barbara. I just hope that all this talk of money doesn't confuse the issue—that this is a great breakthrough in network news. I think there is not a newsman who would have turned down the offer—and for a woman it is an even more unique opportunity (commenting on her ABC contract offer).   (Christian Science Monitor 68:9 April 26, 76)

WALTERS, Barbara. I never asked for a million dollars. They're (ABC) paying me this because this is what I'm worth. And I'm proud I'm worth it.   (Time 107:55 May 3, 76)

WALTERS, Barbara. If it's a woman, it's caustic; if it's a man, it's authoritative. If it's a woman, it's too often pushy, if it's a man it's aggressive in the best sense of the word (commenting on critics who call her brand of interviewing caustic).   (Writer's Digest 56:5 May 76)

WARD, Artemus. Let us all be happy and live within our means, even if we have to borrow the money to do it with.   (Chicago 26:111 Jan 77)

WARHOL, Andy. Art dealers (in reply to the question whom or what is the major influence on photography?).   (Village Voice 20:89 Dec 8, 75)

WARHOL, Andy. Art dealers (in response to the question Whom or what is the major influence on photography?).   (Village Voice 20:89 Dec 8, 75)

WARHOL, Andy. Bad taste makes the day go faster.   (Houston Home/Garden 5:42 Nov 78)

WARHOL, Andy. Good business is the best art.   (Time 106:32 July 28, 75)

WARHOL, Andy. I don't believe in it (death), because you're not around to know that it's happened.   (Time 106:32 July 28, 75)

WARHOL, Andy. I never fall apart because I never fall together.   (Newsweek 86:69 Sept 15, 75)

WARHOL, Andy. In the future everybody will be world famous for at least 15 minutes.   (Time 107:8 May 31, 76)

WARHOL, Andy. Movies are the new novels. No one is going to read anymore. Everyone is going to do movies, because movies are easier to do.   (Texas Monthly 4:42 Aug 76)

WARHOL, Andy. My ideal wife would have a lot of bacon, bring it all home and have a TV station, besides.   (Oui 4:60 May 75)

WARHOL, Andy. Sports figures are to the '70s what movie stars were to the '60s.   (Time 110:65 Nov 21, 77)

WARREN, Earl. A jurist's mind cannot operate in a vacuum.   (Christian Science Monitor 69:27 Aug 3, 77)

WARREN, Earl. Tricky (Richard Nixon) is perhaps the most despicable President this nation has ever had. He was a cheat, a liar and a crook, and he brought my country, which I love, into disrepute. Even worse than abusing his office, he abused the American people.   (Esquire 83:83 April 75)

WARREN, Robert Penn. What is man but his passion?   (Saturday Review 5:19 Dec 78)

WASHINGTON, Booker T., III. Being the sensitive man he was about his race, I think the present day Harlem scene would bring tears to my grandfather's eyes.   (Sepia 26:10 Feb 77)

WASSERMAN, Harvey. Nuclear energy is also a means to keep power—both electrical and otherwise—centralized in the hands of big money.   (Seven Days 1:37 March 14, 77)

WATERS, Craig. About 15 years ago, Jack Rosenberg changed his name to Werner Hans Erhard. His motive for doing so is unknown, but, with the switch, the son of a Jewish restaurant proprietor became an apparent Aryan: a son of history's perpetual victim became an heir apparent to one of history's greatest victimizers. (Boston Magazine 30:48 Sept 75)

WATTENBERG, Ben. How can a nation that believes it hasn't done anything right in the recent past even consider that it can do anything right, or bold, or creative in the immediate future. (Washington Post 72:B1 Feb 15, 77)

WATTENBERG, Ben. There is nothing so powerful as an old idea whose time has come again. (Washingtonian 15:143 Nov 79)

WATTS, Andre. Here lies a man who never played Petrouchka (on his epitaph). (Horizon 20:13 Dec 77)

WAUGH, Evelyn. An artist must be a reactionary. He has to stand out against the tenor of the age and not go flopping along. (Time 113:96 Feb 12, 79)

WAUGH, Evelyn. I regard writing not as investigation of character, but as an exercise in the use of language. (Time 113:96 Feb 12, 79)

WAUGH, Evelyn. It is impudent and exorbitant to demand truth from the lower classes. (Time 110:102 Oct 17, 77)

WAUGH, Evelyn. My children weary me. I can only see them as defective adults; feckless, destructive, frivolous, sensual, humourless. (Time 110:102 Oct 17, 77)

WAUGH, Evelyn. Punctuality is the virtue of the bored. (Time 110:102 Oct 17, 77)

WAUGH, Evelyn. You have no idea how much nastier I would be if I was not a Catholic. Without supernatural aid I would hardly be a human being. (Newsweek 86:119 Nov 24, 75)

WAX, Judith. It's to be expected that in middle age, mortality is not only intimated, but sometimes delivered, that pain and loss are birthday presents nobody asks for. (Los Angeles Times Book Review 2 June 10, 79)

WAYNE, John. I believe in white supremacy until the blacks are educated to a point of responsibility. (Newsweek 93:78 June 25, 79)

WAYNE, John. I stay away from nuances. (Time 113:50 June 25, 79)

WAYNE, John. I'm not an actor, I'm a reactor. I just do what seems natural in a situation. All I got's sincerity and simplicity. (The Tennessean 74:2 June 12, 79)

WAYNE, John. In my opinion Senator Joseph McCarthy was one of the greatest Americans that ever lived. (Guardian Weekly 120:6 June 17, 79)

WAYNE, John. Nobody likes my acting but the public. (The Tennessean 74:2 June 12, 79)

WAYNE, John. Success in films has little to do with acting. I just sell sincerity. And I've been selling the hell out of it since I got going. (Guardian Weekly 120:6 June 17, 79)

WEAVER, Earl. Good ballplayers make good managers, not the other way around. All I can do is help them be as good as they are. (Time 114:65 July 23, 79)

WEICKER, Lowell Palmer. Those who insist on walking backward into the future, with their faces turned resolutely to the past, run a very high risk of falling on their butts. We can not afford to approach the 21st Century with 19th Century foreign policy. (San Francisco Chronicle This World 1977:2 Oct 9, 77)

WEILER, A. H. Nothing is impossible for the man who doesn't have to do it himself. (Washingtonian 14:155 Nov 78)

WEIR, David. The SLA is not only a dream story to the newspapers, it is a dream story to the FBI as well, because it allows them to paint the entire left with the brush of the SLA. (City of San Francisco 9:30 Dec 9, 75)

WEISENFELD, Murray (podiatrist). A runner once came to me and told me that he was in a 55-mile race, and at 35 miles he began to get foot cramps. He asked me what he should do. I told him to see a psychiatrist. (New York Times 125:25 April 16, 76)

WEIZENBAUM, Joseph. A computer will do what you tell it to do, but that may be much different from what you had in mind. (Time 111:45 Feb 20, 78)

WEIZENBAUM, Joseph. We are rapidly losing, have perhaps already lost, physical and mental control of our society. (Omni 2:50 Dec 79)

WEIZMAN, Ezer. Anyone who says he is not emotional is not getting what he should out of life. (Time 112:115 Oct 30, 78)

WEIZMAN, Ezer. I am only responsible for Israel's security, not its sanity (about reports of new Israeli settlements in the Sinai). (Time 111:33 April 3, 78)

WEIZMAN, Ezer. I say to hell with everybody. We're going to have peace with the Gyppos. (Washington Post 314:M1 Oct 15, 78)

WELCH, Raquel. Don't get me wrong. I love being a world-famous sex object. But if you're an artist, you like to use your whole instrument. (People Weekly 5:51 June 21, 76)

WELCH, Raquel. I think the women's lib is only good politically, but sexually I don't think it works. (Chicago Sun-Times 29:22 Feb 20, 76)

WELCH, Robert (founder of the John Birch Society). Every President since Theodore Roosevelt has committed a treasonable act except—maybe—Warren G. Harding, Calvin Coolidge, and Herbert Hoover. (Chicago Tribune 194:14 July 13, 77)

WELK, Lawrence. I like clean ladies and nice ladies. (Playboy 26:26 Oct 79)

WELK, Lawrence. Politics, like music and golf, is best learned at an early age. Having reached the age of 72, I'm afraid it is a little late to change horses in the middle of a stream beset with treacherous currents (declining a draft movement in California for a 1976 presidential bid). (Time 105:81 April 14, 75)

WELLES, Orson. Patty Hearst is the central victim of our time...the best human story in the last thirty years—better than Kane. (Esquire 91:38 Feb 27, 79)

WERBLIN, David A. (Sonny). If you've been around athletes, you know an athlete when you see one, just by their attitude, just by the way they speak. (New York Times 127:C8 Feb 6, 78)

WERTMUELLER, Lina. I'm the last ballbuster left. (Time 107:59 Feb 16, 76)

WEST, Mae. The best way to hold a man is in your arms. (Cosmopolitan 188:268 Feb 80)

WEST, Mae. Between two evils, I always pick the one I never tried before. (Forbes 122:144 Aug 21, 78)

WEST, Mae. He who hesitates is last. (Chicago Tribune 176:2 section II June 25, 78)

WEST, Mae. I never needed Panavision and stereophonic sound to woo the world. I did it in black and white on a screen the size of a postage stamp. Honey, that's talent. (Rolling Stone 245:27 Aug 11, 77)

WEST, Mae. I'm for peace. I have yet to wake up in the morning and hear a man say, I've just had a good war. (Viva 4:26 Aug 77)

WEST, Mae. I've said it before and I'll say it again—I like a man that takes his time. (Coronet 13:37 Sept 75)

WEST, Mae. To err is human—but it feels divine. (Viva 4:24 Jan 77)

WEST, Mae. To me a star is somebody who has a little bit more than somebody else. (In The Know 1:35 Sept 75)

WEST, Mae. Too much of a good thing can be wonderful. (Human Behavior 7:17 May 78)

WEST, Mae. When I'm good, I'm very good; but when I'm bad, I'm better. (Oui 8:82 Jan 79)

WEST, Mae. You should marry for sex or money and you're really lucky if you can get both. (Chicago Tribune 64:1 section 5 Mar 5, 78)

WEST, Morris. In discourse the Italians are the most eloquent people in the world. In action they are either apathetic or impulsive to the point of insanity. (Esquire 89:81 April 25, 78)

WEST, Morris. Stupidity in Italy is an inheritance, built into the system by mad emperors, Bourbon kings, absolutist popes, tyrant dukes, and mafiosi. It is the conviction that change is impossible. (Esquire 89:77 April 25, 78)

WEST, Rebecca. There are jungles of people, and jungles of facts—which make it harder to recognize the great things when they do happen. (New York Times Book Review 14 Oct 2, 77)

WESTMORELAND, William Childs. Despite the final failure of the South Vietnamese, the record of the American military services of never having lost a war is still intact. (Los Angeles Times 94:25 Part 1 Oct 30, 75)

WESTMORELAND, William Childs. The Tet offensive was misrepresented to the American people by the media. It was the last despairing attack by the defeated North Vietnamese. (Saturday Review 6:6 Feb 17, 79)

WESTMORELAND, William Childs. We met the enemy, and he was us. (Rolling Stone 263:41 April 20, 78)

WETZSTEON, Ross. Sex, to paraphrase Clausewitz, is the continuation of war by other means. (Village Voice 20:89 April 28, 75)

WEXLER, Anne. I consider myself a liberal. Always have, always will. (New York Times 128:B14 Nov 24, 78)

WHEELWRIGHT, John Brooks. His death was his best poem (about Harry Crosby). (Village Voice 21:45 Sept 27, 76)

WHITE, Dan. I am not going to be forced out of San Francisco by radicals, social deviates, incorrigibles. (New York Times 128:1 section 4 Dec 3, 78)

WHITE, Dwight. There's no question that I'm schizoid. I might be three or four people. I know I can be evil. (Time 106:62 Dec 8, 75)

WHITE, E. B. Before I start to write, I always treat myself to a nice dry martini. (Writer's Digest 58:25 Oct 78)

WHITE, E. B. A cat sunning himself in the doorway of a barn knows all about solar energy. Why can't man learn? (Newsweek 94:80 Aug 13, 79)

WHITE, E. B. Humor can be dissected, as a frog can, but the thing dies in the process and the innards are discouraging to any but the pure scientific mind. (New York Times Magazine 70 Dec 2, 79)

WHITE, E. B.. New Yorkers temperamentally do not crave comfort and convenience. If they did, they would live elsewhere. (Time 112:20 Aug 21, 78)

WHITE, E. B. No one can write decently who is distrustful of the reader's intelligence. (New York Times 126:C19 Nov 17, 76)

WHITE, E. B. Non-commercial television should address itself to the ideal of excellence, not the ideal of acceptability. (Harper's 259:78 Aug 79)

WHITE, E. B. The way to approach a manuscript is on all fours, in utter amazement. (Washington Post 352:E2 Nov 21, 76)

WHITE, Ed. Losing this game was like having your house robbed and watching it happen (commenting on the Vikings 17-14 defeat by the Cowboys). (New York Times 125:3 Section 5 Jan 4, 76)

WHITE, Kevin. Charismatic leadership is hungered for, but at the same time we fear it. (Time 107:10 Feb 9, 76)

WHITE, Kevin. Everybody knows that Washington, D.C. has no culture—they have to buy it. (Time 113:71 April 23, 79)

WHITE, Kevin. It would be no easier to bus from an Irish to an Italian neighborhood (commenting on how the people of Boston feel about busing). (People Weekly 5:20 May 10, 76)

WHITE, Theodore. Class is a matter of style in leadership. It is the magic that translates the language of the street into the language of history. (Time 111:20 Mar 6, 78)

WHITE, Theodore. If you go back through 2000 years, I guess luck, Marx, and God have made history, the three of them together. (Firing Line 15 July 26, 75)

WHITE, Theodore. It's about time women had their say in the laws governing them—laws that for 5,000 years have been made by old men, mostly with shriveled-up groins, who have long since forgotten what it was like to be young and never knew what it was like to be a woman. (W 7:41 Sept 15-22, 78)

WHITE, Theodore. New York City is a glorious, or rather a tragic, example of 12 years of liberal government. (Firing Line 4 July 26, 75)

WHITE, Theodore. People don't want change—people want more. And I think liberals don't realize that. (Firing Line 9 July 26, 75)

WHITE, Theodore. Politics in America is the binding secular religion. (Firing Line 5 July 26, 75)

WHITE, Theodore. The true crime of Richard Nixon was simple: he destroyed the myth that binds America together, and for this he was driven from power. (Esquire 91:34 Feb 27, 79)

WHITE, William Allen. In education we are striving not to teach youth to make a living, but to make a life. (Kansas City Times 109:11B Feb 4, 77)

WHITEHEAD, Alfred North. Adventure is essential, namely, the search for new perfections. (Atlantic 244:29 Sept 79)

WHITEHEAD, Alfred North. The aims of scientific thought are to see the general in the particular and the eternal in the transitory. (Omni 2:41 Nov 79)

WHITEHEAD, Alfred North. Even perfection will not bear the tedium of indefinite repetition. (Atlantic 244:29 Sept 79)

WHITEHEAD, Alfred North. Nobody has a right to speak more clearly than he thinks. (Washingtonian 15:143 Nov 79)

WHITMAN, Alden. Carter's sermons (on human rights) might be more credible if he had a priority program to end poverty. (Rolling Stone 242:59 June 30, 77)

WHITMAN, Walt. New York is a fine place for a writer to sell his produce, but a poor place to grow it. (New York Times Book Review 9 July 29, 79)

WICKER, Tom. Government expands to absorb revenue—and then some. (Washingtonian 14:155 Nov 78)

WICKER, Tom. My life in journalism has persuaded me that the press too often tries to guard its freedom by shirking its responsibility, and that this leads to default on both. What the press in America needs is less inhibition, not more restraint. (Time 111:E3 May 22, 78)

WICKER, Tom. A reporter should write and his newspaper should print what they know. (Texas Observer 70:9 April 28, 78)

WICKER, Tom. To know things as they are is better than to believe things as they seem. (Reader's Digest 107:121 July 75)

WILDE, Oscar. American women seek in their husbands a perfection which English women seek only in their butlers. (Toronto Globe and Mail 134:6 April 29, 77)

WILDE, Oscar. The discovery of America was the beginning of the death of art. (New West 2:SC-20 Feb 28, 77)

WILDE, Oscar. A gentleman is one who never hurts anyone's feelings unintentionally. (Kansas City Star 97:2F June 5, 77)

WILDE, Oscar. History is gossip but scandal is gossip made tedious by morality. (Chicago Tribune 310:2 section 5 Nov 6, 77)

WILDE, Oscar. I am dying, as I have lived, beyond my means. (Writer's Digest 58:11 Oct 78)

WILDE, Oscar. Modern journalism, by giving us the opinions of the uneducated, keeps us in touch with the ignorance of the community. (New West 2:SC-19 Feb 28, 77)

WILDE, Oscar. Nothing spoils romance so much as a sense of humor in a woman. (Harper's Weekly 3163:10 June 14, 76)

WILDE, Oscar. The one duty we owe to history is to rewrite it. (New West 2:SC-19 Feb 28, 77)

WILDE, Oscar. Young people, nowadays, imagine that money is everything, and when they grow older they know it. (New West 2:SC-19 Feb 28, 77)

WILDER, Billy. As soon as you have chosen a subject for a film, you have already made a success or a failure. (New York 8:43 Nov 24, 75)

WILDER, Billy. France is a country where the money falls apart in your hands and you can't tear the toilet paper. (New York 8:43 Nov 24, 75)

WILDER, Billy. If there's one thing I hate more than not being taken seriously, it's being taken too seriously. (New York 8:43 Nov 24, 75)

WILDER, Gene. Everything I write is a love story and emotionally autobiographical. (Time 107:70 May 30, 77)

WILDER, Gene. It has been my experience that a producer gets more money than anyone else for what is essentially a $6.50-an-hour job. (The Star 4:2 July 26, 77)

WILDER, Roy. Tennis adds years to your life and life to your years. (New York Times 125:5 Section 5 Sept 12, 76)

WILKINS, Mac (1976 Olympic Discus Champion). America expects its athletes to wave a flag and win a medal every four years. But then you're supposed to take off that silly underwear and go out and make a decent living. (Time 107:67 Aug 9, 76)

WILKINS, Roy. If I weren't hopeful, I might as well shoot myself. Hope is the thing the NAACP has brought in its 66 years. (Sepia 25:10 Feb 76)

WILL, George. Education should be primarily an inoculation against the disease of our time, which is disdain for times past. (Washington Post 172:A15 May 26, 77)

WILL, George. Inflation is a great conservatizing issue. (Newsweek 90:36 Nov 7, 77)

WILL, George. When affirmative action came to Ann Arbor and Morningside Heights, dawn came up like thunder. (Newsweek 90:44 Nov 7, 77)

WILL, George. World War II was the last government program that really worked (to the Association of American Publishers). (Washingtonian 10:22 July 75)

WILLIAMS, Dakin. After all, high station in life is earned by the gallantry with which appalling experiences are survived with grace. (Chicago 26:18 Nov 77)

WILLIAMS, Dakin. Political campaigning is like sex. The pleasure is in the pursuit (explaining why he is running for governor of Illinois again). (Chicago 26:16 Nov 77)

WILLIAMS, Edward Bennett. The total egalitarians miss the point. They would divide the wealth equally, impose quotas and ratios in education, in employment, and in the political process, regardless of merit, overlooking the crucial fact that all human progress throughout history owes its origins to the talented and enterprising. (US News & World Report 88:30 Oct 31, 77)

WILLIAMS, Robert. There's nothing wrong with making a buck. Free enterprise is the thing that has made this country go zowee (about the sale of Bicentennial products). (Time 106:73 Sept 29, 75)

WILLIAMS, Tennessee. Men are rather inscrutable to me. (W 8:14 April 13, 79)

WILLIAMS, Tennessee. They teach it (The Glass Menagerie) in college now, and everybody approaches it as though it were a place of worship. Frankly, I fall asleep at times. (Time 106:31 Dec 29, 75)

WILLIAMS, Tennessee. Time is the longest distance between two places. (Omni 2:38 July 80)

WILLS, Garry. Politicians fascinate because they constitute such a paradox: they are an elite that accomplishes mediocrity for the public good. (Time 113:86 April 23, 79)

WILLS, Garry. (The Pope's) theological conservatism undercuts his political liberalism. (Time 114:35 Oct 15, 79)

WILSON, Earl. Middle age is when your clothes no longer fit, and it's you who need the alterations. (Reader's Digest 108:146 Feb 76)

WILSON, Earl. Nature does her best to teach us. The more we overeat, the harder she makes it for us to get close to the table. (Kansas City Times 109:28 Jan 4, 77)

WILSON, Earl. The success of today's rock songs proves one thing—rhyme doesn't pay. (Reader's Digest 112:119 Mar 78)

WILSON, Edmund. Have we ever turned out anything that was comparable artistically to the best German or Russian films? I can think of nothing except Charlie Chaplin, who is his own producer and produces simply himself. (Time 111:63 Jan 2, 78)

WILSON, Harold. (Ian Smith is the) most slippery political customer I've ever negotiated with. (Time 108:37 Oct 11, 76)

WILSON, Harold. It is no longer a humorous matter to point out that in a few years there is a strong possibility that Britain could become a member of OPEC. (Time 106:30 Dec 15, 75)

WILSON, Harold. Once I leave, I leave. I am not going to speak to the man on the bridge, and I am not going to spit on the deck (upon his resignation as Prime Minister of Great Britain). (New York Times 125:14 Mar 17, 76)

WILSON, Harold. Those who subscribe to the Northern Irish Aid Committee, the principal IRA fund-raising organization in the United States, are not financing the welfare of the Irish people, as they might delude themselves. They are financing murder. (Chicago Daily News 298:2 Section 1 Dec 18, 75)

WILSON, Robert Anton. If a man's ideas aren't frightening enough to get him imprisoned, you can be sure he's not really thinking something new and important. (Fate 30:7 Oct 77)

WILSON, Sloan. It is impossible to treat a woman too well. (New York 9:46 May 24, 76)

WILSON, Sloan. A man who wants time to read and write must let the grass grow long. (New York 9:46 May 24, 76)

WILSON, Sloan. A writer's job is sticking his neck out. (Writer's Digest 58:9 Feb 78)

WINCHESTER, Jesse. A war is like a storm; there's nobody to blame, and everybody gets hurt. You've just got to do the best you can. (Mother Jones 2:61 July 77)

WINNER, Michael. Film audiences are people who are seeking light relief in a dark room for an hour and a half. (Chicago Tribune 324:22 section 6 Nov 20, 77)

WINPISINGER, William (union leader). I don't mind being called a lefty. We're being centered to death. (Time 110:52 July 11, 77)

WINPISINGER, William (union leader). I have immense respect for George Meany, but there comes a time when every man passes the apex of his career, and it's all downhill after that. When the polls rate labor just behind Richard Nixon and just ahead of used car salesmen, you know something needs to be changed. (Time 110:22 July 11, 77)

WINPISINGER, William (union leader). In my lifetime, no group has ever gotten justice in this country without lawlessness. So if we want to see change, then we may have to stop having such a high regard for law-and-order. (Time 112:40 Sept 4, 78)

WIRIN, Abraham Lincoln. The rights of all persons are wrapped in the same constitutional bundle as those of the most hated member of the community. (Time 111:94 Feb 20, 78)

WISE, Howard. Great artists and great scientists share many of the same qualities: tenacity, courage, and imagination. (Omni 2:101 April 80)

WISEMAN, Frederick. The final film is a theory about the event, about the subject in the film. (Film Quarterly 31:15 Spring 78)

WOLF, Arnold Jacob. America, where were you when we needed you? And we, where are we now that you need us? (National Catholic Reporter 12:8 July 2, 76)

WOLFE, Tom. You can be denounced from the heavens, and it only makes people interested. (Time 114:82 Sept 24, 79)

WONDER, Stevie. How can you even think of being conceited—with the universe as large as it is? (Penthouse 7:131 Feb 76)

WONDER, Stevie. They (the Beatles) brought all different cultures together. They made White Middle America wake up about those old black artists—the Beatles brought them to people who had never heard of them. And it gave those artists—who were sometimes starving—some money. (Penthouse 7:90 Feb 76)

WONDER, Stevie. What's most beautiful about touring is that I've met some friends in every place I've gone. It always feels to me like I am just playing in someone's living room. (Penthouse 7:92 Feb 76)

WOOD, Natalie. Anyone who says it doesn't hurt when (critics) zap you is not to be believed. (Time 114:101 Dec 10, 79)

WOOD, Robert. Freddie's (Silverman) like a shark's belly. He can't get enough. (Time 110:46 Sept 5, 77)

WOODS, Donald. The level of black anger in my country today is so high, and the determination of whites to resist fair compromise is so strong, that both sides are on a collision course toward a racial civil war. (San Francisco Chronicle This World 1978:2 Feb 5, 78)

WOODWARD, Joanne. You cannot be an actor without being willing to make a fool of yourself. (Chicago Tribune Magazine 38 Aug 7, 77)

WOOLF, Virginia. The art of writing has for backbone some fierce attachment to an idea. (Writer's Digest 58:7 Feb 78)

WOOLF, Virginia. The eyes of others our prisons; their thoughts our cages. (Chicago Tribune 176:2 section II June 25, 78)

WOOLF, Virginia. The history of men's opposition to women's emancipation is more interesting perhaps than the story of that emancipation itself. (Los Angeles Times 97:6 part 4 Feb 3, 78)

WOOLLCOTT, Alexander. I'm tired of hearing it said that democracy doesn't work. Of course it doesn't work. It isn't supposed to work. We are supposed to work it. (Kansas City Times 109:28 Jan 4, 77)

WOTTON, Sir Henry. The aim of architecture is to build well. Well-building hath three conditions: commodity, firmness and delight. (Time 111:63 June 5, 78)

WRIGHT, Frank Lloyd. Houston is an example of what can happen when architecture catches a venereal disease. (Texas Monthly 6:77 Feb 78)

WRIGHT, Frank Lloyd. I have been black and blue in some spot, somewhere, almost all my life from too intimate contact with my own early furniture. (Chicago Tribune 24:1 section 2 Jan 24, 78)

WRIGHT, James. When people are drowning, there is no time to build a better ship. (Chicago Sun-Times 30:2 Feb 2, 77)

WRIGHT, James. The Wright broad rule is that broads ought to be able to type (commenting when asked to state a broad rule for avoiding Congressional sex scandals). (Wall Street Journal 57:1 Dec 31, 76)

WRISTON, Walter. I believe there are no institutional values, only personal values. (Guardian Weekly 124:16 Jan 25, 81)

WRISTON, Walter. To think that the bell does not toll for academic freedom or freedom of the press if economic freedom is shackled is a dangerous illusion. (Time 114:43 Aug 13, 79)

WURF, Jerry. If Jimmy Carter emerges as a strong President and keeps the promises he made in 1976, then there is still time for him to be born again politically. (New York Times 128:A10 July 13, 79)

WYETH, Andrew. Technique is not what interests me. To me, my art is deeply the question of whether or not I can find the theory that expresses the way I feel at a particular time about my own life and my own emotions. (ARTnews 76:43 Dec 76)

WYETH, Andrew. True reality goes beyond reality itself. (Christian Science Monitor 70:24 Sept 28, 78)

WYETH, Jamie. They don't allow anything but realism there. At the end, I told them I could understand their censoring talking and writing but why Art? Their answer was 'Never underestimate the power of painting' (on his recent trip to the Soviet Union). (Wall Street Journal 56:12 Nov 26, 75)

YAMASHITA, Sachio (Painter). Art, color are the vitamins of the soul. (Time 105:8 March 3, 75)

YARBOROUGH, Ralph. This may be the only case on record of a rat swimming toward a sinking ship (commenting on John Connally's announced defection from the Democrats to the Republicans). (New York Times Magazine 50 Aug 8, 76)

YEW, Lee Kuan. The Russians say that there are many different roads to socialism, and that sounds good to new nations. But the United States seems to be saying that there is only one road to democracy. (American Legion Magazine 103:12 Aug 77)

YOSHIMURA, Wendy. I remain high in spirit and strong in my convictions. I extend my special solidarity to all my friends above ground and in the prisons and the Third World (upon being released on bail after 3 months in jail). (Los Angeles Times 95:1 Part 2 Dec 20, 75)

YOUNG, Andrew. After all there are hundreds, perhaps even thousands of people in our (American) prisons, whom I would call political prisoners. I myself was sentenced in Atlanta 10 years ago for having organized the garbage workers there. Yet, three years later, I was a member of the House of Representatives in Georgia. (Guardian Weekly 119:7 July 23, 78)

YOUNG, Andrew. Black folks didn't need much selling on Carter. They have a special kind of radar about whether white folks are for real. (New York 9:91 July 12, 76)

YOUNG, Andrew. Eleven o'clock Sunday morning is still the most segregated hour of the week, and I don't know that anybody can be self-righteous about church integration. (Issues and Answers 2 Nov 14, 76)

YOUNG, Andrew. Georgia is more liberal than New York. (Atlanta 19:60 Nov 79)

YOUNG, Andrew. I don't think affirmative action for blacks requires discrimination against whites. (Sepia 24:10 July 75)

YOUNG, Andrew. I like to get things done, and I don't run from evil. My office has always been open to South Africans. And the meaner and whiter they are, the more I like 'em to come by. (People Weekly 6:30 Dec 27-Jan 3, 77)

YOUNG, Andrew. I really don't feel a bit sorry for anything I have done (on resigning as ambassador to the United Nations). (Time 114:10 Aug 27, 79)

YOUNG, Andrew. I was taught to fight when people called me nigger. That's when I learned that negotiation is better than fighting. (Time 108:13 Dec 27, 76)

YOUNG, Andrew. Influence is like a savings account. The less you use it, the more you've got. (People Weekly 6:30 Dec 27/Jan 3, 77)

YOUNG, Andrew. (Jimmy) Carter does not hand out nickels after a campaign (about political rewards for supporting him). (Time 107:18 June 28, 76)

YOUNG, Andrew. Nigeria is arrogant and Kissinger is arrogant, and so there was a clash. I may be just as arrogant, but I can control it better. (Time 109:44 Feb 21, 77)

YOUNG, Andrew. Nothing is illegal if 100 businessmen decide to do it, and that's true anywhere in the world. (Rolling Stone 235:35 Mar 24, 77)

YOUNG, Andrew. The Russians are the worst racists in the world. (Life 2:117 Dec 79)

YOUNG, Andrew. Sin began with Adam. If you turn the lights out, folks will steal. They'll do that in Switzerland, too. (Rolling Stone 249:33 Oct 6, 77)

YOUNG, Andrew. The truth of the matter is, we as blacks want our cake and want to eat it too. (Chicago Sun-Times Today is Sunday 1:4 June 4, 78)

YOUNG, Loretta. A beautiful face gets you the first five minutes. After that you're on your own. (New Hampshire Profiles 27:18 May 78)

YOUNGQUIST, Wayne. People want leaders with vision rather than programs. Even if conservatism is overtaking liberalism and individualism is prized over collective action, vision is always in demand and often rewarded at the polls. (Time 112:23 Oct 23, 78)

ZACK, Al (spokesman for AFL-CIO). The political and ethical question is whether the word of the President of the United States is any good, and the answer as far as Ford is concerned is still no, even though he has named a good labor secretary (commenting after the nomination of W. J. Usery, Jr. as Secretary of Labor). (Los Angeles Times 95:13 Part 1 Jan 23, 76)

ZAPPA, Frank. The biggest dangers we face today don't even need to sneak past our billion-dollar defense system. They issue the contracts for them. (Rolling Stone 205:22 Jan 29, 76)

ZAPPA, Frank. High school isn't a time and a place. It's a state of mind. (Human Behavior 5:65 Aug 76)

ZAPPA, Frank. It (Boston) is one of the three cities in the world where the girls wear the ugliest shoes. (Boston 70:21 Dec 78)

ZAPPA, Frank. Most rock journalism is people who can't write, interviewing people who can't talk, for people who can't read. (Chicago Tribune 18:12 Jan 18, 78)

ZEFFIRELLI, Franco. You must be as tough as rubber and as soft as steel. (Times Literary Supplement 3969:460 April 28, 78)

ZELZER, Harry. Good music is not as bad as it sounds. (Chicago 27:12 Oct 78)

ZIA UL-HAQ, Mohammad. The army is the only stable institution in Pakistan. (The Observer 9701:13 July 17, 77)

ZIA UL-HAQ, Mohammad. If the Supreme Court says 'acquit him,' I'll acquit him. If it says, 'hang the blighter,' I'll hang him (about Zulfikar Ali Bhutto). (The Observer 9762:8 Oct 1, 78)

ZIA UL-HAQ, Mohammad. With his brain, Bhutto could have been President for life. (The Observer 9762:8 Oct 1, 78)

ZIEGLER, Ronald Louis. Basically, it's the story of a couple of reporters (after seeing All The President's Men). (New York 9:58 April 12, 76)

ZIEGLER, Ronald Louis. I never knowingly lied, but certainly history shows that many things I said were incorrect. (Newsweek 91:22 April 17, 78)

ZIMBALIST, Efrem, Jr. When the lion (J. Edgar Hoover) dies, the rats come out. (Time 106:14 Dec 22, 75)

ZISK, Richie (baseball player). Chicago is the kind of place where, if you fall flat on your face, there's someone to pick you up instead of stomping on your face. (Chicago Tribune 248:20 Sept 5, 77)

ZOLA, Emile. Perfection is such a nuisance that I often regret having cured myself of using tobacco. (Kansas City Star 97:2B July 31, 77)

ZUKOR, Adolph. Look ahead a little and gamble a lot (a formula for success). (Time 107:55 June 21, 76)

ZUMWALT, Elmo R., Jr. A final malady that afflicted—and continues to afflict—the whole Navy, though the surface Navy was and is the greatest sufferer, can be described in one word: Rickover. (Chicago Daily News 92:10 April 16, 76)

SUBJECTS

AARON, HENRY

Lee, Bill (pitcher for the Boston Red Sox). I'm mad at Hank Aaron for deciding to play one more season. I threw him his last home run and thought I would be remembered forever. Now I'll have to throw him another.

ABORTION

Bernardin, Joseph. If the concept of a woman's freedom requires that she have the right to destroy her offspring, then that concept of freedom is brutal and unworthy... Freedom cannot be freedom from personal responsibility. Freedom follows from responsible action.

Blackmun, Harry. There is another world out there, the existence of which the (Supreme) Court, I suspect, either chooses to ignore or fears to recognize. And so the cancer of poverty will continue to grow. (Writing on the decision not to require government financing of abortions).

Carter, James Earl. There are many things in life that are not fair.

Farenthold, Frances Tarlton (Sissy). The right to an abortion has become a class issue, a race issue, a privacy issue and even a consumer issue, but it is above all, our issue (commenting on the National Women's Political Caucus).

Ford, Gerald Rudolph. I share your deep appreciation about the increased irreverence for life (commenting in a speech to the 41st Eucharistic Congress).

Hyde, Henry. There are one million children who are thrown away like Kleenex because someone thinks they are not as valuable as a snail darter (opposing abortions).

Kennedy, Florynce Rae. If men could get pregnant, abortion would be a sacrament.

McLuhan, Marshall. To discuss the dignity of an unborn life is ludicrous (when) the Apocalypse is at hand.

Marshall, Thurgood. (I am) appalled at the ethical bankruptcy of those who preach a right to life that means a bare existence in utter misery for so many.

Mother Teresa, . Those countries with legalized abortions are the poorest countries in the world.

O'Rourke, Joseph. The antiabortionists are antifree, antiwomen and anti-Christian.

ABZUG, BELLA

Abzug, Bella. I may not look like a Senator, but I think I'm what a Senator should look like.

Abzug, Bella. Like Jimmy Carter, I expect to be born again. I may have lost my seat, but my voice, never.

ACADEMIC FREEDOM

Wriston, Walter. To think that the bell does not toll for academic freedom or freedom of the press if economic freedom is shackled is a dangerous illusion.

ACHIEVEMENT

Miller, George William. There is no penalty for overachievement.

ACTING

Burns, George. To be perfectly honest, I don't think acting is very hard. They say the most important thing is to be able to laugh & cry. Well, if I have to cry, I think of my sex life, and if I have to laugh, I think of my sex life.

DeNiro, Robert. You have to earn the right to play a character.

Dunaway, Faye. I've always thought that acting is an art of creating accidents.

Finch, Peter. Acting is fascinating and not an ignoble profession. No one lives more than the actor.

Foster, Jodie. I've never studied acting. My technique is pure instinct. I'm not bragging, but certain kids have the timing and ability to mimic—and others don't. That's the way it is. And it's important not to be self-conscious.

Gielgud, John (attributed by Leslie Caron). Never show your good side—show your faults (instruction to actors).

Hepburn, Katharine. Acting really isn't a very high-class way to make a living, is it?.

Heston, Charlton. Acting is the oldest profession, no matter what claims are made by the other trade.

Jackson, Glenda. Acting is an opportunity to meet other people's minds that you can't get anywhere else.

Newman, Susan. Making movies has nothing to do with acting.

Olivier, Laurence. Acting great parts devours you.

Olivier, Laurence. Acting is a masochistic form of exhibitionism.

Olivier, Laurence. You can't just run. You have to look as if you're running (about acting).

Richardson, Sir Ralph. You've got to perform the role hundreds of times. In keeping it fresh one can become a large, madly humming, demented refrigerator. You go mad (on being in a hit play).

Scott, George C. Most actors, maybe all actors, are not really all that fascinating or brilliant people, aside from their ability to perform on stage or for the camera. If you ask me, they're dull.

Scott, George C. The actor is never rewarded in film. Film stardom is a peripheral and distorted kind of fulfillment.

Stewart, James. The most important thing about acting is to approach it as a craft, not as an art and not as some mysterious type of religion.

Ullmann, Liv. A good director is the same all over the world. A good director is one who provides the inspiration and courage for you to use what is inside you.

Woodward, Joanne. You cannot be an actor without being willing to make a fool of yourself.

Young, Loretta. A beautiful face gets you the first five minutes. After that you're on your own.

ACTORS AND ACTRESSES

Bacall, Lauren. I agree with the Bogart theory that all an actor owes the public is a good performance.

Beaton, Sir Cecil. I think you have to have a strange note of badness if you are to have, to possess goodness (when asked what similarities exist between stars of yesteryear and today).

Burton, Richard. We actors, madmen, are capable of experiencing not just the moment but the nostalgia and anticipation of it.

DeNiro, Robert. You have to earn the right to play a character.

Dietrich, Marlene. Never marry an actress (to Eddie Fisher).

Giannini, Giancarlo. For an actor, it's always difficult to have a wife. It's not hard to be without one.

Gish, Lillian. I don't think actresses have the right to marry and ruin a man's life.

Gordon, Ruth (actress). In the old days, ptomaine poisoning was a cover-all. If you missed a show and you were young, it meant you were having an abortion. If you were old, it meant you were having a face-lift.

Hitchcock, Alfred Joseph. All actors should be treated like cattle.

Hitchcock, Alfred Joseph. Well, I think it's below one's dignity to be an actor (commenting on why he will not appear in films of other directors).

Loren, Sophia. We actors are the damned of the earth.

Mason, James. Talking about my leading ladies is difficult for me if I'm going to be honest. Any opinion I give is bound to offend somebody. So when I want to tread cautiously, I tell people that the best actress I ever worked with was Margaret Rutherford.

Niven, David. Actors don't retire, they just get offered fewer parts.

Olivier, Laurence. Probably every great actor in history was the son of a clergyman.

Stallone, Sylvester. Actors are a walking, throbbing mass of unhealed scar tissue by the time they get anywhere.

West, Mae. To me a star is somebody who has a little bit more than somebody else.

ACUPUNCTURE

Thomas, Lewis. These are bad times for reason, all around. Suddenly, all of the major ills are being coped with by acupuncture. If not acupuncture, it is apricot pits.

ADAMS, ANSEL

Adams, Ansel. Some people belong to a church—everybody needs something to believe in. Conservation is my point of focus.

ADULTERY

Carter, James Earl. Christ says don't consider yourself better than someone else because one guy screws a whole bunch of women while the other guy is loyal to his wife.

ADVENTURE

Buckley, William Frank, Jr. All adventure is now reactionary.

Uemura, Naomi (mountain climber). In an age when technology enables you even to reach the moon, an adventure is only possible where there is no technology.

ADVERTISING

Morley, Robert. Commercials are the last things in life you can count on for a happy ending.

Ogilvey, David. The consumer is not a moron. She is your wife.

ADVICE

Nash, Ogden. People who have what they want are fond of telling people who haven't what they want that they really don't want it.

AESTHETICS

Shapiro, Joseph H. Aesthetics is to art what ornithology is to birds.

Sontag, Susan. Style is the principle of decision in a work of art, the signature of the artist's will.

AFRICA

Amin Dada, Idi. We should not let ourselves be brainwashed by the Western powers that the presence of Soviet technicians in Angola is an indication that the Soviet Union wants to colonize Africa.

Naipaul, V. S. Africa has no future.

Stein, Gertrude. Nothing can, or will, happen in Africa.

AFRICA—POLITICS AND GOVERNMENT

Belafonte, Harry. When African countries got independence, I thought there would be a new morality in the world. The next thing I knew Nigerians were shooting Biafrans, and Idi Amin was on the scene. I thought, 'My God, we're not better than the rest.' There are no super-blacks any more than super-whites. They're only people.

Moynihan, Daniel Patrick. It is no accident, I fear, that this racist murderer (Idi Amin), as one of our leading newspapers (the New York Times) called him this morning, is the head of the Organization of African Unity.

AFRICA—RACE QUESTION

Kaunda, Kenneth. Not every white man is bad.

AFRICANS

Waiyaki, Munyha (Kenyan foreign Minister). We believe that the man (Jimmy Carter) is basically honest. He may not have had too much experience in government, but we don't hold it against him. This was one thing that was said about Africans not too long ago.

AGE

Bergman, Ingrid. I don't dream about my past. I accept my age and make the best of it.

Hayakawa, Samuel Ichiye. There is only one thing age can give you, and that is wisdom.

Levi-Strauss, Claude. Age removes the confusion, only possible in youth, between physical and moral characteristics.

Stein, Gertrude. We are always the same age inside.

AGED

Chevalier, Maurice. Old age is a wonderful thing...when you consider the alternative.

Comfort, Alex. Nobody is safe being prejudiced against what they themselves are going to become (commenting on aging).

Cowley, Malcolm. One compensation of age is simply sitting still.

Lawton, George E. If it is important to give the human animal a good start in life, it is just as important to see that he makes a good finish.

Paige, Satchel. How old would you be if you didn't know how old you was?.

AGING

Bardot, Brigitte. It's better to be old than dead.

Baruch, Bernard Mannes. To me, old age is always 15 years older than I am.

Collins, Judy. Aging does have its rewards.

Comfort, Alex. Nobody is safe being prejudiced against what they themselves are going to become (commenting on aging).

Crawford, Joan. Growing old is no fun. Frankly, if they (senior citizens) say they enjoy it, I think they're either lying through their teeth or they've grown senile.

Hellman, Lillian. In looking about me, in looking at me, I have long believed that few people grow wiser with the years.

Longworth, Alice Roosevelt. The secret of eternal youth is arrested development.

Moreau, Jeanne. Age does not protect you from love. But love, to some extent, protects you from age.

Paige, Satchel. How old would you be if you didn't know how old you was?.

Pierson, L. R. If you're coasting, you're going downhill.

Thomas, Lowell. After the age of 80, everything reminds you of something else.

Wax, Judith. It's to be expected that in middle age, mortality is not only intimated, but sometimes delivered, that pain and loss are birthday presents nobody asks for.

AGNEW, SPIRO THEODORE

Agnew, Spiro Theodore. I'm in possession of some information, which I won't disclose, that leads me to believe that I would be elected to office if I chose to see to it. I don't think my name needs rehabilitation. I did nothing morally wrong in my eyes (commenting May 1, 1977).

AIKEN, CONRAD

Cowley, Malcolm. Conrad Aiken remained just a heavy drinker until he died at 84. By that time he had possibly consumed more gin than anyone else in the world.

AIKEN, GEORGE DAVID

Aiken, George David. I have never seen so many incompetent persons in high office. Politics and legislation have become more mixed and smellier than ever (commenting on the U.S. Senate in his book Aiken: Senate Diary).

AIR CONDITIONING

Vreeland, Diana. Air conditioning is like power and love. In the wrong hands, it'll kill you.

AIR POLLUTION

Ketcham, Brian (architect of New York City's Transportation Control Plan). Everyone is looking for a technological bandaid for the automobile air pollution problem. The answer is walking. It's so logical, it's absurd.

Reagan, Ronald. Eighty percent of air pollution comes from plants and trees.

AIR POLLUTION—TEXAS

Barden, Charles (executive director of the Texas Air Control Board). We prefer economic growth to clean air.

AIR SHIPS

Brown, George, Jr. It is time to take a giant step backward (in suggesting the use of dirigibles instead of airplanes in air travel).

AIR TRAVEL

Brown, George, Jr. It is time to take a giant step backward (in suggesting the use of dirigibles instead of airplanes in air travel).

AIRLINES—SAFETY

Miller, Patricia Robertson. The airlines spell safety with a dollar sign and the FAA practices regulation by death.

AIRPLANES, SUPERSONIC

Abzug, Bella. Like so many of the dreams of the sixties, the dream of supersonic transport aircraft has faded in the deepening problems of its reality.

ALASKA

Denver, John. (Alaska is) not a state it's an experience.

ALASKA—POLITICS AND GOVERNMENT

Udall, Morris King. You're not part of Anchorage society if you support a preservationist bill.

ALBORNOZ, CLAUDIO SANCHEZ

Albornoz, Claudio Sanchez. I have only one word: peace. We have killed each other too much already. Let us reach understanding under a regime of freedom, all of us putting into it what is necessary from each side of the barricade (exiled former president upon returning to Spain).

ALCOHOLIC BEVERAGES

Apollonio, Spencer. When four fishermen get together, there's always a fifth.

Benchley, Nathaniel. Contrary to popular opinion there is not a college education in that bottle; you don't get smarter with every drink you take.

Carter, Billy. I found out water can be drunk straight.

De Vries, Peter. Reality is impossible to take neat, we must dilute it with alcohol.

Fields, W. C. I was in love with a beautiful blonde once—she drove me to drink—'tis the one thing I'm indebted to her for.

Nelson, Willie. To me, a redneck is someone who likes to fight. Whiskey makes you want to fight and marijuana makes you want to listen to music. And marijuana and beer together is probably the greatest truth serum ever.

Shor, Toots. Any bum who can't get drunk by midnight, ain't tryin (commenting on a midnight curfew imposed on nightclubs, bars and restaurants during World War II).

Thurber, James. One martini is all right, two is too many, three is not enough.

ALCOHOLISM

Pierce, Webb. One drink is too many and a million is not enough.

ALCOHOLISM AND AUTHORSHIP

Lehman, Ernest. If writer's block is soluble in alcohol, so is the liver.

ALDA, ALAN

Alda, Alan. If I were a politician, I'd be a decent politician..

ALGREN, NELSON

Algren, Nelson. It's a boomtown. Sixty percent of the people are on welfare. That's my kind of town (about Paterson, New Jersey).

ALI, MUHAMMAD

Ali, Muhammad. America can no longer afford me. Madison Square Garden and other promoters can't bid against whole countries.

Ali, Muhammad. I'm not a Republican or a Democrat. I'm everywhere. I transcend race. I transcend religion. I transcend color. I'm the world's man. I belong to everybody.

Ali, Muhammad. It's hard to be humble when you are as great as I am.

Ali, Muhammad. Service to others is the rent I pay for my room here on earth.

Frazier, Joe. I want him like a hog wants slop (commenting on wanting to fight Muhammad Ali).

ALICE COOPER

Alice Cooper, . Only Tammy Wynette and Alice Cooper know how hard it is to be a woman.

Alice Cooper, . People have the wrong idea of me when they describe me and my music as 'Anti-Establishment'. Bah. I really believe in being Establishment. In fact, I want to be an American Establishment all my own.

Cameron, Clyde (Australian Labor and Immigration Minister). I'm not going to allow a degenerate who could influence the young and weak-minded to enter this country and stage this sort of exhibition here (about Alice Cooper).

ALL THE PRESIDENT'S MEN (MOVING PICTURE)
Ziegler, Ronald Louis. Basically, it's the story of a couple of reporters (after seeing All The President's Men).

ALLEN, GEORGE
Allen, George. Only winners are truly alive. Winning is living. Every time you win, you're reborn. When you lose, you die a little.

ALLEN, WOODY
Allen, Woody. I don't believe in an afterlife, although I am bringing a change of underwear.

Allen, Woody. I have a tough time expressing anger to people. Sometimes I wish I could raise my voice a little, but I just get quiet or become amusing.

Allen, Woody. I have an intense desire to return to the womb. Anybody's.

Allen, Woody. I knew I had problems years ago when they asked me what my religion was and I said, 'Jewish with an explanation'.

Allen, Woody. If my film makes one more person feel miserable, I'll feel I've done my job.

Allen, Woody. It's not that I'm afraid to die, I just don't want to be there when it happens.

Allen, Woody. My aim in life is not to be happy. That's not what life is about. I think life is anxiety and turmoil and struggle.

Allen, Woody. There have been times when I've thought of suicide, but with my luck it'd probably be a temporary solution.

ALLENDE GOSSENS, SALVADOR
Neruda, Pablo. I am writing these quick lines for my memoirs only three days after the unspeakable events took my great comrade, President Allende, to his death. The aggressors' version is that they found clear signs of suicide on his lifeless body. The version published abroad is different. The President of the Republic of Chile was riddled and ripped to pieces by the machine guns of Chile's soldiers, who had betrayed Chile once more (from his book Memoirs).

ALLMAN, GREGG
Allman, Gregg. I'd like Cher to be pregnant all the time.

ALTMAN, ROBERT
Altman, Robert. If I'd gone through school, gotten a good job and not gotten into films, I'd probably be dead today or a drunk.

AMBITION
Norris, Kathleen. If ambition doesn't hurt you, you haven't got it.

AMERICA
Boorstin, Daniel. We suffer primarily not from our vices or our weaknesses, but from our illusions.

Borges, Jorge Luis. America is still the best hope. But the Americans themselves will have to be the best hope too.

Denver, John. I epitomize America.

Douglas, William Orville. The great and invigorating influences in American life have been the unorthodox; the people who challenge an existing institution or way of life, or say and do things that make people think.

Graham, Bill. San Francisco is not a part of America.

Rahv, Philip. Nothing can last in America more than ten years.

Smith, Howard K. The Cubans may be hostile to America, but they love Americans.

Tito, Josip Broz. Frankly speaking, I would not like to live in America. True, there is democracy, in some respects even too much, while in others there is none.

Walden, Phil (President of Capricorn Records). That's the old American way—if you got a good thing, then overdo it.

Wilde, Oscar. The discovery of America was the beginning of the death of art.

AMERICAN FEDERATION OF LABOR AND CONGRESS OF INDUSTRIAL ORGANIZATIONS
Barkan, Al. We're (AFL-CIO) going to have the best-organized, best-financed political force in the history of organized labor. No one else will have what we have. All we need is a candidate.

AMERICAN MUSEUM OF NATURAL HISTORY, NEW YORK
Goelet, Robert G. I can't think of anything I'd rather be doing than serving as president of the museum. I have a personal weakness for fish and birds; I'm nuts for fossils, and I have a healthy respect for poisonous snakes.

AMERICAN PETROLEUM INSTITUTE
American Petroleum Institute, . In an otherwise nostalgic decade, solar energy has eclipsed apple pie and is giving mom a close race for the title of most popular platitude of the seventies.

AMERICAN TELEPHONE AND TELEGRAPH COMPANY
DeButts, John (Chairman of the Board, AT&T). We believe competition works to the disadvantage of the average (telephone) user, and where it does, we are determined to fight it.

AMERICANS
Auden, Wystan Hugh (attributed by Peter Conrad). The economic vice of Europeans is avarice, while that of Americans is waste.

Carter, James Earl. The duty of our generation of Americans is to renew our nation's faith—not focused just against foreign threats, but against the threat of selfishness, cynicism and apathy.

Chandler, A. B. (Happy). We Americans are a peculiar people. We are for the underdog no matter how much of a dog he is.

James, Henry (attributed by William L. Shirer). It's a complex fate, being an American.

Jay, Peter. All I would ask of Americans is that you go on being yourselves—valiant without being fanatical, individualistic without being foolhardy, skeptical without being cynical, openminded without being indecisive, generous without being naive, patriotic without being nationalistic, and good without being perfect.

Lawrence, David Herbert. The essential American soul is hard, stoic, isolate and a killer.

Mansfield, Katherine. Whenever I prepare for a journey, I prepare as though for death. Should I never return, all is in order. This is what life has taught me.

Moore, Clayton. The Lone Ranger was honest, he was a gentleman and he used perfect diction. If I may say so without boasting, I am a great American.

Morrow, Lance. It bewilders Americans to be hated.

Vonnegut, Kurt. Hunter Thompson's disease,...an incurable, fatal malady suffered by those who feel that Americans can be as easily led to beauty as to ugliness, to truth as to public relations, to joy as to bitterness.

AMIN DADA, IDI

Amin Dada, Idi. Hitler was right about the Jews, because the Israelis are not working in the interests of the people of the world, and that is why they burned the Israelis alive with gas in the soil of Germany.

Amin Dada, Idi. I do not want to be controlled by any superpower. I myself consider myself the most powerful figure in the world and that is why I do not let any superpower control me.

Amin Dada, Idi. My face is the most beautiful face in the world.

Amin Dada, Idi. The problem with me is that I am 50 or 100 years ahead of my time. My speed is very fast. Some ministers had to drop out of my government because they could not keep up.

Amin Dada, Idi. When I am criticized by the Western newspapers, it makes me a true son of Africa.

Moynihan, Daniel Patrick. It is no accident, I fear, that this racist murderer (Idi Amin), as one of our leading newspapers (the New York Times) called him this morning, is the head of the Organization of African Unity.

AMUSEMENT PARKS

Kyriazi, Gary. More than ever, people need a place to scream.

ANDERSON, JOHN B.

Anderson, John B. I am a Republican who dares to wear his heart on the left and his wallet on the right.

Anderson, John B. I am not running against General Eisenhower. I am running against Jimmy Carter and Ronald Reagan, and I would respectfully suggest that neither is an Eisenhower.

Anderson, John B. I am willing to do the things that would make me a one-term President.

Bush, George. John Anderson is not a national candidate. He's an anomaly.

Vidal, Gore. Beside Carter and Reagan he (John Anderson) looks like Lincoln. Beside Lincoln he looks like Anderson.

ANDERSON, MIKE

Ozark, Danny. Mike Anderson's limitations are limitless.

ANDERSON, PAUL

Anderson, Paul. Sure, I was once a 97-pound weakling. When I was 4 years old.

ANDERSON, WENDELL

Boschwitz, Rudy. First he appoints himself to the job, and then he doesn't show up for work (about Wendell Anderson).

ANDRETTI, MARIO

Andretti, Mario. I'm my own status symbol.

ANGER

Ford, Gerald Rudolph. Instead of being amiable I can get a little firm with a different tone of my voice and with a little sterner look on my face, but I don't go into an outburst because I think, really, when you go into an outburst, you sort of lose control of your capability to analyze something (commenting on how he shows his anger without creating a scene).

Hoffer, Eric. The mystery of our time is the inability of decent people to get angry. At present, anger and daring have become the monopoly of a band of mindless juvenile terrorists.

Stevenson, Adlai, II. You can tell the size of a man by the size of the thing that makes him mad.

ANGOLA

Amin Dada, Idi. We should not let ourselves be brainwashed by the Western powers that the presence of Soviet technicians in Angola is an indication that the Soviet Union wants to colonize Africa.

Dellums, Ronald V. There are not many Vietnamese constituents in America and that is why it took 12 years to develop a broad base of support against that war. But it won't take 25 million black people 12 years to mobilize against American involvement in Angola.

Reagan, Ronald. Let's face it, the first enemy in Angola is obviously Ronald Reagan.

ANNE, PRINCESS OF GREAT BRITAIN

Anne, Princess of Great Britain, . I would have won if I hadn't fallen off. And that's been the story of my life (commenting in a book Talking About Horses).

Anne, Princess of Great Britain, . Newspaper strikes are a relief.

APARTHEID

Jackson, Jesse. Apartheid is violence by definition.

Paton, Alan. Sometimes, you think of apartheid as a fort. Often it is seen as a prison. But it is really a grave the Afrikanner has dug for himself.

ARAB STATES—POLITICS AND GOVERNMENT

Hussein, King of Jordan, . It's amusing. The Americans have changed Presidents six times since I've been King. And they talk to the Arabs about stability?.

ARABS

Carter, Billy. There's a helluva lot more Arabians than there is Jews.

Dixon, Paul Rand. I understand there are Arabs who are not dirty (responding when asked to retract a racial slur directed at Ralph Nader).

ARAFAT, YASIR

Arafat, Yasir. I have come bearing an olive branch and a freedom fighter's gun. Do not let the olive branch fall from my hand (addressing the United Nations).

Arafat, Yasir. Palestine is my wife.

Begin, Menachem. When I am called a terrorist and Arafat is called a guerilla, I think it is the apex of injustice.

ARBUS, DIANE

Arbus, Diane. I mean it's very subtle and a little embarrassing to me, but I really believe that there are things which nobody would see unless I photographed them.

ARCHITECTURE

Aalto, Alvar. True architecture exists only where man stands in the center.

Burnham, Daniel. Make no little plans.

Hall, Donald. Less is more, in prose as in architecture.

Johnson, Philip. All cultures that can be called cultures have built monuments.

Johnson, Philip. As birds have beautiful plumage, so do we try to have beautiful buildings. There is no other purpose.

Wotton, Sir Henry. The aim of architecture is to build well. Well-building hath three conditions: commodity, firmness and delight.

ARCHITECTURE—HOUSTON

Wright, Frank Lloyd. Houston is an example of what can happen when architecture catches a venereal disease.

ARGENTINA—DESCRIPTION

Borges, Jorge Luis. I have never met a man who was both intelligent and Peronist.

ARGENTINA—POLITICS AND GOVERNMENT

Borges, Jorge Luis. (I am) very glad about the military coup—it will be a pleasure to be free of hoodlums and gangsters and to be governed again by officers and gentlemen (commenting upon his announcement to return to Argentina).

Borges, Jorge Luis. I had a country. I am ashamed of my country today.

Lopez Rega, Jose. I have written a few pages of the prologue in the book of our national destiny. My opponents and the anti-patriots will make it their task to fill an entire volume of fiction (upon being removed from his job as personal secretary to President Isabel Peron).

Peron, Maria Estela Martinez Isabel. If I have to apply five turns of the screw each day for the happiness of Argentina, I will do it.

Videla, Jorge Rafael. A terrorist is not only someone with a gun or a bomb, but anyone who disseminates ideas contrary to Western and Christian civilization.

ARGUMENTS

Beaumarchais, De, Pierre Augustine Caron De. It is not necessary to understand things in order to argue about them.

Sproles, Judy. If there is an opinion, facts will be found to support it.

ARMAMENTS

Edison, Thomas Alva. The day will come when science will create a machine as a force which is so terrible, so infinitely horrifying, that even man, a bellicose being who brings suffering, torment, and death upon his fellows, at the risk of bringing these torments upon himself will shudder with fear and renounce war forever.

ARMSTRONG, LOUIS

Armstrong, Louis. I got a simple rule about everybody. If you don't treat me right, shame on you.

ARMSTRONG, NEIL

Armstrong, Neil A. I believe every human has a finite number of heartbeats. I don't intend to waste any of mine running around doing exercises.

ARNOLD, BENEDICT

Buchwald, Art. Benedict Arnold has been misunderstood. A great general, a ladies' man par excellence and one of the big spenders of the time, he might have been the father of our country if Congress hadn't passed him over for promotion.

ARRAU, CLAUDIO

Arrau, Claudio. Every concert must be an event, never a routine.

ART

Barragan, Luis. Art is made by the alone for the alone.

Brecht, Bertolt. Grub first, art after.

Burden, Chris. Learn how to make counterfeit money. Some of it is really beautiful (advice for budding artists).

Gabo, Naum. Today is the deed.

Ginsberg, Allen. Art is shapely.

Guggenheim, Peggy. I don't like art today, I think it has gone to hell.

Kubrick, Stanley. All you can do is either pose questions or make truthful observations about human behavior. The only morality is not to be dishonest.

Liberman, Alexander. All serious art is against convention.

Malraux, Andre. A minor living art is far more vital than a major dead one.

Miro, Joan. Fools do not make art.

Motherwell, Robert. I think art is one of the few things that bestows very deep meanings to human existence.

Oldenburg, Claes. I am for art that coils and grunts like a wrestler. I am for art that sheds hair. I am for art you can sit on. I am for art you can pick your nose with or stub your toe on.

Oldenburg, Claes. To give birth to form is the only act of man that has any consequence.

Panza di Biumo, Giuseppe. For me, art is the visualization of philosophy.

Picasso, Pablo. Art is lies that tell the truth.

Rauschenberg, Robert. Ideas aren't real estate; they grow collectively, and that knocks out the egotistical loneliness that generally infects art.

Ray, Man. There is no progress in art any more than there is progress in making love. There are simply different ways of doing it.

Rivers, Larry. Is photography art? Art is everything.

Rochberg, George. The business of art is to praise God.

Rubinstein, Artur. You can't generalize about art. A man has no right to the title of artist if he can be compared to another. A condition of the artist is to be a unique personality.

Shapiro, Joseph H. Aesthetics is to art what ornithology is to birds.

Shapiro, Joseph H. Great art is so complex and has so many levels of meaning it carries its own equivocation.

Simpson, David. In the first century A.D., Petronius declared painting dead. In 1934 Moholy-Nagy declared painting dead. In 1970—probably earlier—Robert Morris declared painting dead. Three of many.

Stieglitz, Alfred. Let all the art in the world be destroyed. It will rise again, for the art spirit is inherent in man.

Teasdale, Sara. Art can never mean to a woman what it does to a man. Love means that.

Tharp, Twyla. Art is the only way to run away from home without leaving home.

Warhol, Andy. Good business is the best art.

Yamashita, Sachio (Painter). Art, color are the vitamins of the soul.

ART—MODERNISM

De Chirico, Giorgio. Modernism is dying in all the countries of the world. Let us hope it will soon be just an unhappy memory.

ARTERIOSCLEROSIS

Pritikin, Nathan. Although our results need confirmation, we believe they are the first evidence demonstrating reversal of human arteriosclerosis by diet.

ARTISTS

Albee, Dan. The value of an artistic achievement is inversely proportional to the number of people it appeals to.

Cheever, John. If you are an artist, self-destruction is quite expected of you.

Jong, Erica. Perhaps all artists were, in a sense, housewives: tender of the earth household.

Langlois, Henri. Most people advance through life walking backward. Those artists who face forward are likely to be put in jail—or the madhouse.

Motherwell, Robert. Every intelligent painter carries the whole culture of modern painting in his head. It is his real subject, of which anything he paints is both an hommage and a critique.

Picasso, Pablo. Every child is an artist. The problem is how to remain an artist once he grows up.

Ray, Man. The streets are full of admirable craftsmen, but so few practical dreamers.

Reinhardt, Ad. The eyes are in the head for a reason.

Rubinstein, Artur. You can't generalize about art. A man has no right to the title of artist if he can be compared to another. A condition of the artist is to be a unique personality.

Waugh, Evelyn. An artist must be a reactionary. He has to stand out against the tenor of the age and not go flopping along.

Wise, Howard. Great artists and great scientists share many of the same qualities: tenacity, courage, and imagination.

ARTISTS—SELF PERCEPTION

Steinberg, William. Great conductors do not dance.

THE ARTS

Kramer, Hilton. The way things are going, one expects to hear any day now that virginity is back in style.

Malraux, Andre. A minor living art is far more vital than a major dead one.

Miller, Arthur. I think that you don't take seriously any art that's not dealing finally with whether we are doomed or not.

Musgrave, Thea. In art you have to follow your hunch. You can't play it safe.

THE ARTS—AFRICA

Senghor, Leopold Sedar. Africa will teach rhythm to a world dead with machinery and cannon.

ARTS AND SOCIETY

Bellow, Saul. One can't tell writers what to do. The imagination must find its own path. But one can fervently wish that they—that we—would come back from the periphery. We do not, we writers, represent mankind adequately (excerpt from his Nobel lecture on literature in Stockholm).

Brecht, Bertolt. Grub first, art after.

Malraux, Andre. There cannot be another Michelangelo in today's society because our faith in man is too weak.

THE ARTS—CHICAGO

Solti, Sir Georg. Chicago should erect a statue to me for what I have done.

THE ARTS—CRITICISM

Burns, George (attributed by David Steinberg), . (Critics are) eunuchs at a gang-bang.

Croce, Arlene. Reviewing should function like a Food and Drug Administration, even if that function is largely futile.

Osborne, John. Asking a working writer what he thinks about critics is like asking a lamppost what it feels about dogs.

THE ARTS—RUSSIA

Rostropovich, Mstislav. Music and art are a whole spiritual world in Russia. In Russia when people go to a concert, they don't go to it as an attraction, as an entertainment, but to feel life.

Wyeth, Jamie. They don't allow anything but realism there. At the end, I told them I could understand their censoring talking and writing but why Art? Their answer was 'Never underestimate the power of painting' (on his recent trip to the Soviet Union).

THE ARTS—UNITED STATES

Wilde, Oscar. The discovery of America was the beginning of the death of art.

ASHBERY, JOHN

Ashbery, John. I have a feeling that when people say my poetry is difficult, they mean it's complicated. Well, it probably is, but I don't start out to be as complicated as possible. Life is complicated. I in fact try to simplify it as much as I can.

ASHE, ARTHUR

Ashe, Arthur. I would continue living pretty much as now, except that I would not play tennis as often (in response to 'What would you do with 10 million dollars').

ASIMOV, ISAAC

Asimov, Isaac. A lot of people can write. I have to.

Asimov, Isaac. There's nothing wrong with middle age, but it comes hard to a person who is a child prodigy by profession.

ASPEN, COLORADO

Sandersen, Ann. When I'm in New York I'm homesick for Aspen, and when I'm in Aspen I'm homesick for Aspen.

ASSASSINATION

Kunstler, William. Although I couldn't pull the trigger myself, I don't disagree with murder sometimes, especially political assassinations, which have been a part of political life since the beginning of recorded history.

ASSASSINATION—UNITED STATES

Fromme, Lynette (Squeaky). Anybody can kill anybody.

Kennedy, Edward Moore. If someone in my position doesn't realize the danger, he'd be a fool. But anybody who lets that danger paralyze him is useless (concerning the danger of assassination).

Kennedy, Rose. The temptation to be the one to kill the third Kennedy brother is just too great (on why she doesn't want Ted Kennedy to run for President).

ASSAULT AND BATTERY

Boyles, Tiny. Getting beat up is like eating hot food. After the first bite you don't feel the rest.

ASTAIRE, FRED

Astaire, Fred. I don't dance—ever—and I don't intend to ever again.

ASTOR, NANCY

Astor, Nancy. I married beneath me. All women do.

ASTROLOGY

Anonymous, . Anybody who believes in astrology was probably born under the wrong sign.

ASTROTURF

Allen, Dick. If horses won't eat it, I don't want to play on it.

ATHEISM

Lewis, C. S. A young man who wishes to remain a sound atheist cannot be too careful of his reading. God is, if I may say it, very unscrupulous.

ATHLETES

Arcaro, Eddie. It's hard to get up early when you're wearing silk pajamas (commenting on why rich athletes lose their competitive urge).

Banks, Ernie. I like my players to be married and in debt. That's the way you motivate them.

Garvey, Ed. When you talk about civil liberties in professional sports, it's like talking about virtue in a whorehouse.

Jenner, Bruce. If you want to use the decathlon as a test of total atheletic ability, then I guess I'm the world's greatest athlete. It's as good a test as any, I guess. But that sure doesn't help me when I stand up at a tee and try to hit a golf ball. Then I'm just another guy who can't hit straight.

King, Billie Jean. Amateur athletes have become the pawn of manipulators and big business.

McGuire, Al. I don't know why people question the academic training of a student-athlete. Half the doctors in the country graduated in the bottom half of their class.

Warhol, Andy. Sports figures are to the '70s what movie stars were to the '60s.

Werblin, David A. (Sonny). If you've been around athletes, you know an athlete when you see one, just by their attitude, just by the way they speak.

ATHLETES—UNITED STATES

Wilkins, Mac (1976 Olympic Discus Champion). America expects its athletes to wave a flag and win a medal every four years. But then you're supposed to take off that silly underwear and go out and make a decent living.

ATLANTIS

Cousteau, Jacques Yves. I don't know what to expect. I wouldn't do it if I did. But we know there is something there, and now our task is to find out what (commenting on his search for the legendary lost continent of Atlantis off Greece).

ATOMIC BOMB

Schafly, Phyllis. The atomic bomb is a marvelous gift given to America by a wise god.

ATOMIC POWER

Brown, Edmund Gerald, Jr. I think it's time for the President, certainly the next President, to say no to nuclear power.

Einstein, Albert. To the village square we must carry the facts of atomic energy. From there must come America's voice (commenting in 1946).

Minor, Gregory C. My reason for leaving is a deep conviction that nuclear reactors and nuclear weapons now present a serious danger to the future of all life on this planet (commenting on why he resigned from his position as a managing engineer at a General Electric Company nuclear reactor plant).

Nader, Ralph. This (the Three Mile Island accident) is the beginning of the end of nuclear power in this country.

Penden, Bill. Atomic energy is a future idea whose time is past. Renewable energy is a future idea whose time has come.

Ray, Dixie Lee. A nuclear power plant is infinitely safer than eating, because 300 people choke to death on food every year.

Teller, Edward. Nuclear power is not an option—it is a part of the fight for the survival of freedom.

ATOMIC POWER—FRANCE

Giscard D'Estaing, Valery. Nuclear energy is at the crossroads of the two independences of France: the independence of her defense and the independence of her energy supply.

ATOMIC POWER INDUSTRY

Nader, Ralph. If nuclear power is so safe, why won't the insurance industry insure it?.

Wasserman, Harvey. Nuclear energy is also a means to keep power—both electrical and otherwise—centralized in the hands of big money.

ATOMIC POWER PLANTS

Bridenbaugh, Dale G. From what I've seen, the magnitude of the risks and the uncertainty of the human factor and the genetic unknowns have led me to believe that there should be no nuclear power (commenting after his resignation as manager for performance evaluation and improvement at a General Electric Company plant in California).

Minor, Gregory C. My reason for leaving is a deep conviction that nuclear reactors and nuclear weapons now present a serious danger to the future of all life on this planet (commenting on why he resigned from his position as a managing engineer at a General Electric Company nuclear reactor plant).

Ray, Dixie Lee. A nuclear power plant is infinitely safer than eating, because 300 people choke to death on food every year.

Schlesinger, James Rodney. I would sleep right near the nuclear plant; there is no question about that. It is a comfortable neighbor (affirming his confidence in the safety of nuclear power).

ATOMIC POWER PLANTS—KOREA (REPUBLIC)

Vance, Cyrus R. Our Export-Import Bank is continuing on schedule (to Korea) with its credit and its guarantee of $1 billion for the purchase of nuclear power plants.

ATOMIC WARFARE

Khrushchev, Nikita Sergeevich. The survivors (of a nuclear attack) would envy the dead.

Mountbatten, Louis. If the Third World War is fought with nuclear weapons, the fourth will be fought with bows and arrows.

Sakharov, Andrei Dmitrievich. Thermonuclear warfare has already become a dark reality of modern times, like Auschwitz, the Gulag and Famine.

ATOMIC WEAPONS

Hatfield, Mark. It's in the realm of the unconscionable. It raises the greatest probability and potential of introducing nuclear weaponry into conventional warfare (commenting on the neutron bomb).

Lilienthal, David E. If a great number of countries come to have an arsenal of nuclear weapons, then I'm glad I'm not a young man and I'm sorry for my grandchildren (commenting at hearings of the Senate Government Operations Committee).

Minor, Gregory C. My reason for leaving is a deep conviction that nuclear reactors and nuclear weapons now present a serious danger to the future of all life on this planet (commenting on why he resigned from his position as a managing engineer at a General Electric Company nuclear reactor plant).

ATTICA PRISON

Stokes, Geoffrey. Attica is full of Hurricane Carters who were never champions. Or championed.

AUCHINCLOSS, LOUIS

Auchincloss, Louis. I am neither a satirist nor a cheerleader. I am strictly an observer.

AUDEN, WYSTAN HUGH

Auden, Wystan Hugh. Among those whom I like, I can find no common denominator; but among those whom I love, I can: all of them make me laugh.

AUDIENCES

Hayes, Helen. An audience simply cannot go on reacting indefinitely to a play that doesn't know where it's going.

AUSCHWITZ CONCENTRATION CAMP

Steiner, George. The world of Auschwitz lies outside speech as it lies outside reason.

AUTH, TONY

Auth, Tony. Once in a while when they're expecting a chuckle, I knee them in the groin (explaining his personal cartooning philosophy).

AUTHORS

Abe, Kobo. Once a writer throws away his mask he's finished.

Auden, Wystan Hugh. Biographies of writers, whether written by others or themselves, are always superfluous and usually in bad taste. A writer is a maker, not a man of action.

Borges, Jorge Luis. When the literature of the second half of the 20th century is studied, the names will be different than we hear now. They will have found hidden writers. People who won Nobel prizes will be forgotten. I hope I will be forgotten.

Breslin, Catherine. A freelancer lives at the end of a sawed-off limb.

Cheever, John. If you are an artist, self-destruction is quite expected of you.

Farrell, James T. There's one good kind of a writer—a dead writer.

Fitzgerald, F. Scott. There never was a good biography of a good novelist. There couldn't be. He is too many people, if he's any good.

Johnson, Samuel. No man but a blockhead ever wrote except for money.

Miller, Arthur. I always doubted that writers ever really understand more than anyone else. All you can hope is that maybe you feel a little more.

Moore, Marianne. A writer is unfair when he is unable to be hard on himself.

Parker, Dorothy. An author really hasn't made it until he no longer shows his books to his friends.

Percy, Walker. Every novelist I know is miserable.

Roberts, Dale. He is a man of letters—all of them lower case.

Sexton, Anne. I wonder if the artist ever lives his life—he is so busy recreating it.

Sheed, Wilfrid. One reason the human race has such a low opinion of itself is that it gets so much of its wisdom from writers.

Steinbeck, John. Competing with Hemingway isn't my idea of good business.

Townsend, Peter. It isn't enough any more to write books: publishers expect you to sell them.

Waugh, Evelyn. An artist must be a reactionary. He has to stand out against the tenor of the age and not go flopping along.

Wilson, Sloan. A writer's job is sticking his neck out.

AUTHORS, AMERICAN

Donleavy, J. P. Authors don't have any respect at all in terms of a profession in America—and this is quite a good and stimulating thing.

Mailer, Norman. It's hard to get to the top in America, but it's even harder to stay there.

Susann, Jacqueline. I don't have any peers, as far as writers go.

Vidal, Gore. Most American writers I find phony, but it's a phony country.

AUTHORS—FAME

Schwartz, Delmore. No reputation is more than a snowfall.

AUTHORS—RELATIONS—MOVING PICTURE INDUSTRY

Puzo, Mario. A novelist should never take the movie business seriously.

AUTHORS RIGHTS

Ringer, Barbara A. The basic human rights of individual authors throughout the world are being sacrificed more and more on the altar of the technological revolution.

AUTHORS, RUSSIAN

Amalrik, Andrei. This is not a decision taken freely. I did not want to emigrate to Israel or anywhere else—ever. When a man is born in a country, and is a writer, he does not want to leave—not ever (commenting on his forced emigration to Israel).

AUTHORSHIP

Abe, Kobo. Once a writer throws away his mask he's finished.

Auden, Wystan Hugh. A suffering, a weakness, which cannot be expressed as an aphorism should not be mentioned.

Auden, Wystan Hugh. Literary confessors are contemptible, like beggars who exhibit their sores for money, but not so contemptible as the public that buys their books.

Baker, Russell. Like most writers, I don't read much, at least not good stuff. You can either write or you can read.

Bellow, Saul. Being a writer is a rather dreamy thing. And nobody likes to have the diaphanous tissues torn. One has to protect one's dream space (on learning that he had won the Nobel Prize for Literature).

Bellow, Saul. One can't tell writers what to do. The imagination must find its own path. But one can fervently wish that they—that we—would come back from the periphery. We do not, we writers, represent mankind adequately (excerpt from his Nobel lecture on literature in Stockholm).

Brenan, Gerald. Words are as recalcitrant as circus animals and the unskilled trainer can crack his whip at them in vain.

Cheever, John. Actually, male or female, what a writer has to have are an extraordinary memory, a marvelous ear, and a passion for bringing disparities together.

Cheever, John. It (plot) is a calculated attempt to hold the reader's interest at the sacrifice of moral conviction.

Clemens, Samuel Langhorne. Only kings, editors, and people with tapeworms have the right to use the editorial 'we'.

Cowley, Malcolm. No complete son-of-a-bitch ever wrote a good sentence.

Crichton, Michael. I find facts inhibiting....The more you know, the more you are obliged to the truth. I much prefer not to know.

De Laurentiis, Dino. To make a movie is not like to make a book. A movie is much, much more—not just pushing a pencil in a room.

Doctorow, E. L. In an age that celebrates facts, the writer who begins to break down the line between fact and fiction represents the reassertion of the authority and perception of the individual mind.

Donleavy, J. P. Writing is turning one's worst moments into money.

Eliot, George. I have the conviction that excessive literary production is a social offense.

Ellison, Ralph. People who want to write sociology should not write a novel.

Fowles, John. Fiction is a removing activity. The ghost that haunts all writers is, 'Am I betraying reality?'.

Gordimer, Nadine. The facts are always less than what really happened.

Greenberg, Stanley. Writing isn't an exact science. It is more like chasing a butterfly you're not sure you want to catch.

Hall, Donald. Less is more, in prose as in architecture.

Hellman, Lillian. If I had to give young writers advice, I would say, Don't listen to writers talking about writing or about themselves.

Jong, Erica. I cannibalized real life.

Kafka, Franz. Writing is a sweet and wonderful reward, but for what? In the night it became clear to me, as clear as a child's lesson book, that it is the reward for serving the devil.

Kaselionis, Simas. Writers aren't like mushrooms—you can't grow them.

Lawrence, David Herbert. Never trust the artist. Trust the tale.

Lebowitz, Fran. Having been unpopular in high school is not just cause for book publication.

Lindbergh, Anne Morrow. Writing is thinking. It is more than living, for it is being conscious of living.

MacCarthy, Desmond. A biographer is an artist who is on oath.

McLuhan, Marshall. Most clear writing is a sign that there is no exploration going on. Clear prose indicates an absence of thought.

Mailer, Norman. A writer of the largest dimension can alter the nerves and marrow of a nation.

Nin, Anais. A real writer does not need the publicity that is granted with equal fervor to a toothpaste. A real writer only wants his book to be read by those who want to read it, and if there are 100 of them, it is enough to keep his work alive and sustain his productivity.

O'Connor, Flannery. For a fiction writer, to believe nothing is to see nothing.

Porter, Katherine Anne. Dullness, bitterness, rancor, self-pity, baseness of all kinds can be most interesting material for a story provided these are not also the main elements in the mind of the author.

Rhys, Jean. If you want to write the truth, you must write about yourself.

Roth, Philip. The road to hell is paved with works-in-progress.

Roth, Philip. When you publish a book, it's the world's book. The world edits it.

Singer, Isaac Bashevis. A Marxist has never written a good novel.

Singer, Isaac Bashevis. A writer, like a woman, never knows why people like him, or why people dislike him. We never know.

Singer, Isaac Bashevis. Writers were not born to change the world.

Smith, Red. Writing is very easy. All you do is sit in front of a typewriter keyboard until little drops of blood appear on your forehead.

Steinbeck, John. The profession of book writing makes horse racing seem like a solid, stable business.

Strachey, Lytton. It is perhaps as difficult to write a good life as to live one.

Thomas, Bob. Hemingway had a very strong opinion that writers should not stay in journalism too long. He felt it damaged your sensitivity. I suspect he is right.

Ustinov, Peter. The time to write memoirs is when total recall has not yet invaded the cavities of the mind left empty by the inaction of retirement.

Vidal, Gore. In writing and politicking, it's best not to think about it, just do it.

Vonnegut, Kurt. The work (of writing fiction) is exceedingly tedious. It is like making wallpaper by hand for the Sistine Chapel.

Waugh, Evelyn. I regard writing not as investigation of character, but as an exercise in the use of language.

White, E. B. No one can write decently who is distrustful of the reader's intelligence.

White, E. B. The way to approach a manuscript is on all fours, in utter amazement.

Whitman, Walt. New York is a fine place for a writer to sell his produce, but a poor place to grow it.

Woolf, Virginia. The art of writing has for backbone some fierce attachment to an idea.

AUTHORSHIP SEE ALSO WRITING

AUTHORSHIP—HISTORY

K'ang-Hsi, 1654-1722 (Chinese emperor), . In history one needs the facts, not hollow words or literary elegance.

AUTHORSHIP—POETRY

Sandburg, Carl. Ordering a man to write a poem is like commanding a pregnant woman to give birth to a redheaded child. You can't do it—it's an act of God.

AUTOBIOGRAPHY

Auden, Wystan Hugh. A suffering, a weakness, which cannot be expressed as an aphorism should not be mentioned.

Auden, Wystan Hugh. Literary confessors are contemptible, like beggars who exhibit their sores for money, but not so contemptible as the public that buys their books.

AUTOMOBILE DRIVING

Cobb, Irvin S. I'd rather be late for supper in this world tonight than be in some other world on time for breakfast in the morning.

AUTOMOBILE RACING

Beaumont, Marie-Claude (French automobile racer). Auto racing is a matter of mathematics—timing. Sex has nothing to do with winning a race. You see, the timekeeper's clock ticks at the same speed for a man or a woman.

Newman, Paul. Racing is the best way I know to get away from all the rubbish of Hollywood.

Scott, Wendell. Auto racing, I'm sad to say, is still a white man's sport. It's a shame that a woman got to qualify for Indy before a black man did.

AUTOMOBILES

Ford, Henry, II. This country developed in a particular way because of the automobile, and you can't just push a button and change it.

Randall, Tony. I knew the auto wouldn't last.

Spikol, Art. The fact is that most people don't drive cars that reflect what they are: they drive the closest thing they can find to what they'd like to be.

AUTOMOBILES—POLLUTION

Ketcham, Brian (architect of New York City's Transportation Control Plan). Everyone is looking for a technological bandaid for the automobile air pollution problem. The answer is walking. It's so logical, it's absurd.

AUTOMOBILES—PURCHASING

Iacocca, Lee A. This year the public will have a choice, the likes of which it hasn't had in years. The difference between our cars and GM's is like the difference between a four-foot blonde and a seven-foot brunette.

AUTOMOBILES—USED

Anonymous, . A used car is like a bad woman—no matter how good you treat it, it'll give you more trouble than it's worth.

AUTRY, GENE

Autry, Gene. I'm gonna die with my boots on.

AVARICE

Aron, Jean-Paul. Avarice is the predominant French characteristic because of (our) long peasant history.

AVIATION

Lindbergh, Charles Augustus. It was the combination of an undeveloped science with an art, resulting in adventure for the mind and body that brought stimulation to the spirit (commenting on aviation).

BACON, FRANCIS

Bacon, Francis (British Painter). After all, as existence in a way is so banal, you may as well try to make a kind of grandeur of it rather than be nursed to oblivion.

BAEZ, JOAN

Baez, Joan. I hate getting older, losing my youth. But there's a good side of it. I've left a lot of neuroses behind—stage fright, insecurities, terrors, phobias—that had me dissolved into a puddle of nothing. For anybody who's listening, they don't have to go on forever.

BAGNOLD, ENID

Bagnold, Enid. I wasn't a born writer, but I was born a writer.

BAILEY, F. LEE

Bailey, F. Lee. I defend crime; I'm not in favor of it.

BAILEY, PEARL

Bailey, Pearl. I never ask myself how I do what I do. After all, how does it rain?.

BAKER, HOWARD HENRY

Baker, Howard Henry. In Washington I'm thought of as a conservative, but in Tennessee I'm thought of as a Bolshevik.

BAKER, JOSEPHINE

Davis, Ossie. She was in the nature of a primeval force. She was there and everybody knew it.

Universal. You celebrate her like you celebrate a beautiful sunset (about Josephine Baker).

BAKER, JOY

Baker, Joy (wife of Howard Baker). Politics has nullified my personality.

BAKER, RUSSELL

Baker, Russell. A $10 million windfall? At today's prices, I'd feel almost as rich as I did one day in 1936 when I found a dime on the sidewalk and blew the whole wad on 20 Mary Jane candy bars, a box of jujubes and a double feature. Nowadays, I'd use the $10 million to buy a new suit, subscribe to the opera, get a front-end alignment for my car and take my wife to dinner in a New York restaurant. This would probably use up the whole $10 million, but if there were a few hundred thousand left over, I'd squirrel it away in a sock for my old age, hoping that some evening, when I have been long locked away in a nursing home, it would still have the purchasing power to bribe my caretaker to sneak out to the nearest fast food joint and bring me back a chocolate ice-cream soda (in response to 'What would you do with 10 million dollars').

BALANCHINE, GEORGE

Balanchine, George. I am the mother in this world of dance.

Baryshnikov, Mikhail. With Balanchine I grew up.

BALDNESS

Moss, Stirling. Bald heads are cheap to run and they need very little maintenance.

BALDWIN, ROGER

Baldwin, Roger. I'm a crusader and crusaders don't stop.

BALTIMORE. BASEBALL CLUB (AMERICAN LEAGUE)

Agunga, John (African witch doctor). Publicity. They lost because they turned coming to me into a publicity gimmick. Witchcraft works only by stealth (commenting on why the Baltimore Orioles lost the race in the American League East despite his spells).

BANKHEAD, TALLULAH

Bankhead, Tallulah. Cocaine isn't habit-forming. I should know—I've been using it for years.

Bankhead, Tallulah. I don't know what I am, dahling. I've tried several varieties of sex. The conventional position makes me claustrophobic. And the others give me either a stiff neck or lockjaw.

Bankhead, Tallulah. My heart is as pure as the driven slush.

BANKS AND BANKING
Wriston, Walter. I believe there are no institutional values, only personal values.

BANKS AND BANKING—LAWS AND REGULATIONS
Proxmire, William. Sunlight remains the world's best disinfectant (summing up his feelings on truth in lending and opening the Federal Reserve System to public scrutiny).

BANKS AND BANKING—UNITED STATES
Proxmire, William. Sunlight remains the world's best disinfectant (summing up his feelings on truth in lending and opening the Federal Reserve System to public scrutiny).

Rockefeller, David. One of the great threats to the banking system is excessive disclosure. If banks are required to disclose information on the financial condition of the people we loan money to, this could be very embarrassing and seriously hurtful to our customers. It could make banks so cautious that we wouldn't loan money to anybody except to the triple-A, blue-chip customer.

BAPTISTS
Carter, Rosalynn. When people ask me about Jimmy being a Baptist, and indicate they feel no Baptist can run the country, I just remind them that Harry Truman was a Baptist, and I think he did a great job.

BARDOT, BRIGITTE
Bardot, Brigitte. I leave before being left. I decide.

BARS AND BARROOMS
Shor, Toots. A good saloonkeeper is the most important man in the community.

BARTH, JOHN
Barth, John. My books are allowed to know one another, as children of the same father, but they must lead their lives independently.

BARUCH, BERNARD MANNES
Baruch, Bernard Mannes (attributed by William Flanagan). I buy low and sell high (when asked how he had made a fortune in the stock market).

BARYSHNIKOV, MIKHAIL
Baryshnikov, Mikhail. I am happy in America but I am still a Russian and I hope one day I may go back to dance in Russia.

Baryshnikov, Mikhail. I have no doubts about what I did, but I have regrets. I left behind my friends, my public, my theater and Leningrad, my city, the most beautiful in the world. Now I have a divided soul.

Baryshnikov, Mikhail. With Balanchine I grew up.

BASEBALL
Allen, Dick. If horses won't eat it, I don't want to play on it.

Banks, Ernie. I like my players to be married and in debt. That's the way you motivate them.

Berra, Yogi. In baseball, you don't know nothing.

Bouton, Jim. You see, you spend a good piece of your life gripping a baseball and in the end it turns out that it was the other way around all the time.

Harrelson, Ken. Baseball is the only sport I know that when you're on offense, the other team controls the ball.

Jackson, Reggie. Hitting is better than sex.

Piniella, Lou (New York Yankee outfielder). I cussed him out in Spanish, and he threw me out in English (commenting on an argument he once had with umpire Armando Rodriguez).

Stargell, Willie. They give you a round bat and they throw you a round ball. And they tell you to hit it square (commenting on baseball).

Veeck, Bill. Baseball is the only orderly thing in a very unorderly world. If you get three strikes, even Edward Bennett Williams can't get you off.

BASEBALL—MANAGERS
Curtis, John. Between owners and players, a manager today has become a wishbone.

Weaver, Earl. Good ballplayers make good managers, not the other way around. All I can do is help them be as good as they are.

BASEBALL PLAYERS—HITTING
Rose, Pete. Singles hitters drive Fords. Home-run hitters drive Cadillacs.

BASEBALL—SALARIES, PENSIONS, ETC.
Lane, Frank. Monday got about $125,000 from the Cubs last season and struck out 125 times. He got paid $1,000 a strikeout. This year he'll probably get $250,000 from the Dodgers, which means he's gotten a raise to $2,000 a strikeout.

BASEBALL—UMPIRING
Luciano, Ron. What I really hate about umpiring is that we can never win. We don't walk off a field with a grin on our faces.

Murtaugh, Danny. A bad call (in baseball) is one that goes against you.

Somers, Al. The key to success is a good eye, an even temper and being boss of your game. You should also know where the nearest exit is, and remember to tell the scorekeeper where you want the body sent.

BASIE, WILLIAM (COUNT)
Basie, William (Count). I'll be here until they take me away.

Fuller, Curtis. But there's only one Count Basie. That's all there'll ever be.

BASKETBALL, COLLEGE
McGuire, Al. I want my teams to have my personality—surly, obnoxious and arrogant.

BASKETBALL, PROFESSIONAL
Bradley, Bill. First, I was suspicious of an advertising industry that manufactures needs, then sells products to foster those needs. Second, some offers were coming to me as a "white hope", and that offended me. Third, basketball was an important part of my life. I wanted to keep it pure. Hair sprays and deodorants and popcorn poppers were not basketball (on why he never made TV commercials).

BASKETBALL, PROFESSIONAL—NEGROES
McGuire, Al. The only thing in this country that blacks really dominate, except poverty, is basketball.

BATTLE, BILL

Battle, Bill. Class is, when they run you out of town, to look like you're leading the parade (commenting after being forced out as head football coach at Tennessee).

BEAME, ABRAHAM DAVID

Beame, Abraham David. I believe it would be an act of hypocrisy on my part to participate in any welcoming ceremony with any chief of state who has been a party to the United Nations resolution which seeks to revive a new form of racism as a substitute for the principles of understanding and peaceful negotiations upon which this world body was formed.

Carey, Hugh. I had only two hands all year and one was holding Abe Beame's.

THE BEATLES

McCartney, Paul. You cannot reheat a souffle (commenting on promoter Sid Bernstein's attempt to reunite the Beatles).

Sinatra, Frank, Jr. I rued the day that the Beatles were unfortunately born into this world. They are, in my mind, responsible for most of the degeneration that has happened, not only musically, but in the sense of youth orientation politically, too. They are the people who made it first publicly acceptable to spit in the eye of authority.

Wonder, Stevie. They (the Beatles) brought all different cultures together. They made White Middle America wake up about those old black artists—the Beatles brought them to people who had never heard of them. And it gave those artists—who were sometimes starving—some money.

BEATNIKS

Kupferberg, Tuli. What is a beatnik? Why, it's exactly everything that Herbert Hoover hates.

BEATON, SIR CECIL

Beaton, Sir Cecil. Perhaps the world's second worst crime is boredom; the first is being a bore.

BEATTY, WARREN

McGovern, George Stanley. Warren (Beatty) not only cares about issues, but his judgment is very perceptive.

BEAUTY CONTESTS

Lindgren, Lynn (Ms All-Bare America). I like to expose myself to a diversity of reactions and outcomes (in reply to why she wanted the title of Ms All-Bare America).

BEAUTY, PERSONAL

Chanel, Coco. Youth is something very new: twenty years ago no one mentioned it.

Duffy, Sean. The chance of a meaningful relationship with a member of the opposite sex is inversely proportional to their amount of beauty.

Lamarr, Hedy. Any girl can be glamorous. All you have to do is stand still and look stupid.

Martin, Abe. Beauty is only skin deep, but it's a valuable asset if you're poor or haven't any sense.

Myerson, Bess. You can't be beautiful and hate.

Somers, Suzanne. If you've got it, bump it with a trumpet.

BEAUTY, PERSONAL—MEN

Adams, Alice. I don't like good-looking men—one always thinks they'll be dumb.

Brynner, Yul. If you've got just a plain fat head under your hair, don't shave it or you'll look like a melon.

BEAUVOIR, SIMONE DE

Beauvoir, Simone De. I cannot be angry at God, in whom I do not believe.

BECKETT, SAMUEL

Beckett, Samuel. All I want to do is sit on my ass and fart and think of Dante.

Beckett, Samuel. I turned to writing plays to relieve myself of the awful depression that prose led me into. Life at that time was too demanding, too terrible, and I thought theatre would be a diversion.

Vidal, Gore. Each writer is born with a repertory company in his head. Shakespeare had perhaps 20 players, and Tennessee Williams has about five and Samuel Beckett one—and perhaps a clone of that one. I have ten or so, and that's a lot.

BEER

Carter, Billy. Ah cain't drink this here Reengold beer. The next vice president of the United States is the man who brings me a Pabst Blue Ribbon.

BEGIN, MENACHEM

Begin, Menachem. The life of every man who fights in a just cause is a paradox. He makes war so that there should be peace. He sheds blood so that there should be no more bloodshed. That is the way of the world. A very tragic way beset with terrors. There is no other.

Begin, Menachem. When I am called a terrorist and Arafat is called a guerilla, I think it is the apex of injustice.

Weizman, Ezer. I am only responsible for Israel's security, not its sanity (about reports of new Israeli settlements in the Sinai).

BEHAVIOR (PSYCHOLOGY)

Ace, Jane. Well, time wounds all heels.

Durant, Will. One of the lessons of history is that nothing is often a good thing to do and always a clever thing to say.

Kafka, Franz. In the fight between you and the world, back the world.

BELGIUM—FOREIGN POLICY—AFRICA

Simonet, Henri. France has an African policy which is not ours.

BELIEF AND DOUBT

Burgess, Frank Gelett. If in the last few years you hadn't discarded a major opinion or acquired a new one, check your pulse. You may be dead.

Erhard, Werner. Belief is a disease.

Shields, Mark. I don't think Carter and self-doubt have ever met.

Sitwell, Edith. The public will believe anything, so long as it is not founded on truth.

BELL, GRIFFIN

Bell, Griffin. Former cabinet officers shouldn't be seen or heard.

BELLOW, SAUL

Bellow, Saul. Being a writer is a rather dreamy thing. And nobody likes to have the diaphanous tissues torn. One has to protect one's dream space (on learning that he had won the Nobel Prize for Literature).

Bellow, Saul. I know you think I'm a square, Freifeld, but there's no name for the shape I'm in.

Bellow, Saul. One can't tell writers what to do. The imagination must find its own path. But one can fervently wish that they—that we—would come back from the periphery. We do not, we writers, represent mankind adequately (excerpt from his Nobel lecture on literature in Stockholm).

Bellow, Saul. The child in me is delighted. The adult in me is skeptical (upon receiving the Nobel Prize for Literature).

Freifeld, Sam. Saul Bellow is a great writer who is smaller than life.

BELOFF, NORA

Heath, Edward. She couldn't take down a scoop if you gave it to her at dictation speed (about the London Observer's political correspondent, Nora Beloff).

BENCHLEY, ROBERT

Benchley, Robert. I have tried to know absolutely nothing about a great many things, and I have succeeded fairly well.

BENNY, JACK

Benny, Jack. I'm a simple guy. For a comedian I'm surprisingly normal. I have never been to a psychiatrist and I've only been married once.

BERGMAN, INGMAR

Bergman, Ingmar. Possessiveness is neurotic, but this is how I am.

Fellini, Federico. I know for sure that wherever he goes he will continue to be himself, to speak his voice and to begin from the beginning with exalting sensation (commenting on Ingmar Bergman's self-imposed exile from Sweden).

Palme, Olof. I am deeply sorry if he leaves Sweden, partly because of his artistic ability and partly because he is a good friend (commenting on Ingmar Bergman's plans to leave Sweden permanently).

BERGMAN, INGRID

Bergman, Ingrid. I don't dream about my past. I accept my age and make the best of it.

BERKOWITZ, DAVID

Berkowitz, David. Whatever it is has left me, I've mellowed.

BERNHARDT, SARAH

Jackson, Glenda. Sarah Bernhardt believed in the human will above all things. I can empathize with that. Because I do believe that things can be changed; and by changed, I mean improved, not simply altered.

BEVERLY HILLS, CALIFORNIA

Redford, Robert. If you stay in Beverly Hills too long you become a Mercedes.

Styron, William. I think a great novel could even come out of Beverly Hills.

BHUTTO, ZULFIKAR ALI

Zia Ul-Haq, Mohammad. If the Supreme Court says 'acquit him,' I'll acquit him. If it says, 'hang the blighter,' I'll hang him (about Zulfikar Ali Bhutto).

Zia Ul-Haq, Mohammad. With his brain, Bhutto could have been President for life.

BIKO, STEVE

Anonymous (editorial writer for the Sunday Times, South African newspaper), . As long as this (detention) system survives, men will continue to die mysteriously, and no one will be held accountable. That is what the system was designed to achieve. No South African can say he did not know.

Biko, Steve. Being Black is not a matter of pigmentation, but is a reflection of a mental attitude. Merely by describing yourself as Black you have started to fight against all the forces that seek to use your blackness as a stamp that makes you out as a subservient being.

Kruger, James T. (South African Minister of Justice). I am not glad and I am not sorry about Mr. Biko. He leaves me cold.

BILLY JACK (MOVING PICTURE CHARACTER)

Laughlin, Tom. The youth of this country have only two heroes: Ralph Nader and Billy Jack.

BIOGRAPHY

Auden, Wystan Hugh. Biographies of writers, whether written by others or themselves, are always superfluous and usually in bad taste. A writer is a maker, not a man of action.

Fitzgerald, F. Scott. There never was a good biography of a good novelist. There couldn't be. He is too many people, if he's any good.

MacCarthy, Desmond. A biographer is an artist who is on oath.

Strachey, Lytton. It is perhaps as difficult to write a good life as to live one.

BIRD STUDY

Burroughs, John. If you want to see birds, you must have birds in your heart.

BIRTH CONTROL

Butz, Earl Lauer. He no playa the game, he no maka the rules (in response to Pope Paul's stand on birth control).

BISEXUALITY

Allen, Woody. I can't understand why more people aren't bisexual. It would double your chances for a date on Saturday night.

MacLaine, Shirley. We're bisexual up to the age of 3, but what society won't admit is that we're bisexual most of our lives.

BISMARCK, OTTO, FUERST VON

Gladstone, William Ewart. He (Bismarck) made Germany great and Germans small.

BLACK MUSLIMS

Malcolm X, . This thing with me will be resolved by death and violence.

BLACK, SHIRLEY TEMPLE

Black, Shirley Temple. I'm pleased to be the first woman in 200 years to hold this job. I'm energetic, I'll work hard and I look forward to shaking up anything I see that needs shaking up (commenting on her nomination to be U.S. Chief of Protocol).

O'Neal, Tatum. She (Shirley Temple) wasn't very good. She was fine when she was 6 or 7. But did you notice how she couldn't act when she was 14?.

BLACKBURN, BEN B.

Blackburn, Ben B. If it was up to me, we would go back to public hanging and we would not have trouble collecting rent (advocating public hanging as a remedy for public housing tenants who fall behind in their rent).

BLAIR, ERIC

Blair, Eric. One feels, as with Napoleon, that he is fighting against destiny, that he can't win, and yet that he somehow deserves to. (writing in the New English Weekly, March 21, 1940).

BLAKE, EUBIE

Blake, Eubie. I don't drink, don't carouse and don't fool around with women. These things are all bad for you.

Blake, Eubie. I don't know nothing else but how to write and play music, and I'll never quit until the man counts eight, nine, ten and waves me out.

BLOCH, ROBERT

Bloch, Robert. I haven't had so much fun since the rats ate my baby sister (upon receipt of the World Fantasy Award for his life work—horror stories).

BLOOMINGDALE'S (DEPARTMENT STORE)

Khan, Naved N. Bloomingdale's is more than a store. It is a way of life.

BOCUSE, PAUL

Bocuse, Paul. Your best American restaurants are the Steak Houses,...the ones with the meat in the window. I love a steak with a baked Idaho potato. Delicious.

BOGART, HUMPHREY

Bogart, Humphrey (attributed by Lauren Bacall). I think you (Noel Coward) are wonderful and charming, and if I should ever change from liking girls better, you would be my first thought.

Chandler, Raymond. Bogart can be tough without a gun. Also he has a sense of humor that contains that grating undertone of contempt. Bogart is the genuine article.

BOHR, NIELS

Bohr, Niels. But horseshoes have a way of bringing you luck even when you don't believe in them.

BOLKAN, FLORINDA

Bolkan, Florinda T. The only thing I'm afraid of is getting bored.

BONO, SONNY

Cher, . I left him for a woman: me (commenting on her divorce from Sonny Bono).

BOOK REVIEWERS AND REVIEWING

Barbour, Hugh R. There is nothing like a good negative review to sell a book.

Sheed, Wilfrid. Criticism is what every reviewer would like to write if he had the time.

BOOKS

Dickens, Charles. There are books of which the backs and covers are by far the best parts.

Hemingway, Mary. Books are helpful in bed. But they are not responsive (commenting on widowhood).

Kafka, Franz. A book must be the axe for the frozen sea inside us.

Roth, Philip. When you publish a book, it's the world's book. The world edits it.

Van Doren, Mark (attributed by Robert Giroux). A classic is a book that is never out of print.

BOOKS AND READING

Chamfort, Nicholas. The success of many books is due to the affinity between the mediocrity of the author's ideas and those of the public.

Greene, Graham. God forbid people should read our books to find the juicy passages.

BOOKS—COLLECTORS AND COLLECTING

Prizeman, John. Collecting books is like collecting other people's minds, like having people on the shelves—only, you can just put them away when you want to.

BOOKSELLERS AND BOOKSELLING

Barbour, Hugh R. There is nothing like a good negative review to sell a book.

BOONE, PAT

Boone, Pat. I just can't get it into my head that a cabinet man can tell a bad joke in private and get fired, and then John Dean can tell the same joke to millions and get paid for it (commenting on the Earl Butz resignation).

Boone, Pat. I think my life is a vindication of what Middle America wants.

BOREDOM

Anonymous, . If you're bored in New York, you're boring.

Beaton, Sir Cecil. Perhaps the world's second worst crime is boredom; the first is being a bore.

Birley, Rhoda. Mothers are a great bore.

BORGE, VICTOR

Borge, Victor. I would put it all in escrow and allocate it toward future payments for fuel for the family car (in response to 'What would you do with 10 million dollars').

BORGES, JORGE LUIS

Borges, Jorge Luis. (I am) very glad about the military coup—it will be a pleasure to be free of hoodlums and gangsters and to be governed again by officers and gentlemen (commenting upon his announcement to return to Argentina).

Borges, Jorge Luis. I had a country. I am ashamed of my country today.

Borges, Jorge Luis. When the literature of the second half of the 20th century is studied, the names will be different than we hear now. They will have found hidden writers. People who won Nobel prizes will be forgotten. I hope I will be forgotten.

BOSS RULE

Udall, Morris King. A boss is a political leader who is on somebody else's side.

BOSTON—DESCRIPTION

Friedberg, A. Alan. Boston is a city with champagne tastes and beer pocketbooks.

Zappa, Frank. It (Boston) is one of the three cities in the world where the girls wear the ugliest shoes.

BOULANGER, NADIA

Boulanger, Nadia. I've been a woman for a little more than 50 years, and I've gotten over my original astonishment (upon being asked how it felt to be the first female conductor of the Boston Symphony in 1938).

Boulanger, Nadia. One works or one cannot work—that would be death.

BOUTON, JIM

Lucas, Bill. If he can help us by getting people out, I don't care if he's 120 years old (about Jim Bouton).

BOWEN, ELIZABETH

Bowen, Elizabeth. All your youth you want to have your greatness taken for granted; when you find it taken for granted, you are unnerved.

BOWIE, DAVID

Simels, Steve. David Bowie (is) the single worst thing to happen to rock music since the deaths of Brian Jones, Janis Joplin, and Jimi Hendrix.

BOWLING

Carter, Don. One of the advantages bowling has over golf is that you seldom lose a bowling ball.

BOXING

Ali, Muhammad. America can no longer afford me. Madison Square Garden and other promoters can't bid against whole countries.

Aranoff, Ezra. There's no room for a slow poke in a prize fight.

Foreman, George. Boxing is like jazz. The better it is, the less people appreciate it.

King, Donald. I have risen to the top in the promotion business just as I climbed to the top in the numbers game: by wits and grits and bullshit.

Leonard, Sugar Ray. The era of the trainer or manager talking for the fighter is over. They're not going to do his fighting, so they shouldn't be doing his talking, either.

Louis, Joe. You can run, but you can't hide.

Quarry, Jerry. This will surprise some people because I was at it so long, but the truth of the matter is that I hated boxing. It is a cruel, vicious sport—nothing more than two people trying to kill each other—and the more vicious it gets, the more people like it. I'm not an animal. Maybe that's why I didn't become champion (commenting on embarking on a career as a singer).

BRADLEY, THOMAS

Bradley, Thomas. This isn't a local issue solely between New York and the Ford Administration—all of us are involved (regarding aid to New York City).

BRAIN

Crouch, Dee. At 18,000 feet, you're roughly half as smart as you are at sea level. The lore is that you don't come back from the mountain as smart as when you go up (commenting on the effect of high altitude on the human brain by the doctor with the American Bicentennial Expedition to Mt. Everest).

BRAIN-WASHING

Reich, Walter. If brainwashing is accepted as a defense, we're in for a brainwashing ourselves in regard to our concept of guilt and innocence (commenting on F. Lee Bailey's defense of Patricia Hearst).

BRAINE, JOHN

Braine, John. I believe absolutely in Christian sexual morality, which means that I believe in premarital virginity. Virgins don't get V.D., don't have abortions, don't have illegitimate babies, and aren't forced to get married. And no man, no matter how progressive, has ever objected to his bride being a virgin.

BRAND, STEWART

Brand, Stewart. My expectation is that the sky will fall. My faith is that there's another sky behind it.

BRANDO, MARLON

Brando, Marlon. Acting is an empty profession. I do it for the money because for me there is no pleasure.

Brando, Marlon. I would like to conduct my life and be a part of society that is as good as grass grows. I'd like to be a blade of grass in concert with other blades of grass. Ants do well, sharks and cockroaches. They survive. I'm for survival.

Brando, Marlon. The principal benefit acting has offered me is the money to pay my psychiatrists.

Gabin, Jean. You are a young me (about Marlon Brando).

Houseman, John. There is no question but that Marlon Brando would have been America's Olivier if he had continued in the classical theater.

BRANDT, WILLY

Brandt, Willy. If I had had a shooting iron with me then I would have put an end to it (commenting on his despair during the sex-and-spy scandal revelations that led to his downfall as Chancellor).

BRAZIL

Babenco, Hector. Brazil is a country that can only be understood by metaphors, where the reality of things violently exceeds fiction.

Fernandes, Millor (Brazilian playwright). The horrendous state of our prisons is what prevents them from being occupied by members of our highest society.

Nixon, Richard Milhous. As Brazil goes, so will the rest of the Latin American continent (commenting in 1971).

BREAKFASTS

Gunther, John. All happiness depends on a leisurely breakfast.

BRECHT, BERTOLT

Brecht, Bertolt. I hope that because of my life, the powerful will sleep less comfortably (on his epitaph).

BRESLIN, JIMMY

Breslin, Jimmy. One of the truly great things about being brought up in New York City is that it allows you to go through life with an open mind.

BREZHNEV, LEONID I.

Brezhnev, Leonid I. Modern economics, politics and public affairs are so complex that they can be mastered only by collective understanding.

BRIBERY

Cockburn, Claud. Never underestimate the effectiveness of a straight cash bribe.

Ryan, John. Bribes are just bad business.

BROCK, LOU

Brock, Lou. If you can perceive a goal and then make it happen, you live a dream.

BRONSON, CHARLES

Huston, John. (Charles Bronson is) a hand grenade with the pin pulled.

BROOKS, MEL

Brooks, Mel. I don't think in terms of results. I think: what next insanity can I shock the world with.

Brooks, Mel. To be the funniest has always been my aim. Not the most philosophical, not the most profound, but the funniest.

BROWN, EDMUND GERALD, JR.

Anonymous (California state official), . (Jerry Brown) is the only governor with a foreign policy.

Anonymous (member of Jerry Brown's cabinet), . (Jerry Brown) is the hole in the doughnut. You can't put your finger on him, but he's always there.

Brand, Stewart. (Jerry Brown) is willing to look at new ideas and he has the courage to take risks. I think it's because he did time in a seminary.

Brown, Edmund Gerald, Jr. All I guarantee is a lot of hard work and to tell you what is working and what is not.

Brown, Edmund Gerald, Jr. Are you kidding? Just being governor is a pain in the ass (when asked once if he had Presidential aspirations).

Brown, Edmund Gerald, Jr. California is the place where the rest of the country and the rest of the world look for leadership and I want to keep it that way.

Brown, Edmund Gerald, Jr. If work is more interesting and challenging, people should be paid less. Those are the people who get great psychic rewards: their lives are better because they have the privilege of interesting work.

Brown, Edmund Gerald, Jr. If you want a Governor who makes decisions, then you are going to get a Governor who makes mistakes.

Brown, Edmund Gerald, Jr. I'm not conservative—I'm just cheap.

Brown, Edmund Gerald, Jr. You don't have to do things. Maybe by avoiding doing things you accomplish a lot.

Brown, Edmund Gerald, Jr. You lean a little to the left and then a little to the right in order to always move straight ahead (on the art of governing).

Brown, Willie. Jerry (Brown) likes Jimmy (Carter) about as well as I like Lester Maddox.

Carter, James Earl. (Jerry Brown) is California's way of celebrating the Year of the Child.

Daley, Richard J. He's a young man with his whole future in front of him. You can't blame anyone for being a candidate.

Hoffman, Abbie. I don't trust (Jerry Brown). He has more colors than a Panamanian patio at sunset.

Koch, Edward I. Jerry Brown is not a flake.

Lewis, Jonathan. Most politicians get elected by being all things to all people. Jerry (Brown) survives by being nothing to everyone.

Priolo, Paul. What that guy (Jerry Brown) does is enough to make a grown Republican cry.

Rice, Kathleen Brown. Contrary to his reputation, he is not a flake, and he does have a sense of humor (about Jerry Brown).

Shields, Mark. Jerry Brown is the Renee Richards of American politics.

BROWN, GEORGE S.

Brown, George S. If any citizen of this country is so concerned about his mail being read or is concerned about his presence at a meeting being noted, I'd say we ought to read his mail and we ought to know what the hell he has done.

Brown, George S. They own, you know, the banks in this country, the newspapers. Just look at where the Jewish money is.

Rumsfeld, Donald. The absence of a reprimand should not be taken as an endorsement of inelegant phraseology (commenting at a Pentagon news conference on the controversial statements of General George S. Brown).

BROWN, WILLIE

Brown, Willie. Jerry (Brown) likes Jimmy (Carter) about as well as I like Lester Maddox.

BRUCE, LENNY

Bruce, Lenny. I only said it, man. I didn't do it.

BRYANT, ANITA

Bryant, Anita. God says that someone who practices homosexuality shall not inherit the Kingdom of God. God is very plain on that.

Bryant, Anita. Heaven knows, I wouldn't want to deny anyone their human rights, but I'm not denying their right to be human (commenting on her fight against homosexual rights in Miami).

Costanza, Midge. I'd like to take the two of them (Anita Bryant and Phyllis Schlafly) and make bookends.

Guthrie, Arlo. The difference between Anita Bryant and me may be that she definitely feels that God is on her side, and I have to keep questioning whether I'm on His (upon becoming a Franciscan lay brother).

BUCHWALD, ART

Buchwald, Art. I doubt that I would do anything different from what I am doing right now. First of all, I can't eat any more than I am right now. Second, I would not buy anything more, because I find possessions a pain in the ass. Third, I have a very good relationship with all my relatives and if I started giving them money, I know they would hate me in their hearts. Come to think of it, I am going to have to review your kind offer. I don't want it. It would only screw up my life, which is screwed up enough as it is (in response to 'What would you do with 10 million dollars').

Buchwald, Art. In 80 percent of the countries in the world today, guys like myself would be in jail.

BUCKLEY, WILLIAM FRANK, JR.

Buckley, William Frank, Jr. If people would just take my advice, everything would go well.

BUDDHA AND BUDDHISM

Erhard, Werner. What the Buddhists were saying is this: true nothing is what is. EST is because EST is nothing.

BUDGET

Muchow, David. Budgeting is a black art practiced by bureaucratic magicians.

BUDGET, PERSONAL

Parkinson, C. Northcote. Expenditure rises to meet income.

BUDGET—UNITED STATES

Ichord, Richard. Once you have done the budget, once you get the statistics, it is much like getting down the unvirtuous woman. Once you get her down, you can do anything you want to.

Kirkland, Lane. Any jackass can draw up a balanced budget on paper.

Talmadge, Herman. Virtually everything is under federal control nowadays except the federal budget.

Wicker, Tom. Government expands to absorb revenue—and then some.

BUDGETING

Muchow, David. Budgeting is a black art practiced by bureaucratic magicians.

BUJOLD, GENEVIEVE

Bujold, Genevieve. Caesar was Cleopatra's guru and Guinness was mine.

BUKOVSKY, VLADIMIR

Bukovsky, Vladimir. If I were to answer what sustains us in this struggle, first and foremost is trust, faith in people, faith in the future, and faith in the human values for which we stand (commenting at the White House on Soviet dissidents).

BULGAKOV, MIKHAIL AFANAS'EVICH. THE MASTER AND MARGARITA

Bonner, Yelena (wife of Andrei Sakharov). It (The Master of Margarita) is the perfect theatre for the Moscow intelligentsia. It doles out the truth in small doses, never big enough to cause trouble.

BURDEN, CHRIS

Burden, Chris. Learn how to make counterfeit money. Some of it is really beautiful (advice for budding artists).

BUREAUCRACY

Anonymous (HEW employee), . Being a Democrat or a Republican is just a party affiliation. 'Don't Make Waves' is a religion.

Blumenthal, W. Michael. Most bureaucratic regulations look like Chinese to me—and I can read Chinese.

Friedman, Milton. In this day and age, we need to revise the old saying to read, Hell hath no fury like a bureaucrat scorned.

Hufstedler, Shirley. There is a little nonsense and sloth in the seams and marrow of all human industry.

McCarthy, Eugene Joseph. The only thing that saves us from the bureaucracy is inefficiency. An efficient bureaucracy is the greatest threat to liberty.

Nies, John. The effort expended by the bureaucracy in defending any error is in direct proportion to the size of the error.

Peter, Laurence J. Bureaucracy defends the status quo long past the time when the quo has lost its status.

Reagan, Ronald. The coils woven in that city (Washington, D.C.) are entrapping us all and, as with the Gordian knot, we cannot untie it. We have to cut it with one blow of the sword.

Sidey, Hugh. Bureaucrats are the only people in the world who can say absolutely nothing and mean it.

Sidey, Hugh. One must always remember that freedom from action and freedom from purpose constitute the philosophical bases of creative bureaucracy.

Sidey, Hugh. The measurement of the gestation period of an original thought in a bureaucracy is still pending.

Sidey, Hugh. When a bureaucrat makes a mistake and continues to make it, it usually becomes the new policy.

BURGER KING, INC.

Smith, Donald N (President of Burger King). The individual choice of garnishment of a burger can be an important point to the consumer in this day when individualism, in my mind, is an increasingly important thing to people.

BURGER, WARREN EARL

Burger, Warren Earl. I will never hire a woman clerk. A woman would have to leave work at 6 p.m. and cook dinner for her husband.

Burger, Warren Earl. Perhaps without knowing all the reasons, they were ahead of many others in seeing that something was missing in modern life (commenting on American youth of the '60s).

Dershowitz, Alan. If he (Warren Burger) were one of the Founding Fathers, he would have voted against the Bill of Rights.

BURNS, ARTHUR FRANK

Conable, Barber. Arthur (Burns) is a great politician. He is a master of the pregnant pause. He knows when to clean his pipe. He can answer the most complicated questions with 'I doubt it', and the world is thunderstruck with his wisdom. When he comes to testify before any committee (of Congress), the whole committee shows up. He has the same effect on the members that Henry Kissinger had. He seems to be right.

BURNS, GEORGE

Burns, George. If you tear yourself down, people feel sorry for you, and if they feel sorry for you, they like you.

Burns, George. Now, they say, you should retire at 70. When I was 70 I still had pimples.

Burns, George. To be perfectly honest, I don't think acting is very hard. They say the most important thing is to be able to laugh & cry. Well, if I have to cry, I think of my sex life, and if I have to laugh, I think of my sex life.

Burns, George. When I do go, I plan to take my music with me. I don't know what's out there, but I want to be sure it's in my key.

BURTON, RICHARD

Burton, Richard. I only see a movie when I can't avoid it.

Burton, Richard. I was a homosexual once but not for long. It didn't work, so I gave it up.

Burton, Richard. I was a star from the moment I first walked on the stage.

Taylor, Elizabeth. I love Richard for the extravagant thought but he doesn't have to spoil me any more—just love me (upon the sale of her $1 million pink diamond ring purchased as a wedding gift).

BUSBY, STEVE

Busby, Steve. I throw the ball harder than Nolan Ryan. It just doesn't get there as fast.

BUSH, GEORGE

Anderson, John B. George Bush is just a tweedier version of Ronald Reagan.

Anonymous (aide to George Bush), . George is a bit of a jock.

Bush, George. I am a non-politician, as of now.

Bush, George. I can feel it in my bones. I'm going to be President.

Bush, George. I'll prevail over Reagan because it is right that I prevail.

Connally, John Bowden. All hat and no cattle (about George Bush).

BUSINESS

Booth, Arch. I find these figures impossible to accept (in response to a Peoples Bicentennial Commission's sponsored survey reflecting wide public disenchantment with American business).

Isley, Fred (Manager of public relations, Xerox Corporation). I don't know if the public's negative attitude makes a difference to corporations (in response to a Peoples Bicentennial Commission's sponsored survey reflecting wide public disenchantment with American business).

Lebowitz, Fran. Contrary to popular opinion the hustle is not a new dance step—it is an old business procedure.

LeFevre, William M. There are only two emotions in Wall Street: fear and greed.

Lesher, Richard. We surveyed our members as to what's troubling them. Number one is government. Number two is government. Number three is government and number four is government.

Murphy, Jack (Director of public relations for Exxon). We're not really surprised. But you can just say we have no comment (in response to a Peoples Bicentennial Commission's sponsored survey reflecting wide public disenchantment with American business).

Reagan, Ronald. I don't know of anyone today that has less influence in this country than business.

Riesman, David. The road to the board room leads through the locker room.

Rockefeller, John Davison. A friendship founded on business is better than a business founded on friendship.

Ryan, John. Bribes are just bad business.

Walden, Phil (President of Capricorn Records). That's the old American way—if you got a good thing, then overdo it.

Warhol, Andy. Good business is the best art.

BUSINESS ETHICS

Young, Andrew. Nothing is illegal if 100 businessmen decide to do it, and that's true anywhere in the world.

BUSINESS—INTERNATIONAL ASPECTS

Kugel, Yerachmiel. Ethics is not a branch of economics.

BUSINESS MANAGEMENT AND ORGANIZATION

Drucker, Peter F. So much of what we call management consists in making it difficult for people to work.

Iacocca, Lee A. I never invent anything any more. Everything I do is to meet a law.

Peter, Laurence J. In a hierarchy, every employee tends to rise to the level of his own incompetence.

BUSINESS—PUBLIC RELATIONS

Marcus, Stanley. A businessman can make no worse mistake than to try to use the muscle of the advertising dollar to try to influence the news.

BUSINESS—UNITED STATES

Sawyer, Charles. The United States, like Atlas, is holding up the world. But who holds up Atlas? American business.

BUSINESSMEN

Bogert, Jeremiah M. We've found that frauds often keep a spotless record while too often many otherwise sound business people get careless with credit.

Brooks, Jim. Businessmen commit a fraud when they say they're interested in anything but profit.

Hefner, Hugh Marston. I'm not primarily an entrepreneurial businessman. I'm primarily a playboy philosopher.

Johnson, Nicholas. Most of what I did as a government official was try to encourage more competition, by having smaller enterprises that would truly compete, by removing barriers to entry, by relieving the dependence of business on large government payments and I was opposed at every step and turn of the way, by businessmen.

Lesher, Richard. We surveyed our members as to what's troubling them. Number one is government. Number two is government. Number three is government and number four is government.

McColough, C. Peter. Businessmen's ethics are not any worse than those of the public as a whole. It's just that the businessman is more accountable than any other level of society and is much more likely to be caught in any dereliction of duty or responsibility.

Peter, Laurence J. In a hierarchy, every employee tends to rise to the level of his own incompetence.

Riesman, David. The road to the board room leads through the locker room.

Young, Andrew. Nothing is illegal if 100 businessmen decide to do it, and that's true anywhere in the world.

BUSINESSMEN—GREAT BRITAIN

Charles, Prince of Wales, . Much of British management does not seem to understand the human factor.

BUSINESSMEN—PUBLIC RELATIONS

Marcus, Stanley. A businessman can make no worse mistake than to try to use the muscle of the advertising dollar to try to influence the news.

BUSINESSMEN—TAX DEDUCTIONS

Long, Russell. Entertainment is to the selling business the same thing as fertilizer is to the farming business—it increases the yield (commenting on the three martini lunch).

BUSINESSMEN—UNITED STATES

Mencken, Henry Louis. No one ever went broke underestimating the intelligence of the American people.

BUTZ, EARL LAUER

Boone, Pat. I just can't get it into my head that a cabinet man can tell a bad joke in private and get fired, and then John Dean can tell the same joke to millions and get paid for it (commenting on the Earl Butz resignation).

Butz, Earl Lauer. He no playa the game, he no maka the rules (in response to Pope Paul's stand on birth control).

Butz, Earl Lauer. In California, Mexican farmworkers are no longer allowed to use the short-handled hoes they have for generations; now they are required to use long-handled American-type hoes. This is not because the workers or the farmers want the change; but apparently because the city people, driving by, feel more comfortable watching the workers using the kind of hoes that look good through car windows.

Simon, William E. I've lived through the Saturday Night Massacre and the Sunday Night Massacre. Only Butz and me are left. We'll probably go on Monday.

BYRD, ROBERT

Anonymous, . He (Robert Byrd) makes the trains run on time but the cars are all empty.

Byrd, Robert. West Virginians have always had five friends—God Almighty, Sears Roebuck, Montgomery Ward, Carter's Little Liver Pills and Robert C. Byrd.

BYRNE, JANE

Anonymous (editorial writer for the Chicago Sun-Times), . Chicago redefined clout Tuesday. It's in the hands of the people (upon Jane Byrne's nomination as Chicago's Democratic candidate for mayor).

Byrne, Jane. Diamonds are a girl's best friend, and Federal grants are second.

Byrne, Jane. I'm a Democrat, I believe in the Democratic Party.

Percy, Charles. The Rock of Gibraltar has sunk (upon Jane Byrne's nomination as Chicago's Democratic candidate for mayor).

Talbott, Basil, Jr. Chicago may have nominated its first mayor who goes to a beauty shop, but she is in the city's oldest tradition.

CAAN, JAMES

Caan, James. You know the kind of actor I am? I'm the sort who says before each movie, 'Oh God, give me a break'.

CADDELL, PATRICK

Caddell, Pat. I'm less influential than I'd like to think I am, and a lot more than I deserve.

CAESAR, SID

Coca, Imogene. I've never figured out why we work so well together, except that we both laugh at exactly the same time. (about herself and Sid Caesar).

CAGNEY, JAMES

Cagney, James. Once a song-and-dance man, always a song-and-dance man. Those few words tell as much about me professionally as there is to tell.

CALDER, ALEXANDER

Calder, Alexander. The underlying sense of form in my work has been the system of the universe, or part thereof. For that is a rather large model to work from.

Calder, Alexander. Why do I live in Paris? Because in Paris it's a compliment to be called crazy.

CALDWELL, SARAH

Brooke, Edward William. A dreamer, a genius, a most exciting woman (about Sarah Caldwell).

Gockley, David. Sarah is an administrator only in the sense that no one else can administrate her (about Sarah Caldwell).

CALDWELL, TAYLOR

Caldwell, Taylor. Women irritate me. I've met a few intelligent women—not many. They're usually after a man, that's all.

CALIFANO, JOSEPH

Califano, Joseph, A. Jr. Of course, we recognize the right to dissent. That's what our boys in Vietnam are fighting for. But this shows that the overwhelming majority of American college students and the American public stand fully behind the President in his policy in Vietnam (commenting in 1965 when he accepted for President Johnson an 8-foot petition with 2,500 signatures from students and faculty at American University protesting the Vietnam War).

CALIFORNIA

Didion, Joan. California is a place in which a boom mentality and a sense of Chekhovian loss meet in uneasy suspension.

Starr, Kevin O. An obsession with self-fulfillment proved one of the dangers of the California dream.

Starr, Kevin O. There is no stable intellectual tradition in California except utopianism.

CALIFORNIA—DESCRIPTION

Allen, Fred. California is a great place to live...if you happen to be an orange.

Brown, Edmund Gerald, Jr. In California, you've got to realize one thing: you don't mess around with a man's cars or his guns.

Caen, Herb. What others call kooks we look upon as characters in a charade we smile at (about California).

Redgrave, Vanessa. California is a place with lots of warm weather and lots of cold people.

Smelser, Neil. Californians believe the best is behind them.

CALIFORNIA—POLITICS AND GOVERNMENT

Brown, Edmund Gerald, Jr. California is the place where the rest of the country and the rest of the world look for leadership and I want to keep it that way.

CALLAS, MARIA

Callas, Maria. I hate to be pitied, and I never pitied anyone.

Sills, Beverly. She (Maria Callas) was a pioneer and an inspiration.

CALLEY, WILLIAM LAWS, JR.

Calley, William Laws, Jr. I think I've always been a pacifist.

Calley, William Laws, Jr. I was a coward. I couldn't have backed out (from the My Lai attack) if I wanted to because I believed in this nation.

CALLOWAY, CAB

Calloway, Cab. Women, horses, cars, clothes. I did it all. And do you know what that's called. It's called living.

CAMBODIA

Kissinger, Henry Alfred. Cambodia's agony unfolded with the inevitability of a Greek tragedy.

CAMBODIA—POLITICS AND GOVERNMENT

Norodom Sihanouk, King Of Cambodia (Abdicated 1955), . When they no longer need me, they will spit me out like a cherry pit (about the Khmer Rouge).

CANADA—DESCRIPTION

Trudeau, Pierre Elliott. I'm saying that Canadians as a whole have been trying to get more out of society than they've been putting into it.

CANADA—POLITICS AND GOVERNMENT

Levesque, Rene. The quality of a civilized society is the treatment it affords minorities.

Trudeau, Pierre Elliott. Most Canadians understand that the rupture of their country would be a crime against the history of mankind.

Trudeau, Pierre Elliott. The Tory future is worse than the Liberal past.

CANADA—RELATIONS—UNITED STATES

Meighen, Arthur. We are not in the same boat, but we are pretty much in the same waters.

CANADIANS

Trudeau, Pierre Elliott. I'm saying that Canadians as a whole have been trying to get more out of society than they've been putting into it.

CANCER

Saffiotti, Umberto. Cancer in the last quarter of the 20th century can be considered a social disease, a disease whose causation and control are rooted in the technology and economy of our society.

Salk, Jonas. The best thing to do (for people worried about cancer-causing substances) is quit reading the newspaper.

CANCER—CAUSES

Higginson, John. We now know there are a hundred causes of cancer, and eighty of them are cigarettes.

Newell, Guy. The cancer problem has not been solved, but it has never been more solvable.

CANCER—THERAPY

McNaughton, Andrew. The patient who is suffering from cancer doesn't care if he gets his Laetrile from an angel or a devil.

CANDIDATES, POLITICAL

Railsback, Thomas F. I'm concerned that candidates can often be packaged like wieners, and the best-looking wiener sometimes wins.

CANETTI, ELIAS

Canetti, Elias. ...I have succeeded in grabbing this century by the throat.

CANNES INTERNATIONAL FILM FESTIVAL

Anonymous, . In Cannes, a producer is what any man calls himself if he owns a suit, a tie, and hasn't recently been employed as a pimp.

CAPITAL

Drucker, Peter F. Capital formation is shifting from the entrepreneur who invests in the future to the pension trustee who invests in the past.

CAPITAL INVESTMENTS

Drucker, Peter F. Capital formation is shifting from the entrepreneur who invests in the future to the pension trustee who invests in the past.

CAPITAL PUNISHMENT

Blackburn, Ben B. If it was up to me, we would go back to public hanging and we would not have trouble collecting rent (advocating public hanging as a remedy for public housing tenants who fall behind in their rent).

Fortas, Abe. The law of revenge has its roots in the deep recesses of the human spirit, but that is not a permissible reason for retaining capital punishment.

Gilmore, Gary Mark. Let's do it.

Hoover, John Edgar. The cure for crime is not the electric chair but the high chair.

Reagan, Nancy. I'm in favor of the death penalty—I think it saves lives.

CAPITALISM

Booth, Arch. I find these figures impossible to accept (in response to a Peoples Bicentennial Commission's sponsored survey reflecting wide public disenchantment with American business).

Brandel, Fernand. The preserve of the few, capitalism is unthinkable without society's active complicity.

Butz, Earl Lauer. Our capitalism is no longer capitalism; it is a weakened mixture of government regulations and limited business opportunities.

Castro, Fidel. I don't think the contradictions between capitalism and socialism can be resolved by war. This is no longer the age of the bow and arrow. It's the nuclear age, and war can annihilate us all. The only way to achieve solutions seems to be for the different social systems to coexist.

Forbes, Malcolm. I'd say capitalism's worst excess is in the large number of crooks and tinhorns who get too much of the action.

Galbraith, John Kenneth. Capitalism will survive.

Greenspan, Alan. When I met Ayn Rand, I was a free enterpriser in the Adam Smith sense, impressed with the theoretical structure and efficiency of markets. What she did was to make me see that capitalism is not only efficient and practical, but also moral.

Iguiniz, Javier (Peruvian economist). The growth of capitalism is the same as the growth of world poverty.

Isley, Fred (Manager of public relations, Xerox Corporation). I don't know if the public's negative attitude makes a difference to corporations (in response to a Peoples Bicentennial Commission's sponsored survey reflecting wide public disenchantment with American business).

Janeway, Eliot. The thrill of making a fast buck follows only the thrill of love at first sight. Everyone needs to take an occasional fling with money...and with love.

Levy, Bernard-Henri. Between the barbarity of capitalism, which censures itself much of the time, and the barbarity of socialism, which does not, I guess I might choose capitalism.

Moynihan, Daniel Patrick. The great corporations of this country were not founded by ordinary people. They were founded by people with extraordinary energy, intelligence, ambition, aggressiveness. All those factors go into the primordial capitalist urge.

Murphy, Jack (Director of public relations for Exxon). We're not really surprised. But you can just say we have no comment (in response to a Peoples Bicentennial Commission's sponsored survey reflecting wide public disenchantment with American business).

Sternbach, Leo Henryk. I am not a victim of capitalistic exploitation. If anything, I am an example of capitalistic enlightenment (commenting on his discovery of Valium and Librium and selling of the patent to his employer Hoffman-La Roche at $1 per drug).

Tanner, Jack. Nothing could discredit capitalism more than a decision by the Russians to try it.

Teng, Hsiao-Ping. It doesn't matter whether you climb Mount Everest by its North slope or its South slope as long as you get to the top.

CAPITALISM AND SOCIETY

Kristol, Irving. Many middle-class reformers will find to their surprise, that the populace is going to be quick to bite the hand that aims to feed it. The populace doesn't want to be fed; it wants more freedom to graze on its own.

CAPONE, ALPHONSE

Capone, Alphonse. It rains in Chicago and snows too. But after all home is home.

Capone, Alphonse. Let the worthy citizens of Chicago get their liquor the best way they can. I'm sick of the job. It's a thankless job and full of grief.

Capone, Alphonse. They blamed everything but the Chicago Fire on me.

Capone, Alphonse. When I sell liquor, it's called bootlegging; when my patrons serve it on silver trays on Lake Shore Drive, it's called hospitality.

CAPOTE, TRUMAN

Capote, Truman. I mean I can create any kind of social world I want, anywhere I want.

Capote, Truman. I say I'm a homosexual who has had heterosexual experiences.

Capote, Truman. I'm the greatest genius of all time.

O'Brian, Jack. (Truman Capote is) Jackie Susann with an education.

Vidal, Gore. Truman (Capote) has made lying an art. A *minor* art.

CAPP, AL

Capp, Al. If the strip (Li'l Abner) had any message at all, maybe that was it—leave the goddam world alone and we'll do fine (commenting on the end of Li'l Abner which ran for 43 years).

CARAMANLIS, CONSTANTINE

Caramanlis, Constantine. So we Greeks have been from ancient times: we are skillful at making idols, not that we may worship them, but that we may have the pleasure of destroying them.

CARDIN, PIERRE

Cardin, Pierre. I have to do things differently from anyone else. For that, they say I am crazy.

Cardin, Pierre. The jean. The jean is the destructor. It is a dictator. It is destroying creativity. The jean must be stopped.

CARDS

Algren, Nelson. Never eat at a place called Mom's. Never play cards with a man named Doc. And never lie down with a woman who's got more troubles than you.

CAREW, RODNEY

Carew, Rodney. I baby my bats, treat them like my kids, because using a bat is how I make my living.

Otis, Amos (baseball player). Trying to sneak a pitch past him (Rod Carew) is like trying to sneak the sunrise past a rooster.

CAREY, HUGH

Carey, Hugh. My mind doesn't govern my conscience, my conscience governs my mind.

CAROLINE, PRINCESS OF MONACO

Grace Patricia, Consort of Ranier III, Prince of Monaco, . It's her (daughter Princess Caroline's) happiness that counts. I don't care if she's marrying a commoner.

CARSWELL, HAROLD G.

Scott, Hugh. The worst mistake I made was supporting the Carswell nomination (reflecting on his three decades in Congress).

CARTER, AMY

Taylor, Elizabeth. I do feel sorry for Amy Carter, I know the problems she'll have.

CARTER, BILLY

Carter, Billy. Ah cain't drink this here Reengold beer. The next vice president of the United States is the man who brings me a Pabst Blue Ribbon.

Carter, Billy. I drink liquor out of a cup instead of out of the bottle now (commenting on how his life has been affected by his brother's candidacy for the Presidency).

Carter, Billy. I found out water can be drunk straight.

Carter, Billy. I know more about Libya than the whole State Department put together. I'm going to succeed just by treating them like folks.

Carter, Billy. Jimmy will never tell me to change. His staff may bitch. But to hell with his damn staff.

Carter, Billy. There's a helluva lot more Arabians than there is Jews.

Carter, Billy. Yes sir, I'm a real Southern boy. I got a red neck, white socks, and Blue Ribbon beer.

Carter, Lillian. I tried it once and it gave me diarrhea (about Billy Beer).

Qaddafi, Muammar. If he (Billy Carter) runs for President, we will do what we can to support him.

CARTER, JAMES EARL

Anderson, John B. I am not running against General Eisenhower. I am running against Jimmy Carter and Ronald Reagan, and I would respectfully suggest that neither is an Eisenhower.

Anonymous, . If the President helps me and my candidates next year, I'll help him in 1980. It's as simple as that.

Anonymous (former Presidential adviser), . The President (Jimmy Carter) has a terminal case of meekness.

Anonymous (White House aide), . (Carter's) mental state is about the same as always. He is still the same dull, dogged, determined, nose-to-the-grindstone fellow we all know.

Anonymous (White House staff member), . (Jody) Powell is able to speak for Carter without Carter ever having spoken.

Archer, T. D. Carter very definitely was not prolabor. At a labor gathering, he was a labor man. But if you heard him at the chamber of commerce, he was a chamber man.

Ayers, Brandt. It is much too soon to think of Jimmy Carter as another Jefferson.

Baker, Howard Henry. (Jimmy Carter is) a yellow-pad President.

Block, Herbert L. (Jimmy Carter) looks a little like both Jack Kennedy and Eleanor Roosevelt.

Bond, Julian. Don't let Jimmy Carter pull the peanut butter over your eyes.

Bond, Julian. I think Jimmy Carter wants to be president more than any other person I've ever known. And that is just terrifying.

Bond, Julian. It bothers me to think that a year from now an occasion will come up when some response is called for from him (Jimmy Carter) as President and I have no way of knowing what it would be.

Boone, Pat. Jimmy Carter is a Christian, but he's a McGovern-type Christian, proabortion, prohomosexuality and prolegalizing marijuana.

Brando, Marlon. Carter has done something no other President has done: He has brought into the sharpest contrast the hypocrisy of the U.S. in respect to human rights.

Brock, Bill. If the (1980) election focuses on Carter and his record, Carter will lose.

Broder, David S. The warning flags are flying for front-runner Jimmy Carter. He has simply not been able to consolidate his position in the way a genuinely strong candidate should (commenting on the upcoming Presidential race, 5/23/76).

Brown, Edmund Gerald, Jr. I think Jimmy Carter ought to take the Paraquat out of whatever it is in.

Brown, Willie. Jerry (Brown) likes Jimmy (Carter) about as well as I like Lester Maddox.

Carey, Hugh. My impression was that he (Jimmy Carter) has the Eleanor Roosevelt teeth and she (Rosalynn Carter) has the Eleanor Roosevelt brain.

Carter, Billy. Jimmy will never tell me to change. His staff may bitch. But to hell with his damn staff.

Carter, James Earl. A good old boy is somebody who's compatible with the group. I feel just as much at home around Billy's (his brother's) filling station as I do in the black Baptist Church, as I do with the big-shot Texas businessman.

Carter, James Earl. Christ says don't consider yourself better than someone else because one guy screws a whole bunch of women while the other guy is loyal to his wife.

Carter, James Earl. Civil service reform will be the centerpiece of government reorganization during my term in office.

Carter, James Earl. I can't resign from the human race because there's discrimination, and I don't intend to resign from my own church because there's discrimination.

Carter, James Earl. I have nothing against a community that's made up of people who are Polish, Czechoslovakians, French Canadians or blacks who are trying to maintain the ethnic purity of their neighborhood. This is a natural inclination on the part of the people.

Carter, James Earl. I remember in this room last May someone asked me if my administration was all image and no substance, or style and no substance. Lately the criticisms have been that there is too much substance and not enough style.

Carter, James Earl. I think I earn it (referring to his $200,000 salary).

Carter, James Earl. I would have a fairly steady stream of visitors, just average Americans...to come in and spend a night with us at the White House and eat supper with us.

Carter, James Earl. If I ever lie to you, if I ever betray you, then I want you to leave me (to political supporters).

Carter, James Earl. My name is Jimmy Carter and I'm running for President of the United States.

Carter, James Earl. Our people want a President to be both tough and gentle, both statesman and politician, both dreamer and fighter. You expect him to have the drive to reach the White House, and the wisdom and patience to govern wisely.

Carter, James Earl. The American people and our government will continue our firm commitment to promote respect for human rights not only in our own country but also abroad (to Andrei Sakharov).

Carter, James Earl. The most important skill for any President is leadership. A national leader, to be effective, must have the ability to lead this country and the vision to know where it must be led.

Carter, James Earl. When I chop down this cherry tree it will be the first time I've chopped down a tree and told the truth about it (upon receiving the Atlanta Press Club's I-cannot-tell-a-lie-award).

Carter, James Earl. When I finish my term, I want black people to say that I did more for them in my presidency than any other President in their lifetime.

Carter, James Earl (Attributed by Robert Shrum). I'd be a pretty pathetic nominee if I wasn't able to get rid of Strauss as national chairman.

Carter, Lillian. Jimmy's not sexy, he's my son.

Carter, Rosalynn. The President of the United States cares what I think.

Carter, Rosalynn. When people ask me about Jimmy being a Baptist, and indicate they feel no Baptist can run the country, I just remind them that Harry Truman was a Baptist, and I think he did a great job.

Clifford, Clark. Jimmy Carter has the best mind of any President I have known.

Conable, Barber. The trouble with Carter is he's listening only to God—and God doesn't pay taxes.

Cooks, Stoney (aide to Andrew Young). Liberals want to do it for you. Southerners want to do it with you (commenting on the Carter administration's attempt to involve minorities in the government).

Delisle, Paul (maitre d' of Sans Souci Restaurant). Once we had the Texan. He learned to eat fine French food. The Georgian—he can learn too.

Durkin, John. In New Hampshire today, the Ayatullah Khomeini could beat Carter.

Edwards, James B. I don't believe the South will buy Jimmy Carter. He is nothing more than a Southern-talking George McGovern.

Fallows, James. I came to think that Carter believes fifty things, but no one thing.

Fraser, Douglas. The President is a nice man, an intelligent man and he likes his job. But he doesn't have any fire in his belly.

Fritchey, Clayton. President Carter says he doesn't 'panic in a crisis.' But that's not the problem. The problem is that he panics without a crisis.

Getz, Stan. (Jimmy) Carter is playing it real safe and having only chamber quartets and opera. Let the peanut farmer break out a little and get some jazz at the White House.

Harrington, Michael. I think that we should offer Jimmy Carter our hand to help him fulfill the promises he made. And if he doesn't take our hand, we should give him a shove.

Harris, Louis. Gerald Ford is viewed as more of a man of integrity, for example, than Jimmy Carter is (commenting on the results of his polling of public opinion).

Hatcher, Richard. We've created a Frankenstein's monster with a Southern drawl, a more cultured version of the old Confederate at the schoolhouse door.

Hayakawa, Samuel Ichiye. I lust after women in my heart every hour on the hour. But being so busy in campaigning, I have to settle for that.

Hemenway, Russell. He's (Jimmy Carter) the first president in recent history that would occupy the most important office in the world without any commitment to anybody.

Herndon, Terry. He seemed like a nice little guy with a lot of chutzpah (upon meeting President Carter).

Johnson, Claudia Alta (Taylor). The South is the future. It is the political pivot of the country now. It's very gratifying to see Jimmy Carter become President, to see the South finally win out after all these years.

Kaye, Peter F. (Ford campaign spokesman). Mondale is a 100 per cent bona fide liberal. It gives us a tangible target. We're not just running against this peanut farmer who walks on water.

Kennedy, Edward Moore. I think Mr. Carter has created Ronald Reagan.

Kennedy, Edward Moore. I would be much happier if Carter were successful.

Kennedy, Edward Moore. The press made Jimmy Carter, and now they're trying to destroy him. I'm going to set my own course.

King, Martin Luther, Sr. Surely the Lord sent Jimmy Carter to come on out and bring America back where she belongs.

Kirbo, Charles. He's (Jimmy Carter) got faults, like all of us. He's ambitious. But he's not greedy, and he's considerate.

Kirbo, Charles. I may be wrong, and I may be biased, but I'm sure as hell not uncertain (commenting on his status as advisor to President Carter).

Kirkland, Lane. Carter is your typical, smiling, brilliant, backstabbing, bullshitting, southern nut-cutter.

Kissinger, Henry Alfred. Most administrations come to office believing that they are saving the world. This one believes it created the world (commenting on the Carter administration).

Lance, Thomas Bertram. He (Jimmy Carter) campaigns liberal, but he governs conservative.

Landers, Ann. I believe people want some spiritual leadership. It shows in the primaries; Jimmy Carter. He speaks openly about his religion. They see in him something that offers hope.

Laxalt, Paul D. We are finding that conservatives throughout this country are going to marshal together and present, I think, a formidable political challenge, and comes the general election, personally I think that Ronald Reagan has the potential of putting together the same basic elements against Jimmy Carter that Richard Nixon did in 1972.

McCarthy, Eugene Joseph. If you're in the peanut business you learn to think small (about Jimmy Carter).

McCarthy, Eugene Joseph. Jimmy Carter says he talks to Jesus five times a day. Some of us think he really shouldn't have to bother the Lord that often. He should be able to make some decisions on his own.

McGovern, George Stanley. I will support Jimmy Carter with the same enthusiasm with which he supported the Democratic ticket in 1972.

Maclaine, Shirley. He says his lust is in his heart. I hope it's a little lower (about Jimmy Carter).

Maddox, Lester Garfield. The reason he (Jimmy Carter) says he never lies is because he thinks the truth originates with him.

Maddox, Lester Garfield. There are two Jimmy Carters, one running for president and one governor of Georgia, and let me tell you one thing: if Richard Nixon had gotten his training from Jimmy Carter, he never would have gotten caught.

Mankiewicz, Tom. Whatever Jimmy Carter is asking us to be, Superman is already.

Meany, George. They say Carter is the first businessman ever to sit in the White House. But why did they have to send us a small businessman?.

Moyers, Bill D. He's smiling like a Christian with four aces (about Jimmy Carter).

Nelson, Gaylord. Meeting with Carter, you have the impression you're with a computer taking in information and not giving you any reaction. You don't feel you've met with anybody.

Nesmith, Jeff. Life is a great big monopoly game to Carter, and every piece has to fit in its place—including the press.

New York Times, . The question on Tuesday is not whether there might have been better candidates than those nominated by the two major parties. The only question before the American people is whether they have been given a choice of leadership and prospective policies worthy of their vote. We find the choice clear-cut. We cast our vote for Jimmy Carter.

Phillips, Kevin. I don't see how the (Republican) party can survive a Carter victory because it would wrap up the Southern opportunity for growth. When you take that away, you take away the future of the whole party.

Powell, Jody. How many times did Jimmy Carter say during the campaign he was a fiscal conservative—50,000 times? That's the mistake people have made all along—not believing he means what the hell he says.

Rowan, Carl. Carter turned out to be not a populist but a small-town businessman.

Sadat, Anwar. I have dealt with three presidents, Nixon, Ford and this Carter. I can say that everything is improving.

Sadat, Anwar. The approach of Carter is really something like mine. He is a villager, he is also at ease, and he is also a true believer.

Safire, William. (Jimmy Carter is) the best U.S. President the Soviet Union ever had.

Schindler, Rabbi Alexander. The world isn't used to your (Jimmy Carter's) open diplomacy. It stiffens the back of Israel and raises the expectations of the Arabs, which, once frustrated, will retard rather than bring peace.

Schlesinger, Arthur, Jr. I will support the Democratic ticket, but actually I think they're both a couple of stiffs (commenting on the 1976 Democratic and Republican candidates).

Schlesinger, Arthur, Jr. It is evident that what pretends to be a Democratic administration has deliberately and methodically chosen Republican policies.

Schmidt, Helmut. He (Jimmy Carter) is making (foreign) policy from the pulpit.

Schneiders, Greg. He (Jimmy Carter) is the opposite of macho. He's soft on the outside and hard on the inside.

Shields, Mark. I don't think Carter and self-doubt have ever met.

Sidey, Hugh. Carter must understand that in this city (Washington) we cut red tape lengthwise.

Simon, William E. Surely this (Carter) Administration will go down in history as the worst stewards of the American economy in our lifetime.

Sloane, Harvey. He's maturing like good Kentucky bourbon (about Jimmy Carter).

Sorensen, Theodore Chaikin. To continue fighting for this post, (the directorship of the CIA) which would be my natural inclination, would only handicap the new administration if I am rejected, or handicap my effectiveness if confirmed.

Stapleton, Ruth Carter. I am not going to be the Billy Graham of the Carter administration.

Stone, Isidor Feinstein. (Jimmy Carter) seems to me a conventional moderate conservative, Southern agro-businessman who got elected posing as a barefoot boy populist; a good man, who's doing some things on which he deserves support, but limited in everything but his ambition, which got him to the White House. But he seems more and more the tinkering, fuss-budget engineer. There's no music in him. He can fool people for a while, but he really doesn't know how to inspire. He just doesn't have the gift of greatness, the capacity to speak to the hearts and souls of men.

Strauss, Robert S. There ain't but one good job in this government, and you got it (to Jimmy Carter).

Taylor, Elizabeth. I'm confident that he's (Jimmy Carter) a short-term President.

Tyrrell, R. Emmett, Jr. A new Government took office in Washington, not via bayonets and tanks as is the custom in some of the world's capitals (but) in the Democratic Way...via hyperbole, sham, melodrama and public-spirited mendacity (commenting on the Carter inauguration).

Udall, Morris King. We fought a good fight, now we're here to help Jimmy Carter celebrate his victory (at the Democratic National Convention).

Vidal, Gore. Better the zero of Carter than the minus of Kennedy.

Waiyaki, Munyha (Kenyan foreign Minister). We believe that the man (Jimmy Carter) is basically honest. He may not have had too much experience in government, but we don't hold it against him. This was one thing that was said about Africans not too long ago.

Whitman, Alden. Carter's sermons (on human rights) might be more credible if he had a priority program to end poverty.

Wurf, Jerry. If Jimmy Carter emerges as a strong President and keeps the promises he made in 1976, then there is still time for him to be born again politically.

Young, Andrew. Black folks didn't need much selling on Carter. They have a special kind of radar about whether white folks are for real.

Young, Andrew. (Jimmy) Carter does not hand out nickels after a campaign (about political rewards for supporting him).

CARTER, JAMES EARL—ENERGY PROGRAM

Swearingen, John E. The President has made an emotional appeal to defend a tax program that is indefensible. His energy program involves the largest peacetime tax increase ever imposed on our citizens.

CARTER, JAMES EARL—FAMILY

Carter, Billy. I'm not the Carter that doesn't tell a lie.

CARTER, JAMES EARL—FAMILY—FINANCE, PERSONAL

Carter, James Earl. All personal expenses are paid for out of my own pocket. (We are not) mooching off the American taxpayers (reacting to criticism of the fact that his married son and family live in the White House).

CARTER, JAMES EARL—RELATION WITH THE PRESS

Johnson, Haynes. Jimmy Carter met the press and they were his (commenting after Carter's first press conference as President).

CARTER, JAMES EARL—RELATIONS—RELIGION

Carter, James Earl. I have never detected or experienced any conflict between God's will and my political duties.

CARTER, JAMES EARL—STAFF

Broder, David S. At least half the Carter Cabinet were good bets to be there, no matter which Democrat was nominated and elected.

Carter, James Earl. I look on Senator Mondale, who will be the next Vice President, as my top staff person.

Jordan, Hamilton. If after the inauguration you find a Cy Vance as Secretary of State and Zbigniew Brzezinski (of Columbia University) as head of national security, then I would say we failed. And I'd quit. But that's not going to happen.

Reagan, Ronald. The trouble with (the Carter) administration is that for everybody they got in, it was a step up. They never had it so good.

Sloan, Hugh, Jr. There's a strong parallel between the Carter and Nixon White Houses. I don't think there's going to be another Watergate. But you're relying on a group of eager young people who are going to make mistakes.

CARTER, LILLIAN

Carter, Lillian. I don't know of anybody in my hometown who's destitute. I wouldn't let them be.

Carter, Lillian. I tried it once and it gave me diarrhea (about Billy Beer).

Carter, Lillian. I was born loving everybody.

Carter, Lillian. I'm not a city person, I'm a country hick.

Carter, Lillian. Sometimes when I look at all my children, I say to myself, 'Lillian, you should have stayed a virgin'.

CARTER, ROSALYNN

Carey, Hugh. My impression was that he (Jimmy Carter) has the Eleanor Roosevelt teeth and she (Rosalynn Carter) has the Eleanor Roosevelt brain.

Carter, Rosalynn. I don't mind being called tough. I am strong, and I do have definite ideas and opinions. In the sense that 'tough' means I can take a lot, stand up to a lot, it's a fair description (responding to being called the Steel Magnolia).

Carter, Rosalynn. I find myself in the eye of history. I have influence. And I know it.

Carter, Rosalynn. I have always been more political than (Jimmy).

Carter, Rosalynn. I've always worked hard, and that's why they call me 'The Steel Magnolia'.

Carter, Rosalynn. Jimmy taught me a long time ago that you do the best you can and don't worry about the criticisms. Once you accept the fact that you're not perfect then you develop some confidence.

Carter, Rosalynn. The President of the United States cares what I think.

CARTER, RUBIN (HURRICANE)

Carter, Rubin (Hurricane). The kindest thing I can say about my childhood is that I survived it.

Stokes, Geoffrey. Attica is full of Hurricane Carters who were never champions. Or championed.

CARTIER-BRESSON, HENRI

Cartier-Bresson, Henri. For me the camera is an instrument of intuition and spontaneity, the master of the instant.

CARTLAND, BARBARA
Cartland, Barbara. I'm the only author with 200 virgins in print.

CASH, JOHNNY
Cash, Johnny. I guess the record shows I'm far from perfect—but I want to keep trying.

CASH, KEVIN
Breslin, Jimmy. Nobody ever drank more than Kevin (Cash)—he was a real newspaperman.

CASSIDY, SHAUN
Cassidy, Shaun. I'm no different from what I was before, except that people ask for my autograph and tear off my clothes.

CASTRO, FIDEL
Anonymous (a Cuban), . We don't mind following him blindly because we know Fidel can see everything (commenting on Cuban Prime Minister Fidel Castro).

Castro, Fidel. I don't think the contradictions between capitalism and socialism can be resolved by war. This is no longer the age of the bow and arrow. It's the nuclear age, and war can annihilate us all. The only way to achieve solutions seems to be for the different social systems to coexist.

Quinn, Sally. An attitude of sexuality is as pervasive in Cuba as the presence of Fidel Castro. You can feel sex in the atmosphere, on the street, in conversation, in people's actions. The Cubans seem to be thinking of it much of the time.

Trudeau, Pierre Elliott. He did not talk like a fanatic when he talked about world leaders. Within the framework of his ideology, he's a man of world stature (commenting on Fidel Castro after a visit to Cuba).

CATHOLIC CHURCH
John Paul II, Pope, . It is the right of the faithful not to be troubled by theories and hypotheses that they are not expert in judging or that are easily simplified or manipulated by public opinion.

Lefebvre, Marcel. The church is full of thieves, mercenaries and wolves. During the past 20 years, the Vatican has become the friend of our enemies.

Lefebvre, Marcel. The rite of Mass today is a bastard rite. The sacraments today are bastard sacraments. We want to have prayers like our ancestors. We want to keep the Catholic faith.

Quinlan, Thomas. Church is like a saloon. The doors swing in and the doors swing out. If you don't believe, get the hell out.

CATHOLIC CHURCH IN THE UNITED STATES
Greeley, Andrew. Only a charlatan or a lunatic would be hopeful about the present state of Catholicism.

CATHOLICISM
Waugh, Evelyn. You have no idea how much nastier I would be if I was not a Catholic. Without supernatural aid I would hardly be a human being.

CAUCASIAN RACE
Harrell, John R. The black man's angry, the yellow man's angry. Everybody's angry but the white man, and he's asleep.

Muddy Waters, . Those whites can play instruments real fine. But there's something missing in the singing. They just don't eat enough pinto beans; they haven't had enough hard times.

CAUSATION
Shannon, William V. What is actually happening is often less important than what appears to be happening.

CELEBRITIES—SEXUAL BEHAVIOR
Brando, Marlon. If you're rich and famous you don't have any trouble getting laid.

CENSORSHIP
Irani, C. R. The only protection for a free press is the courage to demand it.

Lear, Norman. Sex and violence are a smokescreen. There are interests in this country that don't care to have fun made about the problems existing in society (concerning the censorship of television).

Rubinstein, Michael. The ultimate blasphemy must be censorship.

CERF, BENNETT
Cerf, Bennett. Everyone has a streak of pure, unadulterated ham. Many won't admit it. I revel in it.

CEZANNE, PAUL
Cezanne, Paul. I am the primitive of the method I have invented.

CHABROL, CLAUDE
Chabrol, Claude. I ask audiences to contemplate a character, not identify with him.

CHAGALL, MARC
Chagall, Marc. I love life more now than I did as a boy, and I will go on loving it more until my last moments.

Chagall, Marc. Me, I do not understand Chagall.

Chagall, Marc. My greatest weakness is America.

Picasso, Pablo. After Matisse, Chagall is the only artist who really knows color.

CHAMBERS, MARILYN
Chambers, Marilyn. Maybe I'll make a Mary Poppins movie and shove the umbrella up my ass.

CHAMPAGNE
Keynes, John Maynard. My only regret in life is that I did not drink more champagne.

CHANCE
Runyon, Damon. All life is six-to-five against.

CHANDLER, RAYMOND
Chandler, Raymond. Every story I write is a fire for you to warm your hands by.

Chandler, Raymond. If my books had been any worse, I should not have been invited to Hollywood...if they had been any better, I should not have come.

CHANGE
Brecht, Bertolt. Because things are the way they are things will not stay the way they are.

Pannenberg, Wolfhart. The greatest deception (of our era is the idea that) political change can satisfy a religious need.

CHAPLIN, CHARLES SPENCER
Chaplin, Charles Spencer. I am known in parts of the world by people who have never heard of Jesus Christ.

Chaplin, Charles Spencer. I can't understand Karl Marx, so how can I be a Communist?.

Chaplin, Charles Spencer. I never thought of the tramp in terms of appeal. He was myself, a comic spirit, something within me that I said I must express.

Chaplin, Charles Spencer. My prodigious sin was and still is, being a nonconformist. Although I am not a Communist, I refused to fall in line by hating them.

Chaplin, Charles Spencer. One cannot do humor without great sympathy for one's fellow man. As the tramp I think I endeared myself through his terrific humility.....

Shaw, George Bernard. (Charlie Chaplin is) the one genius created by the cinema.

Wilson, Edmund. Have we ever turned out anything that was comparable artistically to the best German or Russian films? I can think of nothing except Charlie Chaplin, who is his own producer and produces simply himself.

CHARACTERS AND CHARACTERISTICS

Anonymous, . A clean desk is the sign of a sick mind.

Benchley, Robert. There may be said to be two classes of people in the world: those who constantly divide the people of the world into two classes and those who do not.

Forbes, Malcolm S. A bore is someone who persists in holding his own views after we have enlightened him with ours.

Frost, Robert. Half the world is composed of people who have something to say and can't, and the other half who have nothing to say and keep on saying it.

Herold, Don. Many people have character who have nothing else.

Hitler, Adolf. You know, everybody has a price—and you'd be surprised how low it is.

Kerouac, Jack. Walking on water wasn't built in a day.

Maugham, William Somerset. Only a mediocre person is always at his best.

Meir, Golda. Don't be humble, you're not that great.

Newman, Paul. If you don't have enemies, you don't have character.

Randall, Tony. People don't call you mad or eccentric if you are well-heeled. It's only when you're poor that they call you a nut.....

Shaw, George Bernard. The test of a man's or a woman's breeding is how they behave in a quarrel.

Spinks, Leon. You can take a man out of the ghetto, but you can't take the ghetto out of a man.

Stevenson, Adlai, II. You can tell the size of a man by the size of the thing that makes him mad.

Tanner, Jack. A person without character always does what is right.

CHARACTERS AND CHARACTERISTICS—FRANCE

Aron, Jean-Paul. Avarice is the predominant French characteristic because of (our) long peasant history.

Bell, Helen Choate. The French are a low lot. Give them two more legs and a tail, and there you are.

CHARACTERS AND CHARACTERISTICS—GREAT BRITAIN

Crisp, Quenton. The English think incompetence is the same thing as sincerity.

John, Elton. People in England are so bloody nosey.

Toynbee, Arnold. The Englishman's truly distinctive disease is his cherished habit of waiting until the 13th hour.

CHARACTERS AND CHARACTERISTICS—IRELAND

Byrne, Jane. With the Irish, you know, only the strongest survive

Flanagan, Fionnula. The one thing you must not commit with the Irish is to succeed.

Moynihan, Daniel Patrick. I don't think there's any point in being Irish if you don't know that the world is going to break your heart eventually.

CHARACTERS AND CHARACTERISTICS—ITALY

Mussolini, Benito. It is not impossible to govern Italians. It is merely useless.

West, Morris. In discourse the Italians are the most eloquent people in the world. In action they are either apathetic or impulsive to the point of insanity.

CHARACTERS AND CHARACTERISTICS—MEN

Hufstedler, Shirley. A man cannot be very kind unless he is also very strong.

Rubin, Jerry. Most men act so tough and strong on the outside because on the inside, we are scared, weak, and fragile. Men, not women, are the weaker sex.

Toklas, Alice B. The young men of today seem mostly to be interested in the manner rather than the matter.

Wilde, Oscar. A gentleman is one who never hurts anyone's feelings unintentionally.

CHARACTERS AND CHARACTERISTICS—SOUTH

Allen, Maryon. People in the South love their politics better than their food on the table.

Carter, James Earl. A good old boy is somebody who's compatible with the group. I feel just as much at home around Billy's (his brother's) filling station as I do in the black Baptist Church, as I do with the big-shot Texas businessman.

Jordan, Hamilton. Historically, I think there probably is an inferiority complex associated with being southern.

Wallace, George Corley. Being a southerner is not as much geographical now as it is a state of mind. When I say southern I mean this: people are beginning to realize that big government is not good for the people.

CHARACTERS AND CHARACTERISTICS—UNITED STATES

Acheson, Dean. Americans do at the end of the day what they don't like to do at noon.

Lawrence, David Herbert. The essential American soul is hard, stoic, isolate and a killer.

Rusk, Dean. Americans have a way of doing at the end of the day what they don't want to do at noon.

Sadat, Anwar. I like the way Americans put their feet up on the desk.

CHARLES, PRINCE OF WALES

Charles, Prince of Wales, . I've fallen in love with all sorts of girls—and I fully intend to go on doing so. It's very important to find the right partner. In my position, obviously, the last thing I could possibly entertain is getting divorced.

Charles, Prince of Wales, . What I really need is a good wife.

CHARO

Charo, . It doesn't bother me if I'm called dumb but I do resent it if I'm called slow. You should see how quickly I learned the way to the bank.

CHAVEZ, CESAR

Peretz, Martin. You know, the thing I really disliked most about Chavez was the way he established himself as a tool of the Kennedy elite.

CHEEVER, JOHN

Cheever, John. It (plot) is a calculated attempt to hold the reader's interest at the sacrifice of moral conviction.

CHER

Allman, Gregg. I'd like Cher to be pregnant all the time.

Cher, . I left him for a woman: me (commenting on her divorce from Sonny Bono).

CHICAGO

Capone, Alphonse. It rains in Chicago and snows too. But after all home is home.

Merola, Gaetano. Chicago is merely a place to change trains.

Nettleton, Lois. I'm terribly chauvinistic about this city. Smell the air—it's sexy. Chicago is vital, and it continues to improve.

Zisk, Richie (baseball player). Chicago is the kind of place where, if you fall flat on your face, there's someone to pick you up instead of stomping on your face.

CHICAGO—POLICE

Daley, Richard J. The police are not here to create disorder. They are here to preserve disorder (commenting during the 1968 Democratic Convention in Chicago).

Daley, Richard J. These organizations are fine and legitimate. But what is the matter with (the police) having people in there? (Explaining the secret infiltration of civic organizations by the Chicago Police Department).

CHICAGO—POLITICS AND GOVERNMENT

Anonymous, . Get behind a judge on Monday in case you find yourself in front of him on Tuesday.

Bauler, (Paddy). Chicago ain't ready for reform yet.

Bauler, (Paddy). Take care of the voters first, then you can take care of yourself.

Byrne, Jane. If they care to come with me and accept the fact I'm a candidate, I am willing to work with them (about Chicago's Regular Democratic Organization).

Daley, Richard J. If anything happens to me, you guys stick together. I'm telling you—you guys stick together or everything we've worked for together will be for nothing.

Kelly, Edward J. (Mayor of Chicago, 1933-1947). Franklin Roosevelt was the best precinct captain I ever had.

Royko, Mike. The motto of the (Chicago) City Council is: never do today what somebody else can do today or tomorrow.

CHICAGO—SOCIAL LIFE AND CUSTOMS—PROHIBITION

Capone, Alphonse. When I sell liquor, it's called bootlegging; when my patrons serve it on silver trays on Lake Shore Drive, it's called hospitality.

CHICAGO SYMPHONY ORCHESTRA

Solti, Sir Georg. Chicago should erect a statue to me for what I have done.

CHILDREN

Geisel, Theodor. Adults are obsolete children and the hell with them.

Greenberg, David. An oldtimer is someone who can remember when a naughty child was taken to the woodshed instead of to a psychiatrist.

Greer, Germaine. It's sheer myth that feminists are anti-child—we're the only people who're going to give children a better deal.

Hayakawa, Samuel Ichiye. (Children are) recent immigrants in our midst.

CHILDREN—CLOTHING AND DRESS

Godart, Suzanne. Keep a girl in jeans from 4 to 14, and you'll wind up with a Butch on your hands.

CHILDREN—GROWTH AND DEVELOPMENT

Jung, Carl Gustav. Nothing has a stronger influence on their children than the unlived lives of the parents.

CHILDREN—MANAGEMENT AND TRAINING

Jackson, Jesse. Many of us allow our children to eat junk, watch junk, listen to junk, talk junk, play with junk, and then we're surprised when they come out to be social junkies.

CHILDREN—SEXUAL BEHAVIOR

Tomlin, Lily. I worry about kids today. Because of the sexual revolution they're going to grow up and never know what dirty means.

CHILE—POLITICS AND GOVERNMENT

Neruda, Pablo. I am writing these quick lines for my memoirs only three days after the unspeakable events took my great comrade, President Allende, to his death. The aggressors' version is that they found clear signs of suicide on his lifeless body. The version published abroad is different. The President of the Republic of Chile was riddled and ripped to pieces by the machine guns of Chile's soldiers, who had betrayed Chile once more (from his book Memoirs).

Pinochet, Augusto. When people don't listen to words, they'll listen to deeds.

CHINA (PEOPLE'S REPUBLIC)

Bukovsky, Vladimir. China today is Russia 20 or 30 years ago. She is following in our footsteps, which are those of totalitarianism.

Mansfield, Mike. Treaties are not forever (urging that the United States quit its defense treaty with Taiwan and recognize China).

Mao, Tse-Tung. Revolution is a drama of passion. We did not win the People over by appealing to reason but by developing hope, trust, fraternity.

CHINA (PEOPLE'S REPUBLIC)—DESCRIPTION

Hua, Kuo-Feng. Great disorder across the land leads to great order.

Mao, Tse-tung. Let a hundred schools of thought contend. Let a hundred flowers blossom (in 1956-57).

CHINA (PEOPLE'S REPUBLIC)—MILITARY POLICY

Mao, Tse-Tung. The most important thing is to be strong. With strength, one can conquer others, and to conquer others gives one virtue.

CHINA (PEOPLE'S REPUBLIC)—POLITICS AND GOVERNMENT

Hua, Kuo-Feng. Great disorder across the land leads to great order.

Mao, Tse-Tung. After my death, the rightists may seize power. They will use my words to raise their own banner. (But) they will not rule for long (in a letter to his wife at the start of the Cultural Revolution).

Mao, Tse-tung. By the end of this year, the victory of Socialism will be assured (in 1955).

Mao, Tse-tung. Once all struggle is grasped, miracles are possible.

Teng, Hsiao-Ping. If the masses feel some anger, we must let them express it.

CHINA (PEOPLE'S REPUBLIC)—RELATIONS—COCA-COLA COMPANY

Buchwald, Art. I don't mind 800 million Chinese drinking a bottle (of Coca-Cola) a day, but I don't want them to bring back the empties.

CHOREOGRAPHY

Feld, Eliot. Each time I make a dance, it's like being a virgin.

CHRISTIANITY

Neuhaus, Richard John. Religion had become a silly imitation of what was happening in the marketplace. Christianity lost its nerve to challenge the culture.

CHRISTIANS

Boone, Pat. Jimmy Carter is a Christian, but he's a McGovern-type Christian, proabortion, prohomosexuality and prolegalizing marijuana.

CHRISTIE, AGATHA

Christie, Agatha. If I could write like Elizabeth Bowen, Muriel Spark or Graham Greene, I should jump to high heaven with delight, but I know that I can't.

CHRYSLER CORPORATION

Jones, Reginald. One of the aspects of the free enterprise system is that you should be allowed to succeed, and you should also be allowed to fail (about Chrysler Corporation).

CHURCH AND BELIEF

Sherrill, Henry Knox. Far too many people in the church have very great convictions about very small things.

CHURCH AND RACE PROBLEMS

Carter, James Earl. I can't resign from the human race because there's discrimination, and I don't intend to resign from my own church because there's discrimination.

CHURCH AND STATE

Carter, James Earl. I think the government ought to stay out of the prayer business....

CHURCH ATTENDANCE—SEGREGATION

Young, Andrew. Eleven o'clock Sunday morning is still the most segregated hour of the week, and I don't know that anybody can be self-righteous about church integration.

CHURCH, FRANK

Church, Frank. I've accomplished about all I can in a senatorial career. If SALT II is grounds for my defeat, so be it.

CIGARS

Freud, Sigmund. My cigar is not a symbol. It is only a cigar.

Kipling, Rudyard. A woman is only a woman but a good cigar is a smoke.

CITIES AND TOWNS

Norris, William. Dammit, rebuilding the cities will be one of the great growth industries of the future. It will replace the auto as the big provider of jobs— if we Americans can ever get ourselves organized.

Seidenbaum, Art. A city worrying about image enhancement is like a man considering a wig; each faces the world with a shining inferiority complex.

CITY AND TOWN LIFE

Nyro, Laura. I've always loved the country for the seasons and the city for people and ideas.

Spear, Michael. Launching a new towns program in the early 1970's was like asking the Wright brothers to test their airplane in a hurricane and then concluding, when it crashed, that the invention did not work.

CIVIL DISOBEDIENCE

Berrigan, Daniel. When we get locked up now, there's a sigh of ennui (on the declining state of civil disobedience).

CIVIL RIGHTS

Bukovsky, Vladimir. If I were to answer what sustains us in this struggle, first and foremost is trust, faith in people, faith in the future, and faith in the human values for which we stand (commenting at the White House on Soviet dissidents).

Carter, James Earl. No poor, rural, weak, or black person should ever have to bear the additional burden of being deprived of the opportunity of an education, a job, or simple justice.

Carter, James Earl. The American people and our government will continue our firm commitment to promote respect for human rights not only in our own country but also abroad (to Andrei Sakharov).

Faulk, John Henry. I was taught that the first ten amendments were sacrosanct, that they're the engine by which this society runs and I admire people who cherish them and loathe and despise people who would circumvent and destroy them. So it took no act of courage to do what I did. It was an act of principle. What else would you do? I like to think all American people would do the same thing if they felt the way I did.

Garvey, Ed. When you talk about civil liberties in professional sports, it's like talking about virtue in a whorehouse.

Moynihan, Daniel Patrick. When a person goes to a country and finds their newspapers filled with nothing but good news, he can bet there are good men in jail.

Norris, Clarence (the sole surviving |Scottsboro Boy|). The lesson to Black people, to my children, to everybody, is that you should always fight for your rights even if it costs you your life. Stand up for your rights, even if it kills you (commenting on his struggle to clear his name upon being pardoned by the state of Alabama).

Sakharov, Andrei Dmitrievich. I hope this prize is not only an acknowledgement of my personal merits, but of the merits of all those who fight for human rights (commenting on his Nobel Peace Prize).

Scranton, William W. The only universality that one can honestly associate with the Universal Declaration of Human Rights is universal lip service.

CIVIL RIGHTS—PARAGUAY
Stroessner, Alfredo. Human rights is a Trojan horse of international Communism.

CIVIL RIGHTS—RUSSIA
Anonymous (report in Pravda), . People are not punished for their opinions in the U.S.S.R. The only ones who are prosecuted are those who have indulged in propaganda or anti-Soviet agitation, aiming to weaken the political system in force in our country, or those who broadcast manifestly false bombast whose object is to discredit the Soviet Union.

CIVILIZATION
Dubos, Rene. Each civilization has its own kind of pestilence and controls it only by reforming itself.
Freud, Sigmund. The first human who hurled a curse instead of a weapon against his adversary was the founder of civilization.
Rogers, Will. Any man who thinks civilization has advanced is an egoist.

CIVILIZATION AND LEISURE
Toynbee, Arnold. To be able to fill leisure intelligently is the last product of civilization.

CLARK, JOE
Clark, Joe. If I walked on water, people would say it was because I couldn't swim.

CLEAVER, ELDRIDGE
Cleaver, Eldridge. Prison holds no terror for me (upon his return to the US from self imposed exile).

CLEAVER, KATHLEEN
Cleaver, Kathleen. I'm older and wiser. I've lost my romanticism about revolution in America. I don't say it's inconceivable, but I know that none of us who believed ourselves to be revolutionaries in the '60s can conceive of the form a revolution would take in America.

CLEMENTS, BILL
Clements, Bill. My opponent is in for a real fracas. If he thinks it's going to be some kind of cakewalk, I will assure you he's gotten hold of a hot enchilada.

CLERGY
Graham, Billy. The pressures of being a well-known clergyman are unbelievable, and I'd like to escape to heaven if I could.
Olivier, Laurence. Probably every great actor in history was the son of a clergyman.

CLEVELAND, GROVER
Cleveland, Grover. While the people should patriotically and cheerfully support their government, its functions do not include the support of the people (inaugural address—1893).

CLEVELAND—POLITICS AND GOVERNMENT
Kucinich, Dennis. I'm not antibusiness, just pro-people. The private sector has not been denied a forum here (in Cleveland), only control.

CLOTHING AND DRESS
Voznesensky, Andrei. When Man put on clothes for the first time, he challenged the Lord and became His equal.

CLOTHING AND DRESS—MEN
Gross, Alan. If you see a Gucci loafer in L.A. today, you're looking at the foot of a lawyer.
Hemingway, Margaux. I love men's clothes, but that doesn't make me a weirdo.

CLOTHING AND DRESS—WOMEN
Dickinson, Angie. I dress for women—and I undress for men.

Rykiel, Sonia. Every woman must create her own ambience; it is not I or Yves St. Laurent but the woman who has to create herself and be a unique person.

CLOTHING INDUSTRY
Vollbracht, Michaele. If you have to talk about fashion, then you are not in it.
Vollbracht, Michaele. The fashion industry is like someone with a BB gun: they aim at you, they don't kill you, but they hurt you a hell of a lot.

CLUBS
Marx, Groucho. I wouldn't belong to any club that would have me for a member.

COACHES (ATHLETICS)
Battle, Bill. Class is, when they run you out of town, to look like you're leading the parade (commenting after being forced out as head football coach at Tennessee).

COCA-COLA COMPANY
Sharpe, Cornelia. I think sex is the greatest thing since Coca-Cola.

COCA, IMOGENE
Coca, Imogene. I've never figured out why we work so well together, except that we both laugh at exactly the same time. (about herself and Sid Caesar).

COCAINE
Bankhead, Tallulah. Cocaine isn't habit-forming. I should know—I've been using it for years.

COCHRANE, ELIZABETH
Cochrane, Elizabeth. Life can be a great adventure and I'm going to make it one.

COFFEE
Rappolt, Richard T. It's easier to get people off of heroin than coffee.

COHN, ROY
Cohn, Roy. I only hope that this country remains a place where Steve (Rubell) and I can build what's become a great institution in America and in the world.

COLBY, WILLIAM EGAN
Colby, William Egan. I have definitional problems with the word violence. I don't know what the word violence means.

COLD (DISEASE)
McKuen, Rod. The best remedy for a cold is to go to bed with a good book, or a friend who's read one.

COLICOS, JOHN
Colicos, John. Over the years I have discovered that villains are like blonds—they have more fun (commenting on playing a TV villain).

COLLEGE EDUCATION
Mankiewicz, Frank Fabian. The higher the tuition, the fewer days they spend in school.

COLLEGE EDUCATION, VALUE OF
Duggan, B. To every Ph.D. there is an equal and opposite Ph.D.
King, Billie Jean. Don't go to college if you want to make your living in sports.
Kohler, Jerry. I'd just as soon die in Viet Nam as in the library.

COLLEGE PROFESSORS AND INSTRUCTORS
Bressler, Marvin. There is no crisis to which academics will not respond with a seminar.
Hayakawa, Samuel Ichiye. I must say, I find senators much more interesting people than professors...Professors are too damned specialized.

COLLEGES AND UNIVERSITIES

Dobie, J. Frank. The average Ph.D. thesis is nothing but a transference of bones from one graveyard to another.

Giamatti, A. Bartlett. The university must be a tributary to a larger society, not a sanctuary from it.

Kerr, Clark. Have plenty of football for the alumni, sex for the students, and parking for the faculty.

Kowal, Charles (American astronomer). I enjoy learning things, but a university is the last place in the world to learn anything.

Rhodes, Frank H. T. The great universities are those in which people grow by contact with others in ever-widening circles.

COLLEGES AND UNIVERSITIES—CHEATING (EDUCATION)

Bunting, Josiah. The (West Point honor) code is an anachronism but a good anachronism.

Suskind, Sigmund. Cheating (in colleges) is not endemic, it's epidemic.

COLORADO—POWER RESOURCES

Hart, Gary. Exxon seems to have the idea that it can solve America's energy problems almost totally at Colorado's expense.

COLSON, CHARLES WENDELL

Colson, Charles Wendell. I would do anything that Richard Nixon asks me to do.

COLUMBIA BROADCASTING SYSTEM, INC.

Schorr, Daniel. I think I ended up simply being indigestible (commenting on why he resigned from CBS).

COMEDIANS

Berle, Milton. The best way a new comic can start is to have funny bones.

Tati, Jacques. Comedians speak with their legs.

COMEDY

Allen, Woody. Drama stays with people more, like meat and potatoes, while comedy is a dessert, like meringue.

Burns, George. If you tear yourself down, people feel sorry for you, and if they feel sorry for you, they like you.

Feldman, Marty. Well, any melodrama inverted is good material for a comedy.

COMICS (BOOKS, STRIPS, ETC.)

Pekar, Harvey. A person who can't relate to comic books is like somebody who can't relate to opera. They're both culturally deprived.

COMMERCIAL PRODUCTS

Block, Herbert L. If it's good, they'll stop making it.

COMMITTEES

Emerson, William A., Jr. A foolish consistency is the hobgoblin of small committees.

COMMON SENSE

Stein, Gertrude. Everybody gets so much information all day long that they lose their common sense.

COMMUNES

Leary, Timothy. I don't like hippies. I don't like communes. I despise heroin. I've never participated in an orgy. It may ruin my reputation, but I'm particularly monogamous.

COMMUNICATION

Brown, Edmund Gerald, Jr. Communications erodes provincialism.

Johnson, Lyndon Baines. The most important thing a man has to tell you is what he is not telling you.

Richards, Paul. I don't communicate with players. I tell them what to do. I don't understand the meaning of communication.

Rockwell, Geo. Making something perfectly clear only confuses everybody.

COMMUNISM

Aron, Raymond. Marxism is the opium of the intellectuals.

Brezhnev, Leonid I. Relaxation of international tension by no means eliminates the struggle of ideas.

Carter, James Earl. We are now free of that inordinate fear of Communism which once led us to embrace any dictator who joined us in our fear.

Chaplin, Charles Spencer. My prodigious sin was and still is, being a nonconformist. Although I am not a Communist, I refused to fall in line by hating them.

Falwell, Jerry. Not only should we register them (Communists), but we should stamp it on their foreheads and send them back to Russia. This is a free country.

Hoffman, Abbie. I've adopted a much more orthodox Communist view. I used to say I was an anarchist or maybe a hedonistic Communist, but around the world people understand the force that's fighting for them is Communism. It means the end of sex, love, dope, art, individuality and doing things you want to do.

Kissinger, Henry Alfred. No communist country has solved the problem of succession.

Kruger, James T. (South African Minister of Justice). It remains a fact that a happy person cannot be a communist (asking for reform of his country's race laws).

Monks, John (Oklahoma State Representative). In every country the Communists have taken over, the first thing they do is outlaw cockfighting (opposing a bill that would outlaw cockfighting in Oklahoma).

Ravel, Jean-Francois. Stalinism is the essence of Communism.

Solzhenitsyn, Aleksandr Isaevich. Communism is unregenerate; it will always present a mortal danger to mankind. It is like an infection in the world's organism: it may be dormant, but it will inevitably attack with a crippling disease.

Teng, Hsiao-Ping. It doesn't matter whether you climb Mount Everest by its North slope or its South slope as long as you get to the top.

COMMUNISM—AFRICA

Kaunda, Kenneth. An African in Zimbabwe does not need a communist to tell him that he is not free.

COMMUNISM—CHINA (PEOPLE'S REPUBLIC)

Mao, Tse-Tung. Every Communist must grasp the truth, Political power grown out of the barrel of a gun. Our principle is that the party commands the gun and the gun must never be allowed to command the party.

COMMUNISM—EUROPE

Ford, Gerald Rudolph. Eurocommunism is not, as their propagandists say, Communism with a human face. It is Stalinism in a mask and tyranny in disguise.

COMMUNISM—RELATIONS—JOURNALISTS

Munro, Ross H. Communist countries never expel correspondents for telling lies.

COMMUNISM—RUSSIA

Solzhenitsyn, Aleksandr Isaevich. For us in Russia Communism is a dead dog, while for many people in the West it is still a living lion.

COMPASSION

Humphrey, Hubert Horatio. Life was not meant to be endured, but enjoyed.

COMPETENCE

Boyle, Charles. If not controlled, work will flow to the competent man until he submerges.

COMPETITION

DeButts, John (Chairman of the Board, AT&T). We believe competition works to the disadvantage of the average (telephone) user, and where it does, we are determined to fight it.

COMPETITIONS

Ade, George. Anybody can win—unless there happens to be a second entry.

Minor, Robert. The winning entry is never as good as your own.

Runyon, Damon. The race is not always to the swift, nor the battle to the strong, but that's the way to bet.

COMPROMISE

Battista, O. A. The fellow who says he'll meet you halfway usually thinks he's standing on the dividing line.

COMPUTERS

Drucker, Peter F. The main impact of the computer has been the provision of unlimited jobs for clerks.

Weizenbaum, Joseph. A computer will do what you tell it to do, but that may be much different from what you had in mind.

CONABLE, BARBER

Conable, Barber. The trouble with Carter is he's listening only to God—and God doesn't pay taxes.

CONCEIT

Wonder, Stevie. How can you even think of being conceited—with the universe as large as it is?.

CONCERTS

Wonder, Stevie. What's most beautiful about touring is that I've met some friends in every place I've gone. It always feels to me like I am just playing in someone's living room.

CONCORD, MASSACHUSETTS—POLITICS AND GOVERNMENT

Velleca, Carl. The people will always know where to find me (commenting on his candidacy for Concord, Massachusetts' selectman which originated from his home at the Massachusetts Correctional Institution).

CONDON, RICHARD

Condon, Richard. I'm a man of the marketplace as well as an artist. I am a pawnbroker of myth.

CONDUCT OF LIFE

Adenauer, Konrad. An infallible method for conciliating a tiger is to allow oneself to be devoured.

Adler, Alfred. The chief danger in life is that you may take too many precautions.

Allen, Woody. From childhood I was told never to marry a gentile woman, never to shave on Saturday and, most especially, never to shave a gentile woman on Saturday.

Allen, Woody. The universe is merely a fleeting idea in God's mind—and a pretty uncomfortable thought, particularly if you've just made a down payment on a home.

Anderson, John B. You cannot become weary in well-doing.

Anonymous (Haight-Ashbury Diggers slogan), . Today is the first day of the rest of your life.

Baar, James A. Regardless of what you say or do, some of the people will hate you all of the time.

Blake, Eubie. I don't drink, don't carouse and don't fool around with women. These things are all bad for you.

Bond, Langhorne. The best fertilizer in a pasture is the footprint of the owner.

Braine, John. I believe absolutely in Christian sexual morality, which means that I believe in premarital virginity. Virgins don't get V.D., don't have abortions, don't have illegitimate babies, and aren't forced to get married. And no man, no matter how progressive, has ever objected to his bride being a virgin.

Brooks, Mel. Everything we do in life is based on fear, especially love.

Brown, Edmund Gerald, Jr. There is a limit to the good things we have in this country. We're coming up against those limits. It's really a very salutary exercise to learn to live with them.

Buchwald, Art. Whether it's the best of times or the worst of times, it's the only time you've got.

Burroughs, William S. What you want to do is eventually what you will do anyway. Sooner or later.

Butler, Samuel. In practice it is seldom very hard to do one's duty when one knows what it is, but it is sometimes exceedingly difficult to find this out.

Callaghan, James. I believe all good people should be in bed by 11 o'clock at night.

Cameron, John. When your opponent is down, kick him.

Carlson, Phil. Don't ever try to eat where they don't want to feed you.

Churchill, Sir Winston. Don't argue the difficulties. They argue for themselves.

Ciardi, John. Early to bed and early to rise probably indicates unskilled labor.

Clemens, Samuel Langhorne. Never put off till tomorrow what you can do the day after tomorrow.

Cohodas, Howard L. If it looks too good to be true, it is too good to be true.

Cole, Edward N. Kick the hell out of the status quo.

Collins, John Churton. Half the mistakes in life arise from feeling where we ought to think, and thinking where we ought to feel.

Day, Dorothy. The best thing to do with the best things in life is to give them up.

Dodgson, Charles Lutwidge. If you limit your actions in life to things that nobody can possibly find fault with, you will not do much.

Dubos, Rene. There is a universal tendency, if we can manage it, to do something a little different from what other people are doing.

Eldridge, Paul. Man is always ready to die for an idea, provided that idea is not quite clear to him.

Erhard, Werner. The point is, until its time comes, nothing you do will work. And when its time comes, what you do will work and you will do what works.

Fields, W. C. There comes a time in the affairs of men when you must take the bull by the tail and face the situation.

Ford, Henry, II. Never complain, never explain.

Fresco, Catherine B. If you knew what you were doing, you'd probably be bored.

Fuentes, Carlos. There are two things one never should do after fifty: change wives and give interviews.

Gingrich, Arnold. To stand out, for a man or a magazine, it is necessary to stand for something. Otherwise you stand still.

Gomez, Lefty. If you don't throw it, they can't hit it.

Hagen, Walter. You only get one trip through life, so don't forget to stop and smell the flowers.

Harris, Sydney J. The art of living consists in knowing which impulses to obey and which must be made to obey.

Hayakawa, Samuel Ichiye. If you have ceased to be ready to face the frightening, then you become old. We weren't put on earth to behave like barnacles.

Hefner, Hugh Marston. If a man has a right to find God in his own way, he has a right to go to the Devil in his own way also.

Hemingway, Ernest. The first and final thing you have to do in this world is to last in it and not be smashed by it.

Hill, E. V. Life lived at its best is full of daily forgivin' and forgettin'.

Horowitz, Vladimir. You can't be serious 24 hours a day. You have to take half an hour or an hour a day to be childish.

Hoy, Wayne. If you go slow enough, long enough, you'll be in the lead again.

Hubbard, Elbert. Do not take life too seriously— you will never get out of it alive.

Hubbard, Elbert. Never explain. Your friends do not need it and your enemies will not believe you anyway.

Hubbard, Kin. We're all pretty much alike when we get out of town.

Humphrey, Hubert Horatio. Oh, my friend, it isn't what they take away from you that counts—it's what you do with what you have left.

Johnson, Lyndon Baines. If you don't blow your horn, somebody will steal it.

Kahn, Alfred. If you can't explain what you're doing in simple English, you are probably doing something wrong.

Kesey, Ken. Always stay in your own movie.

Khrushchev, Nikita Sergeevich. Life is short. Live it up.

Kilpatrick, James J. Find out where the people want to go, then hustle yourself around in front of them.

King, Martin Luther, Sr. Nothing that a man does takes him lower than when he allows himself to fall so far as to hate anyone.

Knowles, John H. A sense of humor is the prelude to faith and laughter is the beginning of prayer.

Land, Edwin. Anything worth doing is worth doing to excess.

Lapham, Lewis H. I take for granted Jefferson's dictum that money, not morality, constitutes the principle of commercial nations.

Lewis, Jerry. Only the man who does nothing makes no mistakes.

Liebling, A. J. The people who have something to say don't talk; the others insist on talking.

Longworth, Alice Roosevelt. Fill what's empty. Empty what's full. And scratch where it itches.

Loughrige, Alan Craig. The middle of the road is the best place to get run over.

Louis, Joe. You can run, but you can't hide.

Luce, Clare Boothe (attributed by Paul Dickson). No good deed goes unpunished.

McCarthy, Mary. It really takes a hero to live any kind of spiritual life without religious belief.

Madson, Carlisle. The purchase of any product can be rationalized if the desire to own it is strong enough.

Mandel, Morris. Always put off until tomorrow what you shouldn't do at all.

Mansfield, Mike. The crisis you have to worry about most is the one you don't see coming.

Maugham, William Somerset. The unfortunate thing about this world is that good habits are so much easier to get out of than bad ones.

Mix, Tom (attributed by Heywood Hale Broun). Straight shooters always win.

Montagu, Ashley. The idea is to die young as late as possible.

Morrow, Dwight. One of the troubles is that we judge ourselves by our motives and others by their actions.

Murphy, Gerald. Only the invented part of life was satisfying, only the unrealistic part.

Neizvestny, Ernst. A man should stand on his own two feet, even if he has only one leg.

Nin, Anais. One must thrust out of a finished cycle in life, and that leap is the most difficult to make—to part with one's faith, one's love, when one would prefer to renew the faith and recreate the passion.

Paige, Satchel. Don't look back. Something might be gaining on you.

Paige, Satchel. Go very gently on the vices such as carrying on in society. The social rumble ain't restful.

Paige, Satchel. If your stomach disputes you, lie down and pacify it with cool thoughts.

Paige, Satchel. Keep the juices flowing by jangling around gently as you move.

Peter, Laurence J. If you don't know where you are going, you will probably end up somewhere else.

Quin, Percy Edwards. A man must sometimes rise above principle.

Ram Dass, . If I'm saving the whale, why am I eating tuna fish?.

Rayburn, Sam. Son, always tell the truth. Then you'll never have to remember what you said the last time.

Rayburn, Sam. The three most important words in the English language are wait a minute.

Rockefeller, David. Basically I operate on the principle that you should never do something for yourself that you can get someone else to do for you.

Rogers, Ginger. If you don't stand for something, you will stand for anything.

Roosevelt, Franklin Delano. If you treat people right they will treat you right—90 percent of the time.

Roosevelt, Franklin Delano. When you get to the end of your rope, tie a knot and hang on.

Roosevelt, Theodore. Black care rarely sits behind a rider whose pace is fast enough.

Rumsfeld, Donald. If you try to please everybody, somebody is not going to like it.

Sevareid, Eric. (One should learn) to retain the courage of one's doubts, as well as one's convictions, in this world of dangerously passionate certainties.

Shaw, George Bernard. The man who has never made a mistake will never make anything else.

Shaw, George Bernard. When a stupid man is doing something he is ashamed of, he always decides it is his duty.

Sikinger, Maximilian. It's better to be a hungry coyote than to be a satisfied dog.

Sinatra, Frank. I'm for anything that gets you through the night, be it prayer, tranquilizers or a bottle of Jack Daniels.

Solzhenitsyn, Aleksandr Isaevich. Whenever the tissue of life is woven of legalistic relations, there is an atmosphere of moral mediocrity, paralyzing man's noblest impulses.

Stein, Gertrude. Considering how dangerous everything is, nothing is really frightening.

Stevenson, Adlai, II. It is better to light one candle than to curse the darkness.

Stewart, P. L. When you are in it up to your ears, keep your mouth shut.

Strauss, Robert S. You know, it's awfully easy to tell people to go to hell. But it's another thing to get them there.

Tanner, Jack. A person without character always does what is right.

Terkel, Studs. Take it easy, but take it.

Thatcher, Margaret Hilda. It is important not to be so obsessed with yesterday's danger that we fail to detect today's.

Weizman, Ezer. Anyone who says he is not emotional is not getting what he should out of life.

West, Mae. He who hesitates is last.

West, Mae. To err is human—but it feels divine.

West, Mae. Too much of a good thing can be wonderful.

Wilde, Oscar. A gentleman is one who never hurts anyone's feelings unintentionally.

Williams, Dakin. After all, high station in life is earned by the gallantry with which appalling experiences are survived with grace.

CONDUCTORS (MUSIC)

Copland, Aaron. Conducting is a real sport. You can never guarantee what the results are going to be, so there's always an element of chance. That keeps it exciting.

Levine, James. The audience experience should come from listening, not from noticing the conductor having an eight and a half minute sustained orgasm.

CONFLICT OF GENERATIONS

Brown, Sam. Never trust anybody over 30.

CONFORMITY

Rayburn, Sam. If you want to get along, go along.

CONGRESSMEN

Abourezk, James. When voting on the confirmation of a Presidential appointment, it's always safer to vote against the son of a bitch, because if he's confirmed, it won't be long before he proves how wise you were.

Harris, David. People are ready for a congressman who went to jail before he went to Washington instead of after (commenting on what effect his 20 month jail term for resisting induction would have on his bid for the congressional seat of Pete McCloskey).

CONGRESSMEN—SEXUAL BEHAVIOR

Ray, Elizabeth. I can't type. I can't file. I can't even answer the phone.

CONNALLY, JOHN BOWDEN

Anonymous, . When (John) Connally eats watermelon, (Robert) Strauss spits out the seeds.

Carpenter, Elizabeth. If John Connally had been around at the Alamo, he would have organized Texans for Santa Anna.

Connally, John Bowden. I have very few close friends.

Connally, John Bowden. I hope as long as I live I never lose the desire to participate in public affairs. I've seen the system work today and it has made me more deeply committed to preserving the system (upon his acquittal on bribery charges).

Connally, John Bowden. There's a little larceny in the hearts of all of us.

Crane, Philip. If you asked central casting in Hollywood for somebody to play the role of President, they'd send you John Connally.

Doty, William R. Connally will always be remembered for his bright Nixon button and his weakness for milk shakes.

Ellick, Thomas. If anyone is looking for a replacement for John Wayne as the personification of America, (John Connally) is it.

Evans, Roy. He (John Connally) likes deep rugs and rich people.

Ford, Gerald Rudolph. It's good for America to see that you can get a fair trial in Washington (to Robert S. Strauss upon the acquittal of John Connally).

Kirbo, Charles. Once he (John Connally) gets across that Texas line—he's not much.

Nixon, Richard Milhous. I should have had you for my lawyer and I might still be president (to Edward Bennett Williams upon the acquittal of John Connally).

Nixon, Richard Milhous. Only three men in America understand the use of power. I do. John Connally does. And I guess Nelson does.

Rue, Arnold. I'm always suspicious about anyone from Texas who talks about energy (about John Connally).

Yarborough, Ralph. This may be the only case on record of a rat swimming toward a sinking ship (commenting on John Connally's announced defection from the Democrats to the Republicans).

CONNALLY, MARK

Connally, Mark (son of John Connally). I've seen the political life and I don't want it.

CONRAD, JOSEPH

Conrad, Joseph. The sea is not my subject. Mankind is my subject.

CONSERVATION

Fonda, Jane. Conservation is the religion of the future.

CONSERVATION ASSOCIATIONS

Aspinall, Wayne. The conservation extremists demand too much of our public land for their own private use.

Hodel, Donald. (Environmentalism is) a crusade to stop all development in this country.

CONSERVATION OF RESOURCES

Aspinall, Wayne. The conservation extremists demand too much of our public land for their own private use.

Laird, Melvin. Conservation alone is a slow walk down a dead-end street.

McCormack, Mike. One man's conservation is all to frequently another man's unemployment.

Reagan, Ronald. Once you've seen one redwood, you've seen them all.

CONSERVATISM

Brown, Edmund Gerald, Jr. I'm not conservative—I'm just cheap.

Griffin, Mickey. It's high time the rednecks came back to Washington. There are a hell of a lot more rednecks out there than people who eat crepes suzette.

Hubbard, Elbert. A conservative is a man who is too cowardly to fight and too fat to run.

Moore, Jonathan. We're not getting as conservative as much as we are becoming less liberal.

Rizzo, Frank Lazzaro. A conservative is a liberal who was mugged the night before.

Thatcher, Margaret Hilda. We (Conservatives) believe that you get a responsible society when you get responsible individuals.

Udall, Morris King. (Ronald Reagan and George Wallace) are the twin horsemen of the radical right.

CONSUMER PROTECTION

Butz, Earl Lauer. I don't know why we have to look at every bird that comes down the line. If GM inspected every piston ring the way we inspect chickens, a new Chevrolet would cost $20,000 (responding to consumer pressure for more rigorous government food inspection).

CONSUMERS

Kahn, J. Kesner. Free market competition, freely advertised, is consumerism at its best.

Ogilvey, David. The consumer is not a moron. She is your wife.

CONSUMPTION (ECONOMICS)

Dasmann, Raymond F. We are hooked like junkies, dependent on the drug of wasteful consumption.

Walden, Phil (President of Capricorn Records). That's the old American way—if you got a good thing, then overdo it.

CONTRACTS

Goldwyn, Samuel. A verbal contract isn't worth the paper it's written on.

Minow, Newton. There is no contract you can't get out of for money.

CONVERSATION

Eliot, George. Blessed be the man who, having nothing to say, abstains from giving wordy evidence of the fact.

Frost, Robert. Half the world is composed of people who have something to say and can't, and the other half who have nothing to say and keep on saying it.

Hitchcock, Alfred Joseph. Conversation is the enemy of good wine and food.

Lazar, Swifty. The problem with dull parties is the people who make them up.

COOKERY

Outhier, Louis. You don't get fat from a good kitchen—only from a bad one.

COOKERY—MIDWEST

Pirie, (Mrs) John T., Jr. Great chefs are reluctant to come to the Midwest. They still fear the Indian's tomahawk.

COOKS

Pirie, (Mrs) John T., Jr. Great chefs are reluctant to come to the Midwest. They still fear the Indian's tomahawk.

Szathmary, Louis. If an American chef is pinching anything at 4 A.M., it is his wife's behind (when asked if French chefs were at market at 4 A.M. pinching tomatoes).

COOLIDGE, CALVIN

Coolidge, Calvin. I think the American public wants a solemn ass as a President. And I think I'll go along with them.

COPYRIGHT—UNITED STATES

Ringer, Barbara A. The basic human rights of individual authors throughout the world are being sacrificed more and more on the altar of the technological revolution.

Shields, Gerald R. It is obvious that the photocopying issue is to be decided soon and that the odds favor turning libraries into some sort of reprint warehouse for publisher's products.

CORPORAL PUNISHMENT

Gauld, Joseph. The rod (physical discipline) is only wrong in the wrong hands.

CORPORATIONS

Simon, William E. Corporations are people, too (proposing a new tax break for big businesses).

CORPORATIONS, INTERNATIONAL

Moynihan, Daniel Patrick. (The multinational corporation) is arguably the most creative international institution of the 20th century.

CORSARO, FRANK

Corsaro, Frank. Of course my productions are vulgar. Theater itself is vulgar.

COSMOLOGY

Clarke, Arthur C. The time may come when men control the destinies of the stars.

COST OF LIVING

Glenn, John. Our objective is to prevent the people of this country from getting economically raped (arguing against the decontrol of petroleum prices).

COSTA RICA—FOREIGN POLICY—NICARAGUA

Somoza Debayle, Anastasio. Nicaraguan people will never forget the treason of their Costa Rican friends against their Nicaraguan brothers.

COSTUME DESIGN

Blass, Bill. Design is like the theatre—the bug bites you early.

Halston (costume designer), . A designer is only as good as his clientele. We only suggest things. It is fashionable people who make fashion.

COSTUME DESIGNERS

Vollbracht, Michaele. If you have to talk about fashion, then you are not in it.

COUNCIL ON FOREIGN RELATIONS

Lord, Winston. The Trilateral Commission doesn't secretly run the world. The Council on Foreign Relations does that.

COUNTRY LIFE

Carter, Lillian. I'm not a city person, I'm a country hick.

Nyro, Laura. I've always loved the country for the seasons and the city for people and ideas.

COURAGE

Allen, Woody. In terms of human attributes, what really counts is courage.

Boorstin, Daniel J. The courage we inherit from our Jeffersons and Lincolns and others is not the Solzhenitsyn courage of the true believer, but the courage to doubt.

Hayes, Woody. It isn't the size of the dog in the fight, but the size of the fight in the dog that counts.

McNulty, Franklin L. With adequate integrity, guts can be located.

COUSINS, NORMAN

Cousins, Norman. I am no pessimist. I doubt that any man knows enough to be a pessimist.

COWARD, NOEL

Bogart, Humphrey (attributed by Lauren Bacall). I think you (Noel Coward) are wonderful and charming, and if I should ever change from liking girls better, you would be my first thought.

CREATION

Tanner, Jack. When God created the world, He said it was good. That was His second mistake.

CREATION (LITERARY, ARTISTIC, ETC.)

Adderley, Julian (Cannonball). God smiles on certain individuals, and they get the privilege to have certain beautiful, artistic vibrations pass through them.

Fitzgerald, F. Scott. Having once found the intensity of art, nothing else that can happen in life can ever again seem as important as the creative process.

Hemingway, Ernest. Make a thing as true as possible, and it will live.

Sexton, Anne. Creative people must not avoid the pain that they get dealt.

Steinberg, Saul. The life of the creative man is led, directed and controlled by boredom.

CREDIT

Bogert, Jeremiah M. We've found that frauds often keep a spotless record while too often many otherwise sound business people get careless with credit.

CREDIT UNIONS

Patman, Wright (attributed by James T. Molloy). Next to the church, credit unions do more good for the people than any other institution.

CRICHTON, MICHAEL

Crichton, Michael. I find facts inhibiting....The more you know, the more you are obliged to the truth. I much prefer not to know.

CRIME AND CRIMINALS

Bell, Griffin. I think we have too many crimes, and I definitely have the view that we have too many laws.

Fonda, Jane. It is time to look at crime in the suites, not just in the streets.

Harris, Sydney J. It is not criminals, but laws that are the worst enemy of Law.

Hoover, John Edgar. The cure for crime is not the electric chair but the high chair.

Johnson, Lyndon Baines. Killing, rioting, and looting are contrary to the best traditions of this country.

Jones, Mary Harris (Mother Jones). I asked a man in prison once how he happened to be there and he said he had stolen a pair of shoes. I told him if he had stolen a railroad he would be a United States Senator.

Lacassagne, Jean (19th century French criminologist). Societies have the criminals they deserve.

Maguire, Daniel. Turning the other cheek is an ideal like a horizon to turn to. It is not a practical guide for the police in the Bronx.

Moss, Frank. There comes a certain point when physicians, like other lawbreakers, must be put in jail (commenting on Medicaid and Medicare fraud).

Patterson, L. Ray. The concern of the public (about crime) is not so much for vindictive retribution, but for some retribution.

CRIME AND CRIMINALS—NEW YORK (CITY)

Sobel, Nathan. There's no such thing as organized crime in this city (New York City). There's a little of it in Las Vegas, but that's it.

CRIME AND CRIMINALS—PHILADELPHIA

Rizzo, Frank Lazzaro. The streets are safe in Philadelphia. It's only the people who make them unsafe (when asked his opinion on crime in the streets).

CRIME AND CRIMINALS—RELATIONS—MENTAL HYGIENE

Szasz, Thomas. Just as (mental) illness is not a crime, so crime is not an illness.

CRIME AND CRIMINALS—UNITED STATES

Carlson, Norman A. Until the behavioral sciences can give us clues as to what motivates the criminal offender, we cannot assure rehabilitation. All we can do is offer offenders the opportunity to rehabilitate themselves.

Davis, Edward Michael. America is on the verge of a crime wave like the world has never seen before.

CRIME PREVENTION

Davis, Edward Michael. I think one of the greatest dangers that faces people in this country is the tyrants who would come in and solve your crimes by putting a rock festival in every park.

CRIMINAL JUSTICE, ADMINISTRATION OF

Maguire, Daniel. Turning the other cheek is an ideal like a horizon to turn to. It is not a practical guide for the police in the Bronx.

Patterson, L. Ray. The concern of the public (about crime) is not so much for vindictive retribution, but for some retribution.

CRIMINAL JUSTICE, ADMINISTRATION OF—IRAN

Khomeini, Ayatollah Ruhollah. Criminals should not be tried. They should be killed.

CRITICISM

Lowell, James. A wise skepticism is the first attribute of a good critic.

Maugham, William Somerset. People ask you for criticism, but they only want praise.

Wood, Natalie. Anyone who says it doesn't hurt when (critics) zap you is not to be believed.

CRONKITE, WALTER

Acciari, Larry. Presidents come and go, but Walter Cronkite—he's an institution.

Cronkite, Walter. The very constraint against taking positions is a mark of the professional in journalism, not letting opinions impact on reporting. I've spent a lifetime suppressing them.

Johnson, Lyndon Baines. If Walter Cronkite would say on television what he says on radio, he would be the most powerful man in America.

Sevareid, Eric. People see (Walter) Cronkite as they used to see Eisenhower—the fellow next door who'd invite you to his backyard barbecue, and a world statesman at the same time.

CROSBY, BING

Barber, John. If the gait was stiff the larynx was in superlative order (commenting on the London performance of 72-year-old Bing Crosby).

Berlin, Irving. There wasn't anyone in show business who will be missed as much as Bing Crosby, not only as a performer, but also as a person.

Crosby, Bing. He was an average guy who could carry a tune (on his epitaph).

Crosby, Bing. It (show business) has been my life for 50 years. It's been a long, long pull and I've had great results. I can't complain if it stops tomorrow.

Shore, Dinah. Bing (Crosby) sings like all people think they sing in the shower.

Sinatra, Frank. (Bing Crosby) was the father of my career, the idol of my youth and a dear friend of my maturity.

CROSBY, HARRY

Wheelwright, John Brooks. His death was his best poem (about Harry Crosby).

CUBA

Marquez, Gabriel Garcia. The famous Latin American 'literary boom' is a lie; what is real is the Cuban Revolution.

Smith, Howard K. The Cubans may be hostile to America, but they love Americans.

CUBA—DESCRIPTION

Cruz, Francisco Rodriguez. The biggest crime in Cuba is to think.

Quinn, Sally. An attitude of sexuality is as pervasive in Cuba as the presence of Fidel Castro. You can feel sex in the atmosphere, on the street, in conversation, in people's actions. The Cubans seem to be thinking of it much of the time.

CUBA—FOREIGN RELATIONS—UNITED STATES

Castro, Fidel. I don't think the contradictions between capitalism and socialism can be resolved by war. This is no longer the age of the bow and arrow. It's the nuclear age, and war can annihilate us all. The only way to achieve solutions seems to be for the different social systems to coexist.

CULTURE

Rand, Ayn. The state of today's culture is so low that I do not care to spend my time watching and discussing it.

CURIOSITY

Einstein, Albert (attributed by Yousuf Karsh). Curiosity has its own reason for existence.

CYNICISM

Redford, Robert. I've always had a very low regard for cynicism; I think it is the beginning of dying.

CYPRUS—POLITICS AND GOVERNMENT

Makarios III, Archbishop. I would consort with the devil himself if it would keep Cyprus and its people independent.

DNA

King, Jonathan. There are tremendous fortunes to be made from this new technology (referring to recombinant DNA 'gene-splitting' experiments), and in this case safety and private profit are incompatible.

DALEY, RICHARD J.

Bush, Earl (press aide to Richard J. Daley). Don't print what he says; print what he means (about Richard J. Daley).

Daley, Richard J. It is amazing what they will be able to do once they get the atom harassed.

Daley, Richard J. The police are not here to create disorder. They are here to preserve disorder (commenting during the 1968 Democratic Convention in Chicago).

Daley, Richard J. These organizations are fine and legitimate. But what is the matter with (the police) having people in there? (Explaining the secret infiltration of civic organizations by the Chicago Police Department).

Daley, Richard J. Together we must rise to higher and higher platitudes.

Howlett, Michael. With Daley, you know, it was Daley who always came first; the other guy always came third with Daley, no matter who the other guy was. (Who came second?) Nobody. That was Daley's percentage.

Royko, Mike. Daley is quite good at getting himself elected, but beyond that, he's not much of a political genius anymore.

DALI, SALVADOR

Dali, Salvador. The difference between a madman and me is that I am not mad.

DALLAS. FOOTBALL CLUB (NATIONAL LEAGUE)

White, Ed. Losing this game was like having your house robbed and watching it happen (commenting on the Vikings 17-14 defeat by the Cowboys).

DALTREY, ROGER

Daltrey, Roger. The last thing I wanted to do was have a fist fight with Pete Townshend. Unfortunately, he hit me first with a guitar.

DANCE

Balanchine, George. Ballet is woman.

Balanchine, George. God made men to sing the praises of women. They are not equal to men; they are better.

Balanchine, George (attributed by Merrill Ashley). A new ballet is like putting on a new coat. You have to move around in it awhile before it is comfortable.

Baryshnikov, Mikhail. I am happy in America but I am still a Russian and I hope one day I may go back to dance in Russia.

De Mille, Agnes. Dance today is terrifying.

De Mille, Agnes. If there was the Resurrection, and He danced, I don't think I'd see Him in Swan Lake if I could avoid it.

Hawkins, Erick. Dance is the most beautiful metaphor of existence in the world.

Jamison, Judith. Every dancer lives on the threshold of chucking it.

Makarova, Natalia. Even the ears must dance.

Makarova, Natalia. I am an erotic woman and that's what dance is.

Mata-Hari, . The dance is a poem and each movement a word.

Nagy, Ivan. Ballet is the original women's liberation profession. It is created for females.

Tharp, Twyla. Dancing is like bank robbery, it takes split-second timing.

DANCE THEATER OF HARLEM

Mitchell, Arthur. That's what Dance Theater of Harlem is: classical ballet with soul.

DAVIS, BETTE

Davis, Bette. I divide women into two categories. The female and the broad. Me? I'm a broad.

Davis, Bette. I was always eager to salt a good stew. The trouble is that I was expected to supply the meat and potatoes as well.

DAVIS, CULLEN

Davis, Cullen. You don't know how good it feels to get out of jail.

DAYAN, MOSHE

Dayan, Moshe. I, Moshe Dayan, as an individual am not a coward. But as a Jew I am a very frightened man.

Meir, Golda. Naturally he (Moshe Dayan) has his faults, and like his virtues they are not small ones.

DEAN, JOHN WESLEY, III

Boone, Pat. I just can't get it into my head that a cabinet man can tell a bad joke in private and get fired, and then John Dean can tell the same joke to millions and get paid for it (commenting on the Earl Butz resignation).

Dean, John Wesley, III. I don't have a friend. If I ever get one, I'll come back (responding after being asked to list the name of a reference for a library card application).

Dean, John Wesley, III. I don't want to be known as the all-time snitch.

Liddy, G. Gordon. I think in all fairness to the man, you'd have to put him right up there with Judas Iscariot (about John Dean).

DEATH

Allen, Woody. Death is the big obsession behind all the things I've done.

Allen, Woody. The difference between sex and death is, with death you can do it alone and nobody's going to make fun of you.

Brel, Jacques. Dying is man's only natural act.

Burns, George. When I do go, I plan to take my music with me. I don't know what's out there, but I want to be sure it's in my key.

Franco, Francisco. My God, how hard it is to die.

Gilmore, Gary Mark. Death is the only inescapable, unavoidable, sure thing. We are sentenced to die the day we're born.

Haile Selassie I, Emperor of Ethiopia, . Death changes everything, sweeps everything away. Even mistakes.

Heller, Joseph. I've come to look upon death the same way I look upon root-canal work. Everyone else seems to get through it all right, so it couldn't be too difficult for me.

Hendrix, Jimi. It's funny the way most people love the dead. Once you are dead, you are made for life.

Johnson, Flora. There is nothing like death. Everything that approaches it is metaphor.

Johnson, Samuel. When a man knows he is to be hanged in a fortnight, it concentrates his mind wonderfully.

Lynch, James. If we do not live together, we will die—prematurely—alone.

Malraux, Andre. There is no such thing as death. There is only I who am dying (commenting on death in his novel The Royal Way).

Miller, Henry. Death itself doesn't frighten me because I don't believe it's the end. All my intuitive feelings are that this cannot be the only world. It's too damn short, too ugly and too meaningless.

Redford, Robert. I've always had a very low regard for cynicism; I think it is the beginning of dying.

Roemer, Michael. You can't learn to die as though it were a skill. People die in the way they have lived. Death becomes the expression of everything you are, and you can bring to it only what you have brought to your life.

Smith, James. There ain't no sense in dying before your time is come.

Tolstoy, Leo (attributed by Woody Allen). Any man over 35 for whom death is not the main consideration is a fool.

Warhol, Andy. I don't believe in it (death), because you're not around to know that it's happened.

Wheelwright, John Brooks. His death was his best poem (about Harry Crosby).

DECENTRALIZATION IN GOVERNMENT

Reagan, Ronald. The coils woven in that city (Washington, D.C.) are entrapping us all and, as with the Gordian knot, we cannot untie it. We have to cut it with one blow of the sword.

Wallace, George Corley. Being a southerner is not as much geographical now as it is a state of mind. When I say southern I mean this: people are beginning to realize that big government is not good for the people.

DE CHIRICO, GIORGIO

De Chirico, Giorgio. I paint what I see with my eyes closed.

Soby, James Thrall. Only a few artists in history have been able to create so strange and so original a world as Giorgio De Chirico.

DECISION MAKING (POLITICAL SCIENCE)

Brown, Edmund Gerald, Jr. The power of the executive is like a chess game; there are very few moves that one can make.

Carter, James Earl. Doubts are the stuff of great decisions, but so are dreams.

Cheney, Richard B. Basically, I am skeptical about the ability of government to solve problems, and I have a healthy respect for the ability of people to solve problems on their own.

Felix, Virginia. Decision makers are those who have the greatest vested interest in the decision.

Friedman, Milton. Governments never learn. Only people learn.

Harrington, Michael. We've created a kind of gray, shadowy atmosphere which is 'just don't get us involved.' Well, I think the guy on the street expects us to solve real problems and not just generate the impression of looking busy when we're not doing anything that counts.

Johnson, R. W. Any solution to a problem changes the problem.

Kahn, J. Kesner. When politicians come up with a solution for your problem, you have two problems.

Lao-Tse (Chinese philosopher), . You should govern a great nation as you fry a small fish, with little stirring about.

Marcos, Ferdinand E. It is easier to run a revolution than a government.

Marshall, George C. Anybody who makes a real decision after 4:00 in the afternoon should have his head examined.

Mayer, Jean. The ability to arrive at complex decisions is the hallmark of the educated person.

Ray, Dixie Lee. Anything that the private sector can do, government can do it worse.

Rinfret, Pierre A. Consensus is the security blanket of the insecure.

Shaw, George Bernard. A government that robs Peter to pay Paul can always depend upon the support of Paul.

DECROW, KAREN LIPSHULTZ

DeCrow, Karen Lipshultz. I wasn't a feminist. I just wanted more money (regarding her '67 decision to join the National Organization for Women).

DEDERICH, CHARLES

Dederich, Charles. Anything less than changing the world is Mickey Mouse to me.

DE GAULLE, CHARLES

De Gaulle, Charles. There is no point in taking special precautions when those who want to kill me are as incompetent as those who are supposed to protect me.

Kissinger, Henry Alfred. One had the sense that if (Charles de Gaulle) moved to a window, the center of gravity might shift, and the whole room might tilt everybody into the garden.

DELEGATION OF AUTHORITY

Weiler, A. H. Nothing is impossible for the man who doesn't have to do it himself.

DE MILLE, AGNES

De Mille, Agnes. I am a theater woman. I am not a saint.

De Mille, Agnes. If there was the Resurrection, and He danced, I don't think I'd see Him in Swan Lake if I could avoid it.

DEMOCRACY

Adler, Mortimer. Only democracy has the justice which comes from granting every man the right to participate in his own government.

Adler, Mortimer. Political democracy will not work unless it is accompanied by economic democracy.

Bhutto, Zulfikar Ali. Democracy demands reciprocity.

Brogan, D. W. Democracy is like a raft. It never sinks, but damn it, your feet are always in the water.

Burgess, Anthony. The element of suppression has to exist in any state, but a democracy looks to a sophisticated citizenry that regards the suppression of intolerance as the duty of the individual soul.

Churchill, Sir Winston. It (democracy) is the worst system—except for all those other systems that have been tried and failed.

Einstein, Albert. Let every man be respected as an individual and no man idolized.

Fernandes, Millor (Brazilian playwright). In a democracy we are all equal before the law. In a dictatorship we are all equal before the police.

Kissinger, Henry Alfred. It is necessary for the Western democracies to recapture the sense that they can control their own destiny.

Lapham, Lewis H. Democracy means that you and I must fight. Democracy means a kind of Darwinism for ideas.

Mark, Sir Robert. The real art of policing a free society or a democracy is to win by appearing to lose or at least to win by not appearing to win.

Moynihan, Daniel Patrick. As the lights go out in the rest of the world, they shine all the brighter here.

Nam Duck Woo (Deputy Prime Minister of South Korea), . There is not one developing country in the world where Western democracy really works.

Niebuhr, Reinhold. Man's capacity for justice makes democracy possible, but man's inclination to injustice makes democracy necessary.

Nizer, Louis. I would rather trust 12 jurors with all their prejudices and biases than I would a judge. I think the reason democracy works is because as you multiply judgements, you reduce the incidence of error.

Riesman, David. The question is not whether leadership is obsolete but whether democracy is governable.

Smith, Charles Merrill. In a democracy you can be respected though poor, but don't count on it.

Stevenson, Adlai, II. A free society is one where it is safe to be unpopular.

Stevenson, Adlai, II. Since the beginning of time, governments have been mainly engaged in kicking people around. The astonishing achievement of modern times in the Western world is the idea that the citizens should do the kicking.

Stevenson, Adlai, II. The government must be the trustee for the little man, because no one else will be. The powerful can usually help themselves—and frequently do.

Woollcott, Alexander. I'm tired of hearing it said that democracy doesn't work. Of course it doesn't work. It isn't supposed to work. We are supposed to work it.

DEMOCRATIC PARTY

Bond, Julian. I don't think you'll have to worry that this mental midget, this hillbilly Hitler from Alabama is anywhere near becoming the nominee of the Democratic party.

Broder, David S. At least half the Carter Cabinet were good bets to be there, no matter which Democrat was nominated and elected.

Brown, Rita Mae. I want the American public to discover the difference between the Republican Party and the Democratic Party is the difference between syphillis and gonorrhea.

Byrne, Jane. I'm a Democrat, I believe in the Democratic Party.

Caddell, Patrick. Clearly, God is a Democrat.

Carter, James Earl (Attributed by Robert Shrum). I'd be a pretty pathetic nominee if I wasn't able to get rid of Strauss as national chairman.

Clark, Ramsey. The Democratic Party is a party in name only, not in shared belief.

Fitzhugh, Gilbert W. The Republicans fight like cats and go home and sulk. The Democrats fight like cats, and suddenly there are more cats.

Goldwater, Barry Morris. I don't care if I'm called a Democrat or a Republican as long as I'm in bed with people of the same thinking.

Harriman, Averell. I've had much more fun out of life since I became a Democrat.

Hayakawa, Samuel Ichiye. Republicans are people who, if you were drowning 50 feet from shore, would throw you a 25-foot rope and tell you to swim the other 25 feet because it would be good for your character. Democrats would throw you a 100-foot rope and then walk away looking for other good deeds to do.

Humphrey, Hubert Horatio. I do not want a great political party which nearly lost its soul in Vietnam to sell its soul on busing.

Humphrey, Hubert Horatio. The time has arrived for the Democratic Party to get out of the shadow of states' rights and walk forthrightly into the bright sunshine of human rights (at the 1948 Democratic National Convention).

Jackson, Henry Martin. I think my positions that I have taken are liberal in the best traditions of the Democratic Party.

Kennedy, Edward Moore. I hope to gain the Democratic nomination in 1980. But I also hope to do more—to help give the Democratic Party back its timeless truth.

McGovern, George Stanley. I do not want a great political party which nearly lost its soul in Vietnam to sell its soul on the issue of busing.

McGovern, George Stanley. I will support Jimmy Carter with the same enthusiasm with which he supported the Democratic ticket in 1972.

McGovern, George Stanley. Marching in mindless lockstep is the lowest form of party loyalty.

Mondale, Joan. The issue is Watergate or waterbed. The Democrats do it to their secretaries but the Republicans do it to the country.

Mondale, Walter Frederick. For a workingman or woman to vote Republican this year is the same as a chicken voting for Colonel Sanders.

O'Neill, Thomas P. (Tip). If this were France, the Democratic Party would be five parties.

Simon, William E. My education in the energy realm was not complete until I truly understood the nature of the oil hysteria of the liberal Democrats. It is a symbolic mania sheltered by a profound refusal to look at the facts.

Strauss, Robert S. I'm not going to deliver a candidate to the party, I'm going to deliver a party to the candidate.

Strauss, Robert S. It's a little like makin' love to a gorilla. You don't quit when you're tired—you quit when the gorilla's tired (when asked whether he planned to quit as chairman of the Democratic National Committee).

Udall, Morris King. Obviously the Ford administration is very bad for this country. A Reagan administration would be much worse. I don't anticipate having any trouble supporting a Democratic candidate, whoever it is.

Udall, Morris King. We fought a good fight, now we're here to help Jimmy Carter celebrate his victory (at the Democratic National Convention).

DEMOCRATIC PARTY—CHICAGO

Byrne, Jane. If they care to come with me and accept the fact I'm a candidate, I am willing to work with them (about Chicago's Regular Democratic Organization).

DEMOCRATIC PARTY. NATIONAL CONVENTION, CHICAGO, 1968

Daley, Richard J. The police are not here to create disorder. They are here to preserve disorder (commenting during the 1968 Democratic Convention in Chicago).

DEMOCRATIC PARTY—PRESIDENTIAL CANDIDATES

McGovern, George Stanley. In this campaign, the Democratic Party and its candidates must demand an orderly withdrawal of American forces from Korea within a specified time. It would take no more than a year to leave; it might take as long as the decade of Vietnam to stay and bleed and die and lose. This time let us make peace before the making of a war.

DENIRO, ROBERT

DeNiro, Robert. I'm spending about $600 a week talking to my analyst. I guess that's the price of success.

DeNiro, Robert. There is a certain combination of anarchy and discipline in the way I work.

DENVER, JOHN

Denver, John. I epitomize America.

Simels, Steve. John Denver (is) Johnny Mathis disguised as a hillbilly. He has never written a decent song, his voice is an Irish tenor only a whit less offensive than Dennis Day's, and, as far as I can tell, his only function is to provide adolescent girls with records to cry over in the privacy of their bedrooms.

DEPRESSION, MENTAL

Baker, Russell. Misery no longer loves company. Nowadays it insists upon it.

Roosevelt, Theodore. Black care rarely sits behind a rider whose pace is fast enough.

DEPRESSIONS

Klein, Lawrence. What really scares me is signs of a worldwide slowdown at a time when the economies of the West have become increasingly synchronized.

DESIGN

Noyes, Eliot F (industrial designer). Familiarity breeds acceptance.

Oldenburg, Claes. To give birth to form is the only act of man that has any consequence.

DETENTE (POLITICAL SCIENCE)

Brezhnev, Leonid I. Relaxation of international tension by no means eliminates the struggle of ideas.

Ford, Gerald Rudolph. I don't use the word detente any more. I think what we ought to say is that the United States will meet with the superpowers, the Soviet Union and with China and others, and seek to relax tensions so that we can continue a policy of peace through strength.

Kissinger, Henry Alfred. The cold war was not so terrible and detente was not so exalting.

Morris, Roger. Detente is now suffering from the fact that it was deliberately obscured as diplomacy and oversold as politics.

Russell, Mark. President Ford has thrown the word detente out, and I'm glad he did, because nobody could define it in the first place. Except me. Detente is like going to a wife-swapping party and coming home alone.

Schweiker, Richard. Detente is dead and the Soviets killed it.

Solzhenitsyn, Aleksandr Isaevich. Now they (Russian leaders) don't say we're going to bury you anymore. They say detente.

DEVIL

Graham, Billy. Transcendental Meditation is evil because...it opens space within you for the devil.

Kraus, Karl. The devil is an optimist if he thinks he can make people worse than they are.

DEVRIES, PETER
DeVries, Peter. I love being a writer. What I can't stand is the paperwork.

DICKINSON, ANGIE
Dickinson, Angie. I dress for women—and I undress for men.

DICTATORSHIP
Fernandes, Millor (Brazilian playwright). In a democracy we are all equal before the law. In a dictatorship we are all equal before the police.

Khomeini, Ayatollah Ruhollah. Dictatorship is the greatest sin in the religion of Islam. Fascism and Islamism are absolutely incompatible.

Wallace, George Corley. I don't mind dictatorships abroad provided they are pro-American.

DIET
Pritikin, Nathan. Although our results need confirmation, we believe they are the first evidence demonstrating reversal of human arteriosclerosis by diet.

Wilson, Earl. Nature does her best to teach us. The more we overeat, the harder she makes it for us to get close to the table.

DIETRICH, MARLENE
Hemingway, Ernest. If she (Marlene Dietrich) had nothing but her voice, she could break your heart with it.

DIMAGGIO, JOE
DiMaggio, Joe. I can't take it anymore. I'm not in good enough shape (announcing his retirement as a player in oldtimers' games).

DIPLOMACY
Kissinger, Henry Alfred. A statesman who too far outruns the experience of his people will fail in achieving a domestic consensus, however wise his policies. (On the other hand), a statesman who limits his policies to the experience of his people is doomed to sterility.

Kissinger, Henry Alfred. I think Metternich was an extremely skilled diplomat, but not very creative.

Lippmann, Walter. I think there is a stopping point between globalism and isolationism. The test of statesmanship is to find those stopping points and to act accordingly (comments in a critique of Vietnam policy in 1965).

DIPLOMATS
Brewster, Kingman. A diplomat does not have to be a eunuch.

Kissinger, Henry Alfred. A statesman who too far outruns the experience of his people will fail in achieving a domestic consensus, however wise his policies. (On the other hand), a statesman who limits his policies to the experience of his people is doomed to sterility.

DISARMAMENT
Edison, Thomas Alva. The day will come when science will create a machine as a force which is so terrible, so infinitely horrifying, that even man, a bellicose being who brings suffering, torment, and death upon his fellows, at the risk of bringing these torments upon himself will shudder with fear and renounce war forever.

DISCOVERY
Szent-Gyoergyi von Nagyrapolt, Albert. Discovery consists of seeing what everybody has seen and thinking what nobody has thought.

DISCRIMINATION IN EMPLOYMENT
Kennedy, Florynce Rae. There are a few jobs that actually require a penis or vagina. All other jobs should be open to everybody.

Young, Andrew. I don't think affirmative action for blacks requires discrimination against whites.

DISSENTERS
Moynihan, Daniel Patrick. When a person goes to a country and finds their newspapers filled with nothing but good news, he can bet there are good men in jail.

Terkel, Studs. Dissent is not merely the right to dissent—it is the duty.

DISSENTERS—CHINA (PEOPLE'S REPUBLIC)
Hua, Kuo-Feng. We have such people (dissidents) in a miniscule number. We still have them. Unfortunately, they exist—like thieves, bribe-takers, spectators and other criminals exist. Both are inflicting harm to our society and that is why they should bear punishment in complete accordance with the demands of Soviet law.

DISSENTERS—RUSSIA
Anonymous (report in Pravda), . People are not punished for their opinions in the U.S.S.R. The only ones who are prosecuted are those who have indulged in propaganda or anti-Soviet agitation, aiming to weaken the political system in force in our country, or those who broadcast manifestly false bombast whose object is to discredit the Soviet Union.

Bukovsky, Vladimir. If I were to answer what sustains us in this struggle, first and foremost is trust, faith in people, faith in the future, and faith in the human values for which we stand (commenting at the White House on Soviet dissidents).

DISSENTERS—UNITED STATES
Douglas, William Orville. The great and invigorating influences in American life have been the unorthodox; the people who challenge an existing institution or way of life, or say and do things that make people think.

Young, Andrew. After all there are hundreds, perhaps even thousands of people in our (American) prisons, whom I would call political prisoners. I myself was sentenced in Atlanta 10 years ago for having organized the garbage workers there. Yet, three years later, I was a member of the House of Representatives in Georgia.

DISTRUST
Evtushenko, Evgenii Aleksandrovich. Distrust is the mother of war and political racism.

DIVORCE
Aumont, Jean-Pierre. Marriages are not eternal, so why should divorce be?

Charles, Prince of Wales, . I've fallen in love with all sorts of girls—and I fully intend to go on doing so. It's very important to find the right partner. In my position, obviously, the last thing I could possibly entertain is getting divorced.

Cher, . I left him for a woman: me (commenting on her divorce from Sonny Bono).

John Paul I, Pope, . Divorce is the sword of Damocles hanging over conjugal love: its presence generates uncertainty, fear, suspicion.

Leone, Mama. No one ever filed for divorce on a full stomach.

Lowell, Robert. Almost all good women poets are either divorced or lesbian.

DIXON, PAUL RAND

Dixon, Paul Rand. I understand there are Arabs who are not dirty (responding when asked to retract a racial slur directed at Ralph Nader).

DOBLER, CONRAD

Dobler, Conrad. Religiously speaking, it is an advancement from a Cardinal to a Saint (commenting on his trade from St. Louis to New Orleans football teams).

Dobler, Conrad. Well, 35 million TV viewers know that Karras has a lot of class. And all of it is third (after Alex Karras described him as the dirtiest player in pro football).

DOGS

Lindsay, John Vliet. If you want gratitude, get yourself a dog.

DOLE, ROBERT J.

Butz, Earl Lauer. Oh hell, John, everybody was out by then. You know...it's like the dog who screwed a skunk for a while, until it finally shouted, I've had enough (commenting to Pat Boone and John Dean regarding the lukewarm reception of Robert J. Dole by the delegates of the Republican National Convention).

Carter, Lillian. I don't know why he (President Ford) ever chose Dole when there are so many capable men. I think he's a hatchet man, although he denies it. If he wins and should ever become President, I think I'm going to move to South America.

Dole, Robert J. If you liked Richard Nixon, you'll love Bob Dole.

Dole, Robert J. It may turn out that 1974 was the good year for a Republican to be on the ballot.

Dole, Robert J. Thank goodness whenever I was in the Oval Office I only nodded (commenting on the Watergate tapes).

DOLLAR (MONEY)

Janeway, Eliot. The dollar has become like a hydrant at an international convention of dogs.

DONAHUE, MARK

Donahue, Mark. That last lap, I really didn't want it to end; I wanted it to go on and on (spoken during his short retirement).

DONLEAVY, J. P.

Donleavy, J. P. Nearly everybody who pans my books doesn't get anywhere in the literary trade.

DONOVAN, THOMAS

Rose, Don. One of the reasons I have been in politics so long is to see that there are no more Donovans.

DOUGLAS, WILLIAM ORVILLE

Douglas, William Orville. I have been bothered with incessant and demanding pain which depletes my energy to the extent that I have been unable to shoulder my full share of the burden (upon his resignation from the Supreme Court in a letter to President Ford).

Douglas, William Orville. I haven't been much of a proselytizer on the court. I've got the theory that the only soul I had to save was my own.

DRAMA

Allen, Woody. Drama stays with people more, like meat and potatoes, while comedy is a dessert, like meringue.

Miller, Arthur. I think a play ought to cast a shadow; it ought to be something you can walk around.

Olivier, Laurence. I love comedy every bit as much as tragedy, perhaps more, because the whole scene of humanity is under its roof.

Rudkin, David. The play should liberate itself from the personal origins of the author.

DRAMATIC CRITICISM

Mamet, David. Intellectually, I'd like to think of them (critics) as running-dog conspirators against the institution of art. But they're just jack-offs like the rest of us.

Noto, Lore. Critics are beasts, highly-disturbed people, basically frustrated, totally insincere, and brutalized by the profession they're in. The public should be warned: critics may be harmful to your health.

Ribman, Ronald. Criticism is like an Indian gauntlet. One has to run through it to survive. Critics create an environment of mediocrity.

Schary, Dore. Critics are like mayors of New York; nobody really wants to like them.

DRAMATISTS

Miller, Arthur. Part of being a playwright is being an actor. One way or another, whether surreptitiously or not, a good playwright is an actor.

Papp, Joseph. The true dramatist of our time is a poet; the true poet, a dramatist.

Rudkin, David. The play should liberate itself from the personal origins of the author.

DRAWING

Steinberg, Saul. The doodle is the brooding of the hand.

Steinberg, Saul. Unlike writing, drawing makes up its own syntax as it goes along. The line can't be reasoned in the mind. It can only be reasoned on paper.

DROUGHTS—WEST

Miller, Bill (director of administration for the Denver Water Department). The bad news is that if the drought keeps up within a few years we'll all be drinking reclaimed sewer water. The good news is that there won't be enough to go around.

DRUG INDUSTRY

Kuhn, Maggie (head of the Gray Panthers). What distresses me is that both old and young people are hooked on drugs. Old people are sedated into vegetables with tranquilizers, but the pushers of those drugs—doctors and pharmaceutical houses—are never sent to jail. They have a license to rip off old people and they rip them off every chance they get.

DRUGS

Waits, Tom. Reality is for those who can't face drugs.

DRUGS AND THE AGED

Kuhn, Maggie (head of the Gray Panthers). What distresses me is that both old and young people are hooked on drugs. Old people are sedated into vegetables with tranquilizers, but the pushers of those drugs—doctors and pharmaceutical houses—are never sent to jail. They have a license to rip off old people and they rip them off every chance they get.

DRUNKENNESS

Lewis, Joe E. You're not really drunk if you can lie on the floor without hanging on.

DUCHAMP, MARCEL

Duchamp, Marcel. I was interested in ideas—not in merely visual products. I wanted to put painting once again at the service of the mind.

DUKAKIS, MICHAEL S.

Dukakis, Michael S. If, in fact, I had a windfall of $10 million tax free, I would hire someone to handle all the stupid requests like yours (in response to 'What would you do with 10 million dollars').

DULLES, JOHN FOSTER

Churchill, Sir Winston. Foster Dulles is the only case I know of a bull who carries his china shop with him.

Philby, Kim. John Foster Dulles was a strong personality with views as narrow as a small-gauge railway.

DULLNESS

Read, David H. C. The worst sin is dullness.

DUNAWAY, FAYE

Dunaway, Faye. I've always thought that acting is an art of creating accidents.

DURANT, WILL

Durant, Will. The primary things in my own life have been a wife, a house and some children roaming around us once in a while.

DURANTE, JIMMY

Durante, Jimmy. There's a million good-lookin' guys, but I'm a novelty.

DURKIN, JOHN

Durkin, John. I may not be the smoothest item to come down the turnpike.

DUTY

Butler, Samuel. In practice it is seldom very hard to do one's duty when one knows what it is, but it is sometimes exceedingly difficult to find this out.

Moro, Aldo. I believe I have done my duty to the end (upon the announcement of the resignation of his cabinet).

DYLAN, BOB

Dylan, Bob. I didn't consciously pursue the Bob Dylan myth. It was given to me—by God. Inspiration is what we're looking for. You just have to be receptive to it.

Dylan, Bob. Money doesn't exist because I don't recognize it.

Dylan, Bob. Somebody called me the Ed Sullivan of rock and roll. I don't know what that means, but it sounds right.

EASTWOOD, CLINT

Burton, Richard. Clint (Eastwood) is in the great line of Spencer Tracy and James Stewart and Bob Mitchum. They have a kind of dynamic lethargy. They appear to do nothing and they do everything.

Eastwood, Clint. Everybody talks about love, but the thing that keeps marriage together for me is friendship.

EATING

Leone, Mama. No one ever filed for divorce on a full stomach.

Theroux, Paul. You are not what you eat; but where you eat is who you are.

Wilson, Earl. Nature does her best to teach us. The more we overeat, the harder she makes it for us to get close to the table.

ECHEVERRIA ALVAREZ, LUIS

Echeverria Alvarez, Luis. I would like to have as my successor a person who would continue with the reforms I have begun and carry them much further.

ECOLOGY

Hodel, Donald. (Environmentalism is) a crusade to stop all development in this country.

Richardson, Elliot Lee. There was a time when the seas seemed endless and the skies vast enough to swallow any of the mistakes and errors of man. The world used to be big and men could afford to be small. Now the world is small and men must be big.

Shuttleworth, John. We are still much too preoccupied with taking our machines out into the woods, instead of making a place for the forest in our hearts.

ECONOMIC CONDITIONS

Carter, James Earl. I think the world economy is stable.

Klein, Lawrence. What really scares me is signs of a worldwide slowdown at a time when the economies of the West have become increasingly synchronized.

ECONOMIC FORECASTING

Rinfret, Pierre A. Consensus is the security blanket of the insecure.

ECONOMIC POLICY

Okun, Arthur M. Society can transport money from rich to poor only in a leaky bucket.

Schumacher, Ernst F. Production by the masses, rather than mass production.

ECONOMICS

Allen, Marty. A study of economics usually reveals that the best time to buy anything is last year.

Galbraith, John Kenneth. The study of money, above all other fields of economics, is one in which complexity is used to disguise or evade the truth, not reveal it. Much discussion involves priestly incantation, the same type used by doctors and lawyers to pretend to a sort of difference that excludes other people.

Kugel, Yerachmiel. Ethics is not a branch of economics.

Lapham, Lewis H. I take for granted Jefferson's dictum that money, not morality, constitutes the principle of commercial nations.

Thatcher, Margaret Hilda. There can be no liberty unless there is economic liberty.

Von Hayek, Friedrich. You can have economic freedom without political freedom, but you cannot have political freedom without economic freedom.

ECONOMICS—STUDY AND TEACHING

Schumacher, Ernst F. As a good friend says, most of the modern economics as taught is a form of brain damage.

Schumacher, Ernst F. It's impossible to discuss economic problems without concepts like temptation and seduction. In economics this is translated into free consumer choice.

ECONOMISTS

Drucker, Peter F. In all recorded history there has not been one economist who had to worry about where the next meal would come from.

Schumacher, Ernst F. They're spending their time rearranging the deck chairs on the Titanic (commenting on his fellow economists).

EDER, RICHARD

Eder, Richard. A critic may write for an institution, but he shouldn't be one.

EDISON, THOMAS ALVA

Edison, Thomas Alva. Anything that won't sell, I don't want to invent.

Edison, Thomas Alva. Deafness has been of great advantage to me as my business is thinking.

EDITORS AND EDITING

Perkins, Maxwell. Editors are extremely fallible people, all of them. Don't put too much trust in them (to Taylor Caldwell).

Stevenson, Adlai, II. An editor is someone who separates the wheat from the chaff and then prints the chaff.

Tanner, Jack. An editor has no friends.

EDUCATION

Adler, Mortimer. We are hypocrites if we continue to think that the equality of citizenship belongs to all, but not the equality of educational opportunity.

Ball, George W. (Lyndon Johnson) did not suffer from a poor education, he suffered from the belief that he had a poor education.

Bell, Terrence H. We need to liberalize vocational education—and vocationalize liberal education.

Bok, Derek. If you think education is expensive—try ignorance.

Boulding, Kenneth E. The purpose of education is to transmit information from decrepit old men to decrepit young men.

Dobie, J. Frank. The average Ph.D. thesis is nothing but a transference of bones from one graveyard to another.

Harris, James A. Twenty-three percent of school children are failing to graduate, and another large segment graduate as functional illiterates. If 23 percent of anything else failed—23 percent of the automobiles did not run, 23 percent of the buildings fell down, 23 percent of stuffed ham spoiled—we'd look at the producer. The schools, here, are not blameless.

Kerr, Clark. Naderism has taken over education.

Parker, Gail Thain. We must not be misled by snobbery into thinking that there is only one way to become educated.

White, William Allen. In education we are striving not to teach youth to make a living, but to make a life.

Will, George. Education should be primarily an inoculation against the disease of our time, which is disdain for times past.

EDUCATION—AIMS AND OBJECTIVES

Boulanger, Nadia. Education is to bring people to be themselves, and at the same time, know how to conform to the limits.

Cramer, Jerome. Schools are now asked to do what people used to ask God to do.

EDUCATION—PHILADELPHIA

Rizzo, Frank Lazzaro. We need excellence in public education and if the teachers can't do it, we'll send in a couple of policemen.

EDUCATORS

Macrae, Norman. An anti-growth cult is being taught to a generation of idealistic kids as if it was high moral philosophy or even a religion.

EFFICIENCY, ADMINISTRATIVE

Drucker, Peter F. Look at governmental programs for the past fifty years. Every single one—except for warfare—achieved the exact opposite of its announced goal.

Frankel, Charles. Whatever happens in government could have happened differently, and it usually would have been better if it had.

Parkinson, C. Northcote. Work expands to fill the time allotted to it, or, conversely, the amount of work completed is in inverse proportion to the number of people employed.

Ray, Dixie Lee. Anything that the private sector can do, government can do it worse.

Sidey, Hugh. Bureaucrats are the only people in the world who can say absolutely nothing and mean it.

Sidey, Hugh. Carter must understand that in this city (Washington) we cut red tape lengthwise.

Sidey, Hugh. When a bureaucrat makes a mistake and continues to make it, it usually becomes new policy.

Will, George. World War II was the last government program that really worked (to the Association of American Publishers).

EGALITARIANISM

Williams, Edward Bennett. The total egalitarians miss the point. They would divide the wealth equally, impose quotas and ratios in education, in employment, and in the political process, regardless of merit, overlooking the crucial fact that all human progress throughout history owes its origins to the talented and enterprising.

EGGLESTON, JUSTINE JUDD

Eggleston, Justine Judd. I got tired of people calling me a dirty Jew so I figured I'd settle in the one country (Israel) where dirty Jew means you need a bath.

EGYPT—FOREIGN RELATIONS—ISRAEL

Sadat, Anwar. I am really startled till this moment that the barrier of distrust that has been between us (Egypt and Israel) during the last 30 years has been broken down in 35 hours. Amazing. Really.

EGYPT—FOREIGN RELATIONS—RUSSIA

Sadat, Anwar. The Russians had a Central Committee meeting last summer and decided they could support me but never trust me. I said that was okay—I couldn't trust them either.

Sadat, Anwar. They wanted to exert pressure and to bring me to my knees, but I don't go down on my knees except before God Almighty (speaking about the Soviet Union).

EGYPT—FOREIGN RELATIONS—UNITED STATES

Sadat, Anwar. I have dealt with three presidents, Nixon, Ford and this Carter. I can say that everything is improving.

EHRLICHMAN, JOHN D.

Ehrlichman, John D. I have done my time. I don't think he (Richard Nixon) is ever going to stop doing his time.

EIKERENKOETER, FREDERICK J.

Eikerenkoeter, Frederick J. I indulge myself shamelessly and so should you.

EINSTEIN, ALBERT

Einstein, Albert. Let every man be respected as an individual and no man idolized.

Einstein, Albert. To punish me for my contempt for authority, Fate made me an authority myself.

Einstein, Albert. With fame I become more and more stupid, which of course, is a common phenomenon. There is far too great a disproportion between what one is and what others think one is. With me, every peep becomes a trumpet solo.

EISENHOWER, DWIGHT DAVID
Anderson, John B. I am not running against General Eisenhower. I am running against Jimmy Carter and Ronald Reagan, and I would respectfully suggest that neither is an Eisenhower.

Eisenhower, Dwight David. The path to America's future lies down the middle of the road.

Eisenhower, Mamie Geneva (Doud). I let Ike run the country and I ran the home.

Philby, Kim. Now I can abandon my earlier reserve and call him an idle, ignorant, ungenerous old fraud.

Truman, Harry S. Hell, he (Dwight Eisenhower) probably never paid a medical bill in his life (commenting on Eisenhower's dislike of welfare programs).

EISENHOWER, MAMIE GENEVA (DOUD)
Eisenhower, Mamie Geneva (Doud). I let Ike run the country and I ran the home.

EIZENSTAT, STUART
Jordan, Hamilton. If the President had to fire all but one of us, he probably would keep Stu (Eizenstat).

EKLAND, BRITT
Ekland, Britt. I say I don't sleep with married men, but what I really mean is that I don't sleep with happily married men.

EL SALVADOR—POLITICS AND GOVERNMENT
Arrupe, Pedro (Superior General of the Jesuits). They can become martyrs, but my priests are not going to leave there (El Salvador) because they are with the people.

Romero, Oscar Arnulfo. They can kill me, but the voice of justice will never be stilled.

ELKINS, WEST VIRGINIA—DESCRIPTION
Nessen, Ron. Yes, I think the phone has reached there. They even have indoor toilets (commenting on President Ford's trip to Elkins, West Virginia).

EMIGRATION AND IMMIGRATION LAW
Rohatyn, Felix. We ought to change the sign on the Statue of Liberty to read, 'this time around, send us your rich'.

EMOTIONS
Disraeli, Benjamin. A man is occasionally thankful when he says 'thank you'.

Forbes, Malcolm S. People who never get carried away should be.

Miller, Henry. To the person who thinks with his head, life is a comedy. To those who think with their feelings, or work through their feelings, life is a tragedy.

EMPLOYEES
Peter, Laurence J. In a hierarchy, every employee tends to rise to the level of his own incompetence.

EMPLOYEES, DISMISSAL OF
Galbraith, John Kenneth. Anyone who says he isn't going to resign, four times, definitely will.

EMPLOYEES, PUBLIC
Horowitz, Rachel. If you're a public employee and your job depends on public officials, you have to be in politics.

EMPLOYMENT
Gass, Istvan (Hungarian soccer star). It's not serious work. I don't do anything. In fact, I've never seen a gun (on his job as a soldier).

Norris, William. Dammit, rebuilding the cities will be one of the great growth industries of the future. It will replace the auto as the big provider of jobs—if we Americans can ever get ourselves organized.

Norris, William. We talk a lot about human rights, but I don't know of any human right that is more important than a job.

ENEMIES
Jones, Thomas. Friends may come and go, but enemies accumulate.

ENERGY CONSERVATION
Laird, Melvin. Conservation alone is a slow walk down a dead-end street.

ENGLISH LANGUAGE
Rayburn, Sam. The three most important words in the English language are wait a minute.

ENGLISH LANGUAGE—COMPOSITION
Califano, Joseph A., Jr. Writing things clearly does not necessarily mean writing them short.

ENGLISH LANGUAGE—STUDY AND TEACHING
Botstein, Leon. The English language is dying, because it is not taught.

ENGLISH LANGUAGE—USAGE
Gold, Herbert. The rubber-stamp expression is a rubber stamp even the first time it is pressed into our brains.

ENTERTAINERS
Marx, Minnie. Where else can people who don't know anything make a living (commenting on show business).

ENTERTAINMENT INDUSTRY
Marx, Minnie. Where else can people who don't know anything make a living (commenting on show business).

ENTREPRENEURS
Glassman, James K. As a sit-in veteran and small businessman myself, I'm convinced that entrepreneurship is the last refuge of the trouble-making individual.

Hefner, Hugh Marston. I'm not primarily an entrepreneurial businessman. I'm primarily a playboy philosopher.

ENTREPRENEURS—UNITED STATES
Mencken, Henry Louis. No one ever went broke underestimating the intelligence of the American people.

ENVIRONMENT
Burroughs, John. If you want to see birds, you must have birds in your heart.

Commoner, Barry. When you fully understand the situation it is worse than you think.

ENVIRONMENTAL ACTION (ORGANIZATION)
Helms, Jesse. If Environmental Action had its way, the American people would starve and freeze to death in the dark.

ENVIRONMENTAL MOVEMENT
Breaux, John. If these do-gooders have their way you'll need a permit to turn on a faucet in the bathroom (commenting on environmentalists' causes).

Hagedorn, Tom. As far as I'm concerned, environmentalists and food stamp cheaters are the same thing.

Helms, Jesse. If Environmental Action had its way, the American people would starve and freeze to death in the dark.

Menke-Gluckert, Peter. Environment has become the Viet Nam of the middle class.

ENVIRONMENTAL POLICY

Dasmann, Raymond F. We are hooked like junkies, dependent on the drug of wasteful consumption.

Hodel, Donald. (Environmentalism is) a crusade to stop all development in this country.

EQUALITY

Adler, Mortimer. We are hypocrites if we continue to think that the equality of citizenship belongs to all, but not the equality of educational opportunity.

Armstrong, Louis. I got a simple rule about everybody. If you don't treat me right, shame on you.

Carter, James Earl. No poor, rural, weak, or black person should ever have to bear the additional burden of being deprived of the opportunity of an education, a job, or simple justice.

Jones, Franklin P. One thing in which the sexes are equal is in thinking that they're not.

Kennedy, Florynce Rae. There's no sex to a brain.

Thatcher, Margaret Hilda. Opportunity means nothing unless it includes the right to be unequal.

ERHARD, LUDWIG

Schmidt, Helmut. Talking with him (Ludwig Erhard) is like trying to nail Jell-O to the wall.

ERHARD SEMINARS TRAINING

Erhard, Werner. Belief is a disease.

Erhard, Werner. The goal of the (EST) training is 'getting it,' but you don't 'get it' in the training. You get that you've got it in the training.

ERHARD, WERNER

Waters, Craig. About 15 years ago, Jack Rosenberg changed his name to Werner Hans Erhard. His motive for doing so is unknown, but, with the switch, the son of a Jewish restaurant proprietor became an apparent Aryan: a son of history's perpetual victim became an heir apparent to one of history's greatest victimizers.

ERRORS

Nies, John. The effort expended by the bureaucracy in defending any error is in direct proportion to the size of the error.

ERVIN, SAMUEL JAMES

Ervin, Samuel James. The statute of limitations has already run out on all my past indiscretions. And more unfortunately, I have lost all capacity to commit any more.

ESTES, BILLIE SOL

Estes, Billie Sol. You win by losing, hold on by letting go, increase by diminishing, and multiply by dividing. These are the principles that have brought me success.

ETHICS

Kugel, Yerachmiel. Ethics is not a branch of economics.

ETIQUETTE

Broun, Heywood Hale. If anyone corrects your pronunciation of a word in a public place, you have every right to punch him in the nose.

EUROPE

Boumedieane, Houari. Europe and the U.S. have plundered the natural wealth of the Third World. We should consider whatever contribution the industrialized countries make (to be) a simple restitution of a tiny part of the debt contracted by their odious exploitation.

EUROPE—POLITICS AND GOVERNMENT

Monnet, Jean. The world is divided into those who want to become someone and those who want to accomplish something.

EUROPEANS

Auden, Wystan Hugh (attributed by Peter Conrad). The economic vice of Europeans is avarice, while that of Americans is waste.

EVANGELICALISM

Cockburn, Alexander. Descriptions of sin are what we want at the breakfast table, not admonitions against it.

Coffin, William Sloane. If you get an Evangelical with a social conscience you've got one of God's true saints.

EVANS, CHICK

Evans, Chick. I just hate to think of dying, to not wake up tomorrow and think of another way to hit that golf ball.

EXCESS

Walden, Phil (President of Capricorn Records). That's the old American way—if you got a good thing, then overdo it.

EXERCISE

Nixon, Richard Milhous. One thing I really hate is exercise for exercise's sake.

EXNER, JUDITH CAMPBELL

Sinatra, Frank. Hell hath no fury like a hustler with a literary agent.

EXPENDITURES, PUBLIC

Parkinson, C. Northcote. Expenditure rises to meet income.

EXPERTS

Butler, Nicholas Murray. An expert is one who knows more and more about less and less.

Desae, Morarji. An expert seldom gives an objective view. He gives his own view.

EXPLANATION

Einstein, Albert. Everything should be made as simple as possible, but not simpler.

Hubbard, Elbert. Never explain. Your friends do not need it and your enemies will not believe you anyway.

FACTS

Gordimer, Nadine. The facts are always less than what really happened.

Keyserling, Hermann A. The greatest American superstition is belief in facts.

FAILURE

Anonymous (Murphy's Law), . If anything can go wrong, eventually it will.

Simon, William E. Show me a good loser and I'll show you a loser.

Tomlin, Lily. Why is it we are always hearing about the tragic cases of too much, too soon? What about the rest of us? Too little, too late.

FAITH

Nietzsche, Friedrich Wilhelm. If a man really has strong faith he can indulge in the luxury of skepticism.

Nin, Anais. One must thrust out of a finished cycle in life, and that leap is the most difficult to make—to part with one's faith, one's love, when one would prefer to renew the faith and recreate the passion.

FALLACI, ORIANA

Fallaci, Oriana. An interview is a love story for me. It's a fight. It's a coitus.

Fallaci, Oriana. I doubt very much that my future as an interviewer of powerful people in the United States is a brilliant future if Mr. Kissinger goes on being the President of the United States.

FAME

Bowen, Elizabeth. All your youth you want to have your greatness taken for granted; when you find it taken for granted, you are unnerved.

Emerson, Ralph Waldo. To be great is to be misunderstood.

Gallico, Paul. In place of great literary fame, I've millions of people who care about what I write and who like me. What the hell more do I want?.

Hendrix, Jimi. It's funny the way most people love the dead. Once you are dead, you are made for life.

Lasser, Louise. When you are a celebrity, you are totally a victim.

Lindbergh, Charles Augustus. I've had enough fame for a dozen lives; it's not what it's cracked up to be.

Margolis, Susan. Today the gifted as well as the deranged among us are struggling to be famous the way earlier Americans struggled to be saved.

Morrow, Lance. Celebrities are intellectual fast food.

Morrow, Lance. When fame ceases to bear any relation to worth or accomplishment, then the whole currency of public recognition is debased.

Nabokov, Vladimir. Anonymous praise hurts nobody.

O'Connor, Flannery. (Fame) is a comic distinction shared with Roy Rogers's horse and Miss Watermelon of 1955.

Rubin, Jerry. I'm famous. That's my job.

Tanner, Jack. Fame is empty. But it is better to find that out afterwards.

Wolfe, Tom. You can be denounced from the heavens, and it only makes people interested.

FAMILY

Lance, Thomas Bertram. Folks are serious about three things—their religion, their family, and most of all, their money.

FAMILY LIFE

Crosby, Bing. Family life is the basis for a strong community and a great nation.

Mead, Margaret. At least 50 percent of the human race doesn't want their mother-in-law within walking distance.

Tolstoy, Leo. Happy families are all alike. Every unhappy family is unhappy in its own way (from Anna Karenina).

FANATICISM

Dunne, Finley Peter. A fanatic is a man that does what he thinks the Lord would if He knew all the facts.

FARM LABOR—CALIFORNIA

Butz, Earl Lauer. In California, Mexican farmworkers are no longer allowed to use the short-handled hoes they have for generations; now they are required to use long-handled American-type hoes. This is not because the workers or the farmers want the change; but apparently because the city people, driving by, feel more comfortable watching the workers using the kind of hoes that look good through car windows.

FASCISM

Khomeini, Ayatollah Ruhollah. Dictatorship is the greatest sin in the religion of Islam. Fascism and Islamism are absolutely incompatible.

FASHION

Alsop, Stewart. A fashionable gentleman who much concerns himself with the fashions of gentlemen is neither fashionable nor a gentleman.

Berhanger, Elio. Fashion has become like an old prostitute. Nobody even uses the word elegance anymore.

Cardin, Pierre. Chanel never influenced fashion one bit.

Cardin, Pierre. The jean. The jean is the destructor. It is a dictator. It is destroying creativity. The jean must be stopped.

Rykiel, Sonia. Every woman must create her own ambience; it is not I or Yves St. Laurent but the woman who has to create herself and be a unique person.

Saint Laurent, Yves. Fashions fade, style is eternal.

Saint Laurent, Yves. Haute couture is opera. It is dreams and phantoms and magic.

Vollbracht, Michaele. If you have to talk about fashion, then you are not in it.

FASHION—NEW YORK (CITY)

Vollbracht, Michaele. The fashion industry is like someone with a BB gun: they aim at you, they don't kill you, but they hurt you a hell of a lot.

FATHERS

McKuen, Rod. People are not born bastards. They have to work at it (commenting on his lifelong search to find his father).

Spock, Benjamin. Fathers ought to form a union and win the right to go home early if their children are sick.

FAULK, JOHN HENRY

Faulk, John Henry. I was taught that the first ten amendments were sacrosanct, that they're the engine by which this society runs and I admire people who cherish them and loathe and despise people who would circumvent and destroy them. So it took no act of courage to do what I did. It was an act of principle. What else would you do? I like to think all American people would do the same thing if they felt the way I did.

FAULKNER, WILLIAM

Faulkner, William. I gave the world what it wanted—guts and genitals.

FAWCETT-MAJORS, FARRAH

Fawcett-Majors, Farrah. God balances things out. My theory is that God gives you either straight white teeth with lots of cavities or crooked, stained teeth with no cavities. I have lots of cavities.

Fawcett-Majors, Farrah. I thought Marilyn Monroe was the most beautiful woman in the world and Elizabeth Taylor breathtaking. But when I see myself on the screen I say: Oh, shoot! What are they talking about.

FEAR

Brooks, Mel. Everything we do in life is based on fear, especially love.

King, Martin Luther, Jr. I'm not fearing any man. Mine eyes have seen the glory of the coming of the Lord.

Landor, Walter Savage. Men cannot bear to be deprived of anything they are used to; not even of their fears.

FEDERAL GOVERNMENT

Cranson, Maurice. (Government is) a necessary evil that allows for tyranny by the collectivity over the individual.

Nisbet, Robert. The doctrine of a benevolent state grows stronger. Very big government is not going to disappear.

Reagan, Ronald. The coils woven in that city (Washington, D.C.) are entrapping us all and, as with the Gordian knot, we cannot untie it. We have to cut it with one blow of the sword.

Wallace, George Corley. Being a southerner is not as much geographical now as it is a state of mind. When I say southern I mean this: people are beginning to realize that big government is not good for the people.

FEDERAL-STATE CONTROVERSIES

Hart, Gary. To get the government off your back, get your hands out of the government's pockets.

Wallace, George Corley. Being a southerner is not as much geographical now as it is a state of mind. When I say southern I mean this: people are beginning to realize that big government is not good for the people.

FELDMAN, MARTY

Feldman, Marty. I always feel like a con artist after everything I've done.

FELLINI, FEDERICO

Fellini, Federico. I don't have problems with actors—they have problems with me.

FICTION

Cheever, John. Fiction is our most intimate and acute means of communication.

Dibnah, Stanley. The novel of recent years has become so candid that there are now not many books which are unacceptable to adult readers.

Fowles, John. Fiction is a removing activity. The ghost that haunts all writers is, 'Am I betraying reality?'.

Jong, Erica. I cannibalized real life.

Nabokov, Vladimir. Great novels are above all great fairy tales. Literature does not tell the truth but makes it up.

O'Connor, Flannery. For a fiction writer, to believe nothing is to see nothing.

Porter, Katherine Anne. Dullness, bitterness, rancor, self-pity, baseness of all kinds can be most interesting material for a story provided these are not also the main elements in the mind of the author.

Singer, Isaac Bashevis. A Marxist has never written a good novel.

Singer, Isaac Bashevis. Fiction can entertain and stir the mind; it does not direct it.

Stout, Rex. Writing any kind of fiction is a sort of explosion. When the explosion has taken place, there's no use going around looking at the debris.

Styron, William. I think a great novel could even come out of Beverly Hills.

Vonnegut, Kurt. The work (of writing fiction) is exceedingly tedious. It is like making wallpaper by hand for the Sistine Chapel.

FIELD, MARSHALL, V—FAMILY

Field, Marshall, V. They all started out with nothing in those days, and the biggest crooks won. I was just lucky to come from a line of successful crooks.

FIELDS, W. C.

Fields, W. C. Women are like elephants. They're nice to look at but I wouldn't want to own one.

Rosten, Leo. Any man who hates dogs and babies can't be all bad (about W. C. Fields).

FINANCE, PERSONAL

Cameron, John. In order to get a loan you must first prove you don't need it.

Holmes, Oliver Wendell. Put not your trust in money. Put your money in trust.

Lance, Thomas Bertram. Folks are serious about three things—their religion, their family, and most of all, their money.

Mailer, Norman. My talent is making money, not managing it.

Parker, Charlie. Romance without finance ain't got no chance.

Stevenson, Adlai, II. There was a time when a fool and his money were soon parted, but now it happens to everybody.

FINCH, PETER

Finch, Peter. Acting is fascinating and not an ignoble profession. No one lives more than the actor.

FINKS, JIM

Douglass, Bobby. If you want to keep your beer real cold, put it next to Jim Fink's heart.

FINLEY, CHARLES OSCAR

Finley, Charles Oscar. I always wanted to be a player, but I never had the talent to make the big leagues. So I did the next best thing: I bought a team.

Finley, Charles Oscar. I've never seen so many damned idiots as the owners in sport.

Giles, Warren. (Charlie) Finley wouldn't think God could make a good (baseball) commissioner.

Griffith, Calvin. He's the P.T. Barnum of baseball. (about Charles Oscar Finley).

Symington, Stuart. (Charles Finley) is one of the most disreputable characters to enter the American sports scene.

FIREARMS—LAWS AND REGULATIONS

Davis, Edward Michael. When Brutus gave it to him (Caesar) in the back with that knife, you know if Brutus had a gun they would have talked about gun control. But they didn't pull in knife control or we'd all have to be eating spaghetti all the time.

Hansen, George. Firearms are not the problem. People are.

Koch, Edward I. You're not a nice guy if you have a gun, even if you are a nice guy.

Mankiewicz, Frank Fabian. Since we are not yet serious about guns, let us at least withhold the most costly target (the President).

Reagan, Ronald. Take away the arms of the citizenry and where is its defense.

Thompson, Hunter S. I don't plan to give up any of my guns until the cops give up theirs.

FISHER, EDDIE

Dietrich, Marlene. Never marry an actress (to Eddie Fisher).

FISHER, M. F. K.

Auden, Wystan Hugh. I do not know of anyone in the United States who writes better prose (about M. F. K. Fisher).

FISHERMEN

Apollonio, Spencer. When four fishermen get together, there's always a fifth.

FISHING

Anonymous, . One man's secret uncontrollable vice is another man's total boring drag.

Buchan, John. The charm of fishing is that it is the pursuit of what is elusive but attainable, a perpetual series of occasions for hope.

Hoover, Herbert Clark. Fishing...brings meekness and inspiration, reduces our egotism, soothes our troubles and shames our wickedness. It is discipline in the equality of men—for all men are equal before fish.

Steinbeck, John. Here is no sentiment, no contest, no grandeur, no economics. From the sanctity of this occupation, a man may emerge refreshed and in control of his own soul. He is not idle. He is fishing, alone with himself in dignity and peace. It seems a very precious thing to me.

Talbert, Diron. There ain't but one time to go fishin' and that's whenever you can.

FITZGERALD, F. SCOTT

Fitzgerald, F. Scott. I talk with the authority of failure—Ernest (Hemingway) with the authority of success.

FITZGERALD, ZELDA

Fitzgerald, Zelda. A vacuum can only exist, I imagine, by the things which enclose it.

FITZSIMMONS, FRANK E.

Anonymous (Teamster Union Member), . Look at it this way: Our contract expires in April of 1976, right? If Jimmy Hoffa were running for election against Fitzsimmons in July, 1976, Fitzsimmons would have to bust his tail to negotiate a good contract for us, right? With Jimmy Hoffa gone, he don't have to work so hard, does he?.

Fitzsimmons, Frank E. For those who would say it's time to reform this organization, that it is time that the officers quit selling out the membership of their union, I say to them, go to hell.

Fitzsimmons, Frank E. Personally, I don't think George Meany would know a trade unionist if he tripped over one.

FLANNER, JANET

Flanner, Janet. I'm not one of those journalists with a staff. I don't even have a secretary. I act as a sponge. I soak it up and squeeze it out in ink every two weeks.

FLATTERY

Lindsay, John Vliet. Flattery isn't harmful unless inhaled.

FLIGHT

Dickey, James. Flight is the only truly new sensation that men have achieved in modern history.

FLOOD, CURT

Flood, Curt. I am a man, not a consignment of goods to be bought and sold.

FLYNT, LARRY

Flynt, Althea. I told him 'God may have walked into your life, but $20 million a year just walked out' (to Larry Flynt upon his conversion).

Flynt, Larry. If I'm guilty of anything it's bad taste. I don't think people ought to be put in jail for having bad taste.

Flynt, Larry. If you ask me, yes, I am a born-again Christian. But I am going to continue publishing pornography, and anybody who doesn't like it can go kiss a rope.

Flynt, Larry. I've been all the way to the bottom. There's only one way to go now, and that's up. I'm going to be hustling for the Lord.

Stapleton, Ruth Carter. If Jesus loves Larry Flynt, who am I to turn my back?.

FONDA, HENRY

Fonda, Henry. I don't feel I'm totally a man of integrity. But if there is something in the eyes, a kind of honesty in the face, then I guess you could say that's the man I'd like to be, the man I want to be.

FONDA, PETER

Fonda, Peter. I'm heir to nothing but a legend, which is full of ...air.

FOOD

Curtis, Carl Thomas. In the whole history of the world, whenever a meateating race has gone to war against a non-meateating race, the meat eaters won. It produces superior people.

FOOD HABITS

Wilson, Earl. Nature does her best to teach us. The more we overeat, the harder she makes it for us to get close to the table.

FOOD INDUSTRY—COMPETITION

Tucker, Carol. Competition, you know, is a lot like chastity. It is widely praised, but alas, too little practiced (commenting on her plans as assistant agriculture secretary to seek a healthy shot of competition for the nation's food industry).

FOOD LAW AND LEGISLATION

Tucker, Carol. Competition, you know, is a lot like chastity. It is widely praised, but alas, too little practiced (commenting on her plans as assistant agriculture secretary to seek a healthy shot of competition for the nation's food industry).

FOOD, ORGANIC

Redford, Robert. Health food may be good for the conscience, but Oreos taste a hell of a lot better.

FOOTBALL

Boulding, Kenneth E. Politics is a ritualistic dialectic—a bit like a football game. It doesn't really matter who wins, but you have to pretend it does in order to be part of the whole divine comedy.

Dundes, Alan. Football is a healthy outlet for male-to-male affections just as spin the bottle and post office are healthy outlets for adolescent heterosexual needs.

Hayes, Woody. Football is about the only unifying force left in America today.

Hayes, Woody. It isn't the size of the dog in the fight, but the size of the fight in the dog that counts.

Jones, Bertram Hays. Football plays are like accounting problems. They baffle you at first, but once you've learned the system they're easy.

Mills, Chuck. When it comes to football, God is prejudiced—toward big, fast kids (commenting on religion and football).

FOOTBALL, COLLEGE

Hall, John. The colleges would do better to get rid of the nights and return to Saturday afternoon football the way God and Grantland Rice created it (commenting on college football being played at night).

Mason, Tony. The thing is that 90% of the colleges are abiding by the rules, doing things right. The other 10%, they're going to the bowl games.

Rockne, Knute. You show me a good and gracious loser, and I'll show you a failure!.

FOOTBALL, COLLEGE—TRAINING

Hayes, Woody. When you fight in the North Atlantic, you train in the North Atlantic.

FOOTBALL—GAMBLING

Rozelle, Pete. The world knows no less rational person than a losing bettor (commenting in opposition to efforts to legalize betting on professional football).

FOOTBALL, PROFESSIONAL

Dobler, Conrad. I can say with a clear conscience that I have never knowingly bit another football player. For one thing, I believe in good hygiene (in response to charges that he had bitten a rival player).

Halas, George. You can have a session with your girl friend. What's that last you? Twenty minutes, half an hour? Or you can go out and get stiff with the boys. A few hours, right? But to win a game in the National Football League. That lasts a whole week.

Landry, Tom. Nothing funny ever happens on the football field.

Namath, Joe. I love football. I really love football. As far as I'm concerned, it's the second best thing in the world.

Nye, Blaine. It's not whether you win or lose but who gets the blame (commenting on his football philosophy).

White, Ed. Losing this game was like having your house robbed and watching it happen (commenting on the Vikings 17-14 defeat by the Cowboys).

FORD, CHARLOTTE

Ford, Charlotte. I worked for charity all my life, and now it's kind of fun to work for money.

FORD, GERALD RUDOLPH

Abzug, Bella. Richard Nixon self-impeached himself. He gave us Gerald Ford as his revenge.

Albert, Carl. I wanted to get someone I knew we could beat in the next election (commenting on why he recommended Gerald Ford be appointed to replace Spiro Agnew).

Baker, Howard Henry. I don't understand all the fuss over the Gallup poll (with Reagan leading Ford). President Ford is going to veto it anyway.

Carey, Hugh. It is not becoming of a President to create animosity among the people by pitting one section of the country against another (in response to President Ford's stand on aid to New York City).

Carey, Hugh. It isn't fair when the President of the United States hauls off and kicks the people of the city of New York in the groin, and I'm going to fight back.

Carter, Lillian. I don't know why he (President Ford) ever chose Dole when there are so many capable men. I think he's a hatchet man, although he denies it. If he wins and should ever become President, I think I'm going to move to South America.

Conable, Barber. The country still views him (Gerald Ford) as the guy who is filling the gap between Watergate and the next election.

Dutton, Fred. George Wallace is a more truly democratic candidate than Ford, Humphrey or Jackson. He wants everyone to vote, while they hope to narrow down the voting public.

Ford, Elizabeth (Bloomer). People stop me all the time to urge that my husband run for the presidency, but I'm doing my best to discourage him.

Ford, Gerald Rudolph. Having become Vice President and President without expecting or seeking either, I have a special feeling toward these high offices. To me, the presidency and vice presidency were not prizes to be won, but a duty to be done.

Ford, Gerald Rudolph. I am going to be heard from.

Ford, Gerald Rudolph. I can tell you—and tell you now—that I am prepared to veto any bill that has as its purpose a federal bailout of New York City to prevent a default.

Ford, Gerald Rudolph. I did not take the sacred oath of office to preside over the decline and fall of America.

Ford, Gerald Rudolph. I don't use the word detente any more. I think what we ought to say is that the United States will meet with the superpowers, the Soviet Union and with China and others, and seek to relax tensions so that we can continue a policy of peace through strength.

Ford, Gerald Rudolph. I learned a long time ago in politics, never say never.

Ford, Gerald Rudolph. I share your deep appreciation about the increased irreverence for life (commenting in a speech to the 41st Eucharistic Congress).

Ford, Gerald Rudolph. I'm a better President than a campaigner.

Ford, Gerald Rudolph. Instead of being amiable I can get a little firm with a different tone of my voice and with a little sterner look on my face, but I don't go into an outburst because I think, really, when you go into an outburst, you sort of lose control of your capability to analyze something (commenting on how he shows his anger without creating a scene).

Ford, Gerald Rudolph. It's good for America to see that you can get a fair trial in Washington (to Robert S. Strauss upon the acquittal of John Connally).

Ford, Gerald Rudolph. My motto towards the Congress is communication, conciliation, compromise and cooperation.

Ford, Gerald Rudolph. To the great people of the government of Israel. Excuse me—of Egypt. (Remark at a dinner given in his honor by visiting Egyptian President Anwar Sadat).

Ford, Gerald Rudolph. You can be certain that I have just begun to fight. America's armed forces today are second to none. And I will take whatever steps are necessary to see that they remain second to none.

Ford, Jack. I'll be so glad when this is all over and my father is no longer President (commenting on politics and political campaigning).

Galbraith, John Kenneth. I'm opposed to tax decreases. If the last one had worked Jerry Ford would still be President.

Goldwater, Barry Morris. I have always said if you put Reagan in one hand and Ford in the other hand and turn the lights out, you wouldn't know who the hell you had in either hand, because of their political philosophy.

Goodwin, Richard N. He's not even an accidental president. He's a double-misfortune president— president by grace of the criminal code and modern electronics (about Gerald R. Ford).

Harris, Louis. Gerald Ford is viewed as more of a man of integrity, for example, than Jimmy Carter is (commenting on the results of his polling of public opinion).

Hart, Gary. The race (between Ronald Reagan and Gerald Ford) all boils down to a contest between the philosophies of Herbert Hoover and Calvin Coolidge.

Humphrey, Hubert Horatio. I want the President to be as considerate of New York City and of New York State as he is of countries all over the world. Within the same week that he said no help for New York, he sends us up a program for $5 billion of additional military aid in support assistance for the Middle East.

Johnson, James P. Mr. Chairman, I think the record should show that for the first time since McKinley, we have a Republican President worth shooting (upon hearing of Lynette "Squeaky" Fromme's attack on President Ford).

Kaye, Peter F. (Ford campaign spokesman). Mondale is a 100 per cent bona fide liberal. It gives us a tangible target. We're not just running against this peanut farmer who walks on water.

Keene, David (Reagan aide). Fighting the Ford (presidential campaign) operation is kind of like fighting the Spanish Armada. They're bigger, but they don't maneuver very well.

Loeb, William. I think the total sum of his (Gerald Ford's) incompetency, his failure to lead and to a certain extent his deviousness would in the vernacular sum up to that phrase (that the President of the United States is a jerk), yes.

Magnuson, Warren. Why, if we passed the Ten Commandments, President Ford would veto them. He'd say there were too many or they interfered with foreign policy or something.

Moore, Sara Jane. I did indeed willfully and knowingly attempt to murder Gerald R. Ford, the President of the United States by use of a handgun and would now like to enter a plea of guilty.

O'Neill, Thomas P. (Tip). Since the day he commuted Nixon, he hasn't done anything right (commenting on Congressional rapport with Gerald Ford).

Pastore, John O. This has become a Government by veto. We've got the minority dragging the majority around by the nose.

Rhodes, John J. What the hell would he (Gerald Ford) want to spend the next four years of his life as Vice President for?.

Rockefeller, Nelson Aldrich. After much thought, I have decided further that I do not wish my name to enter into your consideration for the upcoming Republican Vice-Presidential nominee (letter to President Ford).

Rockefeller, Nelson Aldrich. The President (Gerald Ford) is an awfully nice person. He is not by nature a gut fighter. He hasn't had to be. He has been a reconciler.

Russell, Mark. President Ford has thrown the word detente out, and I'm glad he did, because nobody could define it in the first place. Except me. Detente is like going to a wife-swapping party and coming home alone.

Safire, William. Gerald Ford's Presidency was unique in this century for not producing a single memorable phrase.

Schlesinger, Arthur, Jr. I will support the Democratic ticket, but actually I think they're both a couple of stiffs (commenting on the 1976 Democratic and Republican candidates).

Swayduck, Edward. When we examine Ford's political and legislative record, we must ask the crucial question: Is Ford really an Edsel.

Tower, John. You can argue shades of difference all day, yet there is little philosophical difference between Gerald Ford and Ronald Reagan. The important thing is that Mr. Ford is an 'electable' conservative while Mr. Reagan would lose to the Democratic candidate this fall.

Udall, Morris King. Obviously the Ford administration is very bad for this country. A Reagan administration would be much worse. I don't anticipate having any trouble supporting a Democratic candidate, whoever it is.

Zack, Al (spokesman for AFL-CIO). The political and ethical question is whether the word of the President of the United States is any good, and the answer as far as Ford is concerned is still no, even though he has named a good labor secretary (commenting after the nomination of W. J. Usery, Jr. as Secretary of Labor).

FORD, GERALD RUDOLPH—STAFF
Nessen, Ron. I'm a Ron, but not a Ziegler.
Nessen, Ron. Press conferences force more policy decisions than anything else.

FORD, HENRY, II
Bundy, McGeorge. One of the things we've always valued about Henry Ford is candor.

FORD, JACK
Ford, Jack. I'll be so glad when this is all over and my father is no longer President (commenting on politics and political campaigning).

FORD MOTOR COMPANY
Iacocca, Lee A. This year the public will have a choice, the likes of which it hasn't had in years. The difference between our cars and GM's is like the difference between a four-foot blonde and a seven-foot brunette.

FORECASTING
Kojak, Theo. Hindsight is the only exact science.

FOREMAN, GEORGE
Foreman, George. Boxing is like jazz. The better it is, the less people appreciate it.

FOREST CONSERVATION
Reagan, Ronald. Once you've seen one redwood, you've seen them all.

FORGERY

Walpole, Horace. You must renounce imagaination forever if you hope to succeed in plagiarism. Forgery is intention, not invention.

FORM

Oldenburg, Claes. To give birth to form is the only act of man that has any consequence.

FORSTER, E. M.

Forster, E. M. If I had to choose between betraying my country and betraying my friend, I hope I should have the guts to betray my country.

FOSTER, JODIE

Foster, Jodie. Acting has spared me from being a regular everyday kid slob.

Foster, Jodie. I've never studied acting. My technique is pure instinct. I'm not bragging, but certain kids have the timing and ability to mimic—and others don't. That's the way it is. And it's important not to be self-conscious.

FRAMPTON, PETER

Frampton, Peter. I'm not for women's liberation like staunch fem libbers are, but if the old lady is tired and there's a sink full of washing up, I'll do it, you know?.

FRANCE

Bell, Helen Choate. The French are a low lot. Give them two more legs and a tail, and there you are.

Jefferson, Thomas. Every man has two countries—his own and France.

Malle, Louis. It always surprised me that people consider me a French director. I don't like the French. They get on my nerves. They are so pompous and have no humor... They don't adjust to modern civilization at all.

Miller, Henry. I owe everything to the French. I am more close to France than America even though I lived there only 10 years, from 1929 to 1939. Those years in France meant everything to me and formed my whole career.

Wilder, Billy. France is a country where the money falls apart in your hands and you can't tear the toilet paper.

FRANCE—FOREIGN POLICY

Giscard d'Estaing, Valery. The foreign policy of France is not made and will not be made in the newsrooms of some of the international information media. France, her people and her laws have no lessons to receive from anyone, and I invite those who wish to be our friends to refrain from giving us their lessons (commenting about international criticism on the French handling of the release of Abu Daoud, the Palestinian suspected of planning the 1972 Munich Olympic attack on Israeli athletes).

FRANCE—FOREIGN POLICY—AFRICA

Simonet, Henri. France has an African policy which is not ours.

FRANCE—POLITICS AND GOVERNMENT

Anonymous, . The right governs, the left thinks (about French politics).

Giscard D'Estaing, Valery. Nuclear energy is at the crossroads of the two independences of France: the independence of her defense and the independence of her energy supply.

Giscard d'Estaing, Valery. The foreign policy of France is not made and will not be made in the newsrooms of some of the international information media. France, her people and her laws have no lessons to receive from anyone, and I invite those who wish to be our friends to refrain from giving us their lessons (commenting about international criticism on the French handling of the release of Abu Daoud, the Palestinian suspected of planning the 1972 Munich Olympic attack on Israeli athletes).

FRANCO, FRANCISCO

Aregood, Richard. They say only the good die young. Generalissimo Francisco Franco was 82. Seems about right.

Franco, Francisco. I ask forgiveness from all, as I give my most heartfelt forgiveness to those who declared themselves my enemies. I believe and hope that I had no enemies other than those who were enemies of Spain—Spain, which I will love until the last moment and which I promised to serve until my dying breath, which is near.

Franco, Francisco. My God, how hard it is to die.

FRANKEL'S LAW (QUOTATION)

Frankel, Charles. Whatever happens in government could have happened differently, and it usually would have been better if it had.

FRANKLIN, BENJAMIN

Comins, David H. People will accept your idea more readily if you tell them Benjamin Franklin said it first.

FRANKLIN, BONNIE

Franklin, Bonnie. When I was little, my mother always told me my beauty comes from within. Any idiot knows that means you're ugly.

FRAZIER, JOE

Frazier, Joe. I want him like a hog wants slop (commenting on wanting to fight Muhammad Ali).

FREE ENTERPRISE

Harris, Fred. These huge corporations say they favor free enterprise. Well, I want to give them a big dose of it. It's time the J. Paul Gettys, the Nelson Rockefellers and these great big corporations started haulin' their part of the freight. Why, did you know there was one year Rockefeller didn't pay any income taxes. We oughta sue that man for nonsupport.

Iacocca, Lee A. The free-enterprise system has gone to hell.

Kahn, J. Kesner. Free market competition, freely advertised, is consumerism at its best.

Ray, Dixie Lee. Anything that the private sector can do, government can do it worse.

Rockefeller, Nelson Aldrich. Free enterprise is the greatest and most productive system man has ever created. In a modest way, I have been a beneficiary.

FREE SPEECH

Fleishman, Stanley. There are more citizens in jail in the United States today for publishing books, magazines, newspapers, and films than there are in all the countries of the world put together.

Lumbard, J. Edward. In areas of doubt and conflicting considerations, it is thought better to err on the side of free speech.

Moynihan, Daniel Patrick. There is no nation so poor that it cannot afford free speech, but there are few elites which will put up with the bother of it.

FREEDOM

Stravinsky, Igor Fedorovich, . If everything would be permitted to me, I would feel lost in this abyss of freedom.

FREEDOM OF THE PRESS

Buchwald, Art. In 80 percent of the countries in the world today, guys like myself would be in jail.

Douglas, William Orville. The press has a preferred position in our constitutional scheme not to enable it to make money, not to set newsmen apart as a favored class, but to bring fulfillment to the public's right to know.

Gurfein, Murray. A cantankerous press must be suffered by those in authority in order to preserve freedom of expression and the right of the people to know.

Irani, C. R. The only protection for a free press is the courage to demand it.

Jefferson, Thomas. Were it left to me to decide whether we should have government without newspapers or newspapers without government, I should not hesitate a moment to prefer the latter.

Kennedy, Edward Moore. If and when needed, anti-trust laws are ready and able to promote a diverse and competitive press.

Liebling, A. J. Freedom of the press belongs to those who own one.

Moynihan, Daniel Patrick. When a person goes to a country and finds their newspapers filled with nothing but good news, he can bet there are good men in jail.

Rusk, Dean. I don't believe in a code of ethics in the journalism profession, and I don't believe in equal time between the media. If there are abuses toward freedom of the press, then let us correct them thru free speech.

Wriston, Walter. To think that the bell does not toll for academic freedom or freedom of the press if economic freedom is shackled is a dangerous illusion.

FREEDOM (THEOLOGY)

PAUL VI, POPE, . In reality, it is not enough to be free from something. One must be free for someone or something.

FREUD, SIGMUND

Freud, Sigmund. My cigar is not a symbol. It is only a cigar.

FRIEDMAN, MILTON

Friedman, Milton. There is no such thing as a free lunch. That is the sum of my economic theory. The rest is elaboration.

FRIENDSHIP

Carter, Hodding, III. The thing you have to remember about Southerners is that we're always generous and forgiving—with our friends.

Eastwood, Clint. Everybody talks about love, but the thing that keeps marriage together for me is friendship.

Forster, E. M. If I had to choose between betraying my country and betraying my friend, I hope I should have the guts to betray my country.

Gentry, Dave Tyson. True friendship comes when silence between two people is comfortable.

Humphrey, Hubert Horatio. The greatest gift of life is friendship and I have received it.

Jones, Thomas. Friends may come and go, but enemies accumulate.

Rockefeller, John Davison. A friendship founded on business is better than a business founded on friendship.

Truman, Harry S. You want a friend in this life, get a dog.

FROMME, LYNETTE (SQUEAKY)

Fromme, Lynette (Squeaky). I can't be rehabilitated because I haven't done anything wrong.

FUEL INDUSTRY

Hart, Gary. Exxon seems to have the idea that it can solve America's energy problems almost totally at Colorado's expense.

Nader, Ralph. There is not an energy crisis. There is an energy monopoly crisis, too many of the energy decisions are being made by a few large corporations instead of by a broader aggregate of consumer determinants.

Penden, Bill. Atomic energy is a future idea whose time is past. Renewable energy is a future idea whose time has come.

FUEL INDUSTRY—WESTERN STATES

Apodaca, Jerry. Let there be no mistake, the West will not become an energy colony for the rest of the nation.

FULBRIGHT, JAMES WILLIAM

Fulbright, James William. A great nation is peculiarly susceptible to the idea that its power is a sign of God's favor, conferring upon it a special responsibility for other nations—to make them richer and happier and wiser, to remake them, that is, in its own shining image. Power confuses itself with virtue and tends also to take itself for omnipotence (comments made in the 1960s).

FUND RAISING

Shapiro, Joseph H. Nowhere is a man's imagination so fertile as in the discovery of new ways to say no to a man who asks for money.

FUNERALS

Ray, Man. I would like to go to only one funeral, mine.

FUR BEARING ANIMALS

Moore, Mary Tyler. Behind each beautiful wild fur there is an ugly story. It is a brutal, bloody and barbaric story. The animal is not killed—it is tortured. I don't think a fur coat is worth it.

FUR COATS, WRAPS, ETC.

Moore, Mary Tyler. Behind each beautiful wild fur there is an ugly story. It is a brutal, bloody and barbaric story. The animal is not killed—it is tortured. I don't think a fur coat is worth it.

FURNESS, BETTY

Furness, Betty. I'd invest $9 million in Big Mac bonds. It might not really help New York City, but it would not hurt. And if I never saw the money again, what's the difference? I'd still have my $1 million, a figure I can cope with. I would see that some of it got into the hands of a number of people whose problems can be solved with money. I'd try to find one person whose dreams aren't ever going to come true because of lack of money, and I'd pay for those dreams. And then I'd go to Bloomingdale's (in response to 'What would you do with 10 million dollars').

FUTURE

Blair, Eric. If you want a picture of the future, imagine a boot stamping on the human face—forever...and remember that it is forever.

Brecht, Bertolt. Because things are the way they are things will not stay the way they are.

Brown, Edmund Gerald, Jr. We must sacrifice for the future, or else we steal from it.

Buck, Pearl. One faces the future with one's past.

Clarke, Arthur C. The facts of the future can hardly be imagined ab initio by those who are unfamiliar with the fantasies of the past.

Dyson, Freeman. The only certainty in (the) remote future is that radically new things will be happening.

Eiseley, Loren. There is but one way into the future: the technological way.

Fuller, R. Buckminster. The future is a choice between Utopia and oblivion.

Giscard d'Estaing, Valery. The present world crisis is not just a passing perturbation but in reality represents a permanent change. If we examine the major graphic curves that are drawn for the future by the phenomena of our times, you see that all of these curves lead to catastrophe.

Kennedy, Eugene. We not only romanticize the future; we have also made it into a growth industry, a parlor game and a disaster movie all at the same time.

Sanchez, Robert. In looking backward, we must renew our faith in God. In looking forward, we must renew our faith in men.

Warhol, Andy. In the future everybody will be world famous for at least 15 minutes.

GABO, NAUM

Gabo, Naum. Today is the deed.

GABOR, ZSA ZSA

Gabor, Zsa Zsa. I have never hated a man enough to give his diamonds back.

GALLICO, PAUL

Gallico, Paul. In place of great literary fame, I've millions of people who care about what I write and who like me. What the hell more do I want?.

GAMBLING

Anonymous, . All I know is that horses don't bet on people. They would if they knew how much fun it is.

Rozelle, Pete. The world knows no less rational person than a losing bettor (commenting in opposition to efforts to legalize betting on professional football).

GAMES

Harris, Sydney J. The paradox in games is that most games are no fun unless you take them seriously; but when you take them seriously, they cease being games.

GANDHI, INDIRA (NEHRU)

Anonymous (right wing Indian politician), . We are responsible for creating Indira Gandhi. Don't make Indira a demon, we're the culprits—we let the people down. She's the result of us politicians' playing the fool for 25 years and not solving India's problems.

Gandhi, Indira (Nehru). I am one of the sights of Delhi.

Gandhi, Indira (Nehru). I have no recollection of games, children's parties or playing with other children. All my games were political ones—I was, like Joan of Arc, perpetually being burned at the stake.

Gandhi, Indira (Nehru). The people do not care about all that emergency business that is in the newspapers all the time. The poor people are with me. They know that I have always been their friend.

Gandhi, Indira (Nehru). The steps we have taken are to strengthen our democracy (upon suspending civil liberties and imposing press censorship).

Pandit, Vijaya Lakshmi (aunt of Indira Gandhi). The essence of democracy has always been the right to dissent. And it was working in India, though slowly, and perhaps awkwardly. One can't govern simply by clapping into jail everyone who disagrees. Please understand that I'm very proud of Indira. But the good career she has begun is being threatened by all this sorry business of muzzling people and stifling dissent.

GARLAND, JUDY

Garland, Judy. I have gone through hell, I tell you, a hell no one, no person, no man, no beast, not even a fire hydrant could endure.

GARN, JAKE

Garn, Jake. I frankly don't give a damn if a 14-legged bug or the woundfin minnow live or die.

GASTRONOMY

Claiborne, Craig. I think that some people, and I suspect a great number of people, are born with the gustatory equivalent of perfect pitch.

GEMS

Earhart, Amelia. There are two kinds of stones, as everyone knows, one of which rolls.

GENERAL MOTORS CORPORATION

Iacocca, Lee A. This year the public will have a choice, the likes of which it hasn't had in years. The difference between our cars and GM's is like the difference between a four-foot blonde and a seven-foot brunette.

GENERALIZATIONS

Pitman, Keith A. All generalizations are untrue.

GENEROSITY

Disraeli, Benjamin. A man is occasionally thankful when he says 'thank you'.

Skelton, Red. I trust God, my wife, and myself. People take kindness for weakness, and generosity has the form of a sucker.

GENETIC ENGINEERING

Callahan, Daniel. There's no guarantee that high IQ people produce better people or a better society. It is not the retarded kids of the world who produce the wars and destruction.

King, Jonathan. There are tremendous fortunes to be made from this new technology (referring to recombinant DNA 'gene-splitting' experiments), and in this case safety and private profit are incompatible.

GEORGIA—POLITICS AND GOVERNMENT

Young, Andrew. Georgia is more liberal than New York.

GERMANY (FEDERAL REPUBLIC)—FOREIGN RELATIONS

Schmidt, Helmut. We Germans are in the heart of Europe. In any new war, we have everything to lose and nothing to gain.

GERMANY—HISTORY

Gladstone, William Ewart. He (Bismarck) made Germany great and Germans small.

GETTY, JEAN PAUL

Getty, Jean Paul. I suffer no guilt complexes or conscience pangs about my wealth. The Lord may have been disproportionate, but that is how He—or nature, if you like—operates.

Getty, Jean Paul. If you can count your money, you don't have a billion dollars.

GIFTS

Gibbs, Philip. It's better to give than to lend, and it costs about the same.

GILLESPIE, DIZZY

Gillespie, Dizzy. It took me all my life to learn the biggest music lesson of them all—what not to play.

GILMORE, GARY MARK

Gilmore, Gary Mark. Death is the only inescapable, unavoidable, sure thing. We are sentenced to die the day we're born.

Gilmore, Gary Mark. I believe I was given a fair trial. The sentence is proper, and I'm willing to accept it with dignity, like a man (pleading with the Utah Supreme Court to allow him to be executed by a firing squad on schedule).

Gilmore, Gary Mark. You sentenced a man to die—me—and when I accept this most extreme punishment with grace and dignity, the people of Utah want to back down and argue with me about it. You're silly (a note delivered from his death row cell to the Utah State Supreme Court).

GINSBERG, ALLEN

Ginsberg, Allen. I like a varied audience—little old ladies, homosexuals, weirdos.

GIONO, JEAN

Giono, Jean. Reality pushed to its extreme ends in unreality.

GISCARD D'ESTAING, VALERY

Giroud, Francoise. If an atom bomb fell on France, (Valery Giscard d'Estaing) would be there to congratulate himself that there had not been two.

GISH, LILLIAN

Gish, Lillian. I've had the best life of anyone I know, or knew, Dear. And I knew some amazing people.

GIULINI, CARLO MARIA

Giulini, Carlo Maria. I always think I am a very small man. When I shave myself, I look in the mirror and see behind me Beethoven and Brahms.

GIVENCHY, HUBERT DE

Givenchy, Hubert De. After I open a collection and see people trying on my clothes and treating them roughly, I suffer. My dresses are like my family.

THE GLASS MENAGERIE (THEATRICAL PRODUCTION)

Williams, Tennessee. They teach it (The Glass Menagerie) in college now, and everybody approaches it as though it were a place of worship. Frankly, I fall asleep at times.

GLEASON, JACKIE

Dann, Mike. (Jackie) Gleason's one of the most versatile people in the business. He's so brilliant, he's always depressed and bored. Maybe that's why he never seemed to enjoy performing.

Gleason, Jackie. I drank because it removed the warts and blemishes. Not from me but from the people I associated with. It sort of dimmed the lights.

GOD

Allen, Woody. The universe is merely a fleeting idea in God's mind—and a pretty uncomfortable thought, particularly if you've just made a down payment on a home.

Barth, John. God was a pretty good novelist; the only trouble was that He was a realist.

Beauvoir, Simone De. I cannot be angry at God, in whom I do not believe.

Bryant, Anita. God says that someone who practices homosexuality shall not inherit the Kingdom of God. God is very plain on that.

Bryant, Anita. If homosexuality were the normal way, God would have made Adam and Bruce.

Caddell, Patrick. Clearly, God is a Democrat.

Court, Margaret. I will not play any more tournament tennis. If I had been meant to play tennis again, God would have led me to it (commenting upon her permanent retirement from tennis).

Eckhart, Johannes. God becomes and disbecomes.

Einstein, Albert. God may be subtle, but He isn't mean.

Fuller, R. Buckminster. Sometimes I think we're alone. Sometimes I think we're not. In either case, the thought is quite staggering.

Gallup, George. I could prove God statistically.

King, Martin Luther, Jr. I'm not fearing any man. Mine eyes have seen the glory of the coming of the Lord.

Knight, Damon. If there is a universal mind, must it be sane?.

Landry, Tom. God doesn't make any losers.

Lebowitz, Fran. If God had meant for everything to happen at once, he would not have invented desk calendars.

Lewis, C. S. A young man who wishes to remain a sound atheist cannot be too careful of his reading. God is, if I may say it, very unscrupulous.

Orlans, Harold. Logic is a game men play as cats play with balls of string, whereas reality is a game the gods play with us.

Sanchez, Robert. In looking backward, we must renew our faith in God. In looking forward, we must renew our faith in men.

Sandburg, Carl. A baby is God's opinion that the world should go on.

Shaffer, Floyd. I believe it would be healthier if the church could laugh because I believe that God laughs.

Tanner, Jack. When God created the world, He said it was good. That was His second mistake.

Tomlin, Lily. Why is it when we talk to God, we're said to be praying, but when God talks to us, we're schizophrenic?.

Voznesensky, Andrei. When Man put on clothes for the first time, he challenged the Lord and became His equal.

White, Theodore. If you go back through 2000 years, I guess luck, Marx, and God have made history, the three of them together.

GOEBBELS, JOSEPH

Goebbels, Joseph. Nothing is easier than leading the people on a leash. I just hold up a dazzling campaign poster and they jump through it.

Goebbels, Joseph. The Jews are re-emerging. Anyone in a position to do so should kill Jews off like rats. In Germany, thank God, we have already done a fairly complete job. I trust that the world will take its cue from this (from his diary, 1945).

GOELET, ROBERT G.

Goelet, Robert G. I can't think of anything I'd rather be doing than serving as president of the museum. I have a personal weakness for fish and birds; I'm nuts for fossils, and I have a healthy respect for poisonous snakes.

GOLD

Henshaw, Paul C. Gold is how you survive when everything else is down the drain.

GOLDWATER, BARRY MORRIS

Goldwater, Barry Morris. He let this country down, he let his party down. And that's the last time I want to talk about Nixon, ever (summarizing his feelings about Richard Nixon).

Goldwater, Barry Morris. I don't care if I'm called a Democrat or a Republican as long as I'm in bed with people of the same thinking.

Goldwater, Barry Morris. I don't object to a woman doing anything in combat as long as she gets home in time to cook dinner.

Goldwater, Barry Morris. I think there are some things which we don't want to know. Nothing could make the Soviets happier than to see our wonderful intelligence system destroyed (in suggesting that Congressional probes of the CIA be called off).

Goldwater, Barry Morris. This is a great country where anybody can grow up to be President— except me.

Rockefeller, Nelson Aldrich. The best part about being Vice President is presiding over the Senate. Where else could I have Barry Goldwater addressing me as 'Mr. President?'.

GOLDWIN, ROBERT

Goldwin, Robert. The cause I push is a kind of elevated common sense.

GOLDWYN, SAMUEL

Goldwyn, Samuel. If ya wanna send a message, call Western Union.

GOLF

Carter, Don. One of the advantages bowling has over golf is that you seldom lose a bowling ball.

Trevino, Lee. Pressure is playing for ten dollars when you don't have a dime in your pocket.

GOODMAN, BENNY

Goodman, Benny. Everything I own, whatever I have accomplished, all that I am, really, I owe to music.

GOODWIN, RICHARD N.

Moyers, Bill D. Dick Goodwin was no saint, not close, but if there's a hereafter, I'd rather spend it with Goodwin than with Gabriel.

GOSSIP

Dempster, Nigel. If you can't take it (gossip), then don't give it.

Korda, Michael. Gossip, unlike river water, flows both ways.

Lear, Amanda. I hate to spread rumors, but what else can you do with them.

Lilly, Doris. Gossip and manure are only good for one thing—and that's spreading. Gossip doesn't mean a damn thing unless you spread it around.

Seib, Charles. The pettiness and unfairness of gossip masquerading as news is one reason the Washington press is seen by many Americans as vindictive, destructive and often irrelevant.

Wilde, Oscar. History is gossip but scandal is gossip made tedious by morality.

GOVERNMENT

Bismarck, Otto, fuerst von. The less people know about how sausages and laws are made, the better they'll sleep at night.

Jay, Peter. One of the daunting things in the modern world is that the management of this planet would be mind-boggling even if there were only one philosopher-king.

GOVERNMENT AND THE PRESS

Alsop, Joseph. I'm proud they (CIA) asked me (to aid them) and proud to have done it. The notion that a newspaperman doesn't have a duty to his country is perfect balls.

Anderson, Jack. The founding fathers intended us to be watchdogs, not lapdogs.

Aspin, Les. It's a kind of mongoose-cobra relationship (about the press and the CIA).

Chiles, Lawton M., Jr. Half of the reporters in town are looking on you as a Pulitzer Prize to be won (about being a senator).

Cline, Ray S. The only unrestricted intelligence organization in this country is the American press.

Fulbright, James William. If once the press was excessively orthodox and unquestioning of Government policy, it has now become almost sweepingly iconoclastic.

Nessen, Ron. Press conferences force more policy decisions than anything else.

Nixon, Richard Milhous. When news is concerned, nobody in the press is a friend—they are all enemies.

GOVERNMENT AND THE PRESS—GREAT BRITAIN

Knight, Andrew (Editor of The Economist, London). We are a government of opposition, no matter who is in power.

GOVERNMENT EMPLOYEES

Strauss, Robert S. Everybody in government is like a bunch of ants on a log floating down a river. Each one thinks he is guiding the log, but it's really just going with the flow.

GOVERNMENT SPENDING POLICY

Jarvis, Howard. The only way to cut government spending is not to give them the money to spend in the first place.

GOVERNMENTAL INVESTIGATIONS

Mankiewicz, Frank Fabian. The Rockefeller report was the first report that was a smear and whitewash at the same time.

GOVERNORS

Brown, Edmund Gerald, Jr. The power of the executive is like a chess game; there are very few moves that one can make.

GRABLE, BETTY

Grable, Betty. There are only two reasons for my success, and I'm standing on them.

GRAHAM, BILLY

Anonymous (Baptist minister), . To a lot of churchgoing folks in this country, Billy Graham has become nothing less than the nearest thing to Jesus on this earth. He's sort of like Christ's American son.

Graham, Billy. I believe I have demonic forces opposed to me wherever I preach.

Graham, Billy. Nixon in my judgement was a true intellectual.

Graham, Billy. The pressures of being a well-known clergyman are unbelievable, and I'd like to escape to heaven if I could.

Stapleton, Ruth Carter. I am not going to be the Billy Graham of the Carter administration.

GRAHAM, MARTHA

Graham, Martha. Dance is my passion—it's all I really know besides love; a little of both.

GRAND JURY

Campbell, William J. The grand jury is the total captive of the prosecutor, who, if he is candid, will concede that he can indict anybody, at any time, for almost anything, before any grand jury.

GRANDMOTHERS

Rand, Sally. What in heaven's name is so strange about a grandmother dancing nude? I bet lots of grandmothers do it.

GRANT, CARY

Grant, Cary. My formula for living is quite simple. I get up in the morning and go to bed at night. In between times, I occupy myself as best I can.

GRASSO, ELLA

Grasso, Ella. In Connecticut, I'm just an old shoe (describing how she was elected Governor of Connecticut).

GRATITUDE

Lindsay, John Vliet. If you want gratitude, get yourself a dog.

GRAZIANO, ROCKY

Graziano, Rocky. The singin's easy. Memorizin' the words is hard (upon his New York City night club singing debut).

GREAT BRITAIN—DESCRIPTION

Baldwin, James. The range (and rein) of accents on that damp little island make England coherent for the English and totally incomprehensible for everyone else.

Goldsmith, James. We (British) have reached the state where the private sector is that part of the economy the Government controls and the public sector is the part that nobody controls.

GREAT BRITAIN—ECONOMIC CONDITIONS

Thatcher, Margaret Hilda. You cannot have national welfare before someone has created national wealth.

GREAT BRITAIN—ECONOMIC POLICY

Healey, Denis. Mrs. Thatcher is doing for monetarism what the Boston Strangler did for door-to-door salesmen.

GREAT BRITAIN—FOREIGN POLICY

Thatcher, Margaret Hilda. Foreign policy is simply a matter of national self-interest.

GREAT BRITAIN—FOREIGN POLICY—RHODESIA

Thatcher, Margaret Hilda. The British government is wholly committed to genuine black majority rule in Rhodesia.

GREAT BRITAIN—FOREIGN RELATIONS

Macmillan, Harold. A foreign secretary is forever poised between a cliche and an indiscretion.

GREAT BRITAIN—POLITICS AND GOVERNMENT

Howe, Sir Geoffrey. Finance must determine expenditure; expenditure must not determine finance.

Jay, Peter. As a journalist, I have sat for 10 years listening to government spokesmen beating the drum, justifying the unjustifiable, explaining the inexplicable, defending the indefensible. They were doing their jobs, but you could feel the atmosphere of sorrowful skepticism rising.

Thatcher, Margaret Hilda. Britain's progress toward socialism has been an alternation of two steps forward with half a step back.

Thatcher, Margaret Hilda. I never read books.

Thatcher, Margaret Hilda. If a Tory does not believe that private property is one of the main bulwarks of individual freedom, then he had better become a socialist and have done with it.

Thatcher, Margaret Hilda. It is important not to be so obsessed with yesterday's danger that we fail to detect today's.

Thatcher, Margaret Hilda. No one would remember the Good Samaritan if he'd only had good intentions. He had money as well.

Thatcher, Margaret Hilda. We are not short of summits. The only thing we are short of is the results from summits.

Thatcher, Margaret Hilda. What Britain needs is an iron lady.

Wilson, Harold. Once I leave, I leave. I am not going to speak to the man on the bridge, and I am not going to spit on the deck (upon his resignation as Prime Minister of Great Britain).

GREAT BRITAIN—POWER RESOURCES

Davies, Gavin. Like even the best wonder drug, North Sea oil has side effects we (British) don't like.

GREAT BRITAIN—SOCIAL LIFE AND CUSTOMS

Balanchine, George. In England you have to be dignified; if you are awake it is already vulgar.

GREECE—POLITICS AND GOVERNMENT

Caramanlis, Constantine. So we Greeks have been from ancient times: we are skillful at making idols, not that we may worship them, but that we may have the pleasure of destroying them.

GREENE, GAEL

Breslin, Jimmy. If this is what happens when you let them out of the kitchen, I'm all for it (commenting on Gael Greene's first novel Blue Skies, No Candy).

GREENE, GRAHAM

O'Connor, Flannery. What (Graham Greene) does, I think, is try to make religion respectable to the modern unbeliever by making it seedy.

GREENSPAN, ALAN

Greenspan, Alan. When I met Ayn Rand, I was a free enterpriser in the Adam Smith sense, impressed with the theoretical structure and efficiency of markets. What she did was to make me see that capitalism is not only efficient and practical, but also moral.

GREER, GERMAINE

Greer, Germaine. Everyone I know is either married or dotty.

Greer, Germaine. I love men like some people like good food or wine.

GROPPI, JAMES E.

Groppi, James E. Right now, the bus will be my church and the people who board it my parishioners (commenting on his status as a bus driver in Milwaukee after his excommunication from the Catholic Church).

GUCCI (DEPARTMENT STORE)

Gucci, Aldo. We are not businessmen, we are poets.

GUGGENHEIM, PEGGY

Guggenheim, Peggy. I don't like art today, I think it has gone to hell.

GUILT

Beckett, Samuel. There's man all over for you, blaming his boots for the faults of his feet.

Jong, Erica. You don't have to beat a woman if you can make her feel guilty.

Smith, Patti. Jesus died for somebody's sins but not mine.

GUINNESS, SIR ALEC

Bujold, Genevieve. Caesar was Cleopatra's guru and Guinness was mine.

GURNEY, EDWARD JOHN

Gurney, Edward John. Everybody who knows me knows I have a very poor memory.

Gurney, Edward John. I have a feeling of great relief that this long ordeal is finally over, a feeling of great satisfaction that we've beaten these mean, vicious people from the Government. They destroyed a United States Senator, blackened my name and besmirched my character (commenting on his acquittal from the last charge against him in a political shakedown case).

GUTHRIE, ARLO

Guthrie, Arlo. The difference between Anita Bryant and me may be that she definitely feels that God is on her side, and I have to keep questioning whether I'm on His (upon becoming a Franciscan lay brother).

Guthrie, Arlo. The world has shown me what it has to offer...It's a nice plce to visit, but I wouldn't want to live there.

HABIT

Maugham, William Somerset. The unfortunate thing about this world is that good habits are so much easier to get out of than bad ones.

HACKMAN, GENE

Shepherd, Cybill. If you kept seeing Robert Redford stark naked on the screen, would he be a superstar today? No way. Or Gene Hackman showing everything? Their million dollar days would be over. I want to be in a movie where all the men take their clothes off and I don't.

HAGGARD, MERLE

Haggard, Merle. I was born the running kind, with leaving always on my mind.

HAIG, ALEXANDER M

Kissinger, Henry Alfred. One thing I don't want around me is a military intellectual. I don't have to worry about you on that score (to Alexander Haig).

HAIR—CARE

Polykoff, Shirley. If I've only one life, let me live it as a blonde! (advertising slogan).

HAITI—ECONOMIC CONDITIONS

Darbouze, Father, . Dying of hunger and being executed by the government are the same thing.

HAITI—POLITICS AND GOVERNMENT

Darbouze, Father, . Dying of hunger and being executed by the government are the same thing.

HALDEMAN, HARRY ROBBINS

Haldeman, Harry Robbins. I'll approve of whatever will work and am concerned with results—not methods.

HALEY, JACK

Haley, Jack. I don't believe there's no business like show business.

HAMBURGERS

Smith, Donald N (President of Burger King). The individual choice of garnishment of a burger can be an important point to the consumer in this day when individualism, in my mind, is an increasingly important thing to people.

HAPPINESS

Clemens, Samuel Langhorne. The best way to cheer yourself up is to try to cheer somebody else up.

Ephron, Nora. We have lived in an era when happiness was a warm puppy, and the era when happiness was a dry martini, and now we have come to an era when happiness is knowing what your uterus looks like.

Gunther, John. All happiness depends on a leisurely breakfast.

Humphrey, Hubert Horatio. Happiness is contagious, just exactly like being miserable. People have to believe that they can do better. They've got to know that there's somebody that wants to help and work with them, somebody that hasn't tossed in the towel.

Kruger, James T. (South African Minister of Justice). It remains a fact that a happy person cannot be a communist (asking for reform of his country's race laws).

Rubinstein, Artur. Most people ask for happiness on condition. Happiness can only be felt if you don't set any condition.

HARDING, WARREN GAMALIEL

Harding, Warren Gamaliel. Our most dangerous tendency is to expect too much of government, and at the same time to do for it too little (inaugural address—1921).

HARRIMAN, AVERELL

Harriman, Averell. I've had much more fun out of life since I became a Democrat.

Harriman, Averell. The Russians are not nuts, they are not crazy people, they're not Hitler. But they are trying to dominate the world by their ideology and we are killing the one instrument which we have to fight that idealogy, the CIA.

HARRIS, FRED

Harris, Fred. If I had it to do over I would have started out the way I wound up, as more of an iconoclast. There was a feeling when I went to the Senate that if you want to have any influence you had to go along. The truth is just the opposite of that.

Harris, Fred. The basic issue in 1976 is privilege. It's time to take the rich off welfare.

Harris, Fred. You couldn't call it victory because we didn't run that well. But we ran just well enough to keep going so it really wasn't defeat. We didn't know what to call it and we just decided to call it quits (commenting on his decision to end his bid for the Democratic nomination for President).

Troy, Frosty. He's George Wallace without racism (about Fred Harris).

HARRIS, PATRICIA ROBERTS

Harris, Patricia Roberts. If my life has had any meaning at all, it is that those who start out as outcasts can wind up as being part of the system. Maybe others can forget what it was like to be excluded from the dining rooms in this very building, Senator, but I shall not forget (testifying before the Senate Committee on her scheduled nomination for Secretary of Housing and Urban Development).

HARRISON, REX

Harrison, Elizabeth (former wife of Rex Harrison). Rex is the only man in the world who would disdainfully send back the wine in his own home.

HARVARD UNIVERSITY. SCHOOL OF LAW

Morgan, Charles, Jr. If Moses had gone to Harvard Law School and spent three years working on the Hill, he would have written the Ten Commandments with three exceptions and a savings clause.

HATE

Connolly, Cyril. Nothing dates like hate.

Davis, Bette. You've got to know someone pretty well to hate them.

Myerson, Bess. You can't be beautiful and hate.

HAUPTMANN, BRUNO RICHARD

Hauptmann, Bruno Richard. I have said it all, I am innocent. There is nothing else I could tell.

HAYAKAWA, SAMUEL ICHIYE

Hayakawa, Samuel Ichiye. I lust after women in my heart every hour on the hour. But being so busy in campaigning, I have to settle for that.

HAYDEN, THOMAS

Hayden, Thomas. During the 1960s, we fought the pigs. Now we fight the high price of bacon.

Hayden, Thomas. I don't believe that any defense contract ought to be cut in the face of mass unemployment.

Hayden, Thomas. If it weren't for the Bill of Rights people like me would be in jail instead of running for office (commenting on his bid for the Senate).

Hayden, Thomas. The radicalism of the '60's became the fascism of the '70's (responding to heckling from left-wing radicals during a speech on his current campaign for U.S. Senator).

HEARST, PATRICIA CAMPBELL

Hearst, Patricia Campbell. I was sick of the middle-class life I was leading. The SLA members seemed to have some purpose to their lives.

Hearst, Patricia Campbell. I'd really like to travel again—anywhere but Italy. There's too much kidnapping there.

Jimenez, Janey. Just like a bull in the correo, Patty (Hearst) never really had a chance. She was doomed from the beginning.

Johnson, Al (Patricia Hearst's defense attorney). I remember when the Chowchilla kidnapping occurred. Patty (Hearst) said she wondered how long it would take the FBI to indict the 26 children for the crime.

Reich, Walter. If brainwashing is accepted as a defense, we're in for a brainwashing ourselves in regard to our concept of guilt and innocence (commenting on F. Lee Bailey's defense of Patricia Hearst).

Welles, Orson. Patty Hearst is the central victim of our time...the best human story in the last thirty years—better than Kane.

HEATH, EDWARD

Heath, Edward. I started out studying music but very quickly went downhill and into politics.

HEFNER, HUGH MARSTON

Greene, Bob. Indeed, Hugh Hefner is beginning to seem more and more like everyone's kindly and slightly bewildered uncle.

Hefner, Hugh Marston. I'm not primarily an entrepreneurial businessman. I'm primarily a playboy philosopher.

HEIDE, WILMA SCOTT

Heide, Wilma Scott. I do not refer to myself as a housewife for the reason that I did not marry a house.

HEIDEGGER, MARTIN

Heidegger, Martin. He who does not know what homesickness is, cannot philosophize.

HELION, JEAN

Helion, Jean (French painter). I looked through my studio window and I found that the outside world was more beautiful than my picture.

HELL

Friedman, Milton. In this day and age, we need to revise the old saying to read, Hell hath no fury like a bureaucrat scorned.

Hales, E. E. Y. Hell is where you are free to be yourself, and nothing but yourself (commenting in his novel Chariot of Fire).

HELLER, JOSEPH

Heller, Joseph. If I could be clever on demand, I'd still be in advertising.

Puzo, Mario. I never knew anybody so determined to be unhappy (about Joseph Heller).

HELLMAN, LILLIAN

Hellman, Lillian. I cannot and will not cut my conscience to fit this year's fashions (referring to the activities of the House Un-American Activities Committee).

Hellman, Lillian. If I had to give young writers advice, I would say, Don't listen to writers talking about writing or about themselves.

HELM, LEVON

Helm, Levon. Music is medicine, and if the doctor is going to make house calls, he better know how to play.

HELMS, JESSE

Helms, Jesse. If Environmental Action had its way, the American people would starve and freeze to death in the dark.

HELMS, RICHARD MCGARRAH

Helms, Richard McGarrah. If I ever do decide to talk, there are going to be some very embarrassed people in this town, you can bet on that (commenting after testifying to the Watergate Committee on CIA involvement in domestic intelligence operations).

HEMINGWAY, ERNEST

Fitzgerald, F. Scott. I talk with the authority of failure—Ernest (Hemingway) with the authority of success.

Mailer, Norman. Hemingway knew in advance, with a fine sense of timing, that he would have to campaign for himself, that the best tactic to hide the lockjaw of his shrinking genius was to become the personality of our time.

Steinbeck, John. Competing with Hemingway isn't my idea of good business.

Thomas, Bob. Hemingway had a very strong opinion that writers should not stay in journalism too long. He felt it damaged your sensitivity. I suspect he is right.

HEMINGWAY, MARGAUX

Hemingway, Margaux. I love men's clothes, but that doesn't make me a weirdo.

HEMINGWAY, MARY

Hemingway, Mary. I'm too old to waste my time being sentimental.

HEROES

Caputo, Philip J. The impetus or the impulse that makes people heroic in wars is the very thing that can make them monsters.

Einstein, Albert. The world needs heroes and it's better they be harmless men like me than villains like Hitler.

Emerson, Ralph Waldo. Every hero becomes a bore at last.

Laughlin, Tom. The youth of this country have only two heroes: Ralph Nader and Billy Jack.

McCarthy, Mary. It really takes a hero to live any kind of spiritual life without religious belief.

Price, Reynolds. The classical world decided wisely that any human accorded the honors of a hero must be, above all, dead.

HEROIN

Johnson, Sterling. In the heroin business, the Mexicans are the short-order cooks. The French are the chefs.

Rappolt, Richard T. It's easier to get people off of heroin than coffee.

HIGH SCHOOLS

Zappa, Frank. High school isn't a time and a place. It's a state of mind.

HINCKLE, WARREN

Hinckle, Warren. I never know what I am going to do. That's why I'm so valuable (upon the cessation of City of San Francisco Magazine which he edited).

HINDSIGHT

Kojak, Theo. Hindsight is the only exact science.

HIPPIES

Leary, Timothy. I don't like hippies. I don't like communes. I despise heroin. I've never participated in an orgy. It may ruin my reputation, but I'm particularly monogamous.

Leary, Timothy. Successful hippies are on their way to running this country.

Nash, Graham. Serious musicians who read music don't understand what goes on with hippies.

Nelson, Willie. To me, a hippie is a redneck with hair, and a redneck is a hippie with his hair cut off. It's not so much a difference in hair as attitude as to whether a guy is hip or not hip, whether he'd rather talk to you or fight you.

HISTORIANS

Anonymous, . The easiest way to change history is to become a historian.

Braudel, Fernand (French historian). A historian never judges. He is not God. The power the historian has is to make the dead live. It is a triumph over death.

HISTORY

Adenauer, Konrad. History is the sum total of the things that could have been avoided.

Cousins, Norman. History is an accumulation of error.

Faulkner, William. The past is never dead; it is not even past.

Ford, Henry. History is more or less bunk.

Hegel, Georg Wilhelm Friedrich. Peoples and governments have never learned anything from history, or acted on principles deductible from it.

Jefferson, Thomas. I like the dreams of the future better than the history of the past.

K'ang-Hsi, 1654-1722 (Chinese emperor), . In history one needs the facts, not hollow words or literary elegance.

Kelley, Ken. But history is nothing but a chronology of oppressors oppressing the oppressed.

McLuhan, Marshall. Only the vanquished remember history.

Malinowski, Bronislaw. Every historical change creates its mythology.

Nader, Ralph. I'll tell you what the real problem is. We ask people to think, instead of asking them to believe. And history has always gone to those who ask people to believe.

Schlesinger, Arthur, Jr. History can be a high-risk occupation.

West, Rebecca. There are jungles of people, and jungles of facts—which make it harder to recognize the great things when they do happen.

White, Theodore. If you go back through 2000 years, I guess luck, Marx, and God have made history, the three of them together.

Wilde, Oscar. History is gossip but scandal is gossip made tedious by morality.

Wilde, Oscar. The one duty we owe to history is to rewrite it.

HITCHCOCK, ALFRED JOSEPH

Hitchcock, Alfred Joseph. Most people make mystery films. I don't. I make films of suspense. A surprise in a film takes 10 seconds, suspense takes up an hour.

Hitchcock, Alfred Joseph. Well, I think it's below one's dignity to be an actor (commenting on why he will not appear in films of other directors).

Truffaut, Francois. (Alfred Hitchock) considers documentary and reportage the two inherent enemies of the cinema of fiction.

HITCHENS, IVON

Hitchens, Ivon. My pictures are painted to be listened to.

HITLER, ADOLF

Amin Dada, Idi. Hitler was right about the Jews, because the Israelis are not working in the interests of the people of the world, and that is why they burned the Israelis alive with gas in the soil of Germany.

Blair, Eric. One feels, as with Napoleon, that he is fighting against destiny, that he can't win, and yet that he somehow deserves to. (writing in the *New English Weekly,* March 21, 1940).

Wagner, Winifred. If Hitler walked through the door today, I would be just as glad and happy to see and have him here as ever.

HOCHMAN, SANDRA

Hochman, Sandra. I'd rather be hung from clotheslines and washed in laundromats than read in libraries (commenting on her poetry to be printed on clothing and bedsheets).

HOCKEY

Shero, Fred. We know that hockey is where we live, where we can best meet and overcome pain and wrong and death. Life is just a place where we spend time between games.

HOCKEY—VIOLENCE

Hull, Bobby. The idiot owners, the incompetent coaches, the inept players are dragging the game into the mud. They're destroying it with their senseless violence. The game is no pleasure anymore, it's an ordeal (about hockey).

HOCKNEY, DAVID

Hockney, David. I'm a Puritan at heart. I also think I'm the world's most overrated, overpaid artist.

HOFFA, JAMES RIDDLE

Anonymous (Teamster Union Member), . Look at it this way: Our contract expires in April of 1976, right? If Jimmy Hoffa were running for election against Fitzsimmons in July, 1976, Fitzsimmons would have to bust his tail to negotiate a good contract for us, right? With Jimmy Hoffa gone, he don't have to work so hard, does he?.

Fitzsimmons, Frank E. When Hoffa left here (for prison) he said he'd be back in 90 days. That's Hoffa. His ego was as big as this floor.

Hoffa, James Riddle. I don't cheat nobody. I don't lie about nobody. I don't frame nobody. I don't talk bad about people. If I do, I tell 'em. So what the hell's people gonna try to kill me for?.

Hoffa, James Riddle. The only guy who needs a bodyguard is a liar, a cheat, a guy who betrays friendship.

HOFFER, ERIC

Hoffer, Eric. I hang onto my prejudices. They are the testicles of my mind.

Hoffer, Eric. I was never in a hurry in my life. I could hang on to an idea for years, chew on a sentence for months, and I had time to catch fleeting insights.

HOFFMAN, ABBIE

Hoffman, Abbie. It's hard to convince a girl's parents that a revolutionary fugitive with a vasectomy is a good deal.

Hoffman, Abbie. I've adopted a much more orthodox Communist view. I used to say I was an anarchist or maybe a hedonistic Communist, but around the world people understand the force that's fighting for them is Communism. It means the end of sex, love, dope, art, individuality and doing things you want to do.

HOLIDAYS

King, Coretta Scott. There are so many monuments to war, so many testaments to sorrow, I wish America—through a national holiday and the center—would help build one monument of peace (referring to the Dr. Martin Luther King, Jr. Center for Social Change).

HOLLYWOOD, CALIFORNIA

Dunne, John Gregory. Hollywood is the only place where you fail upwards.

Hines, Jack, Jr. (restaurant cashier). Hollywood is the sinkhole of Los Angeles.

Lear, Norman. When I give advice to rising starlets I say, just remember, Hollywood is the land of the definite maybe.

Pisier, Marie-France. People wear resort clothes but actually Hollywood is an enormous factory. People work ten times harder than anywhere else.

Prinze, Freddie. Hollywood is one big whore. It breeds decadence.

Tartikoff, Brandon. Hollywood is like Harvard. Once you're accepted, you can't flunk out.

HOLTZ, LOU

Holtz, Lou. God did not put Lou Holtz on this earth to coach pro football (announcing his resignation as the coach of the New York Jets).

HOLY SPIRIT ASSOCIATION FOR THE UNIFICATION OF WORLD CHRISTIANITY

Moon, Sun Myung. Are Americans that foolish? Can they really be brainwashed by Rev. Moon, a Korean? I know your answer is no. My answer is no, too. No American is so foolish (commenting before congressmen on charges that the Korean evangelist has mind control over young people and forces them to maintain him in luxury).

Moon, Sun Myung. Kings and queens and heads of state will someday bow at my feet. I will conquer and subjugate the world.

HOME

Frost, Robert. Home is the place where when you have to go there, they have to take you in.

HOMOSEXUALITY

Beauvoir, Simone De. In itself, homosexuality is as limiting as heterosexuality: the ideal should be to be capable of loving a woman or a man; either, a human being, without feeling fear, restraint, or obligation.

Bogart, Humphrey (attributed by Lauren Bacall). I think you (Noel Coward) are wonderful and charming, and if I should ever change from liking girls better, you would be my first thought.

Bryant, Anita. God says that someone who practices homosexuality shall not inherit the Kingdom of God. God is very plain on that.

Bryant, Anita. If homosexuality were the normal way, God would have made Adam and Bruce.

Burton, Richard. I was a homosexual once but not for long. It didn't work, so I gave it up.

Capote, Truman. I say I'm a homosexual who has had heterosexual experiences.

Evans, Dale. I cannot sit in judgment of anyone. I have been forgiven a great deal myself. But there are some things that God just does not condone—and homosexuality is just one of them. It says so many times in the Bible.

Hayakawa, Samuel Ichiye. I guess they're entitled to remain as sick as they like as long as they like (commenting on homosexuals).

Loos, Anita. Gentlemen don't prefer blondes. If I were writing that book today, I'd call it 'Gentlemen Prefer Gentlemen'.

Matlovich, Leonard P. They gave me a medal for killing two men and discharged me for loving one.

Schlesinger, Arthur, Jr. 'Gay' used to be one of the most agreeable words in the language. Its appropriation by a notably morose group is an act of piracy.

HOMOSEXUALS—CIVIL RIGHTS

Bryant, Anita. If gays are granted rights, next we'll have to give rights to prostitutes and to people who sleep with St. Bernards and to nailbiters.

HOMOSEXUALS—CIVIL RIGHTS—CALIFORNIA

Briggs, John. When it comes to politics, anything is fair.

HOMOSEXUALS—CIVIL RIGHTS—MIAMI

Bryant, Anita. Heaven knows, I wouldn't want to deny anyone their human rights, but I'm not denying their right to be human (commenting on her fight against homosexual rights in Miami).

HONESTY

Cameron, Simon. An honest politician is one who, when he is bought, will stay bought.

Hunt, Everette Howard. No one is entitled to the truth.

Jennings, Waylon. Honesty is something you can't wear out.

Kubrick, Stanley. All you can do is either pose questions or make truthful observations about human behavior. The only morality is not to be dishonest.

McNulty, Franklin L. With adequate integrity, guts can be located.

HOOVER, JOHN EDGAR

Hoover, John Edgar. The cure for crime is not the electric chair but the high chair.

Johnson, Lyndon Baines. I'd druther have him (J. Edgar Hoover) inside the tent pissin' out than outside pissin' in.

Zimbalist, Efrem, Jr. When the lion (J. Edgar Hoover) dies, the rats come out.

HOPE

Borges, Jorge Luis. America is still the best hope. But the Americans themselves will have to be the best hope too.

Jenkins, Robin. It is not the goodness of saints that makes us feel there is hope for humanity: it is the goodness of obscure men.

Spark, Muriel. People who have hope are sad because they are so often disappointed.

Wilkins, Roy. If I weren't hopeful, I might as well shoot myself. Hope is the thing the NAACP has brought in its 66 years.

HOPE, BOB

Hope, Bob. I don't think I'd do anything if it were a sacrifice.

HOROWITZ, VLADIMIR

Horowitz, Vladimir. You can't be serious 24 hours a day. You have to take half an hour or an hour a day to be childish.

HOSPITALITY

Capone, Alphonse. When I sell liquor, it's called bootlegging; when my patrons serve it on silver trays on Lake Shore Drive, it's called hospitality.

HOSPITALS

Cousins, Norman. A hospital is no place for a person who is seriously ill.

Thomson, Campbell. If it ever was true that a hospital was a charity organization, it no longer is true.

HOUSE DECORATION

Stone, Richard. One privilege of home ownership is the right to have lousy taste and display it.

HOUSTON

Graham, Billy. Most Houstonians will spend eternity in Hell.

Wright, Frank Lloyd. Houston is an example of what can happen when architecture catches a venereal disease.

HOWAR, BARBARA

Howar, Barbara. I'm now fast approaching the age when a woman doesn't fan herself in public.

HUDSON, ROCK

Hudson, Rock. Inside this hulk you see before you is a frustrated song-and-dance man just screaming to get out.

HUGHES, HOWARD ROBARD

Kane, Walter. It is tragic that Howard Hughes had to die to prove that he was alive.

HULL, MA

Hull, Ma. When God sees fit to take me, I want him to take me providing my own way.

HUMOR

Feldman, Marty. Humor is like sex. Those who do it don't talk about it.

Landon, Melville. Levity is the soul of wit.

Rogers, Will. Everything is funny as long as it is happening to somebody else.

White, E. B. Humor can be dissected, as a frog can, but the thing dies in the process and the innards are discouraging to any but the pure scientific mind.

Wilde, Oscar. Nothing spoils romance so much as a sense of humor in a woman.

HUMPHREY, HUBERT HORATIO

Carter, James Earl. (Hubert Humphrey) has been an inspiration and a conscience to us all. His greatest personal attribute was that he really knew how to love.

Dutton, Fred. George Wallace is a more truly democratic candidate than Ford, Humphrey or Jackson. He wants everyone to vote, while they hope to narrow down the voting public.

Humphrey, Hubert Horatio. A man with no tears is a man with no heart.

Humphrey, Hubert Horatio. I guess maybe I am the freest man I have ever been in my life. I seek nothing. I want nothing except one thing: I am going to tell it like it is..

Humphrey, Hubert Horatio. I have no intention to enter any primaries; I will enter no primaries. I am not a candidate for president. I authorize no group to work in my behalf.

Humphrey, Hubert Horatio. I would rather be honestly wrong than to be a deliberate hypocrite.

Humphrey, Hubert Horatio. If I believe in something, I will fight for it with all I have. But I do not demand all or nothing. I would rather get something than nothing. Professional liberals want glory in defeat. The hardest job for a politician today is to have the courage to be moderate.

Humphrey, Hubert Horatio. Life was not meant to be endured, but enjoyed.

Humphrey, Hubert Horatio. One thing I don't need at this stage of my life is to be ridiculous, so I'm not going to do it (explaining his decision not to enter the New Jersey primary).

Humphrey, Hubert Horatio. The greatest gift of life is friendship and I have received it.

Lisagor, Peter. Hubert Humphrey could have gotten a better deal in bankruptcy court (about the 1968 Democratic National Convention).

HUNGER—UNITED STATES

Moynihan, Daniel Patrick. The only reason people in America are starving is because they are idiots, and if they are idiots they deserve to.

HUNT, EVERETTE HOWARD

Hunt, Everette Howard. No one is entitled to the truth.

HUNT, HAROLDSON LAFAYETTE

Hunt, Haroldson Lafayette. Money is just something to make bookkeeping convenient.

HUNTER, ALBERTA

Blake, Eubie. When she (Alberta Hunter) sang the blues, you felt so sorry for her you would want to kill the guy she was singing about.

HUSBANDS

Wilde, Oscar. American women seek in their husbands a perfection which English women seek only in their butlers.

HUSTLER (PERIODICAL)

Ephron, Nora. For those of us who believe that Hustler is a truly obscene magazine, it is a difficult moment. It is one of those cases that makes you search for some loophole (commenting on the Hustler pornography case).

Flynt, Larry. If I'm guilty of anything it's bad taste. I don't think people ought to be put in jail for having bad taste.

Flynt, Larry. We are genuine entertainment with no pretensions. We have proved that barnyard humor has a market appeal.

Steinem, Gloria. If a magazine were published with similar attitudes toward blacks or Jews, it would be immediately shut down by public opinion (commenting on Hustler magazine).

HUTTON, BARBARA

Hutton, Barbara. All the unhappiness in my life has been caused by men.

IDEAS

Comins, David H. People will accept your idea more readily if you tell them Benjamin Franklin said it first.

Harden, Frank. Every time you come up with a terrific idea, you find that someone else thought of it first.

Wattenberg, Ben. There is nothing so powerful as an old idea whose time has come again.

IDEAS, HISTORY OF

Nieh, Jung-chen (Chinese Politburo member). All correct ideas are subject to changes on the basis of time, location and conditions. Otherwise they will become metaphysical ideas.

IDEAS IN ART

Rauschenberg, Robert. Ideas aren't real estate; they grow collectively, and that knocks out the egotistical loneliness that generally infects art.

IDENTITY (PSYCHOLOGY)

Theroux, Paul. You are not what you eat; but where you eat is who you are.

IGNORANCE

Paulucci, Jeno F. It pays to be ignorant, for when you're smart you already know it can't be done.

IMAGINATION

Hugo, Richard. In the world of imagination, all things belong.

Walpole, Horace. You must renounce imagaination forever if you hope to succeed in plagiarism. Forgery is intention, not invention.

IMMIGRANTS IN THE UNITED STATES

Marchesi, Joseph. Only an immigrant can appreciate America (upon revisiting Ellis Island, where he arrived as an immigrant in 1919).

IMMORTALITY

Allen, Woody. I don't believe in an afterlife, although I am bringing a change of underwear.

INCOME

Parkinson, C. Northcote. Expenditure rises to meet income.

INCOME TAX

Galbraith, John Kenneth. I'm opposed to tax decreases. If the last one had worked Jerry Ford would still be President.

Neuman, Alfred E. Today, it takes more brains and effort to make out the Income Tax Form than it does to make the income.

Reagan, Ronald. The entire graduated-income-tax structure was created by Karl Marx.

INDIA—POLITICS AND GOVERNMENT

Anonymous (right wing Indian politician), . We are responsible for creating Indira Gandhi. Don't make Indira a demon, we're the culprits—we let the people down. She's the result of us politicians' playing the fool for 25 years and not solving India's problems.

Gandhi, Indira (Nehru). The freedom of the people cannot be allowed to come in the way of the freedom of the masses.

Gandhi, Indira (Nehru). The steps we have taken are to strengthen our democracy (upon suspending civil liberties and imposing press censorship).

Gandhi, Indira (Nehru). We should be vigilant to see that our march to progress is not hampered in the name of the Constitution.

INDIANA. UNIVERSITY (BASKETBALL)

Cosell, Howard. Indiana should be No. 1. They probably have a bigger payroll than the New York Knicks.

INDIANS OF NORTH AMERICA

Abourezk, James. I was in a refugee camp in Jordan in 1973. I thought if I closed my eyes I could hear the words Pine Ridge. The Indians and the Palestinians are the same—people without power put against the wall by people with power.

Black Elk, . Sometimes I think it might have been better if we had stayed together and made them kill us all.

Hollow, Norman. In the olden days the Indian peoples defended themselves with bows and arrows. Now, politics is the only way our rights can be developed.

INDIANS OF NORTH AMERICA—GOVERNMENT RELATIONS

Anonymous (American Indian Protester), . They made us many promises, more than I can remember, but they never kept but one; they promised to take our land, and they took it (painted in the offices of the Bureau of Indian Affairs during its occupation by Indian protesters).

INDIVIDUAL AND SOCIETY

Borges, Jorge Luis. I think most people are more important than their opinions.

Smith, Donald N (President of Burger King). The individual choice of garnishment of a burger can be an important point to the consumer in this day when individualism, in my mind, is an increasingly important thing to people.

INDIVIDUALISM

Glassman, James K. As a sit-in veteran and small businessman myself, I'm convinced that entrepreneurship is the last refuge of the trouble-making individual.

INFANTS

Sandburg, Carl. A baby is God's opinion that the world should go on.

INFANTS—PURCHASE AND SALE

Schlafly, Phyllis. What's so wrong about that (baby-selling)? If I hadn't been blessed with babies of my own, I would have been happy to have paid thousands of dollars for a baby (commenting in support of the decriminalization of baby-selling).

INFINITY

Cousins, Norman. Infinity converts the possible into the inevitable.

INFLATION (FINANCE)

Abboud, A. Robert. Inflation is a product of—and can only be cured by—the people.

Anderson, John B. Even inflation has taught us to cheat ourselves of the future.

Burns, Arthur Frank. The ultimate consequence of inflation could well be a significant decline of economic and political freedom for the American people.

Carter, James Earl. I guarantee I will not fight inflation with your jobs (to bulding trades tent meeting, San Diego, October 79).

Carter, James Earl. Inflation has become embedded in the very tissue of our economy.

Carter, James Earl. The corrosive effects of inflation eat away at ties that bind us together as a people.

Emminger, Otmar. Inflation is like a dictator. It must be fought before it becomes established, or it is too late.

Friedman, Milton. Inflation is the one form of taxation that can be imposed without legislation.

Hayden, Thomas. During the 1960s, we fought the pigs. Now we fight the high price of bacon.

Lowrey, Bette. Inflation is just a high priced depression.

Meany, George. The fight against inflation must be on the basis of the equality of sacrifice, not the sacrifice of equality.

Miller, George William. Inflation (is) a clear and present danger.

Scammon, Richard. There's nothing wrong with the Republican Party that double-digit inflation won't cure.

Will, George. Inflation is a great conservatizing issue.

INFLUENCE

Young, Andrew. Influence is like a savings account. The less you use it, the more you've got.

INFORMATION

Brown, Edmund Gerald, Jr. Information is the equalizer; it breaks down the hierarchy. A lot of institutions are living in a world that is rapidly passing them by.

Stein, Gertrude. Everybody gets so much information all day long that they lose their common sense.

INFORMATION THEORY

Vallee, Jacques. The theory of space and time is a cultural artifact made possible by the invention of graph paper.

INNOCENCE

Guare, John. Innocence is ignorance where you're not getting caught.

INSANITY

Menninger, Karl. 'Insane' is an expression we psychiatrists don't use until we get to court. Insanity is a question of public opinion.

INSTITUTIONS

Drucker, Peter F. The wonder of modern institutions is not that they work so badly, but that anything works at all.

INTEGRATION

Gruber, Jack. Integration is not something you win at, it's something you work at.

INTELLECT

Miller, Henry. To the person who thinks with his head, life is a comedy. To those who think with their feelings, or work through their feelings, life is a tragedy.

Rumi (Sufi mystic), . Men's minds perceive second causes, but only prophets perceive the action of the First Cause.

INTELLECTUALS

Aron, Raymond. Marxism is the opium of the intellectuals.

Kissinger, Henry Alfred. Intellectuals condemn society for materialism when it is prosperous and for injustice when it fails to ensure prosperity.

Laughlin, Tom. Never trust a man with ideas.

Snow, C. P. Literary intellectuals at one pole—at the other, scientists...Between the two a gulf of mutual incomprehension.

INTELLECTUALS—MOSCOW

Bonner, Yelena (wife of Andrei Sakharov). It (The Master of Margarita) is the perfect theatre for the Moscow intelligentsia. It doles out the truth in small doses, never big enough to cause trouble.

INTELLIGENCE

Penny, J. C. Intelligence is the effort to do the best you can at your particular job; the quality that gives dignity to that job, whether it happens to be scrubbing a floor, or running a corporation.

INTELLIGENCE LEVELS

Adams, Henry Brooks. It is impossible to underrate human intelligence—beginning with one's own.

Callahan, Daniel. There's no guarantee that high IQ people produce better people or a better society. It is not the retarded kids of the world who produce the wars and destruction.

INTELLIGENCE LEVELS—UNITED STATES

Mencken, Henry Louis. No one ever went broke underestimating the intelligence of the American people.

INTELLIGENCE SERVICE—UNITED STATES

Colby, William Egan. From the draft of the committee report that I have seen and the news stories about it, I believe it is totally biased and a disservice to our nation (referring to the report by the House Select Committee on Intelligence).

Colby, William Egan. I'm convinced it's possible to run a secret agency as part of a constitutional society.

Kirkpatrick, Lyman B., Jr. The heart of the matter is that the American people will tolerate what must be done to protect the nation as long as it does not seem to destroy what it is protecting (commenting on what the public will allow from the U.S. Intelligence Community).

Kissinger, Henry Alfred. We must resist the myth that government is a gigantic conspiracy. We cannot allow the intelligence services of the country to be dismantled.

Mondale, Walter Frederick. There must be some fundamental changes in America's intelligence activities or they will fundamentally change America.

Stone, Isidor Feinstein. The biggest menace to American freedom is the intelligence community.

United States. Congress. Senate. Select Committee On Intelligence Operations, . There is no inherent Constitutional authority for the President or any intelligence agency to violate the law.

INTERIOR DECORATION

Rowen, Phyllis. When you grow as a designer, you realize that nothing is forever.

INTERNAL SECURITY

Brown, George S. If any citizen of this country is so concerned about his mail being read or is concerned about his presence at a meeting being noted, I'd say we ought to read his mail and we ought to know what the hell he has done.

INTERNATIONAL BROTHERHOOD OF TEAMSTERS, CHAUFFEURS, WAREHOUSEMEN AND HELPERS OF AMERICA

Anonymous (Teamster Union Member), . Look at it this way: Our contract expires in April of 1976, right? If Jimmy Hoffa were running for election against Fitzsimmons in July, 1976, Fitzsimmons would bust his tail to negotiate a good contract for us, right? With Jimmy Hoffa gone, he don't have to work so hard, does he?.

Fitzsimmons, Frank E. For those who would say it's time to reform this organization, that it is time that the officers quit selling out the membership of their union, I say to them, go to hell.

Fitzsimmons, Frank E. The Teamsters are without peer as an organization dedicated to the service of mankind.

Usery, William J. Even though I don't have a teamsters card, I belong to this club because I believe in it.

INTERNATIONAL RELATIONS

Einstein, Albert. An empty stomach is not a good political adviser.

Goldberg, Arthur Joseph. We need a world in which it is safe to be human.

INTERPERSONAL RELATIONS

Nova, Leo. The other person's attitude depends on which direction the money moves between you.

Ono, Yoko. Keep your intentions in a clear bottle and leave it on the shelf when you rap.

Woolf, Virginia. The eyes of others our prisons; their thoughts our cages.

INTERVIEWING

Fallaci, Oriana. An interview is a love story for me. It's a fight. It's a coitus.

Wallace, Mike. There are no indiscreet questions, there are only indiscreet answers.

Walters, Barbara. If it's a woman, it's caustic; if it's a man, it's authoritative. If it's a woman, it's too often pushy, if it's a man it's aggressive in the best sense of the word (commenting on critics who call her brand of interviewing caustic).

INVESTMENT ADVISERS

Drucker, Peter F. Capital formation is shifting from the entrepreneur who invests in the future to the pension trustee who invests in the past.

IRAN—FOREIGN RELATIONS—UNITED STATES

Banisadr, Abolhassan. In our campaign against the U.S., the hostages are our weakness, not our strength.

Fairlie, Henry. All over Washington, people are now speed-reading the Koran.

IRAN—POLITICS AND GOVERNMENT

Bakhtiar, Shapour. We have replaced an old and corrupt dictatorship with a dictatorship accompanied by anarchy.

Fahd, Prince of Saudi Arabia, . If Iran goes, God help us.

Khomeini, Ayatollah Ruhollah. God has given us all the rules of the game.

Khomeini, Ayatollah Ruhollah. It is impossible to solve Iran's political problems without the disappearance of the Pahlevi dynasty.

Khomeini, Ayatollah Ruhollah. The people of Iran want to be martyrs.

Khomeini, Ayatollah Ruhollah. To vote for anything but an Islamic republic would be a sin.

Khosrowdad, Manouchechr. We know that if the Shah leaves the Communists will come marching.

Mohammed Reza Pahlevi, Shah of Iran. Who would believe that I should work 10 hours a day for 37 years to help my country only to see it go back to the point where I began?.

Mohammed Reza Pahlevi, Shah of Iran, . Those who believe in the Iranian Constitution, the monarchical regime, and the principles of the White Revolution must join the new party. Those who do not are traitors who must either go to prison or leave the country.

IRISH

Byrne, Jane. With the Irish, you know, only the strongest survive.

Flanagan, Fionnula. The one thing you must not commit with the Irish is to succeed.

Moynihan, Daniel Patrick. I don't think there's any point in being Irish if you don't know that the world is going to break your heart eventually.

IRISH REPUBLICAN ARMY

O'Connell, David (one of the IRA's leading tacticians). Put your faith in the Provos and Ireland will be free. We will abolish British rule, we will smash it.

Wilson, Harold. Those who subscribe to the Northern Irish Aid Committee, the principal IRA fund-raising organization in the United States, are not financing the welfare of the Irish people, as they might delude themselves. They are financing murder.

IRWIN, ROBERT

Irwin, Robert. I'm essentially illiterate. I've arrived at all my ideas by sitting on a rock scratching my ass.

ISRAEL

Carter, James Earl. The survival of Israel is not a political issue. It is a moral imperative.

Eban, Abba Solomon. Better to be disliked than pitied.

Eggleston, Justine Judd. I got tired of people calling me a dirty Jew so I figured I'd settle in the one country (Israel) where dirty Jew means you need a bath.

Meir, Golda. It's a sad world. A very sad world. But I'm an optimist. For an Israeli to be a pessimist is a luxury we can't afford. We would have to sit down and die, and that's all. But we don't want to. So we go on. Things will change. You'll see.

United Jewish Appeal, . Speak now, so that we never again pay the price of silence. (appeared as part of an advertisement in the New York Times and the New York Post).

ISRAEL—ECONOMIC CONDITIONS

Arnon, Jacob (Former Israeli Finance Ministry director). There comes a point when defense spending becomes so enormous that it presents just as much danger to our survival as do our Arab enemies.

ISRAEL—FOREIGN POLICY

Fein, Leonard. Israel is squandering recklessly its most critical and natural resource—the good will that many people around the world, and in this country in particular, feel for this gutsy country.

ISRAEL—FOREIGN RELATIONS—ARAB STATES

Arnon, Jacob (Former Israeli Finance Ministry director). There comes a point when defense spending becomes so enormous that it presents just as much danger to our survival as do our Arab enemies.

Sadat, Anwar. I am really startled till this moment that the barrier of distrust that has been between us (Egypt and Israel) during the last 30 years has been broken down in 35 hours. Amazing. Really.

ISRAEL—FOREIGN RELATIONS—EGYPT

Anonymous (American official), . We are so close to a treaty, and yet so far away.

Dayan, Moshe. They (guerrillas) may kill two, five, ten civilians, but they will not destroy the peace treaty with Egypt.

Weizman, Ezer. I say to hell with everybody. We're going to have peace with the Gyppos.

ISRAEL—FOREIGN RELATIONS—UNITED STATES

Dayan, Ehud. Moshe Dayan has exchanged our settlements for peanuts from Jimmy Carter.

ISRAEL—MILITARY POLICY

Begin, Menachem. Europe's rivers are still red with Jewish blood. This Europe cannot teach us how to maintain our security.

ISRAEL—POLITICS AND GOVERNMENT

Arafat, Yasir. In a sense, Menachem Begin is our best ally. We hope he will increase his aggression and his terrorism so that everybody all over the world will discover the ugly face of this Israeli military junta.

Dayan, Moshe. I, Moshe Dayan, as an individual am not a coward. But as a Jew I am a very frightened man.

Fleener, Terre. What the Jewish people endured does not give them the right to visit violence on other people.

Meir, Golda. I wouldn't accept the West Bank and Gaza as part of Israel if they were offered on a silver platter.

Weizman, Ezer. I am only responsible for Israel's security, not its sanity (about reports of new Israeli settlements in the Sinai).

ITALIANS

West, Morris. In discourse the Italians are the most eloquent people in the world. In action they are either apathetic or impulsive to the point of insanity.

ITALY

Hearst, Patricia Campbell. I'd really like to travel again—anywhere but Italy. There's too much kidnapping there.

ITALY—DESCRIPTION

Anselmi, Tina (first Italian woman cabinet member). If people outside Italy have the impression that Italy is always on strike, that is because it is.

ITALY—POLITICS AND GOVERNMENT

Andreotti, Giulio. In politics there is a clause that is always valid: rebus sic stantibus (circumstances being what they are).

Barzini, Luigi. We (Italians) might be the first developed country to turn itself back into an underdeveloped country.

Crespi, Consuelo. In Italy now you want to feel rich and look poor.

Mussolini, Benito. It is not impossible to govern Italians. It is merely useless.

Saragat, Giuseppe. Along-side the body of (Aldo) Moro lies the body of the first Italian republic.

West, Morris. Stupidity in Italy is an inheritance, built into the system by mad emperors, Bourbon kings, absolutist popes, tyrant dukes, and mafiosi. It is the conviction that change is impossible.

JACKSON, GLENDA

Jackson, Glenda. I'm waiting for the day when I wake up and life is a breeze. I used to think that happened when you grew old. But it doesn't. That's just a fantasy.

Simon, John. (Glenda Jackson) has the looks of an asexual harlequin.

JACKSON, HENRY MARTIN

Dutton, Fred. George Wallace is a more truly democratic candidate than Ford, Humphrey or Jackson. He wants everyone to vote, while they hope to narrow down the voting public.

Jackson, Henry Martin. I think my positions that I have taken are liberal in the best traditions of the Democratic Party.

Rockefeller, Nelson Aldrich. I would like to apologize to the Senate of the United States, to its members, and particularly to Senator Jackson for my remarks in an off-the-record meeting. There is no question it was a mistake (apologizing for suggesting that two members of Senator Henry M. Jackson's staff had Communist ties).

Wade, Richard. If you put the top 50 liberals inside a room to stop Henry Jackson, they'd have no troops for the job. Liberals have influence but no power.

JACKSON, REGGIE

Jackson, Reggie. Hitting is better than sex.

Jackson, Reggie. I don't mind getting beaten, but I hate to lose.

Jackson, Reggie. I represent both the overdog and the underdog in society.

Martin, Billy. The two of them (George Steinbrenner and Reggie Jackson) deserve each other. One's a born liar; the other's convicted.

JACOBS, ANDY

Jacobs, Andy. (Ralph) Nader has become a legend in his own mind.

JAGGER, BIANCA

Jagger, Bianca. What do I really want as a woman? I want it all.

JAGGER, MICK

Jagger, Mick. I should think not, judging from Elvis. No, rock 'n' roll music is for adolescents. It's a dead end (responding when asked Can rock stars move toward middle age?).

Jagger, Mick. I'd rather be dead than sing Satisfaction when I'm 45.

Jagger, Mick. Keith and I are two of the nicest people we know.

JAMISON, JUDITH

Jamison, Judith. Every dancer lives on the threshold of chucking it.

JAPAN

Rexroth, Kenneth. The one country I feel at home in is Japan. I don't feel at home here. I don't like a country where traffic cops are armed to the teeth (commenting on life in the U.S.).

JARVIS, HOWARD

Jarvis, Howard. Everyone is entitled to my opinion.

Reeves, Richard. Howard Jarvis is a nut, but in my heart I know he's right.

JAVITS, JACOB KOPPEL

Javits, Marion. I am his mistress. His work is his wife (explaining that she and her husband lead separate lives).

JAVITS, MARION

Javits, Marion. I am his mistress. His work is his wife (explaining that she and her husband lead separate lives).

JEANS

Cardin, Pierre. The jean. The jean is the destructor. It is a dictator. It is destroying creativity. The jean must be stopped.

JEFFERSON, THOMAS

Ayers, Brandt. It is much too soon to think of Jimmy Carter as another Jefferson.

Lapham, Lewis H. I take for granted Jefferson's dictum that money, not morality, constitutes the principle of commercial nations.

JENNER, BRUCE

Jenner, Bruce. If you want to use the decathlon as a test of total atheletic ability, then I guess I'm the world's greatest athlete. It's as good a test as any, I guess. But that sure doesn't help me when I stand up at a tee and try to hit a golf ball. Then I'm just another guy who can't hit straight.

JERUSALEM

Begin, Menachem. Jerusalem will remain undivided for all generations until the end of the world.

JESSYE, EVA

Jessye, Eva. I am no longer the only raisin in the rice pudding.

JESUITS

Arrupe, Pedro (Superior General of the Jesuits). They can become martyrs, but my priests are not going to leave there (El Salvador) because they are with the people.

JESUS CHRIST

Carter, James Earl. Christ says don't consider yourself better than someone else because one guy screws a whole bunch of women while the other guy is loyal to his wife.

Mother Teresa, . Jesus said love one another. He didn't say love the whole world.

Smith, Patti. Jesus died for somebody's sins but not mine.

JEWISH-ARAB RELATIONS

Meir, Golda. We are angriest at the Arabs not because they kill us, but because they force us to kill them.

Rabin, Yitzhak. For me, peace means reconciliation of the Arab countries with the existence of Israel as a Jewish state.

JEWS

Amin Dada, Idi. Hitler was right about the Jews, because the Israelis are not working in the interests of the people of the world, and that is why they burned the Israelis alive with gas in the soil of Germany.

Baroody, J. M. Zionism is racism because it is built on exclusivity. The Jews believe they are a superior race, a chosen people. They believe their home should be in Palestine, the Promised Land. Since when was God in the real-estate business?.

Brando, Marlon. There are so many Jews in creative and executive positions. And Hollywood showed you the crude stereotype of every minority and race—the nigger, the Indian, the Mexican, these portraits reinforced the very attitudes that kept those people down. Many of the people responsible for this were Jews. Didn't they remember what it was like to be down themselves?.

Carter, Billy. There's a helluva lot more Arabians than there is Jews.

Eggleston, Justine Judd. I got tired of people calling me a dirty Jew so I figured I'd settle in the one country (Israel) where dirty Jew means you need a bath.

Goebbels, Joseph. The Jews are re-emerging. Anyone in a position to do so should kill Jews off like rats. In Germany, thank God, we have already done a fairly complete job. I trust that the world will take its cue from this (from his diary, 1945).

United Jewish Appeal, . Speak now, so that we never again pay the price of silence. (appeared as part of an advertisement in the New York Times and the New York Post).

JEWS—IRAN

Anonymous (Iranian Jewish spokesman), . While we will preserve our Jewish tradition, we will also preserve the country's cause, which is, happily, our cause.

Khomeini, Ayatollah Ruhollah. From its very inception, Islam has been afflicted by the Jews.

JEWS—UNITED STATES

Brown, George S. They own, you know, the banks in this country, the newspapers. Just look at where the Jewish money is.

JOBS

Becker, Jules. It is much harder to find a job than to keep one.

McGovern, George Stanley. The longer the title, the less important the job ..

JOHN F. KENNEDY CENTER FOR THE PERFORMING ARTS, WASHINGTON, D.C.

Eckardt, Wolf Von. The only lift you get from this building is when you take the elevator from the basement to the second floor.

JOHN PAUL I, POPE

John Paul I, Pope, . I don't have the wisdom or heart of Pope John or the preparation and culture of Pope Paul—but I am in their place...I hope you will help me with your prayers.

John Paul I, Pope, . If I hadn't been a bishop, I would have wanted to be a journalist.

John Paul I, Pope, . If someone had told me I would be Pope one day, I would have studied harder.

John Paul I, Pope, . Many have forgotten that a theologian is not only he who speaks of God, but he who speaks to God (chastising theologians who he felt had lost their fidelity to the church).

John Paul I, Pope, . The danger for modern man is that he would reduce the earth to a desert, the person to an automaton, brotherly love to planned collectivization, often introducing death where God wishes life.

JOHN PAUL II, POPE

Wills, Garry. (The Pope's) theological conservatism undercuts his political liberalism.

JOHN PAUL II, POPE—RELATIONS—WOMEN

Berrigan, Daniel. (The Pope's) views of women are old-fashioned, and they are probab)y not going to change. We can't have apartheid at the altar.

JOHNS, GLYNNIS

Johns, Glynnis (actress). For me, most relationships with men have been like pregnancies—they last about nine months.

JOHNSON, LYNDON BAINES

Ball, George W. (Lyndon Johnson) did not suffer from a poor education, he suffered from the belief that he had a poor education.

Coughlin, J. Walter (secret service agent for President Johnson). Once, the President and I rode up and down on the White House elevator 21 times because the door wouldn't open, he fired me 42 times before we got out. I finally said, 'I tell you what, Mr. President, you get me off this thing and I'll quit.'.

Delisle, Paul (maitre d' of Sans Souci Restaurant). Once we had the Texan. He learned to eat fine French food. The Georgian—he can learn too.

Harriman, Averell. As I look back, what I regret most was that I wasn't able to influence Johnson to abandon the war in Vietnam. To see that war go on, to find him listening to people with such a completely wrong point of view. Every day there were those whispering in his ear, 'No president ever lost a war.' That was red meat for a Texan.

Johnson, Lyndon Baines. Boys, it is just like the Alamo. Somebody should have by God helped those Texans. I'm going to Viet Nam.

Johnson, Lyndon Baines. I never believed that Oswald acted alone, although I can accept that he pulled the trigger.

Johnson, Lyndon Baines. I never trust a man unless I've got his pecker in my pocket.

Johnson, Lyndon Baines. I'm not going to be the first President to lose a war.

McCarthy, Eugene Joseph (attributed by Daniel Patrick Moynihan). No one ever was associated with (Lyndon Johnson) who was not in the end somehow diminished.

Mitchell, Clarence M., Jr. Lyndon B. Johnson was the greatest American President on civil rights.

Valenti, Jack. I sleep each night a little better, a little more confidently, because Lyndon Johnson is my President.

JOHNSON, NICHOLAS

Johnson, Nicholas. Most of what I did as a government official was try to encourage more competition, by having smaller enterprises that would truly compete, by removing barriers to entry, by relieving the dependence of business on large government payments and I was opposed at every step and turn of the way, by businessmen.

JONES, JAMES THURMAN

Greenfield, Meg. The wages of interracial living is not mass suicide and murder.

Johnson, Wanda. Once I became a member of the inner circle, I realized he was a madman, completely insane (about Jim Jones).

Jones, James Thurman. I am God; there is no other God and religion is the opium of the people.

Jones, Stephan. I can almost say I hate this man because he has destroyed everything I've worked for (about Jim Jones).

JONES, JOHN

Jones, John. I do write poetry but it is no good and I tear it up.

JONES, PRESTON

Jones, Preston. I think I'm a story-teller playwright. But whatever the story is, for me it would always involve "time" because time is not the sun going up and down every day. It is not a clock. It is not a calendar. Time is an eroding, infinite mystery. Time is, in fact, a son-of-a-bitch.

JORDAN, BARBARA

Jordan, Barbara. I'm neither a Black politician, nor a woman politician. Just a politician. A professional politician.

JORDAN, HAMILTON

Anonymous, . When it comes to organization, Hamilton (Jordan) is a one-man slum.

Jordan, Hamilton. If the gossip columnists don't get me, I'll be around. That's on the record.

Jordan, Hamilton. I'm a chauvinist that tries to do better.

Jordan, Hamilton. I'm here for as long as he wants me.

Jordan, Hamilton. One of my strengths is that I know my weaknesses.

Strauss, Robert S. The three most overrated things in Washington are Bob Strauss, home cooking, and Hamilton Jordan's private life.

JOURNALISM

Albert, Claude. You have to love the business (journalism) for what it is, not for what you'd like it to be.

Alexander, Shana. (Journalism) offers the maximum of vicarious living with a minimum of emotional involvement.

Buchwald, Art. In this country, when you attack the Establishment, they don't put you in jail or a mental institution. They do something worse. They make you a member of the Establishment.

Cohen, Richard. The best stories never check out.

Cronkite, Walter. It is not the reporter's job to be a patriot or to presume to determine where patriotism lies. His job is to relate the facts.

Dornfeld, Arnold (attributed by Mike Royko). If your mother says she loves you, check it out (on the journalist's responsibility).

John Paul I, Pope, . If St. Paul returned to the world now as a journalist he would not only direct Reuters but seek time on television.

Krause, Charles. In the jungle, a press card is just another piece of paper.

Marx, Karl. The first freedom of the press consists in this: that it is not a trade (writing in the Neve Rheinische Zeitung, May 19, 1842).

Moyers, Bill D. Of all the myths of journalism, objectivity is the greatest.

Muggeridge, Malcolm. (Journalism) is the ideal profession for those who find power fascinating and its exercise abhorrent.

Nixon, Richard Milhous. The media has abdicated its fact gathering to nonbelieving young people, who seem to want to break down our values.

Rusk, Dean. I don't believe in a code of ethics in the journalism profession, and I don't believe in equal time between the media. If there are abuses toward freedom of the press, then let us correct them thru free speech.

Schorr, Daniel. All news is an exaggeration of life.

Thomas, Bob. Hemingway had a very strong opinion that writers should not stay in journalism too long. He felt it damaged your sensitivity. I suspect he is right.

Thompson, Hunter S. There's no such thing as a 'nice' reporter. That's like saying somebody's a nice liberal.

Wicker, Tom. My life in journalism has persuaded me that the press too often tries to guard its freedom by shirking its responsibility, and that this leads to default on both. What the press in America needs is less inhibition, not more restraint.

Wilde, Oscar. Modern journalism, by giving us the opinions of the uneducated, keeps us in touch with the ignorance of the community.

JOURNALISM—NEW YORK (CITY)

Beame, Abraham David. No New Yorker should take Rupert Murdoch's New York Post seriously any longer. It makes Hustler magazine look like the Harvard (Law) Review.

JOURNALISTIC ETHICS

Alsop, Joseph. I'm proud they (CIA) asked me (to aid them) and proud to have done it. The notion that a newspaperman doesn't have a duty to his country is perfect balls.

Colby, William Egan. (Daniel Schorr) carried out his obligation to the first amendment to the Constitution and to himself as a newsman and should not be punished (commenting the release of the secret House report on United States intelligence operations).

Cronkite, Walter. The very constraint against taking positions is a mark of the professional in journalism, not letting opinions impact on reporting. I've spent a lifetime suppressing them.

Nixon, Richard Milhous. When news is concerned, nobody in the press is a friend—they are all enemies.

Rosenthal, A. M. I don't care if you screw an elephant, just don't cover the circus.

Scheer, Robert. The journalist's job is to get the story by breaking into their offices, by bribing, by seducing people, by lying, by anything else to break through that palace guard.

Schorr, Daniel. To betray a source would be to betray myself, my career and my life. I cannot do it (commenting in his testimony before the Pike committee).

Seib, Charles. The pettiness and unfairness of gossip masquerading as news is one reason the Washington press is seen by many Americans as vindictive, destructive and often irrelevant.

JOURNALISTS

Breslin, Catherine. A freelancer lives at the end of a sawed-off limb.

Dorfman, Dan. To lie to the press on a public matter is, in effect, to lie to the people.

Eisenhower, David. Journalists aren't nearly as interesting as they think they are.

Lippmann, Walter. You are just a puzzled man making notes about what you think.

Mudd, Roger. One of the problems with broadcast journalists is that we have been convinced, sometimes against our better judgment, that we are not reporters but show-business people.

Stone, Isidor Feinstein. The First Amendment gives newspapermen a status and a mandate, an honored place in society, that cannot be matched in England, much less on the European continent. It is peculiarly American. I feel as though I survived an Ice Age and helped to keep this heritage intact.

JUAN CARLOS I, KING OF SPAIN

Maldonado, Jose. For the usurper Juan Carlos, we forsee a war without mercy. Instead of climbing carpeted stairs to the throne, he will be forced to mount the scaffold. Regicide awaits him.

JUDGES

Brandeis, Louis. The most important thing we (judges) do is not doing.

Burger, Warren Earl. We may be well on our way to a society overrun by hordes of lawyers, hungry as locusts, and brigades of judges in numbers never before contemplated.

Dershowitz, Alan. Judges are the weakest link in our system of justice, and they are also the most protected.

Douglas, William Orville. A lifetime diet of the law alone turns judges into dull, dry husks.

Hand, Learned. In a pitilessly consistent democracy, judges would not be making law at all.

Jackson, Robert. We (judges) are not final because we are infallible, but we are infallible because we are final.

Kaufman, Irving. It is not enough for justice to be declared. The judge must assure that justice is done.

Rifkind, Simon. (Judicial) impartiality is an acquired taste, like olives. You have to be habituated to it.

Stevens, John Paul. Judges should impose on themselves the discipline of deciding no more than is before them.

Warren, Earl. A jurist's mind cannot operate in a vacuum.

JUDGES—CHICAGO

Anonymous, . Get behind a judge on Monday in case you find yourself in front of him on Tuesday.

JURY

Nizer, Louis. I would rather trust 12 jurors with all their prejudices and biases than I would a judge. I think the reason democracy works is because as you multiply judgements, you reduce the incidence of error.

JUSTICE

Bennett, Arnold. The price of justice is eternal publicity.

Lukacs, John. I believe human nature doesn't change. I believe very strongly in original sin. I also take a dim view of the pursuit of justice as being the superior value of Western civilization. I think truth is more important than justice.

Niebuhr, Reinhold. Man's capacity for justice makes democracy possible, but man's inclination to injustice makes democracy necessary.

JUSTICE, ADMINISTRATION OF

Baker, Howard Henry. We do more with someone who shoots a cop than someone who assassinates an ambassador.

Brandeis, Louis. The most important thing we (judges) do is not doing.

Dershowitz, Alan. Judges are the weakest link in our system of justice, and they are also the most protected.

Kaufman, Irving. It is not enough for justice to be declared. The judge must assure that justice is done.

McKay, Robert. If war is too important to be left to the generals, surely justice is too important to be left to lawyers.

Newfield, Jack. Justice is a meat grinder.

Nizer, Louis. I would rather trust 12 jurors with all their prejudices and biases than I would a judge. I think the reason democracy works is because as you multiply judgements, you reduce the incidence of error.

Rifkind, Simon. (Judicial) impartiality is an acquired taste, like olives. You have to be habituated to it.

JUSTICE, ADMINISTRATION OF—RUSSIA

Anonymous (report in Pravda), . People are not punished for their opinions in the U.S.S.R. The only ones who are prosecuted are those who have indulged in propaganda or anti-Soviet agitation, aiming to weaken the political system in force in our country, or those who broadcast manifestly false bombast whose object is to discredit the Soviet Union.

JUSTICE, ADMINISTRATION OF—UNITED STATES

Burger, Warren Earl. We may be well on our way to a society overrun by hordes of lawyers, hungry as locusts, and brigades of judges in numbers never before contemplated.

Liddy, G. Gordon. Before going to prison I believed that criticism of the criminal justice system for its treatment of the poor was so much liberal bleating and bunk. I was wrong.

Liddy, G. Gordon. The criminal justice system is breaking down because we, as a nation, have for too long neglected to nourish its heart—the court systems of our country.

Miller, Marvin. The fact that Miss Little was vindicated doesn't mean anything about the judicial system of this state or of the United States. The real reason she was vindicated was the international outcry about Joan Little.

Paul, Jerry. This system doesn't want justice. It wants convictions. That's why, given enough money, I can buy justice. I can win any case in this country, given enough money (upon winning acquittal for Joan Little in her murder trial).

KAFKA, FRANZ

Auden, Wystan Hugh. Had one to name the author who comes nearest to bearing the same kind of relation to our age as Dante, Shakespeare and Goethe bore to theirs, Kafka is the first one would think of.

Kafka, Franz. Writing is a sweet and wonderful reward, but for what? In the night it became clear to me, as clear as a child's lesson book, that it is the reward for serving the devil.

KAHN, ALFRED

Kahn, Alfred. If you can't explain what you're doing in simple English, you are probably doing something wrong.

KAIDA, IVAN IVANOVICH

Kaida, Ivan Ivanovich. First, I was a man without a country, then I was a man without land. Now I am truly rich, for I have both.

KANSAS CITY, MISSOURI—POLITICS AND GOVERNMENT

Prendergast, George Washington. I never took a dime from the public till; it's all been honest graft.

KARRAS, ALEX

Dobler, Conrad. Well, 35 million TV viewers know that Karras has a lot of class. And all of it is third (after Alex Karras described him as the dirtiest player in pro football).

KARSH, YOUSUF

Karsh, Yousuf. Photography is the voice of humanity. And that voice must be heard.

KEATON, DIANE

Brooks, Richard. (Diane Keaton) has more artistic courage than anyone I know.

KELLY, EDWARD J.

Kelly, Edward J. (Mayor of Chicago, 1933-1947). Franklin Roosevelt was the best precinct captain I ever had.

KELLY, GENE

Kelly, Gene. Musicals are my real love. I didn't want to make pictures with messages. I just wanted to make people happy and bring joy.

KENNEDY, EDWARD MOORE

Carey, Hugh. A hard worker but he is perceived otherwise (about Ted Kennedy).

Carter, James Earl. If Kennedy runs, I'll whip his ass.

Culver, John C. Teddy (Kennedy) doesn't want to be President; he just doesn't want anybody else to be President.

Kennedy, Edward Moore. I am glad to be an underdog.

Kennedy, Edward Moore. I hope to gain the Democratic nomination in 1980. But I also hope to do more—to help give the Democratic Party back its timeless truth.

Kennedy, Edward Moore. I would be much happier if Carter were successful.

Kennedy, Edward Moore. If someone in my position doesn't realize the danger, he'd be a fool. But anybody who lets that danger paralyze him is useless (concerning the danger of assassination).

Kennedy, Edward Moore. My father always said: 'If it's on the table, eat it'.

Kennedy, Edward Moore. The press made Jimmy Carter, and now they're trying to destroy him. I'm going to set my own course.

Kennedy, Rose. I never thought I'd live to see the day a Kennedy would have eggs and tomatoes thrown at him in Boston.

Kennedy, Rose. The temptation to be the one to kill the third Kennedy brother is just too great (on why she doesn't want Ted Kennedy to run for President).

Miller, Arthur. There is no solution for him, or us, if we choose him (Ted Kennedy).

Schlesinger, Arthur, Jr. Chappaquiddick is to Kennedy what polio was to FDR. It will make him a better President.

KENNEDY FAMILY

Galella, Ron. I photograph the Kennedys because, like it or not, they are the royalty of America.

Kennedy, Edward Moore. Whatever contributions the Kennedys have made are very much tied into the incredible importance and power of that force in our lives, the family.

KENNEDY, JOAN

Kennedy, Joan. If Ted is elected President of the United States, I will commit myself to the ongoing struggle for women's equality with everything I have and everything I am.

KENNEDY, JOHN FITZGERALD

Aregood, Richard. It's hard to understand all this fuss about John F. Kennedy. After all, Richard Nixon didn't just concentrate on women. He tried to do it to everybody.

Dudney, Bob. The country would have recovered from the death of John Kennedy, but it hasn't recovered yet from the death of Lee Harvey Oswald and probably never will.

Kennedy, John Fitzgerald. And so, my fellow Americans, ask not what your country can do for you; ask what you can do for your country (inaugural address—1961).

Kennedy, John Fitzgerald. Let every nation know, whether it wishes us well or ill, we shall pay any price, bear any burden, meet any hardship, support any friend or oppose any foe to assure the survival and the success of liberty.

Kennedy, John Fitzgerald. The worse I do, the more popular I get.

Kennedy, Robert Francis. At least one half of the days that he (John F. Kennedy) spent on this earth were days of intense physical pain.

Kennedy, Robert Francis (attributed by Bill Moyers). I have myself wondered if we did not pay a very great price for being more energetic than wise about a lot of things, especially Cuba.

Luce, Henry. He seduces me. When I'm with him I feel like a whore (when asked how he felt about John Kennedy).

Monroe, Marilyn. I think I made his back feel better (about John F. Kennedy).

Schlesinger, Arthur, Jr. John Kennedy was a realist brilliantly disguised as a romantic; Robert Kennedy, a romantic stubbornly disguised as a realist.

Schlesinger, Arthur, Jr. One attacked injustices because he found them irrational; the other because he found them unbearable (about John and Robert Kennedy).

Sinatra, Frank. Hell hath no fury like a hustler with a literary agent.

Truman, Harry S. (John Kennedy) had his ear so close to the ground it was full of grasshoppers.

KENNEDY, JOHN FITZGERALD— ASSASSINATION

Hill, Clinton J. If I had reacted just a little bit quicker, I could have (saved Kennedy), I guess, and I'll live with that to my grave.

Johnson, Lyndon Baines. I never believed that Oswald acted alone, although I can accept that he pulled the trigger.

Kennedy, John Fitzgerald. If somebody is going to kill me, they are going to kill me.

Moynihan, Daniel Patrick. I don't think there's any point in being Irish if you don't know that the world is going to break your heart eventually.

Shriver, Eunice. Mistakes were obviously made in terms of the investigation, but I'm satisfied with their conclusions (on the Warren Commission).

KENNEDY, JOSEPH P., III

Kennedy, Joseph P., III. There's no question being a Kennedy can open a lot of doors, but it's also opened a few I didn't want to walk through.

KENNEDY, ROBERT FRANCIS

Eisenhower, Dwight David. It is difficult for me to see a single qualification that the man has for the presidency. I think he is shallow, vain and untrustworthy—on top of which he is indecisive (commenting on Robert Kennedy).

Johnson, Lyndon Baines. The thing I feared from the first day of my presidency was actually coming true. Robert Kennedy had openly announced his intention to reclaim the throne in the memory of his brother.

Schlesinger, Arthur, Jr. If it is necessary for a biographer of Robert Kennedy to regard him as evil, then I am not qualified to be his biographer.

Schlesinger, Arthur, Jr. John Kennedy was a realist brilliantly disguised as a romantic; Robert Kennedy, a romantic stubbornly disguised as a realist.

Schlesinger, Arthur, Jr. One attacked injustices because he found them irrational; the other because he found them unbearable (about John and Robert Kennedy).

Tolson, Clyde. I hopes that someone shoots and kills the son of a bitch (about Robert Kennedy).

KENNEDY, ROSE

Kennedy, Rose. I first met my husband when I was 10 or 12 years old. Unlike many of the kids today, I married for love...the money—that came later.

KEROUAC, JACK

Capote, Truman. It is not writing; it is only typing (about Jack Kerouac).

KEYNES, JOHN MAYNARD

Keynes, John Maynard. My only regret in life is that I did not drink more champagne.

KHOMEINI, AYATOLLAH RUHOLLAH

Khomeini, Ayatollah Ruhollah. We have the ideology to distinguish right from wrong, and we should not hesitate to tell misguided people, here and abroad, what is wrong with them.

Millett, Kate. Male chauvinist is a simple, idiotic way of describing him (Ayatollah Khomeini).

Mohammed Reza Pahlevi, Shah of Iran. Why can't the press see what Marx is doing behind Muhammad's banner?.

Shales, Tom. The Ayatollah Khomeini has the world by the networks.

KIDD, BRUCE

Kidd, Bruce. We should stop preaching about sport's moral values. Sport, after all, isn't Lent. It's a pleasure of the flesh.

KINDNESS

Bovee, Christian. Kindness is a language the dumb can speak and the deaf can hear and understand.

Skelton, Red. I trust God, my wife, and myself. People take kindness for weakness, and generosity has the form of a sucker.

KING, DONALD

King, Donald. I have risen to the top in the promotion business just as I climbed to the top in the numbers game: by wits and grits and bullshit.

KING, MARTIN LUTHER, JR.

King, Coretta Scott. There are so many monuments to war, so many testaments to sorrow, I wish America—through a national holiday and the center—would help build one monument of peace (referring to the Dr. Martin Luther King, Jr. Center for Social Change).

King, Martin Luther, Jr. I'm not fearing any man. Mine eyes have seen the glory of the coming of the Lord.

KING, MARTIN LUTHER, JR.—ASSASSINATION

King, Coretta Scott. I don't have the facts, but at this stage I say it appears there was a conspiracy in the death of my husband.

KINGMAN, DAVID ARTHUR

Kingman, David Arthur. There's no way to be a nice guy and play professional athletics. You have to just go out and be mean.

KING'S LAW (QUOTATION)

King, Larry L. One receives an inverse ratio of romantic opportunities to that which one needs.

KIRBO, CHARLES

Jordan, Hamilton. If Jimmy Carter were running against Charlie Kirbo, I'd vote for Charlie.

Kirbo, Charles. I may be wrong, and I may be biased, but I'm sure as hell not uncertain (commenting on his status as advisor to President Carter).

KISSING

Bergman, Ingrid. A kiss is a lovely trick designed by nature to stop speech when words become superfluous.

KISSINGER, HENRY ALFRED

Fallaci, Oriana. I doubt very much that my future as an interviewer of powerful people in the United States is a brilliant future if Mr. Kissinger goes on being the President of the United States.

Kissinger, Henry Alfred. Among the many claims on American resources, I would put those of Vietnam in alphabetical order.

Kissinger, Henry Alfred. For God's sake, how many swan songs can a lame duck deliver? (commenting on his many farewell ceremonies).

Kissinger, Henry Alfred. I am not here (at the 1980 Republican Convention) as a job seeker.

Kissinger, Henry Alfred. I don't stand on protocol. If you'll just call me excellency (Responding to a newsman who asked how to address the new Secretary of State).

Kissinger, Henry Alfred. I have always thought of foreign policy as bipartisan.

Kissinger, Henry Alfred. I think Metternich was an extremely skilled diplomat, but not very creative.

Kissinger, Henry Alfred. It is true that I enjoyed my celebrity status in my previous position, but I can prove that when I left Washington I wore exactly the same size crown as when I arrived.

Kissinger, Henry Alfred. It's true, as Secretary of State-designate Cy Vance has said, that there will always be a place for me at the State Department. But it's awfully cold down in the basement.

Kissinger, Henry Alfred. My megalomania, of course, reaches levels in which an admission of inadequacy is next to inconceivable (responding to a question of whether or not it is harder to conduct diplomatic negotiations in an election year).

Kissinger, Henry Alfred. Power is the greatest aphrodisiac of all.

Kissinger, Henry Alfred. The longer I am out of office, the more infallible I appear to myself.

Kissinger, Henry Alfred. The main point...in the mechanics of my success comes from the fact that I have acted alone.

Kissinger, Henry Alfred. There cannot be a crisis next week. My schedule is already full.

Kissinger, Henry Alfred. There were some personality disputes which neither of us handled with the elegance and wisdom that perhaps was necessary (commenting on his relationship with former Secretary of Defense James Schlesinger).

Kissinger, Henry Alfred. To me women are no more than a pastime, a hobby. Nobody devotes too much time to a hobby.

Kissinger, Henry Alfred. Two years from now nobody will give a damn if I am up, down or sideways.

Kissinger, Henry Alfred. We are all the president's men, and have got to behave that way.

Kissinger, Henry Alfred. We are making remarkable progress toward an agreement—and toward a nervous breakdown. It's going to be a race to see which will be achieved first (about Middle East peace negotiations).

Kissinger, Henry Alfred. You can give odds of a million to one with Jimmy the Greek because one thing is certain: under no circumstances will I accept a position in a new Administration. It's time for younger men to be given a chance.

Lehrer, Tom. When Henry Kissinger can get the Nobel Peace Prize, what is there left for satire?.

McCarthy, Eugene Joseph. Kissinger won a Nobel Peace Prize for watching a war end that he was for.

Meany, George. Foreign policy is too damned important to be left to the Secretary of State.

Nixon, Richard Milhous. Henry (Kissinger) likes to say outrageous things....he was fascinated by the celebrity set and he liked being one himself.

Phillips, Howard. We hope that Ronald Reagan will not be the third President to work for Henry Kissinger.

Reagan, Ronald. I worry about Kissinger. He needed someone like Nixon to keep him on that tough track. He has to have someone around who can keep him from giving away the store.

Riegle, Donald. Henry Kissinger is pregnant with America's foreign policy, and we're all waiting for him to give birth.

Rosenthal, Benjamin. Kissinger prefers to deal with great men and world leaders, partly because it makes for better history writing. But he must deal with Congress because we reflect the will of the American people.

Shafat, Gershon. Kissinger is a disaster. His priorities are: one, Kissinger; two, the President; three, the U.S. Israel is nowhere among them.

Solzhenitsyn, Aleksandr Isaevich. Mr. Kissinger always has an emergency exit available to him. He can transfer to a university to lecture to credulous youngsters about the art of diplomacy. But the government of the United States will have no emergency exit.

Thomson, Meldrim. Henry Kissinger is the cunning architect of America's planned destruction.

Young, Andrew. Nigeria is arrogant and Kissinger is arrogant, and so there was a clash. I may be just as arrogant, but I can control it better.

KISSINGER, HENRY ALFRED—RELATIONS WITH THE PRESS

Kissinger, Henry Alfred. I will think of you with affection—tinged by exasperation (speaking before the National Press Club).

KLORES, STANLEY

Klores, Stanley. The ordination of women to the priesthood is against the will of God (commenting upon his decision to leave the Protestant Episcopal Church for the Catholic church on the issue of women becoming priests).

KLUGE, ALEXANDER

Kluge, Alexander. German (movie) directors are like airplanes always circling the airport but never landing.

KNIEVEL, EVEL

Knievel, Evel. What I said after the accident about quitting isn't true. That was my body talking over my mind. I plan to try again (recuperating after he and motorcycle failed to clear 13 London buses)..

KNOPF, ALFRED A.

Knopf, Alfred A. It's peculiar. The older I become the more radical I become.

KNOWLEDGE

Butler, Nicholas Murray. An expert is one who knows more and more about less and less.

Clarke, Arthur C. The only way to find the limits of the possible is by going beyond them to the impossible.

Guare, John. Innocence is ignorance where you're not getting caught.

Mayer, Jean. The ability to arrive at complex decisions is the hallmark of the educated person.

Paulucci, Jeno F. It pays to be ignorant, for when you're smart you already know it can't be done.

Perls, Fritz. Learning is discovering that something is possible.

Santayana, George. Our dignity is not in what we do, but in what we understand.

Singer, Isaac Bashevis. The supernatural is like the ocean, while the so-called natural is only a little island on it. And even this little island is a great riddle.

Truman, Harry S. The only things worth learning are the things you learn after you know it all.

Wicker, Tom. To know things as they are is better than to believe things as they seem.

KNOWLEDGE, SOCIOLOGY OF

Snow, C. P. Literary intellectuals at one pole—at the other, scientists...Between the two a gulf of mutual incomprehension.

KOJAK, THEO (TELEVISION CHARACTER)

Kojak, Theo. Hindsight is the only exact science.

KORDA, MICHAEL

Korda, Michael. Accuracy has never been my strongest point.

KOREA (REPUBLIC)

McGovern, George Stanley. We are defending a corrupt dictatorship, as we did to that last shameful day in Saigon (about the Republic of Korea).

KOREA (REPUBLIC)—FOREIGN RELATIONS—UNITED STATES

Park, Tongsun. I'm glad it's all over. They were talking about 150 Congressmen; now it's narrowed to three. The whole thing (Koreagate scandal) was just a syndrome following Watergate.

KORFF, BARUCH

Korff, Baruch. I fully believe that every detractor of President Nixon will come before the bar of justice, whether in this lifetime or later.

KOSINSKI, JERZY

Kosinski, Jerzy. I go to discos for the same reason I visit bars and hospital emergency rooms. They are all graveyards.

KOVIC, RON

Kovic, Ron. The government took the best years of my life away from me and millions of other young men. I just think they're lucky I wrote a book instead of buying a gun.

KREMENTZ, JILL

Krementz, Jill. Can I call you back? (in response to the question 'Is photography art?').

KU KLUX KLAN

Bacon, Mary. We are not just a bunch of illiterate Southern nigger killers. We are good white Christian people working for a white America. When one of your wives or one of your sisters gets raped by a nigger, maybe you'll get smart and join the Klan.

Duke, David. Black people have organizations that fight for black power, and Jews look out for each other. But there isn't anyone except the Klan who will fight for the rights of white people.

Jackson, Jesse. It used to be the Klan in white robes who were the killers, now we've gone from Southern rope to Northern dope.

Marshall, Thurgood. The Ku Klux Klan never dies. They just stop wearing sheets because sheets cost too much.

KUBRICK, STANLEY

Kubrick, Stanley. The essence of dramatic form is to let an idea come over people without its being plainly stated.

KY, NGUYEN CAO

Ky, Nguyen Cao. I was not corrupt. Perhaps that is the only thing I regret. I realized after 14 months in this country the value of money, whether it's clean or dirty.

LABOR AND LABORING CLASSES

Mondale, Walter Frederick. For a workingman or woman to vote Republican this year is the same as a chicken voting for Colonel Sanders.

Terkel, Studs. Working people are brighter than we think. Their jobs may be drab, but they transcend them.

Trachtenberg, Alan. Ellis Island represented the opening American act of one of the most remarkable dramas in all of history: the conversion of agricultural laborers, rural homemakers and traditional craftsmen into urban industrial workers.

LABOR AND LABORING CLASSES—RUSSIA

Anonymous, . As long as the bosses pretend they are paying us a decent wage, we will pretend that we are working (Soviet worker's saying).

LA COSTA, CALIFORNIA

Nizer, Louis. Having fought for the 1st amendment before *Penthouse* was born I wish (the first amendment) was in better hands than a magazine that specializes in close ups of women's orifices (spoken as the attorney for Rancho La Costa in its $630 million libel suit against *Penthouse* magazine.

LAETRILE

McNaughton, Andrew. The patient who is suffering from cancer doesn't care if he gets his Laetrile from an angel or a devil.

Thomas, Lewis. These are bad times for reason, all around. Suddenly, all of the major ills are being coped with by acupuncture. If not acupuncture, it is apricot pits.

LANCE, THOMAS BERTRAM

Bloom, Robert. Nobody wants to be a skunk at a garden party (explaining why his office concealed Bert Lance's past).

Byrd, Robert. The nation cannot afford to have as director of the Office of Management and Budget a man whose personal problems are so great that they detract from the performance of his duties.

LAND, EDWIN

Land, Edwin. I am addicted to at least one good experiment a day.

LANE, MARK

Garry, Charles. Mark Lane knew about everything; the guns, the drugs, the suicide pact—and he never told anyone.

LANGLOIS, HENRI

Langlois, Henri. Most people advance through life walking backward. Those artists who face forward are likely to be put in jail—or the madhouse.

LANGUAGE AND LANGUAGES

Baldwin, James. It (language) is the most vivid and crucial key to identity.

LASSER, LOUISE

Lasser, Louise. The best and worst thing that happened to me in 1976 was that I lived through it.

Lasser, Louise. When you are a celebrity, you are totally a victim.

LATIN AMERICA

Naipaul, V. S. There is a certain 'scum' quality in Latin America. They imagine that if you kill the right people everything will work. Genocide is their history.

LAUDER, ESTEE

Gaussen, Gerard. Mrs. (Estee) Lauder represents what we French admire most about Americans— brains and heart.

LAUGHTER

Auden, Wystan Hugh. Among those whom I like, I can find no common denominator; but among those whom I love, I can: all of them make me laugh.

LAUREN, RALPH

Lauren, Ralph. I can do anything I want.

LAW

Bell, Griffin. I think we have too many crimes, and I definitely have the view that we have too many laws.

Harris, Sydney J. It is not criminals, but laws that are the worst enemy of Law.

Holmes, Oliver Wendell. The life of the law has not been logic; it has been experience.

Silberman, Laurence. The legal process, because of its unbridled growth, has become a cancer which threatens the vitality of our forms of capitalism and democracy.

Solzhenitsyn, Aleksandr Isaevich. Whenever the tissue of life is woven of legalistic relations, there is an atmosphere of moral mediocrity, paralyzing man's noblest impulses.

Trollope, Anthony. Nothing surely is so potent as a law that may not be disobeyed. It has the force of the water drop that hollows the stone.

LAW—PRACTICE—UNITED STATES

Countryman, Vernon (Harvard professor). The bar is still dominated by shortsightedness and self-interest. Spotting change there is like watching a glacier move.

Green, Mark (lawyer). While piously proclaiming an interest in the public good, the bar's Canons of Ethics have operated as Canons of Profits.

LAWYERS

Anonymous (Italian proverb), . A lawsuit is a fruit tree planted in a lawyer's garden.

Auerbach, Jerold S. Equal justice under law (often means) unequal justice under lawyers.

Buchwald, Art. It isn't the bad lawyers who are screwing up the justice system in this country— it's the good lawyers...If you have two competent lawyers on opposite sides, a trial that should take three days could easily last six months.

Burger, Warren Earl. If law-school graduates, like cars, could be recalled for failure to meet commercial standards, the recall rate would be very high on those who go into the courts without substantial added training.

Burger, Warren Earl. We may be well on our way to a society overrun by hordes of lawyers, hungry as locusts, and brigades of judges in numbers never before contemplated.

Countryman, Vernon (Harvard professor). The bar is still dominated by shortsightedness and self-interest. Spotting change there is like watching a glacier move.

Dutton, Fred. Lawyers have become secular priests.

Green, Mark (lawyer). While piously proclaiming an interest in the public good, the bar's Canons of Ethics have operated as Canons of Profits.

Hundley, William G. The worst defense lawyers I know are those who become convinced their clients are innocent.

Keats, John. I think we may class the lawyer in the natural history of monsters.

Kennedy, Florynce Rae. Most lawyers are like whores. They serve the client who puts the highest fee on the table.

McKay, Robert. If war is too important to be left to the generals, surely justice is too important to be left to lawyers.

Nolan, John T. If you outsmart your own lawyer, you've got the wrong lawyer.

Sutton, Willie. I always figured that being a good robber was like being a good lawyer.

Warren, Earl. A jurist's mind cannot operate in a vacuum.

LEADERSHIP

Anonymous, . Two percent don't get the word.

Carter, James Earl. The most important skill for any President is leadership. A national leader, to be effective, must have the ability to lead this country and the vision to know where it must be led.

Clark, Joseph. A leader should not get too far in front of his troops or he will be shot in the ass.

Guerrina, Allan B. In any group of eagles, you will find some turkeys.

Heinfelden, Curt. The scenery only changes for the lead dog.

Kilpatrick, James J. Find out where the people want to go, then hustle yourself around in front of them.

Landers, Ann. I believe people want some spiritual leadership. It shows in the primaries; Jimmy Carter. He speaks openly about his religion. They see in him something that offers hope.

Nader, Ralph. I start with the premise that the function of leadership is to produce more leaders, not more followers.

Qaddafi, Muammar. People are getting killed everywhere by their leaders.

Riesman, David. The question is not whether leadership is obsolete but whether democracy is governable.

Truman, Harry S. The C students run the world.

Truman, Harry S. You know what makes leadership? It is the ability to get men to do what they don't want to do, and like it.

White, Kevin. Charismatic leadership is hungered for, but at the same time we fear it.

White, Theodore. Class is a matter of style in leadership. It is the magic that translates the language of the street into the language of history.

LEAR, AMANDA

Lear, Amanda. I hate to spread rumors, but what else can you do with them.

LEARNING AND SCHOLARSHIP

Frankel, Charles. Scholarship must be free to follow crooked paths to unexpected conclusions.

Truman, Harry S. The only things worth learning are the things you learn after you know it all.

LEARY, TIMOTHY

Kesey, Ken. He (Timothy Leary) is caught like a bone in the throat of the prison system—they can't swallow him and they can't spit him out.

Leary, Timothy. I don't have one nostalgic bone in my body for the 1960's. I have no desire to go back to Woodstock and spend three days in the mud on 'downers'.

LE BRIS, MICHEL

Le Bris, Michel. God is dead, Marx is dead, and I'm not doing all that well myself.

LEBRON, LOLITA

Lebron, Lolita. Until my last breath I will fight for the liberation and freedom of Puerto Rico.

LE CARRE, JOHN

Le Carre, John. I can't live elsewhere; this country (England) is the source for me. I understand the choreography here.

LEDBETTER, HUDDIE

Parks, Gordon. Huddie was meant for music and born for trouble.

LEFEBVRE, MARCEL

Lefebvre, Marcel. Rome, and not I, is in error.

LEFT WING POLITICS

Carmichael, Stokely. The only position for women in the movement is prone.

Garson, Barbara. Elizabeth Gurley Flynn's autobiography reminded me with a jolt that it wasn't until the time of the Stokely Carmichaels, imitated by the Tom Haydens, that women on the left had to fight to get the floor or to get up off of the floor.

Lasch, Christopher. Radicalism in the United States has no great triumphs to record.

Weir, David. The SLA is not only a dream story to the newspapers, it is a dream story to the FBI as well, because it allows them to paint the entire left with the brush of the SLA.

LEGISLATION

Talmadge, Betty. If you love the law and you love good sausage, don't watch either of them being made.

LEISURE

Brenan, Gerald. We are closer to the ants than to the butterflies. Very few people can endure much leisure.

Jerome, Jerome K. It is impossible to enjoy idling thoroughly unless one has plenty of work to do.

Wilson, Sloan. A man who wants time to read and write must let the grass grow long.

LEMON, BOB

Lemon, Bob. I had my bad days on the field, but I didn't take them home with me. I left them in a bar along the way (commenting at his induction into the Baseball Hall of Fame).

LENNON, JOHN

Lennon, John. As usual, there's a great woman behind every idiot (upon winning his permanent residence status in the U.S.).

LESBIANISM

Johnston, Jill. All women are lesbians except those who don't know it yet.

Johnston, Jill. Feminism at heart is a massive complaint. Lesbianism is the solution.

Lowell, Robert. Almost all good women poets are either divorced or lesbian.

LETTERS

Stimson, Henry. Gentlemen do not read each other's mail.

LEVI, EDWARD

Levi, Edward. I would like to be remembered as one who, in a transition period, helped the President in his efforts to restore faith in the operations of government and particularly in the administration of justice.

LEWIS, JOHN L.

Longworth, Alice Roosevelt. He was the best company there ever was (about John L. Lewis).

LIBEL AND SLANDER

Nizer, Louis. Having fought for the 1st amendment before Penthouse was born I wish (the first amendment) was in better hands than a magazine that specializes in close ups of women's orifices (spoken as the attorney for Rancho La Costa in its $630 million libel suit against Penthouse magazine.)

LIBERALISM

Bond, Julian. There's no new right. There's a new left of unbelievably queasy liberals.

Boone, Pat. Jimmy Carter is a Christian, but he's a McGovern-type Christian, proabortion, prohomosexuality and prolegalizing marijuana.

McGovern, George Stanley. The liberals are giving up too soon on the kind of economic and social change that we were trying to bring about in 1972—they want a winner, almost no matter who it is.

Mikva, Abner J. My definition of a liberal is someone who can look at an idea and see that it doesn't work, even if it was a liberal idea.

Rizzo, Frank Lazzaro. A conservative is a liberal who was mugged the night before.

Thompson, Hunter S. There's no such thing as a 'nice' reporter. That's like saying somebody's a nice liberal.

Tonsor, Stephen. New Deal liberals are as dead as a dodo. The only problem is they don't know it.

Wade, Richard. If you put the top 50 liberals inside a room to stop Henry Jackson, they'd have no troops for the job. Liberals have influence but no power.

White, Theodore. New York City is a glorious, or rather a tragic, example of 12 years of liberal government.

White, Theodore. People don't want change— people want more. And I think liberals don't realize that.

LIBERATION THEOLOGY

Esquerra, Maria Antonia (Chicana nun). The theology of liberation in North America will be written by the oppressed.

LIBERTY

Albornoz, Claudio Sanchez. I have only one word: peace. We have killed each other too much already. Let us reach understanding under a regime of freedom, all of us putting into it what is necessary from each side of the barricade (exiled former president upon returning to Spain).

Bernardin, Joseph. If the concept of a woman's freedom requires that she have the right to destroy her offspring, then that concept of freedom is brutal and unworthy... Freedom cannot be freedom from personal responsibility. Freedom follows from responsible action.

Burger, Warren Earl. The very discussion of independence reminds us how much each freedom is dependent on other freedoms.

Church, Frank. If we are to preserve freedom and keep constitutional government alive in America, it cannot be left to a President and his agents alone to decide what must be kept secret. Congress, if it is to check the abuse of executive power, must retain its right to inquiry and independent judgement.

Friedman, Milton. Let me propose that we take as our major motto what I would like to see as an 11th commandment: that everyone shall be free to do good at his own expense.

Gandhi, Indira (Nehru). The freedom of the people cannot be allowed to come in the way of the freedom of the masses.

Giscard D'Estaing, Valery. You do not fear freedom for yourself, do not then fear it for your friends and allies.

Goldwater, Barry Morris. Eternal vigilance is the price of liberty.

MacLeish, Archibald. Freedom is still the last great revolutionary cause.

Madison, James. Liberty is to faction what air is to fire.

Paul VI, Pope, . In reality, it is not enough to be free from something. One must be free for someone or something.

Safire, William. I think that one of Nixon's great contributions to civil liberties was getting caught doing what the two presidents before him got away with.

Sheen, Fulton J. Freedom is the right to do what you ought to do.

Stevenson, Adlai, II. A free society is one where it is safe to be unpopular.

Thatcher, Margaret Hilda. There can be no liberty unless there is economic liberty.

Von Hayek, Friedrich. You can have economic freedom without political freedom, but you cannot have political freedom without economic freedom.

Wriston, Walter. To think that the bell does not toll for academic freedom or freedom of the press if economic freedom is shackled is a dangerous illusion.

LIBRARIANS

Clark, Alan. Librarians are standing in their graves.

Fremont-Smith, Eliot. Booksellers are good at drinking; librarians are better.

LIBRARIES

Clark, Alan. Librarians are standing in their graves.

Dean, John Wesley, III. I don't have a friend. If I ever get one, I'll come back (responding after being asked to list the name of a reference for a library card application).

Fleming, John. Show me your books, and I'll tell you who you are.

Hochman, Sandra. I'd rather be hung from clotheslines and washed in laundromats than read in libraries (commenting on her poetry to be printed on clothing and bedsheets).

Kohler, Jerry. I'd just as soon die in Viet Nam as in the library.

Trezza, Alphonse. The best (publishers') customer in the world is a library. You know why? They don't have the brains to cancel the subscription.

LIBRARIES AND PUBLISHERS

Shields, Gerald R. It is obvious that the photocopying issue is to be decided soon and that the odds favor turning libraries into some sort of reprint warehouse for publisher's products.

LIBYA—FOREIGN RELATIONS—UNITED STATES

Carter, Billy. I know more about Libya than the whole State Department put together. I'm going to succeed just by treating them like folks.

LIDDY, G. GORDON

Liddy, G. Gordon. Before going to prison I believed that criticism of the criminal justice system for its treatment of the poor was so much liberal bleating and bunk. I was wrong.

Liddy, G. Gordon. I have found within myself all I need and all I ever shall need. I am a man of great faith, but my faith is in George Gordon Liddy. I have never failed me.

LIEBLING, A. J.

Shawn, William (attributed by Brendan Gill). Liebling wants to live like a stockbroker, but he doesn't want to be a stockbroker.

LIFE

Adjani, Isabelle. Life is worth being lived but not worth being discussed all the time.

Allen, Woody. The meaning of life is that nobody knows the meaning of life..

Allen, Woody (attributed by Marshall Brickman). Showing up is 80 percent of life.

Anonymous (Haight-Ashbury Diggers slogan), . Today is the first day of the rest of your life.

Ayckbourn, Alan. There are very few people on top of life, and the rest of us don't like them very much.

Blair, Eric. Any life when viewed from the inside is simply a series of defeats.

Camus, Albert. Not only is there no solution but there aren't even any problems.

Carter, James Earl. There are many things in life that are not fair.

Chaplin, Charles Spencer. Life is a tragedy when seen in close-up, but a comedy in long-shot.

Child, Julia. Life itself is the proper binge.

Cochrane, Elizabeth. Life can be a great adventure and I'm going to make it one.

Cousins, Norman. Life is an adventure in forgiveness.

Durant, Will. The primary things in my own life have been a wife, a house and some children roaming around us once in a while.

Eaton, Richard. Life is subject to change without notice.

Ford, Gerald Rudolph. I share your deep appreciation about the increased irreverence for life (commenting in a speech to the 41st Eucharistic Congress).

Goodman, Ellen. It has begun to occur to me that life is a stage I'm going through.

Guevara, Nacha. In life the things you want always arrive after you've stopped waiting.

Haliburton, Thomas C. The great secret of life is to learn lessons, not to teach them.

Hendrix, Jimi. It's funny the way most people love the dead. Once you are dead, you are made for life.

Henry, Julia. Incentive...that's the word for life.

Hubbard, Elbert. Do not take life too seriously—you will never get out of it alive.

Kahn, Alfred. All life is a concatenation of ephemeralities.

Khrushchev, Nikita Sergeevich. Life is short. Live it up.

Kitt, Eartha. There is no greater reward in life than love. The rewards are so tremendous. Even if you don't get love from the person you're giving it to, you get it from somewhere else.

Kristol, Irving. Being frustrated is disagreeable, but the real disasters of life begin when you get what you want.

Larkin, Philip. I see life more as an affair of solitude diversified by company than as an affair of company diversified by solitude.

Lindbergh, Anne Morrow (attributed by Julie Nixon Eisenhower). Life is a gift, given in trust—like a child.

Lindbergh, Charles Augustus. Life is like a landscape. You live in the midst of it, but can describe it only from the vantage point of distance.

Millay, Edna St. Vincent. It is not true that life is one damn thing after another; it's one damn thing over and over.

Miller, Henry. To the person who thinks with his head, life is a comedy. To those who think with their feelings, or work through their feelings, life is a tragedy.

Olivier, Laurence. Living is strife and torment, disappointment and love and sacrifice, golden sunsets and black storms.

O'Malley, Frank Ward. Life is just one damned thing after another.

O'Neill, Eugene. Life is a tragedy, hurrah.

Pirandello, Luigi. Life is little more than a loan shark: it exacts a very high rate of interest for the few pleasures it concedes.

Rattigan, Terrence. What a lovely world we're in, if only we'd let ourselves see it.

Roemer, Michael. You can't learn to die as though it were a skill. People die in the way they have lived. Death becomes the expression of everything you are, and you can bring to it only what you have brought to your life.

Runyon, Damon. All life is six-to-five against.

Sandburg, Carl. Life is like an onion: you peel it off one layer at a time and sometimes you weep.

Sontag, Susan. There are some elements in life—above all, sexual pleasure—about which it isn't necessary to have a position.

Ullmann, Liv. You must put more in your life than a man.

Vallee, Rudy. I thought my freshman English instructor at Yale was crazy when he said life was cold, cruel, rotten, hard and it stinks. But I found out he was right.

Vreeland, Diana. Either one's life is attractive or it isn't.

LIFE ON OTHER PLANETS

Soffer, Gerald. All the signs suggest that life exists on Mars, but we can't find any bodies.

LIFE (PERIODICAL)

Luce, Henry. I thought it was Time's job to make people unhappy and Life's job to make them happy.

LINDBERGH, CHARLES AUGUSTUS

Lindbergh, Charles Augustus. I do not want to be a member of the generation that through blindness and indifference destroys the quality of life on our planet.

Lindbergh, Charles Augustus. I've had enough fame for a dozen lives; it's not what it's cracked up to be.

LINDBERGH, CHARLES AUGUSTUS— KIDNAPPING CASE

Hauptmann, Bruno Richard. I have said it all, I am innocent. There is nothing else I could tell.

LINDGREN, LYNN

Lindgren, Lynn (Ms All-Bare America). I like to expose myself to a diversity of reactions and outcomes (in reply to why she wanted the title of Ms All-Bare America).

LINDSAY, JOHN VLIET

Gotbaum, Victor. (John Lindsay) was elegant where the rest of us had a piece of vulgarity in us. From the start, he was a made-to-order whipping boy.

Lindsay, John Vliet. Every public official should be recycled occasionally (commenting on his post-mayoral activities—as lawyer and TV host).

Moses, Robert. If you elect a matinee idol as mayor, you get a musical-comedy administration.

LIPPMANN, WALTER

Lippmann, Walter. I think there is a stopping point between globalism and isolationism. The test of statesmanship is to find those stopping points and to act accordingly (comments in a critique of Vietnam policy in 1965).

Lippmann, Walter. You are just a puzzled man making notes about what you think.

LIQUOR TRAFFIC—CHICAGO—PROHIBITION

Capone, Alphonse. When I sell liquor, it's called bootlegging; when my patrons serve it on silver trays on Lake Shore Drive, it's called hospitality.

LITERATURE

Blackmur, R. P. Literature exists to remind the powers that be, simple and corrupt as they are, of the turbulence they have to control.

Borges, Jorge Luis. When the literature of the second half of the 20th century is studied, the names will be different than we hear now. They will have found hidden writers. People who won Nobel prizes will be forgotten. I hope I will be forgotten.

Cheever, John. Literature is much more a conversation than a discourse.

Nabokov, Vladimir. Great novels are above all great fairy tales. Literature does not tell the truth but makes it up.

Singer, Isaac Bashevis. Literature is the memory of humanity.

Trilling, Lionel. The particular concern of literature of the last two centuries has been with the self in its standing quarrel with culture.

LITERATURE—LATIN AMERICA

Marquez, Gabriel Garcia. The famous Latin American 'literary boom' is a lie; what is real is the Cuban Revolution.

LITTLE, JOAN

Miller, Marvin. The fact that Miss Little was vindicated doesn't mean anything about the judicial system of this state or of the United States. The real reason she was vindicated was the international outcry about Joan Little.

Paul, Jerry. This system doesn't want justice. It wants convictions. That's why, given enough money, I can buy justice. I can win any case in this country, given enough money (upon winning acquittal for Joan Little in her murder trial).

LOBBYING

Lipsen, Chuck. Folklore has it that the oldest profession is prostitution. I always thought it was lobbying.

LOCAL GOVERNMENT—FEDERAL AID

Moynihan, Daniel Patrick. If welfare reform meant putting arsenic in children's milk, there would be local officials who would settle for that as long as it meant full federal funding.

LOGIC

Mencken, Henry Louis. One horse laugh is worth ten thousand syllogisms.

Orlans, Harold. Logic is a game men play as cats play with balls of string, whereas reality is a game the gods play with us.

LOMBARDO, GUY

Lombardo, Guy. The reason we have lasted so long is that we play music for lovers rather than acrobats.

Lombardo, Guy. When I go, I'll take New Year's Eve with me.

LONE RANGER (RADIO PERSONALITY)

Moore, Clayton. The Lone Ranger was honest, he was a gentleman and he used perfect diction. If I may say so without boasting, I am a great American.

LONELINESS

Feather, William. Loneliness is something you can't walk away from.

Lynch, James. If we do not live together, we will die—prematurely—alone.

Mother Teresa, . Loneliness and the feeling of being unwanted is the most terrible poverty.

LONG, RUSSELL

Hebert, F. Edward. Russell Long could cut your toenails without taking your shoes off.

LONGEVITY

Burns, George. If you want to live a long time you have to smoke cigars, drink martinis and dance close.

Mead, Margaret. One reason women live longer than men is that they can continue to do something they are used to doing, whereas men are abruptly cut off, whether they are admirals or shopkeepers.

LONGWORTH, ALICE ROOSEVELT

Sturm, Joanna. Grandmother (Alice Roosevelt Longworth) certainly is a feminist, but she'd never admit it. She feels it's tacky to identify yourself with a group, and to become overemotional. It's a question of esthetics.

LOPES, DAVE

Lopes, Dave. I don't know where I got the power (to hit a key home run), but maybe it was from the Big Dodger in the Sky.

LOREN, SOPHIA

Loren, Sophia. I will be a very wise and serene old lady. As I get older, I get quieter, because now I know myself better.

Loren, Sophia. I'm a giraffe. I even walk like a giraffe, with a long neck and legs. It's a pretty dumb animal, mind you.

Loren, Sophia. Success has not changed me. I have become more mature with time, but I am that same girl I was 20 years ago.

LOS ANGELES

Anderson, Gary. New York should be saved because without it people would make even more jokes about Los Angeles.

Leary, Timothy. I think climate, atmosphere and environment are tremendously important in your consciousness and your evolution. Southern California is the growing edge of the human species. It is also a media center, where I can transmit my messages. This is where the migrants and the mutants and the future people come, the end point of terrestial migration.

Medlin, James. The most healthy thing in L.A. is to do nothing.

Simon, Neil. When it's 105 in New York City, it's 78 in LA. When it's 20 below in New York City, it's 78 in LA. Of course, there are 11 million interesting people in New York City and only 78 in LA (commenting upon moving to Hollywood).

Stein, Benjamin. L.A. is the original in a gigantic Xerox machine that is spreading its copies everywhere. It is, thus, in a certain sense the center of the universe.

LOS ANGELES—DESCRIPTION

Hines, Jack, Jr. (restaurant cashier). Hollywood is the sinkhole of Los Angeles.

LOS ANGELES—POLICE

Davis, Edward Michael. I always felt the federal government really was out to force me to hire 4-foot-11 transvestite morons.

LOSING

Rockne, Knute. You show me a good and gracious loser, and I'll show you a failure!.

LOUISIANA

Kneece, Jack. They say Louisiana is somewhat like a banana republic, say Guatemala. That's not true. They speak better English in Guatemala.

LOVE

Allen, Woody. Love is the answer. But while you're waiting for the answer, sex raises some pretty good questions.

Auden, Wystan Hugh. Among those whom I like, I can find no common denominator; but among those whom I love, I can: all of them make me laugh.

Baldwin, James. Love does not begin and end the way we seem to think it does. Love is a battle, love is a war; love is a growing up.

Beauvoir, Simone De. In itself, homosexuality is as limiting as heterosexuality: the ideal should be to be capable of loving a woman or a man; either, a human being, without feeling fear, restraint, or obligation.

Brenan, Gerald. When the coin is tossed, either love or lust will fall uppermost. But if the metal is right, under the one will always lie the other.

Brooks, Mel. Everything we do in life is based on fear, especially love.

Charles, Prince of Wales, . Falling madly in love with someone is not necessarily the starting point to getting married.

Ciardi, John. Love is the word used to label the sexual excitement of the young, the habituation of the middle-aged, and the mutual dependence of the old.

Fiedler, Leslie. There can be no terror without the hope for love and love's defeat.

Fields, W. C. I was in love with a beautiful blonde once—she drove me to drink—'tis the one thing I'm indebted to her for.

Freud, Sigmund. One is very crazy when in love.

Janeway, Eliot. The thrill of making a fast buck follows only the thrill of love at first sight. Everyone needs to take an occasional fling with money...and with love.

Kitt, Eartha. There is no greater reward in life than love. The rewards are so tremendous. Even if you don't get love from the person you're giving it to, you get it from somewhere else.

Landers, Ann. Love is the most precious thing in all the world. Whatever figures in second place doesn't even come close.

McCarthy, Mary. One has to believe that love is eternal, even if one knows it is not.

Moreau, Jeanne. Age does not protect you from love. But love, to some extent, protects you from age.

Morgan, Marabel. Love never makes demands. Love is unconditional acceptance of him and his feelings.

Mother Teresa, . Jesus said love one another. He didn't say love the whole world.

Nin, Anais. One must thrust out of a finished cycle in life, and that leap is the most difficult to make—to part with one's faith, one's love, when one would prefer to renew the faith and recreate the passion.

Patton, George S. In war, just as in loving, you've got to keep on shoving.

Russell, Bertrand. I believe myself that romantic love is the source of the most intense delights that life has to offer.

Teasdale, Sara. Art can never mean to a woman what it does to a man. Love means that.

Tomlin, Lily. If love is the answer, could you rephrase the question?.

Truffaut, Francois. In love, women are professionals, men are amateurs.

Viorst, Judith. Brevity may be the soul of wit, but not when someone's saying 'I love you'.

LOVELL, JAMES, JR.

Lovell, James, Jr. I'm convinced that the last human sound on this continent won't be a bang, but a burp (commenting on what will happen if people don't eat less and exercise more.

LOWER CLASSES—GREAT BRITAIN

Waugh, Evelyn. It is impudent and exorbitant to demand truth from the lower classes.

LUBBOCK, TEXAS

Layne, Bobby. Living in a small town (Lubbock) in Texas ain't half bad—if you own it.

LUCAS, GEORGE

Lucas, George. I'm not out to be thought of as a great artist. It's a big world and everybody doesn't have to be significant.

LUCE, HENRY

Long, Earl. Mr. Luce is like a man who owns a shoe store and buys all the shoes to fit himself. Then he expects other people to buy them.

Luce, Henry. He seduces me. When I'm with him I feel like a whore (when asked how he felt about John Kennedy).

Luce, Henry. Make money, be proud of it; make more money, be prouder of it.

LUCK

Anonymous, . You can hide good luck but not misfortune.

Bohr, Niels. But horseshoes have a way of bringing you luck even when you don't believe in them.

LUDLAM, CHARLES

Ludlam, Charles. My work is eclectic not ethnocentric. It is a Rosetta Stone of theatrical conventions.

LUNG CANCER

Fontana, Robert S. Even if everyone quits smoking today, we could still look forward to a legacy of maybe 30,000 lung cancer deaths a year for the next 20 years (commenting on the early findings of a two-year lung cancer study).

LYING

Douglas, Norman. It takes a wise man to handle a lie; a fool had better remain honest.

Jerome, Jerome K. It is always the best policy to speak the truth, unless of course you are an exceptionally good liar.

LYSERGIC ACID DIETHYLAMIDE

Leary, Timothy. We needed drugs like LSD once to make us aware that we could alter our consciousness, do our own rewiring... Today I see drugs like LSD as primitive and at one point necessary evolutionary steps that are rapidly outmoded, like fossil fuels.

MACARTHUR, DOUGLAS

MacArthur, Douglas. It's the orders you disobey that make you famous.

Truman, Harry S. He (Douglas MacArthur) doesn't have a staff, he has a court.

MACARTHUR, JOHN D.

MacArthur, John D. Anybody who knows what he's worth, isn't worth very much (upon being asked how much he was worth).

MacArthur, John D. It's no fun being rich anymore. People are too damned jealous and suspicious of you. They figure anybody that makes as much money as I allegedly have must have cheated somebody.

MCCARTHY, EUGENE JOSEPH

McCarthy, Eugene Joseph. The most important member of the Executive Branch is the press secretary. I will appoint Mort Sahl. He's the only newspaper reader I know in America. I'll have him sit on the White House steps in the morning and catch the New York Times when it's thrown over the fence—and the Washington Post. He will throw the latter back immediately.

McCarthy, Eugene Joseph. The polls show that 10 percent of the public are ready to vote for me even though they don't know I'm running. We hope that figure won't drop when they learn I'm in the race.

MCCARTHY, JOSEPH RAYMOND

Hellman, Lillian. I think (Watergate and the McCarthy Era) are deeply connected, with Mr. Nixon being the connection, the rope that carries it all through.

Wayne, John. In my opinion Senator Joseph McCarthy was one of the greatest Americans that ever lived.

MCCARTNEY, LINDA

McCartney, Linda. Our kids keep asking, what is Daddy going to do when he grows up?.

MCCARTNEY, PAUL

McCartney, Linda. Our kids keep asking, what is Daddy going to do when he grows up?.

MCCULLERS, CARSON

McCullers, Carson. I have more to say than Hemingway, and, God knows, I say it better than Faulkner.

MCGOFF, JOHN

McGoff, John. I am not now, nor have I ever been, an agent or front for any foreign government, including the Republic of South Africa.

MCGOVERN, GEORGE STANLEY

Buckley, William Frank, Jr. Reagan is both too fatalistic and too modest to be a crusader. He doesn't have that darkness around the eyes of a George McGovern.

McGovern, George Stanley. I think it's going to be a fascinating experience...to be required, after twenty years away from the classroom, to systematically organize my thoughts on foreign policy.

McGovern, George Stanley. I will support Jimmy Carter with the same enthusiasm with which he supported the Democratic ticket in 1972.

McGovern, George Stanley. The liberals are giving up too soon on the kind of economic and social change that we were trying to bring about in 1972—they want a winner, almost no matter who it is.

MACHISMO

Gabor, Zsa Zsa. Macho does not prove mucho.

MCHUGH, VICKI

McHugh, Vicki (aide to Rosalynn Carter). I traveled in a Rolls long before Jimmy Carter became President and I don't plan to stop now.

MCINTYRE, BRUCE

McIntyre, Bruce. If the (Washington) Post experience says anything, maybe it's this: being a so-called union-busting paper doesn't interfere with greatness.

MCINTYRE, JAMES

Biggs, Barton. (James McIntyre) is a nice, naive, not terribly bright lawyer from Georgia...without a questioning bone in his body.

MCKUEN, ROD

McKuen, Rod. Having been born a bastard, I feel it has given me a head start on all those people who have spent their lives becoming one.

McKuen, Rod. People are not born bastards. They have to work at it (commenting on his lifelong search to find his father).

MACLAINE, SHIRLEY

MacLaine, Shirley. Sure, I'd play a hooker again, if she got to be Secretary of State.

MacLaine, Shirley. When you know who you are and you realize what you can do, you can do things better at 40 than when you're 20.

MCLUHAN, MARSHALL

McLuhan, Marshall. Most clear writing is a sign that there is no exploration going on. Clear prose indicates an absence of thought.

MADDOX, LESTER GARFIELD

Brown, Willie. Jerry (Brown) likes Jimmy (Carter) about as well as I like Lester Maddox.

MAFIA

Bissell, Richard M. I believe they worked without pay for the most part (on the role of the Mafia in the CIA Castro murder plots).

Pileggi, Nicholas. The best thing that ever happened to the Mafia is that none of them went to the Columbia School of Journalism or read Clay Felker on the importance of the media—so they learn some insight about the way the world really works.

MAFIA—LAS VEGAS

Sobel, Nathan. There's no such thing as organized crime in this city (New York City). There's a little of it in Las Vegas, but that's it.

MAFIA—NEW YORK (CITY)

Sobel, Nathan. There's no such thing as organized crime in this city (New York City). There's a little of it in Las Vegas, but that's it.

MAILER, NORMAN

Mailer, Norman. It is easier not to pay one's mother than not to pay a creditor.

Mailer, Norman. I've made an ass of myself so many times I often wonder if I am one.

MAKARIOS III, ARCHBISHOP

Makarios III, Archbishop. I would consort with the devil himself if it would keep Cyprus and its people independent.

MAKAROVA, NATALIA

Makarova, Natalia. I am an erotic woman and that's what dance is.

MALAMUD, BERNARD

Malamud, Bernard. I write to know the next room of my fate.

MALCOLM X

Malcolm X, . This thing with me will be resolved by death and violence.

MALLE, LOUIS

Malle, Louis. Being a director is like being a thief. You steal bits and pieces of the lives around you, and you put them into a movie.

Malle, Louis. It always surprised me that people consider me a French director. I don't like the French. They get on my nerves. They are so pompous and have no humor... They don't adjust to modern civilization at all.

Malle, Louis. Making a film is a life cycle—like being born, taking first steps, developing relationships. And the end of the shooting is like death in many ways.

MALRAUX, ANDRE

Malraux, Andre. There is no such thing as death. There is only I who am dying (commenting on death in his novel The Royal Way).

MAMET, DAVID

Mamet, David. I want to change the future of American theatre.

MAN

Acton, John Emerich Edward Dalberg. I don't hate humanity. I just don't know them personally.

Asimov, Isaac. We are the only creatures ever to inhabit the Earth who have truly seen the stars.

Beckett, Samuel. There's man all over for you, blaming his boots for the faults of his feet.

Bouza, Anthony. When you watch (ghetto) mothers take their kids to school, en route to a menial job, amid the drunks and junkies, you think maybe there is hope and the human spirit can triumph (commenting upon his retirement from the New York City police department after 23 years).

Castro, Fidel. Men are very fragile. We disappear and go up in smoke for almost any reason.

De Casseres, Benjamin. My studies in speculative philosophy, metaphysics, and science are all summed up in the image of a mouse called man running in and out of every hole in the cosmos hunting for the absolute cheese.

Eiseley, Loren. (Man's) basic and oldest characteristic is that he is a creature of memory, a bridge into the future, a time binder. Without this recognition of continuity, love and understanding between the generations becomes impossible.

Eiseley, Loren. We are changelings...who have slept in wood nests or hissed in the uncouth guise of waddling amphibians. We have played such roles for infinitely longer ages than we have been men.

Faulkner, William. I believe that man will not merely endure: he will prevail (commenting in his 1950 Nobel Prize acceptance speech).

Foreman, Percy. Man's inhumanity to man is only exceeded by woman's inhumanity to woman.

Fulbright, James William. It is one of the perversities of human nature that people have a far greater capacity for enduring disasters than for preventing them, even when the danger is plain and imminent.

Gingrich, Arnold. To stand out, for a man or a magazine, it is necessary to stand for something. Otherwise you stand still.

Humphrey, Hubert Horatio. A man with no tears is a man with no heart.

Jones, David. Man is the only maker, neither beast nor angel share this dignity with him.

Kaida, Ivan Ivanovich. First, I was a man without a country, then I was a man without land. Now I am truly rich, for I have both.

Kraus, Karl. The devil is an optimist if he thinks he can make people worse than they are.

Landor, Walter Savage. Men cannot bear to be deprived of anything they are used to; not even of their fears.

Laszlo, Ervin. The materialistic growth ethic is not an immutable expression of human nature.

Le Carre, John. People are very secretive creatures—secret even from themselves.

Lodge, John Davis. Man is born into the world as a pig and is civilized by women.

Lukacs, John. I believe human nature doesn't change. I believe very strongly in original sin. I also take a dim view of the pursuit of justice as being the superior value of Western civilization. I think truth is more important than justice.

Malraux, Andre. There cannot be another Michelangelo in today's society because our faith in man is too weak.

Morris, Richard B. The United States is still the last best hope of man.

Morrison, Toni. What is curious to me is that bestial treatment of human beings never produces a race of beasts.

Muggeridge, Malcolm. It is only believers in the Fall of Man who can really appreciate how funny men are.

Oldenburg, Claes. To give birth to form is the only act of man that has any consequence.

Orlans, Harold. Logic is a game men play as cats play with balls of string, whereas reality is a game the gods play with us.

Pogo (cartoon character), . We have met the enemy and they is us.

Sanchez, Robert. In looking backward, we must renew our faith in God. In looking forward, we must renew our faith in men.

Santayana, George. Our dignity is not in what we do, but in what we understand.

Solzhenitsyn, Aleksandr Isaevich. Whenever the tissue of life is woven of legalistic relations, there is an atmosphere of moral mediocrity, paralyzing man's noblest impulses.

Thomas, Lewis. We do not, in any real way, run the (world). It runs itself, and we are part of the running.

Valli, Frankie. There's nothing wrong with the world, only the people in it. And the same goes for music.

Voznesensky, Andrei. When Man put on clothes for the first time, he challenged the Lord and became His equal.

Warren, Robert Penn. What is man but his passion?.

MAN—INFLUENCE OF ENVIRONMENT

Leary, Timothy. I think climate, atmosphere and environment are tremendously important in your consciousness and your evolution. Southern California is the growing edge of the human species. It is also a media center, where I can transmit my messages. This is where the migrants and the mutants and the future people come, the end point of terrestial migration.

MAN—INFLUENCE ON NATURE

Beston, Henry. Peace with the earth is the first peace.

Richardson, Elliot Lee. There was a time when the seas seemed endless and the skies vast enough to swallow any of the mistakes and errors of man. The world used to be big and men could afford to be small. Now the world is small and men must be big.

MAN—RESPONSIBILITY

Camus, Albert. Alas, after a certain age every man is responsible for his face.

MANAGEMENT

Anonymous, . Two percent don't get the word.

Lidberg, A. A. Distribute dissatisfaction uniformly.

MANNERS AND CUSTOMS

Guest, Lucy Cochrane (C.Z.). I think manners are the most important thing in life.

MANSFIELD, KATHERINE

Mansfield, Katherine. Whenever I prepare for a journey, I prepare as though for death. Should I never return, all is in order. This is what life has taught me.

MANSFIELD, MIKE

Mansfield, Mike. There is a time to stay and a time to go. Thirty-four years is not a long time but it is time enough (commenting on his retirement from the Senate).

MAO, TSE-TUNG

Mao, Tse-Tung. Every Communist must grasp the truth, Political power grown out of the barrel of a gun. Our principle is that the party commands the gun and the gun must never be allowed to command the party.

Mao, Tse-Tung. I am alone with the masses.

Mao, Tse-Tung. (I am) only a lone monk walking the world with a leaky umbrella.

MARCEAU, MARCEL

Marceau, Marcel. I am a silent witness of my time.

MARCOVICCI, ANDREA

Marcovicci, Andrea. I like to play women who want something for themselves and will fight for it.

MARIJUANA

Brown, Edmund Gerald, Jr. I think Jimmy Carter ought to take the Paraquat out of whatever it is in.

Carter, Billy. Marijuana is like Coors beer. If you could buy the damn stuff at a Georgia filling station, you'd decide you wouldn't want it.

Ford, Steve. Sometimes I'm for it and sometimes I'm against it (on the legalization of marijuana).

Nelson, Willie. To me, a redneck is someone who likes to fight. Whiskey makes you want to fight and marijuana makes you want to listen to music. And marijuana and beer together is probably the greatest truth serum ever.

MARINE POLLUTION

Cousteau, Jacques Yves. Today I don't swim at all because I haven't the time to go 10 to 12 miles offshore to find clean water.

MARKETING

Paulucci, Jeno F. The meek have to inherit the earth—they sure don't know how to market it.

MARRIAGE

Ali, Muhammad. If you want to be equal with me, you can get your own Rolls-Royce, your own house and your own million dollars.

Astor, Nancy. I married beneath me. All women do.

Aumont, Jean-Pierre. Marriages are not eternal, so why should divorce be?.

Brickman, Marshall. Open marriage is nature's way of telling you you need a divorce.

Carter, Lillian. Marriage ain't easy but nothing that's worth much ever is.

Charles, Prince of Wales, . Falling madly in love with someone is not necessarily the starting point to getting married.

Dietrich, Marlene. Never marry an actress (to Eddie Fisher).

Gabor, Zsa Zsa. A man in love is incomplete until he has married. Then he's finished.

Gish, Lillian. I don't think actresses have the right to marry and ruin a man's life.

Gregoire, Menie. Every French male born is convinced that, by definition, he is an expert lover. Many wives tell me that they go to see pornographic movies with their husbands as a way of delicately indicating to them that they don't know as much about lovemaking as they think they do.

Hefferan, Colien. The woman who once saw marriage as a form of security now finds that she can provide her own security.

Heide, Wilma Scott. I do not refer to myself as a housewife for the reason that I did not marry a house.

Kerr, Jean. Marrying a man is like buying something you've been admiring for a long time in a shop window. You may love it when you get it home, but it doesn't always go with everything else in the house.

O'Brian, Hugh. There is quite enough grief when one is alone. Why compound it by getting married? (upon his founding Marriage Anonymous).

Parton, Dolly. A real important thing is that, though I rely on my husband for love, I rely on myself for strength.

Richard, Cliff. Just because someone isn't married doesn't mean he's homosexual.

Rooney, Mickey. Be friends first. If you say 'I love you' in the beginning, it's like using your three best jokes at the start of your act. You have nowhere to go from there (advice on how to ensure a happy marriage).

Saint James, Margo. (We've already) got legalized prostitution: marriage.

Steinem, Gloria. Today a woman without a man is like a fish without a bicycle.

Trudeau, Margaret. It takes two to destroy a marriage.

West, Mae. You should marry for sex or money and you're really lucky if you can get both.

Wilde, Oscar. American women seek in their husbands a perfection which English women seek only in their butlers.

MARS (PLANET)

Soffer, Gerald. All the signs suggest that life exists on Mars, but we can't find any bodies.

MARTIN, BILLY

Flaherty, Joe. It seems that in the baseball world Martin is someone with whom you have an affair or a fling but never a relationship.

Martin, Billy. I can't change now. I guess it's like being a gunfighter. Once you start, you do it for life—until somebody comes along and shoots you down.

MARTIN, MARY

Martin, Mary. Growing old is boring. It's boring to lose your hair or your eyesight or to go to the dentist and have teeth put in. Though I can't help thinking I'm still 19. I wouldn't have missed my life for anything, but I wouldn't go back for anything.

MARTINIS

Thurber, James. One martini is all right, two is too many, three is not enough.

MARTYRDOM

Schorr, Daniel. The joys of martyrdom are considerably overrated.

MARX, GROUCHO

Marx, Groucho. I never forget a face, but in your case I'll make an exception.

Marx, Groucho. I wouldn't belong to any club that would have me for a member.

Marx, Groucho. Not since 'David Copperfield' have I read such a stirring and inspiring life story (commenting on his own book Groucho and Me).

MARX, KARL

Chaplin, Charles Spencer. I can't understand Karl Marx, so how can I be a Communist?.

White, Theodore. If you go back through 2000 years, I guess luck, Marx, and God have made history, the three of them together.

MARXISM

Singer, Isaac Bashevis. A Marxist has never written a good novel.

MARY HARTMAN, MARY HARTMAN (TELEVISION PROGRAM)

Vidal, Gore. To understand Mary Hartman is to understand America. If Tiberius had watched the show, he would still be alive today.

MARZULLO, VITO

Marzullo, Vito. It's not that I lie. It's just that I don't know the difference sometimes.

MASON, JAMES

Mason, James. Talking about my leading ladies is difficult for me if I'm going to be honest. Any opinion I give is bound to offend somebody. So when I want to tread cautiously, I tell people that the best actress I ever worked with was Margaret Rutherford.

MASS

Lefebvre, Marcel. The rite of Mass today is a bastard rite. The sacraments today are bastard sacraments. We want to have prayers like our ancestors. We want to keep the Catholic faith.

MASS MEDIA

Clay, William. Whenever I see certain elements in the press show favoritism to a Black man running for a position of power, I know there's a nigger in the woodpile somewhere.

Schorr, Daniel. I'm fighting for freedom of the press, and maybe I should also be fighting for freedom *from* the press.

MASS MEDIA—UNITED STATES

Ravitz, Justin Charles. I understand the function of American media. Essentially, they exist to please their advertisers.

MATERIALISM

Laszlo, Ervin. The materialistic growth ethic is not an immutable expression of human nature.

MATTER

Elgin, Duane S (futurologist). Once you discover that space doesn't matter, or that time can be traveled through at will so that time doesn't matter, and that matter can be moved by consciousness so that matter doesn't matter—well, you can't go home again.

MAUGHAM, WILLIAM SOMERSET

Churchill, Sir Winston (attributed by Michael Korda). Willie (W. Somerset Maugham) may be an old bugger, but by God, he's never tried to bugger me.

MAXWELL, ELSA

Flanner, Janet. She (Elsa Maxwell) was built for crowds. She has never come any closer to life than the dinner table.

MAYS, WILLIE

Mays, Willie. I think I was the best baseball player I ever saw.

MEAD, MARGARET

Bohannan, Paul. Margaret Mead was, in fact, a centipede; she had that many shoes.

Mead, Margaret. I expect to die someday but I'll never retire.

MEANS, JACQUELINE

Means, Jacqueline. We have spent so many years meeting and debating on this when we could have been doing other things. I'm glad it's over so that I can be able to get to work with the ministry (commenting on the ordination of women in the Protestant Episcopal Church).

MEANY, GEORGE

Dole, Robert J. George Meany could run for President. But why should he step down?.

Fitzsimmons, Frank E. Personally, I don't think George Meany would know a trade unionist if he tripped over one.

Winpisinger, William (union leader). I have immense respect for George Meany, but there comes a time when every man passes the apex of his career, and it's all downhill after that. When the polls rate labor just behind Richard Nixon and just ahead of used car salesmen, you know something needs to be changed.

MEDICAL LAWS AND LEGISLATION

Moss, Frank. There comes a certain point when physicians, like other lawbreakers, must be put in jail (commenting on Medicaid and Medicare fraud).

MEDICAL SERVICE

Barnard, Christiaan. There is one message I would give to young doctors and that is that the goal of medicine is not to prolong life. It is to alleviate suffering and improve the quality of life.

MEDICAL SERVICE, COST OF

Thomson, Campbell. If it ever was true that a hospital was a charity organization, it no longer is true.

MEDICAL SERVICE—UNITED STATES

Anonymous, . The socialization of medicine is coming...the time now is here for the medical profession to acknowledge that it is tired of the eternal struggle for advantage over one's neighbor (editorial comment in the Journal of the American Medical Association, 1914).

Crichton, Michael. I think we can all agree that American medicine, the way it is now, is not successful. But there's no evidence that the Government can run anything. If you like the Post Office, you'll like socialized medicine.

MEDICARE

Moss, Frank. There comes a certain point when physicians, like other lawbreakers, must be put in jail (commenting on Medicaid and Medicare fraud).

MEDICINE

Thomas, Lewis. These are bad times for reason, all around. Suddenly, all of the major ills are being coped with by acupuncture. If not acupuncture, it is apricot pits.

MEDICINE—PRACTICE—UNITED STATES

Anonymous, . The socialization of medicine is coming...the time now is here for the medical profession to acknowledge that it is tired of the eternal struggle for advantage over one's neighbor (editorial comment in the Journal of the American Medical Association, 1914).

Cousins, Norman. A hospital is no place for a person who is seriously ill.

MEDIOCRITY

Miller, George William. Don't rationalize mediocrity.

MEDITATION

Elgin, Duane S (futurologist). Once you discover that space doesn't matter, or that time can be traveled through at will so that time doesn't matter, and that matter can be moved by consciousness so that matter doesn't matter—well, you can't go home again.

Graham, Billy. Transcendental Meditation is evil because...it opens space within you for the devil.

Van De Wetering, Janwillem. I've meditated for thousands of hours now, and I still don't know nothing. It's disgusting.

MEEKNESS

Allen, Woody. The lion and the calf shall lie down together, but the calf won't get much sleep.

Getty, Jean Paul. The meek shall inherit the earth, but not its mineral rights.

MEIR, GOLDA

Meir, Golda. I may not have been a great prime minister, but I would have been a great farmer.

MEMORY

Cabell, James Branch. There is no memory with less satisfaction in it than the memory of some temptation we resisted.

MEN

Addams, Jane. I do not believe that women are better than men. We have not wrecked railroads, nor corrupted legislatures, nor done many unholy things that men have done; but then we must remember that we have not had the chance.

Bardot, Brigitte. Men are beasts and even beasts don't behave as they do.

Castro, Fidel. Men are very fragile. We disappear and go up in smoke for almost any reason.

Disraeli, Benjamin. A man is occasionally thankful when he says 'thank you'.

Jackson, Jesse. I suggest to you boys you are not a man because you make a baby. You are a man because you protect a baby (urging pupils at Martin Luther King Junior High School to develop pride through education).

Luce, Clare Boothe. There aren't many women now I'd like to see as President—but there are fewer men.

Needham, Richard J. Men are foolish, they think money should be taken from the rich and given to the poor. Women are sensible, they think money should be taken from the rich and given to them.

Peterson, Esther. If a man fights his adversaries, he's called determined. If a woman does it, she's frustrated.

Sanchez, Robert. In looking backward, we must renew our faith in God. In looking forward, we must renew our faith in men.

Schreiner, Olive. We are men or women in the second place, human beings in the first.

Thatcher, Margaret Hilda. If you want anything said, ask a man; if you want anything done, ask a woman.

Truffaut, Francois. I am reproached because my men (in films) aren't adults, but in my life, I have not met many men who are adults.

Williams, Tennessee. Men are rather inscrutable to me.

MEN—BEHAVIOR

DeVore, Irven. Males are a vast breeding experiment run by females.

Stevenson, Adlai, II. Man does not live by words alone, despite the fact that sometimes he has to eat them.

MEN—FRANCE

Gregoire, Menie. Every French male born is convinced that, by definition, he is an expert lover. Many wives tell me that they go to see pornographic movies with their husbands as a way of delicately indicating to them that they don't know as much about lovemaking as they think they do.

MEN—POWER (SOCIAL SCIENCES)

Soeder, Karin (Sweden's first woman Foreign Minister). Men care about power because for them power is linked to sexual performance. Women achieve positions of power out of a need to do something, not because we need reassurance.

MEN—PSYCHOLOGY

Alsop, Stewart. A fashionable gentleman who much concerns himself with the fashions of gentlemen is neither fashionable nor a gentleman.

Beauvoir, Simone De. In itself, homosexuality is as limiting as heterosexuality: the ideal should be to be capable of loving a woman or a man; either, a human being, without feeling fear, restraint, or obligation.

Gabor, Zsa Zsa. A man in love is incomplete until he has married. Then he's finished.

Gabor, Zsa Zsa. Macho does not prove mucho.

Hufstedler, Shirley. A man cannot be very kind unless he is also very strong.

Mead, Margaret. Women, it is true, make human beings, but only men can make men.

MENOTTI, GIAN CARLO

MENOTTI, Gian Carlo. I am almost 66, and I have to start fighting the shadow of death. When I see darkness coming, I turn on the stage lights and don't worry about the cost of electricity.

MENTAL HYGIENE

Janov, Arthur. The world is having a nervous breakdown. Valium is the only glue that holds it together.

MERCOURI, MELINA

Mercouri, Melina. I have been playing a woman with a past since I was five years old.

MERCURY POISONING

Train, Russell E. Economic, social and environmental costs and benefits of the continued use (of mercurial pesticides) are not sufficient to outweigh the risk to man or the environment (commenting on the EPA immediate ban on production of virtually all pesticides containing mercury).

METTERNICH, KLEMENS WENZEL NEPOMUK LOTHAR, VON, PRINCE

Kissinger, Henry Alfred. I think Metternich was an extremely skilled diplomat, but not very creative.

MEXICO

Fuentes, Carlos. Mexicans have always asked themselves why a people so close to God should be so near the United States.

MEXICO—FOREIGN RELATIONS—UNITED STATES

Portillo, Jose Lopez. We will have to be tied by geography as long as the world goes round; we already are tied by history; we also would like to be tied by good will.

MEXICO—POLITICS AND GOVERNMENT

Anonymous (U.S. official), . What happens when you combine capital and corruption is simply more corruption (about Mexico).

Echeverria Alvarez, Luis. I would like to have as my successor a person who would continue with the reforms I have begun and carry them much further.

Riding, Alan. Never commit yourself fully to anyone; always leave numerous options open; be all things to all men, and, keep your true sentiments well hidden (rule number 1 of long-term survival in Mexican politics).

MEYER, RUSS

Meyer, Russ. My films are like a reptile you beat with a club. You think you've killed it, but then you turn around and it gets you in the ankle.

MEYERS, VICTOR ALOYSIUS

Meyers, Victor Aloysius (former Lieutenant Governor of California). Habitually I go without a vest so that I can't be accused of standing for the vested interests.

MIAMI

Benes, Bernardo. God gave us our geography and Fidel Castro gave us our biculturalism (about Miami).

MIAMI—DESCRIPTION

Arboleya, Carlos. History will write Miami's (Florida) future in Spanish and English.

MIDDLE AGE

Asimov, Isaac. There's nothing wrong with middle age, but it comes hard to a person who is a child prodigy by profession.

Dundee, Chris. Middle age is when you start for home about the same time you used to start for somewhere else.

Howar, Barbara. I'm now fast approaching the age when a woman doesn't fan herself in public.

MacLaine, Shirley. When you know who you are and you realize what you can do, you can do things better at 40 than when you're 20.

Reagan, Ronald. Middle age is when you're faced with two temptations and you choose the one that will get you home by 9:30 (commenting on the 27th anniversary of his 39th birthday).

Wax, Judith. It's to be expected that in middle age, mortality is not only intimated, but sometimes delivered, that pain and loss are birthday presents nobody asks for.

Wilson, Earl. Middle age is when your clothes no longer fit, and it's you who need the alterations.

MIDDLE CLASSES—UNITED STATES

Wonder, Stevie. They (the Beatles) brought all different cultures together. They made White Middle America wake up about those old black artists—the Beatles brought them to people who had never heard of them. And it gave those artists—who were sometimes starving—some money.

MIDDLE EAST

Begin, Menachem. This region isn't Switzerland.

MIDDLE EAST—FOREIGN RELATIONS

Assad, Hafez. Step-by-step might be all right if the steps were giant steps, but they are tortoise steps.

Kissinger, Henry Alfred. We are making remarkable progress toward an agreement—and toward a nervous breakdown. It's going to be a race to see which will be achieved first (about Middle East peace negotiations).

MIDDLE EAST—PEACE AND MEDIATION

Sadat, Anwar. The dogs can go on barking—but they will not stop the caravan (about Arab critics of the Egypt-Israeli Peace Treaty).

MIDDLE EAST—POLITICS AND GOVERNMENT

Anonymous, . The Arabs cannot make war without the Egyptians, but they cannot make peace without the Palestinians.

Arafat, Yasir. I have very few cards, but I have the strongest cards.

Arafat, Yasir. Palestine is the cement that holds the Arab world together, or it is the explosive that blows it apart.

Carter, James Earl. I have never met an Arab leader that in private professed the desire for an independent Palestinian state.

Dayan, Moshe. Of course, if you want to make peace, you don't talk to your friends. You talk to your enemies. But the question is whom do we want to make peace with—not just who are our enemies (explaining his objections to negotiating with the PLO).

Dayan, Moshe. You cannot get the Arab opinion by sitting and talking to Jews.

Eban, Abba Solomon. You cannot have peace without risks.

Hussein, King of Jordan, . It's amusing. The Americans have changed Presidents six times since I've been King. And they talk to the Arabs about stability?.

MIDLER, BETTE

Midler, Bette. (Fans) make me think that maybe there's more to me than I know.

Midler, Bette. I adore deceit and don't give a damn about being misrepresented (in interviews). But I will not be made to sound boring to the thousands that are convinced I am, if not Jackie O, certainly the next best thing.

Midler, Bette. I want to be a legend.

Midler, Bette. The worst part of having success is to try finding someone who is happy for you.

MIGRATION, INTERNAL—CALIFORNIA

Leary, Timothy. I think climate, atmosphere and environment are tremendously important in your consciousness and your evolution. Southern California is the growing edge of the human species. It is also a media center, where I can transmit my messages. This is where the migrants and the mutants and the future people come, the end point of terrestial migration.

MIKULSKI, BARBARA A.

Mikulski, Barbara A. Some people like to raise flowers; I like to raise hell, I want to be the Amelia Earhart of Congress. I want to fly into the areas of the unknown, like she did, for the fun of it.

MILITARY ASSISTANCE

Sakata, Michita. Security is like sun, water or air. When they are plentiful you don't appreciate their value.

MILITARY INTELLIGENCE

Marx, Groucho. Military intelligence is a contradiction in terms.

MILITARY SERVICE AS A PROFESSION

Haig, Alexander M. Military service and public service are not unakin.

MILLER, ANN

Miller, Ann. All my life I've tried to be an eight-by-ten glossy.

MILLER, ARNOLD

Miller, Arnold (U.M.W. President). Julius Caesar had his Brutus but I've got about a hundred Brutuses. The problems I have are not with the membership, it's with the elected officials and the staff.

MILLER, ARTHUR

Miller, Arthur. I've always written in the back of my head for the great unwashed.

Miller, Arthur. Part of being a playwright is being an actor. One way or another, whether surreptitiously or not, a good playwright is an actor.

MILLER, GEORGE WILLIAM

Miller, George William. There is no penalty for overachievement.

MILLER, HENRY

Miller, Henry. Death itself doesn't frighten me because I don't believe it's the end. All my intuitive feelings are that this cannot be the only world. It's too damn short, too ugly and too meaningless.

Miller, Henry. I owe everything to the French. I am more close to France than America even though I lived there only 10 years, from 1929 to 1939. Those years in France meant everything to me and formed my whole career.

Miller, Henry. I'm going to beat those bastards (when asked how he would write his epitaph).

MILLIONAIRES

Shor, Toots. I don't want to be a millionaire, I just want to live like one.

MILLS, CHUCK

Mills, Chuck. I give the same halftime speech over and over. It works best when my players are better than the other coach's players.

MILLS, WILBUR DAIGH

Mills, Wilbur Daigh. I'd go for days at a time and not remember what I'd done. Especially 1974, I don't remember much of 1974 at all.

Mills, Wilbur Daigh. I'm not the man of steel I thought I was.

MILNES, RICHARD MONCKTON

Milnes, Richard Monckton. My exit is the result of too many entrees.

MIND

Knight, Damon. If there is a universal mind, must it be sane?.

MINELLI, LIZA

Simon, John. I always thought Miss (Liza) Minelli's face deserving—of first prize in the beagle category.

MINERAL RIGHTS

Getty, Jean Paul. The meek shall inherit the earth, but not its mineral rights.

MINGUS, CHARLES

Mingus, Charles. Don't call me a jazz musician. The word jazz means nigger, discrimination, second-class citizenship, the back-of-the-bus bit.

MINIMUM WAGE

Reagan, Ronald. The minimum wage has caused more misery and unemployment than anything since the Great Depression.

MINNESOTA. FOOTBALL CLUB (NATIONAL LEAGUE)

White, Ed. Losing this game was like having your house robbed and watching it happen (commenting on the Vikings 17-14 defeat by the Cowboys).

MINNESOTA. UNIVERSITY (FOOTBALL)

Stoll, Cal. We finally got Nebraska where we want them—off the schedule.

MINORITIES—EQUAL RIGHTS

Henderson, Vivian Wilson. We have programs for combatting racial discrimination, but not for combatting economic class distinctions.

MIRACLES

Brenan, Gerald. Miracles are like jokes. They relieve our tension suddenly by setting us free from the chain of cause and effect.

MISERY

Baker, Russell. Misery no longer loves company. Nowadays it insists upon it.

MISFORTUNE

Anonymous, . You can hide good luck but not misfortune.

MISTAKES

Peter, Laurence J. In the country of the blind, the one-eyed King can still goof up.

Shaw, George Bernard. The man who has never made a mistake will never make anything else.

MITCHELL, JOHN

Mitchell, John. All that crap, you're putting it in the paper? It's all been denied. Katie Graham's gonna get her tit caught in a big fat wringer if that's published.

Mitchell, John. Henceforth, don't call me, I'll call you (on release from Federal prison).

Mitchell, John. It could have been a hell of a lot worse. He could have sentenced me to spend the rest of my life with Martha Mitchell (commenting on his Watergate-related jail sentence).

Mitchell, John. It's nice to be back in Alabama (upon entering prison at Maxwell Air Force Base).

MITCHELL, MARTHA

Nixon, Richard Milhous. If it hadn't been for Martha, there'd have been no Watergate.

MITCHUM, ROBERT

Mitchum, Robert. I do films for the greatest return, for the least effort.

MOBS—PSYCHOLOGY

Houde, Camillien. A mob is like a river—it never runs uphill.

MOHAMMED REZA PAHLEVI, SHAH OF IRAN

Khalkhali, Ayatollah. Even if this traitor Shah hides himself in a corner of the White House, we shall get him out and kill him.

Khomeini, Ayatollah Ruhollah. It is impossible to solve Iran's political problems without the disappearance of the Pahlevi dynasty.

Kissinger, Henry Alfred. The Shah (of Iran) was—despite the travesties of retroactive myth—a dedicated reformer.

Mohammed Reza Pahlevi, Shah Of Iran, . I will not rule. I will reign.

Mohammed Reza Pahlevi, Shah of Iran, . I'm not just another dictator. I'm a hereditary monarch.

Mohammed Reza Pahlevi, Shah of Iran, . Nobody can overthrow me—I have the power.

Nixon, Richard Milhous. If the United States doesn't stand up for our friends when they are in trouble, we're going to wind up without any friends.

MONDALE, JOAN

Mondale, Joan. Fritz (Walter Mondale) says I never make a decision without consulting him. He's right. I consult—and then do what I want to.

MONDALE, WALTER FREDERICK

Carter, James Earl. I look on Senator Mondale, who will be the next Vice President, as my top staff person.

Humphrey, Hubert Horatio. I have a feeling he (Walter Mondale) was born under the right star.

Kaye, Peter F. (Ford campaign spokesman). Mondale is a 100 per cent bona fide liberal. It gives us a tangible target. We're not just running against this peanut farmer who walks on water.

McCarthy, Eugene Joseph. He (Fritz Mondale) has the soul of a vice-president.

Mondale, Joan. Fritz (Walter Mondale) says I never make a decision without consulting him. He's right. I consult—and then do what I want to.

Mondale, Walter Frederick. Everybody thinks it's easy to be appointed. It's the toughest of all. You have to get 100 percent of the vote.

Mondale, Walter Frederick. I saw where Joe Califano gave up $500,000 a year to become HEW secretary; Mike Blumenthal, $400,000 to become Treasury secretary; and Cy Vance, $250,000 to become secretary of state. As far as I can tell, I'm the only one who took the job because I needed the money.

MONDAY, RICK

Lane, Frank. Monday got about $125,000 from the Cubs last season and struck out 125 times. He got paid $1,000 a strikeout. This year he'll probably get $250,000 from the Dodgers, which means he's gotten a raise to $2,000 a strikeout.

MONEY

Galbraith, John Kenneth. (Money) ranks with love as man's greatest source of joy. And it ranks with death as his greatest source of anxiety. It differs from an automobile, a mistress, and cancer in being equally important to those who have it and those who don't. So when you watch people in a supermarket, you're seeing people in touch with their deepest emotions.

Galbraith, John Kenneth. The study of money, above all other fields of economics, is one in which complexity is used to disguise or evade the truth, not reveal it. Much discussion involves priestly incantation, the same type used by doctors and lawyers to pretend to a sort of difference that excludes other people.

Holmes, Oliver Wendell. Put not your trust in money. Put your money in trust.

Hunt, Haroldson Lafayette. Money is just something to make bookkeeping convenient.

Janeway, Eliot. The thrill of making a fast buck follows only the thrill of love at first sight. Everyone needs to take an occasional fling with money...and with love.

Ky, Nguyen Cao. I was not corrupt. Perhaps that is the only thing I regret. I realized after 14 months in this country the value of money, whether it's clean or dirty.

Luce, Henry. Make money, be proud of it; make more money, be prouder of it.

Snow, C. P. Money is not so important as a pat on the head.

Stein, Gertrude. Money is always there but the pockets change; it is not in the same pockets after a change, and that is all there is to say about money.

Wallace, Clinton. Money is the means by which you can purchase everything but happiness and health, and will pay your ticket to all places but Heaven.

Wilde, Oscar. Young people, nowadays, imagine that money is everything, and when they grow older they know it.

MONEY—INTERNATIONAL ASPECTS

Janeway, Eliot. The dollar has become like a hydrant at an international convention of dogs.

MONNIER, VALENTINE

Monnier, Valentine. I'm not a big deal yet, but I will be.

MONROE, MARILYN

Monroe, Marilyn. I think I made his back feel better (about John F. Kennedy).

MOON—EXPLORATION

Armstrong, Neil A. That's one small step for man, one giant leap for mankind (upon stepping on the Moon).

MOON, KEITH

Altham, Keith. (Keith Moon's death) was not suicide. If Keith wanted to do that, he would get into a sports car and drive through a brick wall.

Moon, Keith. Some of the things I've done, I couldn't have anything but the reputation of being a lunatic.

MOON, SUN MYUNG

Moon, Sun Myung. Are Americans that foolish? Can they really be brainwashed by Rev. Moon, a Korean? I know your answer is no. My answer is no, too. No American is so foolish (commenting before congressmen on charges that the Korean evangelist has mind control over young people and forces them to maintain him in luxury).

Moon, Sun Myung. God has been very good to me.

Moon, Sun Myung. God sent me to America in the role of a doctor.

Moon, Sun Myung. Kings and queens and heads of state will someday bow at my feet. I will conquer and subjugate the world.

Moon, Sun Myung. The time will come when my words will serve as law.

Moon, Sun Myung. Without me, on earth everything will be nullified.

MOORE, HENRY

Moore, Henry. Some people ask me why I live and work in the country. Space, light and distance are three good reasons.

MOORE, MARIANNE

Moore, Marianne. A writer is unfair when he is unable to be hard on himself.

MOORE, ROGER

Moore, Roger. My real attitude toward women is this, and it hasn't changed because of any movement or anything: basically, women like to be treated as sex objects.

MOORE, SARA JANE

Moore, Sara Jane. I did indeed willfully and knowingly attempt to murder Gerald R. Ford, the President of the United States, by use of a handgun and would now like to enter a plea of guilty.

MORAL ATTITUDES

Braine, John. I believe absolutely in Christian sexual morality, which means that I believe in premarital virginity. Virgins don't get V.D., don't have abortions, don't have illegitimate babies, and aren't forced to get married. And no man, no matter how progressive, has ever objected to his bride being a virgin.

MORMONS AND MORMONISM

Kimball, Spencer W. (President of the Mormon Church). Too many people have forgotten the first commandment—be fruitful and multiply.

MORO, ALDO

Moro, Aldo. I believe I have done my duty to the end (upon the announcement of the resignation of his cabinet).

Saragat, Giuseppe. Along-side the body of (Aldo) Moro lies the body of the first Italian republic.

MOROCCO—FOREIGN RELATIONS—SPAIN

Hassan II, King of Morocco, . I am convinced that the march has fulfilled its mission and reached its goal, and we must therefore return to our point of departure (commenting upon Morocco's march into the Spanish Sahara).

MOROCCO—POLITICS AND GOVERNMENT

Hassan II, King of Morocco, . I do not want to frustrate my subjects because a people is not a toy.

MOSCOW—DESCRIPTION

Bonner, Yelena (wife of Andrei Sakharov). It (The Master of Margarita) is the perfect theatre for the Moscow intelligentsia. It doles out the truth in small doses, never big enough to cause trouble.

MOSES

Morgan, Charles, Jr. If Moses had gone to Harvard Law School and spent three years working on the Hill, he would have written the Ten Commandments with three exceptions and a savings clause.

MOTHER TERESA

Mother Teresa, . I am unworthy (upon winning the Nobel Peace Prize).

MOTHERS

Birley, Rhoda. Mothers are a great bore.

Duncan, Isadora. With what a price we pay for the glory of motherhood.

Lasch, Christopher. The mother's power originates in the imposition of her own madness on everybody else.

MOTHERS AND SONS

Carter, Lillian. How could Jimmy criticize me? I am his momma.

MOTHERWELL, ROBERT

Motherwell, Robert. I think art is one of the few things that bestows very deep meanings to human existence.

MOTORCYCLE RACING

Aldana, Dave. It's kind of like tumbling around inside a giant clothes dryer (commenting on what it's like falling off a motorcycle at 150 mph).

MOUNT EVEREST

Crouch, Dee. At 18,000 feet, you're roughly half as smart as you are at sea level. The lore is that you don't come back from the mountain as smart as when you go up (commenting on the effect of high altitude on the human brain by the doctor with the American Bicentennial Expedition to Mt. Everest).

MOUNTAINEERING

Crouch, Dee. At 18,000 feet, you're roughly half as smart as you are at sea level. The lore is that you don't come back from the mountain as smart as when you go up (commenting on the effect of high altitude on the human brain by the doctor with the American Bicentennial Expedition to Mt. Everest).

MOUNTBATTEN, LOUIS

Mountbatten, Louis. I can't think of a more wonderful thanksgiving for the life I have had than that everyone should be jolly at my funeral.

Mountbatten, Louis. I loathe all manifestations of extremism and I believe we should strive, above all else, for the dignity and human rights of mankind, regardless of race, color and creed.

MOVING PICTURE ACTORS AND ACTRESSES

Lear, Norman. When I give advice to rising starlets I say, just remember, Hollywood is the land of the definite maybe.

Loren, Sophia. The mob that adores you is the most wonderful tribute there can be.

Scott, George C. The actor is never rewarded in film. Film stardom is a peripheral and distorted kind of fulfillment.

MOVING PICTURE AUDIENCES

Chabrol, Claude. I ask audiences to contemplate a character, not identify with him.

Winner, Michael. Film audiences are people who are seeking light relief in a dark room for an hour and a half.

MOVING PICTURE AUTHORSHIP

Puzo, Mario. (Film writing) is the most crooked business that I've ever had any experience with. You can get a better shake in Vegas than you can in Hollywood.

MOVING PICTURE INDUSTRY

Brando, Marlon. There are so many Jews in creative and executive positions. And Hollywood showed you the crude stereotype of every minority and race—the nigger, the Indian, the Mexican, these portraits reinforced the very attitudes that kept those people down. Many of the people responsible for this were Jews. Didn't they remember what it was like to be down themselves?.

Dunne, John Gregory. Hollywood is the only place where you fail upwards.

Kael, Pauline. Hollywood is the only place where you can die of encouragement.

Lear, Norman. When I give advice to rising starlets I say, just remember, Hollywood is the land of the definite maybe.

Mekas, Jonas. Avant-garde film doesn't want to and can't be part of any business.

Sellers, Peter. The older I get, the less I like the film industry and the people in it. In fact, I'm at a stage where I almost loathe them.

Tanen, Ned (former Hollywood agent). There's no orphan like the movie that doesn't work; a hit movie has 90 fathers.

MOVING PICTURE INDUSTRY—WAGES

Hunter, Ross. Every one of us in Hollywood is overpaid.

MOVING PICTURES

Burton, Richard. I only see a movie when I can't avoid it.

Costa-Gavras, . Film is the only way now to reach out to people all around the world. The time of the book is over.

Davis, Bette. My contention is that producers won't make repulsive films if the public don't got to see them.

De Laurentiis, Dino. To make a movie is not like to make a book. A movie is much, much more—not just pushing a pencil in a room.

Fassbinder, Rainer Werner. I long for a little naivete but there's none around.

Fonda, Jane. I think that every movie is political.

Gish, Lillian. Films are the greatest force ever to move the hearts and minds of the world.

Gish, Lillian. Movies have to answer a great deal for what the world is today.

Greenfeld, Josh. Cinema is a form of Danish.

Herzog, Werner. You should look straight at a film; that's the only way to see one. Film is not the art of scholars but of illiterates.

Hitchcock, Alfred Joseph. Most people make mystery films. I don't. I make films of suspense. A surprise in a film takes 10 seconds, suspense takes up an hour.

Monaco, James. Film has come of age as an art, probably because television now receives the brunt of contempt from the remaining proponents of an elite culture.

Newman, Susan. Making movies has nothing to do with acting.

Rossellini, Roberto. I believe that the cinema has failed in its mission of being the art of our century.

Shepherd, Cybill. If you kept seeing Robert Redford stark naked on the screen, would he be a superstar today? No way. Or Gene Hackman showing everything? Their million dollar days would be over. I want to be in a movie where all the men take their clothes off and I don't.

Stein, Gertrude. One of the great things about not going to movies is that you get lots of surprises.

Truffaut, Francois. They (tomorrow's films) will resemble the men who make them, and the number of spectators will be about equal to the number of the director's friends. They will be an act of love.

Vidor, King. Good films, like good wine, improve with age.

Warhol, Andy. Movies are the new novels. No one is going to read anymore. Everyone is going to do movies, because movies are easier to do.

Wiseman, Frederick. The final film is a theory about the event, about the subject in the film.

Zukor, Adolph. Look ahead a little and gamble a lot (a formula for success).

MOVING PICTURES—DIRECTORS

Bertolucci, Bernardo. To make a film it is not necessary to know anything technical at all. It will all come with time.

Kluge, Alexander. German (movie) directors are like airplanes always circling the airport but never landing.

Kubrick, Stanley. All you can do is either pose questions or make truthful observations about human behavior. The only morality is not to be dishonest.

Spielberg, Steven. My advice to anyone who wants to be a movie director is to make home movies. I started out by shooting 8 millimeter home movies with neighbors and friends.

Ullmann, Liv. A good director is the same all over the world. A good director is one who provides the inspiration and courage for you to use what is inside you.

MOVING PICTURES, EXPERIMENTAL

Mekas, Jonas. Avant-garde film doesn't want to and can't be part of any business.

MOVING PICTURES—FINANCE

Hitchcock, Alfred Joseph. I wouldn't be able to sleep nights if I thought I had to spend even $10 million on a picture...When you work with a smaller budget, you're forced to use ingenuity and imagination and you almost always come up with a better picture.

MOVING PICTURES—PORNOGRAPHY

Hope, Bob. I think we're running out of perversions to put in film, and I'm looking forward to it (on pornographic movies).

MOVING PICTURES—PORNOGRAPHY—FRANCE

Gregoire, Menie. Every French male born is convinced that, by definition, he is an expert lover. Many wives tell me that they go to see pornographic movies with their husbands as a way of delicately indicating to them that they don't know as much about lovemaking as they think they do.

MOVING PICTURES—PRODUCTION AND DIRECTION

Altman, Robert. Every time you make a film, you live a full lifetime.

Altman, Robert. Making movies is like playing baseball—the fun is the playing.

Anonymous, . In Cannes, a producer is what any man calls himself if he owns a suit, a tie, and hasn't recently been employed as a pimp.

Lehmen, Ernest. Very few people realize, when they go to a movie theatre and want to be entertained, what sort of blood has flowed in order that they might have a good time.

Malle, Louis. Being a director is like being a thief. You steal bits and pieces of the lives around you, and you put them into a movie.

Malle, Louis. Making a film is a life cycle—like being born, taking first steps, developing relationships. And the end of the shooting is like death in many ways.

Spielberg, Steven. Directing a movie with Truffaut on the set is like having Renoir around when you're still painting by numbers.

Tati, Jacques. Comedians speak with their legs.

Wilder, Billy. As soon as you have chosen a subject for a film, you have already made a success or a failure.

Wilder, Gene. It has been my experience that a producer gets more money than anyone else for what is essentially a $6.50-an-hour job.

Zeffirelli, Franco. You must be as tough as rubber and as soft as steel.

MOWAT, FARLEY

Mowat, Farley. Everything outrages me that outrages nature—and most of what modern man does outrages nature.

MOYERS, BILL D.

Moyers, Bill D. Dick Goodwin was no saint, not close, but if there's a hereafter, I'd rather spend it with Goodwin than with Gabriel.

MOYNIHAN, DANIEL PATRICK

Abzug, Bella. He's a political opportunist, an intellectual mercenary (commenting on her opponent, in the Democratic primary for Senator for New York, Daniel Patrick Moynihan).

Moynihan, Daniel Patrick. I would consider it dishonorable to leave this post (as chief United States delegate to the U.N.) and run for any office, and I hope it would be understood that if I do, the people, the voters to whom I would represent myself in such circumstances, would consider me as having said in advance that I am a man of no personal honor to have done so.

Moynihan, Daniel Patrick. The only reason people in America are starving is because they are idiots, and if they are idiots they deserve to.

Moynihan, Daniel Patrick. What kind of a prick are you? (to Ron Gollobin, reporter for WCVD-TV, Boston).

MOZAMBIQUE—POLITICS AND GOVERNMENT

Machel, Samora (President of Mozambique). We cannot tolerate a bourgeoisie in Mozambique, even a black one.

MUHAMMAD, WALLACE D.

Muhammad, Wallace D. I doubt if the Pope knows as much about Scripture as I do. I may not be the best orator, I may not have gone very far in school, but I am the boldest nigger you ever saw.

MUNICIPAL FINANCE

Burton, John C (New York City's Deputy Mayor for Finance). It's time that financial types developed a greater tolerance for imprecision, because that's the way the world is.

Carey, Hugh. I cannot deny that there is a contagion in New York which is about to sweep across the nation.

MUNITIONS

Cummings, Sam. The arms business is founded on human folly. That is why its depths will never be plumbed, and why it will go on forever.

Cummings, Sam. The plainest print cannot be read through a solid gold sovereign—or a ruble or a golden eagle (about attempts to control arms exports).

Cummings, Sam. There are huge new markets opening up; soon there will be the rearming of China, as everybody knows. And then Russia. And then Europe again. There's no end to it.

Haig, Alexander M. The arms race is the only game in town.

MURDER

Kunstler, William. Although I couldn't pull the trigger myself, I don't disagree with murder sometimes, especially political assassinations, which have been a part of political life since the beginning of recorded history.

Margaret Rose, Princess of Great Britain, . Things have come to a pretty pass when somebody of our type murders his nanny. They're so hard to come by these days (commenting on Lord Lucan, accused of murdering his children's nanny).

MURDOCH, IRIS

Murdoch, Iris. A bad review is even less important than whether it is raining in Patagonia.

MURDOCH, RUPERT

Beame, Abraham David. No New Yorker should take Rupert Murdoch's New York Post seriously any longer. It makes Hustler magazine look like the Harvard (Law) Review.

Murdoch, Rupert. I cannot avoid the temptation of wondering whether there is any other industry (than newspaper publishing) in this country which seeks to presume so completely to give the customer what he does not want.

MURPHY'S LAW (QUOTATION)

Ade, George. Anybody can win—unless there happens to be a second entry.

Albee, Dan. The value of an artistic achievement is inversely proportional to the number of people it appeals to.

Alito, Noelie. The shortest distance between two points is under construction.

Allen, Agnes. Almost anything is easier to get into than to get out of.

Allen, Agnes. When all else fails, read the instructions.

Anonymous (attributed by George F. Will), . The chance of the bread falling buttered-side-down is directly proportional to the cost of the carpet.

Anonymous (Corollary to Murphy's Law), . Everything will take longer than you think it will.

Anonymous (corollary to Murphy's Law), . If everything appears to be going well, you have obviously overlooked something.

Anonymous (corollary to Murphy's Law), . If there is a possibility of several things going wrong, the one that will go wrong is the one that will do the most damage.

Anonymous (corollary to Murphy's Law), . If you play with a thing long enough, you will surely break it.

Anonymous (Corollary to Murphy's Law), . Nothing is as easy as it looks.

Anonymous (Murphy's Law), . If anything can go wrong, eventually it will.

Berra, Yogi. You can observe a lot just by watching.

Carswell, James. Whenever man comes up with a better mousetrap, nature invariably comes up with a better mouse.

Clemens, Samuel Langhorne. Only kings, editors, and people with tapeworms have the right to use the editorial 'we'.

Conner, Caryl. All avocados in all stores will always be rock-hard the day you want to make guacamole.

Corry, Carolyn M. Paper is always strongest at the perforations.

Czapko, Laura. No child throws up in the bathroom.

Duffy, Sean. The chance of a meaningful relationship with a member of the opposite sex is inversely proportional to their amount of beauty.

Emerson, Eric. The second is never as good as the first.

Epstein, Thomas A. With extremely few exceptions, nothing is worth the trouble.

Felix, Virginia. Decision makers are those who have the greatest vested interest in the decision.

Frank, Mark R. One's ability to perform a given task competently decreases in proportion to the number of people watching.

Hofstader, Douglas. It always takes longer than you expect, even when you take Hofstader's Law into account.

Labue, Charles. A natural child is always conceived as soon as one is adopted.

Leibowitz, Irv. When hammering a nail, you will never hit your finger if you hold the hammer with both hands.

Main, Michael. For every action there is an equal and opposite government program.

Mathis, Andrew W. It's bad luck to be superstitious.

Minor, Robert. The winning entry is never as good as your own.

Morton, W. C., Jr. If rats are experimented upon, they will develop cancer.

Nova, Leo. The other person's attitude depends on which direction the money moves between you.

Ogden, David A. If you don't appreciate the amount of luxuries your budget can afford, you are getting paid far too much.

Parker, Tim. Originality begets conformity.

Parkins, Tom. Anything that happens enough times to irritate you will happen at least once more.

Poulsen, Brad. When anything is used to its full potential, it will break.

Runyon, Damon. The race is not always to the swift, nor the battle to the strong, but that's the way to bet.

Ryan, Eddie. The amount of time it takes to deliver a letter is directly proportional to the price of the stamp.

Sproles, Judy. If there is an opinion, facts will be found to support it.

Stewart, P. L. When you are in it up to your ears, keep your mouth shut.

Stone, David. One man's 'simple' is another man's 'huh'?.

Teague, Freeman, Jr. Nothing is so simple it cannot be misunderstood.

MUSGRAVE, THEA

Musgrave, Thea. In art you have to follow your hunch. You can't play it safe.

MUSIC

Arrau, Claudio. Every concert must be an event, never a routine.

Musgrave, Thea. In art you have to follow your hunch. You can't play it safe.

Nelson, Willie. My definition of music is anything that sounds good to the ear. If a peanut rolling across the floor sounds good, that's music.

Nyiregyhazi, Ervin. Music is a wonderful way of life but a terrible career.

Rubinstein, Artur. Composing a concert is like composing a menu. I believe in musical digestion.

Stokowski, Leopold. Music appeals to me for what can be done with it.

Valli, Frankie. There's nothing wrong with the world, only the people in it. And the same goes for music.

MUSIC—APPRECIATION

Copland, Aaron. The ideal listener, above all else, possesses the ability to lend himself to the power of music.

Levine, James. The audience experience should come from listening, not from noticing the conductor having an eight and a half minute sustained orgasm.

Reich, Steve. You must love music or be a duck.

Thomson, Virgil. Music in any generation is not what the public thinks of it but what the musicians make of it.

MUSIC—APPRECIATION—YOUTH

Sidlin, Murry. Young people are visually sophisticated but often musically illiterate.

MUSIC, BLUEGRASS

Brown, Don. (Bluegrass) becomes an addiction—just like any other grass, I suppose.

MUSIC, BLUES

Muddy Waters, . Those whites can play instruments real fine. But there's something missing in the singing. They just don't eat enough pinto beans; they haven't had enough hard times.

Standish, David. The blues hasn't died out; it's turned white.

MUSIC, CLASSICAL

Stokowski, Leopold. Every rehearsal must be better than the last. Every concert must be better than the last. We must never be satisfied because upwards in quality is quality without limit.

Zelzer, Harry. Good music is not as bad as it sounds.

MUSIC, DISCO

Mann, Herbie. Don't let your taste get in the way of reaching a broader audience.

MUSIC, FOLK

Broonzy, Bill (Big). It's all folk music, cause horses don't sing (in response to Studs Terkel's question, are the Blues folk music).

MUSIC, JAZZ

Broonzy, Bill (Big). It's all folk music, cause horses don't sing (in response to Studs Terkel's question, are the Blues folk music).

Foreman, George. Boxing is like jazz. The better it is, the less people appreciate it.

Getz, Stan. (Jimmy) Carter is playing it real safe and having only chamber quartets and opera. Let the peanut farmer break out a little and get some jazz at the White House.

Mogull, Artie (President of United Artists Records). I'll make two predictions: big bands will not come back, and Dolly Parton will continue to be the only girl singer with big tits to sell records.

Rollins, Sonny. Music is an open sky.

Simone, Nina. Jazz lets black people know, everytime they hear it, that they have their hands on the pulse of life.

Sousa, John Philip. Jazz will endure as long as people hear it through their feet instead of their brains.

MUSIC, JAZZ—WOMEN
Simon, George T. Only God can make a tree and only men can play good jazz.

MUSIC, POPULAR
Stokowski, Leopold. The history of popular music shows that it is the true art form of the people.

MUSIC, ROCK
Dylan, Bob. Rock and roll ended with Little Anthony and the Imperials.

Jagger, Mick. I should think not, judging from Elvis. No, rock 'n' roll music is for adolescents. It's a dead end (responding when asked Can rock stars move toward middle age?).

Nash, Graham. Serious musicians who read music don't understand what goes on with hippies.

Simels, Steve. David Bowie (is) the single worst thing to happen to rock music since the deaths of Brian Jones, Janis Joplin, and Jimi Hendrix.

Smith, Patti. Not even boot camp is as tough as being in rock and roll.

Wilson, Earl. The success of today's rock songs proves one thing—rhyme doesn't pay.

MUSIC, ROCK—FESTIVALS
Davis, Edward Michael. I think one of the greatest dangers that faces people in this country is the tyrants who would come in and solve your crimes by putting a rock festival in every park.

MUSIC, ROCK—JOURNALISM
Zappa, Frank. Most rock journalism is people who can't write, interviewing people who can't talk, for people who can't read.

MUSIC—UNITED STATES
Maazel, Lorin. Too many concerts are given by too many orchestras. You get the professionalism of mediocrity, and it grinds on like some kind of dreadful machine that never stops.

MUSICAL COMEDIES, REVUES, ETC.
Ade, George. A good musical comedy consists largely of disorderly conduct occasionally interrupted by talk.

MUSICIANS
Nyiregyhazi, Ervin. Music is a wonderful way of life but a terrible career.

Spivey, Victoria. Musicians today are sloppier than I ever seen them. And the most of them, the worst notes they make, the greater they seem to become.

MUSICIANS—CONDUCT OF LIFE
Segovia, Andres. Artists who say they practice eight hours a day are liars or asses.

MUSICIANS, ROCK
Hall, Daryl. It's socially immoral for a white person to act like a black person.

Perry, Joe. The only aging rock star is a dead one.

Plant, Robert. The lifestyle of rock 'n' roll is to live well and take a good woman.

MYTHOLOGY
Tanner, Jack. What is counted as truth in one age is counted as myth in the next.

NABOKOV, VLADIMIR
Nabokov, Vladimir. I am an American writer, born in Russia and educated in England, where I studied French literature before spending 15 years in Germany.

NADER, RALPH
Dixon, Paul Rand. I understand there are Arabs who are not dirty (responding when asked to retract a racial slur directed at Ralph Nader).

Jacobs, Andy. (Ralph) Nader has become a legend in his own mind.

Laughlin, Tom. The youth of this country have only two heroes: Ralph Nader and Billy Jack.

NAIVETE
Fassbinder, Rainer Werner. I long for a little naivete but there's none around.

NAMATH, JOE
Namath, Joe. I can't wait until tomorrow. Why not? Cause I get better looking every day.

Namath, Joe. I love football. I really love football. As far as I'm concerned, it's the second best thing in the world.

NAMIBIA—DESCRIPTION
Botha, Pieter W. I believe SWAPO is not interested in elections. They are only interested in foisting their ideas on the people of SouthWest Africa at the point of a gun.

NARCOTICS
Ehrlichman, John D. Narcotics suppression is a very sexy political issue.

Leary, Timothy. I don't like hippies. I don't like communes. I despise heroin. I've never participated in an orgy. It may ruin my reputation, but I'm particularly monogamous.

NARCOTICS AND NEGROES
Jackson, Jesse. It used to be the Klan in white robes who were the killers, now we've gone from Southern rope to Northern dope.

NASSER, GAMAL ABDEL
Nasser, Gamal Abdel. Blow for blow, slap for slap. I don't act, I react.

NATIONAL ASSOCIATION FOR THE ADVANCEMENT OF COLORED PEOPLE
Wilkins, Roy. If I weren't hopeful, I might as well shoot myself. Hope is the thing the NAACP has brought in its 66 years.

NATIONAL BROADCASTING COMPANY
Goodman, Julian. As the pioneering network, as the first network, we like to think of ourselves as the network with some class (commenting on NBC).

NATIONAL ENQUIRER (NEWSPAPER)
Pope, Generoso, Jr. A Pulitzer Prize ain't going to win us (the National Enquirer) two readers.

NATIONALISM
Einstein, Albert. Nationalism is an infantile disease. It is the measles of mankind.

NATURE IN ART
Helion, Jean (French painter). I looked through my studio window and I found that the outside world was more beautiful than my picture.

NAVRATILOVA, MARTINA
Navratilova, Martina. My wish is to have enough money so that I never have to play another set of tennis if I don't want to.

NEBRASKA. UNIVERSITY (FOOTBALL)
Stoll, Cal. We finally got Nebraska where we want them—off the schedule.

NECESSITY
Hall, Keith W. The word 'necessary' seldom is.

NEED (PSYCHOLOGY)
Kirkup, Jon. The sun goes down just when you need it the most.

NEGRO MUSICIANS

Wonder, Stevie. They (the Beatles) brought all different cultures together. They made White Middle America wake up about those old black artists—the Beatles brought them to people who had never heard of them. And it gave those artists—who were sometimes starving—some money.

NEGRO POLITICIANS

Clay, William. Whenever I see certain elements in the press show favoritism to a Black man running for a position of power, I know there's a nigger in the woodpile somewhere.

NEGROES

Barrow, Willie. It's easier being black than being a woman.

Brooke, Edward William. If my years in public life have taught me anything, it is that nothing in this nation is separate but equal. Nothing could be worse for our country and our children than the resurrection of this immoral and illegal doctrine.

Carter, James Earl. When I finish my term, I want black people to say that I did more for them in my presidency than any other President in their lifetime.

Hall, Daryl. It's socially immoral for a white person to act like a black person.

Hooks, Benjamin Lawson. We are not looking for Jimmy Carter or any other white man to deliver black people but for black people to deliver themselves.

Jackson, Maynard. If Richard Nixon were black, he would be catching so much hell, he would rather be in jail.

Killens, John O. Let's stop titillating white people. No matter what we black folks do, we always wind up as entertainers.

King, Billie Jean. Tennis is still a rich suburban game. Whites identify with tennis and hockey. Blacks identify with basketball and music.

McGuire, Al. The only thing in this country that blacks really dominate, except poverty, is basketball.

Maheu, Robert. I can summarize my attitude about employing more Negroes very simply. I think it is a wonderful idea for somebody else, somewhere else. I know this is not a very praiseworthy point of view, but I feel that Negroes have already made enough progress to last the next hundred years.

Muse, Clarence. The public believed in the Negro's voice, but not in his intelligence.

Norris, Clarence (the sole surviving |Scottsboro Boy|). The lesson to Black people, to my children, to everybody, is that you should always fight for your rights even if it costs you your life. Stand up for your rights, even if it kills you (commenting on his struggle to clear his name upon being pardoned by the state of Alabama).

Scott, William. The only reason we need zip codes is because niggers can't read.

Simone, Nina. Jazz lets black people know, everytime they hear it, that they have their hands on the pulse of life.

Young, Andrew. The truth of the matter is, we as blacks want our cake and want to eat it too.

NEGROES AND POLITICS

Belafonte, Harry. When African countries got independence, I thought there would be a new morality in the world. The next thing I knew Nigerians were shooting Biafrans, and Idi Amin was on the scene. I thought, 'My God, we're not better than the rest.' There are no super-blacks any more than super-whites. They're only people.

Butz, Earl Lauer. I'll tell you why you can't attract coloreds. Because coloreds only want three things. You know what they want? I tell you what coloreds want. It's three things: first, a tight pussy; second, loose shoes; and third, a warm place to shit. That's all (responding to a question from Pat Boone and explaining why the Republican Party didn't attract more blacks—reported by John Dean).

Cooks, Stoney (aide to Andrew Young). Liberals want to do it for you. Southerners want to do it with you (commenting on the Carter administration's attempt to involve minorities in the government).

NEGROES—CIVIL RIGHTS

Eisenhower, Dwight David. These are not bad people... All they are concerned about is to see that their sweet little girls are not required to sit in schools alongside some big overgrown Negroes.

Wilkins, Roy. If I weren't hopeful, I might as well shoot myself. Hope is the thing the NAACP has brought in its 66 years.

NEGROES—CIVIL RIGHTS—HISTORY

Borrows, Lee (resident of Harlem). That 'Roots' ain't nothin. If they ever told it like it was, the riots would start again.

NEGROES—ECONOMIC CONDITIONS

Jackson, Jesse. In a hot war we (Blacks) die first; in a cold war, we starve first.

Jackson, Jesse. We too often condemn blacks who succeed and excel, calling them Uncle Toms. The ideal ought to be for all of us to succeed and excel.

NEGROES—EDUCATION

Jackson, Jesse. A school system without parents at its foundation is just like a bucket with a hole in it.

Jackson, Jesse. Affirmative action is a moot point if you don't learn to read and write.

Jackson, Jesse. What does it matter if we have a new book or an old book, if we open neither?.

NEGROES—EMPLOYMENT

Bond, Julian. It is almost as though we were climbing a molasses mountain dressed in snowshoes, while everyone else rides a rather rapid ski lift to the top (about Black unemployment).

Hooks, Benjamin Lawson. There's a great lie abroad that black people don't want to work. I have an idea. You give us the jobs and we'll give you the welfare and see how you like that for a while.

Maheu, Robert. I can summarize my attitude about employing more Negroes very simply. I think it is a wonderful idea for somebody else, somewhere else. I know this is not a very praiseworthy point of view, but I feel that Negroes have already made enough progress to last the next hundred years.

NEGROES—PSYCHOLOGY

Flood, Curt. Being black is always having people being cautious about what they call you.

Robeson, Paul (attributed by John E. Mitchell). My problem is not to counteract the white man's prejudice against the Negro. That does not matter. I have set myself to educate my brother to believe in himself.

NEGROES—SEGREGATION—CHICAGO

Hauser, Philip M. (Chicago) has lace pants in the front, and soiled drawers behind.

NEGROES—SEGREGATION—PLAINS, GEORGIA

Carter, Billy. Bunch of damned hypocrites down there at that Baptist church. The only time I ever go is when one of the kids is baptized.

King, Clennon. It shows how beautiful Southern people are—they may growl and grimace, but they're the sweetest white folks on earth (commenting on the decision by the Plains Baptist Church to integrate).

NEGROES—SOCIAL CONDITIONS

Borrows, Lee (resident of Harlem). That 'Roots' ain't nothin. If they ever told it like it was, the riots would start again.

Washington, Booker T., III. Being the sensitive man he was about his race, I think the present day Harlem scene would bring tears to my grandfather's eyes.

NEGROES—UNITED STATES

Cleaver, Eldridge. Black people need to realize very fundamentally that they are full and equal citizens of the U.S. We can no longer 'fence straddle' about where we are going. We're as much a part of the United States as any Rockefeller.

Mays, Benjamin. If this (country) is a melting pot, I don't want the Negro to melt away.

NEIGHBORHOODS

Carter, James Earl. I have nothing against a community that's made up of people who are Polish, Czechoslovakians, French Canadians or blacks who are trying to maintain the ethnic purity of their neighborhood. This is a natural inclination on the part of the people.

NELSON, WILLIE

Nelson, Willie. My definition of music is anything that sounds good to the ear. If a peanut rolling across the floor sounds good, that's music.

Nelson, Willie. To write songs, I usually need a reason. Like not having any money.

NESSEN, RON

Nessen, Ron. I'm a Ron, but not a Ziegler.

NEUROSES

Clark, Alex. It's always darkest just before the lights go out.

NEUTRON BOMB

Hatfield, Mark. It's in the realm of the unconscionable. It raises the greatest probability and potential of introducing nuclear weaponry into conventional warfare (commenting on the neutron bomb).

NEW JERSEY—DESCRIPTION

Greenfeld, Josh. New Jersey looks like the back of an old radio.

NEW ORLEANS—DESCRIPTION

Monaghan, Jim. I guess every day in New Orleans is like a B-movie.

NEW YORK (CITY)

Anderson, Gary. New York should be saved because without it people would make even more jokes about Los Angeles.

Anonymous, . If you're bored in New York, you're boring.

Anonymous (Indian Leader), . Guilt feelings have plagued us all. We knew it was a bad investment when we sold it (responding to New York City's threatened bankruptcy with an offer to buy back the land for $24).

Bradley, Thomas. This isn't a local issue solely between New York and the Ford Administration—all of us are involved (regarding aid to New York City).

Breslin, Jimmy. One of the truly great things about being brought up in New York City is that it allows you to go through life with an open mind.

Burns, Arthur Frank. While I have not yet reached the conclusion that Federal financial assistance is necessary (to New York City), I am closer to such a conclusion than I have been in the past.

Carey, Hugh. I cannot deny that there is a contagion in New York which is about to sweep across the nation.

Carey, Hugh. It is not becoming of a President to create animosity among the people by pitting one section of the country against another (in response to President Ford's stand on aid to New York City).

Ellison, Jessie. New York should be saved because we live there even when we live somewhere else.

Emerson, William A., Jr. New Yorkers are an endangered species.

Gallagher, Bill. The first thing they cut were night classes to teach English to migrants. You have to ask whether the motives are fiscal or political. It seems to me that we have our priorities backward—we are paying the banks, and trying to deal with the needs of the people last.

Gannett, Lewis. The great days in New York were just before you got there.

Goldberger, Paul. Other cities consume culture, New York creates it.

Humphrey, Hubert Horatio. I want the President to be as considerate of New York City and of New York State as he is of countries all over the world. Within the same week that he said no help for New York, he sends us up a program for $5 billion of additional military aid in support assistance for the Middle East.

Koch, Edward I. New York is a place of bounding, exuberant diversity.

Maddox, Lester Garfield. The thing I don't like about New York is the tendency to reward bums and penalize hard work.

Proxmire, William. If New York has one quality, it is the fantastic brass—that ability to con you into buying the Brooklyn Bridge.

Reeves, Richard. New Yorkers are so optimistic that there's going to be some kind of bailout. There's no such thing as a bailout. The options now are total disaster or Washington taking control of the city. It's really the beginning of the end of local government in this country.

Rivers, Joan. My favorite city in the world is New York. Sure it's dirty—but like a beautiful lady smoking a cigar.

Rohatyn, Felix. I feel like somebody who tries to check into a hospital and keeps getting referred to the cemetery (about New York funding problems).

Simon, Neil. When it's 105 in New York City, it's 78 in LA. When it's 20 below in New York City, it's 78 in LA. Of course, there are 11 million interesting people in New York City and only 78 in LA (commenting upon moving to Hollywood).

White, E. B.. New Yorkers temperamentally do not crave comfort and convenience. If they did, they would live elsewhere.

White, Theodore. New York City is a glorious, or rather a tragic, example of 12 years of liberal government.

Whitman, Walt. New York is a fine place for a writer to sell his produce, but a poor place to grow it.

NEW YORK (CITY)—DEBT

Burton, John C (New York City's Deputy Mayor for Finance). It's time that financial types developed a greater tolerance for imprecision, because that's the way the world is.

Carey, Hugh. I had only two hands all year and one was holding Abe Beame's.

Carey, Hugh. It isn't fair when the President of the United States hauls off and kicks the people of the city of New York in the groin, and I'm going to fight back.

Ford, Gerald Rudolph. I can tell you—and tell you now—that I am prepared to veto any bill that has as its purpose a federal bailout of New York City to prevent a default.

Friedman, Milton. New York City's financial crisis was possibly the best thing to happen in this country in a long time.

Packwood, Robert. We haven't got an obligation to bail those liars out (in accusing New York City officials of deliberately lying to the Senate Banking Committee).

Reagan, Ronald. I have included in my morning and evening prayers every day the prayer that the Federal Government not bail out New York.

Simon, William E. We're going to sell New York to the Shah of Iran. It's a hell of an investment (during New York City's financial crisis).

NEW YORK (CITY)—DESCRIPTION

Bouza, Anthony. When you watch (ghetto) mothers take their kids to school, en route to a menial job, amid the drunks and junkies, you think maybe there is hope and the human spirit can triumph (commenting upon his retirement from the New York City police department after 23 years).

Dryansky, G. Y. Paris is becoming more vulgar, New York more refined.

NEW YORK (CITY)—ELLIS ISLAND

Trachtenberg, Alan. Ellis Island represented the opening American act of one of the most remarkable dramas in all of history: the conversion of agricultural laborers, rural homemakers and traditional craftsmen into urban industrial workers.

NEW YORK (CITY)—HARLEM—DESCRIPTION

Washington, Booker T., III. Being the sensitive man he was about his race, I think the present day Harlem scene would bring tears to my grandfather's eyes.

NEW YORK (CITY)—HISTORY

Tweed, William Marcy (Boss). I've tried to do some good, even if I have not had good luck.

NEW YORK (CITY)—POLITICS AND GOVERNMENT

Reeves, Richard. The people of New York have no political leader.

NEW YORK (STATE)—POLITICS AND GOVERNMENT

Fink, Stanley. There are times when reasonable people come to no solution.

Reeves, Richard. The people of New York have no political leader.

Young, Andrew. Georgia is more liberal than New York.

NEW YORK TIMES

Eder, Richard. A critic may write for an institution, but he shouldn't be one.

New York Times, . The question on Tuesday is not whether there might have been better candidates than those nominated by the two major parties. The only question before the American people is whether they have been given a choice of leadership and prospective policies worthy of their vote. We find the choice clear-cut. We cast our vote for Jimmy Carter.

Ochs, Adolph Simon. When a tabloid prints it, that's smut. When the Times prints it, that's sociology.

Sarris, Andrew. We New Yorkers are the most naive and provincial people in the world to put so much faith not in princes and priests, but in a mere publication (about the New York Times).

NEWMAN, PAUL

Newman, Paul. I figure that on my tombstone, it's going to say, 'He was a terrific actor until one day his eyes turned brown'.

Newman, Paul. Racing is the best way I know to get away from all the rubbish of Hollywood.

Newman, Paul. There's no way that what people see on celluloid has anything to do with me.

NEWSPAPER PUBLISHERS AND PUBLISHING

McIntyre, Bruce. If the (Washington) Post experience says anything, maybe it's this: being a so-called union-busting paper doesn't interfere with greatness.

Murdoch, Rupert. I cannot avoid the temptation of wondering whether there is any other industry (than newspaper publishing) in this country which seeks to presume so completely to give the customer what he does not want.

Wicker, Tom. A reporter should write and his newspaper should print what they know.

NEWSPAPERS

Anne, Princess of Great Britain, . Newspaper strikes are a relief.

Bagnold, Enid. The state of the world depends on one's newspaper.

Cockburn, Alexander. Descriptions of sin are what we want at the breakfast table, not admonitions against it.

Daley, Richard J. But then you can never go as low as a newspaper. A newspaper is the lowest thing there is.

Gold, Herbert. Never trust a newspaper over 10.

Jefferson, Thomas. Were it left to me to decide whether we should have government without newspapers or newspapers without government, I should not hesitate a moment to prefer the latter.

Moynihan, Daniel Patrick. When a person goes to a country and finds their newspapers filled with nothing but good news, he can bet there are good men in jail.

Spaulding, Jim. When newspapers write about themselves, they lie.

NEWSPAPERS AND TELEVISION

Bellows, Jim. Newspapers were 15 years too late in awakening to TV. If newspapers had done their jobs, TV Guide would not have been successful, and newspapers would have had more readers than advertisers.

Chancellor, John. Television is good at the transmission of experience. Print is better at the transmission of facts.

NEWSPAPERS—PHILADELPHIA

Rizzo, Frank Lazzaro. If you want fiction, read the news pages; if you want facts, read the comic pages.

NEWSPAPERS—RELATIONS—TRADE UNIONS

McIntyre, Bruce. If the (Washington) Post experience says anything, maybe it's this: being a so-called union-busting paper doesn't interfere with greatness.

NEWSPAPERS—SECTIONS, COLUMNS, ETC.

Lippmann, Walter. You are just a puzzled man making notes about what you think.

NEWTON, C. M.

Newton, C. M. When you're hired, you're fired—the date just hasn't been filled in yet.

NGUYEN-VAN-THIEU

Ky, Nguyen Cao. Remember, we lost the war not because of your fault but because of bad leadership. Tell your children and grandchildren we are exiled because of Nguyen Van Thieu. Remember that name. He is the most despicable man in the world (visiting Vietnamese refugees in Camp Pendleton, California).

Nguyen-van-Thieu (former President of South Vietnam), . I am resigning, but I am not deserting.

Tran-van-Huong, . Thieu ran away from destiny; it has now come to me.

NIKOLAIS, ALWIN

Nikolais, Alwin. Whatever I do reflects the fact that I am an American. It reflects the freedom, the history and the creativity that is possible here.

NIN, ANAIS

Nin, Anais. A real writer does not need the publicity that is granted with equal fervor to a toothpaste. A real writer only wants his book to be read by those who want to read it, and if there are 100 of them, it is enough to keep his work alive and sustain his productivity.

1970'S

Epstein, Joseph. A few things ought to be said on behalf of the 1970's—not the least among them that they weren't the 1960's.

Hayden, Thomas. The radicalism of the '60's became the fascism of the '70's (responding to heckling from left-wing radicals during a speech on his current campaign for U.S. Senator).

Sahl, Mort. In the forties, to get a girl you had to be a GI or a jock. In the fifties, to get a girl you had to be Jewish. In the sixties, to get a girl you had to be black. In the seventies, to get a girl you've got to be a girl.

Salmore, Stephen. In the 1960s, the burden of proof against change rested with those accepting the status quo. In the 1970s, the burden of proof rests with those who want change.

1978

Howe, Sir Geoffrey. Nineteen seventy-eight has been the year of the bloody-minded.

1975

Nixon, Richard Milhous. We have very little leadership in our country today (1975).

1960S

Brand, Stewart. I thought the sixties went on too long.

Dickstein, Morris. The history of the sixties was written as much in the Berkeley Barb as in the New York Times.

Hayden, Thomas. The radicalism of the '60's became the fascism of the '70's (responding to heckling from left-wing radicals during a speech on his current campaign for U.S. Senator).

Leary, Timothy. I don't have one nostalgic bone in my body for the 1960's. I have no desire to go back to Woodstock and spend three days in the mud on 'downers'.

Salmore, Stephen. In the 1960s, the burden of proof against change rested with those accepting the status quo. In the 1970s, the burden of proof rests with those who want change.

Vreeland, Diana. It was a small revolution and not bloody thank God. But it was a revolution, and for the first time youth went out to life, instead of waiting for life to come to them, which is the difference between the '60s and any other decade I've lived in (commenting on the flower children).

NIVEN, DAVID

Niven, David. I have a face that is a cross between two pounds of halibut and an explosion in an old clothes closet.

Niven, David. I've taken up the Bible again, somewhat in the spirit of W.C. Fields—looking for loopholes.

NIXON, PATRICIA RYAN

Nixon, Patricia Ryan. I gave up everything I've ever loved (commenting in 1960 on the price of political life).

NIXON, RICHARD MILHOUS

Abzug, Bella. Richard Nixon self-impeached himself. He gave us Gerald Ford as his revenge.

Aregood, Richard. It's hard to understand all this fuss about John F. Kennedy. After all, Richard Nixon didn't just concentrate on women. He tried to do it to everybody.

Beard, Peter. Nixon is what America deserved and Nixon is what America got.

Carpenter, Elizabeth. If John Connally had been around at the Alamo, he would have organized Texans for Santa Anna.

Dean, John Wesley, III. Last summer I reread *1984*, and after several years at the Nixon White House, it made fascinating, almost frightening reading.

De Gaulle, Sandra. Everyone in the world loves him except the Americans (about Richard Nixon).

De Marco, Frank. That would be like hearing from a call girl who gave you a dose (when asked if he had heard from ex-president Nixon lately—his former tax client).

Dole, Robert J. If you liked Richard Nixon, you'll love Bob Dole.

Ehrlichman, John D. I have done my time. I don't think he (Richard Nixon) is ever going to stop doing his time.

Ervin, Samuel James. Nobody I know wanted to see Nixon go to jail, (but) there's an old saying that mercy but murders, pardoning those that kill.

Goldwater, Barry Morris. He let this country down, he let his party down. And that's the last time I want to talk about Nixon, ever (summarizing his feelings about Richard Nixon).

Goldwater, Barry Morris. There are only so many lies you can take, and now there has been one too many. Nixon should get his ass out of the White House—today (after leaving a conference with Nixon before his resignation as president).

Graham, Billy. I stopped in San Clemente last month and spent an hour with him. He's more like his old self before he became President. He's joking, he's kidding, he's laughing a lot.

Graham, Billy. I was shocked and surprised. This was a Nixon I didn't know (commenting on the language used on some of the Nixon tapes).

Graham, Billy. Nixon in my judgement was a true intellectual.

Hellman, Lillian. I think (Watergate and the McCarthy Era) are deeply connected, with Mr. Nixon being the connection, the rope that carries it all through.

Jackson, Maynard. If Richard Nixon were black, he would be catching so much hell, he would rather be in jail.

Kennedy, John Fitzgerald. He's got no class (about Richard Nixon).

Kissinger, Henry Alfred. It was hard to avoid the impression that Nixon, who thrived on crisis, also craved disasters.

Kissinger, Henry Alfred. One thing I have never understood is how he became a politician. He really dislikes people. He hated to meet new people (about Richard Nixon).

Kissinger, Henry Alfred. We are all the president's men, and have got to behave that way.

Korff, Baruch. I fully believe that every detractor of President Nixon will come before the bar of justice, whether in this lifetime or later.

Lacovara, Philip. Nixon having resigned without formal prosecution has carried into his retirement a presumption of formal innocence, which was ratified by Ford's pardon. He is accepted in polite society—not as the felon he unquestionably was.

Liddy, G. Gordon. When the prince approaches his lieutenant, the proper response of the lieutenant to the prince is Fiat volutas tua, (thy will be done)...I think I delayed things substantially. The prince was prince for a longer period of time (when asked if he would do that kind of work again for a President and if he felt he had taken the blame for Watergate in vain).

Maddox, Lester Garfield. There are two Jimmy Carters, one running for president and one governor of Georgia, and let me tell you one thing: if Richard Nixon had gotten his training from Jimmy Carter, he never would have gotten caught.

Mao, Tse-Tung. What's wrong with taping a conversation when you happen to have a tape recorder with you? Most people in America love playing with tape recorders. (about Richard Nixon).

Marx, Groucho. Nixon is a scoundrel. He belongs in the penitentiary. That's where he belongs. And that's where he'd be if a deal hadn't been made.

Mitchell, John. Watch what we do, not what we say (commenting in 1969 on the direction of the Nixon administration).

Moyers, Bill D. Nixon systematically robbed the country of its ability and willingness to trust the President.

Moynihan, Daniel Patrick. Nixon understood more about liberals than liberals ever understood about him.

Nixon, Richard Milhous. Call it paranoia, but paranoia for peace isn't that bad (commenting on the wiretapping of government officials and journalists to discover leaks of confidential information during the Vietnam war).

Nixon, Richard Milhous. I brought myself down. I have impeached myself.

Nixon, Richard Milhous. I let down my friends. I let down the country....I let the American people down....(But) if they want me to get down and grovel on the floor, no. Never (commenting in his first David Frost interview on Watergate).

Nixon, Richard Milhous. I should have had you for my lawyer and I might still be president (to Edward Bennett Williams upon the acquittal of John Connally).

Nixon, Richard Milhous. I'm not a loveable man (on his explanation of why the press kept picking on him).

Nixon, Richard Milhous. In our own lives, let each of us ask—not just what will government do for me, but what can I do for myself (inaugural address—1973).

Nixon, Richard Milhous. It is quite obvious that there are certain inherently governmental actions which, if undertaken by the sovereign in protection of...the nation's security, are lawful, but which if undertaken by private citizens are not (commenting to the Senate Intelligence Committee on his authorization of covert CIA efforts to prevent Chilean President Allende's election in 1970).

Nixon, Richard Milhous. My political life is over.

Nixon, Richard Milhous. One thing I really hate is exercise for exercise's sake.

Nixon, Richard Milhous. Only three men in America understand the use of power. I do. John Connally does. And I guess Nelson does.

Nixon, Richard Milhous. Some people say I didn't handle it properly and they're right. I screwed it up. And I paid the price (about Watergate).

Nixon, Richard Milhous. The media has abdicated its fact gathering to nonbelieving young people, who seem to want to break down our values.

Nixon, Richard Milhous. (Watergate) was worse than a crime, it was a blunder.

Nixon, Richard Milhous. Writing is the toughest thing I've ever done.

Nixon, Richard Milhous (attributed by Robert J. Dole). It's always hard to lose the close ones—if it's a big one—but when it's close, everyone is looking around, you know, the cannibals come out and try to assess what happened.

Rockwell, Geo. Making something perfectly clear only confuses everybody.

Safire, William. I think that one of Nixon's great contributions to civil liberties was getting caught doing what the two presidents before him got away with.

Schneiders, Greg. For all his flaws and faults, as a manager he (Nixon) did a good job.

Scott, Hugh. I had a will to believe (in Nixon's innocence), but they didn't show me all the documents. I was led into making statements on incomplete evidence. I was trying to be fair when I was personally deeply disturbed.

Sirica, John J. I hope no political party will ever stoop so low as to embrace the likes of Richard Nixon again.

Sirica, John J. Nixon should have been indicted.

Stevenson, Adlai, II. Nixon is the kind of politician who would cut down a redwood tree, then mount the stump for a speech on conservation.

Truman, Harry S. That Richard Nixon, boys, is a no-good lying son of a bitch (commenting during one of his Presidential press conferences).

Warren, Earl. Tricky (Richard Nixon) is perhaps the most despicable President this nation has ever had. He was a cheat, a liar and a crook, and he brought my country, which I love, into disrepute. Even worse than abusing his office, he abused the American people.

White, Theodore. The true crime of Richard Nixon was simple: he destroyed the myth that binds America together, and for this he was driven from power.

Ziegler, Ronald Louis. I never knowingly lied, but certainly history shows that many things I said were incorrect.

NIXON, RICHARD MILHOUS—CONDUCT OF LIFE

Peter, Laurence J. If two wrongs don't make a right, try three (Nixon's principle).

NIXON, RICHARD MILHOUS—STAFF

Colson, Charles Wendell. I would do anything that Richard Nixon asks me to do.

Connally, John Bowden. I don't subscribe to the notion that everyone around President Nixon was tarnished.

Haldeman, Harry Robbins. I'll approve of whatever will work and am concerned with results—not methods.

NKOMO, JOSHUA

Nkomo, Joshua. We are not the beasts and villains we are painted to be.

NOBEL PRIZES

Bellow, Saul. The child in me is delighted. The adult in me is skeptical (upon receiving the Nobel Prize for Literature).

McCarthy, Eugene Joseph. Kissinger won a Nobel Peace Prize for watching a war end that he was for.

Mother Teresa, . I am unworthy (upon winning the Nobel Peace Prize).

Sakharov, Andrei Dmitrievich. I hope this prize is not only an acknowledgement of my personal merits, but of the merits of all those who fight for human rights (commenting on his Nobel Peace Prize).

Sakharov, Andrei Dmitrievich. I regard this as a challenge to world public opinion. I have always been trusted and I do not believe there are grounds to think that I have committed a state crime (upon the denial of permission to travel to Oslo, Norway to receive the Nobel Peace Prize).

Sakharov, Andrei Dmitrievich. To keep one's self-respect, one must act in accordance with the general human longing for peace, for true detente, for genuine disarmament (in his message accepting the Nobel Peace Prize).

Tiselius, Arne. The world is full of people who should get the Nobel Prize but haven't got it and won't get it.

NONVIOLENCE

Corrigan, Mairead. Our world is rushing towards disaster. But it's not too late to prove the power of love...we've got to prove that the way of nonviolence can bring social change (from her Nobel Peace Prize acceptance speech).

NORODOM SIHANOUK, KING OF CAMBODIA (ABDICATED 1955)

Norodom Sihanouk, King Of Cambodia (Abdicated 1955), . When they no longer need me, they will spit me out like a cherry pit (about the Khmer Rouge).

NORTH AMERICA

McLuhan, Marshall. North America looks, as usual, grim.

NORTHERN IRELAND

O'Connell, David (one of the IRA's leading tacticians). Put your faith in the Provos and Ireland will be free. We will abolish British rule, we will smash it.

Wilson, Harold. Those who subscribe to the Northern Irish Aid Committee, the principal IRA fund-raising organization in the United States, are not financing the welfare of the Irish people, as they might delude themselves. They are financing murder.

NORTHERN IRELAND—DESCRIPTION

Holland, Jack. The tragedy of Northern Ireland is that it is now a society in which the dead console the living.

NORTHERN IRELAND—POLITICS AND GOVERNMENT

Anonymous, . Northern Ireland has too many Catholics and twice as many Protestants, but very few Christians.

Rose, Richard. Even an atheist must be a Protestant atheist or Catholic atheist in order to have status in the society (commenting on life in Northern Ireland).

NORTHERN IRELAND—RELIGION

Anonymous, . Northern Ireland has too many Catholics and twice as many Protestants, but very few Christians.

NORTHERN IRISH AID COMMITTEE

Wilson, Harold. Those who subscribe to the Northern Irish Aid Committee, the principal IRA fund-raising organization in the United States, are not financing the welfare of the Irish people, as they might delude themselves. They are financing murder.

NOTHING (PHILOSOPHY)

Durant, Will. One of the lessons of history is that nothing is often a good thing to do and always a clever thing to say.

NUDISM

Shepherd, Cybill. If you kept seeing Robert Redford stark naked on the screen, would he be a superstar today? No way. Or Gene Hackman showing everything? Their million dollar days would be over. I want to be in a movie where all the men take their clothes off and I don't.

NUREEV, RUDOLF

Nureev, Rudolf. I do not try to dance better than anyone else. I only try to dance better than myself.

Nureev, Rudolf. I'm 40 years old. It's time to indulge, to be foolish if I wish.

NURSEMAIDS

Margaret Rose, Princess of Great Britain, . Things have come to a pretty pass when somebody of our type murders his nanny. They're so hard to come by these days (commenting on Lord Lucan, accused of murdering his children's nanny).

NYE, BLAINE

Nye, Blaine. It's not whether you win or lose but who gets the blame (commenting on his football philosophy).

NYIREGYHAZI, ERVIN

Nyiregyhazi, Ervin. Music is a wonderful way of life but a terrible career.

OATES, JOYCE CAROL

Oates, Joyce Carol. Sometimes my work is very savage, very harsh. But so is life. My material is not sordid, it's just a realistic reflection of a society that is in turmoil.

OBESITY

Bernstein, Al. Obesity can't be laughed off.

Connolly, Cyril. Imprisoned in every fat man a thin one is wildly signalling to be let out.

Gleason, Jackie. Thin people are beautiful, but fat people are adorable.

Leachman, Cloris. Fat people pollute the esthetic environment.

Outhier, Louis. You don't get fat from a good kitchen—only from a bad one.

OBEY, DAVID R.

Obey, David R. Joe McCarthy made me an independent, Stevenson made me a Liberal, and Eisenhower made me a Democrat.

Obey, David R. Politics is the only thing I really cared about, except the Green Bay Packers.

OBSCENITY (LAW)

Fleishman, Stanley. There are more citizens in jail in the United States today for publishing books, magazines, newspapers, and films than there are in all the countries of the world put together.

Stevens, John Paul. One of the strongest arguments against regulating obscenity through criminal law is the inherent vagueness of the obscenity concept.

OCCUPATIONS

Becker, Jules. It is much harder to find a job than to keep one.

OFFICES—ETIQUETTE

McArthur, Robert. Never imply that they care whether your socks match; and never forget that they do.

OFFICIAL SECRETS

Anderson, Thomas J. The only secrets the American government has are the secrets it keeps from its own people.

Chiles, Lawton M., Jr. Secrecy in government has become synonymous, in the public mind, with deception by the government.

Seale, Bobby. Those who know don't talk; and those who talk don't know.

OHIO. KENT STATE UNIVERSITY, KENT

Capp, Al. The martyrs at Kent State were the kids in National Guard uniforms.

Rhodes, James. They are the worst type of people we harbor in America, worse than brown shirts and the Communist element (concerning the Kent State demonstrators).

O'KEEFFE, GEORGIA

O'Keeffe, Georgia. I'll paint what I see but I'll paint it big to say what is to me the wideness and wonder of the world as I live it.

OKLAHOMA—POLITICS AND GOVERNMENT

Monks, John (Oklahoma State Representative). In every country the Communists have taken over, the first thing they do is outlaw cockfighting (opposing a bill that would outlaw cockfighting in Oklahoma).

OKLAHOMA. UNIVERSITY—FOOTBALL

Cross, George L. We want to build a university the football team can be proud of.

OLDENBURG, CLAES

Oldenburg, Claes. I am for art that coils and grunts like a wrestler. I am for art that sheds hair. I am for art you can sit on. I am for art you can pick your nose with or stub your toe on.

OLIVIER, LAURENCE

Glenville, Peter. Compared to ordinary men with ordinary ambitions, Larry (Olivier) was a sea monster.

Olivier, Laurence. I am an actor because that is all I am qualified to do.

Olivier, Laurence. I love comedy every bit as much as tragedy, perhaps more, because the whole scene of humanity is under its roof.

Olivier, Laurence. I think I would have liked to have been a farmer. Earth and greasepaint are a very good mix.

Olivier, Laurence. I'm not sure what I'm like and I'm not sure I want to know.

Olivier, Laurence. My worst performance was as Father Christmas. I didn't fool my children. They said, 'We know you're not Daddy' Christmas. You're Daddy.

OLYMPIC GAMES

Cosell, Howard. I think the Moscow Games will be a disaster—and the last Olympics.

Wilkins, Mac (1976 Olympic Discus Champion). America expects its athletes to wave a flag and win a medal every four years. But then you're supposed to take off that silly underwear and go out and make a decent living.

OLYMPIC GAMES, 1980

Sakharov, Andrei Dmitrievich. Every spectator or athlete who comes to the Olympics will be giving indirect support to Soviet military policies.

Toomey, Bill. We would be naive to place track and field ahead of world events. Sports cannot live outside reality.

OMNISCIENCE

Santayana, George. Fanatics are those people who know what they are doing is what God would be doing if He only had all the facts.

ONASSIS, JACQUELINE LEE (BOUVIER) KENNEDY

Jong, Erica. If Jackie Kennedy did not exist, the press would have to invent her.

Onassis, Jacqueline Lee (Bouvier) Kennedy. I always wanted to be some kind of writer or newspaper reporter. But after college—I did other things.

Vidal, Gore. I would pay off those publications that report the doings and expenditures of Madame Onassis. Never to read about her again would not only be socially beneficial but would, I am sure, stem the rising tide of world communism (in response to 'What would you do with 10 million dollars').

O'NEILL, EUGENE

O'Neill, Eugene. Born in a hotel room—and God damn it—died in a hotel room.

O'NEILL, THOMAS P. (TIP)

Kennedy, Edward Moore. Tip O'Neill can communicate more with a wink and a nod than most politicians can in a two-hour speech.

O'Neill, Thomas P. (Tip). Since the day he commuted Nixon, he hasn't done anything right (commenting on Congressional rapport with Gerald Ford).

ONO, YOKO

Lennon, John. As usual, there's a great woman behind every idiot (upon winning his permanent residence status in the U.S.).

OPERA

Liebermann, Rolf. Running an opera is like running a restaurant. If the boss is not there, the food gets bad and the service even worse.

Pekar, Harvey. A person who can't relate to comic books is like somebody who can't relate to opera. They're both culturally deprived.

OPERA SINGERS

Callas, Maria. To be an opera singer, you have to be an actress.

Tourel, Jennie. You see, it isn't just boiled potatoes, what I do.

OPPORTUNITY

Thatcher, Margaret Hilda. Opportunity means nothing unless it includes the right to be unequal.

OPPRESSION

Kelley, Ken. But history is nothing but a chronology of oppressors oppressing the oppressed.

OPTIMISM

Chesterton, Gilbert Keith. Optimism: the noble temptation to see too much in everything.

Martin, Abe. Being an optimist after you've got everything you want doesn't count.

Oppenheimer, J. Robert. The optimist thinks this is the best of all possible worlds, and the pessimist knows it.

Ullmann, Peter. Pessimism was a Victorian luxury. I think nowadays you have to be optimistic—even if the facts are completely opposed to your viewpoint and ridiculous and unrealistic.

Ustinov, Peter. An optimist is someone who knows exactly how sad and bad the world can be.

ORCHESTRAS

Maazel, Lorin. Too many concerts are given by too many orchestras. You get the professionalism of mediocrity, and it grinds on like some kind of dreadful machine that never stops.

ORGANIZATION OF PETROLEUM EXPORTING COUNTRIES

Perez, Carlos Andres (President of Venezuela). The increase of petroleum prices is by no means a selfish act of OPEC members for the exclusive benefit of their countries. It represents the irrevocable decision to dignify the terms of trade, to revalue raw materials and other basic products of the third world.

Wilson, Harold. It is no longer a humorous matter to point out that in a few years there is a strong possibility that Britain could become a member of OPEC.

ORGANIZATIONS

Drucker, Peter F. The only things that evolve by themselves in an organization are disorder, friction and malperformance.

OSWALD, LEE HARVEY

Dudney, Bob. The country would have recovered from the death of John Kennedy, but it hasn't recovered yet from the death of Lee Harvey Oswald and probably never will.

Johnson, Lyndon Baines. I never believed that Oswald acted alone, although I can accept that he pulled the trigger.

OUTDOOR LIFE—NEW YORK (CITY)

Lebowitz, Fran. The outdoors is what you have to pass through to get from your apartment into a taxicab.

PAGE, GERALDINE

Page, Geraldine. The sadness I feel is that half my life or more is over, the list of films so short, and the people won't see all of what I could have shown them.

PAINTERS

Motherwell, Robert. Every intelligent painter carries the whole culture of modern painting in his head. It is his real subject, of which anything he paints is both an hommage and a critique.

PAINTING

Cezanne, Paul. Painting from nature is not copying the object; it is realizing one's sensations.

Delacroix, Eugene. A taste for simplicity cannot endure for long.

Duchamp, Marcel. I was interested in ideas—not in merely visual products. I wanted to put painting once again at the service of the mind.

Rothko, Mark. There is no such thing as a good painting about nothing.

Ruda, Edwin (Artist). I find it incredible that after 25,000 years of art and 5,000 years of written history—after all that visual hindsight and explication—the gulf between image and word persists the way it does. Only 25 years ago abstract painters were being asked why they painted the way they did; now the question seems to be: why paint at all?.

Simpson, David. In the first century A.D., Petronius declared painting dead. In 1934 Moholy-Nagy declared painting dead. In 1970—probably earlier—Robert Morris declared painting dead. Three of many.

PAINTING—REALISM

Wyeth, Andrew. True reality goes beyond reality itself.

PAKISTAN—POLITICS AND GOVERNMENT

Zia Ul-Haq, Mohammad. The army is the only stable institution in Pakistan.

PALESTINE

Arafat, Yasir. Palestine is my wife.

Arafat, Yasir. Palestine is the cement that holds the Arab world together, or it is the explosive that blows it apart.

Arafat, Yasir. There is nothing greater than to die for Palestine's return.

PALESTINE LIBERATION ORGANIZATION

Arafat, Yasir. I have come bearing an olive branch and a freedom fighter's gun. Do not let the olive branch fall from my hand (addressing the United Nations).

Arafat, Yasir. I have very few cards, but I have the strongest cards.

Arafat, Yasir. In a sense, Menachem Begin is our best ally. We hope he will increase his aggression and his terrorism so that everybody all over the world will discover the ugly face of this Israeli military junta.

Arafat, Yasir. We (the PLO) do not want to destroy any people. It is precisely because we have been advocating coexistence that we have shed so much blood.

Arafat, Yasir. When you put a cat in a corner, it will scratch.

Dayan, Moshe. Of course, if you want to make peace, you don't talk to your friends. You talk to your enemies. But the question is whom do we want to make peace with—not just who are our enemies (explaining his objections to negotiating with the PLO).

Hatem, Abu. We will force the United States to recognize (us). Without the Palestine Liberation Organization there is not going to be any peace in the Middle East.

Peres, Shimon. Stroking a tiger (the P.L.O.) will not make it a pussycat.

PALESTINIAN ARABS

Abourezk, James. I was in a refugee camp in Jordan in 1973. I thought if I closed my eyes I could hear the words Pine Ridge. The Indians and the Palestinians are the same—people without power put against the wall by people with power.

Arafat, Yasir. Palestine is the cement that holds the Arab world together, or it is the explosive that blows it apart.

Carter, James Earl. I have never met an Arab leader that in private professed the desire for an independent Palestinian state.

Tawil, Raymonde. We (Palestinians) are like grass. The more you cut it, the more it will grow.

PALEY, WILLIAM

Von Hoffman, Nicholas. If he (William Paley) is remembered at all, it will be as the man who gave America 'Hee Haw'.

PANAMA CANAL

Anonymous (U.S. diplomat), . If Torrijos had not worked his charm on the senators, the (Panama Canal) treaties would simply be a dead letter.

Buckley, William Frank, Jr. We should be big enough to grant a little people what we ourselves fought for 200 years ago (commenting on the Panama Canal).

Goldwater, Barry Morris. I would have said that we should fight for the (Panama) canal if necessary. But the Viet Nam years have taught me that we wouldn't. So we might as well hand it over.

Reagan, Ronald. Treaties invite nationalization.

Roosevelt, James. My uncle Teddy stole it, my father Franklin kept it going, and as far as I'm concerned they can now give it back (commenting on the Panama Canal).

Torrijos, Omar. In truth, the (Panama Canal Zone) treaty is like a little pebble which we shall be able to carry in our shoe for 23 years, and that is better than the stake we have had to carry in our hearts.

PANAMA—FOREIGN RELATIONS—UNITED STATES

Torrijos, Omar. In truth, the (Panama Canal Zone) treaty is like a little pebble which we shall be able to carry in our shoe for 23 years, and that is better than the stake we have had to carry in our hearts.

PARAGUAY—POLITICS AND GOVERNMENT

Stroessner, Alfredo. Human rights is a Trojan horse of international Communism.

PARANOIA

Sanders, Ed. Just because you're paranoid doesn't mean they're not trying to get you.

PARENT-CHILD RELATIONSHIP

Colette, Sidonie Gabrielle Claudine. It is not a bad thing that children should occasionally, and politely, put parents in their place.

Jung, Carl Gustav. Nothing has a stronger influence on their children than the unlived lives of the parents.

Needham, Richard J. You should treat your children as strangers whom you happen to like. If, that is, you happen to like them.

Schlafly, Phyllis. 'Equal parenting' does not work—the maternal tuning in never turns off.

PARENTS

Schlafly, Phyllis. 'Equal parenting' does not work—the maternal tuning in never turns off.

PARIS

Calder, Alexander. Why do I live in Paris? Because in Paris it's a compliment to be called crazy.

PARIS—DESCRIPTION

Anonymous (French politician), . It seems that the more Paris resembles New York, the more anti-American we become.

Dryansky, G. Y. Paris is becoming more vulgar, New York more refined.

Harriss, Joseph. Parisians have always recognized the human need for the superfluous.

PARK, TONGSUN

Park, Tongsun. I want to tell you what I have done in Washington constitutes an American success story on a small scale.

Park, Tongsun. Some people enjoy making other people happy. I like to entertain. I am concerned that we have no Perle Mesta. We should have somebody in the private sector who plays the role of catalyst to bring people together. I like to do my share.

PARKINSON'S LAW (QUOTATION)

Johnson, Haynes. As work and space expand and collide they breed their own reaction.

Parkinson, C. Northcote. Nonsense expands so as to fill the space available (Corollary to Parkinson's Law).

Parkinson, C. Northcote. Work expands to fill the time allotted to it, or, conversely, the amount of work completed is in inverse proportion to the number of people employed.

PARSONS, BETTY

Kuhn, Annette. To be 75, sailing, cracking a bone, and wanting to go sailing again as soon as this trifle is healed—that's my idea of a good life.

PARTON, DOLLY

Mogull, Artie (President of United Artists Records). I'll make two predictions: big bands will not come back, and Dolly Parton will continue to be the only girl singer with big tits to sell records.

Parton, Dolly. I know my hair is out of the '60s, my clothes are '50s and the shoes I wear are from the '40s. But I like looking like I came out of a fairy tale.

Parton, Dolly. If people think I'm a dumb blonde because of the way I look, then they're dumber than they think I am.

Parton, Dolly. When I sit back in my rocker, I want to have done it all.

PARTRIDGE, ERIC

Partridge, Eric. I always wanted to become a writer, and I consider myself to be one.

PAST (TIME)

Faulkner, William. The past is never dead; it is not even past.

PASTORE, JOHN O.

Pastore, John O. I've always been weary of people who stayed on too long—stalwarts in their day who end up being held up by their staff. I don't want to mention any names. I wouldn't let that happen to me.

PATERSON, NEW JERSEY

Algren, Nelson. It's a boomtown. Sixty percent of the people are on welfare. That's my kind of town (about Paterson, New Jersey).

PATRONAGE, POLITICAL

Lincoln, Abraham. Sitting here, where all the avenues to public patronage seem to come together in a knot, it does seem to me that our people are fast approaching the point where it can be said that seven-eighths of them are trying to find out how to live at the expense of the other eighth.

PAUL, SAINT

John Paul I, Pope, . If St. Paul returned to the world now as a journalist he would not only direct Reuters but seek time on television.

PAUL VI, POPE

Butz, Earl Lauer. He no playa the game, he no maka the rules (in response to Pope Paul's stand on birth control).

PEACE

Albornoz, Claudio Sanchez. I have only one word: peace. We have killed each other too much already. Let us reach understanding under a regime of freedom, all of us putting into it what is necessary from each side of the barricade (exiled former president upon returning to Spain).

Beston, Henry. Peace with the earth is the first peace.

Brzezinski, Zbigniew. We live in a world in which there will be many local conflicts, in which all the major powers will exercise self-restraint, because they have to exercise self-restraint in the nuclear...it will be a sign of the maturity of the American people and of the growing wisdom of the American people if we adjust ourselves to the notion that in our age there is a twilight zone between war and peace and that this twilight zone of limited wars is going to be very much a feature of our lifetime.

Carter, James Earl. In war, we offer our very lives as a matter of routine. We must be no less daring, no less steadfast, in the pursuit of peace.

Corrigan, Mairead. Our world is rushing towards disaster. But it's not too late to prove the power of love...we've got to prove that the way of nonviolence can bring social change (from her Nobel Peace Prize acceptance speech).

Edison, Thomas Alva. The day will come when science will create a machine as a force which is so terrible, so infinitely horrifying, that even man, a bellicose being who brings suffering, torment, and death upon his fellows, at the risk of bringing these torments upon himself will shudder with fear and renounce war forever.

Hua, Kuo-Feng. Peace cannot be got by begging. War cannot be averted by yielding.

Sakharov, Andrei Dmitrievich. To keep one's self-respect, one must act in accordance with the general human longing for peace, for true detente, for genuine disarmament (in his message accepting the Nobel Peace Prize).

Stevenson, Adlai, II. The journey of a thousand leagues begins with a single step. So we must never neglect any work of peace within our reach, however small.

West, Mae. I'm for peace. I have yet to wake up in the morning and hear a man say, I've just had a good war.

PEACE—MIDDLE EAST

Anonymous, . The Arabs cannot make war without the Egyptians, but they cannot make peace without the Palestinians.

Eban, Abba Solomon. You cannot have peace without risks.

Kissinger, Henry Alfred. The absence of alternatives (in the Middle East) clears the mind marvelously.

McLuhan, Marshall. That was the human family sitting down together. It passed history unexpectedly (about Anwar Sadat's first visit to Israel).

Rabin, Yitzhak. For me, peace means reconciliation of the Arab countries with the existence of Israel as a Jewish state.

PECKINPAH, SAM

Kristofferson, Kris. Sam (Peckinpah) is like an old dog you sometimes have to apologize for.

PELE

Pele, . God has been kind to me. Three World Cups and now a championship in America. I can die now.

PENN, IRVING

Penn, Irving. I rate myself out of combat—as something between a painter and an old-time photographer. But if I were to define myself, I'd say I was the least specialized of all photographers. I need a balanced diet.

PENTHOUSE (PERIODICAL)

Nizer, Louis. Having fought for the 1st amendment before *Penthouse* was born I wish (the first amendment) was in better hands than a magazine that specializes in close ups of women's orifices (spoken as the attorney for Rancho La Costa in its $630 million libel suit against *Penthouse* magazine.

PEOPLE'S BICENTENNIAL COMMISSION

Booth, Arch. I find these figures impossible to accept (in response to a Peoples Bicentennial Commission's sponsored survey reflecting wide public disenchantment with American business).

Isley, Fred (Manager of public relations, Xerox Corporation). I don't know if the public's negative attitude makes a difference to corporations (in response to a Peoples Bicentennial Commission's sponsored survey reflecting wide public disenchantment with American business).

Murphy, Jack (Director of public relations for Exxon). We're not really surprised. But you can just say we have no comment (in response to a Peoples Bicentennial Commission's sponsored survey reflecting wide public disenchantment with American business).

PEREZ, MANUEL BENITEZ

Perez, Manuel Benitez. Bullfighting is an animal inside me, and it is one that I cannot dominate—it dominates me.

PERFECTION

Whitehead, Alfred North. Adventure is essential, namely, the search for new perfections.

Whitehead, Alfred North. Even perfection will not bear the tedium of indefinite repetition.

Zola, Emile. Perfection is such a nuisance that I often regret having cured myself of using tobacco.

PERIODICALS

Gingrich, Arnold. To stand out, for a man or a magazine, it is necessary to stand for something. Otherwise you stand still.

PERIODICALS—COVERS

Stolley, Richard. Young sells better than old, pretty sells better than ugly, music sells better than television, television better than movies, and politics doesn't sell at all.

PERKINS, FRANCES

Perkins, Frances (former Secretary of Labor). Being a woman has only bothered me in climbing trees.

PERKINS, MAXWELL

Perkins, Maxwell. Editors are extremely fallible people, all of them. Don't put too much trust in them (to Taylor Caldwell).

Perkins, Maxwell. It is always better to give a little less than the reader wants, than more (to Ray Stannard Baker).

Perkins, Maxwell. You have to throw yourself away when you write (to Elizabeth Lemmon).

PERON, MARIA ESTELA MARTINEZ ISABEL

Borges, Jorge Luis. (I am) very glad about the military coup—it will be a pleasure to be free of hoodlums and gangsters and to be governed again by officers and gentlemen (commenting upon his announcement to return to Argentina).

Peron, Maria Estela Martinez Isabel. The country is suffering internal and external aggression from journalistic terrorism and defamatory rumors. My state of health is not a sufficient reason to try unethically and against the popular will to strip me of my legitimate authority.

PERSISTENCE

Billings, Josh. Consider the postage stamp: its usefulness consists in the ability to stick to one thing till it gets there.

PERSONALITY

Anonymous, . You can hide good luck but not misfortune.

Erhard, Werner. You are perfect exactly the way you are.

Pagnol, Marcel. The most difficult secret for a man to keep is the opinion he has of himself.

Read, David H. C. The worst sin is dullness.

Schwab, Charles M. Personality is to a man what perfume is to a flower.

PERSUASION (PSYCHOLOGY)

Comins, David H. People will accept your idea more readily if you tell them Benjamin Franklin said it first.

PERSUASION (RHETORIC)

Comins, David H. People will accept your idea more readily if you tell them Benjamin Franklin said it first.

PESSIMISM

Brzezinski, Zbigniew. Pessimism is a luxury that policymakers can't afford because pessimism, on the part of people who try to shape events, can become a self-fulfilling prophecy.

Cousins, Norman. I am no pessimist. I doubt that any man knows enough to be a pessimist.

Oppenheimer, J. Robert. The optimist thinks this is the best of all possible worlds, and the pessimist knows it.

Ullmann, Peter. Pessimism was a Victorian luxury. I think nowadays you have to be optimistic—even if the facts are completely opposed to your viewpoint and ridiculous and unrealistic.

PETER PRINCIPLE (QUOTATION)

Peter, Laurence J. In a hierarchy, every employee tends to rise to the level of his own incompetence.

Peter, Laurence J. Most hierarchies were established by men who now occupy the upper levels, thus depriving women of an equal opportunity to achieve their levels of incompetence.

Peter, Laurence J. The cream rises until it sours.

PETROLEUM—GREAT BRITAIN

Wilson, Harold. It is no longer a humorous matter to point out that in a few years there is a strong possibility that Britain could become a member of OPEC.

PETROLEUM INDUSTRY

Adams, Cecil. The average oilman has the moral development of a newt.

Bayh, Birch Evans. I am tired of the oil companies determining the price of everything we use that is made from petroleum. I want to break up the monopolistic control they have from the time they punch a hole in the ground to putting gas in the tank.

Bayh, Birch Evans. If there is one symbol of the Establishment ripping off the people, it is the oil companies.

Carter, James Earl. As is the case in time of war there is potential war profiteering in the impending energy crisis. This could develop with the passing months as the biggest rip-off in history.

Dirksen, Everett. The oil can is mightier than the sword.

Ehrlich, Paul. The petrochemical industry is at about the intellectual and moral level of the people who sell heroin to high school kids.

Glenn, John. Our objective is to prevent the people of this country from getting economically raped (arguing against the decontrol of petroleum prices).

Long, Russell. Those who defame us, curse us, abuse us and lie about us, would be in one hell of a fix without us (about energy producers).

Rockefeller, John Davison, III. I don't have a whole lot of faith in what the oil companies say.

Schlesinger, James Rodney. They (the oil companies) are just as much victims of the shortage as we are; indeed, more the victims.

PETROLEUM—PIPE LINES—ALASKA

Patton, Edward L. Almost everyone who views the (Alaska) pipeline agrees that it is not a visual abomination. In fact, I predict that it will be a leading tourist attraction.

PETROLEUM—PRICES

Amouzegar, Jamshid (Iran's Interior Minister). The substantive issue is not whether the oil price has gone up too rapidly; the real issue is whether or not the world is willing to realize that the era of cheap and abundant energy is over.

Bayh, Birch Evans. I am tired of the oil companies determining the price of everything we use that is made from petroleum. I want to break up the monopolistic control they have from the time they punch a hole in the ground to putting gas in the tank.

Bayh, Birch Evans. If there is one symbol of the Establishment ripping off the people, it is the oil companies.

Hayakawa, Samuel Ichiye. Let gas go to $1.50, even $2 per gallon. A lot of poor don't need gas because they are not working.

Perez, Carlos Andres (President of Venezuela). The increase of petroleum prices is by no means a selfish act of OPEC members for the exclusive benefit of their countries. It represents the irrevocable decision to dignify the terms of trade, to revalue raw materials and other basic products of the third world.

PETROLEUM SUPPLY

Anonymous (Federal Trade Commission memo), . The current gasoline shortage may be contrived.

O'Leary, John. There isn't a gasoline shortage. There's a driving surplus.

Wagner, Robert. A person's state of happiness is almost directly related to the amount of gas in his tank.

PETROLEUM SUPPLY—TEXAS

Hubbard, Harry. Making Texans stand in line for gas is like making Kansans stand in line for wheat.

PHILADELPHIA—DESCRIPTION

Rizzo, Frank Lazzaro. The streets are safe in Philadelphia. It's only the people who make them unsafe (when asked his opinion on crime in the streets).

PHILADELPHIA. HOCKEY CLUB (NATIONAL LEAGUE)

Shero, Fred. We know that hockey is where we live, where we can best meet and overcome pain and wrong and death. Life is just a place where we spend time between games.

PHILADELPHIA—POLITICS AND GOVERNMENT

Rizzo, Frank Lazzaro. Just wait, after November you'll have a front row seat because I'm gonna make Attila the Hun look like a faggot (to several friends).

PHILIPPINES

Beveridge, Albert J. The Philippines are ours forever. They are not capable of self-government. How could they be? They are not of a self-governing race (comments made in 1900).

PHILIPPINES—POLITICS AND GOVERNMENT

Marcos, Ferdinand E. I would like to return the Filipino to what he was before he was altered and modified by the softness of Western and other ways.

PHILOSOPHY

Adler, Mortimer. Philosophy is everybody's business.

De Casseres, Benjamin. My studies in speculative philosophy, metaphysics, and science are all summed up in the image of a mouse called man running in and out of every hole in the cosmos hunting for the absolute cheese.

Haldane, J. B. S. I suspect that there are more things in heaven and earth than are dreamed of, or can be dreamed of, in any philosophy.

Harris, Sydney J. Any philosophy that can be 'put in a nutshell' belongs there.

Heidegger, Martin. He who does not know what homesickness is, cannot philosophize.

Panza di Biumo, Giuseppe. For me, art is the visualization of philosophy.

PHILOSOPHY—FRANCE

Le Bris, Michel. God is dead, Marx is dead, and I'm not doing all that well myself.

PHOBIAS

Clark, Alex. It's always darkest just before the lights go out.

PHONOGRAPH RECORD INDUSTRY

Walden, Phil (President of Capricorn Records). That's the old American way—if you got a good thing, then overdo it.

PHOTOGRAPHERS

Cunningham, Imogen. In my professional life as a portrait photographer, I've found very often people can't face themselves. They can't live with the faces they were born with. It's not a nice occupation to try to please people with their faces..

Ray, Man. The streets are full of admirable craftsmen, but so few practical dreamers.

PHOTOGRAPHY

Bourke-White, Margaret. Know your subject thoroughly, saturate yourself with your subject, and your camera will take you by the hand.

Cartier-Bresson, Henri. For me the camera is an instrument of intuition and spontaneity, the master of the instant.

Cartier-Bresson, Henri. The camera is a weapon. It's not a propaganda means, but it's a way of shouting the way you feel.... It's an affirmation. It's like the last three words of 'Ulysses' of James Joyce. It's 'Yes, yes, yes!'.

Cunningham, Imogen. In my professional life as a portrait photographer, I've found very often people can't face themselves. They can't live with the faces they were born with. It's not a nice occupation to try to please people with their faces..

Evans, Walker. Photography isn't a matter of taking pictures. It's a matter of having an eye.

Giono, Jean. Reality pushed to its extreme ends in unreality.

Karsh, Yousuf. Photography is the voice of humanity. And that voice must be heard.

Krementz, Jill. Can I call you back? (in response to the question 'Is photography art?').

Misrach, Richard. The primary illusion of photography is fact—its apparent literal transcription of the world. Thus, it becomes interesting when a body of photographs describes a world that is both convincing and authentic, and at the same time nonexistent.

Ray, Man. I have always preferred inspiration to information (commenting on photography).

Rivers, Larry. Is photography art? Art is everything.

Sontag, Susan. Nobody ever discovered ugliness through photographs. But many, through photographs, have discovered beauty.

Steichen, Edward. The mission of photography is to explain man to man and each man to himself.

Warhol, Andy. Art dealers (in reply to the question whom or what is the major influence on photography?).

Warhol, Andy. Art dealers (in response to the question Whom or what is the major influence on photography?).

PHYSICAL FITNESS

Lovell, James, Jr. I'm convinced that the last human sound on this continent won't be a bang, but a burp (commenting on what will happen if people don't eat less and exercise more.

PHYSICIAN AND PATIENT

Schweitzer, Albert (attributed by Norman Cousins). We are at our best when we give the doctor who resides within each patient a chance to go to work.

PHYSICIANS

McGuire, Al. I don't know why people question the academic training of a student-athlete. Half the doctors in the country graduated in the bottom half of their class.

Moss, Frank. There comes a certain point when physicians, like other lawbreakers, must be put in jail (commenting on Medicaid and Medicare fraud).

PHYSICIANS—CHICAGO

Haughton, James (Cook County Hospital Director). The residents and interns (who struck the Cook County Hospital for 18 days) are the same young people who tore up colleges five years ago.

PHYSICIANS—PSYCHOLOGY

Cooley, Denton. A successful surgeon should be a man who, when asked to name the three best surgeons in the world, would have difficulty deciding on the other two.

PIANISTS

Arrau, Claudio. Every concert must be an event, never a routine.

PICASSO, PABLO

Picasso, Jacqueline. Living with Picasso was like living with a blowtorch; he was a consuming flame.

Picasso, Pablo. Every child is an artist. The problem is how to remain an artist once he grows up.

Picasso, Pablo. For me there are only two kinds of women—goddesses and doormats.

PIERCE, WEBB

Pierce, Webb. One drink is too many and a million is not enough.

PINERO, MIGUEL

Pinero, Miguel. I'd like to die with my back against the wall and two guns smokin'.

PINIELLA, LOU

Piniella, Lou (New York Yankee outfielder). I cussed him out in Spanish, and he threw me out in English (commenting on an argument he once had with umpire Armando Rodriguez).

PIPPIN, HORACE

Pippin, Horace (folk artist). Pictures just come to my mind and then I tell my heart to go ahead.

PITCHING (BASEBALL)

Busby, Steve. I throw the ball harder than Nolan Ryan. It just doesn't get there as fast.

Gomez, Lefty. If you don't throw it, they can't hit it.

PITTSBURGH. FOOTBALL CLUB (NATIONAL LEAGUE)

Fugett, Jean. I always thought of Pittsburgh as a dirty city, a crude city and a blue-collar town. And that's exactly what I think of their football team (commenting after the Super Bowl game).

PITY

Eban, Abba Solomon. Better to be disliked than pitied.

Ryan, Cornelius. The mathematics of self-pity can be raised to infinity.

PLAGIARISM

Walpole, Horace. You must renounce imagaination forever if you hope to succeed in plagiarism. Forgery is intention, not invention.

PLAINS, GEORGIA—DESCRIPTION

Carter, Lillian. I don't know of anybody in my hometown who's destitute. I wouldn't let them be.

PLANNING

Brown, Edmund Gerald, Jr. The reason why everybody likes planning is because nobody has to do anything.

Feather, William. No plan is worth a damn unless somebody makes it work.

Leopold, Aldo. The first prerequisite of intelligent tinkering is to save all the pieces.

Peter, Laurence J. If you don't know where you are going, you will probably end up somewhere else.

Van Derbur, Marilyn (former Miss America). The vital, successful people I have met all had one common characteristic. They had a plan.

PLAYBOY ENTERPRISES, INC.

Lownes, Victor. This company is doing a good business, if we can only stop pissing away the profits.

PLAYBOY (PERIODICAL)

Hefner, Hugh Marston. If I told you, for example that Playboy, in its 22 years, was one of the major things that contributed to the women's movement, you might find it a mindboggler, but it happens to be true.

PLEASURE

Allen, Woody. The meaning of life is that nobody knows the meaning of life..

POETRY

Auden, Wystan Hugh. Poetry makes nothing happen.

Bishop, Elizabeth. Poetry shouldn't be used as a vehicle for any personal philosophy.

Hochman, Sandra. I'd rather be hung from clotheslines and washed in laundromats than read in libraries (commenting on her poetry to be printed on clothing and bedsheets).

Kavanagh, Patrick. Whatever will live must touch the heart of the mob in some way.

Marsh, Jean. I think poetry is like a diary: people don't tend to write anything in it until something awful happens.

POETRY—RUSSIA

Mandelstam, Osip. Poetry is respected only in this country (Russia)—people are killed for it. There's no place where more people are killed for it.

POETS

Fowles, John. Cherish the poet; there seemed many great auks till the last one died.

Papp, Joseph. The true dramatist of our time is a poet; the true poet, a dramatist.

Pritchett, V. S. It is the role of the poet to look at what is happening in the world and to know that quite other things are happening.

Sexton, Anne. I wonder if the artist ever lives his life—he is so busy recreating it.

Wagner, Richard. A poet is nothing if not someone who knows without having made a study.

POLICE

Behan, Brendan. I have never seen a situation so dismal that a policeman couldn't make it worse.

Cleaver, Eldridge. A black pig, a white pig, a yellow pig, a pink pig—a dead pig is the best pig of all. We encourage people to kill them (in 1970).

Fernandes, Millor (Brazilian playwright). In a democracy we are all equal before the law. In a dictatorship we are all equal before the police.

Mark, Sir Robert. The real art of policing a free society or a democracy is to win by appearing to lose or at least to win by not appearing to win.

POLITICAL CAMPAIGNS

Railsback, Thomas F. I'm concerned that candidates can often be packaged like wieners, and the best-looking wiener sometimes wins.

POLITICAL CAMPAIGNS—TEXAS

Clements, Bill. My opponent is in for a real fracas. If he thinks it's going to be some kind of cakewalk, I will assure you he's gotten hold of a hot enchilada.

POLITICAL PRISONERS

Moynihan, Daniel Patrick. When a person goes to a country and finds their newspapers filled with nothing but good news, he can bet there are good men in jail.

POLITICAL SCIENCE

Lao-Tse (Chinese philosopher), . You should govern a great nation as you fry a small fish, with little stirring about.

POLITICIANS

Abourezk, James. If you want to curry favor with a politician, give him credit for something someone else did.

Alda, Alan. If I were a politician, I'd be a decent politician..

Anonymous, . A statesman is a dead politician.

Bauler, (Paddy). Take care of the voters first, then you can take care of yourself.

Bhutto, Zulfikar Ali. A politician is like a spring flower: he blossoms, he blooms, and a time comes for him to fade.

Burgess, Anthony. We need beauty queens more than politicians.

Bush, Earl (press aide to Richard J. Daley). Don't print what he says; print what he means (about Richard J. Daley).

Caddell, Patrick. I don't know any politician in America who could run against himself and win.

Cameron, Simon. An honest politician is one who, when he is bought, will stay bought.

Eckhardt, Nadine. Most politicians are just little men who couldn't get it up in high school.

Greenfield, Jeff. You will get what you want if you vote for the candidate who says exactly the opposite of what you most deeply believe.

Hayakawa, Samuel Ichiro. Before World War II in Japan they killed off all the older politicians. All that were left were the damn fools who attacked Pearl Harbor. I think that this country needs elder statesmen too.

Johnson, Claudia Alta (Taylor). A politician ought to be born a foundling and remain a bachelor.

Johnson, Lyndon Baines. I never trust a man unless I've got his pecker in my pocket.

Kahn, J. Kesner. When politicians come up with a solution for your problem, you have two problems.

Khrushchev, Nikita Sergeevich. Politicians are the same the world over: they promise to build a bridge even where there is no river.

Menninger, Karl. The jail is a horrible institution manned by amateurs and politicians.

Meyers, Victor Aloysius (former Lieutenant Governor of California). Habitually I go without a vest so that I can't be accused of standing for the vested interests.

Moynihan, Daniel Patrick. Most politicians have a right to feel morally superior to their constituencies.

Ridgeway, Matthew B. Candidates are no better or worse than those who choose and elect them, and therein lies the answer to what we are to become.

Roth, William V., Jr. Public confidence and trust in the federal government are low not only because of Watergate or our experience in Vietnam, but also because too many politicians have promised more than the government can deliver.

Simon, William E. Bad politicians are sent to Washington by good people who don't vote.

Simons, Frank. There is but one way for a newspaperman to look on a politician, and that is down.

Strauss, Robert S. If you're in politics, you're a whore anyhow. It doesn't make any difference who you sleep with.

Truman, Harry S. The C students run the world.

Unruh, Jesse. If I had slain all my political enemies, I wouldn't have any friends today.

Wills, Garry. Politicians fascinate because they constitute such a paradox: they are an elite that accomplishes mediocrity for the public good.

Youngquist, Wayne. People want leaders with vision rather than programs. Even if conservatism is overtaking liberalism and individualism is prized over collective action, vision is always in demand and often rewarded at the polls.

POLITICIANS—CONDUCT OF LIFE

Hayakawa, Samuel Ichiye. I think it's too much to expect of an elected official to condemn himself to a fully ascetic life, as if he were a priest. But whatever he does he must do with utmost discretion.

POLITICIANS—RELATION WITH THE PRESS

Dorfman, Dan. To lie to the press on a public matter is, in effect, to lie to the people.

POLITICIANS—SEXUAL BEHAVIOR

Mondale, Joan. The issue is Watergate or waterbed. The Democrats do it to their secretaries but the Republicans do it to the country.

Wright, James. The Wright broad rule is that broads ought to be able to type (commenting when asked to state a broad rule for avoiding Congressional sex scandals).

POLITICIANS—UNITED STATES

Burns, George. Too bad that all the people who know how to run the country are busy driving taxicabs and cutting hair.

POLITICIANS—WIVES

Nixon, Patricia Ryan. I gave up everything I've ever loved (commenting in 1960 on the price of political life).

POLITICS

Abourezk, James. Don't worry about your enemies, it's your allies who will do you in (in politics).

Abourezk, James. In politics, people will do whatever is necessary to get their way.

Abourezk, James. Politics is like the farmer's dog. If you run too fast you get nipped in the ass. If you stand still too long you get screwed.

Andreotti, Giulio. In politics there is a clause that is always valid: rebus sic stantibus (circumstances being what they are).

Anonymous, . To err is human; to blame it on the other party is politics.

Baker, Joy (wife of Howard Baker). Politics has nullified my personality.

Barkley, Alben. Three months is a generation in politics.

Bauler, (Paddy). Take care of the voters first, then you can take care of yourself.

Bellow, Saul. I see politics—ultimately—as a buzzing preoccupation that swallows up art and the life of the spirit.

Boulding, Kenneth E. Politics is a ritualistic dialectic—a bit like a football game. It doesn't really matter who wins, but you have to pretend it does in order to be part of the whole divine comedy.

Briggs, John. When it comes to politics, anything is fair.

Brown, Edmund Gerald, Jr. Issues are the last refuges of scoundrels.

Brown, Edmund Gerald, Jr. The first rule of politics is to be different.

Brown, Edmund Gerald, Jr. You lean a little to the left and then a little to the right in order to always move straight ahead (on the art of governing).

Brown, Sam. Never offend people with style when you can offend them with substance.

Cohen, Mark B. Nothing can so alienate a voter from the political system as backing a winning candidate.

Connally, John Bowden (attributed by Henry Alfred Kissinger). You will be measured in (Washington D.C.) by the enemies you destroy. The bigger they are, the bigger you are.

Connally, Mark (son of John Connally). I've seen the political life and I don't want it.

Crane, Philip. It's always better to stand on your principles and lose than to lose your principles and win.

Drinan, Robert. Politics is the formation of public morality.

Edwards, Shelton. The way to get somewhere in politics is to find a crowd that's going some place and get in front of it.

Ford, Gerald Rudolph. I learned a long time ago in politics, never say never.

Heller, Joseph. No one governs. Everyone performs. Politics has become a social world.

Hillman, Sidney. Politics is the science of how who gets what, when and why.

Horowitz, Rachel. If you're a public employee and your job depends on public officials, you have to be in politics.

Humphrey, Hubert Horatio. Politics isn't a matter of making love. It's making choices.

Humphrey, Hubert Horatio. The biggest corruption in politics, friends, is not money. It's publicity.

Jagger, Mick. Politics, like the legal system, is dominated by old men.

Kapiloff, Larry. I believe that politics is 90 percent the profession of cowards.

Kelley, Stanley. Last guys don't finish nice.

Kennedy, Florynce Rae. If the ass is protecting the system, ass-kicking should be undertaken regardless of the sex, ethnicity, or charm of the ass involved.

Kissinger, Henry Alfred. Competing pressures tempt one to believe that an issue deferred is a problem avoided; more often it is a crisis invited.

Kissinger, Henry Alfred. I have always thought of foreign policy as bipartisan.

Koch, Edward I. It happens that intellectual honesty is not the coin of the realm in politics.

Lao-Tse (Chinese philosopher), . You should govern a great nation as you fry a small fish, with little stirring about.

McCarthy, Eugene Joseph. If you've been in this business for 28 years, you don't like to leave the institutions in worse shape than you found them (explaining his rationale for staying in politics).

McGovern, George Stanley. Marching in mindless lockstep is the lowest form of party loyalty.

Mathias, Charles McCurdy. People tend to want to follow the beaten path. The difficulty is that the beaten path doesn't seem to be leading anywhere.

Mikva, Abner J. Someone once said that politics is like poker—it's only fun when you play for a trifle more than you can afford to lose.

Nixon, Patricia Ryan. I gave up everything I've ever loved (commenting in 1960 on the price of political life).

Nixon, Richard Milhous. There is one thing solid and fundamental in politics—the law of change. What's up today is down tomorrow.

Nixon, Richard Milhous (attributed by Robert J. Dole). It's always hard to lose the close ones—if it's a big one—but when it's close, everyone is looking around, you know, the cannibals come out and try to assess what happened.

Okun, Arthur M. The world is not safe for incumbents.

Pannenberg, Wolfhart. The greatest deception (of our era is the idea that) political change can satisfy a religious need.

Rayburn, Sam. A whore's vote is just as good as a debutante's.

Reagan, Ronald. As a matter of fact, Nancy never had any interest in politics or anything else when we got married (denying charges that his wife is the real political power in the family).

Reagan, Ronald. I finally figured out this politics. It's like show business. You start with a big opening act, coast, and close with a great crescendo.

Reeves, Richard. Politics is sex in a hula-hoop.

Rogers, Will. The trouble with practical jokes is that very often they get elected.

Roosevelt, Franklin Delano. Nothing just happens in politics. If something happens you can be sure it was planned that way.

Rumsfeld, Donald. If you try to please everybody, somebody is not going to like it.

Sears, John. Politics is motion and excitement.

Sears, John. You never really win anything in politics. All you get is a chance to play for higher stakes and perform at a higher level.

Stevenson, Adlai, II. Good government cannot exist side by side with bad politics: the best government is the best politics.

Stevenson, Adlai, III. I don't think ideas are incompatible with political reality.

Stevenson, Robert Louis. Politics is perhaps the only profession for which no preparation is thought necessary.

Stolley, Richard. Young sells better than old, pretty sells better than ugly, music sells better than television, television better than movies, and politics doesn't sell at all.

Talmadge, Betty. There's not much difference between selling a ham and selling a political idea.

Thompson, James. It is better to make fun of yourself than let your opponent do it for you.

Unruh, Jesse. Money is the mother's milk of politics.

Vidal, Gore. In writing and politicking, it's best not to think about it, just do it.

Voigt, Jon. Things don't have to be about politics to be political.

Walker, Jimmy. A reformer is a guy who rides through a sewer in a glass-bottomed boat.

White, Kevin. Charismatic leadership is hungered for, but at the same time we fear it.

White, Theodore. Politics in America is the binding secular religion.

Williams, Dakin. Political campaigning is like sex. The pleasure is in the pursuit (explaining why he is running for governor of Illinois again).

POLITICS, CORRUPTION IN

Aregood, Richard. It's hard to understand all this fuss about John F. Kennedy. After all, Richard Nixon didn't just concentrate on women. He tried to do it to everybody.

Cameron, Simon. An honest politician is one who, when he is bought, will stay bought.

Ervin, Samuel James. The statute of limitations has already run out on all my past indiscretions. And more unfortunately, I have lost all capacity to commit any more.

Prendergast, George Washington. I never took a dime from the public till; it's all been honest graft.

POLITICS, CORRUPTION IN—ILLINOIS

Powell, Paul. I can smell the meat a-cookin'. If you can't get a meal, take a sandwich (advice to lawmakers).

POLITICS, CORRUPTION IN—NEW YORK (CITY)

Tweed, William Marcy (Boss). I've tried to do some good, even if I have not had good luck.

POLITICS—SOUTH

Allen, Maryon. People in the South love their politics better than their food on the table.

POLLUTION

Gardner, Brian. Polluters must be made to pay so much that the fines—continuously leveled until the pollution stops—are so high that not to pollute is a cheaper alternative.

POOR

Bouza, Anthony. When you watch (ghetto) mothers take their kids to school, en route to a menial job, amid the drunks and junkies, you think maybe there is hope and the human spirit can triumph (commenting upon his retirement from the New York City police department after 23 years).

Churchill, Sir Winston. You don't make the poor richer by making the rich poorer.

Liddy, G. Gordon. Before going to prison I believed that criticism of the criminal justice system for its treatment of the poor was so much liberal bleating and bunk. I was wrong.

Poirot, Paul L. Multiplying wealth is by far the fastest way to help the poor. Dividing the wealth and subsidizing poverty is the fastest way to starve everyone.

Smith, Charles Merrill. In a democracy you can be respected though poor, but don't count on it.

POOR—UNITED STATES

McHarg, Ian. Give us your poor and oppressed and we will give them Harlem and the Lower East Side, Bedford-Stuyvesant, the South Side of Chicago, and the North of Philadelphia—or, if they are very lucky, Levittown.

POPES

Kung, Hans. The Pope needs a think tank, no, a brain trust, around him, instead of the court theologians who now surround him.

PORNOGRAPHY

Ephron, Nora. For those of us who believe that Hustler is a truly obscene magazine, it is a difficult moment. It is one of those cases that makes you search for some loophole (commenting on the Hustler pornography case).

Goldstein, Al. When it comes to pornography, I know two kinds of people: those who don't know what they're talking about, and those who don't know what they're missing.

Wallace, George Corley. The Supreme Court has to write a hundred pages on what pornography is. The average man who works in a steel mill can tell you right off whether that's filth or not.

PORTER, COLE

Merman, Ethel. (Cole Porter) sang like a hinge.

PORTUGAL—POLITICS AND GOVERNMENT

Azevedo, Pinheiro de. People power becomes tyranny when it is not united under a body of law.

Goncalves, Vasco dos Santos. It is not simple to be a member of a government team whose duration is expressed in days.

Soares, Mario. Troikas never work. They haven't worked since Roman times.

POSTAL SERVICE—UNITED STATES

Goldwater, Barry Morris. A book should not be charged the same rate for mailing as a brick.

POUND, EZRA

Pound, Ezra. At seventy, I realized that instead of being a lunatic, I was a moron.

POVERTY

Ali, Muhammad. Wars on nations are fought to change maps, but wars on poverty are fought to map change.

Harris, Patricia Roberts. Poverty is not so much the absence of money as the absence of aspiration, of the knowledge that it is possible to go anywhere else.

Mother Teresa, . Loneliness and the feeling of being unwanted is the most terrible poverty.

Poirot, Paul L. Multiplying wealth is by far the fastest way to help the poor. Dividing the wealth and subsidizing poverty is the fastest way to starve everyone.

POWELL, JODY

Anonymous (White House staff member), . (Jody) Powell is able to speak for Carter without Carter ever having spoken.

Powell, Jody. After getting kicked out (of the Air Force Academy) for cheating, politics seemed like the next best thing.

Powell, Jody. I probably had a political philosophy at one point, but I don't think about political philosophy any more.

POWELL, PAUL

Powell, Paul. I can smell the meat a-cookin'. If you can't get a meal, take a sandwich (advice to lawmakers).

POWER RESOURCES

Adelman, Morris A. (economist). The (energy) gap is like the horizon, always receding as you walk, ride, or fly toward it.

Amouzegar, Jamshid (Iran's Interior Minister). The substantive issue is not whether the oil price has gone up too rapidly; the real issue is whether or not the world is willing to realize that the era of cheap and abundant energy is over.

Carter, James Earl. No one should mistake the energy problem for what it is—a fundamental crisis that threatens Americans and America's way of life.

Davies, Denzil. Oil is a wasting asset, and if you don't invest (its revenues) in profitable assets, you'll be left with nothing.

Laird, Melvin. Conservation alone is a slow walk down a dead-end street.

Nader, Ralph. There is not an energy crisis. There is an energy monopoly crisis, too many of the energy decisions are being made by a few large corporations instead of by a broader aggregate of consumer determinants.

Penden, Bill. Atomic energy is a future idea whose time is past. Renewable energy is a future idea whose time has come.

Reagan, Ronald. The problem isn't a shortage of fuel, it's a surplus of government.

Udall, Morris King. I am saying we have to make fundamental changes in this country, that we are at the end of an era of cheap energy and resources, that the 70's and 80's are going to be a time of adaptation.

POWER (SOCIAL SCIENCES)

Abe, Kobo. In the love for the weak there is always an intent to kill.

Addams, Jane. I do not believe that women are better than men. We have not wrecked railroads, nor corrupted legislatures, nor done many unholy things that men have done; but then we must remember that we have not had the chance.

Allen, Woody. The lion and the calf shall lie down together, but the calf won't get much sleep.

Brown, Edmund Gerald, Jr. The power of the executive is like a chess game; there are very few moves that one can make.

Brzezinski, Zbigniew. Power is very intangible. It's nothing to be liked for its own sake. But...if you use power in a responsible way, then power is something one can enjoy.

Canetti, Elias. To be the last man to remain alive is the deepest urge of every real seeker after power.

Carr, Jesse. Being powerful is like being a lady. If you have to tell people you are, you ain't.

Cater, Douglass. If power corrupts, being out of power corrupts absolutely.

Evans, Medford. It usually takes disciplined organization to dislodge entrenched power.

Fulbright, James William. A great nation is peculiarly susceptible to the idea that its power is a sign of God's favor, conferring upon it a special responsibility for other nations—to make them richer and happier and wiser, to remake them, that is, in its own shining image. Power confuses itself with virtue and tends also to take itself for omnipotence (comments made in the 1960s).

Kissinger, Henry Alfred. Power is the greatest aphrodisiac of all.

Lao-Tse (Chinese philosopher), . You should govern a great nation as you fry a small fish, with little stirring about.

Nixon, Richard Milhous. Only three men in America understand the use of power. I do. John Connally does. And I guess Nelson does.

Novick, Julius. It is a well-known and infuriating fact of life that in any relationship, if one party really and truly does not give a damn, that party will inevitably have the upper hand. Indifference is power (ask any cat).

Shanker, Albert. Power is a good thing. It is better than powerlessness.

Soeder, Karin (Sweden's first woman Foreign Minister). Men care about power because for them power is linked to sexual performance. Women achieve positions of power out of a need to do something, not because we need reassurance.

Young, Andrew. Influence is like a savings account. The less you use it, the more you've got.

PRAISE

Nabokov, Vladimir. Anonymous praise hurts nobody.

Post, Emily. An overdose of praise is like 10 lumps of sugar in coffee; only a very few people can swallow it.

PRAYER

Tomlin, Lily. Why is it when we talk to God, we're said to be praying, but when God talks to us, we're schizophrenic?.

PREJUDICE

Comfort, Alex. Nobody is safe being prejudiced against what they themselves are going to become (commenting on aging).

James, William. A great many people think they are thinking when they are merely rearranging their prejudices.

PRESENT (TIME)

Boorstin, Daniel J. The contemporary time is always the best time to live. It is a mistake to say the best age is one without problems.

Faulkner, William. The past is never dead; it is not even past.

PRESIDENTIAL CAMPAIGNS

Broder, David S. Anybody who wants the presidency so much that he'll spend two years organizing and campaigning for it is not to be trusted with the office.

Brown, Edmund Gerald, Jr. In this business a little vagueness goes a long way.

Kissinger, Henry Alfred. My impression is that there is unanimity on the course that we are pursuing. It would be a tragedy if during this election year we did not find some means to put some restraint on our domestic debates in the field of foreign policy.

McCarthy, Eugene Joseph. Vice-presidential candidates just clutter up the campaign. We should not ask the country to make two judgements. Everyone knows Vice-Presidents have no influence on Presidents, once elected. Presidents' wives have much more influence. Perhaps we should have the candidates' wives debate.

Thompson, Mike. Franklin Roosevelt couldn't be nominated today. A Bruce Jenner could beat him.

PRESIDENTIAL CAMPAIGNS—1976

Ford, Gerald Rudolph. There is no Soviet domination of Eastern Europe and there never will be under a Ford Administration.

Kaye, Peter F. (Ford campaign spokesman). Mondale is a 100 per cent bona fide liberal. It gives us a tangible target. We're not just running against this peanut farmer who walks on water.

PRESIDENTIAL CAMPAIGNS—1980

Brock, Bill. If the (1980) election focuses on Carter and his record, Carter will lose.

Kennedy, Edward Moore. I am glad to be an underdog.

Kennedy, Edward Moore. I think Mr. Carter has created Ronald Reagan.

Reagan, Ronald. This is not a campaign; it's a crusade.

PRESIDENTIAL CANDIDATES

Barkan, Al. We're (AFL-CIO) going to have the best-organized, best-financed political force in the history of organized labor. No one else will have what we have. All we need is a candidate.

Hart, Gary. The race (between Ronald Reagan and Gerald Ford) all boils down to a contest between the philosophies of Herbert Hoover and Calvin Coolidge.

Jackson, Jesse. The absence of (George) Wallace is not the presence of justice.

McCloskey, Paul N. I don't believe there are any reasoning powers behind the programmed articulation of Ronald Reagan and I would like to test this thesis in open debate.

McGovern, George Stanley. Any candidate who says or implies that by supporting him the voters can stop the buses will prove as President to be either a liar or a violator of the Constitution.

McGovern, George Stanley. I will support Jimmy Carter with the same enthusiasm with which he supported the Democratic ticket in 1972.

PRESIDENTS—INAUGURAL ADDRESSES—1893

Cleveland, Grover. While the people should patriotically and cheerfully support their government, its functions do not include the support of the people (inaugural address—1893).

PRESIDENTS—INAUGURAL ADDRESSES—1921

Harding, Warren Gamaliel. Our most dangerous tendency is to expect too much of government, and at the same time to do for it too little (inaugural address—1921).

PRESIDENTS—INAUGURAL ADDRESSES—1933

Roosevelt, Franklin Delano. Our true destiny is not to be ministered unto but to minister to ourselves and to our fellow men (inaugural address—1933).

PRESIDENTS—INAUGURAL ADDRESSES—1961

Kennedy, John Fitzgerald. And so, my fellow Americans, ask not what your country can do for you; ask what you can do for your country (inaugural address—1961).

PRESIDENTS—INAUGURAL ADDRESSES—1973

Nixon, Richard Milhous. In our own lives, let each of us ask—not just what will government do for me, but what can I do for myself (inaugural address—1973).

PRESIDENTS—UNITED STATES

Broder, David S. Anybody who wants the presidency so much that he'll spend two years organizing and campaigning for it is not to be trusted with the office.

Carter, James Earl. I think the President is the only person who can change the direction or attitude of our nation.

Carter, James Earl. Our people want a President to be both tough and gentle, both statesman and politician, both dreamer and fighter. They expect him to have the drive to reach the White House, and the wisdom and patience to govern wisely.

Carter, James Earl. The most important skill for any President is leadership. A national leader, to be effective, must have the ability to lead this country and the vision to know where it must be led.

Church, Frank. The Presidency is no place for on-the-job training. I've always advocated the politics of substance, not the politics of style.

Ford, Gerald Rudolph. Most of the important things that happen in the world happen in the middle of the night.

Harlow, Bryce N. Our only protection against the presidency is the character of the president.

Humphrey, Hubert Horatio. I guess maybe I am the freest man I have ever been in my life. I seek nothing. I want nothing except one thing: I am going to tell it like it is..

Hussein, King of Jordan, . It's amusing. The Americans have changed Presidents six times since I've been King. And they talk to the Arabs about stability?.

Kennedy, Edward Moore. I *know* I cannot run for President now, and I've accepted that. It took a certain discipline and adjustment, but I've settled this with myself.

Kennedy, John Fitzgerald. I know that when things don't go well, they like to blame the President, and that is one of the things presidents are paid for.

Luce, Clare Boothe. There aren't many women now I'd like to see as President—but there are fewer men.

McCarthy, Eugene Joseph. Vice-presidential candidates just clutter up the campaign. We should not ask the country to make two judgements. Everyone knows Vice-Presidents have no influence on Presidents, once elected. Presidents' wives have much more influence. Perhaps we should have the candidates' wives debate.

Moyers, Bill D. It isn't wisdom or intelligence that influences a President, it's opportunity.

Nixon, Richard Milhous. Knowing a little about everything won't work. Knowing a great deal about important things is essential (for Presidents).

Nixon, Richard Milhous. The next President's qualifications should be tested against foreign policy. If he fails there, we all fail.

Reston, James. Old men running for the Presidency of the United States are like old men who take young brides. It's an exciting idea for a while but it seldom works.

Safire, William. I think that one of Nixon's great contributions to civil liberties was getting caught doing what the two presidents before him got away with.

Stevenson, Adlai, II. By the time a man is nominated for the Presidency of the United States, he is no longer worthy to hold the office.

Stoessinger, John G. The President holds our future in his hands. His personality may be our destiny.

Strauss, Robert S. There ain't but one good job in this government, and you got it (to Jimmy Carter).

Thompson, Hunter S. I don't think incompetence is any excuse for being a dumb President.

Thompson, Mike. Franklin Roosevelt couldn't be nominated today. A Bruce Jenner could beat him.

United States. Congress. Senate. Select Committee On Intelligence Operations, . There is no inherent Constitutional authority for the President or any intelligence agency to violate the law.

Vidal, Gore. Any man who can win a contemporary presidential campaign ought not to be President.

Vidal, Gore. As now set up, the best one can hope for in a President is that he not be entirely insane.

Welch, Robert (founder of the John Birch Society). Every President since Theodore Roosevelt has committed a treasonable act except—maybe—Warren G. Harding, Calvin Coolidge, and Herbert Hoover.

PRESIDENTS—UNITED STATES—POWERS AND DUTIES

Brown, Edmund Gerald, Jr. You don't have to do things. Maybe by avoiding doing things you accomplish a lot.

Church, Frank. If we are to preserve freedom and keep constitutional government alive in America, it cannot be left to a President and his agents alone to decide what must be kept secret. Congress, if it is to check the abuse of executive power, must retain its right to inquiry and independent judgement.

Ford, Gerald Rudolph. A President should never promise more than he can deliver and a President should always deliver everything that he's promised.

Nixon, Richard Milhous. It is quite obvious that there are certain inherently governmental actions which, if undertaken by the sovereign in protection of...the nation's security, are lawful, but which if undertaken by private citizens are not (commenting to the Senate Intelligence Committee on his authorization of covert CIA efforts to prevent Chilean President Allende's election in 1970).

Rockefeller, Nelson Aldrich. Congressional actions in the past few years, however well intentioned, have hamstrung the presidency and usurped the presidential prerogative in the conduct of foreign affairs.

PRESIDENTS—UNITED STATES—PRESS SECRETARY

McCarthy, Eugene Joseph. The most important member of the Executive Branch is the press secretary. I will appoint Mort Sahl. He's the only newspaper reader I know in America. I'll have him sit on the White House steps in the morning and catch the New York Times when it's thrown over the fence—and the Washington Post. He will throw the latter back immediately.

PRESIDENTS—UNITED STATES—PROTECTION

Mankiewicz, Frank Fabian. Since we are not yet serious about guns, let us at least withhold the most costly target (the President).

Starr, Kevin O. Perhaps if we find a way to save our Presidents, we can find a way to save ourselves.

PRESIDENTS—UNITED STATES—STAFF

Mikulski, Barbara A. Pete Preppy looks through his yearbook, calls up Mike Macho, and says, "Got anyone good for State?" "Sure," answers Mike. "Try Tom Terrifico." (On "the old boy network" of hiring practices in Washington, D.C.).

PRESIDENTS—UNITED STATES—WIVES

Johnson, Claudia Alta (Taylor). The First Lady is an unpaid public servant elected by one person: her husband.

McCarthy, Eugene Joseph. Vice-presidential candidates just clutter up the campaign. We should not ask the country to make two judgements. Everyone knows Vice-Presidents have no influence on Presidents, once elected. Presidents' wives have much more influence. Perhaps we should have the candidates' wives debate.

PRESLEY, ELVIS

Jagger, Mick. I should think not, judging from Elvis. No, rock 'n' roll music is for adolescents. It's a dead end (responding when asked Can rock stars move toward middle age?).

Jarvis, Felton (Elvis Presley's producer), . It's like someone just came up and told me there aren't going to be any more cheeseburgers in the world (commenting on Elvis Presley's death).

Kennedy, Caroline. His face seemed swollen and his sideburns reached his chin (writing about Elvis Presley's corpse).

Lewis, Jerry Lee. That dead son of a gun is still riding on my coattails (about Elvis Presley).

Presley, Elvis. I don't know anything about music. In my line I don't have to.

Smith, Sam. He stood on his own (about Elvis Presley).

PRESS

Jefferson, Thomas. Nature has given to man no other means (than the press) of sifting out the truth either in religion, law, or politics.

Nixon, Richard Milhous. When news is concerned, nobody in the press is a friend—they are all enemies.

PRETTY BABY (MOVING PICTURE)

Malle, Louis. Pretty Baby is a picture about child prostitution in which everybody else is the victim.

PRICES

Glenn, John. Our objective is to prevent the people of this country from getting economically raped (arguing against the decontrol of petroleum prices).

PRIESTS

John Paul II, Pope, . Priesthood is forever—we do not return the gift once given.

PRINCETON, NEW JERSEY

Einstein, Albert. Princeton is a wonderful little spot. A quaint and ceremonious village of puny demigods on stilts.

PRINCIPLE (PHILOSOPHY)

Lapham, Lewis H. I take for granted Jefferson's dictum that money, not morality, constitutes the principle of commercial nations.

PRISONS

Dean, John Wesley, III. Prisons are emotional zoos filled with paranoids, manic depressives, homosexuals, schizophrenics and assorted fruits and vegetables without labels.

Menninger, Karl. The jail is a horrible institution manned by amateurs and politicians.

PRISONS—BRAZIL

Fernandes, Millor (Brazilian playwright). The horrendous state of our prisons is what prevents them from being occupied by members of our highest society.

PRIVACY, RIGHT OF

Brown, George S. If any citizen of this country is so concerned about his mail being read or is concerned about his presence at a meeting being noted, I'd say we ought to read his mail and we ought to know what the hell he has done.

Goldwater, Barry Morris, Jr. Without a sense of privacy, the Bill of Rights' guarantees cease to function.

Linewes, David. We are an information-spoiled society. It's been so easy to collect that we just keep on collecting. Tens of millions of names are being pushed around from one organization to another for whatever purposes they want them, and we don't know anything about it.

Stimson, Henry. Gentlemen do not read each other's mail.

PROBLEM SOLVING

Anderson, Paul. I have yet to see any problem, however complicated, which, when you looked at it in the right way, did not become still more complicated.

Mencken, Henry Louis. For every human problem, there is a neat, plain solution—and it is always wrong.

Paulucci, Jeno F. It pays to be ignorant, for when you're smart you already know it can't be done.

Sevareid, Eric. The chief cause of problems is solutions.

PRODUCTION

Murphy, Thomas A. (Chairman of General Motors Corporation). For years the motto of organized labor was said to be the single word 'more'. It has not changed, but now we also hear talk of 'less'—not less wages, not less benefits, but less work. The public will see—must see—that less work not balanced by increased productivity really means more cost.

PRODUCTION STANDARDS

Schultze, Charles. If you can't measure output, then you measure input.

PROFESSIONALISM

Von Hoffman, Nicholas. Professionalism is a cheap and easy way of disciplining labor.

PROFIT

Brooks, Jim. Businessmen commit a fraud when they say they're interested in anything but profit.

Janeway, Eliot. The thrill of making a fast buck follows only the thrill of love at first sight. Everyone needs to take an occasional fling with money...and with love.

PROGRESS

Adenauer, Konrad. History is the sum total of the things that could have been avoided.

Eiseley, Loren. There is but one way into the future: the technological way.

Jenkins, Robin. It is not the goodness of saints that makes us feel there is hope for humanity: it is the goodness of obscure men.

King, Coretta Scott. There is a spirit and a need and a man at the beginning of every great human advance. Each of these must be right for that particular moment of history, or nothing happens.

Nash, Ogden. Progress might have been all right once, but it's gone on too long.

Rogers, Will. Any man who thinks civilization has advanced is an egoist.

Williams, Edward Bennett. The total egalitarians miss the point. They would divide the wealth equally, impose quotas and ratios in education, in employment, and in the political process, regardless of merit, overlooking the crucial fact that all human progress throughout history owes its origins to the talented and enterprising.

PRONUNCIATION

Broun, Heywood Hale. If anyone corrects your pronunciation of a word in a public place, you have every right to punch him in the nose.

PROPAGANDA

Goebbels, Joseph. Nothing is easier than leading the people on a leash. I just hold up a dazzling campaign poster and they jump through it.

PROPERTY

Didion, Joan. I think nobody owns land until their dead are in it.

PROPHETS

Rumi (Sufi mystic), . Men's minds perceive second causes, but only prophets perceive the action of the First Cause.

PROSTITUTION

Lipsen, Chuck. Folklore has it that the oldest profession is prostitution. I always thought it was lobbying.

Reagan, Ronald. You know, politics has been called the second oldest profession. Sometimes there is a similarity to the first.

Saint James, Margo. (We've already) got legalized prostitution: marriage.

Sinatra, Frank. Hell hath no fury like a hustler with a literary agent.

PROTESTANT EPISCOPAL CHURCH

Means, Jacqueline. We have spent so many years meeting and debating on this when we could have been doing other things. I'm glad it's over so that I can be able to get to work with the ministry (commenting on the ordination of women in the Protestant Episcopal Church).

PRYOR, RICHARD

Tomlin, Lily. Of all the actors working now, he (Richard Pryor) is the one who has the most instant rapport with his audience.

PSYCHIATRISTS

Brando, Marlon. The principal benefit acting has offered me is the money to pay my psychiatrists.

Montagu, Ashley. Most psychiatrists need to have their heads examined. Analysis, it has been said, is the study of the id by the odd.

PSYCHIATRY

Greenberg, David. An oldtimer is someone who can remember when a naughty child was taken to the woodshed instead of to a psychiatrist.

Montagu, Ashley. Most psychiatrists need to have their heads examined. Analysis, it has been said, is the study of the id by the odd.

PUBLIC OFFICE

Kissinger, Henry Alfred. High office teaches decision making, not substance. It consumes intellectual capital; it does not create it.

PUBLIC OPINION

Brown, Sam. Never offend people with style when you can offend them with substance.

Roth, William V., Jr. Public confidence and trust in the federal government are low not only because of Watergate or our experience in Vietnam, but also because too many politicians have promised more than the government can deliver.

Rowse, A. L. Most people's opinions are of no value at all.

PUBLIC SCHOOLS AND RELIGION

Reagan, Ronald. If we get the federal government out of the classroom, maybe we'll get God back in.

PUBLIC SCHOOLS—DESEGREGATION

Clark, Kenneth. Integration is a painful job. It is social therapy, and like personal therapy it is not easy.

Wallace, George Corley. I draw the line in the dust and toss the gauntlet before the feet of tyranny. And I say, segregation now. Segregation tomorrow. Segregation forever.

PUBLIC SCHOOLS—PHILADELPHIA

Rizzo, Frank Lazzaro. We need excellence in public education and if the teachers can't do it, we'll send in a couple of policemen.

PUBLIC SERVICE

Schlesinger, Arthur, Jr. The higher loyalty, it has always seemed to me, is to truth, public enlightenment, and history.

PUBLIC WELFARE

Califano, Joseph A., Jr. If you put a cookie jar on the shelf and leave a kid in the room, he's going to get at that jar. We've got a lot of people out there eating cookies (on the existing welfare system).

Moynihan, Daniel Patrick. Work is no longer considered to be a form of punishment as applied to women. A liberal constituency no longer finds work unattractive.

Schorr, Alvin (director of New York City's Community Service Society). Poor people are losing more money to which they are entitled by law because of callous and hostile welfare administration than they are getting from all the fraud that is charged. There is a welfare Watergate to be looked into, but the poor have no special prosecutor.

PUBLIC WELFARE—FEDERAL AID

Moynihan, Daniel Patrick. If welfare reform meant putting arsenic in children's milk, there would be local officials who would settle for that as long as it meant full federal funding.

PUBLISHERS AND PUBLISHING

Coover, Robert. You make a million or you don't even get printed.

Costa-Gavras, . Film is the only way now to reach out to people all around the world. The time of the book is over.

Hochmann, John L. After all, publishing is a business, literature is a happy accident.

Philipson, Morris. The commercial publisher says of his book, this is no good but it'll make a lot of money. The university publisher says, this is good and it won't make money.

Rosenthal, Arthur J. If I had a book on the bestseller list I'd suspect I was doing something wrong (commenting on his role as director of the Harvard University Press).

Talese, Gay. Lawyers have become the third force in publishing. I see them as the new enemy.

Townsend, Peter. It isn't enough any more to write books: publishers expect you to sell them.

PUERTO RICO—POLITICS AND GOVERNMENT

Lebron, Lolita. Until my last breath I will fight for the liberation and freedom of Puerto Rico.

PULITZER PRIZES

Ashbery, John. I have a feeling that when people say my poetry is difficult, they mean it's complicated. Well, it probably is, but I don't start out to be as complicated as possible. Life is complicated. I in fact try to simplify it as much as I can.

PUNCTUALITY

Waugh, Evelyn. Punctuality is the virtue of the bored.

PURCHASING

Allen, Marty. A study of economics usually reveals that the best time to buy anything is last year.

QADDAFI, MUAMMAR

Qadafi, Muammar. She does not interfere in politics (commenting on his wife's best quality).

QUALITY

Block, Herbert L. If it's good, they'll stop making it.

QUARRY, JERRY

Quarry, Jerry. This will surprise some people because I was at it so long, but the truth of the matter is that I hated boxing. It is a cruel, vicious sport—nothing more than two people trying to kill each other—and the more vicious it gets, the more people like it. I'm not an animal. Maybe that's why I didn't become champion (commenting on embarking on a career as a singer).

QUINLAN, KAREN ANNE
Muir, Robert. The single most important quality Karen Anne Quinlan has is life. This court will not authorize that life to be taken away from her.

QUOTATIONS
Chapman, Robert W. A quotation, like a pun, should come unsought, and then be welcomed only for some propriety or felicity justifying the intrusion (from "The Art of Quotation").

RABIN, YITZHAK
Scott, William. What's this Gaza stuff? I never have understood that (to Israeli Prime Minister Yitzhak Rabin).

RACE DISCRIMINATION
Carter, James Earl. I can't resign from the human race because there's discrimination, and I don't intend to resign from my own church because there's discrimination.

Harris, Patricia Roberts. If my life has had any meaning at all, it is that those who start out as outcasts can wind up as being part of the system. Maybe others can forget what it was like to be excluded from the dining rooms in this very building, Senator, but I shall not forget (testifying before the Senate Committee on her scheduled nomination for Secretary of Housing and Urban Development).

RACE RELATIONS
Gruber, Jack. Integration is not something you win at, it's something you work at.

RACIAL DIFFERENCES
Roosevelt, Theodore. All the great masterful races have been fighting races.

RADICALISM
Brown, Elaine. I may not be saying 'off the mother-fucking pigs' anymore, but I'm still talking about serious political change. Who cares who takes credit? The Panthers? The Democrats? As long as the work gets done.

Hayden, Thomas. The radicalism of the '60's became the fascism of the '70's (responding to heckling from left-wing radicals during a speech on his current campaign for U.S. Senator).

Lasch, Christopher. Radicalism in the United States has no great triumphs to record.

Lynd, Staughton. The best way to be a radical in America would be to be so much a part of the situation in which you were that you didn't need to be a radical. You could just live the situation as opposed to coming in and organizing it.

RADIO ADVERTISING
Thompson, Lord Roy Herbert. My favorite music is the sound of radio commercials at $10 a whack.

RADIO BROADCASTING
Newman, Edwin. I believe some silence is helpful to thought. And I believe to some extent radio and television discourage thought and reflection.

RADNER, GILDA
Radner, Gilda. I grew up in front of a television set, and now I'm growing old inside one.

RADZIWILL, LEE
Radziwill, Lee. I do hope to get married someday.

RAM DASS
Ram Dass, . If I'm saving the whale, why am I eating tuna fish?.

RAND, AYN
Greenspan, Alan. When I met Ayn Rand, I was a free enterpriser in the Adam Smith sense, impressed with the theoretical structure and efficiency of markets. What she did was to make me see that capitalism is not only efficient and practical, but also moral.

RAND, SALLY
Rand, Sally. What in heaven's name is so strange about a grandmother dancing nude? I bet lots of grandmothers do it.

RAPE
Brownmiller, Susan. It (rape) is nothing more or less than a conscious process of intimidation by which all men keep all women in a state of fear.

RATTIGAN, TERRENCE
Rattigan, Terrence. I could never see why craftsmanship should be equated with insincerity.

Rattigan, Terrence. What a lovely world we're in, if only we'd let ourselves see it.

RAUSCHENBERG, ROBERT
Rauschenberg, Robert. Painting relates to both art and life. I try to act in the gap between the two.

RAY, MAN
Ray, Man. I would like to go to only one funeral, mine.

Ray, Man. The pursuit of liberty and the pursuit of pleasure—that takes care of my whole art.

REACTIONARIES
Mao, Tse-Tung. All reactionaries are paper tigers.

READING
Lewis, C. S. A young man who wishes to remain a sound atheist cannot be too careful of his reading. God is, if I may say it, very unscrupulous.

Puzo, Mario. I find that the only thing that really stands up, better than gambling, better than booze, better than women, is reading.

Warhol, Andy. Movies are the new novels. No one is going to read anymore. Everyone is going to do movies, because movies are easier to do.

REAGAN, NANCY
Reagan, Ronald. As a matter of fact, Nancy never had any interest in politics or anything else when we got married (denying charges that his wife is the real political power in the family).

REAGAN, RONALD
Anderson, John B. I am not running against General Eisenhower. I am running against Jimmy Carter and Ronald Reagan, and I would respectfully suggest that neither is an Eisenhower.

Baker, Howard Henry. I don't understand all the fuss over the Gallup poll (with Reagan leading Ford). President Ford is going to veto it anyway.

Brock, Bill. Reagan has this remarkable ability to project decency, a sense of knowing where he is and where he is going.

Buckley, William Frank, Jr. Reagan is both too fatalistic and too modest to be a crusader. He doesn't have that darkness around the eyes of a George McGovern.

Bush, George. I'll prevail over Reagan because it is right that I prevail.

Connally, John. He (Ronald Reagan) communicates with his constituents, and they fill in the blanks. He leaves a thought with people that they can flesh out.

Derrow, Martin. Ronald Reagan is the prototype American politician of the '70s: mindless, witless, positionless and worthless.

Ford, Gerald Rudolph. (Governor Ronald Reagan) doesn't dye his hair; he's just prematurely orange.

Galvin, William. Instead of bemoaning what Government does to business, Reagan attacked what Government is doing to people. It's a strategy, and one which, as a Democrat, frightens me.

Goldwater, Barry Morris. I have always said if you put Reagan in one hand and Ford in the other hand and turn the lights out, you wouldn't know who the hell you had in either hand, because of their political philosophy.

Hart, Gary. The race (between Ronald Reagan and Gerald Ford) all boils down to a contest between the philosophies of Herbert Hoover and Calvin Coolidge.

Howar, Barbara. I just can't bring myself to believe this country will ever elect a president with orange hair (commenting on Ronald Reagan's election prospects).

Keene, David (Reagan aide). Fighting the Ford (presidential campaign) operation is kind of like fighting the Spanish Armada. They're bigger, but they don't maneuver very well.

Kennedy, Edward Moore. I think Mr. Carter has created Ronald Reagan.

Laxalt, Paul D. We are finding that conservatives throughout this country are going to marshal together and present, I think, a formidable political challenge, and comes the general election, personally I think that Ronald Reagan has the potential of putting together the same basic elements against Jimmy Carter that Richard Nixon did in 1972.

McCloskey, Paul N. I don't believe there are any reasoning powers behind the programmed articulation of Ronald Reagan and I would like to test this thesis in open debate.

MacLaine, Shirley. He (Ronald Reagan) is a true velvet fascist, really smooth.

Morton, Rogers Clark Ballard. Governor Reagan's announcement (of choosing Senator Schweicker as his running mate) appears to be an effort to exchange the second highest office in the land for a handful of delegates.

Phillips, Howard. We hope that Ronald Reagan will not be the third President to work for Henry Kissinger.

Reagan, Maureen. I am the most vociferous of all his detractors in our family regarding his candidacy (commenting on her father's candidacy for President).

Reagan, Nancy. My life began with Ronnie.

Reagan, Ronald. I always grew up believing that if you build a better mousetrap, the world will beat a path to your door. Now if you build a better mousetrap the government comes along with a better mouse.

Reagan, Ronald. I don't believe in the old tradition of picking someone at the opposite end of the political spectrum because he can get some votes you can't get yourself (on choosing a running mate, July 9, 1976).

Reagan, Ronald. I don't have an ideology. I think ideology is a scare word. Ideology is Marxism and Leninism, Hitlerism or something of the kind.

Reagan, Ronald. I don't think my positions have changed at all.

Reagan, Ronald. I sometimes think Adam and Eve were Russians. They didn't have a roof over their head, nothing to wear, but they had one apple between them and they thought that was Paradise.

Reagan, Ronald. I think an image has been created that I don't care about the underprivileged. Anyone who knows me knows that's not true; I'm a pushover for a hard-luck story.

Reagan, Ronald. (In movies) I was usually the steady, sincere suitor—the one the girl finally turned to.

Reagan, Ronald. Let's face it, the first enemy in Angola is obviously Ronald Reagan.

Reagan, Ronald. Once you've seen one redwood, you've seen them all.

Reagan, Ronald. Thou shalt not criticize other Republicans.

Reagan, Ronald. You can vote with your feet in this country. If a state is mismanaged you can move (commenting on the possibility that some states might substitute inadequate programs for the Federal ones he would like to eliminate).

Stevens, Robert S. Ronald Reagan badly ruined the Republican party in California.

Tower, John. You can argue shades of difference all day, yet there is little philosophical difference between Gerald Ford and Ronald Reagan. The important thing is that Mr. Ford is an 'electable' conservative while Mr. Reagan would lose to the Democratic candidate this fall.

Udall, Morris King. Obviously the Ford administration is very bad for this country. A Reagan administration would be much worse. I don't anticipate having any trouble supporting a Democratic candidate, whoever it is.

Udall, Morris King. (Ronald Reagan and George Wallace) are the twin horsemen of the radical right.

Unruh, Jesse. As a Governor, Reagan was better than most Democrats would concede, though not nearly as good as most Republicans like to think.

Vidal, Gore. Reagan may not be all man, but he sure is all boy. Just what the country needs.

REAL ESTATE INVESTMENT
Koslow, Ron. What marijuana was to the Sixties, real estate is to the Seventies.

REALITY
Baker, Howard Henry. There are animals crashing around in the forest. I can hear them but I can't see them (about the Watergate investigation).

Baker, Russell. Inanimate objects are classified scientifically into three major categories—those that don't work, those that break down, and those that get lost.

Cohodas, Howard L. If it looks too good to be true, it is too good to be true.

De Vries, Peter. Reality is impossible to take neat, we must dilute it with alcohol.

Giono, Jean. Reality pushed to its extreme ends in unreality.

Orlans, Harold. Logic is a game men play as cats play with balls of string, whereas reality is a game the gods play with us.

Waits, Tom. Reality is for those who can't face drugs.

Wyeth, Andrew. True reality goes beyond reality itself.

REASON

Fink, Stanley. There are times when reasonable people come to no solution.

REASONER, HARRY

Reasoner, Harry. Confirming my long-time nonsexist grace and courtesy, I suggest we just do it alphabetically by last names (commenting on the billing of the co-anchor news team of Harry Reasoner and Barbara Walters).

REBOZO, CHARLES GREGORY

Rebozo, Charles Gregory. Never again. (In response to the question if he plans to dabble in politics).

REDDY, HELEN

Wald, Jeffrey. I don't *think* I made her a star. I *know* I did (about Helen Reddy).

REDFORD, ROBERT

Fonda, Jane. (Robert Redford) is, and remains, a bourgeois in the worst sense of the word.

Redford, Robert. Health food may be good for the conscience, but Oreos taste a hell of a lot better.

Redford, Robert. I've always had a very low regard for cynicism; I think it is the beginning of dying.

Saint John, Adela Rogers. Poor little man, they made him out of lemon Jello and there he is. He's honest and he's hard-working. But he's not great (commenting on Robert Redford).

Shepherd, Cybill. If you kept seeing Robert Redford stark naked on the screen, would he be a superstar today? No way. Or Gene Hackman showing everything? Their million dollar days would be over. I want to be in a movie where all the men take their clothes off and I don't.

REDNECKS

Nelson, Willie. To me, a hippie is a redneck with hair, and a redneck is a hippie with his hair cut off. It's not so much a difference in hair as attitude as to whether a guy is hip or not hip, whether he'd rather talk to you or fight you.

Nelson, Willie. To me, a redneck is someone who likes to fight. Whiskey makes you want to fight and marijuana makes you want to listen to music. And marijuana and beer together is probably the greatest truth serum ever.

REED, LOU

Reed, Lou. I'm like an Elvis Presley with brains, or Bob Dylan with looks.

REEVE, CHRISTOPHER

Reeve, Christopher. Women keep asking me if I really am Superman. My reply to them is, 'only if you're Lois Lane'.

REFORM

Carter, James Earl. I think the President is the only person who can change the direction or attitude of our nation.

REFUGEES, VIETNAMESE

Hung, Tran Van (Vietnamese refugee). We are shrubs, planted in a new place, needing care and water to grow again.

Ky, Nguyen Cao. We Vietnamese are the newest refugees in your history. We know your country is a land of immigrants. Your sons and daughters fought to keep Vietnam free, and we Vietnamese wish to earn your respect and friendship. We wish not to be hawks or doves, but eagles.

Phan Hien (Deputy Prime Minister of Vietnam), . We are ready to do our best to facilitate departures.

REGULATION

Emery, Fred J. Regulation is the substitution of error for chance.

RELATIVITY THEORY

Einstein, Albert. Sit with a pretty girl for an hour, and it seems like a minute; sit on a hot stove for a minute, and it seems like an hour—that's relativity.

RELIGION

Lance, Thomas Bertram. Folks are serious about three things—their religion, their family, and most of all, their money.

McCarthy, Mary. It really takes a hero to live any kind of spiritual life without religious belief.

Neuhaus, Richard John. Religion had become a silly imitation of what was happening in the marketplace. Christianity lost its nerve to challenge the culture.

Pannenberg, Wolfhart. The greatest deception (of our era is the idea that) political change can satisfy a religious need.

Schuller, Robert. The church is in the business of retailing religion.

Shaffer, Floyd. I believe it would be healthier if the church could laugh because I believe that God laughs.

White, Theodore. Politics in America is the binding secular religion.

REPORTERS AND REPORTING

Wicker, Tom. A reporter should write and his newspaper should print what they know.

REPUBLICAN PARTY

Anderson, John B. We (Republicans) are a staid and proper bunch.

Brock, Bill. This (Republican) party is a new party—we are on our way up.

Brown, Rita Mae. I want the American public to discover the difference between the Republican Party and the Democratic Party is the difference between syphillis and gonorrhea.

Butz, Earl Lauer. I'll tell you why you can't attract coloreds. Because coloreds only want three things. You know what they want? I tell you what coloreds want. It's three things: first, a tight pussy; second, loose shoes; and third, a warm place to shit. That's all (responding to a question from Pat Boone and explaining why the Republican Party didn't attract more blacks—reported by John Dean).

Carter, James Earl. (Republicans are) men of narrow vision who are afraid of the future and whose leaders are inclined to shoot from the hip.

Dolan, Terry. The Republican Party is a fraud. It's a social club where rich people go to pick their noses.

Dole, Robert J. A Republican has to have a sense of humor because there are so few of us.

Dole, Robert J. If you liked Richard Nixon, you'll love Bob Dole.

Dole, Robert J. It may turn out that 1974 was the good year for a Republican to be on the ballot.

Dole, Robert J. With all respect, Connally, Goldwater and Rockefeller are great men but they don't indicate any forward thrust in our party. We've got to start building from the bottom up instead of the top down.

Fitzhugh, Gilbert W. The Republicans fight like cats and go home and sulk. The Democrats fight like cats, and suddenly there are more cats.

Goldwater, Barry Morris. I don't care if I'm called a Democrat or a Republican as long as I'm in bed with people of the same thinking.

Hart, Gary. The race (between Ronald Reagan and Gerald Ford) all boils down to a contest between the philosophies of Herbert Hoover and Calvin Coolidge.

Hayakawa, Samuel Ichiye. Republicans are people who, if you were drowning 50 feet from shore, would throw you a 25-foot rope and tell you to swim the other 25 feet because it would be good for your character. Democrats would throw you a 100-foot rope and then walk away looking for other good deeds to do.

McCarthy, Eugene Joseph. The Republican Party is a lower form of plant life, like moss on a rock. It has very low vitality—green in the summer, slightly gray in the winter—but it never dies. If the Republicans had any decency, they'd just go away.

Mondale, Joan. The issue is Watergate or waterbed. The Democrats do it to their secretaries but the Republicans do it to the country.

Mondale, Walter Frederick. For a workingman or woman to vote Republican this year is the same as a chicken voting for Colonel Sanders.

Pastore, John O. This has become a Government by veto. We've got the minority dragging the majority around by the nose.

Percy, Charles. We have to get the (Republican) Party out of the country clubs, out of a Caucasian atmosphere, away from the Anglo-Saxon approach. As long as the Republican Party takes a Neanderthal point of view, I don't see why it deserves to win.

Phillips, Kevin. I don't see how the (Republican) party can survive a Carter victory because it would wrap up the Southern opportunity for growth. When you take that away, you take away the future of the whole party.

Reagan, Ronald. Thou shalt not criticize other Republicans.

Reeves, Richard. The GOP has been reduced to aging Sinclair Lewis characters, white Protestants, small tycoons, and shopkeepers from small places.

Rhodes, John J. If the Republicans split this year I think Republicans will deserve the fate they will get, which is resounding defeat.

Rockefeller, Nelson Aldrich. After much thought, I have decided further that I do not wish my name to enter into your consideration for the upcoming Republican Vice-Presidential nominee (letter to President Ford).

Rockefeller, Nelson Aldrich. I think the Republican Party is only going to be an effective party if it reflects the best interests of the American people, and traditionally that is in the center. That is where our country has always been. That is where the Republican Party has won.

Scammon, Richard. There's nothing wrong with the Republican Party that double-digit inflation won't cure.

Scott, Ulric. An Independent-Republican is an elephant that is trying to forget.

Simon, William E. The Republican Party today is inert, flattened into a jellied inconsistency by a half century of compromises of principle. It may even deserve to die.

Stevenson, Adlai, II. I have been tempted to make a proposal to our Republican friends: that if they stop telling lies about us, we would stop telling the truth about them.

Tower, John. You can argue shades of difference all day, yet there is little philosophical difference between Gerald Ford and Ronald Reagan. The important thing is that Mr. Ford is an 'electable' conservative while Mr. Reagan would lose to the Democratic candidate this fall.

Yarborough, Ralph. This may be the only case on record of a rat swimming toward a sinking ship (commenting on John Connally's announced defection from the Democrats to the Republicans).

REPUBLICAN PARTY—CALIFORNIA
Stevens, Robert S. Ronald Reagan badly ruined the Republican party in California.

REPUBLICAN PARTY. NATIONAL CONVENTION, DETROIT, 1980
Kissinger, Henry Alfred. I am not here (at the 1980 Republican Convention) as a job seeker.

REPUBLICAN PARTY. NATIONAL CONVENTION, KANSAS CITY, 1976
Butz, Earl Lauer. Oh hell, John, everybody was out by then. You know...it's like the dog who screwed a skunk for a while, until it finally shouted, I've had enough (commenting to Pat Boone and John Dean regarding the lukewarm reception of Robert J. Dole by the delegates of the Republican National Convention).

REPUBLICAN PARTY—RELATIONS—WOMEN
Crisp, Mary D. We are about to bury the rights of over 100 million American women under a heap of platitudes.

RESPECTABILITY
Buchan, Alastair. Respectability depends on whose side you're on. To the Turks, Lawrence of Arabia was a terrorist.

RESTAURANTS
Algren, Nelson. Never eat at a place called Mom's. Never play cards with a man named Doc. And never lie down with a woman who's got more troubles than you.

RESTAURANTS—FRANCHISE SYSTEM
Anonymous, . We do it all for you (McDonald's jingle).

RESTAURANTS—UNITED STATES
Bocuse, Paul. Your best American restaurants are the Steak Houses,...the ones with the meat in the window. I love a steak with a baked Idaho potato. Delicious.

RETIREMENT
Agnelli, Giovanni. At twenty, it would be fun to retire. It's silly at sixty. At sixty, what can you do anymore?.

Barringer, John W. I was president of the Pittsburgh & Lake Erie but they fired.

Burns, George. Now, they say, you should retire at 70. When I was 70 I still had pimples.

Mead, Margaret. One reason women live longer than men is that they can continue to do something they are used to doing, whereas men are abruptly cut off, whether they are admirals or shopkeepers.

Niven, David. Actors don't retire, they just get offered fewer parts.

Pepper, Claude. Mandatory retirement arbitrarily severs productive persons from their livelihood, squanders their talent, scars their health, strains an already overburdened Social Security system and drives many elderly persons into poverty and despair.

Ustinov, Peter. The time to write memoirs is when total recall has not yet invaded the cavities of the mind left empty by the inaction of retirement.

REVENGE

Fortas, Abe. The law of revenge has its roots in the deep recesses of the human spirit, but that is not a permissible reason for retaining capital punishment.

REVOLUTIONISTS

Lenin, Vladimir Il'ich. The propagandist transmits many ideas to one or more persons; the agitator transmits only one or a few ideas, but transmits them to a whole lot of people.

Sinclair, John. You can't make a revolution if you have to make a living.

REVOLUTIONISTS, CAMBODIAN

Norodom Sihanouk, King Of Cambodia (Abdicated 1955), . When they no longer need me, they will spit me out like a cherry pit (about the Khmer Rouge).

REVOLUTIONS

Bella, Ben. It is an illusion to think you can have a revolution without prisons.

Cleaver, Kathleen. I'm older and wiser. I've lost my romanticism about revolution in America. I don't say it's inconceivable, but I know that none of us who believed ourselves to be revolutionaries in the '60s can conceive of the form a revolution would take in America.

Goebbels, Joseph. Whoever can conquer the streets will one day conquer the state, for every form of power politics and any dictatorially run state has its roots in the streets.

Kennedy, John Fitzgerald (attributed by David Reckford). Those who make peaceful revolution impossible make violent revolution inevitable.

Levy, Bernard-Henri. The only successful revolution of this century is totalitarianism.

Mao, Tse-Tung. Revolution is a drama of passion. We did not win the People over by appealing to reason but by developing hope, trust, fraternity.

Marcos, Ferdinand E. It is easier to run a revolution than a government.

Marley, Bob. It takes a revolution to make a solution.

Sinclair, John. You can't make a revolution if you have to make a living.

REVOLUTIONS—AFGHANISTAN

Rahim, Abdur. The war (in Afghanistan) is like a good love affair. All the action happens at night.

REVOLUTIONS—NICARAGUA

Somoza Debayle, Anastasio. I am a tied donkey fighting with a tiger.

REWARDS, PRIZES, ETC.

Snow, C. P. Money is not so important as a pat on the head.

REXROTH, KENNETH

Rexroth, Kenneth. The one country I feel at home in is Japan. I don't feel at home here. I don't like a country where traffic cops are armed to the teeth (commenting on life in the U.S.).

REYNOLDS, BURT

Reynolds, Burt. I want to lead a quiet, pseudointellectual life and go out and direct a picture two times a year. You can only hold your stomach in for so many years.

Reynolds, Burt. I'm trying very subtly and subliminally to ease myself away from Billy Clyde Puckett and toward Cary Grant. I may be the most unsophisticated Cary Grant in 20 years, but I'm going to get there.

RHODESIA SEE ALSO ZIMBABWE

RHODES, JAMES

Rhodes, James. They are the worst type of people we harbor in America, worse than brown shirts and the Communist element (concerning the Kent State demonstrators).

RHODESIA—DESCRIPTION

Anonymous (African ambassador), . The only way to true majority rule (in Zimbabwe) is by force of arms.

RHODESIA—POLITICS AND GOVERNMENT

Anonymous (an American mercenary in Rhodesia), . If I shot a black in Australia or New Zealand or anywhere else in the world, they'd put me in jail for 20 years. Here I can do it legally.

Kaunda, Kenneth. A new Zimbabwe (Rhodesia) can only be born out of the barrel of a gun.

Muzorewa, Bishop Abel. I do not want Zimbabwe ever to become another banana republic.

Muzorewa, Bishop Abel. I question whether God himself would wish me to hide behind the principles of non-violence while innocent persons were being slaughtered.

Muzorewa, Bishop Abel. We are not here in a spirit of give and take—we have come here to take, to take our country (comment made at the Geneva Conference on Rhodesia).

Nkomo, Joshua. I do not think the British know what genuine majority rule is.

Owen, David. The government (of Rhodesia) under the Constitution may well be multiracial, but the power structure will be white.

Smith, Ian Douglas. Everything is fine in Rhodesia.

Smith, Ian Douglas. I am not prepared to think in terms of color (speaking about black v. white rule in Rhodesia).

Smith, Ian Douglas. I do not believe in black majority rule in Rhodesia—not in a thousand years.

Smith, Ian Douglas. I don't accept anybody as a mediator. When you are dealing with your future, in other words your life, I don't think you can place this in the hands of anybody (rejecting Secretary of State Henry Kissinger's suggestion that Harold Wilson could act as a mediator in the Rhodesian crisis).

Smith, Ian Douglas. I have got to admit that things haven't gone quite the way I wanted.

Smith, Ian Douglas. No African rule in my lifetime. The white man is the master of Rhodesia, has built it, and intends to keep it (comment made in 1964).

Smith, Ian Douglas. We never have had a policy in Rhodesia to hand over our country to any black majority and, as far as I am concerned, we never will (commenting in March, 1976).

RHODESIA—RACE QUESTION

Nkomo, Joshua. There's no such thing to me as whites.

Nyerere, Julius Kamberage. South Africa is no
different from Rhodesia. The struggle by blacks
in both countries is exactly the same—for
majority rule. So what happens in Rhodesia will
happen in South Africa.

Smith, Ian Douglas. I do not believe in black
majority rule in Rhodesia—not in a thousand
years.

Smith, Ian Douglas. We may lose in the end, but I
think it's better to lose while you're standing up
and fighting than crawling out on your knees
(commenting on his fight to continue white rule in
Rhodesia).

RHYS, JEAN

Rhys, Jean. If you want to write the truth, you
must write about yourself.

RICH

Baltzell, Edward Digby, Jr. I believe in inherited
wealth. Society needs to have some people who
are above it all.

Churchill, Sir Winston. You don't make the poor
richer by making the rich poorer.

Gill, Brendan. The rich have no need to pronounce
words correctly. They can leave all that to their
lawyers and accountants.

Harris, Fred. The basic issue in 1976 is privilege.
It's time to take the rich off welfare.

Hubbard, Kin. It must be great to be rich and let
the other fellow keep up appearances.

MacArthur, John D. Anybody who knows what he's
worth, isn't worth very much (upon being asked
how much he was worth).

MacArthur, John D. It's no fun being rich anymore.
People are too damned jealous and suspicious
of you. They figure anybody that makes as much
money as I allegedly have must have cheated
somebody.

Poirot, Paul L. Multiplying wealth is by far the
fastest way to help the poor. Dividing the wealth
and subsidizing poverty is the fastest way to
starve everyone.

Shor, Toots. I don't want to be a millionaire, I just
want to live like one.

RICH—SEXUAL BEHAVIOR

Brando, Marlon. If you're rich and famous you
don't have any trouble getting laid.

RICH—SOCIAL LIFE AND CUSTOMS

Lear, Amanda. I've come to realize that as soon
as you get rich and famous, you stop picking up
the bills. And as long as you're poor and
struggling, you have to pay for everything.

RICHARD, KEITH

Jagger, Mick. Keith and I are two of the nicest
people we know.

RICHARDS, PAUL

Richards, Paul. I don't communicate with players. I
tell them what to do. I don't understand the
meaning of communication.

RICHARDSON, ELLIOT LEE

Richardson, Elliot Lee. I may be at this very
moment entering the Guiness Book of Records
as the most sworn-in of Americans. If I hadn't
been moving so fast from place to place, I might
well have become the most sworn-at of
Americans.

Richardson, Elliot Lee. You don't have to be
Jewish to like being on the Supreme Court.

RICKOVER, HYMAN GEORGE

Rickover, Hyman G. I never start to like a man
until I tell him off three or four times a day.

Zumwalt, Elmo R., Jr. A final malady that
afflicted—and continues to afflict—the whole
Navy, though the surface Navy was and is the
greatest sufferer, can be described in one word:
Rickover.

RIGGS, BOBBY

Riggs, Bobby. Gals are super, but I haven't
changed my opinion of them: I still like them best
in the bedroom and the kitchen.

RIGHT AND WRONG

Royster, Vermont. When things go wrong
somewhere, they are apt to go wrong
everywhere.

RIMBAUD, ARTHUR

Rimbaud, Arthur. My greatest fear is that people
will see me as I see them.

RIOTS

Borrows, Lee (resident of Harlem). That 'Roots'
ain't nothin. If they ever told it like it was, the
riots would start again.

Johnson, Lyndon Baines. Killing, rioting, and
looting are contrary to the best traditions of this
country.

RITTER, JOHN

Ritter, John. Luckily, as an actor I can still be an
adolescent.

RIZZO, FRANK LAZZARO

Rizzo, Frank Lazzaro. Just wait, after November
you'll have a front row seat because I'm gonna
make Attila the Hun look like a faggot (to several
friends).

Rizzo, Frank Lazzaro. Male chauvinist? I'm sure
that title don't fit me because I was a leader with
men.

Rizzo, Frank Lazzaro. This city could never pay
Frank Rizzo back for what I've done—slept on
floors, no holidays, no vacation. I knew I was the
difference between destruction and disorder.

Rizzo, Frank Lazzaro. When I see the American
flag, my blood still runs cold.

ROADS

Alito, Noelie. The shortest distance between two
points is under construction.

ROBBERY

Sutton, Willie. I always figured that being a good
robber was like being a good lawyer.

ROBBINS, HAROLD

Robbins, Harold. I'm the best novelist in the world.

ROBESON, PAUL

Robeson, Paul (attributed by John E. Mitchell). My
problem is not to counteract the white man's
prejudice against the Negro. That does not
matter. I have set myself to educate my brother
to believe in himself.

ROBINSON, FRANK

Robinson, Frank. It's nice to come into town and
be referred to as the manager of the Cleveland
Indians instead of as the first black manager.

ROBINSON, JACKIE

Kahn, Roger. His (Jackie Robinson) race was
humanity, and he did a great deal for us.

ROCKEFELLER, DAVID

Rockefeller, David. Although I work downtown, my family does have something of a stake in a small parcel of land which abuts Fifth Avenue (commenting on Rockefeller Center and his ties to the Fifth Avenue area in New York City).

ROCKEFELLER FAMILY

Rockefeller, David. Although I work downtown, my family does have something of a stake in a small parcel of land which abuts Fifth Avenue (commenting on Rockefeller Center and his ties to the Fifth Avenue area in New York City).

ROCKEFELLER, JOHN DAVISON, III

Rockefeller, John Davison, III. I don't have a whole lot of faith in what the oil companies say.

Rockefeller, John Davison, III. The name Rockefeller does not connote a revolutionary, and my life situation has fostered a careful, cautious attitude that verges on conservatism. I am not given to errant causes.

Rockefeller, John Davison III (attributed by an aide). I am too rich to steal.

ROCKEFELLER, NELSON ALDRICH

Capote, Truman. He's like a good brand of cereal—nothing is wrong, but nothing is particularly appetizing (commenting on Nelson Rockefeller).

Harris, Fred. These huge corporations say they favor free enterprise. Well, I want to give them a big dose of it. It's time the J. Paul Gettys, the Nelson Rockefellers and these great big corporations started haulin' their part of the freight. Why, did you know there was one year Rockefeller didn't pay any income taxes. We oughta sue that man for nonsupport.

Kissinger, Henry Alfred. Nelson Rockefeller was the greatest American I have ever known.

Nixon, Richard Milhous. Only three men in America understand the use of power. I do. John Connally does. And I guess Nelson does.

Rockefeller, Nelson Aldrich. After much thought, I have decided further that I do not wish my name to enter into your consideration for the upcoming Republican Vice-Presidential nominee (letter to President Ford).

Rockefeller, Nelson Aldrich. Being a Rockefeller is like living in a goldfish bowl. The goldfish get used to it and so do we.

Rockefeller, Nelson Aldrich. Free enterprise is the greatest and most productive system man has ever created. In a modest way, I have been a beneficiary.

Rockefeller, Nelson Aldrich. I don't think I'm cut out to be a number 2 type of guy.

Rockefeller, Nelson Aldrich. I would like to apologize to the Senate of the United States, to its members, and particularly to Senator Jackson for my remarks in an off-the-record meeting. There is no question it was a mistake (apologizing for suggesting that two members of Senator Henry M. Jackson's staff had Communist ties).

Rockefeller, Nelson Aldrich. The best part about being Vice President is presiding over the Senate. Where else could I have Barry Goldwater addressing me as 'Mr. President?'.

ROCKNE, KNUTE

Rockne, Knute. You show me a good and gracious loser, and I'll show you a failure!.

RODGERS, RICHARD

Martin, Mary. He's (Richard Rodgers) the one person I will never, never wash out of my hair.

Rodgers, Richard. When the lyrics are right, it's easier for me to write a tune than to bend over and tie my shoelaces.

RODRIGUEZ, ARMANDO

Piniella, Lou (New York Yankee outfielder). I cussed him out in Spanish, and he threw me out in English (commenting on an argument he once had with umpire Armando Rodriguez).

RODRIGUEZ, CHI CHI

Rodriguez, Chi Chi. After all these years it's still embarrassing for me to play on the American golf tour. Like the time I asked my caddie for a sand wedge and he comes back 10 minutes later with a ham on rye (commenting on his Puerto Rican Spanish accent).

ROLLING STONES (MUSICAL GROUP)

Kokonien, Vladimir. The group do nothing to help people achieve self-perfection. They lack glamour, novelty and sparkle. They are unattractive and they have no originality (upon rejecting the Rolling Stones' request to perform in the USSR).

ROLLINS, SONNY

Occhiogrosso, Peter. Sonny Rollins is the Vladimir Nabokov of the tenor saxophone.

ROMANCE

Dubus, Andre. Romance dies hard, because its very nature is to want to live.

Parker, Charlie. Romance without finance ain't got no chance.

Russell, Bertrand. I believe myself that romantic love is the source of the most intense delights that life has to offer.

Viorst, Judith. Brevity may be the soul of wit, but not when someone's saying 'I love you'.

Wilde, Oscar. Nothing spoils romance so much as a sense of humor in a woman.

ROME

Lebowitz, Fran. Rome is a very loony city in every respect. One needs but spend an hour or two there to realize that Fellini makes documentaries.

RONSTADT, LINDA

Ronstadt, Linda. I'm so disorganized, what I really need is a good wife.

ROONEY, MICKEY

Rooney, Mickey. A lot of people have asked me how short I am. Since my last divorce, I think I'm about $100,000 short.

Rooney, Mickey. I'm the only man who has a marriage license made out To Whom It May Concern.

ROOSEVELT, ELEANOR

Black, Shirley Temple. I admired Mrs. Roosevelt enormously for two things in particular: her capacity for hard work and her overwhelming interest in the field of human rights.

Carey, Hugh. My impression was that he (Jimmy Carter) has the Eleanor Roosevelt teeth and she (Rosalynn Carter) has the Eleanor Roosevelt brain.

ROOSEVELT, FRANKLIN DELANO

Kelly, Edward J. (Mayor of Chicago, 1933-1947). Franklin Roosevelt was the best precinct captain I ever had.

Roosevelt, Franklin Delano. Our true destiny is not to be ministered unto but to minister to ourselves and to our fellow men (inaugural address—1933).

Rossiter, Clinton. The essence of (Franklin) Roosevelt's Presidency was his airy eagerness to meet the age head on.

ROOTS (TELEVISION PROGRAM)

Borrows, Lee (resident of Harlem). That 'Roots' ain't nothin. If they ever told it like it was, the riots would start again.

ROREM, NED

Rorem, Ned. I have suffered far less from being a homosexual than I have from being a composer.

ROSENBLOOM, CARROLL

Rosenbloom, Carroll. I never did really care for working. I don't know why anyone would work if they didn't have to.

ROSSINI, GIOACCHINO

Rossini, Gioacchino. Give me a laundry list, and I will set it to music.

ROSTROPOVICH, MSTISLAV

Ozawa, Seiji. Slave (Mstislav Rostropovich) doesn't interpret, he feels. His music is really his character. He is conducting his life.

Rostropovich, Mstislav. I don't even know why my hands do certain things sometimes. They just grab for the notes.

Rostropovich, Mstislav. The cello is like an imperfect woman whom you love for her imperfections. Through the cello I can speak with my own personal voice, without intermediaries between me and the audience.

Rostropovich, Mstislav. When I play for an audience, I feel that I am making my confession to those people.

ROTHSCHILD, MARIE-HELEN DE

Rothschild, Marie-Helene De. I'm not a bit ashamed of being rich. I think it's very healthy to have big parties now and again, like they did in history.

ROWEN, PHYLLIS

Rowen, Phyllis. When you grow as a designer, you realize that nothing is forever.

ROWSE, A. L.

Rowse, A. L. I've always thought of myself as a parallel to D.H. Lawrence.

ROYALTY—ENGLAND

Russell, John Robert (Duke of Bedford). You Americans have this lovely notion about English royalty. You think the prince marries the princess and they go off to live happily ever after in a beautiful castle. In reality the prince is trying to get that lovely 300-year-old roof to stop leaking.

RUBIN, JERRY

Rubin, Jerry. I'm famous. That's my job.

RUBINSTEIN, ARTUR

Rubinstein, Artur. I need to be surrounded by (beautiful women). They don't have to be anything special, I can enjoy looking at the legs of a stupid woman.

Rubinstein, Artur. I'm not a drug fiend, I'm not a drunkard, but I am the laziest man I ever met.

Rubinstein, Artur. To get as old as I am (91) one must drink a glass of whiskey every morning, smoke a long cigar and chase beautiful girls.

Rubinstein, Artur. When I was young I used to have successes with women because I was young. Now I have successes with women because I am old. Middle age was the hard part.

RUCKLESHAUS, JILL

Ruckelshaus, Jill. It occurred to me when I was 13 and wearing white gloves and Mary Janes and going to dancing school, that no one should have to dance backwards all their lives.

RULES

Conner, Caryl. All avocados in all stores will always be rock-hard the day you want to make guacamole.

Faber, Harold. If there isn't a law, there will be.

Jackson, Jack. No rule is ever so good, or so well written, or covers so many contingencies, that it can't be replaced by another, much better, more appropriate rule (with the exception of this rule).

Pitman, Keith A. All generalizations are untrue.

RUMANIA—FOREIGN POLICY

Ceausescu, Nicolae. We are an independent Rumania and we will always remain an independent Rumania.

RUNNING

Sheehan, George A. To know running is to know life.

Weisenfeld, Murray (podiatrist). A runner once came to me and told me that he was in a 55-mile race, and at 35 miles he began to get foot cramps. He asked me what he should do. I told him to see a psychiatrist.

RUSSELL, ROSALIND

Russell, Rosalind. Flops are a part of life's menu, and I'm never a girl to miss out on any of the courses.

RUSSIA

Buchwald, Art. The day you leave Russia is the happiest day of your life.

Bukovsky, Vladimir. China today is Russia 20 or 30 years ago. She is following in our footsteps, which are those of totalitarianism.

Churchill, Sir Winston. Russia is a riddle wrapped in an enigma.

Reagan, Ronald. I sometimes think Adam and Eve were Russians. They didn't have a roof over their head, nothing to wear, but they had one apple between them and they thought that was Paradise.

Wyeth, Jamie. They don't allow anything but realism there. At the end, I told them I could understand their censoring talking and writing but why Art? Their answer was 'Never underestimate the power of painting' (on his recent trip to the Soviet Union).

RUSSIA—DESCRIPTION

Greene, Graham. There is far more religious faith in Russia than in England.

Mandelstam, Osip. Poetry is respected only in this country (Russia)—people are killed for it. There's no place where more people are killed for it.

Rostropovich, Mstislav. Music and art are a whole spiritual world in Russia. In Russia when people go to a concert, they don't go to it as an attraction, as an entertainment, but to feel life.

Solzhenitsyn, Aleksandr Isaevich. For us in Russia Communism is a dead dog, while for many people in the West it is still a living lion.

Teng, Hsiao-Ping. You can sign all the treaties you want, but you cannot trust the Russians.

RUSSIANS IN ISRAEL

Amalrik, Andrei. This is not a decision taken freely. I did not want to emigrate to Israel or anywhere else—ever. When a man is born in a country, and is a writer, he does not want to leave—not ever (commenting on his forced emigration to Israel).

RUTHERFORD, MARGARET

Mason, James. Talking about my leading ladies is difficult for me if I'm going to be honest. Any opinion I give is bound to offend somebody. So when I want to tread cautiously, I tell people that the best actress I ever worked with was Margaret Rutherford.

RYAN, NOLAN

Busby, Steve. I throw the ball harder than Nolan Ryan. It just doesn't get there as fast.

RYUN, JIM

Ryun, Jim. Christ spoke to me. He said I had fought a good fight, run a good race and it was finished (commenting on how he decided to retire).

SADAT, ANWAR

Assad, Hafez. Sadat is a traitor to his own people and the Arab nation.

Beame, Abraham David. I believe it would be an act of hypocrisy on my part to participate in any welcoming ceremony with any chief of state who has been a party to the United Nations resolution which seeks to revive a new form of racism as a substitute for the principles of understanding and peaceful negotiations upon which this world body was formed.

Eastland, James O. I didn't know that guy was a nigger (about Anwar Sadat).

Kissinger, Henry Alfred. Sadat is the greatest (statesman) since Bismarck.

Nasser, Gamal Abdel. Sadat's greatest ambition is to own a big automobile and have the government pay for the gasoline (commenting on Sadat as Vice President of Egypt).

Sadat, Anwar. No one ever knows what I am thinking, not even my own family. I go alone.

Sadat, Anwar. The Russians had a Central Committee meeting last summer and decided they could support me but never trust me. I said that was okay—I couldn't trust them either.

Sadat, Anwar. They wanted to exert pressure and to bring me to my knees, but I don't go down on my knees except before God Almighty (speaking about the Soviet Union).

Saiqua (Palestinian organization), . Sadat has committed the ugliest treason in the history of the Arab nation, so the blood of the traitor must be shed. He will be followed to the farthest corners of the world until his death sentence is carried out (upon Anwar Sadat's visit to Israel).

SADAT, ANWAR—VISIT TO JERUSALEM, 1977

McLuhan, Marshall. That was the human family sitting down together. It passed history unexpectedly (about Anwar Sadat's first visit to Israel).

SAFETY

Thurber, James. There is no safety in numbers, or in anything else.

SAFIRE, WILLIAM

Reeves, Richard. I'm not enamored of his (William Safire) political viewpoint, which is sometimes to the right of Genghis Khan. But, hell, I read him because I have to. He's not predictable.

Safire, William. My business (is) writing informed polemics—with a satisfying zap.

SAHL, MORT

McCarthy, Eugene Joseph. The most important member of the Executive Branch is the press secretary. I will appoint Mort Sahl. He's the only newspaper reader I know in America. I'll have him sit on the White House steps in the morning and catch the New York Times when it's thrown over the fence—and the Washington Post he will throw the latter back immediately.

Sahl, Mort. The more you stay the same, the more they say you've changed.

SAILING

Kuhn, Annette. To be 75, sailing, cracking a bone, and wanting to go sailing again as soon as this trifle is healed—that's my idea of a good life.

SAINTS

Marty, Martin E. A saint has to be a misfit. A person who embodies what his culture considers typical or normal cannot be exemplary.

SAKHAROV, ANDREI DMITRIEVICH

Sakharov, Andrei Dmitrievich. I hope this prize is not only an acknowledgement of my personal merits, but of the merits of all those who fight for human rights (commenting on his Nobel Peace Prize).

Sakharov, Andrei Dmitrievich. I regard this as a challenge to world public opinion. I have always been trusted and I do not believe there are grounds to think that I have committed a state crime (upon the denial of permission to travel to Oslo, Norway to receive the Nobel Peace Prize).

Sakharov, Andrei Dmitrievich. To keep one's self-respect, one must act in accordance with the general human longing for peace, for true detente, for genuine disarmament (in his message accepting the Nobel Peace Prize).

SALINGER, J. D.

Salinger, J. D. Some of my best friends are children. In fact, all of my best friends are children.

SALVATION

Hellman, Lillian. I don't understand personal salvation. It seems to me a vain idea.

SAN ANTONIO, TEXAS

Greenberg, Mike. Half of San Antonio's population is of Mexican descent; the other half just eats that way.

SAN FRANCISCO

Graham, Bill. San Francisco is not a part of America.

SANS SOUCI (RESTAURANT), WASHINGTON, D.C.

Delisle, Paul (maitre d' of Sans Souci Restaurant). Once we had the Texan. He learned to eat fine French food. The Georgian—he can learn too.

SAROYAN, WILLIAM

Saroyan, William. I would rather write, even pompously, than celebrate meaninglessness.

Saroyan, William. 1977 was one hell of a year. I didn't die.

SASSOON, VIDAL

Sassoon, Vidal. I call myself a lucky barber.

SATIRE

Kaufman, George. Satire is what closes Saturday night.

Lehrer, Tom. When Henry Kissinger can get the Nobel Peace Prize, what is there left for satire?.

SAUDI ARABIA—POLITICS AND GOVERNMENT

Bani-Assadi, Hossein. Islam has no kings.

Feisal, King of Saudi Arabia, . If anyone feels wrongly treated, he has only himself to blame for not telling me. What higher democracy can there be.

SAVALAS, TELLY

Savalas, Telly. I am a loud, extraverted friendly person, but never rude.

SAVING AND SAVINGS

Ward, Artemus. Let us all be happy and live within our means, even if we have to borrow the money to do it with.

SAVORY, ALLEN

Savory, Allen (former Rhodesian MP). The prime minister (Ian Smith) has the rare ability to make people believe things they know for a fact are untrue.

SCANDAL

Wilde, Oscar. History is gossip but scandal is gossip made tedious by morality.

SCHEER, ROBERT

Scheer, Robert. The journalist's job is to get the story by breaking into their offices, by bribing, by seducing people, by lying, by anything else to break through that palace guard.

SCHIZOPHRENIA

Tomlin, Lily. Why is it when we talk to God, we're said to be praying, but when God talks to us, we're schizophrenic?.

SCHLAFLY, PHYLLIS

Costanza, Midge. I'd like to take the two of them (Anita Bryant and Phyllis Schlafly) and make bookends.

Schlafly, Phyllis. What's so wrong about that (baby-selling)? If I hadn't been blessed with babies of my own, I would have been happy to have paid thousands of dollars for a baby (commenting in support of the decriminalization of baby-selling).

SCHLESINGER, ARTHUR, JR.

Schlesinger, Arthur, Jr. I will support the Democratic ticket, but actually I think they're both a couple of stiffs (commenting on the 1976 Democratic and Republican candidates).

Schlesinger, Arthur, Jr. If it is necessary for a biographer of Robert Kennedy to regard him as evil, then I am not qualified to be his biographer.

SCHLESINGER, JAMES RODNEY

Fonda, Jane. Putting Energy Secretary James Schlesinger in charge of nuclear power is like putting Dracula in charge of a blood bank.

Kissinger, Henry Alfred. There were some personality disputes which neither of us handled with the elegance and wisdom that perhaps was necessary (commenting on his relationship with former Secretary of Defense James Schlesinger).

Schlesinger, James Rodney. Any time the President of the United States asks one to do a job that's doable, it's one's obligation to do it (explanation of why he agreed to help create a national energy policy).

SCHMIDT, HELMUT

Scheuch, Erwin. (Helmut) Schmidt is an above-average average German.

SCHOOL CHILDREN—TRANSPORTATION FOR INTEGRATION

Clark, Kenneth. Integration is a painful job. It is social therapy, and like personal therapy it is not easy.

Greeley, Andrew. (Busing) is not designed to bring justice to blacks or to improve education. It is intended rather to punish whites for their past racial prejudice. You punish whites by playing chess with their children.

Humphrey, Hubert Horatio. I do not want a great political party which nearly lost its soul in Vietnam to sell its soul on busing.

Jackson, Henry Martin. It is a misguided social experiment and it is failing and we ought to stop it (about busing).

McGovern, George Stanley. Any candidate who says or implies that by supporting him the voters can stop the buses will prove as President to be either a liar or a violator of the Constitution.

McGovern, George Stanley. I do not want a great political party which nearly lost its soul in Vietnam to sell its soul on the issue of busing.

Mondale, Walter Frederick. You should know that my position has always been that I have not been an advocate of busing to achieve racial balance. What I have resisted is the repeal of the 14th Amendment that prohibits discrimination in our school system. I think that is the only honorable and legal position that can be taken.

SCHOOL CHILDREN—TRANSPORTATION FOR INTEGRATION—BOSTON

White, Kevin. It would be no easier to bus from an Irish to an Italian neighborhood (commenting on how the people of Boston feel about busing).

SCHOOLS

Harris, James A. Twenty-three percent of school children are failing to graduate, and another large segment graduate as functional illiterates. If 23 percent of anything else failed—23 percent of the automobiles did not run, 23 percent of the buildings fell down, 23 percent of stuffed ham spoiled—we'd look at the producer. The schools, here, are not blameless.

SCHORR, DANIEL

Colby, William Egan. (Daniel Schorr) carried out his obligation to the first amendment to the Constitution and to himself as a newsman and should not be punished (commenting the release of the secret House report on United States intelligence operations).

Salant, Richard S. In view of the adversary situation in which Dan Schorr is placed in pending government investigations, he has agreed with CBS that he be relieved of all reporting duties for an indefinite period.

Schorr, Daniel. I think I ended up simply being indigestible (commenting on why he resigned from CBS).

Schorr, Daniel. I'm fighting for freedom of the press, and maybe I should also be fighting for freedom *from* the press.

Schorr, Daniel. The joys of martyrdom are considerably overrated.

Schorr, Daniel. To betray a source would be to betray myself, my career and my life. I cannot do it (commenting in his testimony before the Pike committee).

SCHRADER, PAUL

Schrader, Paul. I like to fire a movie like a bullet. Then I stay with it until it hits its target.

SCHUMACHER, ERNST F.

Schumacher, Ernst F. People always called me a crank, but I didn't carry any resentment about that because it is an excellent thing, a crank. It is not expensive, it is relatively nonviolent, and it causes revolutions.

SCHUMAN, WILLIAM

Schuman, William. In my own music, I'm alone, absolutely alone.

SCHWEIKER, RICHARD S.

Morton, Rogers Clark Ballard. Governor Reagan's announcement (of choosing Senator Schweicker as his running mate) appears to be an effort to exchange the second highest office in the land for a handful of delegates.

Reagan, Ronald. I don't believe in the old tradition of picking someone at the opposite end of the political spectrum because he can get some votes you can't get yourself (on choosing a running mate, July 9, 1976).

SCIENCE

Alves, Reuben. Science is what it is not what scientists think they do.

Bragg, W. L. The essence of science lies not in discovering facts but in discovering new ways of thinking about them.

Clarke, Arthur C. When a distinguished but elderly scientist says that something is possible he is almost certainly right. When he says it is impossible, he is very probably wrong.

Clemens, Samuel Langhorne. There is something fascinating about science. One gets such wholesale returns of conjecture out of such trifling investments of fact.

De Casseres, Benjamin. My studies in speculative philosophy, metaphysics, and science are all summed up in the image of a mouse called man running in and out of every hole in the cosmos hunting for the absolute cheese.

Whitehead, Alfred North. The aims of scientific thought are to see the general in the particular and the eternal in the transitory.

SCIENCE FICTION

Le Guin, Ursula. If science fiction becomes respectable, it may die.

SCIENCE—RESEARCH

Einstein, Albert. When a man after long years of searching chances upon a thought which discloses something of the beauty of this mysterious universe, he should not therefore be personally celebrated. He is already sufficiently paid by his experience of seeking and finding.

SCIENTISTS

Eysenck, H. J. Scientists, especially when they leave the particular field in which they have specialized, are just as ordinary, pig-headed and unreasonable as anybody else.

Snow, C. P. Literary intellectuals at one pole—at the other, scientists...Between the two a gulf of mutual incomprehension.

Wise, Howard. Great artists and great scientists share many of the same qualities: tenacity, courage, and imagination.

SCOTT, HUGH

Scott, Hugh. I had a will to believe (in Nixon's innocence), but they didn't show me all the documents. I was led into making statements on incomplete evidence. I was trying to be fair when I was personally deeply disturbed.

Scott, Hugh. The worst mistake I made was supporting the Carswell nomination (reflecting on his three decades in Congress).

SCOTT, WILLIAM

Anonymous (State Department Spokesman), . It will take us two years to repair the damage Scott did in these couple of weeks (commenting on Senator Scott's "fact-finding" tour of the Middle East).

Goldwater, Barry Morris. If he (William Scott) were any dumber, he'd be a tree.

Scott, William. The only reason we need zip codes is because niggers can't read.

Scott, William. What's this Gaza stuff? I never have understood that (to Israeli Prime Minister Yitzhak Rabin).

SCREW (PERIODICAL)

Dershowitz, Alan. Screw is a despicable magazine, but that's what the First Amendment was designed to protect.

SCULPTURE

Moore, Henry. Looking at sculpture teaches people to use their inborn sense of form, to improve their own surroundings, to make life marvelous.

Moore, Henry. Sculpture should always at first sight have some obscurities and further meanings. People should want to go on looking and thinking.

Oldenburg, Claes. To give birth to form is the only act of man that has any consequence.

SECRET SERVICE—UNITED STATES

Moore, George C. No, we never gave it a thought (in response to whether the FBI had ever discussed the constitutional or legal authority for its Cointelpro Program).

SECRETS

Le Carre, John. People are very secretive creatures—secret even from themselves.

Seale, Bobby. Those who know don't talk; and those who talk don't know.

SECURITY (PSYCHOLOGY)

Greer, Germaine. Security is when everything is settled, when nothing can happen to you; security is a denial of life.

Herzberg, Donald. Never leave hold of what you've got until you've got hold of something else.

Rinfret, Pierre A. Consensus is the security blanket of the insecure.

SEGREGATION

Eisenhower, Dwight David. These are not bad people... All they are concerned about is to see that their sweet little girls are not required to sit in schools alongside some big overgrown Negroes.

Thurmond, Strom. There are not enough laws on the books of the nation, nor can there be enough laws, to break down segregation in the South (commenting in 1948 as he accepted the presidential nomination of the Dixiecrat Party).

SEGREGATION IN EDUCATION

Wallace, George Corley. Segregation is a moot question, and integration is the law of the land. It is a moot question, and therefore we don't want to go back, nor make any attempt to change what is now a fact accomplished.

SELF EVALUATION

Bailey, Pearl. There's a period of life when we swallow a knowledge of ourselves and it becomes either good or sour inside.

Pagnol, Marcel. The most difficult secret for a man to keep is the opinion he has of himself.

Rogers, Ginger. If you don't stand for something, you will stand for anything.

SELF PERCEPTION

De Gaulle, Charles. We may as well go to the moon, but that's not very far. The greatest distance we have to cover still lies within us.

Roosevelt, Eleanor. No one can make you feel inferior without your consent.

Sartre, Jean-Paul. We can only see the somber recesses in our selves if we try to become transparent to others.

Shields, Mark. I don't think Carter and self-doubt have ever met.

Vanderbilt, Amy. One face to the world, another at home makes for misery.

Wicker, Tom. To know things as they are is better than to believe things as they seem.

SELLERS, PETER

Sellers, Peter. The older I get, the less I like the film industry and the people in it. In fact, I'm at a stage where I almost loathe them.

SENATORS

Abourezk, James. When voting on the confirmation of a Presidential appointment, it's always safer to vote against the son of a bitch, because if he's confirmed, it won't be long before he proves how wise you were.

Hayakawa, Samuel Ichiye. I must say, I find senators much more interesting people than professors...Professors are too damned specialized.

SENATORS—WIVES

Baker, Joy (wife of Howard Baker). Politics has nullified my personality.

SENGHOR, LEOPOLD SEDAR

Senghor, Leopold Sedar. Africa will teach rhythm to a world dead with machinery and cannon.

SERVANTS

Stotesbury, E. T. A good servant should never be in the way and never out of the way.

SETON, ELIZABETH, SAINT

Feeney, Leonard. The first American girl who 'made good' according to God's exact standards (about Elizabeth Seton).

SEVAREID, ERIC

Chancellor, John. Eric (Sevareid) never told people what he thought, but what he learned.

SEX

Allen, Woody. I have an intense desire to return to the womb. Anybody's.

Allen, Woody. Love is the answer. But while you're waiting for the answer, sex raises some pretty good questions.

Allen, Woody. The difference between sex and death is, with death you can do it alone and nobody's going to make fun of you.

Bankhead, Tallulah. I don't know what I am, dahling. I've tried several varieties of sex. The conventional position makes me claustrophobic. And the others give me either a stiff neck or lockjaw.

Bunuel, Luis. Sex without sin is like an egg without salt.

Burgess, Anthony. Women cannot help moving, and men cannot help being moved.

Dury, Ian. Sex is about as important as a cheese sandwich.

Feldman, Marty. Humor is like sex. Those who do it don't talk about it.

Goldstein, Al. A hard-on is its own redeeming value.

Menninger, Karl. Sex and sexuality never made anyone ill and never made anyone feel guilty. It is the hate and destructiveness concealed in them which produce strange aberrations and bitter regret.

Namath, Joe. I love football. I really love football. As far as I'm concerned, it's the second best thing in the world.

Paz, Octavio. The soul has become a department of sex, and sex has become a department of politics.

Reagan, Ronald. Human beings are not animals, and I do not want to see sex and sexual differences treated as casually and amorally as dogs and other beasts treat them. I believe this could happen under the ERA.

Reeves, Richard. Politics is sex in a hula-hoop.

Sharpe, Cornelia. I think sex is the greatest thing since Coca-Cola.

Sontag, Susan. There are some elements in life—above all, sexual pleasure—about which it isn't necessary to have a position.

Thomas, Marlo. Nothing is either all masculine or all feminine except sex.

Turner, R. E. (Ted). Lots of sex for everybody, that's a solution to the world's problems.

Vidal, Gore. Sex is politics.

SEX—CUBA

Quinn, Sally. An attitude of sexuality is as pervasive in Cuba as the presence of Fidel Castro. You can feel sex in the atmosphere, on the street, in conversation, in people's actions. The Cubans seem to be thinking of it much of the time.

SEX (PSYCHOLOGY)

Masters, William Howell. Males have made asses of themselves writing about female sexual experience.

Wetzsteon, Ross. Sex, to paraphrase Clausewitz, is the continuation of war by other means.

SEXUAL BEHAVIOR

Behan, Brendan. I think anything is all right provided it is done in private and doesn't frighten the horses.

Capote, Truman. I say I'm a homosexual who has had heterosexual experiences.

Greene, Bob. Indeed, Hugh Hefner is beginning to seem more and more like everyone's kindly and slightly bewildered uncle.

Hefner, Hugh Marston. I'm not primarily an entrepreneurial businessman. I'm primarily a playboy philosopher.

Hemingway, Mary. Books are helpful in bed. But they are not responsive (commenting on widowhood).

Leary, Timothy. I don't like hippies. I don't like communes. I despise heroin. I've never participated in an orgy. It may ruin my reputation, but I'm particularly monogamous.

Sontag, Susan. There are some elements in life—above all, sexual pleasure—about which it isn't necessary to have a position.

Tomlin, Lily. I worry about kids today. Because of the sexual revolution they're going to grow up and never know what dirty means.

SEXUAL ETHICS

Braine, John. I believe absolutely in Christian sexual morality, which means that I believe in premarital virginity. Virgins don't get V.D., don't have abortions, don't have illegitimate babies, and aren't forced to get married. And no man, no matter how progressive, has ever objected to his bride being a virgin.

SHAKESPEARE, WILLIAM

Vidal, Gore. Each writer is born with a repertory company in his head. Shakespeare had perhaps 20 players, and Tennessee Williams has about five and Samuel Beckett one—and perhaps a clone of that one. I have ten or so, and that's a lot.

SHANKER, ALBERT

Shanker, Albert. Power is a good thing. It is better than powerlessness.

SHAW, GEORGE BERNARD

Shaw, George Bernard. My method is to take utmost trouble to find the right thing to say, and then to say it with the utmost levity.

SHCHARANSKY, ANATOLY

Shcharansky, Anatoly. I am happy that I have lived honestly and in peace with my conscience, and never lied even when I was threatened with death.

SHEEN, MARTIN

Sheen, Martin. I don't believe in God, but I do believe that Mary was His mother.

SHEPHERD, CYBILL

Shepherd, Cybill. If you kept seeing Robert Redford stark naked on the screen, would he be a superstar today? No way. Or Gene Hackman showing everything? Their million dollar days would be over. I want to be in a movie where all the men take their clothes off and I don't.

SHOFNER, JIM

Henry, Orville. He's such a nice guy. But if they had a Naive Bowl, he would coach both sides (about TCU's football coach Jim Shofner).

SICILY

Dolci, Danilo. We in Sicily are still parched by the sun, plagued by poverty and milked by the Mafia.

SICK

Knowles, John H. Over 99 percent of us are born healthy and made sick as a result of personal misbehavior and environmental conditions.

SICKNESS

Camus, Albert. Illness is a convent which has its rule, its austerity, its silences, and its inspirations.

Knowles, John H. Over 99 percent of us are born healthy and made sick as a result of personal misbehavior and environmental conditions.

SILENCE

Gentry, Dave Tyson. True friendship comes when silence between two people is comfortable.

SILLS, BEVERLY

Sills, Beverly. My voice has served me very well, and I would like to be able to put it to bed, so that it can go quietly and with pride (upon her announcement that she would retire in 1980).

Sills, Beverly. When I go on the talk shows, I project what I am—an intelligent and well-educated girl from Brooklyn.

SILVERMAN, FRED

Wood, Robert. Freddie's (Silverman) like a shark's belly. He can't get enough.

SIMON, WILLIAM E.

Simon, William E. I've lived through the Saturday Night Massacre and the Sunday Night Massacre. Only Butz and me are left. We'll probably go on Monday.

Simon, William E. We're going to sell New York to the Shah of Iran. It's a hell of an investment (during New York City's financial crisis).

SIN

Lukacs, John. I believe human nature doesn't change. I believe very strongly in original sin. I also take a dim view of the pursuit of justice as being the superior value of Western civilization. I think truth is more important than justice.

Young, Andrew. Sin began with Adam. If you turn the lights out, folks will steal. They'll do that in Switzerland, too.

SINATRA, FRANK

Anka, Paul. I didn't want to find a horse's head in my bed (explaining why he allowed Frank Sinatra to first record My Way).

Sinatra, Frank. I am a symmetrical man, almost to a fault.

SINCLAIR, UPTON

Sinclair, Upton. I tried to touch America's conscience and all I did was hit it in the stomach (commenting on the effect of his novel The Jungle).

SINGER, ISAAC BASHEVIS

Singer, Isaac Bashevis. I never forget that I am only a storyteller.

Singer, Isaac Bashevis. I'm a pessimist with cheerfulness. It's a riddle even to me, but this is how I am.

Singer, Isaac Bashevis. I'm before everything else a writer, not just Jewish, and I'm not doing it with some illusion that I'm going to do great things. I just feel that I have to tell a story.

SINGERS

Eckstine, Billy. If your popularity is based on a gimmick, like plunking a guitar with your teeth to taunting the audience with obscenities, better grab the money and run. You'll never last.

SINGLE PEOPLE

O'Brian, Hugh. There is quite enough grief when one is alone. Why compound it by getting married? (upon his founding Marriage Anonymous).

SKELTON, RED

Skelton, Red. I trust God, my wife, and myself. People take kindness for weakness, and generosity has the form of a sucker.

SKEPTICISM

Nietzsche, Friedrich Wilhelm. If a man really has strong faith he can indulge in the luxury of skepticism.

SKIN—CARE AND HYGIENE

Swanson, Gloria. It's hereditary, all in the genes. But no one can have skin like a baby's bottom if they're going to stuff that hole in their face with chocolate and banana splits.

SKIS AND SKIING

Anonymous, . If God had meant for Texans to ski, He would have made bullshit white.

Ford, Gerald Rudolph. We skiers know that falling down isn't important; it's getting up again.

SKYLAB

Fraser, Malcolm. Receiving Skylab is an honor we would happily have foregone.

SLANG

Sandburg, Carl. Slang is language that takes off its coat, spits on its hands, and goes to work.

SLEEP

Lebowitz, Fran. Sleep is death without the responsibility.

SLICK, GRACE

Lowe, Nick. (Grace Slick) is like somebody's mom who's had a few too many drinks at a cocktail party.

SLUMS

Agnew, Spiro Theodore. If you've seen one slum, you've seen them all.

SMALL TOWN LIFE—TEXAS

Layne, Bobby. Living in a small town (Lubbock) in Texas ain't half bad—if you own it.

SMITH, IAN DOUGLAS

Savory, Allen (former Rhodesian MP). The prime minister (Ian Smith) has the rare ability to make people believe things they know for a fact are untrue.

Smith, Ian Douglas. I do not believe in black majority rule in Rhodesia—not in a thousand years.

Smith, Ian Douglas. We may lose in the end, but I think it's better to lose while you're standing up and fighting than crawling out on your knees (commenting on his fight to continue white rule in Rhodesia).

Smith, Ian Douglas. We never have had a policy in Rhodesia to hand over our country to any black majority and, as far as I am concerned, we never will (commenting in March, 1976).

Wilson, Harold. (Ian Smith is the) most slippery political customer I've ever negotiated with.

SMITH, JACLYN

Ladd, Cheryl. Jaclyn (Smith) is the only girl I know that has the body of a go-go dancer and the mind of an angel.

SMITH, MAGGIE

Smith, Maggie. I'm always very relieved to be somebody else, because I'm not sure at all who I am.

SMITH, MARGARET CHASE

Smith, Margaret Chase. We live together. I don't make any apologies (explaining her relationship with William C. Smith, Jr.).

SMITH, PATTI

Smith, Patti. As far as I'm concerned, being any gender is a drag.

Smith, Patti. I want every faggot, grandmother, five-year-old and Chinaman to be able to hear my music and say YEAH.

SMITH, W. EUGENE

Smith, W. Eugene. I carry a torch with my camera.

Smith, W. Eugene. I torture myself to make it all come out as deep and honest as I can.

SMOKING

Fontana, Robert S. Even if everyone quits smoking today, we could still look forward to a legacy of maybe 50,000 lung cancer deaths a year for the next 20 years (commenting on the early findings of a two-year lung cancer study).

Higginson, John. We now know there are a hundred causes of cancer, and eighty of them are cigarettes.

SOCIAL CHANGE

Brown, Elaine. I may not be saying 'off the mother-fucking pigs' anymore, but I'm still talking about serious political change. Who cares who takes credit? The Panthers? The Democrats? As long as the work gets done.

Corrigan, Mairead. Our world is rushing towards disaster. But it's not too late to prove the power of love...we've got to prove that the way of nonviolence can bring social change (from her Nobel Peace Prize acceptance speech).

Dubos, Rene. Each civilization has its own kind of pestilence and controls it only by reforming itself.

Jackson, Glenda. Sarah Bernhardt believed in the human will above all things. I can empathize with that. Because I do believe that things can be changed; and by changed, I mean improved, not simply altered.

Mao, Tse-Tung. All reactionaries are paper tigers.

Weizenbaum, Joseph. We are rapidly losing, have perhaps already lost, physical and mental control of our society.

SOCIAL CLASSES

Orton, Joe. All classes are criminal today. We live in an age of equality.

SOCIAL CLASSES—UNITED STATES

Henderson, Vivian Wilson. We have programs for combatting racial discrimination, but not for combatting economic class distinctions.

SOCIAL INTERACTION

Fields, W. C. There comes a time in the affairs of men when you must take the bull by the tail and face the situation.

SOCIAL PROBLEMS

Junot, Philippe. Society's ills come from people having lost the taste for enjoyment.

SOCIAL VALUES

Eliot, Thomas Stearns. Those who say they give the public what it wants begin by underestimating public taste and end by debauching it.

Ferris, Earle. There's nothing neither good nor bad that can't be made more so.

Loy, Myrna. Nobody seems to like each other anymore.

Muggeridge, Malcolm. Western society suffers from a largely unconscious collective death wish.

Murphy, Thomas Aquinas. There's a desire today for more security and for a risk-free society. But that becomes a choiceless society, not a free society.

Spikol, Art. The fact is that most people don't drive cars that reflect what they are: they drive the closest thing they can find to what they'd like to be.

SOCIALISM

Castro, Fidel. I don't think the contradictions between capitalism and socialism can be resolved by war. This is no longer the age of the bow and arrow. It's the nuclear age, and war can annihilate us all. The only way to achieve solutions seems to be for the different social systems to coexist.

Davis, Angela. I'm not pessimistic about change in this country. I'm convinced that this country will one day be socialist.

Humphrey, Hubert Horatio. Compassion is not weakness and concern for the unfortunate is not socialism.

Levy, Bernard-Henri. Between the barbarity of capitalism, which censures itself much of the time, and the barbarity of socialism, which does not, I guess I might choose capitalism.

Mehta, Asoka. Socialism is an attractive goal, but concentration of power is as dangerous as concentration of capital.

SOCIALISM—GREAT BRITAIN

Thatcher, Margaret Hilda. Britain's progress toward socialism has been an alternation of two steps forward with half a step back.

SOCIALISM—SWEDEN

Anonymous (Swedish banker), . Our (Swedish) socialists don't care who owns the cow so long as the government gets most of the milk.

SOCIALISM—UNITED STATES

Anonymous, . The socialization of medicine is coming...the time now is here for the medical profession to acknowledge that it is tired of the eternal struggle for advantage over one's neighbor (editorial comment in the Journal of the American Medical Association, 1914).

SOCIETY

Townshend, Pete. The way all societies are is that some people get, and some people don't.

Weizenbaum, Joseph. We are rapidly losing, have perhaps already lost, physical and mental control of our society.

SOLAR ENERGY

American Petroleum Institute, . In an otherwise nostalgic decade, solar energy has eclipsed apple pie and is giving mom a close race for the title of most popular platitude of the seventies.

Porter, Sir George. If sunbeams were weapons of war, we would have had solar energy centuries ago.

White, E. B. A cat sunning himself in the doorway of a barn knows all about solar energy. Why can't man learn?.

SOLDIER OF FORTUNE (PERIODICAL)

Fenson, Mel. We're aimed at people interested in the sport of hunting—hunting for animals or hunting for people (commenting as Marketing Director on the aims of the periodical Soldier of Fortune).

SOLDIERS

Gass, Istvan (Hungarian soccer star). It's not serious work. I don't do anything. In fact, I've never seen a gun (on his job as a soldier).

Terrell, Douglas. In Europe, it's easy to instill pride (in the Army); on the border they can see the enemy. In the States, they see McDonald's.

SOLITUDE

Lueders, Edward. Solitude leads to amplitude.

SOLTI, SIR GEORG

Solti, Sir Georg. Chicago should erect a statue to me for what I have done.

SOLZHENITSYN, ALEKSANDR ISAEVICH

Boorstin, Daniel J. The courage we inherit from our Jeffersons and Lincolns and others is not the Solzhenitsyn courage of the true believer, but the courage to doubt.

Levy, Bernard-Henri. Solzhenitsyn is the Shakespeare of our time, the only one who knows how to point out the monsters.

SOMOZA DEBAYLE, ANASTASIO

Anonymous (Nicaraguan woman), . Five earthquakes—what Somoza has done to us, not even five earthquakes could do.

Somoza Debayle, Anastasio. I was born in Nicaragua, I am Nicaraguan, and I will live here forever. Those who want me to go will have to push me out by force.

SONGS

Guthrie, Woody. You can't write a good song about a whorehouse unless you been in one.

SOREL, EDWARD

Sorel, Edward. At what I do, I am the best there is.

Sorel, Edward. For the past 15 years I've been making cartoons that in one way or another suggest that America is educated by incompetents, governed by hypocrites, and ruled by the military industrial complex.

SORENSEN, THEODORE CHAIKIN

McGovern, George Stanley. We can mark it down that the ghost of Joe McCarthy still stalks this land (commenting on the treatment of Theodore Sorensen as Carter's nominee for the directorship of the CIA).

Sorensen, Theodore Chaikin. To continue fighting for this post, (the directorship of the CIA) which would be my natural inclination, would only handicap the new administration if I am rejected, or handicap my effectiveness if confirmed.

SOUTH

Carter, Hodding, III. The thing you have to remember about Southerners is that we're always generous and forgiving—with our friends.

Cooks, Stoney (aide to Andrew Young). Liberals want to do it for you. Southerners want to do it with you (commenting on the Carter administration's attempt to involve minorities in the government).

Edwards, James B. I don't believe the South will buy Jimmy Carter. He is nothing more than a Southern-talking George McGovern.

Johnson, Claudia Alta (Taylor). The South is the future. It is the political pivot of the country now. It's very gratifying to see Jimmy Carter become President, to see the South finally win out after all these years.

SOUTH AFRICA

Kriel, Anneline (Miss World of 1975). (South Africa is) a great country and a lot of changes are going on. In all the government buildings the black and white separate signs are down and in the major hotels and restaurants too.

SOUTH AFRICA—DESCRIPTION

Barnard, Christiaan. Compared with Harlem, Soweto is paradise.

SOUTH AFRICA—POLITICS AND GOVERNMENT

Anonymous (editorial writer for the Sunday Times, South African newspaper), . As long as this (detention) system survives, men will continue to die mysteriously, and no one will be held accountable. That is what the system was designed to achieve. No South African can say he did not know.

Botha, Pieter W. I believe SWAPO is not interested in elections. They are only interested in foisting their ideas on the people of SouthWest Africa at the point of a gun.

Buthelezi, Gatsha (Zulu Chief). I shudder for my country, and I shudder for all its people. The whole white population will, in the final analysis, be answerable for the sins that are committed in their name by those they have elected to determine not only their destiny but ours.

Buthelezi, Gatsha (Zulu Chief). South Africa is one country. It has one destiny. Those who are attempting to divide the land of our birth are attempting to stem the tide of history.

Coulson, Gail. In South Africa all of us, for one reason or another, are living behind bars—blacks and whites, good guys, bad guys, everybody.

Jackson, Jesse. People in South Africa only have the Bible as a constitution.

Lewis, Anthony. In making a prison for others, the Afrikaners have imprisoned themselves.

Paton, Alan. Sometimes, you think of apartheid as a fort. Often it is seen as a prison. But it is really a grave the Afrikanner has dug for himself.

SOUTH AFRICA—RACE QUESTION

Biko, Steve. Being Black is not a matter of pigmentation, but is a reflection of a mental attitude. Merely by describing yourself as Black you have started to fight against all the forces that seek to use your blackness as a stamp that makes you out as a subservient being.

Kruger, James T. (South African Minister of Justice). It remains a fact that a happy person cannot be a communist (asking for reform of his country's race laws).

Nyerere, Julius Kamberage. South Africa is no different from Rhodesia. The struggle by blacks in both countries is exactly the same—for majority rule. So what happens in Rhodesia will happen in South Africa.

Paton, Alan. Sometimes, you think of apartheid as a fort. Often it is seen as a prison. But it is really a grave the Afrikanner has dug for himself.

Woods, Donald. The level of black anger in my country today is so high, and the determination of whites to resist fair compromise is so strong, that both sides are on a collision course toward a racial civil war.

SOUTHERN METHODIST UNIVERSITY (FOOTBALL)

Muir, Bill. If the meek are going to inherit the earth, our offensive linemen are going to be land barons.

SPACE

Elgin, Duane S (futurologist). Once you discover that space doesn't matter, or that time can be traveled through at will so that time doesn't matter, and that matter can be moved by consciousness so that matter doesn't matter—well, you can't go home again.

Joubert, Joseph. Space is to place as eternity is to time.

Schmitt, Harrison. Space represents the kind of resource for the human spirit that North America was three hundred years ago: a new stimulus for the spirit of freedom.

Vallee, Jacques. The theory of space and time is a cultural artifact made possible by the invention of graph paper.

SPACE, OUTER—EXPLORATION

Leary, Timothy. There's no way you're going to have full employment in this country without a war or space migration... Only in space can we take steps in our evolution... Only there will we be able to expand intelligence and the human life span...

Von Braun, Werner. I look forward to the day when mankind will join hands to apply the combined technological ingenuity of all nations to the exploration and utilization of outer space for peaceful uses.

SPAIN—HISTORY—CIVIL WAR, 1936-1939

Ibarruri, Dolores (Spanish Civil War activist). It is better to die on your feet than live on your knees.

SPAIN—POLITICS AND GOVERNMENT

Callaghan, James. Spain's self-inflicted isolation is brought about not just by a single act of brutality, but by injustices over a generation or more.

Juan Carlos I, King of Spain, . No human life should be put in danger when just and disinterested solutions are offered and when cooperation and understanding are sought among peoples.

SPANISH SAHARA

Hassan II, King of Morocco, . I am convinced that the march has fulfilled its mission and reached its goal, and we must therefore return to our point of departure (commenting upon Morocco's march into the Spanish Sahara).

SPEECH

Rayburn, Sam. No one has a finer command of language than the person who keeps his mouth shut.

SPIELBERG, STEVEN

Spielberg, Steven. My advice to anyone who wants to be a movie director is to make home movies. I started out by shooting 8 millimeter home movies with neighbors and friends.

Spielberg, Steven. The most expensive habit in the world is celluloid, not heroin, and I need a fix every few years.

SPIRITUAL LEADERSHIP

Landers, Ann. I believe people want some spiritual leadership. It shows in the primaries; Jimmy Carter. He speaks openly about his religion. They see in him something that offers hope.

SPITZ, MARK

Spitz, Mark. I was a porpoise out of water. I was not prepared for the adulation I received. I could not handle the world.

SPORTS

Allen, George. Only winners are truly alive. Winning is living. Every time you win, you're reborn. When you lose, you die a little.

Broun, Heywood Hale. Sport is a preparation for more sport and not a businessmen's ROTC.

Finley, Charles Oscar. I've never seen so many damned idiots as the owners in sport.

Garvey, Ed. When you talk about civil liberties in professional sports, it's like talking about virtue in a whorehouse.

Kidd, Bruce. We should stop preaching about sport's moral values. Sport, after all, isn't Lent. It's a pleasure of the flesh.

King, Billie Jean. Amateur athletes have become the pawn of manipulators and big business.

Rozelle, Pete. Sporting events give people time off from the problems of the world.

Warhol, Andy. Sports figures are to the '70s what movie stars were to the '60s.

SPORTS JOURNALISM

Sherrod, William Forrest (Blackie). Sportswriting is just like driving a taxi. It ain't the work you enjoy. It's the people you run into.

STAFFORD, JEAN

Stafford, Jean. I write for myself and God and a few close friends.

STALLONE, SYLVESTER

Stallone, Sylvester. I make my living with my mind. My muscles I consider merely machinery to carry my mind around.

STAPLETON, RUTH CARTER

Stapleton, Ruth Carter. I am not going to be the Billy Graham of the Carter administration.

STARGELL, WILLIE

Tanner, Chuck. Having Willie Stargell on your ball club is like having a diamond ring on your finger.

STATE GOVERNMENTS

Burns, John. We expect very little of our (state) legislatures, and they continually live up to our expectations.

Reagan, Ronald. You can vote with your feet in this country. If a state is mismanaged you can move (commenting on the possibility that some states might substitute inadequate programs for the Federal ones he would like to eliminate).

STATESMEN

Kissinger, Henry Alfred. A statesman who too far outruns the experience of his people will fail in achieving a domestic consensus, however wise his policies. (On the other hand), a statesman who limits his policies to the experience of his people is doomed to sterility.

STATISTICS

Gallup, George. I could prove God statistically.

STEEL INDUSTRY

Kennedy, John Fitzgerald. My father always told me that steel men were sons-of-bitches, but I never realized till now how right he was (in the 1962 steel-price confrontation).

STEINBECK, JOHN

Steinbeck, John. Competing with Hemingway isn't my idea of good business.

STEINBERG, SAUL

Rosenberg, Harold. In linking art to the modern consciousness, no artist is more relevant than Steinberg.

Rosenberg, Harold. Steinberg's art is a parade of fictitious personages, geometric shapes, items of household equipment, personified furniture, each staged in a fiction of what it is—or in a dream of being something else.

Steinberg, Saul. Performance bores me. What interests me is the invention. I like to make a parody of bravura.

STEINBRENNER, GEORGE

Martin, Billy. The two of them (George Steinbrenner and Reggie Jackson) deserve each other. One's a born liar; the other's convicted.

STENGEL, CHARLES DILLON (CASEY)

Stengel, Charles Dillon (Casey). Oldtimers weekends and airplane landings are alike. If you can walk away from them they're successful (after the annual Oldtimers Day at Shea Stadium).

STERNBACH, LEO HENRYK

Sternbach, Leo Henryk. I am not a victim of capitalistic exploitation. If anything, I am an example of capitalistic enlightenment (commenting on his discovery of Valium and Librium and selling of the patent to his employer Hoffman-La Roche at $1 per drug).

STEVENS, JOHN PAUL

Stevens, John Paul. It's always been my philosophy to decide cases on the narrowest grounds possible and not to reach out.

Stevens, John Paul. Judges should impose on themselves the discipline of deciding no more than is before them.

STEVENSON, ADLAI, II

Stevenson, Adlai, II. I have often thought that if I had any epitaph that I would rather have more than another, it would be to say that I had disturbed the sleep of my generation.

Stevenson, Adlai, II. It is better to light one candle than to curse the darkness.

STEVENSON, ADLAI, III

Stevenson, Adlai, III. I've been called my great-grandfather's grandson, my father's son and at times even my wife's husband. Now, they're calling me Mayor Daley's pet rock.

STOCK EXCHANGES—NEW YORK EXCHANGE

Graham, Benjamin. (The stock market is) a Falstaffian joke that frequently degenerates into a madhouse.

STOCKS

Levin, S. Jay. Stocks do not move unless they are pushed.

STOKOWSKI, LEOPOLD

Stokowski, Leopold. Every rehearsal must be better than the last. Every concert must be better than the last. We must never be satisfied because upwards in quality is quality without limit.

Stokowski, Leopold. I don't believe in tradition. It is a form of laziness.

Stokowski, Leopold. Music appeals to me for what can be done with it.

STONE, EDWARD DURRELL

Eckardt, Wolf Von. The only lift you get from this building is when you take the elevator from the basement to the second floor.

STONE, ISIDORE FEINSTEIN

Stone, Isidor Feinstein. The First Amendment gives newspapermen a status and a mandate, an honored place in society, that cannot be matched in England, much less on the European continent. It is peculiarly American. I feel as though I survived an Ice Age and helped to keep this heritage intact.

STONEHENGE

Moore, Henry. Stonehenge is not a building, it is a carving.

STOPPARD, TOM
Stoppard, Tom. I suppose my purpose as a playwright, if such a thing can be stated at all, has been to marry the play of ideas with comedy or farce.

STOWE, HARRIET BEECHER
Lincoln, Abraham. So this is the little lady who made this big war (comment upon meeting Harriet Beecher Stowe).

STRATEGIC ARMS LIMITATION TALKS
Biden, Joseph. Half the people don't know the difference between SALT and pepper.
Brezhnev, Leonid I. God will not forgive us if we fail (about Strategic Arms Limitation Talks).
Helms, Jesse. It's very clear that the Russians have taken us to the cleaners. If this is the best the Administration can do, I suggest a SALT-free diet.
McGovern, George Stanley. I will not vote for the illusion of arms control.

STRAUSS, ROBERT S.
Anonymous, . When (John) Connally eats watermelon, (Robert) Strauss spits out the seeds.
Carter, James Earl (Attributed by Robert Shrum). I'd be a pretty pathetic nominee if I wasn't able to get rid of Strauss as national chairman.
Strauss, Robert S. I didn't come to town yesterday on a load of watermelons.
Strauss, Robert S. I'm not going to deliver a candidate to the party, I'm going to deliver a party to the candidate.
Strauss, Robert S. It's a little like makin' love to a gorilla. You don't quit when you're tired—you quit when the gorilla's tired (when asked whether he planned to quit as chairman of the Democratic National Committee).
Strauss, Robert S. The three most overrated things in Washington are Bob Strauss, home cooking, and Hamilton Jordan's private life.

STRAVINSKY, VERA
Stravinsky, Vera. When people ask me what I want for my birthday, I always say, 'Time, time, time'.

STRESS
Selye, Hans. Stress is the nonspecific response of the body to any demand.

STRIKES—ITALY
Anselmi, Tina (first Italian woman cabinet member). If people outside Italy have the impression that Italy is always on strike, that is because it is.

STRIKES—NEWSPAPERS
Graham, Katharine. This company (The Washington Post) is not now and never has been antiunion.

STROUT, RICHARD
Broder, David S. He (Richard Strout) must get out of bed every day as if it's his first chance to set the world right.

STUDENT MILITANTS
Glassman, James K. As a sit-in veteran and small businessman myself, I'm convinced that entrepreneurship is the last refuge of the trouble-making individual.

STUDENTS
Borges, Jorge Luis. (American students) read only what they must to pass, or what the professors choose. Otherwise they are totally dedicated to television, to baseball and to football.

STUDIO 54 (DISCOTHEQUE), NEW YORK (CITY)
Cohn, Roy. I only hope that this country remains a place where Steve (Rubell) and I can build what's become a great institution in America and in the world.

STUPIDITY
Miller, Arthur. The paranoia of stupidity is always the worst, since its fear of destruction by intelligence is reasonable.

STYLE
Sontag, Susan. Style is the principle of decision in a work of art, the signature of the artist's will.

SUCCESS
Albee, Dan. The value of an artistic achievement is inversely proportional to the number of people it appeals to.
Alderson, M. H. If at first you don't succeed, you are running about average.
Anonymous (Murphy's Law), . If anything can go wrong, eventually it will.
Bucy, Fred. Nothing is ever accomplished by a reasonable man.
Cozzens, James Gould. The longer I watch men and life, the surer I get that success whenever more than minor comes of luck alone. By comparison, no principles, ideas, goals, and standards of conduct matter much in an achieving of it.
Eckstine, Billy. If your popularity is based on a gimmick, like plunking a guitar with your teeth to taunting the audience with obscenities, better grab the money and run. You'll never last.
Ephron, Nora. For a lot of women, the women's movement has just given them a political rationalization for their fear of success.
Graham, Benjamin. Never having to balance your checkbook (a definition of financial success).
Kissinger, Henry Alfred. Each success only buys an admission ticket to a more difficult problem.
Midler, Bette. The worst part of having success is to try finding someone who is happy for you.
Paulucci, Jeno F. It pays to be ignorant, for when you're smart you already know it can't be done.
Simon, William E. Show me a good loser and I'll show you a loser.
Slater, Jim. As you get better at a thing it gets less interesting.
Tomlin, Lily. Sometimes I worry about being a success in a mediocre world.
Tomlin, Lily. Why is it we are always hearing about the tragic cases of too much, too soon? What about the rest of us? Too little, too late.
Van Derbur, Marilyn (former Miss America). The vital, successful people I have met all had one common characteristic. They had a plan.
Vidal, Gore. It is not enough to succeed, a friend must also fail.
Zukor, Adolph. Look ahead a little and gamble a lot (a formula for success).

SUCCESS—IRELAND
Flanagan, Fionnula. The one thing you must not commit with the Irish is to succeed.

SUICIDE
Allen, Woody. There have been times when I've thought of suicide, but with my luck it'd probably be a temporary solution.

Sheed, Wilfrid. Suicide is the sincerest form of criticism life gets.

Wheelwright, John Brooks. His death was his best poem (about Harry Crosby).

SULLIVAN, ED
Dylan, Bob. Somebody called me the Ed Sullivan of rock and roll. I don't know what that means, but it sounds right.

SUSANN, JACQUELINE
Susann, Jacqueline. I don't have any peers, as far as writers go.

SUTTON, WILLIE
Sutton, Willie. I always figured that being a good robber was like being a good lawyer.

SWAN LAKE (BALLET)
De Mille, Agnes. If there was the Resurrection, and He danced, I don't think I'd see Him in Swan Lake if I could avoid it.

SWITZERLAND
Rossy, Paul (former vice chairman, Swiss Banking Commission). God, after all, created Switzerland for one purpose—to be the clearinghouse of the world.

Young, Andrew. Sin began with Adam. If you turn the lights out, folks will steal. They'll do that in Switzerland, too.

SYMBIONESE LIBERATION ARMY
Hearst, Patricia Campbell. I was sick of the middle-class life I was leading. The SLA members seemed to have some purpose to their lives.

Weir, David. The SLA is not only a dream story to the newspapers, it is a dream story to the FBI as well, because it allows them to paint the entire left with the brush of the SLA.

SYNANON (ORGANIZATION)
Dederich, Charles. Nonviolence was a position. We can change positions anytime we want to (about Synanon).

TAIWAN
Mansfield, Mike. Treaties are not forever (urging that the United States quit its defense treaty with Taiwan and recognize China).

TALENT
Jong, Erica. Everyone has talent. What is rare is the courage to follow the talent to the dark place where it leads.

TALMADGE, HERMAN
Talmadge, Herman. At no time did I maintain a cash hoard in the pocket of an overcoat or anywhere else.

Talmadge, Herman. I took my personal problems to the bottle rather than to my Maker.

Talmadge, Herman. The people of Georgia did not elect me to be a bookkeeper.

TASTE (AESTHETICS)
Quant, Mary. Good taste is death, vulgarity life.

Stone, Richard. One privilege of home ownership is the right to have lousy taste and display it.

Warhol, Andy. Bad taste makes the day go faster.

TAX RETURNS
Neuman, Alfred E. Today, it takes more brains and effort to make out the Income Tax Form than it does to make the income.

TAXATION
Colbert, Jean Baptiste. The art of taxation consists in so plucking the goose as to obtain the largest possible amount of feathers with the smallest possible amount of hissing.

Friedman, Milton. Inflation is the one form of taxation that can be imposed without legislation.

Galbraith, John Kenneth. I'm opposed to tax decreases. If the last one had worked Jerry Ford would still be President.

Holmes, Oliver Wendell. Taxes are the price that society pays for civilization.

Simon, William E. Corporations are people, too (proposing a new tax break for big businesses).

Wicker, Tom. Government expands to absorb revenue—and then some.

TAXATION—CALIFORNIA
Gann, Paul. We're only asking the government to live within our means (favoring California's Proposition 4).

Jarvis, Howard. I didn't promise anybody that Prop 13 would reduce rent.

TAXATION—UNITED STATES
Galbraith, John Kenneth. The (tax) revolt of the affluent, which now has politicans so frightened, is not a violent thing. The response in the ghettoes if life there is allowed further to deteriorate might be different.

Simon, William E. We're going to have a taxpayers' revolt if we don't begin to make the tax system more simple, more understandable, so that everyone knows that everybody is paying his fair share.

Swearingen, John E. The President has made an emotional appeal to defend a tax program that is indefensible. His energy program involves the largest peacetime tax increase ever imposed on our citizens.

TAYLOR, ELIZABETH
Taylor, Elizabeth. I do feel sorry for Amy Carter, I know the problems she'll have.

Taylor, Elizabeth. I love Richard for the extravagant thought but he doesn't have to spoil me any more—just love me (upon the sale of her $1 million pink diamond ring purchased as a wedding gift.

Taylor, Elizabeth. When people say: she's got everything, I've only one answer: I haven't had tomorrow.

TEACHERS
Adams, Henry Brooks. A teacher affects eternity; he can never tell where his influence stops.

TEACHING
Shanker, Albert. Teaching is no longer seen as a woman's job. Teaching is seen as a tough, exciting place where things are happening.

TECHNOLOGICAL CHANGE
Clarke, Arthur C. Experience has shown that the most important results of any technological breakthrough are those that are not obvious.

TECHNOLOGY AND CIVILIZATION
Clarke, Arthur C. Any sufficiently advanced technology is undistinguishable from magic.

Clarke, Arthur C. Experience has shown that the most important results of any technological breakthrough are those that are not obvious.

TECHNOLOGY TRANSFER
Clarke, Arthur C. Experience has shown that the most important results of any technological breakthrough are those that are not obvious.

TELEPHONE COMPANIES

DeButts, John (Chairman of the Board, AT&T). We believe competition works to the disadvantage of the average (telephone) user, and where it does, we are determined to fight it.

TELEVISION

Allen, Fred. Television is a triumph of equipment over people, and the minds that control it are so small that you could put them in a gnat's navel with room left over for two caraway seeds and an agent's heart.

Allen, Fred. Television is chewing gum for the eyes.

Arledge, Roone. The single biggest problem of television is that everyone talks so much.

Arlen, Michael J. Every civilization creates its own cultural garbage and ours is television (commenting in his book The View from Highway 1).

Arlen, Michael J. TV is a kind of language that people have learned how to read.

Baker, Russell. Televiso ergo sum—I am televised, therefore I am.

Boorstin, Daniel J. Just as the printing press five centuries before had begun to democratize learning, now the television set would democratize experience, incidentally changing the very nature of what was newly shared.

Canby, Vincent. Bland has always been big in television.

Chayefsky, Paddy. Television is democracy at it's ugliest.

McLuhan, Marshall. Television is not a visual medium.

McLuhan, Marshall. TV is addictive. It's a drug.

Mead, Margaret. For the first time the young are seeing history being made before it is censored by their elders (in defense of TV).

Minow, Newton. The most important educational institution in the country is not Harvard or Yale or Caltech—it's television.

Monaco, James. Film has come of age as an art, probably because television now receives the brunt of contempt from the remaining proponents of an elite culture.

Newman, Edwin. I believe some silence is helpful to thought. And I believe to some extent radio and television discourage thought and reflection.

O'Connor, John J. Exposure to television is not necessarily fatal.

Reeves, Richard. (Television is) our new environment and, like the weather, it often determines whether we stay home or not.

Reeves, Richard. Television, of course, is dangerous. But that does not mean it is necessarily bad.

Seeger, Pete. TV must become our council fire, our town hall.

TELEVISION ADVERTISING

Bradley, Bill. First, I was suspicious of an advertising industry that manufactures needs, then sells products to foster those needs. Second, some offers were coming to me as a "white hope", and that offended me. Third, basketball was an important part of my life. I wanted to keep it pure. Hair sprays and deodorants and popcorn poppers were not basketball (on why he never made TV commercials).

Wald, Richard. California understands the real purpose of television is to collect a crowd of advertisers.

TELEVISION ADVERTISING AND POLITICS

O'Toole, John E. Most packaged goods are minor products (and) the consumer's most effective response to a disparity between an advertising claim and reality is never to buy the product again. When you buy a political candidate as a result of his advertising, you're stuck with the purchase for four years—with results that can be far more devastating than not getting your teeth as white as you had hoped.

TELEVISION AUDIENCES

Sevareid, Eric. There is an immense amount of biased listening and inaccurate listening (commenting on TV news audiences).

Wald, Richard. California understands the real purpose of television is to collect a crowd of advertisers.

TELEVISION AUTHORSHIP

Oliansky, Joel. TV writing is the country of the blind where the one-eyed man is king.

TELEVISION BROADCASTING

Arledge, Roone. The single biggest problem of television is that everyone talks so much.

Howard, Robert T. The family hour seems to have become just another cop-out used by creative people to explain their failure.

Lear, Norman. Sex and violence are a smokescreen. There are interests in this country that don't care to have fun made about the problems existing in society (concerning the censorship of television).

TELEVISION BROADCASTING—NEWS

Anderson, Jack. The networks don't recognize a story until it's in the New York Times. They aren't competent; they're incompetent.

Chancellor, John. Television is good at the transmission of experience. Print is better at the transmission of facts.

Friendly, Fred. The news is the one thing networks can point to with pride. Everything else they do is crap, and they know it.

Friendly, Fred. TV still basically indexes rather than reports the news.

Hewitt, Don. People are finding that truth is more fascinating than fiction.

Leonard, Bill. This is the major leagues. They didn't turn the Sistine Chapel over to the first guy who walked in off the street. They turned it over to Michelangelo (Defending network television's policy of rejecting news documentaries from outside sources).

MacNeil, Robert. TV has created a nation of news junkies who tune in every night to get their fix on the world.

Murrow, Edward R (attributed by Charles Kuralt). Just because you speak in a voice loud enough to be heard over television by 16 million people, that doesn't make you any smarter than you were when you spoke loudly enough to be heard only at the other end of the bar.

Savitch, Jessica. The thing you need most in this business (TV journalism) is stamina.

Sevareid, Eric. The problem is not so much finding out what the news is, it's making sense of it.

Walters, Barbara. I just hope that all this talk of money doesn't confuse the issue—that this is a great breakthrough in network news. I think there is not a newsman who would have turned down the offer—and for a woman it is an even more unique opportunity (commenting on her ABC contract offer).

TELEVISION BROADCASTING, NONCOMMERCIAL

Rich, Lee. Public broadcasting has become a joke. They spend more time fighting with each other than they do putting shows on the air.

White, E. B. Non-commercial television should address itself to the ideal of excellence, not the ideal of acceptability.

TELEVISION BROADCASTING—PROGRAMMING

Lear, Norman. TV executives don't make decisions based on their own sense of showmanship. They make decisions based on fear.

TELEVISION BROADCASTING—PROGRAMS

Hall, Monty. You can learn more about America by watching one half-hour of Let's Make a Deal than you can by watching Walter Cronkite for an entire month.

TELEVISION CHARACTERS

Colicos, John. Over the years I have discovered that villains are like blonds—they have more fun (commenting on playing a TV villain).

TELEVISION PERFORMERS

Moyers, Bill D. TV personalities are like celluloid. They're very perishable.

TELEVISION PROGRAMS

Logan, Ben. TV is hydraulic. You push down violence and up pops exploitative sex.

Randall, Tony. (Television is) producing such crap that the public is going to get tired of it very, very fast. It's garbage. But crap is my real word for it. I am supposed to be an intelligent, educated man, but I can't find a better word for it.

TELLER, EDWARD

Teller, Edward. I am forever described as the father of the H-bomb. I would much prefer to be known as the father of two wonderful children.

TEMPTATION

Cabell, James Branch. There is no memory with less satisfaction in it than the memory of some temptation we resisted.

Talbert, Bob. Resisting temptation is easier when you think you'll probably get another chance later on.

TENNIS

Anonymous, . Tennis isn't a matter of life and death—it's more important than that (sign at the John Gardiner Tennis Clinic, Warren, Vermont).

Court, Margaret. I will not play any more tournament tennis. If I had been meant to play tennis again, God would have led me to it (commenting upon her permanent retirement from tennis).

King, Billie Jean. Tennis is still a rich suburban game. Whites identify with tennis and hockey. Blacks identify with basketball and music.

Wilder, Roy. Tennis adds years to your life and life to your years.

TERROR

Fiedler, Leslie. There can be no terror without the hope for love and love's defeat.

Hitchcock, Alfred Joseph. There is no terror in a bang, only in the anticipation of it.

TERRORISM

Buchan, Alastair. Respectability depends on whose side you're on. To the Turks, Lawrence of Arabia was a terrorist.

John Paul II, Pope, . There is but one thing more dangerous than sin: the murder of man's sense of sin.

TERRORISM—GREAT BRITAIN

Mark, Sir Robert (chief of London's police force). To be perfectly blunt about it, what we are saying is that we are prepared to sacrifice the life of the hostages, if it comes to that. The only way to deal with these people is to make no deals at all (commenting on the British response to terrorists).

TERRORISM—ITALY

Crespi, Consuelo. In Italy now you want to feel rich and look poor.

Saragat, Giuseppe. Along-side the body of (Aldo) Moro lies the body of the first Italian republic.

TERRORISM—NETHERLANDS

Anonymous (member of the South Moluccan community), . Before and after each death, they prayed that God would forgive them. After every killing they wept a long time (explaining that the hijackers of a train in the Netherlands are deeply religious men, doing what they think they must).

Fonteijn, Abraham J (chief of Netherlands' police force). There is one basic approach and that is never give in (summarizing his government's response to terrorism).

TEXANS

Anonymous, . If God had meant for Texans to ski, He would have made bullshit white.

Dugger, Ronnie. To be from Texas will always have a kind of gusto to it.

TEXAS

Layne, Bobby. Living in a small town (Lubbock) in Texas ain't half bad—if you own it.

Samuels, John S., III. Texas is sort of an opera.

TEXAS—POLITICS AND GOVERNMENT

Barden, Charles (executive director of the Texas Air Control Board). We prefer economic growth to clean air.

TEXTBOOKS

Falwell, Jerry. Textbooks are Soviet propaganda.

THARP, TWYLA

Tharp, Twyla. I sometimes find structure a riot.

THATCHER, MARGARET HILDA

Healey, Denis. Mrs. Thatcher is doing for monetarism what the Boston Strangler did for door-to-door salesmen.

Thatcher, Margaret Hilda. I am controversial. That means I stand for something.

Thatcher, Margaret Hilda. I represent the workers, not the shirkers.

Thatcher, Margaret Hilda. I'm not a consensus politician, or a pragmatic politician, but a conviction politician.

Thatcher, Margaret Hilda. I've got fantastic stamina and great physical strength, and I've a woman's ability to stick to a job and get on with it when everyone else walks off and leaves it.

Thatcher, Margaret Hilda. Opportunity means nothing unless it includes the right to be unequal.

Thatcher, Margaret Hilda. Patience is not one of my obvious virtues.

Thatcher, Margaret Hilda. What Britain needs is an iron lady.

THEATER

De Mille, Agnes. The theater gives us one rule: don't be a bore.

Hayes, Helen. An audience simply cannot go on reacting indefinitely to a play that doesn't know where it's going.

Hayes, Helen. There is no racial or religious prejudice among people in the theater. The only prejudice is against bad actors, especially successful ones.

Kaufman, George. Satire is what closes Saturday night.

Mamet, David. I want to change the future of American theatre.

Simon, John. I love plays, but I love them in a different way. I'm not blind. I don't gush. I love the theater as it might be.

THEATRICAL PRODUCTION AND DIRECTION

Kubrick, Stanley. The essence of dramatic form is to let an idea come over people without its being plainly stated.

THEOLOGY

Esquerra, Maria Antonia (Chicana nun). The theology of liberation in North America will be written by the oppressed.

John Paul I, Pope, . Those who treat theology as a human science rather than a sacred science, or exaggerate their freedom lack faith.

THOMAS, CAITLIN

Thomas, Caitlin (wife of Dylan Thomas). Dylan wanted us to be young and unwise forever—to be permanently naughty children. He managed this by killing himself with booze, but I was left to grow old.

THOMAS, DYLAN

Thomas, Caitlin (wife of Dylan Thomas). Dylan wanted us to be young and unwise forever—to be permanently naughty children. He managed this by killing himself with booze, but I was left to grow old.

Thomas, Dylan. I've had eighteen straight whiskies. I think that is the record.

THOMAS, LOWELL

Thomas, Lowell. After the age of 80, everything reminds you of something else.

Thomas, Lowell. The best years have been all of my years.

THOMPSON, HUNTER S.

Thompson, Hunter S. I'm basically a lazy person. And proud of it.

Vonnegut, Kurt. Hunter Thompson's disease,...an incurable, fatal malady suffered by those who feel that Americans can be as easily led to beauty as to ugliness, to truth as to public relations, to joy as to bitterness.

THOMPSON, LORD ROY HERBERT

Thompson, Lord Roy Herbert. I am in business to make money, and I buy more newspapers to make more money to buy more newspapers.

Thompson, Lord Roy Herbert. My favorite music is the sound of radio commercials at $10 a whack.

Thompson, Lord Roy Herbert. No leisure, no pleasure, just work (commenting on the secret of his success).

THOUGHT AND ACTION

Bergson, Henri. Think like a man of action, and act like a man of thought.

Bruce, Lenny. I only said it, man. I didn't do it.

Fitzgerald, F. Scott. The test of a first-rate intelligence is the ability to hold two opposed ideas in the mind at the same time, and still retain the ability to function.

THOUGHT AND THINKING

Bergson, Henri. Think like a man of action, and act like a man of thought.

Eldridge, Paul. Man is always ready to die for an idea, provided that idea is not quite clear to him.

Fitzgerald, F. Scott. The test of a first-rate intelligence is the ability to hold two opposed ideas in the mind at the same time, and still retain the ability to function.

Ford, Henry. Thinking is the hardest work there is—which is probably the reason why so few engage in it.

Goncalves, Vasco dos Santos. Emotion is not incompatible with lucidity.

Harden, Frank. Every time you come up with a terrific idea, you find that someone else thought of it first.

James, William. A great many people think they are thinking when they are merely rearranging their prejudices.

* Kroc, Ray. If you think small, you'll stay small.

Laker, Freddie. The man that doesn't change his mind doesn't think.

Lippmann, Walter. When all think alike, no one is thinking.

Marquis, Don. If you make people think they're thinking, they'll love you; but if you really make them think, they'll hate you.

Newman, Edwin. I believe some silence is helpful to thought. And I believe to some extent radio and television discourage thought and reflection.

Whitehead, Alfred North. Nobody has a right to speak more clearly than he thinks.

Wilson, Robert Anton. If a man's ideas aren't frightening enough to get him imprisoned, you can be sure he's not really thinking something new and important.

THURMOND, STROM

Thurmond, Strom. There are not enough laws on the books of the nation, nor can there be enough laws, to break down segregation in the South (commenting in 1948 as he accepted the presidential nomination of the Dixiecrat Party).

TIFFANY'S, INC.

Hoving, Walter (Chairman of Tiffany's). Give the customer what Tiffany likes, because what it likes, the public ought to like.

TIME

Elgin, Duane S (futurologist). Once you discover that space doesn't matter, or that time can be traveled through at will so that time doesn't matter, and that matter can be moved by consciousness so that matter doesn't matter—well, you can't go home again.

Jones, Preston. I think I'm a story-teller playwright. But whatever the story is, for me it would always involve "time" because time is not the sun going up and down every day. It is not a clock. It is not a calendar. Time is an eroding, infinite mystery. Time is, in fact, a son-of-a-bitch.

Lewis, C. S. All that is not eternal is eternally out of date.

Vallee, Jacques. The theory of space and time is a cultural artifact made possible by the invention of graph paper.

Williams, Tennessee. Time is the longest distance between two places.

TIME (PERIODICAL)

Luce, Henry. I thought it was Time's job to make people unhappy and Life's job to make them happy.

TIME, USE OF

Rayburn, Sam. The three most important words in the English language are wait a minute.

TOBACCO

Zola, Emile. Perfection is such a nuisance that I often regret having cured myself of using tobacco.

TOMLIN, LILY

Tomlin, Lily. Sometimes I worry about being a success in a mediocre world.

TORRIJOS, OMAR

Anonymous (U.S. diplomat), . If Torrijos had not worked his charm on the senators, the (Panama Canal) treaties would simply be a dead letter.

TOSCANINI, ARTURO

Toscanini, Arturo. I kissed my first woman and smoked my first cigarette on the same day; I've never had time for tobacco since.

TOTALITARIANISM

Levy, Bernard-Henri. The only successful revolution of this century is totalitarianism.

TOUREL, JENNIE

Tourel, Jennie. You see, it isn't just boiled potatoes, what I do.

TOWNSHEND, PETE

Daltrey, Roger. The last thing I wanted to do was have a fist fight with Pete Townshend. Unfortunately, he hit me first with a guitar.

TRACK ATHLETICS

Weisenfeld, Murray (podiatrist). A runner once came to me and told me that he was in a 55-mile race, and at 35 miles he began to get foot cramps. He asked me what he should do. I told him to see a psychiatrist.

TRADE UNIONS

Barkan, Al. We're (AFL-CIO) going to have the best-organized, best-financed political force in the history of organized labor. No one else will have what we have. All we need is a candidate.

Fitzsimmons, Frank E. Personally, I don't think George Meany would know a trade unionist if he tripped over one.

Meany, George. Everything in this world that affects life, liberty and happiness is the business of the American trade union movement.

Murphy, Thomas A. (Chairman of General Motors Corporation). For years the motto of organized labor was said to be the single word 'more'. It has not changed, but now we also hear talk of 'less'—not less wages, not less benefits, but less work. The public will see—must see—that less work not balanced by increased productivity really means more cost.

Sadlowski, Ed. I guess maybe I'm a romantic, but I look on the American labor movement as a holy crusade, which should be the dominant force in this country to fight for the workingman and the underdog and make this a more just society.

Winpisinger, William (union leader). I don't mind being called a lefty. We're being centered to death.

Winpisinger, William (union leader). I have immense respect for George Meany, but there comes a time when every man passes the apex of his career, and it's all downhill after that. When the polls rate labor just behind Richard Nixon and just ahead of used car salesmen, you know something needs to be changed.

Winpisinger, William (union leader). In my lifetime, no group has ever gotten justice in this country without lawlessness. So if we want to see change, then we may have to stop having such a high regard for law-and-order.

TRADE UNIONS—GREAT BRITAIN

Callaghan, James. I was brought up to believe that free collective bargaining was the milk of the gospel. (But) if I went into the witness box today, having watched its operation over many years, I could not with honesty declare that it produced either justice for the weak or fairness between different groups.

TRADE UNIONS—ITALY

Anselmi, Tina (first Italian woman cabinet member). If people outside Italy have the impression that Italy is always on strike, that is because it is.

TRADE UNIONS—UNITED STATES

Kirkland, Lane. All sinners belong in the church; all citizens owe fealty to their country; and all true unions belong in the American Federation of Labor and Congress of Industrial Organizations.

TRAN-VAN-HUONG

Tran-van-Huong, . Thieu ran away from destiny; it has now come to me.

TRANSCENDENTAL MEDITATION

Graham, Billy. Transcendental Meditation is evil because...it opens space within you for the devil.

TRANSLATIONS AND TRANSLATING

Seymour, Steven. Translations are like women. When they are pretty, chances are they won't be very faithful.

TRAVEL

Disraeli, Benjamin. Travel teaches toleration.

Theroux, Paul. Travel is glamorous only in retrospect.

TRAVEL WITH CHILDREN

Benchley, Robert. Traveling with children corresponds roughly to traveling third class in Bulgaria.

TREATIES

De Gaulle, Charles. Treaties fade as quickly as young girls and roses.

TRILATERAL COMMISSION

Lord, Winston. The Trilateral Commission doesn't secretly run the world. The Council on Foreign Relations does that.

TROLLOPE, ANTHONY

James, Henry. (Anthony Trollope's) great, his inestimable merit was a complete appreciation of the usual.

TRUDEAU, MARGARET

Trudeau, Margaret. I was not so much a hippy as a failed hippy; a hippy without a cause.

Trudeau, Margaret. If I don't feel like wearing a bra I don't wear one. I'd never let my nipples show at a state function, though—I'd be frightened the old men would have heart attacks.

TRUFFAUT, FRANCOIS

Spielberg, Steven. Directing a movie with Truffaut on the set is like having Renoir around when you're still painting by numbers.

TRUMAN, HARRY S.

Carter, Rosalynn. When people ask me about Jimmy being a Baptist, and indicate they feel no Baptist can run the country, I just remind them that Harry Truman was a Baptist, and I think he did a great job.

Truman, Harry S. I never did give anybody hell. I just told the truth, and they thought it was hell.

Truman, Harry S. I vote for the better man. He is the democratic nominee.

TRUST

Frain, Andy. Never trust a man with a mustache or a man who carries an umbrella.

Johnson, Lyndon Baines. I never trust a man unless I've got his pecker in my pocket.

TRUSTS AND TRUSTEES

Holmes, Oliver Wendell. Put not your trust in money. Put your money in trust.

TRUTH

Barrymore, John. There's something about a closet that makes a skeleton terribly restless.

Hunt, Everette Howard. No one is entitled to the truth.

Huxley, Thomas. It is the customary fate of new truths to begin as heresies and to end as superstitions.

Jerome, Jerome K. It is always the best policy to speak the truth, unless of course you are an exceptionally good liar.

Keyserling, Hermann A. The greatest American superstition is belief in facts.

Leary, Timothy. You have to remember, the truth is funny.

Lukacs, John. I believe human nature doesn't change. I believe very strongly in original sin. I also take a dim view of the pursuit of justice as being the superior value of Western civilization. I think truth is more important than justice.

Norman, Edward. Truth does not cease because people give up believing it.

Rayburn, Sam. Son, always tell the truth. Then you'll never have to remember what you said the last time.

Santayana, George. Sometimes we have to change the truth in order to remember it.

Shaw, Henry Wheeler. As scarce as truth is, the supply has always been in excess of the demand.

Sitwell, Edith. The public will believe anything, so long as it is not founded on truth.

Strachey, Lytton. Uninterpreted truth is as useless as buried gold.

Tanner, Jack. What is counted as truth in one age is counted as myth in the next.

TURNER, R.E. (TED)

Turner, R. E. (Ted). If being against stuffiness and pompousness and bigotry is bad behavior, then I plead guilty.

TWEED, WILLIAM MARCY (BOSS)

Tweed, William Marcy (Boss). I've tried to do some good, even if I have not had good luck.

TWENTIETH CENTURY

Mailer, Norman. Ego is the word of the century.

Remarque, Erich Maria. Not to laugh at the 20th century is to shoot yourself.

Rowse, A. L. This filthy 20th century. I hate its guts.

Solzhenitsyn, Aleksandr Isaevich. Hastiness and superficiality are the psychic disease of the 20th century.

UDALL, MORRIS KING

Udall, Morris King. I am against vice in every form, including the Vice Presidency (responding to questions concerning the possibility of his accepting a vice presidential nomination).

Udall, Morris King. Obviously the Ford administration is very bad for this country. A Reagan administration would be much worse. I don't anticipate having any trouble supporting a Democratic candidate, whoever it is.

Udall, Morris King. The voters are the people who have spoken—the bastards (consoling his campaign workers with a story of what a politician, beaten in a close, hard-fought election once said).

Udall, Morris King. We fought a good fight, now we're here to help Jimmy Carter celebrate his victory (at the Democratic National Convention).

UGANDA—POLITICS AND GOVERNMENT

Amin Dada, Idi. I do not want people in government to play with other people's housewives.

Lule, Yusufu. Our strength and our success will depend on our unity.

UNDERDEVELOPED AREAS

Abdullah, Ismail Sabry. No nation, no matter how rich, can develop another country.

Boumedieane, Houari. Europe and the U.S. have plundered the natural wealth of the Third World. We should consider whatever contribution the industrialized countries make (to be) a simple restitution of a tiny part of the debt contracted by their odious exploitation.

McNamara, Robert Strange. It's not a frustration that my speeches have less impact on the U.S. It's a frustration that the U.S. has not, I think, given proper weight to the developing countries, even in its own narrow national interest.

Nam Duck Woo (Deputy Prime Minister of South Korea), . There is not one developing country in the world where Western democracy really works.

UNEMPLOYED

Becker, Jules. It is much harder to find a job than to keep one.

UNEMPLOYMENT

Hayden, Thomas. I don't believe that any defense contract ought to be cut in the face of mass unemployment.

UNEMPLOYMENT—RELIEF MEASURES

Leary, Timothy. There's no way you're going to have full employment in this country without a war or space migration... Only in space can we take steps in our evolution... Only there will we be able to expand intelligence and the human life span...

Reagan, Ronald. Unemployment insurance is a prepaid vacation plan for freeloaders.

UNITED FARM WORKERS UNION

Chavez, Cesar. We will win in the end. We learned many years ago that the rich may have the money, but the poor have the time.

Davis, Edward Michael. Now I don't think you can necessarily equate Farm Workers with people with unusual sexual preference, but I suppose you could call them united fruit workers.

UNITED MINE WORKERS

Miller, Arnold (U.M.W. President). Julius Caesar had his Brutus but I've got about a hundred Brutuses. The problems I have are not with the membership, it's with the elected officials and the staff.

UNITED NATIONS

Buckley, William Frank, Jr. The General Assembly long ago abdicated the authority to cause uproar. Do you get mad at the Bronx Zoo? We shouldn't pull out of the United Nations. We shouldn't stop debating in the General Assembly. But we should stop voting in it—permanently (upon the anti-Zionist vote in the UN General Assembly).

Crane, Philip. It is suicidal to pay the bills for an organization (the United Nations) whose goal has become world revolution, the stimulation of terrorist violence, and the destruction of the West.

Moynihan, Daniel Patrick. Even our sense of peoplehood grows uncertain as ethnic assertions take their implacable toll on the civic assumption of unity.

Moynihan, Daniel Patrick. For some time now, the United Nations has been showing a seemingly compulsive urge so to outrage those very principles on which it was founded, as to suggest that a sinister transmutation has occurred in an organism that yet enough remembers its own beginnings as to be revulsed by what it has become and somehow to seek expatriation in bringing on its own doom (upon the UN vote to equate Zionism with racism).

Moynihan, Daniel Patrick. If the U.N. didn't exist, it would be impossible to invent it.

Moynihan, Daniel Patrick. Totalitarianism is bad, gangsterism is worse, but capitulationism is the worst of all.

Richard, Ivor. The U.N. will not abolish sin, but it can make it more difficult for the sinner.

Waldheim, Kurt. The post of Secretary General is at the same time one of the most fascinating and one of the most frustrating jobs in the world, encompassing, as it does, the height of human aspiration and the depth of human frailty.

Wallace, George Corley. We told you years ago that the U.N. was a no-'count outfit.

UNITED STATES

Bell, Griffin. I think we have too many crimes, and I definitely have the view that we have too many laws.

Billington, James. Violence is not only "as American as cherry pie," it is likely to remain a la mode for some time to come.

Borges, Jorge Luis. America is still the best hope. But the Americans themselves will have to be the best hope too.

Boumedieane, Houari. Europe and the U.S. have plundered the natural wealth of the Third World. We should consider whatever contribution the industrialized countries make (to be) a simple restitution of a tiny part of the debt contracted by their odious exploitation.

Brooke, Edward William. If my years in public life have taught me anything, it is that nothing in this nation is separate but equal. Nothing could be worse for our country and our children than the resurrection of this immoral and illegal doctrine.

Brown, Edmund Gerald, Jr. People are ready to make sacrifices for the betterment of this country, but only on a basis that we all bear up the burdens and bear under them on an equal basis, and that is not happening today.

Brown, Edmund Gerald, Jr. There is a limit to the good things we have in this country. We're coming up against those limits. It's really a very salutary exercise to learn to live with them.

Buckley, William Frank, Jr. The General Assembly long ago abdicated the authority to cause uproar. Do you get mad at the Bronx Zoo? We shouldn't pull out of the United Nations. We shouldn't stop debating in the General Assembly. But we should stop voting in it—permanently (upon the anti-Zionist vote in the UN General Assembly).

Butz, Earl Lauer. Our capitalism is no longer capitalism; it is a weakened mixture of government regulations and limited business opportunities.

Chagall, Marc. My greatest weakness is America.

Chandler, A. B. (Happy). We Americans are a peculiar people. We are for the underdog no matter how much of a dog he is.

Davis, Angela. I'm not pessimistic about change in this country. I'm convinced that this country will one day be socialist.

Denver, John. I epitomize America.

Ehrlichman, John D. We operate in this country, and in the media and the courts, on a situational ethics base.

Falwell, Jerry (fundamentalist minister). Not only should we register them (Communists), but we should stamp it on their foreheads and send them back to Russia. This is a free country.

Ford, Gerald Rudolph. I did not take the sacred oath of office to preside over the decline and fall of America.

Ford, Henry, II. This country developed in a particular way because of the automobile, and you can't just push a button and change it.

Fuentes, Carlos. Mexicans have always asked themselves why a people so close to God should be so near the United States.

Hofstadter, Richard. The United States was the only country in the world that began with perfection and aspired to progress.

Hubbard, Elbert. This will never be a civilized country until we spend more money for books than we do for chewing gum.

Hungate, William. The electorate knows more and believes less and expresses it louder than at any time in history.

Jones, Mary Harris (Mother Jones). I asked a man in prison once how he happened to be there and he said he had stolen a pair of shoes. I told him if he had stolen a railroad he would be a United States Senator.

Kaida, Ivan Ivanovich. First, I was a man without a country, then I was a man without land. Now I am truly rich, for I have both.

Kennedy, John Fitzgerald. If we are strong, our strength will speak for itself. If we are weak, words will be no help.

Keyserling, Hermann A. The greatest American superstition is belief in facts.

Kissinger, Henry Alfred. The American body politic is basically healthy. Our people want to believe in their government.

Kovic, Ron. The government took the best years of my life away from me and millions of other young men. I just think they're lucky I wrote a book instead of buying a gun.

Ky, Nguyen Cao. I was not corrupt. Perhaps that is the only thing I regret. I realized after 14 months in this country the value of money, whether it's clean or dirty.

Lynd, Staughton. The best way to be a radical in America would be to be so much a part of the situation in which you were that you didn't need to be a radical. You could just live the situation as opposed to coming in and organizing it.

McGovern, George Stanley. Thoughtful Americans understand that the highest patriotism is not a blind acceptance of official policy, but a love of one's country deep enough to call her to a higher standard.

McHarg, Ian. Give us your poor and oppressed and we will give them Harlem and the Lower East Side, Bedford-Stuyvesant, the South Side of Chicago, and the North of Philadelphia—or, if they are very lucky, Levittown.

McNamara, Robert Strange. It's not a frustration that my speeches have less impact on the U.S. It's a frustration that the U.S. has not, I think, given proper weight to the developing countries, even in its own narrow national interest.

Marchesi, Joseph. Only an immigrant can appreciate America (upon revisiting Ellis Island, where he arrived as an immigrant in 1919).

Martin, Abe. What this country needs is a good five-cent cigar.

Mauldin, Bill. We have more provincialism and bigotry and superstition and prejudice per square mile than almost any other nation.

Mencken, Henry Louis. No one ever went broke underestimating the intelligence of the American people.

Miyazawa, Kiichi (Foreign Minister of Japan). What you have lost is not a war but a cause, and your credibility has not really suffered because it is widely known that the people you were trying to help could not really help themselves.

Montaner, Carlos Alberto. The U.S. is a neurotic Midas who homogenizes everything he touches.

Morris, Richard B. The United States is still the last best hope of man.

Moynihan, Daniel Patrick. As the lights go out in the rest of the world, they shine all the brighter here.

Nader, Ralph. I'll tell you what the real problem is. We ask people to think, instead of asking them to believe. And history has always gone to those who ask people to believe.

Ravenal, James C. The American Century is over. The era of American dominance and control, heralded by Henry Luce and established in the wake of World War II, lasted only 25 years. Of course, everyone knows that it is over. But our policy-makers have not absorbed this message, and our nation has not begun to adjust to its implications and consequences.

Reagan, Ronald. I always grew up believing that if you build a better mousetrap, the world will beat a path to your door. Now if you build a better mousetrap the government comes along with a better mouse.

Reagan, Ronald. I don't know of anyone today that has less influence in this country than business.

Rexroth, Kenneth. The one country I feel at home in is Japan. I don't feel at home here. I don't like a country where traffic cops are armed to the teeth (commenting on life in the U.S.).

Rockefeller, Nelson Aldrich. Free enterprise is the greatest and most productive system man has ever created. In a modest way, I have been a beneficiary.

Sevareid, Eric. We are a turbulent society but a stable republic. The mind goes blank at the thought of a world without one such power.

Smith, Howard K. The Cubans may be hostile to America, but they love Americans.

Udall, Morris King. I am saying we have to make fundamental changes in this country, that we are at the end of an era of cheap energy and resources, that the 70's and 80's are going to be a time of adaptation.

Vidal, Gore. To understand Mary Hartman is to understand America. If Tiberius had watched the show, he would still be alive today.

Voigt, Jon. The real dream (of America) is that with independence there is more strength and more beauty.

Wattenberg, Ben. How can a nation that believes it hasn't done anything right in the recent past even consider that it can do anything right, or bold, or creative in the immediate future.

Will, George. World War II was the last government program that really worked (to the Association of American Publishers).

Wolf, Arnold Jacob. America, where were you when we needed you? And we, where are we now that you need us?.

UNITED STATES. AIR FORCE
Matlovich, Leonard P. They gave me a medal for killing two men and discharged me for loving one.

UNITED STATES—APPROPRIATION AND EXPENDITURES
Wicker, Tom. Government expands to absorb revenue—and then some.

UNITED STATES—ARMED FORCES
Ford, Gerald Rudolph. You can be certain that I have just begun to fight. America's armed forces today are second to none. And I will take whatever steps are necessary to see that they remain second to none.

UNITED STATES. BUREAU OF INDIAN AFFAIRS
Tayac, Turkey (Chief of the Piscataway Indians). They don't know about Indians any more than a buzzard knows about ice cream (about the Bureau of Indian Affairs).

UNITED STATES—CENTENNIAL CELEBRATIONS, ETC.
Williams, Robert. There's nothing wrong with making a buck. Free enterprise is the thing that has made this country go zowee (about the sale of Bicentennial products).

UNITED STATES. CENTRAL INTELLIGENCE AGENCY
Agee, Philip. The CIA claims that secrecy is necessary to hide what it's doing from the enemies of the United States. I claim that the real reason for secrecy is to hide what the CIA is doing from the American people.

Agee, Philip. The CIA is nothing more than the secret police of American capitalism, plugging up leaks in the political dam night and day so that shareholders of U.S. companies operating in poor countries can continue enjoying their rip-off.

Alsop, Joseph. I'm proud they (CIA) asked me (to aid them) and proud to have done it. The notion that a newspaperman doesn't have a duty to his country is perfect balls.

Angleton, James. Our generation believed that you go in naked and you leave naked (about working for the CIA).

Aspin, Les. It's a kind of mongoose-cobra relationship (about the press and the CIA).

Bissell, Richard M. I believe they worked without pay for the most part (on the role of the Mafia in the CIA Castro murder plots).

Colby, William Egan. By the way, *did* you ever work for the CIA? (to Bob Woodward upon agreeing to issue an official denial that Woodward had ever worked for the CIA).

Colby, William Egan. I'm convinced it's possible to run a secret agency as part of a constitutional society.

Ford, Gerald Rudolph. We cannot improve this agency by destroying it (commenting on the CIA at the installation ceremony for George Bush as director).

Goldwater, Barry Morris. I think there are some things which we don't want to know. Nothing could make the Soviets happier than to see our wonderful intelligence system destroyed (in suggesting that Congressional probes of the CIA be called off).

Harriman, Averell. The Russians are not nuts, they are not crazy people, they're not Hitler. But they are trying to dominate the world by their ideology and we are killing the one instrument which we have to fight that ideology, the CIA.

Harris, Fred. We've got to dismantle the monster (about the CIA).

Helms, Richard McGarrah. I think he was yielding to that human impulse of the greater good (explaining why the CIA scientist in charge of the Chemical Weapons Division did not destroy shellfish toxin as ordered by President Nixon).

Helms, Richard McGarrah. If I ever do decide to talk, there are going to be some very embarrassed people in this town, you can bet on that (commenting after testifying to the Watergate Committee on CIA involvement in domestic intelligence operations).

Helms, Richard McGarrah. We're not in the Boy Scouts (about the Central Intelligence Agency).

McGovern, George Stanley. We can mark it down that the ghost of Joe McCarthy still stalks this land (commenting on the treatment of Theodore Sorensen as Carter's nominee for the directorship of the CIA).

Mankiewicz, Frank Fabian. The Rockefeller report was the first report that was a smear and whitewash at the same time.

Mondale, Walter Frederick. It shows above all that Americans are no good at all at killing, lying and covering up and I'm glad that's the case (on CIA assassination attempts on foreign leaders).

Mondale, Walter Frederick. There must be some fundamental changes in America's intelligence activities or they will fundamentally change America.

Osborn, Kenneth Barton. There *are* icebergs, and we are the Titanic (about the Central Intelligence Agency).

Sorensen, Theodore Chaikin. To continue fighting for this post, (the directorship of the CIA) which would be my natural inclination, would only handicap the new administration if I am rejected, or handicap my effectiveness if confirmed.

Terkel, Studs. I would like to see the end of institutional brutalities and stupidities. I would like to see the abolition of the CIA, which symbolizes those things, and I would like people to look at the FBI as the secret police system it is, rather than something sacred.

UNITED STATES. COMMISSION ON CIA ACTIVITIES WITHIN THE UNITED STATES

Mankiewicz, Frank Fabian. The Rockefeller report was the first report that was a smear and whitewash at the same time.

UNITED STATES. CONGRESS

Abourezk, James. The bigger the appropriations bill, the shorter the debate.

Church, Frank. If we are to preserve freedom and keep constitutional government alive in America, it cannot be left to a President and his agents alone to decide what must be kept secret. Congress, if it is to check the abuse of executive power, must retain its right to inquiry and independent judgement.

Cohen, William. Congress is designed to be slow and inefficient because it represents the total diversity of this country.

Connally, John Bowden. The power of this country, in spite of all the misconceptions that exist, is in the Congress of the United States and not in the White House.

Ford, Gerald Rudolph. My motto towards the Congress is communication, conciliation, compromise and cooperation.

Harrington, Michael. We've created a kind of gray, shadowy atmosphere which is 'just don't get us involved.' Well, I think the guy on the street expects us to solve real problems and not just generate the impression of looking busy when we're not doing anything that counts.

Jones, Charles. A shift of power (toward Congress) that started because of Nixon's arrogance has continued because of Carter's artlessness.

Pastore, John O. This has become a Government by veto. We've got the minority dragging the majority around by the nose.

Rockefeller, Nelson Aldrich. Congressional actions in the past few years, however well intentioned, have hamstrung the presidency and usurped the presidential prerogative in the conduct of foreign affairs.

Rogers, Will. There is good news from Washington today. The Congress is deadlocked and can't act.

Rosenthal, Benjamin. Kissinger prefers to deal with great men and world leaders, partly because it makes for better history writing. But he must deal with Congress because we reflect the will of the American people.

Wright, James. The Wright broad rule is that broads ought to be able to type (commenting when asked to state a broad rule for avoiding Congressional sex scandals).

UNITED STATES. CONGRESS. HOUSE

Bauman, Robert E. Anytime the House is in session the American people are probably in danger.

Hastings, James F. I came up to age 49 without having a great deal to show for it. Taking a look around at the next 12 to 14 years of productive life, I decided I couldn't spend it here under the circumstances and frustrations I see in this legislative body (upon his mid-term resignation as a U.S. congressman).

Schroeder, Patricia. We need some nannies around here for the boys. We need some warm milk, we need some cookies, and then maybe we can have a little better decorum in this body and be able to deal with a little more substance (about the House of Representatives).

UNITED STATES. CONGRESS. HOUSE. SELECT COMMITTEE ON INTELLIGENCE

Colby, William Egan. From the draft of the committee report that I have seen and the news stories about it, I believe it is totally biased and a disservice to our nation (referring to the report by the House Select Committee on Intelligence).

UNITED STATES. CONGRESS. SENATE

Aiken, George David. I have never seen so many incompetent persons in high office. Politics and legislation have become more mixed and smellier than ever (commenting on the U.S. Senate in his book Aiken: Senate Diary).

Byrd, Robert. The Senate is very much like a violin. The sound will change with the weather, the dampness, the humidity. The Senate is a place of great moods.

Harris, Fred. If I had it to do over I would have started out the way I wound up, as more of an iconoclast. There was a feeling when I went to the Senate that if you want to have any influence you had to go along. The truth is just the opposite of that.

Humphrey, Hubert Horatio. The Senate is a place filled with goodwill and good intentions, and if the road to hell is paved with them, then it's a pretty good detour.

Kennedy, Edward Moore. The people I respected most in the Senate—Phil Hart, for example—said you measure accomplishments not by climbing mountains, but by climbing molehills.

Pastore, John O. I've always been weary of people who stayed on too long—stalwarts in their day who end up being held up by their staff. I don't want to mention any names. I wouldn't let that happen to me.

Rockefeller, Nelson Aldrich. I would like to apologize to the Senate of the United States, to its members, and particularly to Senator Jackson for my remarks in an off-the-record meeting. There is no question it was a mistake (apologizing for suggesting that two members of Senator Henry M. Jackson's staff had Communist ties).

Rockefeller, Nelson Aldrich. The best part about being Vice President is presiding over the Senate. Where else could I have Barry Goldwater addressing me as 'Mr. President?'.

UNITED STATES—CONGRESS—STAFF

Ray, Elizabeth. I can't type. I can't file. I can't even answer the phone.

UNITED STATES—CONSTITUTION

Douglas, William Orville. The press has a preferred position in our constitutional scheme not to enable it to make money, not to set newsmen apart as a favored class, but to bring fulfillment to the public's right to know.

Jefferson, Thomas. Our peculiar security is the possession of a written constitution. Let us not make it a blank paper by construction.

Jordan, Barbara. My faith in the Constitution is whole—complete—total.

Marshall, John. The peculiar circumstances of the moment may render a measure more or less wise, but cannot render it more or less constitutional.

Wirin, Abraham Lincoln. The rights of all persons are wrapped in the same constitutional bundle as those of the most hated member of the community.

UNITED STATES—CONSTITUTION— AMENDMENTS

Faulk, John Henry. I was taught that the first ten amendments were sacrosanct, that they're the engine by which this society runs and I admire people who cherish them and loathe and despise people who would circumvent and destroy them. So it took no act of courage to do what I did. It was an act of principle. What else would you do? I like to think all American people would do the same thing if they felt the way I did.

Reagan, Ronald. Human beings are not animals, and I do not want to see sex and sexual differences treated as casually and amorally as dogs and other beasts treat them. I believe this could happen under the ERA.

UNITED STATES—CONSTITUTION— AMENDMENTS—FIRST AMENDMENT

Cline, Ray S. The First Amendment is not the central purpose of our Constitution.

Dershowitz, Alan. Screw is a despicable magazine, but that's what the First Amendment was designed to protect.

Ephron, Nora. For those of us who believe that Hustler is a truly obscene magazine, it is a difficult moment. It is one of those cases that makes you search for some loophole (commenting on the Hustler pornography case).

UNITED STATES—CONSTITUTION—BILL OF RIGHTS

Goldwater, Barry Morris, Jr. Without a sense of privacy, the Bill of Rights' guarantees cease to function.

Hayden, Thomas. If it weren't for the Bill of Rights people like me would be in jail instead of running for office (commenting on his bid for the Senate).

UNITED STATES. DEPARTMENT OF DEFENSE

McCarthy, Eugene Joseph. The selling of arms is now one of the principal occupations of the Defense Department.

UNITED STATES. DEPARTMENT OF ENERGY

Orben, Robert. I feel that if God had really wanted us to have enough oil, He never would have given us the Department of Energy.

UNITED STATES. DEPARTMENT OF HEALTH, EDUCATION, AND WELFARE. OFFICE OF EDUCATION

Ryor, John (National Education Association president). It's just about as useless as a back pocket in a shirt (commenting on the value of the U.S. Office of Education).

UNITED STATES. DEPARTMENT OF LABOR

Usery, William J. Even though I don't have a teamsters card, I belong to this club because I believe in it.

UNITED STATES. DEPARTMENT OF STATE

Cooper, Chester L. There are a lot of ambitious guys who are neither bright nor able, yet they do well. The guy who's willing to cancel his wife's birthday party is the guy who's likely to become an assistant secretary of state.

UNITED STATES—DESCRIPTION

Boorstin, Daniel. We suffer primarily not from our vices or our weaknesses, but from our illusions.

Buchwald, Art. As the economy gets better, everything else gets worse.

Commoner, Barry. Our system today no more resembles free enterprise than a freeway resembles a dirt road.

Douglas, William Orville. The great and invigorating influences in American life have been the unorthodox; the people who challenge an existing institution or way of life, or say and do things that make people think.

Eisenhower, Dwight David. It has been the tough-minded optimist whom history has proved right in America.

Erish, Andrew. America is 90 percent corn.

Fairlie, Henry. The once rambunctious American spirit of innovation and adventurousness is today being paralyzed by the desire to build a risk-free society.

Foley, Thomas S. There is a mood in this country that government action is not necessarily always the perfect solution to social problems.

Hellman, Lillian. We have no national memory.

Jordan, Hamilton. Perhaps the strongest feeling in this country today (1972) is the general distrust and disillusionment of government and politicians at all levels.

Morgan, Ted. One has come to America to get a sense of life's possibilities.

Rahv, Philip. Nothing can last in America more than ten years.

Sawyer, Charles. The United States, like Atlas, is holding up the world. But who holds up Atlas? American business.

Solzhenitsyn, Aleksandr Isaevich. To defend oneself, one must also be ready to die; there is little such readiness in a society raised in the cult of material well-being.

UNITED STATES—ECONOMIC CONDITIONS

Carter, James Earl. There is nothing for nothing.

Harris, Fred. Our current economic problems are not a failure of the system, they are a failure of economic leadership.

Iacocca, Lee A. I don't want to mislead anyone or to spread false hope—unemployment is awful. From the bottom of the trough we're in, it's a long climb back to business as usual. Even with all the qualification, however, things are getting better, not worse.

Laffer, Arthur. The U.S. is the fastest 'undeveloping' country in the world.

Simon, William E. Surely this (Carter) Administration will go down in history as the worst stewards of the American economy in our lifetime.

Volcker, Paul A. The standard of living of the average American has to decline.

UNITED STATES—ECONOMIC RELATIONS—EUROPE

Rothschild, Emma. For the last 20 years, America's influence on Europe has had more to do with food and animal feed than with high politics or low diplomacy.

UNITED STATES—ECONOMIC RELATIONS—VIETNAM

Kissinger, Henry Alfred. Among the many claims on American resources, I would put those of Vietnam in alphabetical order.

UNITED STATES—ENERGY POLICY

Simon, William E. My education in the energy realm was not complete until I truly understood the nature of the oil hysteria of the liberal Democrats. It is a symbolic mania sheltered by a profound refusal to look at the facts.

UNITED STATES. FEDERAL AVIATION ADMINISTRATION

Miller, Patricia Robertson. The airlines spell safety with a dollar sign and the FAA practices regulation by death.

UNITED STATES. FEDERAL BUREAU OF INVESTIGATION

Johnson, Al (Patricia Hearst's defense attorney). I remember when the Chowchilla kidnapping occurred. Patty (Hearst) said she wondered how long it would take the FBI to indict the 26 children for the crime.

Kelley, Clarence M. If we are to have any degree of success in solving the cases now confronting us in terrorist, espionage, and other major security matters, we must have all the tools available to us—including electronic surveillance (suggesting before a Palm Beach, California civic group that Congress authorize the use of wiretaps and bugs for the FBI).

Moore, George C. No, we never gave it a thought (in response to whether the FBI had ever discussed the constitutional or legal authority for its Cointelpro Program).

Morgan, Charles, Jr. If I were in New York and I were on the other side of the law...I would think about moving somewhere else fast.

Terkel, Studs. I would like to see the end of institutional brutalities and stupidities. I would like to see the abolition of the CIA, which symbolizes those things, and I would like people to look at the FBI as the secret police system it is, rather than something sacred.

Weir, David. The SLA is not only a dream story to the newspapers, it is a dream story to the FBI as well, because it allows them to paint the entire left with the brush of the SLA.

UNITED STATES. FEDERAL BUREAU OF INVESTIGATION—RELATIONS—ORAL SEX

Hoover, John Edgar. I regret to say that we of the FBI are powerless to act in cases of oral-genital intimacy, unless it has in some way obstructed interstate commerce.

UNITED STATES. FEDERAL COMMUNICATIONS COMMISSION

Johnson, Nicholas. Most of what I did as a government official was try to encourage more competition, by having smaller enterprises that would truly compete, by removing barriers to entry, by relieving the dependence of business on large government payments and I was opposed at every step and turn of the way, by businessmen.

UNITED STATES—FOREIGN OPINION

Morrow, Lance. It bewilders Americans to be hated.

UNITED STATES—FOREIGN POLICY

Brown, Harold. A lesson we learned from Viet Nam is that we should be very cautious about intervening in any place where there's a poor political base for our presence.

Brzezinski, Zbigniew. A big country like the U.S. is not like a speedboat on a lake. It can't veer suddenly to the right or left. It's like a large ship. There's continuity to its course.

Brzezinski, Zbigniew. By the time we're through, the world will have been reordered.

Brzezinski, Zbigniew. Pessimism is a luxury that policymakers can't afford because pessimism, on the part of people who try to shape events, can become a self-fulfilling prophecy.

Carter, James Earl. I am against any creation of a separate Palestinian state.

Carter, James Earl. We are now free of that inordinate fear of Communism which once led us to embrace any dictator who joined us in our fear.

Eaton, Cyrus S. We must either learn to live with the Communists or resign ourselves to perish with them.

Giscard D'Estaing, Valery. You do not fear freedom for yourself, do not then fear it for your friends and allies.

Graff, Henry. Vance is a practitioner of turtle diplomacy.

Kennedy, Edward Moore. We cannot afford a foreign policy based on the pangs of unrequitted love.

Kennedy, John Fitzgerald. Domestic policy can only defeat us; foreign policy can kill us.

Kennedy, John Fitzgerald. Let every nation know, whether it wishes us well or ill, we shall pay any price, bear any burden, meet any hardship, support any friend or oppose any foe to assure the survival and the success of liberty.

Kissinger, Henry Alfred. I have always thought of foreign policy as bipartisan.

Kissinger, Henry Alfred. My impression is that there is unanimity on the course that we are pursuing. It would be a tragedy if during this election year we did not find some means to put some restraint on our domestic debates in the field of foreign policy.

McGovern, George Stanley. I think it's going to be a fascinating experience...to be required, after twenty years away from the classroom, to systematically organize my thoughts on foreign policy.

Meany, George. Foreign policy is too damned important to be left to the Secretary of State.

Moynihan, Daniel Patrick. Totalitarianism is bad, gangsterism is worse, but capitulationism is the worst of all.

Reagan, Ronald. I'm beginning to wonder if the symbol of the United States pretty soon isn't going to be an ambassador with a flag under his arm climbing into the escape helicopter.

Reagan, Ronald. The (Carter) administration doesn't know the difference between being a diplomat and a doormat.

Reagan, Ronald. Treaties invite nationalization.

Riegle, Donald. Henry Kissinger is pregnant with America's foreign policy, and we're all waiting for him to give birth.

Rogers, William D. Making foreign policy is a little bit like making pornographic movies. It's more fun doing it than watching it.

Rosenthal, Benjamin. Kissinger prefers to deal with great men and world leaders, partly because it makes for better history writing. But he must deal with Congress because we reflect the will of the American people.

Schlesinger, James Rodney. The American role in maintaining a worldwide military balance is better understood in Moscow than it is in this country.

Schmidt, Helmut. He (Jimmy Carter) is making (foreign) policy from the pulpit.

Weicker, Lowell Palmer. Those who insist on walking backward into the future, with their faces turned resolutely to the past, run a very high risk of falling on their butts. We can not afford to approach the 21st Century with 19th Century foreign policy.

Yew, Lee Kuan. The Russians say that there are many different roads to socialism, and that sounds good to new nations. But the United States seems to be saying that there is only one road to democracy.

UNITED STATES—FOREIGN POLICY—CIVIL RIGHTS

Vance, Cyrus R. In pursuing a human rights policy, we must always keep in mind the limits of our power and of our wisdom.

UNITED STATES—FOREIGN POLICY—CUBA

Benes, Bernardo. It is up to Jimmy Carter to say, 'Yes, I believe in human rights' (on President Castro's offer to let political prisoners to come to the United States).

Eaton, Cyrus S. I've been going to Cuba for 60 years. I think our policy is wrong there, just as it was in Vietnam (discussing his planned invitation to visit Cuba).

UNITED STATES—FOREIGN POLICY—RUSSIA

Solzhenitsyn, Aleksandr Isaevich. Mr. Kissinger always has an emergency exit available to him. He can transfer to a university to lecture to credulous youngsters about the art of diplomacy. But the government of the United States will have no emergency exit.

UNITED STATES—FOREIGN POLICY—VIETNAM

Kissinger, Henry Alfred. Among the many claims on American resources, I would put those of Vietnam in alphabetical order.

UNITED STATES—FOREIGN POPULATION

Trachtenberg, Alan. Ellis Island represented the opening American act of one of the most remarkable dramas in all of history: the conversion of agricultural laborers, rural homemakers and traditional craftsmen into urban industrial workers.

UNITED STATES—FOREIGN RELATIONS

Brzezinski, Zbigniew. We live in a world in which there will be many local conflicts, in which all the major powers will exercise self-restraint, because they have to exercise self-restraint in the nuclear...it will be a sign of the maturity of the American people and of the growing wisdom of the American people if we adjust ourselves to the notion that in our age there is a twilight zone between war and peace and that this twilight zone of limited wars is going to be very much a feature of our lifetime.

Ford, Gerald Rudolph. I don't think the United States should ever involve itself in the internal situation in any country.

Fulbright, James William. A great nation is peculiarly susceptible to the idea that its power is a sign of God's favor, conferring upon it a special responsibility for other nations—to make them richer and happier and wiser, to remake them, that is, in its own shining image. Power confuses itself with virtue and tends also to take itself for omnipotence (comments made in the 1960s).

Giscard D'Estaing, Valery. You do not fear freedom for yourself, do not then fear it for your friends and allies.

Harris, Fred. Sometimes it seems we are willing to prop up any two-bit dictator who can afford the price of a pair of sunglasses.

Kissinger, Henry Alfred. We are not going around looking for opportunities to prove our manhood.

Lippmann, Walter. I think there is a stopping point between globalism and isolationism. The test of statesmanship is to find those stopping points and to act accordingly (comments in a critique of Vietnam policy in 1965).

Rockefeller, Nelson Aldrich. Congressional actions in the past few years, however well intentioned, have hamstrung the presidency and usurped the presidential prerogative in the conduct of foreign affairs.

Wallace, George Corley. I don't mind dictatorships abroad provided they are pro-American.

UNITED STATES—FOREIGN RELATIONS— ANGOLA

Dellums, Ronald V. There are not many Vietnamese constituents in America and that is why it took 12 years to develop a broad base of support against that war. But it won't take 25 million black people 12 years to mobilize against American involvement in Angola.

Diggs, Charles C. As an American, I regret that the United States has allowed the Soviet Union to become identified as the principal supporter of African liberation.

Kissinger, Henry Alfred. If we do not meet the Russian challenge now at modest cost we will find it necessary to do so further down the road when it will be more costly and more dangerous (commenting on why U.S. aid is needed in Angola).

UNITED STATES—FOREIGN RELATIONS—ARAB STATES

Arafat, Yasir. The future of the United States of America, the American interest in this part of the world, is with the Arab people, not with Israel.

UNITED STATES—FOREIGN RELATIONS—ASIA

Marcos, Ferdinand E. Not only the occurrences in Vietnam, but the aspirations of the new nations in Asia seem to have brought about a changed situation which challenges the historic commitment of the United States to the peace and stability of the region.

UNITED STATES—FOREIGN RELATIONS— BRAZIL

Nixon, Richard Milhous. As Brazil goes, so will the rest of the Latin American continent (commenting in 1971).

UNITED STATES—FOREIGN RELATIONS—CHINA (PEOPLE'S REPUBLIC)

Mao, Tse-Tung. If the Americans do not recognize us in 1,000 years, they will recognize us in 1,001 years.

Mao, Tse-Tung. Sometimes we have only to fart to stir Americans into moving a battleship or two or even a whole fleet.

UNITED STATES—FOREIGN RELATIONS—CUBA

Kennedy, Robert Francis (attributed by Bill Moyers). I have myself wondered if we did not pay a very great price for being more energetic than wise about a lot of things, especially Cuba.

UNITED STATES—FOREIGN RELATIONS— ISRAEL

Anonymous (State Department Spokesman), . It will take us two years to repair the damage Scott did in these couple of weeks (commenting on Senator Scott's "fact-finding" tour of the Middle East).

Arafat, Yasir. The future of the United States of America, the American interest in this part of the world, is with the Arab people, not with Israel.

Carter, James Earl. I'd rather commit political suicide than hurt Israel.

Carter, James Earl. The survival of Israel is not a political issue. It is a moral imperative.

Neff, Donald. To state it crudely, it appears that since the U.S. cannot negotiate peace in the Middle East, it will buy it.

Scott, William. What's this Gaza stuff? I never have understood that (to Israeli Prime Minister Yitzhak Rabin).

Shafat, Gershon. Kissinger is a disaster. His priorities are: one, Kissinger; two, the President; three, the U.S. Israel is nowhere among them.

UNITED STATES—FOREIGN RELATIONS— KOREA (REPUBLIC)

McGovern, George Stanley. In this campaign, the Democratic Party and its candidates must demand an orderly withdrawal of American forces from Korea within a specified time. It would take no more than a year to leave; it might take as long as the decade of Vietnam to stay and bleed and die and lose. This time let us make peace before the making of a war.

UNITED STATES—FOREIGN RELATIONS—LATIN AMERICA

Reagan, Ronald. The Latin American countries have a respect for *macho*. I think if the United States reacts with firmness and fairness, we might not earn their love, but we would earn their respect.

UNITED STATES—FOREIGN RELATIONS— MEXICO

Castaneda, Jorge. We would like to see the U.S. treat us (Mexico) as an adult country capable of managing our own affairs.

Portillo, Jose Lopez. Mexico is neither on the list of United States priorities nor on that of United States respect.

UNITED STATES—FOREIGN RELATIONS— MIDDLE EAST

Kissinger, Henry Alfred. All the Russians can offer is war, but we can bring the peace (commenting on the Mideast situation).

Schindler, Rabbi Alexander. The world isn't used to your (Jimmy Carter's) open diplomacy. It stiffens the back of Israel and raises the expectations of the Arabs, which, once frustrated, will retard rather than bring peace.

UNITED STATES—FOREIGN RELATIONS— NICARAGUA

Vaky, Viron Peter. No negotiation, mediation or compromise can be achieved any longer with a Somoza government.

UNITED STATES—FOREIGN RELATIONS— PANAMA

Goldwater, Barry Morris. I would have said that we should fight for the (Panama) canal if necessary. But the Viet Nam years have taught me that we wouldn't. So we might as well hand it over.

UNITED STATES—FOREIGN RELATIONS— PHILIPPINES

Beveridge, Albert J. The Philippines are ours forever. They are not capable of self-government. How could they be? They are not of a self-governing race (comments made in 1900).

UNITED STATES—FOREIGN RELATIONS— RUSSIA

Ford, Gerald Rudolph. Detente means moderate and restrained behavior between two superpowers—not a license to fish in troubled waters.

Harriman, Averell. People read into 'detente' a situation that doesn't exist. They get 'detente' mixed up with 'rapprochement'. Detente means the relaxation of tensions between nations. My experience is that the Russians are suspicious as hell, but Brezhnev is absolutely committed to peace. It takes patience. If we let the Pentagon have its way, we'll have war.

Kissinger, Henry Alfred. If we do not meet the Russian challenge now at modest cost we will find it necessary to do so further down the road when it will be more costly and more dangerous (commenting on why U.S. aid is needed in Angola).

Kissinger, Henry Alfred. The cold war was not so terrible and detente was not so exalting.

Morris, Roger. Detente is now suffering from the fact that it was deliberately obscured as diplomacy and oversold as politics.

Nixon, Richard Milhous. We are now in a war called peace.

UNITED STATES—FOREIGN RELATIONS— SOUTH AFRICA

Vorster, John. It's fast reaching the state where we feel that the United States wants to prescribe to us (South Africa) how we should run our country internally and that is of course unacceptable to us. It is a fool who doesn't listen to advice but nobody can allow outsiders however well-intentioned, whatever their motives, to meddle in their internal affairs.

UNITED STATES—HISTORY—CIVIL WAR

Lincoln, Abraham. So this is the little lady who made this big war (comment upon meeting Harriet Beecher Stowe).

UNITED STATES—INTELLECTUAL LIFE

Boorstin, Daniel J. The courage we inherit from our Jeffersons and Lincolns and others is not the Solzhenitsyn courage of the true believer, but the courage to doubt.

Rand, Ayn. The state of today's culture is so low that I do not care to spend my time watching and discussing it.

Sills, Beverly. We have taste, and if we like something we should be verbal about it. We are behind Europe in only one way and that is in government subsidization (commenting on why Americans should be proud of their own culture).

UNITED STATES. LIBRARY OF CONGRESS

MacLeish, Archibald. What we know to be man is in these stacks (about the Library of Congress).

UNITED STATES MILITARY ACADEMY, WEST POINT

Bunting, Josiah. The (West Point honor) code is an anachronism but a good anachronism.

MacArthur, Douglas. Duty, honor, country: Those three hallowed words reverently dictate what you want to be, what you can be, and what you will be...The long gray line has never failed us (at the U.S. Military Academy at West Point, May 12, 1962).

UNITED STATES—MILITARY POLICY

Anonymous, . Any country that goes to this much trouble to account for every soldier it loses probably ought not to fight a war.

Haig, Alexander M. The arms race is the only game in town.

Hayden, Thomas. I don't believe that any defense contract ought to be cut in the face of mass unemployment.

Kissinger, Henry Alfred. We now face the challenge of the early '80s with forces designed in the '60s.

Kissinger, Henry Alfred. We should have bombed the hell out of them the minute we got into office (a week after the 1973 Vietnam peace agreement).

McGovern, George Stanley. He who tugs Uncle Sam's beard too hard risks reprisal from the mightiest nation on the face of this earth.

Reagan, Ronald. Of the four wars in my lifetime, none came about because the U.S. was too strong.

Schlesinger, James Rodney. The American role in maintaining a worldwide military balance is better understood in Moscow than it is in this country.

Schroeder, Patricia. When men talk about defense, they always claim to be protecting women and children, but they never ask the women and children what they think.

UNITED STATES—MILITARY POLICY—IRAN

Khomeini, Ayatollah Ruhollah. We (Iran) did not need these armaments in the past; we will not be in need of them in the future (about U.S. arms).

UNITED STATES. NATIONAL SECURITY AGENCY

Rockefeller, Nelson Aldrich. It depends on who you're talking to. If you're talking to the head of the KGB and you happen to be overheard, and you're Jane Fonda or somebody else, there's no reason you shouldn't be overheard if somebody has the capability to overhear you—which I don't know if they do or not (commenting on electronic surveillance by the National Security Agency).

UNITED STATES. NAVY

Zumwalt, Elmo R., Jr. A final malady that afflicted—and continues to afflict—the whole Navy, though the surface Navy was and is the greatest sufferer, can be described in one word: Rickover.

UNITED STATES—POLITICS AND GOVERNMENT

Abourezk, James. Anybody who really changed things for the better in this country could never be elected President anyway.

Acheson, Dean. Americans do at the end of the day what they don't like to do at noon.

Anonymous, . If the President helps me and my candidates next year, I'll help him in 1980. It's as simple as that.

Anonymous (HEW employee), . Being a Democrat or a Republican is just a party affiliation. 'Don't Make Waves' is a religion.

Baker, Bobby. It's very important for the American people to know who's buying their politicians.

Baron, Alan. We have divided the presidential election process from the governing process.

Bauman, Robert E. Anytime the House is in session the American people are probably in danger.

Beard, Peter. Nixon is what America deserved and Nixon is what America got.

Boorstin, Daniel J. Our national politics has become a competition for images or between images, rather than between ideals.

Brown, Edmund Gerald, Jr. All I guarantee is a lot of hard work and to tell you what is working and what is not.

Brown, Edmund Gerald, Jr. Government isn't a religion. It shouldn't be treated as such. It's not God; it's human, fallible people feathering their nest most of the time.

Brown, Edmund Gerald, Jr. In this business a little vagueness goes a long way.

Brown, Edmund Gerald, Jr. The nation is not governable without new ideas.

Brown, Elaine. I may not be saying 'off the mother-fucking pigs' anymore, but I'm still talking about serious political change. Who cares who takes credit? The Panthers? The Democrats? As long as the work gets done.

Caddell, Patrick. I don't know any politician in America who could run against himself and win.

Carter, James Earl. I remember in this room last May someone asked me if my administration was all image and no substance, or style and no substance. Lately the criticisms have been that there is too much substance and not enough style.

Carter, James Earl. In war, we offer our very lives as a matter of routine. We must be no less daring, no less steadfast, in the pursuit of peace.

Carter, James Earl. The American people and our government will continue our firm commitment to promote respect for human rights not only in our own country but also abroad (to Andrei Sakharov).

Carter, James Earl. We must face a time of national austerity.

Church, Frank. If we are to preserve freedom and keep constitutional government alive in America, it cannot be left to a President and his agents alone to decide what must be kept secret. Congress, if it is to check the abuse of executive power, must retain its right to inquiry and independent judgement.

Clay, William. Whenever I see certain elements in the press show favoritism to a Black man running for a position of power, I know there's a nigger in the woodpile somewhere.

Cleaver, Kathleen. I'm older and wiser. I've lost my romanticism about revolution in America. I don't say it's inconceivable, but I know that none of us who believed ourselves to be revolutionaries in the '60s can conceive of the form a revolution would take in America.

Cleveland, Grover. While the people should patriotically and cheerfully support their government, its functions do not include the support of the people (inaugural address—1893).

Colby, William Egan. I'm convinced it's possible to run a secret agency as part of a constitutional society.

Davis, Edward Michael. I always felt the federal government really was out to force me to hire 4-foot-11 transvestite morons.

Dean, John Wesley, III. Washington is a much better place if you are asking questions rather than answering them.

Derrow, Martin. Ronald Reagan is the prototype American politician of the '70s: mindless, witless, positionless and worthless.

Dole, Robert J. It may turn out that 1974 was the good year for a Republican to be on the ballot.

Dorfman, Dan. To lie to the press on a public matter is, in effect, to lie to the people.

Dudney, Bob. The country would have recovered from the death of John Kennedy, but it hasn't recovered yet from the death of Lee Harvey Oswald and probably never will.

Ehrlichman, John D. If I wanted to do some candidate a dirty trick, I'd endorse him. Maybe I'll go campaign for Lowell Weicker.

Ehrlichman, John D. Narcotics suppression is a very sexy political issue.

Eisenhower, Dwight David. The path to America's future lies down the middle of the road.

Fallows, James. I'm inclined to doubt this government can be changed, by Carter or any other President.

Fleishman, Stanley. There are more citizens in jail in the United States today for publishing books, magazines, newspapers, and films than there are in all the countries of the world put together.

Foley, Thomas S. There is a mood in this country that government action is not necessarily always the perfect solution to social problems.

Ford, Gerald Rudolph. My motto towards the Congress is communication, conciliation, compromise and cooperation.

Gardner, John. Instead of the United States being run by a well-knit behind-the-scenes power group, it is whipsawed by a great multiplicity of special interests.

Goldwater, Barry Morris. He let this country down, he let his party down. And that's the last time I want to talk about Nixon, ever (summarizing his feelings about Richard Nixon).

Goldwin, Robert. The cause I push is a kind of elevated common sense.

Greenfield, Jeff. You will get what you want if you vote for the candidate who says exactly the opposite of what you most deeply believe.

Griffin, Mickey. It's high time the rednecks came back to Washington. There are a hell of a lot more rednecks out there than people who eat crepes suzette.

Harding, Warren Gamaliel. Our most dangerous tendency is to expect too much of government, and at the same time to do for it too little (inaugural address—1921).

Harlow, Bryce N. Our only protection against the presidency is the character of the president.

Harris, Fred. Our current economic problems are not a failure of the system, they are a failure of economic leadership.

Hastings, James F. I came up to age 49 without having a great deal to show for it. Taking a look around at the next 12 to 14 years of productive life, I decided I couldn't spend it here under the circumstances and frustrations I see in this legislative body (upon his mid-term resignation as a U.S. congressman).

Hayakawa, Samuel Ichiye. Before World War II in Japan they killed off all the older politicians. All that were left were the damn fools who attacked Pearl Harbor. I think that this country needs elder statesmen too.

Hayden, Thomas. The radicalism of the '60's became the fascism of the '70's (responding to heckling from left-wing radicals during a speech on his current campaign for U.S. Senator).

Heller, Joseph. No one governs. Everyone performs. Politics has become a social world.

Henderson, Vivian Wilson. We have programs for combatting racial discrimination, but not for combatting economic class distinctions.

Hollow, Norman. In the olden days the Indian peoples defended themselves with bows and arrows. Now, politics is the only way our rights can be developed.

Holtzman, Elizabeth. Government follows Newton's law of physics. Objects stay at rest until they're pushed.

Ichord, Richard. Once you have done the budget, once you get the statistics, it is much like getting down the unvirtuous woman. Once you get her down, you can do anything you want to.

Jones, Charles. A shift of power (toward Congress) that started because of Nixon's arrogance has continued because of Carter's artlessness.

Jones, Mary Harris (Mother Jones). I asked a man in prison once how he happened to be there and he said he had stolen a pair of shoes. I told him if he had stolen a railroad he would be a United States Senator.

Kennedy, Edward Moore. The people I respected most in the Senate—Phil Hart, for example—said you measure accomplishments not by climbing mountains, but by climbing molehills.

Kennedy, John Fitzgerald. And so, my fellow Americans, ask not what your country can do for you; ask what you can do for your country (inaugural address—1961).

Kissinger, Henry Alfred. There are times when the national interest is more important than the law (commenting on suggestions that the U.S. cut off military aid to Turkey for making illegal use of American arms in Cyprus).

Landers, Ann. I believe people want some spiritual leadership. It shows in the primaries; Jimmy Carter. He speaks openly about his religion. They see in him something that offers hope.

Lasch, Christopher. Radicalism in the United States has no great triumphs to record.

Laxalt, Paul D. We are finding that conservatives throughout this country are going to marshal together and present, I think, a formidable political challenge, and comes the general election, personally I think that Ronald Reagan has the potential of putting together the same basic elements against Jimmy Carter that Richard Nixon did in 1972.

Leary, Timothy. Successful hippies are on their way to running this country.

Lisagor, Peter. Washington is a place where the truth is not necessarily the best defense. It surely runs a poor second to the statute of limitations.

McCarthy, Eugene Joseph. The two-party system has given this country the war of Lyndon Johnson, the Watergate of Nixon, and the incompetence of Carter. Saying we should keep the two-party system simply because it is working is like saying the Titanic voyage was a success because a few people survived on life rafts.

McGovern, George Stanley. The liberals are giving up too soon on the kind of economic and social change that we were trying to bring about in 1972—they want a winner, almost no matter who it is.

McGovern, George Stanley. We can mark it down that the ghost of Joe McCarthy still stalks this land (commenting on the treatment of Theodore Sorensen as Carter's nominee for the directorship of the CIA).

Magnuson, Warren. Why, if we passed the Ten Commandments, President Ford would veto them. He'd say there were too many or they interfered with foreign policy or something.

Main, Michael. For every action there is an equal and opposite government program.

Marchetti, Victor. Ours is not yet a totalitarian government, but it is an elitist democracy—and becoming more so every year.

Mathias, Charles McCurdy. People tend to want to follow the beaten path. The difficulty is that the beaten path doesn't seem to be leading anywhere.

Mathias, Charles McCurdy. That's what the American system is all about: to keep power divided, to prevent a small core from either pole suddenly thrusting its decisions on the country.

Mitchell, John. Watch what we do, not what we say (commenting in 1969 on the direction of the Nixon administration).

Mondale, Walter Frederick. If you are sure you understand everything that is going on, you are hopelessly confused.

Morgan, Charles, Jr. If Moses had gone to Harvard Law School and spent three years working on the Hill, he would have written the Ten Commandments with three exceptions and a savings clause.

Moynihan, Daniel Patrick. Work is no longer considered to be a form of punishment as applied to women. A liberal constituency no longer finds work unattractive.

Nader, Ralph. The speed of exit of a civil servant is directly proportional to the quality of his service.

Nessen, Ron. Press conferences force more policy decisions than anything else.

Nixon, Richard Milhous. In our own lives, let each of us ask—not just what will government do for me, but what can I do for myself (inaugural address—1973).

Nixon, Richard Milhous. It is quite obvious that there are certain inherently governmental actions which, if undertaken by the sovereign in protection of...the nation's security, are lawful, but which if undertaken by private citizens are not (commenting to the Senate Intelligence Committee on his authorization of covert CIA efforts to prevent Chilean President Allende's election in 1970).

Nixon, Richard Milhous. There is one thing solid and fundamental in politics—the law of change. What's up today is down tomorrow.

Nixon, Richard Milhous. We are a compromised country at the moment (1975).

Nixon, Richard Milhous. We have very little leadership in our country today (1975).

O'Neill, Thomas P. (Tip). If this were France, the Democratic Party would be five parties.

Peters, Charles. In Washington, bureaucrats confer, the President proclaims and the Congress legislates, but the impact on reality is negligible, if evident at all.

Ravenal, James C. The American Century is over. The era of American dominance and control, heralded by Henry Luce and established in the wake of World War II, lasted only 25 years. Of course, everyone knows that it is over. But our policy-makers have not absorbed this message, and our nation has not begun to adjust to its implications and consequences.

Reagan, Ronald. I believe that government is the problem, not the answer.

Reagan, Ronald. The coils woven in that city (Washington, D.C.) are entrapping us all and, as with the Gordian knot, we cannot untie it. We have to cut it with one blow of the sword.

Reagan, Ronald. You know, politics has been called the second oldest profession. Sometimes there is a similarity to the first.

Rebozo, Charles Gregory. Never again. (In response to the question if he plans to dabble in politics).

Reston, James. Washington has no memory.

Rhodes, John J. If the Republicans split this year I think Republicans will deserve the fate they will get, which is resounding defeat.

Ridgeway, Matthew B. Candidates are no better or worse than those who choose and elect them, and therein lies the answer to what we are to become.

Robeson, Paul. American democracy is Hitler Fascism.

Roosevelt, Franklin Delano. Government has the definite duty to use all its power and resources to meet new social problems with new social controls.

Roosevelt, Franklin Delano. Our true destiny is not to be ministered unto but to minister to ourselves and to our fellow men (inaugural address—1933).

Roosevelt, Franklin Delano. The only way to do anything in the American government is to bypass the Senate (returning from Yalta).

Roth, William V., Jr. Public confidence and trust in the federal government are low not only because of Watergate or our experience in Vietnam, but also because too many politicians have promised more than the government can deliver.

Sanders, Ed. Just because you're paranoid doesn't mean they're not trying to get you.

Simon, William E. In the United States today, we already have more government than we need, more government than most people want, and certainly more government than we are willing to pay for.

Simon, William E. Washington is the only city where sound travels faster than light.

Singlaub, John K. I don't know if it's capriciousness, inconsistency or naivete, but I have a feeling that with the present Administration there isn't anybody in charge (commenting on the Carter administration).

Steinfels, Peter. Rather than getting the government they want, the people should want the government they get; they should be retutored to fit its current capacities.

Stevenson, Adlai, II. It is better to light one candle than to curse the darkness.

Stevenson, Adlai, III. I don't think ideas are incompatible with political reality.

Stevenson, Adlai, III. The nation was never exalted to high levels of endeavor by reorganization plans and zero-based budgeting. In fact, the strong Presidents may have been least occupied by matters of management. A great President has an agenda for the nation.

Stone, Isidor Feinstein. The biggest menace to American freedom is the intelligence community.

Strauss, Robert S. Everybody in government is like a bunch of ants on a log floating down a river. Each one thinks he is guiding the log, but it's really just going with the flow.

Strout, Richard. (American Democracy is) the only governmental vehicle on earth that has two steering wheels: one for the President, one for the Congress. You never can tell who's driving.

Terkel, Studs. Dissent is not merely the right to dissent—it is the duty.

Tito, Josip Broz. Frankly speaking, I would not like to live in America. True, there is democracy, in some respects even too much, while in others there is none.

Tyrrell, R. Emmett, Jr. A new Government took office in Washington, not via bayonets and tanks as is the custom in some of the world's capitals (but) in the Democratic Way...via hyperbole, sham, melodrama and public-spirited mendacity (commenting on the Carter inauguration).

Udall, Morris King. A boss is a political leader who is on somebody else's side.

Udall, Morris King. (Ronald Reagan and George Wallace) are the twin horsemen of the radical right.

Wade, Richard. If you put the top 50 liberals inside a room to stop Henry Jackson, they'd have no troops for the job. Liberals have influence but no power.

White, Kevin. Charismatic leadership is hungered for, but at the same time we fear it.

White, Theodore. People don't want change—people want more. And I think liberals don't realize that.

White, Theodore. Politics in America is the binding secular religion.

Will, George. When affirmative action came to Ann Arbor and Morningside Heights, dawn came up like thunder.

Winpisinger, William (union leader). I don't mind being called a lefty. We're being centered to death.

Wolf, Arnold Jacob. America, where were you when we needed you? And we, where are we now that you need us?.

Woollcott, Alexander. I'm tired of hearing it said that democracy doesn't work. Of course it doesn't work. It isn't supposed to work. We are supposed to work it.

Wright, James. When people are drowning, there is no time to build a better ship.

Zappa, Frank. The biggest dangers we face today don't even need to sneak past our billion-dollar defense system. They issue the contracts for them.

Ziegler, Ronald Louis. I never knowingly lied, but certainly history shows that many things I said were incorrect.

UNITED STATES—RACE QUESTION

Hooks, Benjamin Lawson. If we don't solve this race problem, this country isn't going to ever rest in peace.

Moynihan, Daniel Patrick. The time may have come when the issue of race could benefit from a period of 'benign neglect' (to Richard Nixon in 1970).

UNITED STATES—SOCIAL CONDITIONS

Galbraith, John Kenneth. The (tax) revolt of the affluent, which now has politicans so frightened, is not a violent thing. The response in the ghettoes if life there is allowed further to deteriorate might be different.

King,, Coretta Scott. America's jobless cannot "wait". Not only because waiting is no solution and not only because waiting has social consequences that are frightening to contemplate, but because to do nothing when we have the capacity to act is morally and socially wrong.

Mikulski, Barbara A. America is not a melting pot. It is a sizzling cauldron. The ethnic worker is fooled into thinking that blacks are getting everything.

UNITED STATES—SOCIAL CONDITIONS—FOREIGN OPINION

Brzezinski, Zbigniew. America still provides to most people in the world the most attractive social condition (even if not the model), and that remains America's special strength.

UNITED STATES—SOCIAL LIFE AND CUSTOMS

Kramer, Hilton. The way things are going, one expects to hear any day now that virginity is back in style.

Walden, Phil (President of Capricorn Records). That's the old American way—if you got a good thing, then overdo it.

UNITED STATES. SUPREME COURT

Nixon, Richard Milhous. Presidents come and go, but the Supreme Court, through its decisions, goes on forever.

Richardson, Elliot Lee. You don't have to be Jewish to like being on the Supreme Court.

Scott, Hugh. The worst mistake I made was supporting the Carswell nomination (reflecting on his three decades in Congress).

UNITED STATES. SUPREME COURT—ABORTION DECISIONS

Blackmun, Harry. There is another world out there, the existence of which the (Supreme) Court, I suspect, either chooses to ignore or fears to recognize. And so the cancer of poverty will continue to grow. (Writing on the decision not to require government financing of abortions).

UNITED STEELWORKERS OF AMERICA

Sadlowski, Ed. There's a fire in the steelworkers union, and I'm not gonna piss on it.

UNIVERSAL DECLARATION OF HUMAN RIGHTS

Scranton, William W. The only universality that one can honestly associate with the Universal Declaration of Human Rights is universal lip service.

UNIVERSE

Allen, Woody. The universe is merely a fleeting idea in God's mind—and a pretty uncomfortable thought, particularly if you've just made a down payment on a home.

Eddington, Arthur. The stuff of the universe is mind stuff.

Haldane, J. B. S. I suspect that there are more things in heaven and earth than are dreamed of, or can be dreamed of, in any philosophy.

Hoyle, Fred. There is a coherent plan in the universe, though I don't know what it's a plan for.

UNIVERSITY PRESSES

Philipson, Morris. The commercial publisher says of his book, this is no good but it'll make a lot of money. The university publisher says, this is good and it won't make money.

Rosenthal, Arthur J. If I had a book on the bestseller list I'd suspect I was doing something wrong (commenting on his role as director of the Harvard University Press).

UNRUH, JESSE

Unruh, Jesse. If I had slain all my political enemies, I wouldn't have any friends today.

UPPER CLASSES

Baltzell, Edward Digby, Jr. The masses who have no roots are far less dangerous to a society than an elite with no roots.

Baltzell, Edward Digby, Jr. When class authority declines, money talks.

UPPER CLASSES—GREAT BRITAIN

Margaret Rose, Princess of Great Britain, . Things have come to a pretty pass when somebody of our type murders his nanny. They're so hard to come by these days (commenting on Lord Lucan, accused of murdering his children's nanny).

UPSTAIRS, DOWNSTAIRS (TELEVISION PROGRAM)

Marsh, Jean. I wouldn't have wanted to be an upstairs or a downstairs woman: I would have wanted to be a man. The women weren't allowed to do anything (commenting on English life in the television program Upstairs, Downstairs).

USERY, WILLIAM J.

Usery, William J. Even though I don't have a teamsters card, I belong to this club because I believe in it.

USTINOV, PETER

Ustinov, Peter. I just don't know what my image is and I don't want to know. If you arrive at the point where the man looking back at you in the mirror is more important than the man who is looking into the mirror, then you might as well pack up.

UTAH. UNIVERSITY (FOOTBALL)

Lovat, Tom. Last night I sat down and tried to think about the highlights from last year and I fell asleep (Utah football coach commenting on his 1-10 season).

VAGUENESS

Brown, Edmund Gerald, Jr. In this business a little vagueness goes a long way.

VALIUM

Janov, Arthur. The world is having a nervous breakdown. Valium is the only glue that holds it together.

VALUES

Haskins, Caryl. It's funny that we often value what is rare and specialized. What is truly precious is what is common and unspecialized.

Wriston, Walter. I believe there are no institutional values, only personal values.

VANCE, CYRUS R.

Graff, Henry. Vance is a practitioner of turtle diplomacy.

VATICAN—FOREIGN RELATIONS—POLAND

John Paul II, Pope, . Our times demand not to enclose ourselves in inflexible borders, especially when human good is concerned.

VEECK, BILL

Veeck, Bill. I'd like to be devious, but I can't find it in myself.

VELLECA, CARL

Velleca, Carl. The people will always know where to find me (commenting on his candidacy for Concord, Massachusetts' selectman which originated from his home at the Massachusetts Correctional Institution).

VICE-PRESIDENTIAL CANDIDATES

Laxalt, Paul D. Our polls show that every prospective bride is a drag on the (Republican) ticket, except Jerry Ford. That would be a political marriage made in heaven.

VICE-PRESIDENTS—UNITED STATES

Anonymous, . The vice-presidency is like a Sally Quinn or Oriana Fallaci interview. Each one thinks it's going to be better for him than it was for the others.

Bush, George. Everyone says they are going to reinvent the wheel, that their Vice President is going to be in on developing North-South strategy and other great projects. But it never happens. Two years later, you wake up and find he's still going to funerals.

Carter, James Earl. I look on Senator Mondale, who will be the next Vice President, as my top staff person.

McCarthy, Eugene Joseph. Vice-presidential candidates just clutter up the campaign. We should not ask the country to make two judgements. Everyone knows Vice-Presidents have no influence on Presidents, once elected. Presidents' wives have much more influence. Perhaps we should have the candidates' wives debate.

Mondale, Walter Frederick. There is no way on earth people can take the Vice-president of the United States seriously (originally quoted by columnist Jim Klobuchar in the Minneapolis Tribune in 1974).

Rockefeller, Nelson Aldrich. The best part about being Vice President is presiding over the Senate. Where else could I have Barry Goldwater addressing me as 'Mr. President?'.

VIDAL, GORE

Vidal, Gore. Each writer is born with a repertory company in his head. Shakespeare had perhaps 20 players, and Tennessee Williams has about five and Samuel Beckett one—and perhaps a clone of that one. I have ten or so, and that's a lot.

Vidal, Gore. I no more want to see the world end than Swift wanted to eat Irish babies.

Vidal, Gore. I would pay off those publications that report the doings and expenditures of Madame Onassis. Never to read about her again would not only be socially beneficial but would, I am sure, stem the rising tide of world communism (in response to 'What would you do with 10 million dollars').

VIETNAM—POLITICS AND GOVERNMENT

Ho Chi Minh, . It is better to sniff French dung for a while than to eat China's all our lives.

Nguyen-Van-Thieu (former President of South Vietnam), . A coalition (government) is like a sugar-coated poison pill. When the sugar melts, the poison kills you.

VIETNAMESE

Ky, Nguyen Cao. Never believe what any Vietnamese tells you, including me (commenting in 1966).

VIETNAMESE IN THE UNITED STATES

Ky, Nguyen Cao. We Vietnamese are the newest refugees in your history. We know your country is a land of immigrants. Your sons and daughters fought to keep Vietnam free, and we Vietnamese wish to earn your respect and friendship. We wish not to be hawks or doves, but eagles.

VIETNAMESE WAR, 1957-1975

Brown, Harold. A lesson we learned from Viet Nam is that we should be very cautious about intervening in any place where there's a poor political base for our presence.

Bundy, McGeorge. The history of the Vietnam war, properly understood, will testify not to the dangers of excessive presidential power but to the perils of secretiveness (comment made at the end of his own role in the war in October 1973).

Califano, Joseph, A. Jr. Of course, we recognize the right to dissent. That's what our boys in Vietnam are fighting for. But this shows that the overwhelming majority of American college students and the American public stand fully behind the President in his policy in Vietnam (commenting in 1965 when he accepted for President Johnson an 8-foot petition with 2,500 signatures from students and faculty at American University protesting the Vietnam War).

Colby, William Egan. America got into Viet Nam and then decided that there are some things we can't do. Well, I think we didn't do it right. But I think we could have done it.

Ford, Gerald Rudolph. Unfortunately the United States did not carry out its commitment in the supplying of military hardware and economic aid to South Vietnam. I wish we had. I think if we had, this present tragic situation in South Vietnam would not have occurred.

Grass, Gunter. If you don't face it, it means two things: you lost the war and you've also lost the ability to make clear why it happened.

Harriman, Averell. As I look back, what I regret most was that I wasn't able to influence Johnson to abandon the war in Vietnam. To see that war go on, to find him listening to people with such a completely wrong point of view. Every day there were those whispering in his ear, 'No president ever lost a war.' That was red meat for a Texan.

Humphrey, Hubert Horatio. I do not want a great political party which nearly lost its soul in Vietnam to sell its soul on busing.

Humphrey, Hubert Horatio. We made judgements about that part of the world based on our experience in Europe. We were a world power with a half-world knowledge.

Johnson, Lyndon Baines. Boys, it is just like the Alamo. Somebody should have by God helped those Texans. I'm going to Viet Nam.

Johnson, Lyndon Baines. If you have a mother-in-law with only one eye, and that eye is in the middle of her forehead, you don't keep her in the living room (in response to why he had not told Congress more of what he knew to be the truth about Vietnam).

Johnson, Lyndon Baines. I'm not going to be the first President to lose a war.

Kissinger, Henry Alfred. It is idiotic to talk about negotiations if we are really serious. The only thing we are doing that is positive, that puts pressure on the enemy, is killing Viet Cong—we would have to stop killing Viet Cong during negotiations and right then we would lose the only bargaining counter we have (comments made in January of 1967).

Kissinger, Henry Alfred. We should have bombed the hell out of them the minute we got into office (a week after the 1973 Vietnam peace agreement).

Kohler, Jerry. I'd just as soon die in Viet Nam as in the library.

Ky, Nguyen Cao. Remember, we lost the war not because of your fault but because of bad leadership. Tell your children and grandchildren we are exiled because of Nguyen Van Thieu. Remember that name. He is the most despicable man in the world (visiting Vietnamese refugees in Camp Pendleton, California).

McCarthy, Eugene Joseph. Kissinger won a Nobel Peace Prize for watching a war end that he was for.

Miyazawa, Kiichi (Foreign Minister of Japan). What you have lost is not a war but a cause, and your credibility has not really suffered because it is widely known that the people you were trying to help could not really help themselves.

Paringaux, Roland-Pierre (French journalist). The two parts of Viet Nam are like Sparta and Byzantium; they are like two ingredients of a sweet and sour sauce, difficult to mix so that it will remain tasty for all.

Reagan, Ronald. We could pave the whole country and put parking stripes on it and still be home by Christmas (about winning the Vietnamese War).

Rockefeller, Nelson Aldrich. It's already too late to do anything about it (South Vietnam). I guess a lot of Vietnamese are going to die. For us, we go on living.

Westmoreland, William Childs. Despite the final failure of the South Vietnamese, the record of the American military services of never having lost a war is still intact.

Westmoreland, William Childs. The Tet offensive was misrepresented to the American people by the media. It was the last despairing attack by the defeated North Vietnamese.

Westmoreland, William Childs. We met the enemy, and he was us.

VIETNAMESE WAR, 1957-1975—ATROCITIES— MY LAI

Calley, William Laws, Jr. I was a coward. I couldn't have backed out (from the My Lai attack) if I wanted to because I believed in this nation.

VIETNAMESE WAR, 1957-1975—PROTESTS, DEMONSTRATIONS ETC., AGAINST—KENT, OHIO

Capp, Al. The martyrs at Kent State were the kids in National Guard uniforms.

Rhodes, James. They are the worst type of people we harbor in America, worse than brown shirts and the Communist element (concerning the Kent State demonstrators).

VIOLENCE

Billington, James. Violence is not only "as American as cherry pie," it is likely to remain a la mode for some time to come.

Colby, William Egan. I have definitional problems with the word violence. I don't know what the word violence means.

John Paul II, Pope, . Violence always delays the day of justice (to the IRA).

VIOLENCE IN MOVING PICTURES

Marvin, Lee. There's too much damned violence on the screen. I don't go for it. Some of those producers and directors need some sense bashed into their heads.

VIOLENCE IN TELEVISION
Miller, Arthur. Violence is the last refuge of scoundrels (commenting on TV violence).

VIOLIN
Stern, Isaac. You don't realize how close it is to you, how much it is a part of your body, until it is gone (about the violin).

VIRGINIA. UNIVERSITY (FOOTBALL)
Randle, Sonny (football coach at the University of Virginia). We've stopped recruiting young men who want to come here to be students first and athletes second.

VIRGINITY
Braine, John. I believe absolutely in Christian sexual morality, which means that I believe in premarital virginity. Virgins don't get V.D., don't have abortions, don't have illegitimate babies, and aren't forced to get married. And no man, no matter how progressive, has ever objected to his bride being a virgin.

Kramer, Hilton. The way things are going, one expects to hear any day now that virginity is back in style.

VIVA
Viva, . I'm so gullible that Hitler probably could have led me around by the nose.

VOCATIONAL EDUCATION
Bell, Terrence H. We need to liberalize vocational education—and vocationalize liberal education.

VOLLBRACHT, MICHAELE
Vollbracht, Michaele. The fashion industry is like someone with a BB gun: they aim at you, they don't kill you, but they hurt you a hell of a lot.

VOLUNTEER SERVICE
Ali, Muhammad. Service to others is the rent I pay for my room here on earth.

Myrdal, Gunnar. It is natural for the ordinary American when he sees something wrong to feel not only that there should be a law against it but also that an organization should be formed to combat it.

VORONEL, NINA
Voronel, Nina. Soviet life is so absurd that when I write realistically, it becomes the theatre of the absurd.

VOTING
Mondale, Walter Frederick. For a workingman or woman to vote Republican this year is the same as a chicken voting for Colonel Sanders.

WAGES
Ogden, David A. If you don't appreciate the amount of luxuries your budget can afford, you are getting paid far too much.

WALDHEIM, KURT
Waldheim, Kurt. The post of Secretary General is at the same time one of the most fascinating and one of the most frustrating jobs in the world, encompassing, as it does, the height of human aspiration and the depth of human frailty.

WALES
Hepburn, Katharine. First God made England, Ireland and Scotland. That's when He corrected His mistakes and made Wales.

WALKING
Ketcham, Brian (architect of New York City's Transportation Control Plan). Everyone is looking for a technological bandaid for the automobile air pollution problem. The answer is walking. It's so logical, it's absurd.

Stengel, Charles Dillon (Casey). If you walk backward you'll find out that you can go forward and people won't know if you're coming or going.

WALL STREET
Baruch, Bernard Mannes (attributed by William Flanagan). I buy low and sell high (when asked how he had made a fortune in the stock market).

Graham, Benjamin. (The stock market is) a Falstaffian joke that frequently degenerates into a madhouse.

LeFevre, William M. There are only two emotions in Wall Street: fear and greed.

WALLACE, CORNELIA
Wallace, Cornelia. I'm the Rocky Stallone of Alabama politics.

WALLACE, GEORGE CORLEY
Bond, Julian. I don't think you'll have to worry that this mental midget, this hillbilly Hitler from Alabama is anywhere near becoming the nominee of the Democratic party.

Dutton, Fred. George Wallace is a more truly democratic candidate than Ford, Humphrey or Jackson. He wants everyone to vote, while they hope to narrow down the voting public.

Griffin, Mickey. It's high time the rednecks came back to Washington. There are a hell of a lot more rednecks out there than people who eat crepes suzette.

Jackson, Jesse. The absence of (George) Wallace is not the presence of justice.

Udall, Morris King. (Ronald Reagan and George Wallace) are the twin horsemen of the radical right.

Wallace, Cornelia. I don't believe George needs a family. He just needs an audience.

Wallace, George Corley. I don't mind dictatorships abroad provided they are pro-American.

Wallace, George Corley. Let 'em call me a racist in the press. It don't make any difference. Hell, I want 'em to. 'Cause if you want to know the truth, race is what's gonna win this thing for us.

Wallace, George Corley. Segregation is a moot question, and integration is the law of the land. It is a moot question, and therefore we don't want to go back, nor make any attempt to change what is now a fact accomplished.

Wallace, George Corley. The viewpoints I expressed eight years ago now are expressed by all the candidates. They are expressed by a majority of the American people, and they are going to prevail in 1976 whether I'm around or not.

WALTERS, BARBARA

Reasoner, Harry. Confirming my long-time nonsexist grace and courtesy, I suggest we just do it alphabetically by last names (commenting on the billing of the co-anchor news team of Harry Reasoner and Barbara Walters).

Walters, Barbara. I always told people that if I ever had a million dollars my dream was to stay up every night reading trashy novels and sleep until noon.

Walters, Barbara. I just hope that all this talk of money doesn't confuse the issue—that this is a great breakthrough in network news. I think there is not a newsman who would have turned down the offer—and for a woman it is an even more unique opportunity (commenting on her ABC contract offer).

Walters, Barbara. I never asked for a million dollars. They're (ABC) paying me this because this is what I'm worth. And I'm proud I'm worth it.

Walters, Barbara. If it's a woman, it's caustic; if it's a man, it's authoritative. If it's a woman, it's too often pushy, if it's a man it's aggressive in the best sense of the word (commenting on critics who call her brand of interviewing caustic).

WAR

Begin, Menachem. The life of every man who fights in a just cause is a paradox. He makes war so that there should be peace. He sheds blood so that there should be no more bloodshed. That is the way of the world. A very tragic way beset with terrors. There is no other.

Brzezinski, Zbigniew. We live in a world in which there will be many local conflicts, in which all the major powers will exercise self-restraint, because they have to exercise self-restraint in the nuclear...it will be a sign of the maturity of the American people and of the growing wisdom of the American people if we adjust ourselves to the notion that in our age there is a twilight zone between war and peace and that this twilight zone of limited wars is going to be very much a feature of our lifetime.

Buchwald, Art. There is entirely too much talk about going to war these days.

Caputo, Philip J. The impetus or the impulse that makes people heroic in wars is the very thing that can make them monsters.

Curtis, Carl Thomas. In the whole history of the world, whenever a meateating race has gone to war against a non-meateating race, the meat eaters won. It produces superior people.

Edison, Thomas Alva. The day will come when science will create a machine as a force which is so terrible, so infinitely horrifying, that even man, a bellicose being who brings suffering, torment, and death upon his fellows, at the risk of bringing these torments upon himself will shudder with fear and renounce war forever.

Evtushenko, Evgenii Aleksandrovich. Distrust is the mother of war and political racism.

Haig, Alexander M. The next war could be a come-as-you-are party.

Hua, Kuo-Feng. Peace cannot be got by begging. War cannot be averted by yielding.

Kuan, Han-Ch'ing. What characterizes the current world situation is decidedly not an irreversible process of detente but the approaching danger of a new world war.

Mountbatten, Louis. If the Third World War is fought with nuclear weapons, the fourth will be fought with bows and arrows.

Patton, George S. In war, just as in loving, you've got to keep on shoving.

West, Mae. I'm for peace. I have yet to wake up in the morning and hear a man say, I've just had a good war.

Winchester, Jesse. A war is like a storm; there's nobody to blame, and everybody gets hurt. You've just got to do the best you can.

WAR—CASUALITIES

Anonymous, . Any country that goes to this much trouble to account for every soldier it loses probably ought not to fight a war.

WARHOL, ANDY

Capote, Truman. He's a sphinx without a secret (commenting on Andy Warhol).

Warhol, Andy. I never fall apart because I never fall together.

Warhol, Andy. My ideal wife would have a lot of bacon, bring it all home and have a TV station, besides.

WASHINGTON, BOOKER T.

Washington, Booker T., III. Being the sensitive man he was about his race, I think the present day Harlem scene would bring tears to my grandfather's eyes.

WASHINGTON, D.C.

Corcoran, Thomas. Whenever this town loses positive direction, it means something is struggling to be born in the nation—there is a wind coming (about Washington, D.C.).

Dean, John Wesley, III. Washington is a much better place if you are asking questions rather than answering them.

Dutton, Fred. Washington is like a woman who is always waiting to be seduced.

McCree, Wade. Washington is the only town in the world where sound travels faster than light.

Simon, John. The culture of the nation's capital would seem to be a capital joke.

White, Kevin. Everybody knows that Washington, D.C. has no culture—they have to buy it.

WASHINGTON, D.C.—DESCRIPTION

Connally, John Bowden (attributed by Henry Alfred Kissinger). You will be measured in (Washington D.C.) by the enemies you destroy. The bigger they are, the bigger you are.

Fairlie, Henry. All over Washington, people are now speed-reading the Koran.

Simon, William E. Washington is the only city where sound travels faster than light.

WASHINGTON, D.C.—SOCIAL LIFE AND CUSTOMS

Quinn, Sally. Washington society is ruled with unwavering severity by a handful of aging widows, dowagers and old maids who subsist on fortunes inherited from robber-baron husbands or corrupt political daddies.

WASHINGTON POST

Graham, Katharine. This company (The Washington Post) is not now and never has been antiunion.

Mitchell, John. All that crap, you're putting it in the paper? It's all been denied. Katie Graham's gonna get her tit caught in a big fat wringer if that's published.

WATER PURIFICATION

Anonymous (Environmental Protection Agency official), . Sludge is the most serious dilemma we face in wastewater treatment. It's Catch-22. The cleaner we make the water, the more sludge we create.

WATER TREATMENT PLANTS

Anonymous (Environmental Protection Agency official), . Sludge is the most serious dilemma we face in wastewater treatment. It's Catch-22. The cleaner we make the water, the more sludge we create.

WATERGATE CASE

Baker, Howard Henry. There are animals crashing around in the forest. I can hear them but I can't see them (about the Watergate investigation).

Butz, Earl Lauer. It was stupid—like General Motors breaking into Ford to steal Edsel plans (commenting on Watergate, in the long term).

Colson, Charles Wendell. The only good guys to emerge from Watergate are those self-justified, upright fellows writing their own accounts. Since everyone has written a book, the sum of all the books is that no one was guilty, just everyone else.....

Dean, John Wesley, III. Last summer I reread *1984*, and after several years at the Nixon White House, it made fascinating, almost frightening reading.

Dole, Robert J. Thank goodness whenever I was in the Oval Office I only nodded (commenting on the Watergate tapes).

Hellman, Lillian. I think (Watergate and the McCarthy Era) are deeply connected, with Mr. Nixon being the connection, the rope that carries it all through.

Liddy, G. Gordon. When the prince approaches his lieutenant, the proper response of the lieutenant to the prince is Fiat volutas tua, (thy will be done)...I think I delayed things substantially. The prince was prince for a longer period of time (when asked if he would do that kind of work again for a President and if he felt he had taken the blame for Watergate in vain).

Magruder, Jeb Stuart. I lost my moral compass.

Mitchell, John. All that crap, you're putting it in the paper? It's all been denied. Katie Graham's gonna get her tit caught in a big fat wringer if that's published.

Nixon, Richard Milhous. History will justifiably record that my handling of the Watergate crisis was an unmitigated disaster.

Nixon, Richard Milhous. If it hadn't been for Martha, there'd have been no Watergate.

Nixon, Richard Milhous. Some people say I didn't handle it properly and they're right. I screwed it up. And I paid the price (about Watergate).

Nixon, Richard Milhous. (Watergate) was worse than a crime, it was a blunder.

Scott, Hugh. I had a will to believe (in Nixon's innocence), but they didn't show me all the documents. I was led into making statements on incomplete evidence. I was trying to be fair when I was personally deeply disturbed.

Trudeau, Pierre Elliott. The atmosphere of Watergate has polluted the atmosphere of other democratic countries. Nobody trusts anybody anymore.

Ziegler, Ron Louis. Basically, it's the story of a couple of reporters (after seeing All The President's Men).

WATERGATE SPECIAL PROSECUTION FORCE

Lacovara, Philip. Nixon having resigned without formal prosecution has carried into his retirement a presumption of formal innocence, which was ratified by Ford's pardon. He is accepted in polite society—not as the felon he unquestionably was.

WATERGATE TAPES

Dole, Robert J. Thank goodness whenever I was in the Oval Office I only nodded (commenting on the Watergate tapes).

Graham, Billy. I was shocked and surprised. This was a Nixon I didn't know (commenting on the language used on some of the Nixon tapes).

Nixon, Patricia Ryan. If they had been my tapes, would have burned or destroyed them because they were like a private diary, not public property.

WATERS, ETHEL

Graham, Billy. In her own way she (Ethel Waters) did as much for race relations as any American in the 20th Century.

WATTS, ANDRE

Watts, Andre. Here lies a man who never played Petrouchka (on his epitaph).

WATTS TOWERS, LOS ANGELES

Rodia, Simon. I had in mind to do something big and I did (about the Watts Towers).

WAUGH, EVELYN

Waugh, Evelyn. You have no idea how much nastier I would be if I was not a Catholic. Without supernatural aid I would hardly be a human being.

WAUGH, EVELYN—CHILDREN

Waugh, Evelyn. My children weary me. I can only see them as defective adults; feckless, destructive, frivolous, sensual, humourless.

WAYNE, JOHN

Simon, John. Every era gets the leader it deserves; John Wayne is ours.

Wayne, John. I believe in white supremacy until the blacks are educated to a point of responsibility.

Wayne, John. I stay away from nuances.

Wayne, John. I'm not an actor, I'm a reactor. I just do what seems natural in a situation. All I got's sincerity and simplicity.

Wayne, John. Nobody likes my acting but the public.

Wayne, John. Success in films has little to do with acting. I just sell sincerity. And I've been selling the hell out of it since I got going.

WEALTH

Baltzell, Edward Digby, Jr. I believe in inherited wealth. Society needs to have some people who are above it all.

Baltzell, Edward Digby, Jr. When class authority declines, money talks.

Getty, Jean Paul. I suffer no guilt complexes or conscience pangs about my wealth. The Lord may have been disproportionate, but that is how He—or nature, if you like—operates.

Getty, Jean Paul. If you can count your money, you don't have a billion dollars.

Getty, Jean Paul. Remember, a billion dollars isn't worth what it used to be.

Graham, Benjamin. Never having to balance your checkbook (a definition of financial success).

MacArthur, John D. Anybody who knows what he's worth, isn't worth very much (upon being asked how much he was worth).

Mellon, Paul. One of the main things money provides is privacy.

Poirot, Paul L. Multiplying wealth is by far the fastest way to help the poor. Dividing the wealth and subsidizing poverty is the fastest way to starve everyone.

Vanderbilt, William K. Inherited wealth is a real handicap to happiness. It is as certain a death to ambition as cocaine is to morality.

WELCH, RAQUEL

Welch, Raquel. Don't get me wrong. I love being a world-famous sex object. But if you're an artist, you like to use your whole instrument.

Welch, Raquel. I think the women's lib is only good politically, but sexually I don't think it works.

WELD, TUESDAY

Rosenfield, Paul. (Tuesday Weld is) too much a '60's character to be a 70's star, but she'll always work: When they need an eccentric, they call Tuesday.

WELK, LAWRENCE

Welk, Lawrence. I like clean ladies and nice ladies.

Welk, Lawrence. Politics, like music and golf, is best learned at an early age. Having reached the age of 72, I'm afraid it is a little late to change horses in the middle of a stream beset with treacherous currents (declining a draft movement in California for a 1976 presidential bid).

WELLES, ORSON

Mankiewicz, Herman. There but for the grace of God goes God (about Orson Welles).

WERTMUELLER, LINA

Melato, Mariangela. She's like 25 men. I've never seen so monstrous a vitality (about Lina Wertmueller).

Walker, Alexander (British critic). She (Lina Wertmueller) is a female misogynist masquerading as a political crusader.

Wertmueller, Lina. I'm the last ballbuster left.

WEST, MAE

West, Mae. Between two evils, I always pick the one I never tried before.

West, Mae. I never needed Panavision and stereophonic sound to woo the world. I did it in black and white on a screen the size of a postage stamp. Honey, that's talent.

West, Mae. I'm for peace. I have yet to wake up in the morning and hear a man say, I've just had a good war.

West, Mae. When I'm good, I'm very good; but when I'm bad, I'm better.

WESTERN FILMS

Autry, Gene. We had no violence when I did the westerns, just fist fights and comedy.

WEXLER, ANNE

Wexler, Anne. I consider myself a liberal. Always have, always will.

WHISKEY

Nelson, Willie. To me, a redneck is someone who likes to fight. Whiskey makes you want to fight and marijuana makes you want to listen to music. And marijuana and beer together is probably the greatest truth serum ever.

WHITE, DAN

White, Dan. I am not going to be forced out of San Francisco by radicals, social deviates, incorrigibles.

WHITE, DWIGHT

White, Dwight. There's no question that I'm schizoid. I might be three or four people. I know I can be evil.

WHITE, E. B.

White, E. B. Before I start to write, I always treat myself to a nice dry martini.

WIDOWS

Hemingway, Mary. Books are helpful in bed. But they are not responsive (commenting on widowhood).

WILDE, OSCAR

Wilde, Oscar. I am dying, as I have lived, beyond my means.

WILDER, BILLY

Wilder, Billy. If there's one thing I hate more than not being taken seriously, it's being taken too seriously.

WILDER, GENE

Wilder, Gene. Everything I write is a love story and emotionally autobiographical.

WILLIAMS, EDWARD BENNETT

Nixon, Richard Milhous. I should have had you for my lawyer and I might still be president (to Edward Bennett Williams upon the acquittal of John Connally).

Veeck, Bill. Baseball is the only orderly thing in a very unorderly world. If you get three strikes, even Edward Bennett Williams can't get you off.

WILLIAMS, TENNESSEE

Brando, Marlon. If there are men who have a clean soul, he's (Tennessee Williams) one of them.

Vidal, Gore. Each writer is born with a repertory company in his head. Shakespeare had perhaps 20 players, and Tennessee Williams has about five and Samuel Beckett one—and perhaps a clone of that one. I have ten or so, and that's a lot.

Williams, Tennessee. Men are rather inscrutable to me.

Williams, Tennessee. They teach it (The Glass Menagerie) in college now, and everybody approaches it as though it were a place of worship. Frankly, I fall asleep at times.

WILSON, HAROLD

Wilson, Harold. Once I leave, I leave. I am not going to speak to the man on the bridge, and I am not going to spit on the deck (upon his resignation as Prime Minister of Great Britain).

WINNING

Allen, George. Only winners are truly alive. Winning is living. Every time you win, you're reborn. When you lose, you die a little.

Lombardi, Vince. Winning isn't everything. It is the only thing.

Rockne, Knute. You show me a good and gracious loser, and I'll show you a failure!.

WINPISINGER, WILLIAM

Winpisinger, William (union leader). I don't mind being called a lefty. We're being centered to death.

WIRE TAPPING

Kelley, Clarence M. If we are to have any degree of success in solving the cases now confronting us in terrorist, espionage, and other major security matters, we must have all the tools available to us—including electronic surveillance (suggesting before a Palm Beach, California civic group that Congress authorize the use of wiretaps and bugs for the FBI).

Mao, Tse-Tung. What's wrong with taping a conversation when you happen to have a tape recorder with you? Most people in America love playing with tape recorders. (about Richard Nixon).

Rockefeller, Nelson Aldrich. It depends on who you're talking to. If you're talking to the head of the KGB and you happen to be overheard, and you're Jane Fonda or somebody else, there's no reason you shouldn't be overheard if somebody has the capability to overhear you—which I don't know if they do or not (commenting on electronic surveillance by the National Security Agency).

WISDOM

Hayakawa, Samuel Ichiye. There is only one thing age can give you, and that is wisdom.

Hellman, Lillian. In looking about me, in looking at me, I have long believed that few people grow wiser with the years.

Levi-Strauss, Claude. Age removes the confusion, only possible in youth, between physical and moral characteristics.

WISEMAN, FREDERICK

Wiseman, Frederick. The final film is a theory about the event, about the subject in the film.

WITCHCRAFT

Agunga, John (African witch doctor). Publicity. They lost because they turned coming to me into a publicity gimmick. Witchcraft works only by stealth (commenting on why the Baltimore Orioles lost the race in the American League East despite his spells).

WIVES

Ronstadt, Linda. I'm so disorganized, what I really need is a good wife.

Warhol, Andy. My ideal wife would have a lot of bacon, bring it all home and have a TV station, besides.

WOLFE, THOMAS

Mailer, Norman. (Thomas Wolfe was) the greatest five-year-old who ever lived.

O'Connor, Flannery. Anybody that admires Thomas Wolfe can be expected to like good fiction only by accident.

WOMEN

Abzug, Bella. Women are still conceived on television and radio as being creatures of consumption who run around squeezing toilet paper and worrying about the taste of their coffee. And that's the role that many of them are prepared to believe they still have to carry forward.

Addams, Jane. I do not believe that women are better than men. We have not wrecked railroads, nor corrupted legislatures, nor done many unholy things that men have done; but then we must remember that we have not had the chance.

Barrow, Willie. It's easier being black than being a woman.

Beauvoir, Simone De. One is not born a woman, one becomes one.

Buckley, Pat. Women were born to be taken care of by men—I do think that's the law of the universe.

Carr, Jesse. Being powerful is like being a lady. If you have to tell people you are, you ain't.

Cleaver, Eldridge. If it came down to the choice between a woman and a radio, I'd choose a radio. It brings the outside world in.

Durant, Will. The primary things in my own life have been a wife, a house and some children roaming around us once in a while.

Durant, Will. We are living in a time when woman thinks she has been emancipated, but I'm afraid that's a complimentary way of saying she's been industrialized.

Fields, W. C. Women are like elephants. They're nice to look at but I wouldn't want to own one.

Fontaine, Joan. The physical side of being a woman is detestable.

Ford, Elizabeth (Bloomer). A liberated woman is one who feels confident in herself, and is happy in what she is doing. She is a person who has a sense of self. I think it all comes down to freedom of choice.

Foreman, Percy. Man's inhumanity to man is only exceeded by woman's inhumanity to woman.

Hearst, Austine. After 40, a woman needs a lover and a good facelift. And after 50, cash.

Johnston, Jill. All women are lesbians except those who don't know it yet.

Kipling, Rudyard. A woman is only a woman but a good cigar is a smoke.

Kissinger, Henry Alfred. To me women are no more than a pastime, a hobby. Nobody devotes too much time to a hobby.

Koon, Larry. Women are best suited for secretarial work, decorating cakes and counter sales, like selling lingerie.

Lamarr, Hedy. Any girl can be glamorous. All you have to do is stand still and look stupid.

Lennon, John. As usual, there's a great woman behind every idiot (upon winning his permanent residence status in the U.S.).

Luce, Clare Boothe. There aren't many women now I'd like to see as President—but there are fewer men.

MacLaine, Shirley. I want women to be liberated and still be able to have a nice ass and shake it.

Masters, William Howell. Males have made asses of themselves writing about female sexual experience.

Mead, Margaret. One reason women live longer than men is that they can continue to do something they are used to doing, whereas men are abruptly cut off, whether they are admirals or shopkeepers.

Mitford, Nancy. Sisters stand between one and life's cruel circumstances.

Mohammed Reza Pahlevi, Shah of Iran, . In a man's life, women count only if they're beautiful and graceful and know how to stay feminine.

Moore, Roger. My real attitude toward women is this, and it hasn't changed because of any movement or anything: basically, women like to be treated as sex objects.

Needham, Richard J. Men are foolish, they think money should be taken from the rich and given to the poor. Women are sensible, they think money should be taken from the rich and given to them.

Perkins, Frances (former Secretary of Labor). Being a woman has only bothered me in climbing trees.

Peterson, Esther. If a man fights his adversaries, he's called determined. If a woman does it, she's frustrated.

Picasso, Pablo. For me there are only two kinds of women—goddesses and doormats.

Polykoff, Shirley. If I've only one life, let me live it as a blonde! (advertising slogan).

Riggs, Bobby. Gals are super, but I haven't changed my opinion of them: I still like them best in the bedroom and the kitchen.

Rubinstein, Artur. I need to be surrounded by (beautiful women). They don't have to be anything special, I can enjoy looking at the legs of a stupid woman.

Schreiner, Olive. We are men or women in the second place, human beings in the first.

Skinner, Cornelia Otis. A woman's virtue is man's greatest invention.

Smith, Alexis. Women who are only involved with how they look are always dull.

Thatcher, Margaret Hilda. If you want anything said, ask a man; if you want anything done, ask a woman.

Tucker, Sophie. From birth to age 18, a girl needs good parents. From 18 to 35, she needs good looks. From 35 to 55, she needs a good personality. From 55 on, she needs good cash.

Vanderbilt, Gloria. A woman can never be too thin or too rich.

Vizinczey, Stephen. No girl, however intelligent and warmhearted, can possibly know or feel half as much at 20 as she will at 35.

Vreeland, Diana. Show me a fashionable woman, and I will show you a woman who accomplished something.

Wilde, Oscar. Nothing spoils romance so much as a sense of humor in a woman.

Wilson, Sloan. It is impossible to treat a woman too well.

WOMEN, AMERICAN

Wilde, Oscar. American women seek in their husbands a perfection which English women seek only in their butlers.

WOMEN AND FASHION

Vreeland, Diana. Show me a fashionable woman, and I will show you a woman who accomplished something.

WOMEN AND MEN

Algren, Nelson. Never eat at a place called Mom's. Never play cards with a man named Doc. And never lie down with a woman who's got more troubles than you.

Balanchine, George. God made men to sing the praises of women. They are not equal to men; they are better.

Bardot, Brigitte. Men are beasts and even beasts don't behave as they do.

Bergman, Ingmar. Possessiveness is neurotic, but this is how I am.

Bocuse, Paul. The only place for them (women) is in bed. Anyone who doesn't change his woman every week or so lacks imagination.

Brown, Phyllis George. A smart woman will suggest things to a man and let him take the credit.

Buckley, Pat. Women were born to be taken care of by men—I do think that's the law of the universe.

Burger, Warren Earl. I will never hire a woman clerk. A woman would have to leave work at 6 p.m. and cook dinner for her husband.

Burgess, Anthony. Women cannot help moving, and men cannot help being moved.

Caldwell, Taylor. Women irritate me. I've met a few intelligent women—not many. They're usually after a man, that's all.

Carmichael, Stokely. The only position for women in the movement is prone.

Cleaver, Eldridge. If it came down to the choice between a woman and a radio, I'd choose a radio. It brings the outside world in.

Curtis, Tony. There's simply no other way for a man to feel his manliness, his kingliness if you will, than to be loved by a beautiful woman.

DeCrow, Karen Lipshultz. I like the companionship of men. I don't want to cut myself off from half the human race.

Derek, John. I always get along fine with my women, as soon as they recognize that I am God.

DeVore, Irven. Males are a vast breeding experiment run by females.

Dietrich, Marlene. Once a woman has forgiven her man, she must not reheat his sins for breakfast.

Duffy, Sean. The chance of a meaningful relationship with a member of the opposite sex is inversely proportional to their amount of beauty.

French, Marilyn. Men believe men are central to women's lives, and they're not—even when they become economically central, even psychologically, when we have to please them. Children are the center of a woman's life. Work is always central. When you have children, they become your work, your opus.

Gabor, Zsa Zsa. A man in love is incomplete until he has married. Then he's finished.

Hepburn, Katharine. Sometimes I wonder if men and women really suit each other. Perhaps they should live next door and just visit now and then.

Jones, Franklin P. One thing in which the sexes are equal is in thinking that they're not.

Jong, Erica. You don't have to beat a woman if you can make her feel guilty.

Khomeini, Ayatollah Ruhollah. A Moslem woman must be at the man's disposition for anything he may desire, and she may not refuse him without a religiously valid reason. When she is married to a Moslem man, she becomes his chattel.

King, Larry L. One receives an inverse ratio of romantic opportunities to that which one needs.

Leone, Mama. No one ever filed for divorce on a full stomach.

Little Richard, . Real women don't want to climb telephone poles.

Lodge, John Davis. Man is born into the world as a pig and is civilized by women.

Loos, Anita. Gentlemen don't prefer blondes. If I were writing that book today, I'd call it 'Gentlemen Prefer Gentlemen'.

Mabley, Moms. A woman is a woman until the day she dies, but a man's a man only as long as he can.

Marsh, Jean. We're not sent into this life to be alone, but two-by-two, like in the ark.

Mature, Victor. Apparently, the way to a girl's heart is to saw her in half.

Miller, Ann. No matter what you've achieved, if you're not loved (by a man), Honey, you ain't nothin' but a hound dog.

Morgan, Marabel. It is only when a woman surrenders her life to her husband, reveres and worships him, and is willing to serve him, that she becomes really beautiful to him.

Morgan, Marabel. Love never makes demands. Love is unconditional acceptance of him and his feelings.

Nash, Ogden. Marriage is the alliance of two people, one of whom never remembers birthdays and the other never forgets them.

Novick, Julius. It is a well-known and infuriating fact of life that in any relationship, if one party really and truly does not give a damn, that party will inevitably have the upper hand. Indifference is power (ask any cat).

Pritchett, V. S. There are rules for old men who are in love with young girls, all the stricter when the young girls are in love with them. It has to be played as a game.

Runyon, Damon. Man's only weapon against a woman is his hat. He should grab it and run.

Schroeder, Patricia. When men talk about defense, they always claim to be protecting women and children, but they never ask the women and children what they think.

Smith, Patti. As far as I'm concerned, being any gender is a drag.

Steinem, Gloria. The first problem for all of us, men and women, is not to learn, but to unlearn.

Steinem, Gloria. Today a woman without a man is like a fish without a bicycle.

Ullmann, Liv. You must put more in your life than a man.

Wertmueller, Lina. I'm the last ballbuster left.

West, Mae. I've said it before and I'll say it again—I like a man that takes his time.

West, Mae. The best way to hold a man is in your arms.

Wilson, Sloan. It is impossible to treat a woman too well.

Woolf, Virginia. The history of men's opposition to women's emancipation is more interesting perhaps than the story of that emancipation itself.

WOMEN AND POLITICS

Carmichael, Stokely. The only position for women in the movement is prone.

Ruckelshaus, Jill. When you write stories about the women's movement now, don't look for us in the street. We have gone to the statehouse (to the National Press Club).

WOMEN AS ASTRONAUTS

Lovell, James, Jr. We will fly women into space and use them the same way we use them on Earth—and for the same purpose.

WOMEN AS AUTOMOBILE RACING DRIVERS

Beaumont, Marie-Claude (French automobile racer). Auto racing is a matter of mathematics—timing. Sex has nothing to do with winning a race. You see, the timekeeper's clock ticks at the same speed for a man or a woman.

Guthrie, Janet. I am a racing driver who happens to be a woman.

WOMEN AS CRIMINALS

Ianni, Francis (American Sociologist). As in business, politics and education, there will be equal opportunities in crime. You can't have Bella Abzugs without Bonnie Parkers.

WOMEN AS JOURNALISTS

Walters, Barbara. If it's a woman, it's caustic; if it's a man, it's authoritative. If it's a woman, it's too often pushy, if it's a man it's aggressive in the best sense of the word (commenting on critics who call her brand of interviewing caustic).

WOMEN AS POETS

Lowell, Robert. Almost all good women poets are either divorced or lesbian.

WOMEN AS POLITICIANS

Byrne, Jane. Diamonds are a girl's best friend, and Federal grants are second.

WOMEN AS PRIESTS

Paul VI, Pope, . The real reason (for the ban on women priests) is that Christ, giving the church its fundamental constitution, its theological anthropology subsequently always followed by church tradition, ordained it thus: That in a choir of human voices there shall be tenors and sopranos.

WOMEN AS SOLDIERS

Goldwater, Barry Morris. I don't object to a woman doing anything in combat as long as she gets home in time to cook dinner.

WOMEN—CIVIL RIGHTS

Farenthold, Frances Tarlton (Sissy). The right to an abortion has become a class issue, a race issue, a privacy issue and even a consumer issue, but it is above all, our issue (commenting on the National Women's Political Caucus).

WOMEN—EMPLOYMENT

Hefferan, Colien. The woman who once saw marriage as a form of security now finds that she can provide her own security.

Kaida, Yuju. Women company employees are like desserts. If you consider company work as a meal, men employees are the main dishes, and women employees are desserts. If a company has to slash the cost of food, the first thing it has to cut is a dessert.

Moynihan, Daniel Patrick. Work is no longer considered to be a form of punishment as applied to women. A liberal constituency no longer finds work unattractive.

Steinem, Gloria. The average secretary in the U.S. is better educated than the average boss.

WOMEN, ENGLISH

Wilde, Oscar. American women seek in their husbands a perfection which English women seek only in their butlers.

WOMEN—EQUAL RIGHTS

Bartholomew, Summer (Miss U.S.A.--1975). I believe in equal pay for equal jobs, but not communal toilets or anything like that.

Chapman, Marshall. As far as I'm concerned, feminists have done to women what the Baptists did to religion.

Farley, Lin. A feminist is a woman who knows she's oppressed, who responds to that oppression by fighting it, and who realizes that she can change nothing alone; she is a sister. She believes in herself and the power of women, she sees the necessity for struggle and she likes to win, in other words, she is completely un-feminine.

Friedan, Betty. The women's liberation movement was only a waystation. The questions we face now cannot be solved by women alone. Thinking must come in cooperation with old people, young people, heart-attack prone executives, trade unionists, blacks and other minorities. I feel a great anxiety now about the collision between the increased aspirations of women and the erosion of support for affirmative action programs and equal rights.

Garson, Barbara. Elizabeth Gurley Flynn's autobiography reminded me with a jolt that it wasn't until the time of the Stokely Carmichaels, imitated by the Tom Haydens, that women on the left had to fight to get the floor or to get up off of the floor.

Gillespie, Marcia Ann. I did not stand up for my rights as a black person in America to be told that I have to sit down because I'm a woman.

Gray, Francine du Plessix. Women are the only exploited group in history who have been idealized into powerlessness.

Hellman, Lillian. Nobody can argue any longer about the rights of women. It's like arguing about earthquakes.

Johnston, Jill. Feminism at heart is a massive complaint. Lesbianism is the solution.

Jong, Erica. It seems to me that sooner or later, all intelligent women become feminists.

Kennedy, Joan. If Ted is elected President of the United States, I will commit myself to the ongoing struggle for women's equality with everything I have and everything I am.

Nagy, Ivan. Ballet is the original women's liberation profession. It is created for females.

Reagan, Ronald. Human beings are not animals, and I do not want to see sex and sexual differences treated as casually and amorally as dogs and other beasts treat them. I believe this could happen under the ERA.

Seaman, Barbara. (A feminist is) a woman who is for women, which does not mean being against men.

Steinem, Gloria. Feminism means that each woman has power over her own life and can decide what to do for herself.

Thomas, Marlo. A man has to be Joe McCarthy to be called ruthless. All a woman has to do is put you on hold.

White, Theodore. It's about time women had their say in the laws governing them—laws that for 5,000 years have been made by old men, mostly with shriveled-up groins, who have long since forgotten what it was like to be young and never knew what it was like to be a woman.

WOMEN—HISTORY—GREAT BRITAIN

Marsh, Jean. I wouldn't have wanted to be an upstairs or a downstairs woman: I would have wanted to be a man. The women weren't allowed to do anything (commenting on English life in the television program Upstairs, Downstairs).

WOMEN—OCCUPATIONAL MOBILITY

Peter, Laurence J. Most hierarchies were established by men who now occupy the upper levels, thus depriving women of an equal opportunity to achieve their levels of incompetence.

WOMEN—POWER (SOCIAL SCIENCES)

Soeder, Karin (Sweden's first woman Foreign Minister). Men care about power because for them power is linked to sexual performance. Women achieve positions of power out of a need to do something, not because we need reassurance.

WOMEN—PSYCHOLOGY

Asimov, Isaac. Women tend to be dirtier but less clever than men. I don't know why, but they can be surprisingly vulgar (about women and limericks).

Beauvoir, Simone De. In itself, homosexuality is as limiting as heterosexuality: the ideal should be to be capable of loving a woman or a man; either, a human being, without feeling fear, restraint, or obligation.

Ephron, Nora. For a lot of women, the women's movement has just given them a political rationalization for their fear of success.

Ephron, Nora. We have lived in an era when happiness was a warm puppy, and the era when happiness was a dry martini, and now we have come to an era when happiness is knowing what your uterus looks like.

Gabor, Zsa Zsa. You're never too young to be younger.

Greer, Germaine. Security is when everything is settled, when nothing can happen to you; security is a denial of life.

Jong, Erica. You don't have to beat a woman if you can make her feel guilty.

Mature, Victor. Apparently, the way to a girl's heart is to saw her in half.

Sahl, Mort. In the forties, to get a girl you had to be a GI or a jock. In the fifties, to get a girl you had to be Jewish. In the sixties, to get a girl you had to be black. In the seventies, to get a girl you've got to be a girl.

Steinem, Gloria. A pedestal is as much a prison as any small space.

WOMEN—SUCCESS

Goode, William J. Success is sexy (about women).

WOMEN—WASHINGTON, D.C.

Wright, James. The Wright broad rule is that broads ought to be able to type (commenting when asked to state a broad rule for avoiding Congressional sex scandals).

WOMEN'S LIBERATION MOVEMENT

Abzug, Bella. Women are still conceived on television and radio as being creatures of consumption who run around squeezing toilet paper and worrying about the taste of their coffee. And that's the role that many of them are prepared to believe they still have to carry forward.

Buchwald, Art. The women's liberation movement has affected my sex life: I haven't had any since it started.

Chapman, Marshall. As far as I'm concerned, feminists have done to women what the Baptists did to religion.

Charles, Prince of Wales, . Women's liberationists rather annoy me because they tend to argue all the time and start calling you a male chauvinist pig and, frankly, it becomes rather uncivilized.

Ephron, Nora. For a lot of women, the women's movement has just given them a political rationalization for their fear of success.

Friedan, Betty. The women's liberation movement was only a waystation. The questions we face now cannot be solved by women alone. Thinking must come in cooperation with old people, young people, heart-attack prone executives, trade unionists, blacks and other minorities. I feel a great anxiety now about the collision between the increased aspirations of women and the erosion of support for affirmative action programs and equal rights.

Greer, Germaine. It's sheer myth that feminists are anti-child—we're the only people who're going to give children a better deal.

Hefner, Hugh Marston. If I told you, for example that Playboy, in its 22 years, was one of the major things that contributed to the women's movement, you might find it a mindboggler, but it happens to be true.

Meyner, Helen. Let the best man win, whomever she may be.

Ringer, Robert. The women behind the (women's liberation) movement want the same thing all group leaders want and have wanted through history: ego assuagement.

Ruckelshaus, Jill. It occurred to me when I was 13 and wearing white gloves and Mary Janes and going to dancing school, that no one should have to dance backwards all their lives.

Ruckelshaus, Jill. When you write stories about the women's movement now, don't look for us in the street. We have gone to the statehouse (to the National Press Club).

Schlafly, Phyllis. Ask yourself: When you are rescued from the third floor of a burning building, do you want to be carried down the ladder by a man or a woman?.

Schlafly, Phyllis. 'Equal parenting' does not work—the maternal tuning in never turns off.

Welch, Raquel. I think the women's lib is only good politically, but sexually I don't think it works.

WOMEN'S LIBERATION MOVEMENT—HISTORY
Anthony, Susan B. Failure is impossible.

Woolf, Virginia. The history of men's opposition to women's emancipation is more interesting perhaps than the story of that emancipation . itself.

WOODWARD, BOB
Colby, William Egan. By the way, *did* you ever work for the CIA? (to Bob Woodward upon agreeing to issue an official denial that Woodward had ever worked for the CIA).

WOODWARD, BOB AND BERNSTEIN, CARL. THE FINAL DAYS
Bernstein, Carl. Let me say no one has successfully challenged the accuracy of this book (The Final Days) or any single assertion in it.

WORDS
Compton-Burnett, Ivy. We must use words as they are used or stand aside from life.

Schlesinger, Arthur, Jr. 'Gay' used to be one of the most agreeable words in the language. Its appropriation by a notably morose group is an act of piracy.

WORK
Anonymous (Corollary to Murphy's Law), . Everything will take longer than you think it will.

Anonymous (Corollary to Murphy's Law), . Nothing is as easy as it looks.

Boyle, Charles. If not controlled, work will flow to the competent man until he submerges.

Brown, Edmund Gerald, Jr. If work is more interesting and challenging, people should be paid less. Those are the people who get great psychic rewards: their lives are better because they have the privilege of interesting work.

Drucker, Peter F. So much of what we call management consists in making it difficult for people to work.

Galbraith, John Kenneth. No ethic is as ethical as the work ethic.

Hull, Ma. When God sees fit to take me, I want him to take me providing my own way.

Jerome, Jerome K. It is impossible to enjoy idling thoroughly unless one has plenty of work to do.

McCarthy, Eugene Joseph. Work is the only kind of property many people have in America.

Parkinson, C. Northcote. Work expands to fill the time allotted to it, or, conversely, the amount of work completed is in inverse proportion to the number of people employed.

Thompson, Lord Roy Herbert. No leisure, no pleasure, just work (commenting on the secret of his success).

Weiler, A. H. Nothing is impossible for the man who doesn't have to do it himself.

Wilson, Sloan. A man who wants time to read and write must let the grass grow long.

WORK—RUSSIA
Anonymous, . As long as the bosses pretend they are paying us a decent wage, we will pretend that we are working (Soviet worker's saying).

WORLD POLITICS
Brzezinski, Zbigniew. We live in a world in which there will be many local conflicts, in which all the major powers will exercise self-restraint, because they have to exercise self-restraint in the nuclear...it will be a sign of the maturity of the American people and of the growing wisdom of the American people if we adjust ourselves to the notion that in our age there is a twilight zone between war and peace and that this twilight zone of limited wars is going to be very much a feature of our lifetime.

Evtushenko, Evgenii Aleksandrovich. Distrust is the mother of war and political racism.

Ford, Gerald Rudolph. Most of the important things that happen in the world happen in the middle of the night.

Gasich, Welko (Vice President of Northrop Aircraft Corporation). Until we have a bona fide world police force, it's still Dodge City and everyone wants a rifle over his door.

Goldberg, Arthur Joseph. We need a world in which it is safe to be human.

Khomeini, Ayatollah Ruhollah. All western governments are just thieves. Nothing but evil comes from them.

Kuan, Han-Ch'ing. What characterizes the current world situation is decidedly not an irreversible process of detente but the approaching danger of a new world war.

Lord, Winston. The Trilateral Commission doesn't secretly run the world. The Council on Foreign Relations does that.

Moynihan, Daniel Patrick. As the lights go out in the rest of the world, they shine all the brighter here.

Solzhenitsyn, Aleksandr Isaevich. The entire period from 1945 to 1975 can be viewed as another world war that was lost by the West without a battle.

Thomas, Lewis. We do not, in any real way, run the (world). It runs itself, and we are part of the running.

Truman, Harry S. The C students run the world.

WORLD WAR, 1939-1945

Will, George. World War II was the last government program that really worked (to the Association of American Publishers).

WORRY

Allen, Woody. The lion and the calf shall lie down together, but the calf won't get much sleep.

Moore, Mary Tyler. Worrying is a necessary part of life.

WORTH

Arden, Elizabeth. Nothing that costs only a dollar is worth having.

Haskins, Caryl. It's funny that we often value what is rare and specialized. What is truly precious is what is common and unspecialized.

Hunt, Nelson Bunker. People who know how much they're worth aren't usually worth that much.

WRIGHT, FRANK LLOYD—FURNITURE

Wright, Frank Lloyd. I have been black and blue in some spot, somewhere, almost all my life from too intimate contact with my own early furniture.

WRITING

Brenan, Gerald. Words are as recalcitrant as circus animals and the unskilled trainer can crack his whip at them in vain.

Califano, Joseph A., Jr. Writing things clearly does not necessarily mean writing them short.

Cowley, Malcolm. No complete son-of-a-bitch ever wrote a good sentence.

Crichton, Michael. I find facts inhibiting....The more you know, the more you are obliged to the truth. I much prefer not to know.

Doctorow, E. L. In an age that celebrates facts, the writer who begins to break down the line between fact and fiction represents the reassertion of the authority and perception of the individual mind.

Doctorow, E. L. There is no longer any such thing as fiction or nonfiction; there's only narrative.

Hall, Donald. Less is more, in prose as in architecture.

Kafka, Franz. Writing is a sweet and wonderful reward, but for what? In the night it became clear to me, as clear as a child's lesson book, that it is the reward for serving the devil.

Lindbergh, Anne Morrow. Writing is thinking. It is more than living, for it is being conscious of living.

McLuhan, Marshall. Most clear writing is a sign that there is no exploration going on. Clear prose indicates an absence of thought.

Nixon, Richard Milhous. Writing is the toughest thing I've ever done.

Perkins, Maxwell. It is always better to give a little less than the reader wants, than more (to Ray Stannard Baker).

Perkins, Maxwell. You have to throw yourself away when you write (to Elizabeth Lemmon).

Roth, Philip. The road to hell is paved with works-in-progress.

Steinbeck, John. The profession of book writing makes horse racing seem like a solid, stable business.

Waugh, Evelyn. I regard writing not as investigation of character, but as an exercise in the use of language.

Woolf, Virginia. The art of writing has for backbone some fierce attachment to an idea.

WRITING SEE ALSO AUTHORSHIP

WYETH, ANDREW

Wyeth, Andrew. Technique is not what interests me. To me, my art is deeply the question of whether or not I can find the theory that expresses the way I feel at a particular time about my own life and my own emotions.

WYNETTE, TAMMY

Alice Cooper, . Only Tammy Wynette and Alice Cooper know how hard it is to be a woman.

YANKEE STADIUM, NEW YORK

Mantle, Mickey. There was a great, dark mystery about it when I first came here from Oklahoma. I still get goose-pimples just walking inside it. Now I think this is about the prettiest ball park I ever saw (commenting at the reopening of Yankee Stadium).

YOSHIMURA, WENDY

Yoshimura, Wendy. I remain high in spirit and strong in my convictions. I extend my special solidarity to all my friends above ground and in the prisons and the Third World (upon being released on bail after 3 months in jail).

YOUNG, ANDREW

Carter, James Earl. Any claims or allegations that American Jewish leaders or anyone else urged me to ask Andy (Young) for his resignation are absolutely and totally false.

Young, Andrew. I like to get things done, and I don't run from evil. My office has always been open to South Africans. And the meaner and whiter they are, the more I like 'em to come by.

Young, Andrew. I really don't feel a bit sorry for anything I have done (on resigning as ambassador to the United Nations).

Young, Andrew. I was taught to fight when people called me nigger. That's when I learned that negotiation is better than fighting.

Young, Andrew. Nigeria is arrogant and Kissinger is arrogant, and so there was a clash. I may be just as arrogant, but I can control it better.

YOUTH

Burger, Warren Earl. Perhaps without knowing all the reasons, they were ahead of many others in seeing that something was missing in modern life (commenting on American youth of the '60s).

Cartland, Barbara. Being 18 is like visiting Russia. You're glad you've had the experience, but you'd never want to repeat it.

Chanel, Coco. Youth is something very new: twenty years ago no one mentioned it.

Longworth, Alice Roosevelt. The secret of eternal youth is arrested development.

Macrae, Norman. An anti-growth cult is being taught to a generation of idealistic kids as if it was high moral philosophy or even a religion.

White, William Allen. In education we are striving not to teach youth to make a living, but to make a life.

Wilde, Oscar. Young people, nowadays, imagine that money is everything, and when they grow older they know it.

ZIEGLER, RONALD LOUIS

Nessen, Ronald. I'm a Ron, but not a Ziegler.

Ziegler, Ronald Louis. I never knowingly lied, but certainly history shows that many things I said were incorrect.

ZIMBABWE—CIVIL RIGHTS

Kaunda, Kenneth. An African in Zimbabwe does not need a communist to tell him that he is not free.

Nkomo, Joshua. There's no such thing to me as whites.

ZIMBABWE—DESCRIPTION

Anonymous (African ambassador), . The only way to true majority rule (in Zimbabwe) is by force of arms.

ZIONISM

Baroody, J. M. Zionism is racism because it is built on exclusivity. The Jews believe they are a superior race, a chosen people. They believe their home should be in Palestine, the Promised Land. Since when was God in the real-estate business?.

Moynihan, Daniel Patrick. Even our sense of peoplehood grows uncertain as ethnic assertions take their implacable toll on the civic assumption of unity.

Wallace, George Corley. We told you years ago that the U.N. was a no-'count outfit.

ZUKOR, ADOLPH

Zukor, Adolph. Look ahead a little and gamble a lot (a formula for success).